The 1934 St. Louis Cardinals
The World Champion Gas House Gang

Edited by Charles F. Faber
Associate Editors: Russell Lake, Leonard Levin, and Bill Nowlin
Photo Editor: Joseph Wancho

Society for American Baseball Research, Inc.
Phoenix, AZ

THE 1934 ST. LOUIS CARDINALS
The World Champion Gas House Gang
Edited by Charles F. Faber
Associate editors: Russell Lake, Leonard Levin, and Bill Nowlin
Photo Editor: Joseph Wancho
Copyright © 2014 Society for American Baseball Research, Inc.

All rights reserved. Reproduction in whole or in part without permission is prohibited.

ISBN 978-1-933599-731
(Ebook ISBN 978-1-933599-748)
Design and Production: Gilly Rosenthol, Rosenthol Design

Photo Credits:
Retro Images Archive (George Brace Collection) - pages 2, 45, 48, 51, 57, 62, 74, 86, 96, 108, 112, 118, 145, 156, 161, 170, 176, 196, 205, 216, 223, 230, 263.
National Baseball Hall of Fame – front cover, and pages 18, 21, 46, 69, 78, 102, 131, 138, 166, 185, 191, 202, 211, 233, 238, 243, 250, 259.
Baseball-Reference.com – page 149.

The Society for American Baseball Research, Inc.
4455 E. Camelback Road, Ste. D-140
Phoenix, AZ 85018
Phone: (800) 969-7227 or (612) 343-6455

Web: www.sabr.org
Facebook: Society for American Baseball Research
Twitter: @SABR

Table of Contents

Acknowledgments 1
Introduction by Charles F. Faber 2
   and Joseph Wancho
Brief History of the pre-1934 Cardinals 4
   by Parker J. Bena
Assembling the Team by John J. Watkins 12
Sportsman's Park by Scott Ferkovich 17
St. Louis in 1934 by Eric Aron 25
1934 St. Louis Cardinals Season Timeline 29
The Cardinals in the 1934 Pennant Race 41
   by Charles F. Faber
The 1934 World Series 44
   by Matthew Silverman

The Players
Tex Carleton by Gregory H. Wolf 51
Ripper Collins by Cort Vitty 57
Pat Crawford by Gregory H. Wolf 62
Kiddo Davis by Don Harrison 69
Spud Davis by Andy Sturgill 74
Dizzy Dean by Joseph Wancho 78
Paul Dean by Paul Geisler 86
Bill DeLancey by Thomas Ayers 96
Leo Durocher by Jeffrey Marlett 102
Frankie Frisch by Fred Stein 108
Chick Fullis by Jack Morris 112
Burleigh Grimes by Charles F. Faber 118
Jesse Haines by Gregory H. Wolf 131
Bill Hallahan by Gregory H. Wolf 138
Francis Healy by Greg Erion 145

Clarence Heise by J. G. Preston 149
Jim Lindsey by Alan Cohen 156
Pepper Martin by Norm King 161
Joe Medwick by Charles F. Faber 166
Buster Mills by Bill Nowlin 170
Jim Mooney by Charlie Weatherly 176
   and Gregory H. Wolf
Gene Moore by Greg Erion 185
Ernie Orsatti by Lawrence Baldassaro 191
Flint Rhem by Nancy Snell Griffith 196
Lew Riggs by Bob Webster 202
Jack Rothrock by Bill Nowlin 205
Dazzy Vance by Charles F. Faber 211
Bill Walker by Gregory H. Wolf 216
Burgess Whitehead by C. Paul Rogers III 223
Jim Winford by Clayton J. Trutor 230
Red Worthington by Jimmy Keenan 233

Executives
Sam Breadon by Mark Armour 238
Bill DeWitt by Dwayne Isgrig 243
Branch Rickey by Andy McCue 250

Coaches
Mike Gonzalez by Joseph Girard 259
Buzzy Wares by Charles F. Faber 265

Postscript by Charles F. Faber 268

Contributors 269

Acknowledgements

THIS BOOK IS entirely the product of volunteers—thirty-five members of the Society for American Baseball Research, all passionate enthusiasts for the game, dedicated researchers, and talented writers. The associate editors—Bill Nowlin, Russ Lake, and Leonard Levin—contributed their editorial skill, knowledge of baseball, and meticulous attention to detail, making this book far better than it could have been without benefit of their wise counsel. Their diligence ensures that our readers can have confidence in the accuracy of what they read. In addition to serving as an Associate Editor, Bill Nowlin was a willing and capable mentor to this neophyte editor. He was always available to help me navigate unfamiliar terrain.

A special note of thanks goes to Joseph Wancho. This project benefited greatly in its early stages from his encouragement and contributions. Without Joe's assistance at inception, this book might never have been written. Joe has also served as Photo Editor, securing and selecting photographs to be used in the book. In these efforts he has been assisted by John Horne of the National Baseball Hall of Fame and Matt Grace of Planet Giant, among others.

The invaluable help of Zachariah Webb in dealing with computer issues is deeply appreciated. It has been a pleasure to work with him.

The biographies of Branch Rickey and Leo Durocher were originally published in Lyle Spitz, ed., *The Team That Forever Changed Baseball and America* (Lincoln, University of Nebraska Press, 2012.) The piece on Burleigh Grimes is adapted from Charles F. Faber and Richard B. Faber, *Spitballers: The Last Legal Hurlers of the Wet One* (Jefferson, NC: McFarland, 2006.) An earlier version of the essay by the late Fred Stein on Frankie Frisch appeared in the SABR BioProject.

— Charles F. Faber

Introduction

By Charles F. Faber and Joseph Wancho

THE 1934 ST. Louis Cardinals were one of the most colorful crews ever to play the National Pastime. Sportswriters delighted in assigning nicknames to the players, based on their real or imagined qualities. What a cast of characters it was! None was more picturesque than Pepper Martin, the "Wild Horse of the Osage," who ran the bases with reckless abandon, led his teammates in off-the-field hi-jinks, and organized a hillbilly band called the Mississippi Mudcats, in which he played guitar. He was quite a baseball player, the star of the 1931 World Series and a significant contributor to the 1934 championship. The harmonica player for the Mudcats was the irrepressible Dizzy Dean. Full of braggadocio, Dean delivered on his boasts by winning 30 games in 1934, the last National League hurler to achieve that feat. Dizzy and his brother Paul accounted for all of the Cardinal victories in the 1934 World Series. Some writers tried to pin the moniker Daffy on Paul, but that name didn't fit the younger and much quieter brother. The club's hitters were led by the New Jersey strong boy, Joe "Ducky" Medwick, who hated the nickname, preferring to be called "Muscles." Presiding over this aggregation was the "Fordham Flash", Frankie Frisch.

Rounding out the club were worthies bearing such nicknames as Ripper, "Leo the Lip," Spud, Kiddo, Pop, Dazzy, Ol' Stubblebeard, Wild Bill, Buster, Chick, Red, and Tex. Some of these were aging stars, past their prime, and others were youngsters, on their way up. Together they comprised a championship ball club.

The club earned lasting fame as the "Gas House Gang." Our authors have uncovered various explanations of the origin of the term, some of which will be presented in the text. Ironically, the nickname was not given to the Redbirds until the year following their

Team photo of the 1934 St. Louis Cardinals.

spectacular 1934 season. *The Dizziest Season*, edited by H.G. Fleming, is a compilation of articles and anecdotes written by National League beat writers covering the St. Louis Cardinals in 1934. Through the entire book, there is no mention of "Gas House Gang". How the name came to be, by whom and where, is open to much dispute. The only sure bet is that it was first used widely in 1935.

The Cards were a team of fast-talking, hard-nosed players who played the game well and to the hilt. Good, tough ballplayers that didn't let up, leaving their supreme effort on the field day in and day out. If your uniform was clean at the end of a ballgame, well, then you were just not playing "Gas House" brand of baseball. The team was assembled with as lively a bunch of free-spirited players ever played the game. They were indeed a formidable squad.

St. Louis won a hard-fought pennant race with New York, and they trailed the Giants by 2 1/2 games in the final week of the season. But the Giants dropped their last five games and the Cards swept Cincinnati in a season-ending four-game series to win the flag by a margin of two games. Dizzy and Paul Dean won the last three games, as the duo surrendered one run between them. Diz was often considered the ringleader of the team. He tells the following tale about a doubleheader at Ebbets Field in 1934, with Paul and himself as the starting pitchers. "Frisch was giving us instructions, telling me how to pitch to Tony Cuccinello and Linus Frey and Sam Leslie and Ralph Boyle and all the other Dodgers and I give him an argument on everyone. I finally said, 'Let's stop this silly business, Frank. Don't you think it's kind of silly for an ordinary second baseman like you to be telling a great pitcher like me how to pitch to anybody?' Frank almost had a stroke. He told us to go out and pitch the way we wanted, he didn't care if we did get out ears pinned back."

The story of this great team deserves to be told. *"The 1934 St. Louis Cardinals"* is a biographical sketch of the entire Cardinals team. Included are bios ranging from Hall-of-Famers Dean, Durocher, Frisch, Grimes, Haines, Medwick, Rickey, and Vance to All-Stars Ripper Collins and Pepper Martin, to bench players like Kiddo Davis and Francis Healy. There are also stories about Sportsman's Park, the history of the club, and the 1934 World Series, as well as bios of the coaching staff and key front office personnel.

Please accept our invitation to get to know these men, relive an important part of baseball history, and to acquaint yourself with many untold stories of the 1934 St. Louis Cardinals. This book is written entirely by members of the Society for American Baseball Research (SABR). It is their superb research and writing that make this book a must in any baseball fan's library.

Pre-1934 St. Louis Cardinals History

By Parker J. Bena

MANY A FAN of the baseball team now known as the St. Louis Cardinals has been seen walking around wearing some item of clothing proclaiming the date of the establishment of their beloved Cardinals as 1892. Is that date correct? No. The history of professional baseball in St. Louis actually goes back a lot further than that.

In January of 1876, a group of businessmen led by William A. Hulbert met at the Galt House hotel in Louisville, Kentucky, intending to create a new professional baseball league called the Western League.[1] The idea was spearheaded by groups in four cities, Chicago, St. Louis, Cincinnati, and Louisville. In order for the new league to succeed, it was decided that more Eastern cities were needed in the league. In February 1876 Hulbert and Charles A. Fowle (representing the interests of the St. Louis club) met with delegates from Boston, New York, Philadelphia, and Hartford at the Grand Central Hotel in New York. They formed the National League of Professional Base Ball Clubs, an organization that operates to this day as the National League. The new league would include among its teams, the St. Louis Brown Stockings and the Chicago White Stockings (now the Cubs)—the continuation of a baseball rivalry that started in the old National Association when the two teams took the field against each other for the first time on May 6, 1875.[2] The rivalry also continues to this day.

The baseball rivalry between St. Louis and Chicago was born out of a civic rivalry. St. Louis had long been the largest population center in the Midwest because of its river-borne commerce, However, it would soon be overtaken by Chicago because of the latter's increasing ties to the railroad industry.[3]

The Brown Stockings did very well in the National League's inaugural season of 1876, finishing third behind the White Stockings and the Hartford Dark Blues with a record of 45-19. The main highlight of their season was provided by pitcher George Washington "Grin" Bradley who on July 15 pitched the league's first no-hit, no-run game, a 2-0 victory over Tommy Bond and the Dark Blues.[4] Bradley posted a record of 45-19 with a 1.23 ERA and 16 shutouts. The Brown Stockings slumped badly in 1877, slipping to 28-32. This was perhaps in no small part due to star pitcher Bradley moving on to the Chicago team.

The Brown Stockings also collapsed financially and dropped out of the National League at the end of the season—probably due to a gambling scandal that had plagued the league in its second season. Starting in 1878, the Brown Stockings operated as a semipro team. Several players, including outfielder Ned Cuthbert (a participant in Bradley's no-hitter[5]) decided to stay in St. Louis.

Enter Chris Von der Ahe. The German-born Von der Ahe was a beer baron and the owner of the Golden Lion Saloon at Grand Boulevard and St. Louis Avenue, just two blocks from the ballpark.[6] Cuthbert, one of the regulars at the Golden Lion, convinced Von der Ahe that vast riches awaited the man who could tie baseball and concessions together.[7] Von der Ahe later recalled, "It was 'Eddie' who talked me into baseball. … He picked me out, and, for months, he talked league baseball, until he convinced me there was something in it."[8]

On November 2, 1881, Von der Ahe met with ownership groups from Baltimore, Cincinnati, Louisville, Philadelphia, and Pittsburgh at the Hotel Gibson in Cincinnati and they formed the American Association. The new league played games on Sundays and encouraged the sale of beer and liquor at its ballparks. In another direct challenge to the National League, the American Association charged its patrons 25 cents instead of the 50 cents charged by the older, more established league. The owners of all six clubs had ties to the brewing industry.[9] Because of this, the American Association became known as "The Beer and Whiskey League." The Brown Stockings became one of the six charter franchises of the new league along with the Baltimore Orioles, Cincinnati Red Stockings, Louisville Eclipse, Philadelphia Athletics, and Pittsburgh Alleghenys. The franchise now known as the St. Louis

Cardinals was born. Aside from the Brown Stockings, three teams that played in the old American Association still operate: the Alleghenys (now the Pirates), the Red Stockings (now the Reds), and the Brooklyn Atlantics, who joined in 1884 (now the Los Angeles Dodgers).

The reconstituted Brown Stockings, managed by Von der Ahe's old drinking buddy, Ned Cuthbert (who was also the team's left fielder), took the field for the first time in St. Louis on May 2, 1882, and defeated Louisville, 9-7. The team finished fifth in its inaugural American Association season with a 37-43 record.[10] The 1883 team engaged in a hard fight for the pennant with the Philadelphia Athletics, but ended up losing the pennant by one game. Irish-born pitcher Tony Mullane had one of the greatest pitching seasons in franchise history, winning 35 games and finishing in the top five in nearly every pitching category.[11]

The Brown Stockings (or Browns as they were sometimes known) quickly became the Beer and Whiskey League's flagship franchise and Chris Von der Ahe became its showman owner. The team's stars included Cuthbert, second baseman Yank Robinson, first baseman Charlie Comiskey, third baseman Arlie Latham, pitchers Jumbo McGinnis, Silver King, and Bob Caruthers, pitcher/outfielder Dave Foutz, and Cuthbert's successor in left field, Tip O'Neill, who became baseball's first Canadian-born superstar.

O'Neill had an amazing season in 1887—perhaps the finest season statistically in the franchise's history. He had a .492 average, 275 hits, 52 doubles, 19 triples, 14 home runs, 123 RBIs, a .492 batting average, and a .691 slugging percentage. However, O'Neill was the beneficiary of a short-lived scoring rule: bases on balls were counted as hits. Due to the over-abundance of .400 hitters, the rule was changed in 1888 and the change was made retroactive to the 1887 campaign. This resulted in the loss of 50 hits and 57 points on O'Neill's batting average. His hit total was cut to 225 and his batting average was lowered to .435, figures that have been accepted by the major leagues ever since. O'Neill became the first Triple Crown winner in franchise history and, as of 2014 was the only player to lead a professional league in doubles, triples, and home runs in the same season.[12] The following year O'Neill repeated as batting champion despite the fact that his average fell 100 points to .335.

Chris Von der Ahe was something of a visionary. Displaying a spirit of innovation well ahead of his time, he envisioned the ballpark he would build for his team as a multipurpose entertainment complex with "a cricket field … a baseball diamond, cinder paths for 'sprinters,' a handball court, bowling alleys, and everything of that sort." Sportsmen who were passionate about shooting contributed to the development of the new facility, intending to hold weekly shooting events at the grounds under the auspices of the St. Louis Gun Club, hence the name for the new facility—Sportsman's Park.[13]

In 1885 the Browns began a run of four consecutive American Association pennants, which made them baseball's first dynasty. They would meet the champions of the National League in a postseason contest known as the World's Series with the winner being declared world's champion. In 1885 the Brown Stockings met the Chicago White Stockings (now the Cubs), but the outcome was disputed and no winner was declared. In 1886 the two teams met again and St. Louis prevailed, four games to two, giving the city its first professional baseball championship. They repeated as American Association champions the next two years but were defeated in the World's Series, in 1887 by the Detroit Wolverines in an epic 12-city extravaganza 10 games to 5; and in 1888 to the New York (now San Francisco) Giants, six games to five.

Alfred H. Spink, one of the founders of *The Sporting News*, once wrote of the Brown Stockings: "The team was the wonder of the baseball world for many a day. The players were not stalwart looking, but rather slight and slim-waisted and when they met heavy nines like Chicago and Detroit they suffered on the field in comparison. Nonetheless, the Browns played wonderful and speedy ball and … they knew how to win ball games."[14]

The years that followed were mostly lean. After the 1891 season, the American Association folded and the Brown Stockings, along with Louisville, Baltimore, and Washington, were absorbed into the National League for the 1892 season (hence the date on many a Cardinal fan's clothing). In 1898 the franchise hit rock bottom, losing a franchise-record 111 games. The ballpark was destroyed by a fire on April 16.[15] Von der Ahe had risked his fortune to build the ballpark, and went deeply into debt as a result. In 1899 he lost his team as well when it was sold to brothers Frank and Stanley Robison,[16] who also owned the National League's Cleveland Spiders. At that time, there were no rules against owners holding stock in more than one team. Deciding that they could make more money in St. Louis, the Robisons transferred the best Cleveland players, including pitcher Cy Young, outfielder Jesse Burkett, and shortstop Bobby Wallace, to St. Louis. The 1899 team (renamed the Perfectos) finished fifth in the 12-team National League with a record of 84-67. The Cleveland Spiders finished dead last with a record of 20-134 — the worst record in baseball history. They were disbanded after the season.

The 1900 season offered a glimmer of hope for the St. Louis team and its fans as there were five future Hall of Famers on the roster that year. Besides Burkett, Wallace, and Young, the team now included catcher Wilbert Robinson and third baseman John McGraw. That season the team adopted the nickname Cardinals. (Frank Robison's daughter Helene Robison Britton remarked that the team's new uniform socks were "a lovely shade of cardinal.") The new hope quickly faded as various ailments (including a nasty spiking incident and boils) kept McGraw out of action for lengthy stretches. The team was largely a disappointment on the field as it finished fifth in the eight-team National League with a 65-75 record.

After the 1900 campaign, three of the Cardinals' star players, McGraw, Robinson, and Young, defected to the brand-new American League. (An urban legend, whose truth has never been established, had McGraw and Robinson throwing their Cardinals uniforms out of a train and into the Mississippi River as they headed back east.)

Despite the defections, the club fared a little better in 1901, with a record of 76-64, good enough for fourth place. Burkett and Wallace jumped to the American League after the season. And St. Louis became a two-team city when the Milwaukee Brewers of the American League moved to St. Louis and became the Browns.

After 1901 the Cardinals continued to experience no real success on the field. In 1908 they won only 49 games and lost 105, the worst record posted by a Cardinals team in the 20th century. That season, the Cardinals were what writer Cait Murphy termed "everybody's punching bag." Things started out bad on Opening Day and got worse from there. The Pirates won the opener 3-1 despite committing four errors. The Cardinals, for their part, made six.[17] On April 20, in a game that typified the Cardinals' frustrations in 1908, Bugs Raymond pitched a one-hitter against the eventual Cubs but lost 2-0 as Chicago scored its two runs in the sixth inning on two walks, an error, and a single.[18] On September 25 Frank Robison died from a stroke at the age of 54. His brother Stanley took over control of the team. (The 1908 team was the last Cardinals team as of 2014 to have lost 100 or more games in a season.)

The Cardinals acquired catcher Roger Bresnahan from the Giants on December 12, 1908, and named him player-manager. For the next two seasons, the Cardinals fared little better than they had in 1908. In 1911 the Cardinals posted a 75-74 record, good for fifth place and their first winning season since 1901. Before the season, on March 24, Stanley Robison died of heart failure at 54 and control of the team passed to Frank's daughter, Helene Robison Britton, who became the first female owner of a major sports franchise in North America. Britton ruled the team with an iron fist and players, sportswriters, and fans alike dubbed her the Queen Bee. The 1912 team could not duplicate its success from 1911 and Bresnahan quickly fell out of favor with the new owner. After the season, he was fired and replaced by Mrs. Britton's favorite player, second baseman Miller Huggins.

The 1915 season offered Cardinals fans a glimpse into their team's promising future. Rogers Hornsby, who became the greatest right-handed hitter in National League history, saw his first big-league action on September 10.

Mrs. Britton grew tired of running the team, and sold it to a group of investors led by James Jones in March 1917. Among the investors was a transplanted New Yorker named Sam Breadon, who got rich selling cars in St. Louis and initially bought four shares of stock for $200.[19] One of the first moves the new owners made was to hire as club president Branch Rickey, a University of Michigan Law School graduate who had been the manager of the crosstown rival Browns. While with the Cardinals, Rickey began what evolved into the modern farm system: developing players within the organization instead of purchasing expensive veterans.

The team began to show signs of life under the new ownership. In 1917 the Cardinals finished third in the National League with a record of 82-70. However, Miller Huggins left after the season to manage the New York Yankees (and eventually cement his place in the Baseball Hall of Fame). In the war-shortened 1918 season the Cardinals fell to the cellar, finishing with a record of 51-78 under new manager Jack Hendricks. After the season Rickey fired Hendricks and took over the manager's job himself, stepping down as team president but remaining the general manager.[20]

Rickey's player development system laid the foundations for future Cardinal success. The organization produced players like outfielders Heinie Mueller and Ray Blades, pitcher Jesse Haines, and first baseman Jim Bottomley. Under Rickey, Hornsby's career began to take off; his statistics rivaled those of Babe Ruth. But Breadon, who bhy then had become majority owner, saw that Rickey was over-extending himself in the dual role and confined him, despite Rickey's protests, to general manager duties. Hornsby became the manager.

The team started off slowly in 1926, not reaching the .500 mark until May 22, when their record stood at 18-18. On June 22 the Cardinals made a crucial move, picking up veteran pitcher Grover Cleveland Alexander from the Chicago Cubs on waivers. About the same time the Cardinals acquired outfielder Billy Southworth from the Giants for outfielder Heinie Mueller. The Cardinals were now developing into a legitimate contender. After adding Alexander and Southworth, the team surged into the pennant race.

With a 6-4 win over the Giants at the Polo Grounds on September 24, the Cardinals clinched their first National league pennant and their first title of any kind since 1888 (when they lost the World's Series to the Giants). As the Cardinals prepared to face the mighty New York Yankees in the World Series, Rogers Hornsby's mother died. Hornsby decided to postpone her funeral until after the Series. As he told a group of reporters, "It was her greatest ambition to have me play in the World Series. My aunt told me that the last thing my mother had said was that I play in the World Series come what may."[21]

The World Series opened at Yankee Stadium on Saturday, October 2. The Yankees struck first, winning 2-1 as Herb Pennock tossed a complete game. Bill Sherdel took the loss. The Cardinals won the next day as home runs by Southworth and shortstop Tommy Thevenow powered their attack. Alexander struck out 10 while going the distance in the 6-2 victory.

In St. Louis the Cardinals won Game Three as Haines threw a shutout and hit a home run in the 4-0 Cardinal win. The Yankees got back even the next day as Ruth homered three times in the 10-5 Yankee win. In Game Five Bill Sherdel and Pennock both went the distance as the Yankees prevailed, 3-2 in 10 innings. The Cardinals stood one game from elimination as the Series moved back to Yankee Stadium.

Before Game Six, Hornsby delivered a speech that was meant to get his players refocused: "If we don't do it today, there ain't any more Series. But there is going to be more Series. We've got to win today and we've got to win tomorrow. So get out there, fight your heads off, knock the ball down the pitcher's throat, and don't concede a thing."[22] The Cardinals humbled the Yankees, 10-2, as Alexander went the distance for the second time. As hard as he pitched that day, he celebrated even harder that night.

October 10 dawned cold, dark, and overcast. Only 38,093 people showed up for Game Seven. Jesse Haines started for the Cardinals against Waite Hoyt. The Yankees drew first blood on a Ruth home run in the third—his fourth of the Series. The Cardinals struck back with three runs in the fourth. The Yankees added a tally in the sixth. The Cardinals led, 3-2. The stage was set.

Alexander was in the bullpen nursing his hangover from the night before. In the bottom of the seventh inning, Haines was beginning to tire. The bases were loaded and Tony Lazzeri was coming up. Sherdel was warming up, but Hornsby wanted Alexander. Hornsby recalled, "I trotted about halfway out to the outfield to meet Alex. 'Well, the bases are full,' I told him. 'Lazzeri's up and there ain't no place to put him.'"[23] As Alexander himself recalled, "I wasn't worried about the spot I was in. Naw. You know, I always had one motto, and it was this: 'I'm a better pitcher than you are a hitter.' I carried that idea into every game. Besides, Lazzeri hadn't bothered me in the Series. Of course, if he'd a hit one, it wouldn't have been so good. But, he didn't."[24] Lazzeri took Alexander's first pitch for a ball. The next one was a strike. He got hold of the third pitch and it looked like a sure grand slam, but the ball was foul by about ten inches. Strike two. Alexander then threw a fastball. Lazzeri swung late and missed. Strike three. The side was retired in the Yankees' seventh. Alexander retired the Yankees in order in the eighth and the Cardinals were scoreless in the top of the ninth. Alexander was still on the mound for the Yankees' half of the ninth. He got Earle Combs and Mark Koenig on grounders to third. Then came the heart of the Yankee order—Ruth, Bob Meusel, and Gehrig. Ruth drew a walk, and was the potential tying run. As Alexander threw a low curve to Meusel, Ruth broke for second. Catcher Bob O'Farrell threw a strike to Hornsby at second to nail Ruth. It was all over. The Cardinals had their first championship in 40 years! The city of St. Louis went wild.

Hornsby's joy proved to be short-lived. He was critical of owner Breadon whenever he disagreed with his policies. He wanted a three-year contract, but Breadon was offering a one-year, $50,000 deal, which would have made Hornsby the second highest paid player in baseball behind Babe Ruth. On December 20, 1926, Breadon traded Hornsby to the New York Giants for second baseman Frankie Frisch and pitcher Jimmy Ring. It was said that Hornsby's taste for gambling was a factor in the trade as Breadon had requested that he stop betting on horse races. (Hornsby owned 12.5 percent of the stock in the Cardinals, and major-league rules prevented a player from owning stock in one club while playing for another. Hornsby wound up getting $110,000 for his stock—$86,000 from Breadon, $12,000 from the Giants and $2,000 from the other clubs.)[?] The deal was completed on April 8, 1927.[25]

Meanwhile, catcher Bob O'Farrell, who had been voted the National League's Most Valuable Player in 1926, had been named Hornsby's successor as the Cardinals' player-manager.

Cardinal fans hoped for a second consecutive championship in 1927, but it was not be. The club won 92 games, three more than in 1926, but Pittsburgh finished in first place by 1 1/2 games. After the season O'Farrell was dropped as manager, but he remained as the catcher. His replacement was Bill McKechnie, who had managed the Pirates to a World Series victory in 1925.

After the disappointment of 1927, the Cardinals and their fans hoped things would be different in 1928. They were. The Cardinals took over first place on June 15 and stayed there the rest of the season. McKechnie coaxed another good season out of the aging Alexander (16-9, 3.36 ERA). Sunny Jim Bottomley hit 31 home runs and drove in 136 runs, left fielder Chick Hafey hit .337, and Frisch became the glue of the infield and hit .300. The Cardinals won 95 games and clinched the pennant on the next-to-last day of the season.

For the Cardinals, the 1928 World Series was something of an anticlimax. They faced their foes from 1926, the Yankees, and this time they were no match for the Murderers' Row lineup as they fell in four straight games. Babe Ruth and Lou Gehrig led the Yankee attack, combining to hit seven home runs. Ruth hit three (all of them in Game Four) and Gehrig hit four (one in Game Two, two in Game Three, and one in Game Four). Despite giving Cardinals fans their second pennant in three years, Bill McKechnie was shown the door after the season. He was replaced by Billy Southworth, who had been managing the Cardinals' top farm team in Rochester.

The 1929 club started off fairly well and was in first place as late as June 18. They lost to the Cubs that day 13-6, and began a skid in which they won only one of their next 16 games. A 9-5 loss at home to the Cubs on June 28 put the team in fourth place, which is where they stayed for the rest of the season. Southworth was fired in midseason and McKechnie was brought back. There was one last highlight left for Pete Alexander: On August 10 he pitched four scoreless innings in relief and got the win as the Cardinals defeated the Phillies

11-9 in 11 innings. The win was the 373rd and last of his storied career, tying him with Christy Mathewson for the most career pitching victories in the National League. The 1929 Cardinals finished fourth with a record of 78-74, 20 games out of first. After the season McKechnie was replaced as manager by Gabby Street.

The Cardinals started off slowly under Street in 1930, but they started to catch fire for a brief period in late May. They were up by a half-game on May 27 but, in almost a direct parallel to the previous season, they went into another horrendous skid, winning only two of their next 16 games. The team struggled for most of the year, but then took off in the final two months, winning 44 of its final 57 games. On September 16 a 1-0 victory over Brooklyn at Ebbets Field put them in first place to stay. Then they won 10 of their final 12 games to finish with a 92-62 record. Jesse Haines pitched the Cardinals to a 10-5 pennant-clinching win against Pittsburgh at home two days before the end of the season. In the season's final game, a glimpse into the future was offered by a brash young right-handed pitcher from Springdale, Arkansas, Dizzy Dean, who pitched a 3-1, complete-game victory over the Pirates.

There was still the matter of the World Series. The Cardinals faced the Philadelphia Athletics, who were in the midst of a run that took them to three consecutive pennants and one world championship. The A's boasted a powerful lineup that many said was every inch the equal of the Yankees'. Mickey Cochrane, the catcher, batted .357. First baseman Jimmie Foxx and outfielder Al Simmons combined for 73 home runs and 321 RBIs. Lefty Grove was the team's best pitcher, going 28-5 with a 2.54 ERA. George Earnshaw won 22 games. The Cardinals had a powerful lineup themselves; all eight of their starting position players hit over .300. As a team the Cardinals batted .314. (Baseball's moguls had juiced up the offense that season, and individual and team averages were high.)

The World Series opened at Shibe Park in Philadelphia on October 1 with the A's winning the first two games. The Series shifted to St. Louis for Games Three, Four, and Five. In Game Three, Wild Bill Hallahan pitched a seven-hit shutout to give the Cardinals a 5-0 win. The next day Haines pitched a four-hitter to win, 3-1, and even the Series at two games apiece. The A's won Game Five, 2-0, and, back at Shibe Park they captured the Series with a 7-1 victory. Bottomley, who had made a spectacular catch of a Jimmie Foxx foul pop when he leaped into the box seats in the sixth inning of Game Three, had an otherwise miserable Series, going 1-for-22.

Street returned as the Cardinals skipper in 1931. This time, except for a couple of brief stretches, it was a wire-to-wire finish as the Cardinals cruised to their fourth pennant in six seasons. They finished with a record of 101-53, becoming the first team in franchise history to win 100 or more games in a season.

On September 20 Street caught the first three innings of a 6-1 loss to the Brooklyn Robins at home. He came to bat once before giving way to Mike Gonzalez. At 48 years and 355 days old, it was Street's first major-league game since 1912. (Gonzalez, himself 40 years old, caught in parts of 15 games that season before beginning his long coaching career.)

The Cardinals again faced Philadelphia in the World Series. The lineups for both squads were largely the same, but the outcome was different. The Series opened at Sportsman's Park and, as in the previous season, the A's drew first blood with a 6-2 victory. The Cardinals drew even with a 2-0 win the next day as Pepper Martin scored the second run on a squeeze bunt by Charlie Gelbert.

When the Series shifted to Philadelphia, the Cardinals took Game Three as Burleigh Grimes beat the A's, 5-2. Martin had a single and a double and scored twice. The A's evened the Series in Game Four as Earnshaw pitched a two-hit shutout to win 3-0. Martin got both Cardinals hits. The Cardinals won Game Five, 5-1, as Martin had three hits, including a home run, and drove in four runs. The A's evened the Series with an 8-1 romp in Game Six, but the Cardinals closed it out with a 4-2 win in Game Seven. Martin was the star of the Series, batting .500 with 12 hits, 5 stolen bases, and 5 RBIs. His all-out hustle had earlier earned him the nickname Wild Horse of the Osage.

The Cardinals were never a factor in the 1932 pennant race as they slipped below .500, posting a record of 72-82 and finishing in a tie for sixth place, 18 games behind the pennant-winning Cubs. One highlight of the dismal season was the return of Dizzy Dean to the big leagues. Dean burst onto the scene with a record of 18-15, 191 strikeouts, and a 3.30 ERA. That season also saw the big-league debut of 20-year-old outfielder Joe Medwick. In a 26-game "cup of coffee," Medwick batted .349 with 2 home runs and 12 RBIs.

The 1933 Cardinals fared somewhat better. They stumbled out of the gate, losing nine of 14 games, but staged a midseason rally and were in first place by one game on June 4 after a 4-2 win over the Reds at Crosley Field. They were tied for the lead as late as June 17 after a 17-2 shellacking of the Reds in Cincinnati, but faded and finished in fifth place, 9 1/2 games behind the pennant-winning New York Giants. They still posted a winning record at 82-71.

Dizzy Dean was 20-18 with 199 strikeouts, a 3.04 ERA, and a league-leading 26 complete games. On July 30 he set a major-league record by striking out 17 hitters in 6-2 win over the Cubs. Dizzy liked to coin colorful quotes for whatever situation he was in. When he was asked about his record-setting performance, he said: "Shoot! If I'da known I was settin' a record, I'da gotten me more strikeouts."

Two moves made during the 1933 season helped to shape the future of the Gas House Gang. On May 7 the Cardinals traded pitchers Paul Derringer and Allyn Stout and third baseman Sparky Adams to the Cincinnati Reds for shortstop Leo Durocher, pitchers Jack Ogden and Dutch Henry, and catcher Butch Henline. Durocher exhibited the fiery, combative nature that came to define the Gas House Gang, and became the team's captain.

On July 24, after the Cardinals had lost nine out of 12 games, Gabby Street told Rickey he felt he was losing control of the team. Rickey said, "Name the players and I'll trade them. If you don't discipline them now, they'll run you right out of your job."[26] After naming the players he felt were at the root of the problem, Street said, "I'm through, Branch. I'm pushed."[27]

Sam Breadon decided to fire Street. Frankie Frisch tried to get Breadon to let Street finish out the season. He recalled: "I said, 'Mr. Breadon, why don't you just let Gabby finish out the season? We've only got about two months more and it wouldn't be such a blow to him if the change were made in the winter months."[28]

Breadon replied, "I am going to make a change, Frank. The club is out of hand. Gabby doesn't have control of the situation as he did in 1930 and 1931. I'd like you to try your hand at it. During the remaining two months, you can be studying what you'd like to do next year. I think it is the wisest course."[29]

So Frisch was named the player-manager of the St Louis Cardinals for their historic 1934 season.

Sources

Achorn, Edward, *The Summer of Beer and Whiskey* (New York: Public Affairs Books, 2013).

Anderson, Dave, *More Than Merkle* (Lincoln: University of Nebraska Press, 2000).

Cash, Jon David, *Before They Were Cardinals: A History of Major League Baseball in 19th Century St. Louis* (Columbia, Missouri: University of Missouri Press, 2002).

Doutrich, Paul E., *The Cardinals and the Yankees, 1926: A Classic Season and St. Louis in Seven* (Jefferson, North Carolina: McFarland & Company Publishers, Inc., 2011).

Felber, Bill, et al., *Inventing Baseball: The 100 Greatest Games of the Nineteenth Century* (Phoenix: Society for American Baseball Research, 2013).

Golenbock, Peter, *The Spirit of St. Louis: A History of the St. Louis Cardinals and Browns* (New York: HarperCollins Publishers, Inc. 2000).

Heindry, John, *The Gashouse Gang* (New York: Public Affairs Books, 2007).

Hetrick, J. Thomas, *Chris Von der Ahe and the St. Louis Browns* (Lanham, Maryland: Scarecrow Press, 1999).

Murphy, Cait, *Crazy '08* (New York: Harper Collins Publishers, 2007).

Snyder, John, *Cardinals Journal* (Cincinnati: Clerisy Press, 2010)

Sugar, Bert Randolph, *The Baseball Trivia Book to End All Baseball Trivia Books … Promise!* (New York: Freundlich Books, 1986)

"Ken Burns' Baseball. Inning Five. Shadow Ball," (Washington: PBS Video, 1994).

baseball-reference.com

retrosheet.org

Notes

1. Jon David Cash, *Before They Were Cardinals: A History of Major League Baseball in 19th Century St. Louis*, 27. Hereafter cited as Cash.
2. Cash, 9.
3. Ibid.

4   Bill Felber et al., *Inventing Baseball: The 100 Greatest Games of the Nineteenth Century,* 100. Hereafter cited as SABR.

5   SABR, 102.

6   J. Thomas Hetrick, *Chris Von der Ahe and the St. Louis Browns,* 53.

7   Cash, 60.

8   Ibid.

9   Cash, 64.

10 John Snyder, *Cardinals Journal,* 12. Hereafter cited as Snyder.

11 Edward Achorn, *The Summer of Beer and Whiskey,* 267-68. Hereinafter cited as Achorn.

12 Snyder, 37.

13 Achorn, 13.

14 Achorn, 253.

15 Snyder, 84.

16 Snyder, 87.

17 Cait Murphy, *Crazy '08,* 68. Hereafter cited as Murphy.

18 Snyder, 123.

19 Peter Golenbock, *The Spirit of St. Louis: A History of the St. Louis Cardinals and Browns,* 88. Hereafter cited as Golenbock.

20 Ibid.

21 Paul E. Doutrich, *The Cardinals and Yankees, 1926,* 153.

22 Golenbock, 111.

23 Golenbock, 115.

24 Golenbock, 114.

25 Snyder, 214.

26 Golenbock, 164.

27 Golenbock, 165.

28 Ibid.

29 Ibid.

Assembling the Gas House Gang

By John J. Watkins

WHEN BRANCH RICKEY returned to the St. Louis Cardinals after briefly serving in the Army during World War I, the club was broke. Although he scraped together $10,000 to purchase the contract of pitcher Jesse Haines from the Class AA Kansas City Blues after the 1919 season, Rickey knew that his small-market team lacked the gate receipts to compete with the likes of the New York Giants and Yankees in buying top players from the three largest minor leagues, which were then exempt from the player draft. When an owner of a team in one of these leagues learned of Rickey's interest in a player, he would simply invite one of the large-market clubs to outbid the cash-strapped Cardinals.

It was in this environment that Rickey conceived of the modern farm system. "Good farmer that he was," historian Harold Seymour observed, "Rickey decided to grow his own crop on his own land."[1] With funds available from new owner Sam Breadon's shrewd sale of decrepit Robison Field and his lease of Sportsman's Park on favorable terms from the Browns, Rickey began putting together a network of minor-league teams owned by the Cardinals for development of players. Those with talent could be used to restock the St. Louis roster as needed, traded to other teams for quality players, or sold outright for a handsome profit.

The Cardinals began in late 1919 by purchasing a half-interest in the Fort Smith, Arkansas, franchise in the Western Association (then a Class D league). The following spring, the club acquired an 18 percent interest in the Houston Buffaloes of the Texas League (then Class B). Next came a 50 percent share in the Syracuse Stars of the Class AA International League in early 1921. Rickey soon arranged to buy the other half-interest in the Syracuse club, and by 1925 St. Louis owned 90 percent of the stock in the Houston team, by then in Class A. Three years later, having dumped Syracuse in favor of Rochester, New York, St. Louis owned seven clubs spanning all levels of the minors and controlled 203 minor-league players.[2]

The farm system paid off for the Cardinals on the field and at the bank. St. Louis won six National League pennants and four World Series championships from 1922 through 1942, Rickey's last season. During the same period, the sale of surplus players to other clubs added an estimated $2 million to the Cardinals' bottom line. Largely because of these sales, St. Louis realized a profit more than twice that of any other National League club between 1925 and 1950 despite paid attendance much smaller than that of the Cubs, Dodgers, and Giants.[3]

Predictably, Rickey assembled the 1934 team, later dubbed the Gas House Gang, using the method he had envisioned when building the St. Louis minor-league network. Sid Keener, sports editor of the *St. Louis Star-Times*, viewed the Cardinals' World Series triumph over Detroit as a victory for "the chain-store system." The St. Louis club was put together "largely with material from its farms," Keener wrote, estimating that direct player acquisition costs did "not exceed $40,000."[4] On further review 80 years later, his assessment holds up rather well.

Of the 21 St. Louis players on the World Series roster,[5] ten came up through the Cardinals' farm system, and four were obtained by trades for players that the system had developed. Of the remaining seven players, four were acquired by contract purchases and three in trades that did not involve players from the St. Louis organization.

From the farm system came pitchers Dizzy Dean, Paul Dean, Tex Carleton, and Bill Hallahan, outfielders Joe Medwick and Ernie Orsatti, third baseman Pepper Martin, first baseman Ripper Collins, catcher Bill DeLancey, and utility infielder Burgess Whitehead. Trades of other farm products landed pitchers Bill Walker and Jim Mooney, outfielder Chick Fullis, and shortstop Leo Durocher, while other trades secured the services of player-manager Frankie Frisch, outfielder Jack Rothrock, and catcher Spud Davis. In addition to Jesse Haines, who had pitched for St. Louis since 1920, the other players acquired via contract purchase were pitcher Dazzy Vance, reserve infielder-pinch hitter Pat Crawford, and bullpen catcher Francis Healy.

The Cardinals stocked their farm system with players discovered by a far-flung network of scouts, most of whom worked part-time, and identified at tryout camps open to all comers. The Dean brothers, for instance, were signed by scout Don Curtis, whose regular job was as a brakeman on the Missouri, Kansas & Texas railroad line.[6] Medwick was signed as an 18-year-old off the New Jersey sandlots and Hallahan as a 19-year-old pitching for the Corona Typewriter Company's team in Groton, New York.[7] DeLancey broke in at Class C Shawnee, Oklahoma, at age 18 and four years later was the Cardinals' regular catcher, having taken over from the veteran Davis midway through the 1934 season.[8]

Martin's raw talent was recognized at a tryout camp in Greenville, Texas, where he arrived on a freight train a few days after he lost his first professional job with a team in his native Oklahoma when the league folded. Although Martin signed with the Class D Greenville club and played 27 games there, chief scout Charley Barrett of the Cardinals kept tabs on him and recommended that Rickey buy his contract.[9] The Cardinals did so, for $500.[10] At the other end of the spectrum, Whitehead made the jump from the University of North Carolina to Class AA ball at Columbus, Ohio, in the American Association.[11]

Scouts spotted some players toiling in the lower minors. Carleton, for example, initially signed with the Texarkana Twins in the Class D East Texas League in 1925 after two years at Texas Christian University. Following a contract dispute he moved to the Marshall Indians in the same league and was recommended to the Cardinals by scout Jack Ryan.[12] Similarly, Orsatti was plucked from Cedar Rapids, Iowa, of the Class D Mississippi Valley League, where he had landed in 1925 after a six-game stint in the Pacific Coast League arranged by film star Buster Keaton, for whom Orsatti had worked as a stand-in.[13]

Collins might be included in this group with an asterisk, as St. Louis acquired his contract when it purchased the Rochester club in the International League.[14] He had twice hit better than .300 in the lower minors but blossomed into a fearsome hitter in the Cardinals' organization. At Rochester, the Ripper batted .315 with 38 home runs in 1929 and .376 with 40 home runs in 1930.

By trade, St. Louis secured Durocher's services in a six-player deal with Cincinnati in early May 1933. For the Reds, the key to the transaction was pitcher Paul Derringer, who had come up through the Cardinals' farm system, although third baseman Sparky Adams, originally purchased from Pittsburgh in 1929, was also included.[15] In a four-player trade, St. Louis obtained pitchers Bill Walker and Jim Mooney from the New York Giants in 1932 for catcher Gus Mancuso and pitcher Ray Starr, both of whom had originally been signed by the Cardinals organization.[16]

The deal for the fourth player in this group was circuitous. St. Louis obtained Fullis, who platooned with Orsatti in center field, at the June 15 trading deadline in a transaction that sent center fielder Kiddo Davis to the Philadelphia Phillies. Davis had come to St. Louis during spring training in a trade with the New York Giants for holdout George Watkins, who had hit .309 over the previous four seasons as the Cardinals' regular right fielder. Watkins was a product of the St. Louis farm system, having been signed from the Houston amateur leagues.[17]

Of the seven other players, two were vital to the team's success: Frankie Frisch, the second baseman and manager, and Jack Rothrock, the right fielder. Both were acquired by trades that did not involve players from the St. Louis "chain store."

In December 1926, the Cardinals traded Rogers Hornsby, who had just led the club to its first World Series championship, to the New York Giants for the Bronx-born and Fordham-educated Frisch and journeyman pitcher Jimmy Ring. The blockbuster deal angered St. Louis fans — Sam Breadon received death threats[18] — but their attitude changed as Frisch helped the Redbirds to three pennants and a World Series title over the next five seasons. Shortly after Frisch played in the first All-Star team game in 1933, he became the Cardinals' player-manager.

Rothrock, a switch-hitter who had begun his major-league career with the Boston Red Sox, came to the

Cardinals from the Chicago White Sox in November 1932 with infielder Carey Selph to complete a deal made on September 11 for outfielder Evar Swanson. He spent the 1933 season at Class AA Columbus, where he hit .347 and made the all-star team. When the Cardinals traded George Watkins to the Giants during spring training in 1934, Rothrock stepped into the right-field spot.[19]

St. Louis initially obtained Spud Davis, who opened the season as the number one catcher, from Buffalo in the 1927 Rule 5 draft but traded him to Philadelphia in May 1928 in a deal to obtain catcher Jimmie Wilson. The clubs swapped the two players again after the 1933 season, with Wilson becoming player-manager of the Phillies and Davis returning to the Cardinals.

Pitchers Haines and Vance were both nearing the end of careers that would lead to the Hall of Fame. The Cardinals' purchase of Haines' contract for $10,000 after the 1919 season marked the last time that Rickey would spend such a significant sum for a minor-league player during his tenure in St. Louis.[20] Vance, a star with Brooklyn in the 1920s, was traded to St. Louis before the 1933 season. He finished 6-2 for the fifth-place Cardinals but was waived in February 1934 and picked up by Cincinnati. When the Redbirds' pitching staff was stretched thin in late June, however, Vance returned to St. Louis via the waiver wire.

Crawford, a graduate of Davidson College, broke in with the New York Giants in 1929 and was traded to Cincinnati shortly after the 1930 season began. When the Reds traded him to Hollywood of the Pacific Coast League in November, he announced that he would retire and further his education, forcing Cincinnati to send another player to Hollywood to complete the deal. In the spring of 1931, shortly after the Cardinals had purchased the Columbus franchise from Cincinnati, Columbus general manager Larry MacPhail worked out an arrangement whereby Crawford could attend Ohio State part-time to obtain his master's degree.[21] Though retired, he remained under the Reds' control, and St. Louis paid Cincinnati $5,000 for his contract.[22] After two seasons with Columbus, Crawford joined the Cardinals in 1933.

In far simpler transaction, St. Louis purchased the 23-year-old Healy's contract from the New York Giants in early May. He had spent the 1933 season in the minors after having played sparingly for the Giants from 1930-1932.

Ten other players dotted on the St. Louis roster during the season, most making only cameo appearances. Of this group, six came from the Cardinals' farm system, including pitchers Clarence Heise (0-0) and Jim Winford (0-2),[23] third baseman Lew Riggs (two games, one at-bat),[24] and outfielder Buster Mills (.236 in 29 games). Mills, a four-sport letterman at the University of Oklahoma, caught the eye of Cardinals chief scout Charley Barrett when the Sooner baseball team played Washington University in St. Louis. Barrett wanted to sign him but mistakenly inked a different player because of a teammate's erroneous identification. Mills later signed with Cleveland but eventually wound up in the St. Louis farm system.[25]

Pitcher Flint Rhem (1-0) and outfielder Red Worthington (one at-bat) can also be so categorized, although in 1934 they arrived in St. Louis from other clubs. The Cardinals signed Rhem, who played at Clemson University and in the tough South Carolina textile leagues, in 1924. With the exception of 1929, which he spent at Rochester, he was with the Cardinals from 1925 through 1931. St. Louis sold his contract to the Phillies in June 1932 but repurchased it in February 1934.[26] Worthington was signed by the Cardinals organization in 1925 while touring with a semipro team shortly after he had graduated high school.[27] After he had worked his way up to Rochester, the Cardinals sold his contract to the Boston Braves, and he spent 1931-1933 and most of 1934 with that club. St. Louis picked him up off waivers on September 11, 1934, and three days later, he struck out as a pinch hitter in a loss to the Giants at the Polo Grounds. It was his only appearance for the Cardinals and his last major-league game.

Another of the ten players, the aforementioned Kiddo Davis (.303 in 16 games), was obtained by trade for a product of the St. Louis farm system. According to speculation at the time, that may have also been the case with another outfielder, Gene Moore (.278 in 9 games). On paper, Moore was acquired in January 1933 when the Reds sold his contract to the Houston Buffs.[28] Reports in *The Sporting News* and other newspapers, however, suggested that he was one of nine additional Cincinnati players sent to the St. Louis organization as part of deal for first baseman Jim Bottomley the previous month.[29] Formally, the Reds had traded only pitcher Ownie Carroll and outfielder Estel Crabtree for Sunny Jim.[30]

One player's contract was purchased outright: pitcher Jim Lindsey (0-1), acquired in early June from the St. Paul Saints of the Class AA American Association. Lindsey, who at age 26 went from the Louisiana sandlots to the Cleveland Indians in 1922, had been with St. Louis from 1930-32. The Cardinals' Columbus farm team sold his contract to Cincinnati in February 1934,[31] and in late May the Reds traded him to St. Paul. A few days later St. Louis bought his contract.[32]

Also on his second tour of duty with the Cardinals was Burleigh Grimes (2-1), who had signed as a free agent in July 1933. St. Louis obtained Grimes in mid-June 1930 in a trade with the Boston Braves, and the last legal spitballer won 13 games as the Cardinals mounted a furious stretch drive to clinch the pennant. In 1931, he was on the mound for two St. Louis wins in the World Series against the powerful Philadelphia Athletics, including the seventh game. With Dizzy Dean waiting in the wings, the Cardinals traded Grimes to the Cubs two months later. But when St. Louis needed pitching help in 1933, the club signed him the day after Chicago released him.[33]

How did Sid Keener of the *St. Louis Star-Times* determine that the Cardinals assembled the Gas House Gang for less than $40,000 in direct player acquisition costs? Here are his numbers: Jesse Haines — $10,000 to Kansas City; Leo Durocher — $7,500, the amount paid to Pittsburgh for Sparky Adams, who went to Cincinnati in trade for Durocher; Pat Crawford — $5,000 to Cincinnati; Dazzy Vance — $4,000, the waiver price, to Cincinnati; Francis Healy — $4,000, the waiver price, to the New York Giants; and Jack Rothrock — $3,000 to the Chicago White Sox, for a total of $33,500.[34]

This list is not complete, but the omissions probably do not increase the total to much past $40,000. As mentioned, the cost of Pepper Martin's minor-league contract was $500.[35] The cash outlay for Frankie Frisch was $600, the amount that St. Louis paid in 1915 to buy Rogers Hornsby's contract from a Class D club in Texas, the Denison Railroaders.[36] Red Worthington's one pinch-hit appearance cost $4,000, the waiver price paid to the Braves, although the Cardinals' Rochester farm club probably sold his contract to Boston for a higher sum four years earlier. For four other contract purchases — Lindsey, Moore, Orsatti, and Rhem — the amount is unknown.

Even if the direct costs were, say, $45,000, by one measure the St. Louis National Baseball Club, Inc., tripled its money. Its share of the 1934 World Series proceeds was $144,238.57.[37]

Notes

1   Harold Seymour, *Baseball: The Golden Age* (New York: Oxford University Press, 1971), 414.

2   Lee Lowenfish, *Branch Rickey: Baseball's Ferocious Gentleman* (Lincoln, Nebraska: University of Nebraska Press: 2007), 82, 123; Jim Mandelaro and Scott Pitoniak, *Silver Seasons: The Story of the Rochester Red Wings* (Syracuse, New York: Syracuse University Press, 1996), 23; Arthur Mann, *Branch Rickey: American in Action* (Boston: Houghton Mifflin Co., 1957), 109-10, 112; J. Roy Stockton, *The Gas House Gang and a Couple of Other Guys* (New York: A.S. Barnes & Co., 1945), 22; *Organized Baseball*, Report of the Subcommittee on Study of Monopoly Power of the Committee on the Judiciary, 82d Congress, 1st Sess. (May 27, 1952), 63 (testimony of Branch Rickey).

3   *Organized Baseball*, op cit., 95 (estimate for 1922 through 1941), citing Sid Keener, "Baseball's Rags-to-Riches Story — The Cards," *St. Louis Star-Times* (January 15-21, 1946); Seymour, op cit., 415.

4   "Scribbled by Scribes," *The Sporting News* (October 25, 1934), 4.

5   "Thumb-Nail Sketches of Cards and Tigers," *The Sporting News* (October 4, 1934), 3.

6   Robert Gregory, *Diz: The Story of Dizzy Dean and Baseball During the Great Depression* (New York: Viking, 1992), 36; Robert E. Hood, *The Gashouse Gang* (New York: William Morrow & Co., 1976), 74-75; Mann, op cit., 159.

7   Hood, op cit., 170, 220-21; Stockton, op cit., 29.

8   "Juvenile Card Star," *The Sporting News* (July 19, 1934), 1; Bob Broeg, *The Pilot Light and the Gas House Gang* (St. Louis: Bethany Press, 1980), 126.

9   Thomas Barthel, *Pepper Martin: A Baseball Biography* (Jefferson, North Carolina: McFarland & Co., 2003), 17-19.

10 Lieb, op cit., 150.

11 P.R. White, "Cardinals Grooming Whitehead on Farm as Eventual Successor to Frankie Frisch," *The Sporting News* (March 19, 1932), 8.

12 Gregory Wolf, "Tex Carleton," SABR Baseball Biography Project (Society for American Baseball Research), http://sabr.org/bioproj/person/80d4f848.

13 Obituary, Ernie Orsatti, *The Sporting News* (September 21, 1968), 36.

14 Stockton, op cit., 29.

15 Lowenfish, op cit., 229. St. Louis also traded St. Louis pitcher Allyn Stout, who had risen through the ranks of the Cardinals' farm system. The other Reds were pitchers Dutch Henry and Jack Ogden, former major leaguers then in the minors.

16 The Giants also sent two veterans, catcher Bob O'Farrell and outfielder Ethan Allen, to St. Louis in the deal, but neither was on the Cardinals' 1934 roster. St. Louis traded O'Farrell, a member of the Redbirds' 1926 World Series championship team, and pitcher Syl Johnson to Cincinnati in January 1934 for pitcher Glenn Spencer, who spent the season in the minors. The following month, the Cardinals sold Allen's contract to the Phillies.

17 Harry T. Brundidge, "Brother Sacrificed Chance for Diamond Career to Give Like Opportunity to George Watkins, Cards' Outfielder," *The Sporting News* (November 5, 1931), 5.

18 Lowenfish, op cit., 173.

19 Bill Nowlin, "Jack Rothrock," SABR Baseball Biography Project (Society for American Baseball Research), http://sabr.org/bioproj/person/6551658d.

20 Lowenfish, op cit., 110.

21 Hood, op cit., 192-94.

22 "Scribbled by Scribes," op cit.

23 Heise signed with St. Louis in 1928 and began his career that season at Laurel, Mississippi, in the Class D Cotton States League. Philip Singerman, "Field of Dreams This Baseball Season, These Three Men Share Life in the Minor Leagues," *Orlando Sentinel* (August 11, 1985), 9; Baseball-Reference.com, http://www.baseball-reference.com/minors/team.cgi?id=400f8627 (listing "Heise?" on the roster). Winford came up through the St. Louis organization, starting in 1929 with Scottdale in the Class C Middle Atlantic League. Baseball-Reference.com, http://www.baseball-reference.com/minors/team.cgi?id=13da87df. Heise was also at Scottdale that season.

24 Riggs attended the University of North Carolina, where he played basketball and baseball. The Cardinals signed him for $2,500 after the spring term of 1930. Whitney Martin, "Riggs to Draw Third Straight Series Check," *Spartanburg Herald* (September 30, 1941), 6.

25 Bill Nowlin, "Buster Mills," SABR Baseball Biography Project (Society for American Baseball Research), http://sabr.org/bioproj/person/89af0f16.

26 Nancy Snell Griffth, "Flint Rhem," SABR Baseball Biography Project (Society for American Baseball Research), http://sabr.org/bioproj/person/97c73ab1.

27 Obituary, Robert (Red) Worthington, *The Sporting News* (December 28, 1963), 26.

28 "Gene Moore Shipped to Texas League Ball Team," *Rochester Democrat-Chronicle* (January 11, 1933), 11.

29 Tom Swope, "11 Reds Have Moved in Cincy-Cards Deals," *The Sporting News* (January 26, 1933), 3; Sam Murphy, "Knickerbocker Gains 10 Pounds," *New York Sun* (January 30, 1933), 22.

30 Lowenfish, op cit., 118-19.

31 "Recruits to Swell Red Training Squad," *The Sporting News* (February 22, 1934), 2.

32 The next day, June 23, the Cardinals sent Flint Rhem to Syracuse. "Highlights of the Week," *The Sporting News* (June 14, 1934), 4.

33 "Burleigh Grimes Signs with Cards for Rest of Year," *St. Petersburg Times* (August 1, 1933), 8; "National League," *The Sporting News* (August 3, 1933), 8.

34 "Scribbled by Scribes," op cit. To reach $40,000, Keener included "a generous guess" of the "small expense accounts" submitted by St. Louis scouts "for their travels and incidentals."

35 Lieb, op cit., 150.

36 Charles C. Alexander, *Rogers Hornsby: A Biography* (New York: Henry Holt & Co., 1995), 20.

37 "Facts on the Series," *The Sporting News* (October 11, 1934), 7.

Sportsman's Park (St. Louis)

By Scott Ferkovich

IN BASEBALL HISTORY there have been certain street corners that through the years have become synonymous with the ballparks located at them. At the corner of Michigan and Trumbull was Detroit's Tiger Stadium. 21st and Lehigh was Shibe Park in Philadelphia. Findlay and Western was Cincinnati's Crosley Field. On the South Side of Chicago, 35th and Shields was Comiskey Park. Today, Clark and Addison carries on this tradition with Wrigley Field. To old-time baseball fans in St. Louis, there is another hallowed corner that can be added to the list: Grand and Dodier. From the days when amateur baseball clubs first laid out a rough diamond there in the mid-1860s until the Cardinals played their final game at Busch Stadium a century later, the fabled corner on the north side of St. Louis was witness to some great baseball.

In the 19th century several teams called Grand and Dodier home. The first professional circuit, the National Association of Professional Baseball Players, had a St. Louis entry in 1875, known as the Brown Stockings. They played at a park called the Grand Avenue Ball Grounds, which was really nothing fancier than a single grandstand for the paying customers. The league folded after that year.

The park's name was changed to Sportsman's Park in 1876 with the arrival of the St. Louis Brown Stockings, a charter member of the new National League. After the 1877 season, the Brown Stockings went bankrupt, and the city was without a professional baseball team for four years.

In 1882 the new American Association was formed, with yet another St. Louis Brown Stockings team. Soon the name was shortened to Browns. The team fielded some of the strongest teams of the decade, finishing first from 1885 through 1888. They were led by young player-manager Charles Comiskey. The team's owner was German-American saloonkeeper Chris von der Ahe, who renovated Sportsman's Park. By keeping ticket prices low, the Browns were annually among the league leaders in attendance, and their fans were left over with more money to spend on beer at games. Von der Ahe was a born promoter. In an effort to sell even more brew, he put up a beer garden in the right-field corner at Sportsman's Park, which, oddly enough, was in play. Eventually the rules were changed so that a ball hit into the beer garden was a home run.

The American Association folded after 1891, and the Browns rejoined the National League. Grand and Dodier, however, sat vacant for the remainder of the decade, as the Browns moved to another location in the city.

With the dawning of the new century came an upstart new "major" league, Ban Johnson's American League, which featured an entry in Milwaukee called the Brewers. After struggling their only year in the Cream City, 1901, the franchise moved to St. Louis, changed its name to the Browns, and played at the newly refurbished Sportsman's Park at Grand and Dodier.

Like most venues of the era, Sportsman's Park was a wooden structure, susceptible to fires. But in the winter of 1908-09, the Browns' ballpark underwent an extensive renovation, and by Opening Day of 1909 it featured a double-decked (and fireproof) concrete and steel grandstand. A covered single-deck grandstand extended down the left-field line. The outfield was ringed by single-decked wooden bleachers. The seating capacity was listed as 24,040. That same summer two new ballparks built of reinforced concrete and structural steel opened: Shibe Park in Philadelphia and Forbes Field in Pittsburgh. Within the next few years, many new teams would build comparable modern stadiums. The era of the Classic Ballpark had begun.

Also calling Sportsman's Park home during this time was the St. Louis University football team, under legendary coach Eddie Cochems. Football historians will quickly identify him as the originator of an offense built around the forward pass, which revolutionized the game. In 1906 the team finished with an 11-0 record, taking advantage of the forward pass to outscore its opponents, 407-11.

From 1920 to 1953 Sportsman's Park was the home of both the Cardinals and Browns. The park on North Grand Blvd. was renamed Busch Stadium in 1953 after the original tenants, the St. Louis Browns, moved to Baltimore.

The National League's St. Louis Cardinals, the descendants of the Brown Stockings, had for years played at League Park, an outmoded and inadequate facility (the last wooden park, in fact, used by a major-league team). In July 1920 the Cardinals and Browns owner Phil Ball worked out an arrangement that allowed the Cardinals to move into Sportsman's Park as tenants. The Cardinals' offices were located at 3623 Dodier, the Browns' around the corner at 2911 North Grand. Both teams called Sportsman's Park home until the Browns left town for Baltimore after the 1953 season. As a result of the constant use, the field was perennially one of the worst in baseball.

The end of World War I brought an attendance boom to baseball in the early 1920s. To make room for more fans, Ball spent $500,000 to renovate the old ballpark. By the end of 1925 the park had taken on the form that it would assume for the rest of its days. The second deck now ran all the way down both foul lines. The old wooden bleachers in the outfield were replaced by concrete stands, including a covered pavilion from the right-field foul line to the center-field bleachers. The outfield distances were 351 feet to left field, 426 to dead center, and a mere 310 feet to right. The seating capacity was listed as 30,500. Sportswriter Red Smith called it "a garish, county fair sort of layout." The short distance to the right-field fence necessitated the addition in 1929 of one of the quirkiest features of the park: A 25-foot screen atop the 11 1/2-foot wall that extended 156 feet toward center, ending at the 354-foot mark in right-center. A batted ball that hit the screen was in play. (Years later, Cardinal great Stan Musial described the effects of the screen: "[It] made it much more interesting. The ball would fly out there and the runner didn't know if it was going to hit the screen, go over it, or how it would bounce."[1]) Because of the short distance to right, outfielders tended to play shallow, and thus had a better shot of throwing out runners at third or home on singles.)

The move by the Cardinals to bigger and better digs was the catalyst that forever changed the landscape of professional baseball in St. Louis. It was perhaps the most fortuitous decision the Cardinals franchise ever made. For the first two decades of the 20th century, neither the Browns nor the Cardinals fielded particularly competitive teams. After their second-place finish in their inaugural American League season in 1902, the Browns never placed that high again until 1922. The Cardinals, meanwhile, didn't fare much better, never topping third place from 1900 to 1925. But relocating to Sportsman's Park allowed Sam Breadon, the owner of the Cardinals, to sell League Park, the club's former home. Branch Rickey, the team's manager at the time, used the money to create baseball's first farm system. By being able to develop homegrown talent on minor-league teams that they owned, the Cardinals became one of the more progressive teams in baseball. As a result, the fortunes of the two St. Louis teams went in opposite directions. From 1926, when the Cardinals went to their first World Series, until early in the 1966 season, when they abandoned the Sportsman's Park neighborhood, the club went to the fall classic ten times, winning seven times. The Browns, meanwhile, became a byword for futility, a franchise that seemingly fell off the baseball radar for decades.

The Browns came close to a pennant in 1922, but lost out to the Yankees by one game. They never seriously contended again during the decade, but featured some exciting players. Slugging left fielder Ken Williams led the league in home runs (39) and RBIs (155) in 1922, and hit .326 in his ten years as a Brown. Center fielder Baby Doll Jacobson was a consistent .300 hitter and RBI man in these years. On the mound, the Browns had one of the best baseball names ever, in Urban Shocker. The right-handed Shocker was a fine pitcher for the club from 1918 to 1924, winning 126 games, with four straight 20-win seasons. But the biggest star ever to don a Browns uniform was first baseman George Sisler. Gorgeous George played with the Browns from 1915 to 1927 (he missed 1923 with illness), hitting .344 during those years, twice topping the .400 mark. His 1922 season was stunning: He led the league in average (.420), hits (246), runs (134), triples (18), and stolen bases (51). His OPS (on-base average plus slugging average) was 1.061. Sisler was elected to the Hall of Fame in 1939.

While the Cardinals never led the league in attendance in their years at Sportsman's Park, they did draw over a million fans in 13 different seasons. They annually outdrew their landlords by large margins. The highest single-season attendance for the Cardinals at Sportsman's Park was 1,430,676 in 1949, when they missed the pennant in a tight race with the Dodgers. The Browns, meanwhile, never topped the million mark at Grand and Dodier. Their highest single-season total was 712,918 in 1922. In a four-year stretch from 1933 to 1936, they drew fewer than 100,000 fans in a season three times, with a ridiculously low 80,922 in 1935. Even in the pennant-winning year of 1944, they attracted 508,644, fifth out of the eight American League teams.

By the middle of the 1920s, the Cardinals were beginning to come into their own as a franchise. Rogers Hornsby had emerged as perhaps the greatest right-handed hitter of all time. Certainly you cannot argue against a lifetime .358 batting average and 301 home runs. In 1926, with Hornsby as player-manager, the Cardinals reached the World Series for the first time, prevailing in seven games over the New York Yankees. In Game Four at Sportsman's Park, Babe Ruth hit three home runs, one of which cleared the pavilion roof in right field. Two years later the Babe had another three-homer game at Grand and Dodier, in Game Four of the 1928 Series, which the Yankees swept. A second Cardinals world championship followed in 1931, capping a season in which the club topped 100 victories for the first time.

Perhaps no Cardinals team is as fondly remembered as the Gas House Gang of 1934. Depression Era America fell in love with this colorful collection of hard-nosed, rough-and-tumble players who always seemed to have the dirtiest uniforms on the field.

The player-manager of the Gas House Gang was second baseman Frankie Frisch, known as the Fordham Flash for his having attended Fordham University, and his speed while starring in collegiate sports. At shortstop was scrappy Leo Durocher, a player as famous for his propensity for wearing flashy suits as for his refusal to back down from anyone who challenged him. He wasn't much of a hitter at the dish. Babe Ruth, in fact, had referred to him as the All-American Out. The batting order also boasted first baseman Ripper Collins, a Triple Crown winner in 1934 with a .333 average, 35 homers, and 128 RBIs; future Hall of Famer Joe "Ducky" Medwick also topped 100 RBIs, and added 18 home runs and a .319 average; and Pepper Martin, the hustling third baseman.

But the biggest star of the Gas House Gang was a farmboy from Lucas, Arkansas, Dizzy Dean. With a blazing fastball, the 24-year-old Dean won 30 games that year, the last National League pitcher to do so. His brother Paul won 19. Dizzy's meteoric career was cut short by injury, but it nonetheless warranted election to the Hall of Fame in 1953. He was brash, confident, and talented. But he also had a country-boy charm about him, and could tell a tale with the best of them, a quality that later helped him to forge a long career as a baseball broadcaster.

The Gas House Gang won 95 games in 1934, edging the New York Giants by two games. Their American League opponents in the World Series were the Detroit Tigers. One of baseball's most amusing fables emerged from this postseason. In Game Four, at Sportsman's Park, Dizzy was inserted as a pinch-runner at first base in the fourth inning. Trying to break up a double play, he was plunked in the forehead by the baseball on the relay throw to first base. A collective groan could be heard through Sportsman's Park as Dean lay unconscious for several moments on the field. He was carried off and taken to the hospital, before eventually being released. According to legend, a newspaper headline the next day ran, "X-Rays of Dean's Head Show Nothing." Game Seven was noteworthy for the near-riot that occurred at Navin Field in Detroit after a hard slide by Medwick into Detroit's third baseman, Marv Owen. The Gas House Gang won the last game in a blowout, 11-0, to take the world championship. The Dean brothers each won two games.

After the Depression, more and more ballparks were being outfitted with modern public-address systems. But not so at Sportsman's Park. For years announcers had to make the best of it by shouting into a megaphone while dashing around the perimeter of the field. Finally, in 1937, Sportsman's Park installed an electronic public-address system, one of the last ballparks to do so.

Starting in the 1930s, radio station KMOX began broadcasting Cardinals and Browns games. Because it was a 50,000-watt clear-channel station, games from Sportsman's Park could be heard throughout the Midwest and much of the South. This helped the Cardinals (they and the Browns were at the time the westernmost major-league teams) to develop a strong fan base throughout the nation's midsection. In 1945 broadcasting legend Harry Caray began calling games from his perch in the broadcasting booth behind home plate at Sportsman's Park. He would go on to call Cardinals games for 25 seasons before going to the White Sox and then the Cubs. One of the primary sponsors of the St. Louis broadcasts was locally brewed Griesedieck beer.

People attending games at Grand and Dodier in the 1930s would not have been able to avoid noticing the park's loudest fan. Mrs. Mary Ott, known as the Horse Lady, would tug at her ears and let out a neigh at the top of her lungs, much to the chagrin of umpires, opposing players, and the unfortunate people sitting in front of her.

In 1940 lights were installed at the ballpark. The Browns played the first night game there, on May 24, drawing a crowd of 24,827, their biggest home attendance of the season. The Cardinals played their first contest under the lights on June 4, in front of 23,500 spectators, also the most at home they would draw that year. With the sweltering hot, humid St. Louis summers, players and fans could appreciate the novelty (and the relief) of playing at night. On April 18, 1950, the Cardinals became the first team to hold their home opener at night..

From 1942 to 1946, the Cardinals experienced a stretch of excellence that saw them go to the fall classic

Sportsman Park hosted the 1944 World Series, an "All St. Louis" affair featuring the Cardinals and Browns.

four times, winning three of them. Their win totals in 1942, '43, and '44 were 106, 105, and 105. Stan Musial emerged as a star during this period, and the Cardinals were fortunate that he missed only one year, 1945, due to World War II. Stan the Man went on to have a long and storied career at Grand and Dodier, finishing with a .331 career batting average, 475 home runs, and what was then the most lifetime hits by a National Leaguer.

The war years were lean ones for baseball, as many stars of the game were called to serve Uncle Sam. As a result, teams were forced to fill their depleted rosters with castoffs, retreads, or unknowns who during normal times would most likely be toiling in the minor leagues. One-armed Pete Gray, who played for the Browns in 1945, came to be a symbol of wartime baseball. Despite (or because of) the roster attrition, however, the unthinkable happened in 1944. The St. Louis Browns, who had had only four winning seasons in the prior 20 years,

won the American League pennant. They started strong out of the gate, winning their first nine games. They also got hot at the end, when they had to win, going 11-1 in their final 12 games, including a four-game sweep of the Yankees on the final weekend. It came down to the last game of the season at Sportsman's Park. The Browns entered the October 1 game tied with Detroit for the top spot. Before a crowd of 35,518, the largest regular-season Browns crowd ever at Grand and Dodier, they prevailed over New York, 5-2, while the Tigers lost in Detroit to the Washington Senators. The Browns were the champions of the American League, with a record of 89-65. They wound up facing the Cardinals in the only All-St. Louis World Series ever. The Browns came up short, four games to two, in what was dubbed the Streetcar Series. It was the lone World Series appearance in the long history of the Browns.

One of the most famous plays ever at Sportsman's Park occurred in Game Seven of the 1946 World Series, which featured the Cardinals against the Boston Red Sox. In the bottom of the eighth inning, with the score tied, 3-3, the Cardinals' Enos Slaughter led off with a single. The next two batters made outs, then Harry "The Hat" Walker, who got his nickname because he would constantly tug at the bill of his cap between pitches, poked a solid hit to left-center. Boston center fielder Leon Culberson ambled over, fielded it routinely, and lobbed the ball to shortstop Johnny Pesky, neither of them expecting Slaughter to continue around third and run home. Pesky perhaps hesitated just a second before gunning the ball to catcher Roy Partee. The throw was a bit up the third-base line, but it didn't matter. Slaughter slid into home safely. Many have speculated down the ages that Pesky's slight hesitation allowed Slaughter to score. In the end, it proved to be the winning run of the World Series. Before the Series started, it had been billed as a showdown between the two biggest stars on either club, Ted Williams of the Red Sox and Stan Musial of the Cardinals. Neither hit particularly well in the Series, however. Williams batted .200, while Musial was slightly better at .222.

Sportsman's Park was the last ballpark in the majors to maintain a Jim Crow section. Until the 1944 season black patrons could sit only in the right-field pavilion. But by 1947 the Browns became only the third big-league team (after the Dodgers and the Indians) to field a black player. The team had purchased two players from the Negro Leagues' Kansas City Monarchs, infielder Hank Thompson and outfielder Willard Brown. The 21-year-old Thompson didn't do much for St. Louis, playing in only 27 games with no home runs, but he did go on to have some good years with the New York Giants. Brown, who was 32, played in only 21 big-league games, hitting .179. In 2006, however, he was enshrined in Cooperstown for his achievements in the Negro Leagues.

After their World Series appearance in 1944, the Browns finished third the next year with a record of 81-70. It was the final .500 season in their history. In July 1951, in the midst of a 102-loss season, the team was purchased by one of baseball's foremost impresarios ever, Bill Veeck. A master of promotion and theatrics, Veeck pulled off perhaps his most famous stunt on August 19, 1951, between games of a Sunday doubleheader with the Tigers. A big birthday cake was wheeled onto the field. Suddenly, a 3-foot 7-inch midget by the name of Eddie Gaedel popped out, to the delight of the crowd. Had the promotion ended there, it would have been forgotten. But it didn't, and it wasn't. When the second game got under way, Frank Saucier was scheduled to lead off the bottom of the first inning for the Browns. The fans were shocked to see Gaedel come trotting up to home plate as a pinch-hitter. When nonplussed home-plate umpire Ed Hurley asked Browns manager Zack Taylor what the big idea was, Taylor presented the man in blue with a standard player contract with Gaedel's signature on it. Veeck knew the umps wouldn't appreciate his sense of humor, so he had had the contract prepared beforehand and sent to the league office after it had closed. Hurley had to comply, and Gaedel was allowed to bat. Tigers pitcher Bob Cain threw four straight balls, and the midget took his base. Gaedel got a standing ovation from the crowd as he was removed for a pinch-runner. His uniform number, 1/8, is on display at the Baseball Hall of Fame.

Veeck and his family lived in an apartment of his own making under the stands at Sportsman's Park. He had high hopes that his promotional acumen would help to increase attendance and allow the Browns to compete with the Cardinals. Veeck himself was by no means a wealthy man, and the team operated on a shoestring budget. Among his other promotional stunts was Grandstand Managers Day, when fans in one section were given placards with words like "bunt," "steal," "swing," and "pull the pitcher." They would hold the cards up at strategic points in the game, and the players on the field had to obey the fans' decisions.

Promotions aside, the Browns didn't improve any on the field during Veeck's reign. He did sign former Negro Leagues star Satchel Paige in 1951. Paige was in his mid-40s at the time. He pitched three seasons for the Brownies, winning 18 and losing 23.

In 1953 the Anheuser-Busch brewery, maker of Budweiser beer, purchased the Cardinals, with August "Gussie" Busch, Jr. becoming team president. Veeck knew he couldn't compete with Busch's deep pockets. He tried unsuccessfully to move the Browns to greener pastures in Milwaukee. When that didn't work, he promptly sold Sportsman's Park to Busch. The tables were now turned; the Cardinals were the landlords and the Browns were the tenants.

Busch wanted to change the name of Sportsman's Park to Budweiser Stadium, but the league balked at having a ballpark named after a beer. Busch instead changed the name to Busch Stadium, after which the brewery introduced Busch Bavarian Beer in 1955. Thus, instead of naming the ballpark after a beer, they tried a different tack and named a beer after the ballpark.

By the 1953 season, it was a foregone conclusion that Veeck would be moving the Browns out of town the next season. The highlight of the year at Grand and Dodier came on May 6. Bobo Holloman, a 30-year-old career minor leaguer, pitched a no-hitter against the Philadelphia Athletics in his first major-league start, the only player ever to do so.

The final game for the Browns in St. Louis came on September 27, 1953. The club lost its 100th game of the season, in front of an intimate gathering of 3,174 fans. Jim Dyck hit a fly ball to center for the last at-bat ever by a St. Louis Brown. By Opening Day 1954, Veeck had sold the team, and the new owners had moved it to Baltimore. The Cardinals now had St. Louis all to themselves.

The old ballpark at Grand and Dodier may have had a new name, but by the 1950s Busch Stadium was in definite need of sprucing up. Years of hands-off stewardship by the Browns had left the place in a state of neglect. Gussie Busch spent over a million dollars to brighten up the ballpark. He closed the center-field bleachers and replaced them with more eye-appealing shrubbery. Every seat in the house was either repaired or replaced. Dugouts and clubhouses were renovated and expanded. Busch was also responsible for installing one of the more distinctive features of the park during its remaining years: an electronic Anheuser-Busch eagle perched atop the scoreboard in left field. After every home run, the eagle would flap its electronic wings.

Stan "The Man" Musial was the brightest star to shine at Grand and Dodier for more than two decades. From his first season, 1941, until he retired after the 1963 season Musial won no fewer than seven National League batting titles, finishing his career with the most (at the time) career hits in the NL (3,630). During his tenure, the Cardinals went to four World Series, winning three of them.

In its history Sportsman's Park played host to three All-Star Games, in 1940, 1948, and 1957. The 1957 contest involved a ballot-box stuffing controversy. Overly zealous Cincinnati fans had voted all but one of the Redlegs' position players to the game. The only non-Redleg to get voted onto the squad was Musial. Commissioner Ford Frick replaced starting Cincinnati outfielders Gus Bell and Wally Post with Hank Aaron and Willie Mays, and then decided that for future All-Star Games fans would not be casting any more ballots. Starters would now be decided by players, managers, and coaches. This policy lasted until 1970, when the vote was given back to the fans.

By the late 1950s, serious discussions began to take place about a new ballpark. Despite Gussie Busch's improvements, the stadium had begun to deteriorate. The public perception of Busch Stadium was the same as that of many other urban ballparks during this period. For one thing, the neighborhood was become increasingly dangerous. Also, the United States was becoming a car culture; people preferred to drive to baseball games, rather than take buses or trolleys as they had in previous decades. Busch Stadium, with its lack of parking, could not accommodate them. In 1964 ground was broken for what would be the future Busch Memorial Stadium, in downtown St. Louis.

That same year the Cardinals captured the pennant by one game on the last day of the season after a thrilling three-way pennant race with the Phillies and the Reds. Thanks to Philadelphia's classic late-season collapse, in which they blew the 6 1/2-game lead they had with 12 games left to play, St. Louis went on to face the New York Yankees in the World Series. The seventh game featured Bob Gibson on the hill for the Cardinals at Busch Stadium. Gibson threw a complete game as St. Louis won by a final score of 7-5. This last championship team in Sportsman's Park's history was just on the cusp of greatness. Gibson would emerge as the most intimidating pitcher in an era filled with many of them. Lou Brock, Curt Flood, and Orlando Cepeda ignited the Redbirds' lineup in the second half of the decade. The club returned to the World Series at their new downtown stadium in 1967 and 1968.

Grand and Dodier was also the home of the St. Louis football Cardinals starting in 1960, after the franchise relocated from Chicago. The NFL's Cardinals never went to the playoffs in their six seasons at Busch Stadium. Bill and Charles Bidwill, the owners of the team, threatened to pull up stakes and move the team to Atlanta, having become disenchanted with the old ballpark and frustrated with the slow progress on the new stadium. The city eventually persuaded the Bidwill brothers to stay.

The Cardinals were scheduled to move into the new Busch Memorial Stadium for Opening Day 1966. But construction delays forced the team to continue to play at the old Busch for the first ten home games of the season. The end finally came on Sunday, May 8, an afternoon affair against San Francisco, which the Giants won 10-5. The final home run was hit by Willie Mays in the top of the ninth inning. In the bottom of the ninth, the Cardinals' Alex Johnson made the last out, hitting into a double play. Considering the occasion, a surprisingly modest crowd of 17,503 showed up. The team had had a disappointing 1965 season, and was in eighth place and playing very poorly at the beginning of 1966, which probably led to the modest crowd. There was not much "final game" fanfare for Busch Stadium; the Cardinals had scheduled a downtown parade later that day to celebrate the new stadium, and was genuinely happy to get out of the Sportsman's Park neighborhood. The ballpark area had become run-down and dangerous. A young fan was shot and killed during an armed robbery while he was hurrying to the 1964 opener. (After the May 8 game, home plate was dug up, and a few fans unbolted and carried out sections of seats, while many were content with a scoop of the outfield warning track to take home for a souvenir.)

Within six months the old ballpark at Grand and Dodier succumbed to the wrecking ball. After demolition, all that remained was the playing field. As a goodwill gesture, Gussie Busch transferred the real-estate title to the Metropolitan St. Louis Boys' Club. At this writing the grass athletic field was being used by the Boys & Girls Clubs of Greater St. Louis. A sign there noted the site of Sportsman's Park in St. Louis.

Sources

Benson, Michael, *Ballparks of North America: A Comprehensive Historical Reference to Baseball Grounds, Yards and Stadiums, 1845 to Present* (Jefferson, North Carolina, and London: McFarland & Company, 2009).

Feldmann, Doug, *Dizzy & The Gas House Gang: The 1934 Cardinals and Depression-Era Baseball* (Jefferson, North Carolina, and London: McFarland & Company, 2000).

Gillette, Gary, and Eric Enders, *Big League Ballparks: The Complete Illustrated History* (New York: Metro Books, 2009).

Jordan, David M., *Closing 'Em Down: Final Games at Thirteen Classic Ballparks* (Jefferson, North Carolina, and London: McFarland & Company, 2010).

Leventhal, Josh, *Take Me Out to the Ballpark.* (New York: Black Dog & Leventhal Publishers, 2011).

Smith, Ron. *The Ballpark Book: A Journey Through the Fields of Baseball Magic* (St. Louis: The Sporting News, 2000).

The Sporting News

Baseball-Reference.com

Notes

1 Ron Smith, *The Ballpark Book: A Journey Through the Fields of Baseball Magic*, 289-90.

St. Louis in 1934

By Eric Amon

In 1934 St. Louis was mired in a deep economic depression. That year was one of the worst in modern economic history, not only in St. Louis but throughout the United States and much of the world. The collapse of the US stock market on October 24, 1929, known as Black Tuesday, is usually cited as the start of the Great Depression, a time of hardship and suffering that lasted for many years.

The Depression affected nearly every aspect of American life. The effects of the 1929 crash trickled down to every street corner in the city. One of the largest Hoovervilles in the nation was built in 1930 in St. Louis. It had its own mayor, churches, and social institutions. (The slapdash shantytowns called Hoovervilles were wryly named after Herbert Hoover, who was the president when the market crashed.) The St. Louis Hooverville was funded by private donors and existed until 1936. Meanwhile, when they could afford to do so, St. Louisans tried to forget their troubles by spending a rare relaxing afternoon at the ballpark or an evening of theater at the Kiel Auditorium. With the repeal of Prohibition in 1933, the city's bars finally openly carried legal, locally brewed Budweiser beer.

The 1930 Census showed a population of 821,960 for St. Louis, ranking it seventh in the nation. This was a sharp decline from 1900, when the city was ranked fourth. However, the numbers are somewhat misleading, a result of an action confining the city's growth to the area it had occupied in the horse-and-buggy days. Since the city of St. Louis broke from St. Louis County in 1876 in what was known as the Great Divorce, the city has been unable to extend its boundaries. Reconsolidation of city and county was put to the voters a couple of times, most notably in 1926. The belief was that a unified population center would improve businesses, roads, water, and schools. While the city favored it, county voters turned it down.

St. Louis was hit hard by the Great Depression. By 1933 the city had lost half of its manufacturing output and 35 percent of its population. Thirty percent of the whites and an astonishing 80 percent of African-Americans were without jobs or underemployed. Blacks comprised one-tenth of the city's population, but one-fourth of the unemployed.

David Grant described the employment situation for most St. Louis African-Americans: "They had no white collar jobs; they had all the slop wagons with the mules; they had all the mops, and slop buckets, and that's all they had. They had one assistant city counselor. … These officeholders would make their black employees do work at their homes such as cutting their grass and being their butler.[1]

Racial segregation was a hodgepodge in St. Louis in 1934. The schools were segregated, but the libraries were not. Blacks were excluded from white hotels, restaurants, barber shops, and dance halls. Department stores were open to all, and blacks were not confined to back seats of buses and streetcars. African-Americans were restricted to the balconies of theaters that admitted them. Segregation prevailed at ballgames and other sporting events. Sportsman's Park was a notoriously segregated stadium for decades. Until the mid-1950s, black patrons were confined to the 2,400 right-field pavilion seats and were not allowed to purchase grandstand tickets.[2]

Hard times were worsened by the Dust Bowl of 1934, the worst manmade disaster in American history. On May 10, 1934, the rest of the world began to know at first hand about the dust storms of the Great Plains. "A gigantic cloud of dust, 1,500 miles long, 900 miles across and two miles high, buffeted and smothered almost one-third of the nation today," the United Press reported.[3]

St. Louisans suffered in the summer of 1934 when temperatures reached at least 100 degrees on 29 days—the high was 111—and killed 420 people. With little rain, crops wilted and trees died. The Mississippi River barely had enough water for commercial boats and trading, further damaging the local economy.

In the depths of the Depression, Commissioner Kenesaw Mountain Landis said, "Steel, factories, railroads, newspapers, agriculture, baseball. We all rode down together, and we'll ride back together."⁴ The commissioner was right. The nation did ride out the Depression, although it took a long, long time. Baseball survived in St. Louis. Because the Cardinals (and the less successful Browns) were the Southernmost and Westernmost major-league clubs and there were no other teams remotely close, the Redbirds gained a regional following unlike that of any other team. This was largely due to the advent of radio, specifically KMOX in St. Louis, which was heard throughout the Midwest and the South and created diehard fans for decades. Contrary to the fears of Cardinals owner Sam Breadon, who blacked out some broadcasts, airing the games did not depress attendance. It had the opposite effect. Entire families were listening to games together, and many wanted to see a game in person if they could afford it.

Nearly all major-league teams experienced financial losses in the years after the stock market crash of 1929. In 1934 the Browns averaged only 1,517 fans per game.⁵

More than half of all minor-league clubs active in 1929 had folded by the mid-'30s. Despite these losses, and with clubs doing whatever they could to cut costs and attract fans, the major leagues played a full schedule throughout the Depression.

Attendance at major-league games dropped from more than 9.5 million in 1929 to less than 7 million in 1934. Between 1929 and 1934, players' salaries dropped 25 percent. Despite being a two-team city, the Cardinals might be considered the only relevant franchise in town. In 1934 the Cardinals drew 325,056 fans, while the Browns drew a comparatively minuscule 115,305. It is no wonder that the Browns at one point considered a move to the West Coast. (Their plight gave rise to the saying about St. Louis: First in shoes, first in booze, and last in the American League.)

Blue-collar fans spent their hard-earned cash to go to games and escape their daily existence. Times were so tough that it was not uncommon for young men at the ballpark to eat a nickel hot dog as their only meal for the day.⁶

Even before baseball was truly devastated by the effects of the crippling Depression, Breadon took steps in 1930 to bring in more fans. By scheduling Sunday doubleheaders at Sportsman's Park, he could provide more wholesome entertainment to an entire family. "In the days of the automobile, movies, and radio I found we had to give the fans of Missouri and southern Illinois, to say nothing of our St. Louis fans, more than a two-hour show to bring them to the park on Sunday; we had to give them a full afternoon's entertainment," Breadon said.⁷

Some publications called for teams to adapt to changing times by selling more 50-cent bleacher seats than $1 grandstand tickets that nobody could afford. "Each of us deserves some form of recreation," said a 1933 article in the *Washington Post*. "It serves as a good, all-around tonic; it eases the strain of the daily grind; it helps to freshen the mind and sharpen the wit."⁸

Cardinals fans loved their team of ragtag "gamers" who played in dirty uniforms and had almost a rough and tough early football mentality. They viewed the Yankees and Giants as having a "corporate culture,"⁹ and being out of touch with the common fan.

The 1934 World Series between the Cardinals and the Detroit Tigers was significant for many reasons. It was the first fall classic in 15 years not to feature an East Coast team. In addition, both St. Louis and Detroit were ravaged by effects of the Depression. Detroit was suffering from layoffs in the automobile industry, while St. Louis was affected by both the collapse of the wheat-belt economy from the Dust Bowl and river-borne trade that came to a virtual halt due to drought.

Baseball wasn't the only game in town during the Gas House days. In those years St. Louis fielded teams in professional football (the Gamers 1931-1934) and hockey (the St. Louis Eagles 1934-1935). The St. Louis Arena, located west of downtown, was completed in 1929. It seated 18,000 for a variety of cultural and sporting events. With lengthy travel limited to trains in the 1930s, St. Louis had a hard time getting and keeping professional sports franchises.

St. Louis had hosted a Negro National League team, the Stars, but they folded in 1931. The club, which joined the league in 1921, had been a powerhouse. From 1928 to 1931 the Stars won three pennants in four years. Over the years its players included Hall of Famers Cool Papa Bell, Mule Suttles, and Willie Wells. Stars Park, built in 1922, seated 10,000 and was one of the few ballparks built exclusively for Negro League baseball.

In 1934, in the heart of the Depression, St. Louis dedicated two new structures to house cultural events. To great fanfare, the Municipal Auditorium and Community Center opened on April 14, 1934. A parade, which included American Legion drummers and the Knights of Columbus, celebrated the opening of the building at Market and 14th Streets. Mayor Bernard Dickmann "rode with the mounted police on his favorite chestnut, Big Boy."[10] The project had been financed through the passage of a bond issue in 1923, a time of greater prosperity. The auditorium, Mayor Dickmann said, was "designed to enrich the people's lives and increase their enjoyment and … add to the attractiveness and popularity of our city as it will bring to us great conventions and cultural activities."[11]

Also completed in 1934 was the St. Louis Opera House, which seated 3,563 (the Municipal Auditorium seated 9,300). What made the building unique was its back-to-back stages, which could be combined as was done when President Truman visited St. Louis in 1950.

One of the Democratic Party's major planks in the 1932 election called for the repeal of the 18th Amendment, which had instituted Prohibition in 1920. Repealing Prohibition, the party hoped would lead to an increase in jobs in the brewing industry, which would snowball and help improve the economy. American farmers would also benefit from increased wheat, barley, and rye production.

If it was not the Cardinals who helped boost morale, then it was certainly the repeal of Prohibition in 1933 that gave St. Louisans something to celebrate. Before the Prohibition era, breweries, along with shoemaking, had been among the chief industries in the Gateway City. During Prohibition brewers had to be creative about how to stay in business. Some sold non-alcoholic beer, while others sold refrigerators. Repeal officially took effect on December 5, 1933. Most breweries were back in business by 1934.

The St. Louis landmark most familiar to Americans at present is the Gateway Arch. Its beginnings go back to 1934. The Jefferson National Expansion Association, a committee chaired by St. Louis attorney Luther Ely Smith was formed to explore the establishment of a memorial to Thomas Jefferson on the city's riverfront. A year later, voters approved that a $7.5 million bond issue for the project. President Franklin D. Roosevelt authorized the US Interior Department Interior to work on the project. Sadly, Smith did not live to see his dream become a reality; he died in 1951. The Arch was completed on October 28, 1965. It stands as a proud tribute to Thomas Jefferson and the brave pioneers who made this nation what it is today.

Sources

Alexander, Charles C., *Breaking the Slump: Baseball in the Depression Era* (New York: Columbia University Press, 2002).

Brewer, John Stephen, *A Compartmentalized Life* (Bloomington, Indiana: XLibris Corporation, 2011).

Campbell, Tracy, *The Gateway Arch: A Biography* (New Haven: Yale University Press, 2013).

Corzine, Nathan M., *American Game; American Mirror: Baseball, Beer, the Media, and American Culture, 1933-54*. (Master of Arts thesis, University of Missouri-Columbia, 2004).

Feldmann, Doug, *Dizzy and the Gas House Gang: The 1934 St. Louis Cardinals and Depression-Era Baseball* (Jefferson, North Carolina: McFarland, 2000).

Lieb, Frederick G., *The St. Lois Cardinals* (New York: G.P. Putnam's Sons, 1944).

Primm, James Neal, *Lion of the Valley: St. Louis, Missouri, 1764-1980* (St. Louis: Missouri History Museum Press, 1998).

Stein, Lana, *St. Louis Politics: The Triumph of Tradition* (St. Louis: Missouri History Museum Press, 2002).

Hastings (Nebraska) *Tribune*

St. Louis Post-Dispatch

Washington Post

baseball-reference.com.

Pro-football-reference.com.

Notes

1   George Grant, interview by Richard Resh, Oral History Program, University of Missouri, St. Louis, August 24, 1970.

2   John Stephen Brewer, *A Compartmentalized Life*, 12.

3   *Hastings* (Nebraska) *Tribune*, May 11, 1934.

4   Doug Feldmann, *Dizzy and the Gas House Gang: The 1934 St. Louis Cardinals and Depression Era Baseball*, 2.

5   baseball-reference.com.

6   Feldmann, 15,

7   Frederick G. Lieb, *The St. Lois Cardinals*, 80.

8   *Washington Post*, May 22, 1933.

9   Feldmann, 12.

10 *St. Louis Post Dispatch*, April 10, 2011.

11 Ibid.

1934 St. Louis Cardinals Season Timeline
By Joseph Wancho

April 17, at St. Louis
St. Louis opens the season against Pittsburgh and Dizzy Dean pitches the Cards to a 7-1 victory. Joe Medwick homers and drives in three runs.

April 18, at St. Louis
Pittsburgh edges St. Louis, 7-6, as Larry French gets the win. Pie Traynor, Gus Suhr, and Cookie Lavagetto smack home runs for the Pirates.

April 19, at St. Louis
The Pirates thump St. Louis, 14-4. Five Bucs (Paul Waner, Pie Traynor, Arky Vaughan, Gus Suhr, and Cookie Lavagetto) each collect two RBIs. The Cardinals commit five errors, leading to seven unearned runs.

April 21, at St. Louis
Despite striking out 11 batters, Tex Carleton is the hard-luck loser, 2-1, to Charlie Root and the Chicago Cubs. The Cubs score the winning run in the top of the ninth inning, when Chuck Klein singles to plate Woody English. Charlie Root homers off Carleton in the third inning.

April 22, at St. Louis
The Cubs hold a hit parade at Sportsman's Park, as every player in their lineup gets at least one hit for a total of 22 safeties during a 15-2 bashing of St. Louis. Chuck Klein and Tuck Stainback each drive in three runs. Lon Warneke goes the distance, pitching a one-hitter for the win. Gabby Hartnett hits a home run off Clarence Heise in the ninth inning. (It was the Cardinals relief pitcher's only major-league game.)

April 24, at Pittsburgh
Freddie Lindstrom uncorks a three-run homer over the left-field wall at Forbes Field. The blast is hit off Jesse Haines in the bottom of the ninth inning to give the Pirates a 5-4 win.

April 26, at Pittsburgh
The Cardinals put the brakes on their five-game losing streak as Bill Hallahan wins, 10-1, over Pittsburgh. Hallahan backs his performance with two RBIs and Spud Davis jacks a three-run homer.

April 27, at Chicago
Gabby Hartnett's single in the 11th inning scores Kiki Cuyler to ice the game for the Cubs, a 3-2 victory. Lon Warneke claims his third victory of the young season.

April 28, at Chicago
Guy Bush strikes out eight and goes the distance for his third win in the 7-1 Cubs victory. Chicago's Chuck Klein homers and drives in three runs to lead the offense.

April 29, at Chicago
St. Louis tops the Cubs, 9-4, as Bill Walker gets his first win of the season. Ripper Collins and Buster Mills each drill two-run home runs.

April 30, at St. Louis
The Cards return home and put on their hitting shoes, tallying 17 hits in a 10-6 win over Cincinnati. Spud Davis and Pepper Martin collect two RBIs each and Burleigh Grimes wins in relief.

National League standings at month's end

Team Name	G	W	L	T	PCT	GB
Chicago Cubs	12	10	2	0	.833	-
New York Giants	11	8	3	0	.727	1.5
Boston Braves	12	6	5	1	.545	3.5
Pittsburgh Pirates	10	5	5	0	.500	4.0
Brooklyn Dodgers	12	5	6	1	.455	4.5
St. Louis Cardinals	11	4	7	0	.364	5.5
Cincinnati Reds	11	3	8	0	.273	6.5
Philadelphia Phillies	11	3	8	0	.273	6.5

May 1, at St. Louis
The Cards rally twice to win 3-2 in 11 innings over Cincinnati. Burleigh Grimes is credited with the win in relief for the second consecutive game. The win is the last in the major leagues for the last legal spitballer to record a victory. Ripper Collins's smacks two solo shots - the first one in the ninth inning and the second in the eleventh inning. Both homers even the score.

Burgess Whitehead's single to score Bill DeLancey wins it in the eleventh inning.

May 2, at St. Louis
St. Louis holds off the Reds again, winning 4-1. Frankie Frisch goes 2-for-4 and drives in two runs. Tex Carleton gets his first victory of the season.

May 3, at St. Louis
The Cardinals beat the Phillies 8-7 as Paul Dean notches his first major-league win in relief. Joe Medwick hits a grand slam in the fourth frame, and Ripper Collins knocks in two runs in the sixth with a double.

May 4, at St. Louis
Ladies Day at Sportsman's Park brings an estimated 2,000 women fans to the ballgame. They were not disappointed as the home team wins, 3-1, with Bill Walker getting the win. Medwick hits his fifth home run, in the sixth inning. In a personnel move, catcher Francis Healy is purchased from the New York Giants.

May 5, at St. Louis
Dizzy Dean strikes out seven to even his record at 2-2 as the Cardinals win their seventh straight, 7-1 over the Phillies. Ripper Collins hits a three-run homer in the third inning, and six Cards stroke doubles (Pepper Martin, Collins, Jack Rothrock, Buster Mills, Spud Davis, and Joe Medwick).

May 6, at St. Louis
The Cardinals win streak is snapped at seven games as they drop a 3-2 decision to the Boston Braves. Joe Mowry's eighth-inning solo shot off Grimes is the difference.

May 7, at St. Louis
Joe Medwick's bases-loaded double in the third inning and Jack Rothrock's two-run homer in the fifth inning stake the Cardinals to a 10-0 lead after seven innings, and they win, 10-5. Tex Carleton claims the win to even his record at 2-2.

May 8, at St. Louis
St. Louis trails Boston by four runs after three innings, but two RBIs each from Ripper Collins and Ernie Orsatti lead the Cardinals' offensive attack as they win, 5-4. Jesse Haines gets the win in relief, pitching 6⅓ scoreless innings.

May 9, at St. Louis
Dizzy Dean scatters five hits and strikes out seven, shutting out the Giants, 4-0. Four different players knock in a run each.

May 10, at St. Louis
The Cards nip the Giants, 5-4, and are now tied with New York in third place. Five Cardinals (Leo Durocher, Jack Rothrock, Spud Davis, Pepper Martin, and Frank Frisch) pace the offense with two hits apiece. Jim Mooney picks up the win in relief.

May 11, at St. Louis
Paul Dean defeats Carl Hubbell, as the Cards win by a 3-2 margin in ten innings. Jack Rothrock singles in pinch-runner Ernie Orsatti with the winning run.

May 12, at St. Louis
The Giants salvage one win in the series, upending the Cards, 6-4. New York scores five runs in the last two innings, the big blow coming on a bases-loaded double by Travis Jackson. Mel Ott drives in two runs. Tex Carleton is saddled with the loss; his record drops to 2-3.

May 13, at St. Louis
Dizzy Dean notches his fourth victory of the season and the offense pounds out 18 hits against four Dodgers pitchers. Jack Rothrock goes 3-for-4 with four RBIs. The 12-7 win lands the Cardinals in third place, 1 1/2 games behind Pittsburgh.

May 15, at St. Louis
Brooklyn nips St. Louis, 6-5, taking control by scoring three runs in the eighth inning. The inning is highlighted by a double steal, as Lonnie Frey steals home and Danny Taylor swipes second base off Dizzy Dean and Spud Davis. Spitball pitcher Burleigh Grimes is released by St. Louis.

May 17, at Boston
Spud Davis and Frank Frisch each homer and drive in two runs as the Cardinals beat the Braves 5-3. Paul Dean goes the distance, striking out five and raising his record to 3-0.

May 18, at Boston
The Braves defeat St. Louis 6-2 as Fred Frankhouse wins to raise his record to 5-1. Marty McManus steals two bases and collects two RBIs. Jim Winford takes the loss.

May 19, at Boston
Tex Carleton evens his record at 3-3 with a narrow 2-1 win over Boston. Tex scatters three hits and Joe Medwick and Ripper Collins account for the two Cardinal RBIs.

May 20, at New York
The Cardinals shell Carl Hubbell for seven runs in five innings in a 9-5 win. Dizzy Dean coasts to his fifth victory. Medwick blasts a two-run homer into the upper tier at the Polo Grounds in the fifth inning. Kiddo Davis and Ripper Collins also hit homers.

May 21, at New York
Scheduled Giants starter Freddie Fitzsimmons is injured before the game when Cardinal Jim Mooney loses the grip on his bat and it strikes Freddie in the kidneys. Joe Bowman is pressed into action and defeats the Redbirds 5-2. Travis Jackson strokes a two-run homer and Blondy Ryan also drives in two runs for the victors.

May 22, at New York
With the score 4-4 in the ninth inning and Cardinals on second and third, Giants manager Bill Terry elects to walk Frank Frisch and face Joe Medwick. Medwick triples and the Cards win, 7-4. Paul Dean strikes out six and raises his record to 4-0.

May 23, at Brooklyn
Ray Benge raises his record to 3-0 as the Dodgers beat St. Louis, 5-3. Three errors by the Cardinals lead to two unearned runs. Hack Wilson walks twice and drives in two runs for Brooklyn. Says Dodgers manager Casey Stengel of St. Louis, "Not a championship club. Frisch isn't what he once was, and the shortstop [Durocher] can't hit, they have one good hitting catcher [Davis] and one swell outfielder [Medwick]."

May 24, at Brooklyn
Buster Mills pinch-hits for Ernie Orsatti in the seventh inning and doubles home two runs. Leo Durocher also doubles home two runs and the Cards top the Dodgers, 7-3. Tex Carleton wins to push his record to 4-3.

May 27, at Philadelphia
The Cards need extra innings to dispatch the Phillies, 5-2. Dizzy Dean raises his record to 6-2, and aids his cause with a home run in the tenth despite 40-mph winds howling through the Baker Bowl.

May 28, at Philadelphia
Bill Hallahan wins his second game in a 10-0 thrashing of Philadelphia to complete a two-game sweep. The Phillies turned five double plays. Jack Rothrock, Spud Davis, and Ernie Orsatti each knock in two runs to lead the Cardinals' offense. The win vaulted the Cardinals into first place, a game over the Pirates.

May 30, at Cincinnati
The Cardinals sweep a doubleheader from the Reds at Crosley Field, winning 9-6 in the opener and 9-2 in the nightcap. Paul Dean gets his fifth victory in the first game as Bill DeLancey is the offensive hero, going 4-for-5 with four RBIs. Tex Carleton wins his fifth to complete the double dip. Six players (Carleton, Spud Davis, Jack Rothrock, Frank Frisch, Joe Medwick, and Ripper Collins) each get a double. The Cardinals remained in first place, a half-game over the Giants.

May 31, at Cincinnati
The Cardinals win their sixth game in a row as they edge the Reds 3-2 in ten innings to complete the three-game series sweep. Frank Frisch's double in the tenth inning is the difference as Flint Rhem wins his first game of the season.

National League standings at month's end

Team Name	G	W	L	T	PCT	GB
St. Louis Cardinals	38	25	13	0	.658	-
Chicago Cubs	41	25	16	0	.610	1.5
New York Giants	41	25	16	0	.610	1.5
Boston Braves	37	20	16	1	.556	4.0
Pittsburgh Pirates	36	20	16	0	.556	4.0
Brooklyn Dodgers	39	16	22	1	.421	9.0
Philadelphia Phillies	35	11	24	0	.314	12.5
Cincinnati Reds	35	8	27	0	.229	15.5

June 1, at Pittsburgh
Dizzy Dean claimed he had a sore arm, but really was in a dispute with management over the contract of brother Paul. Bill Hallahan takes the hill in his place and the Cards drop a 4-3 game to the Pirates. Pittsburgh scored three runs in the ninth inning, giving Waite Hoyt his second win.

June 2, at Pittsburgh
In a doubleheader, Dizzy Dean strikes out six and coasts to his seventh win in a 13-4 win in the first game. Ripper Collins goes 3-for-4 with a pair of home runs, three runs scored, and seven RBIs to pace the offense. In the second contest, the Pirates avenge the loss with a 6-3 victory. Paul Dean, summoned from the bullpen in the eighth inning to face Wally Roettger with the bases loaded, gives up a triple. Roettger has five RBIs in the game.

June 3, at Pittsburgh
Heinie Meine pitches Pittsburgh to a 4-2 win for his third victory. Four players tally an RBI for the Bucs. Pepper Martin hits a two-run homer in the seventh inning.

June 5, at St. Louis
St. Louis returns home and Paul Dean strikes out seven to raise his record to 6-0 in a 6-3 win over the Cubs. Dean backs his performance with a double and an RBI, while Ripper Collins knocks in two runs for the Cards. They are percentage points ahead of the Giants for the National League lead.

June 6, at St. Louis
With the Cubs and Cardinals knotted, 6-6, Joe Medwick tries to score on a Ripper Collins double in the bottom of the 12th but is called out at the plate by umpire Charles Rigler. Manager Frisch races from the dugout and nearly comes to blows with Rigler. Rigler's mask crashes against Frisch's jaw and there is a lot of pushing and shoving. After order is restored, the Cubs score six times in the 13th inning to come away with the 12-6 win.

June 7, at St. Louis
The Cubs win their second straight from the Cardinals as Jim Weaver strikes out eight for his third win. Babe Herman's single to score Billy Herman in the third inning is the lone run in the 1-0 victory.

June 8, at St. Louis
The Cardinals rights the ship with a 6-2 win over the Pirates behind Tex Carleton, who records his sixth win. Ripper Collins unloads for his 12th home run in the third inning, and Frankie Frisch drives in two runs with a double.

June 10, at St. Louis
Dizzy Dean goes to 8-2 as the Cards nip the Pirates, 3-2. Ripper Collins hits his 13th homer in the fourth inning, and doubles and scores the go-ahead run in the eighth inning.

June 12, at St. Louis
For the third game in a row, Ripper Collins hits a homer, this time a three-run blast in the seventh inning. Pepper Martin also homers. Paul Dean goes the distance, striking out five in the 7-3 win over Boston. His record stands at 7-0.

June 13, at St. Louis
Fred Frankhouse blanks the Cards on six hits in Boston's 9-0 win. He raises his record to 9-2, and backs his effort with two hits and two RBIs. Buck Jordan and Wally Berger also drive in a pair of runs each. The Cardinals commit five errors, four by Durocher.

June 14, at St. Louis
The Cards beat Boston in a slugfest, 12-9. The teams combined for 34 hits. Frisch, DeLancey, and Durocher homer, with Durocher's a grand slam. Tex Carleton gets his seventh victory, with relief help from Paul Dean.

June 15, at St. Louis
The Braves blast St. Louis, 10-4. Boston pounds out 19 hits as Ed Brandt goes the distance to even his record at 5-5. Buck Jordan smashes two doubles and drives in three runs. Wally Berger and Hal Lee each drive in a pair of runs. The Cardinals trade part-time outfielder Kiddo Davis to Philadelphia for outfielder Chick Fullis.

June 16, at St. Louis
The Phillies beat the Cardinals for the first time this season, handing Dizzy Dean his third loss. Dolph

Camilli hits two solo shots off Dean and Johnny Moore drives in three runs in Philadelphia's 8-3 victory.

June 17, at St. Louis
The Cardinals get back on the winning track, sweeping a doubleheader from Philadelphia, 6-0 and 7-5. Paul Dean runs his record to 8-0, striking out seven and scattering five hits. Durocher goes 2-for-4 with three RBIs. In the second game, Dizzy Dean picks up his ninth win, pitching two innings of relief. Newcomer Chick Fullis smacks a pinch-hit double with the bases loaded that plates two runs in the bottom of the seventh frame to pull the Cards ahead. After Dizzy shuts down the Phillies in the top of the eighth, the Cardinals bat in the bottom of the inning before the game is called because of darkness.

June 19, at St. Louis
The Phillies outlast St. Louis, 10-8, as Paul Dean, pitching in relief, loses his first game. The extra-inning contest is decided in the 12th inning when Johnny Moore's single, Dolph Camilli's triple, and a double by Curt Davis provide the margin of victory.

June 20, at St. Louis
Brooklyn defeats the Redbirds 9-5 behind Van Lingle Mungo's seven strikeouts. He gets his 11th win. Tony Cuccinello goes 3-for-4 and drives in four runs to pace the Dodgers' attack. The Cardinals are now firmly entrenched in second place, trailing New York by five games.

June 21, at St. Louis
Dizzy Dean wins his tenth as St. Louis bests Brooklyn, 9-2. Joe Medwick and Ripper Collins both homer. The Giants are shut out by the Cubs, cutting their lead over St. Louis to four games.

June 22, at St. Louis
Paul Dean registers ten K's in his ninth win as the Cardinals beat the Dodgers, 7-2. Frank Frisch, Joe Medwick, and Ripper Collins each collect two RBIs.

June 23, at St. Louis
Trailing by four runs, the Cardinals hang a five-run sixth inning on the Dodgers and come away with a 5-4 victory. Dizzy Dean wins his 11th with three innings in relief. Ernie Orsatti smacks a bases-loaded double to plate two runs and pinch-hitter Pat Crawford singles in two runs. St. Louis sells pitcher Flint Rhem to the Braves.

June 24, at St. Louis
On a hot summer day when the temperature reaches 100 degrees, the Giants beat the Cardinals, 9-7. The Giants score six runs in the top of the fifth inning. Each pitching staff records only one strikeout.

June 25, at St. Louis
The Giants make it two in a row with a 10-7 win. The win pushes New York to a 3 1/2-game advantage over the third-place Cardinals. Carl Hubbell goes the distance for his 11th win. Bill Terry, Mel Ott, and Travis Jackson drive in two runs each. St. Louis claims pitcher Dazzy Vance on waivers from Cincinnati.

June 26, at St. Louis
The Cardinals strike back with a 13-7 win over New York. Ripper Collins goes 4-for-5 with four RBIs. Jack Rothrock, Spud Davis, and Chick Fullis drive in two runs apiece. Paul Dean goes the distance for his tenth win.

June 27, at St. Louis
The Cardinals beat the Giants 8-7 to split the four-game series as Dizzy Dean wins his 12th game. Bill DeLancey goes 2-for-5 and has the big hit, a home run in the bottom of the ninth inning. Dean, who pitches 8⅔ innings before giving way to Jim Mooney, is credited with the win even though Mooney was the pitcher of record.

June 29, at Cincinnati
The Reds steamroll the Cards, 7-1, as Paul Derringer picks up his fourth win. Adam Comorosky and Tony Piet drive in a pair of runs each.

June 30, at Cincinnati
The Reds make it two straight over the Cardinals with an 11-4 shellacking. Si Johnson wins his fifth game while Paul Dean suffers his second defeat, again in a relief role. The Reds score nine times in the bottom of the eighth inning, all the runs scoring with two out.

The Cardinals close out June in third place, trailing the Giants by three games and the Cubs by two.

National League standings at month's end

Team Name	G	W	L	T	PCT	GB
New York Giants	67	42	25	0	.627	-
Chicago Cubs	68	41	26	1	.612	1.0
St. Louis Cardinals	65	38	27	0	.585	3.0
Pittsburgh Pirates	64	34	29	1	.540	6.0
Boston Braves	66	35	30	1	.538	6.0
Brooklyn Dodgers	68	27	40	1	.403	15.0
Philadelphia Phillies	66	24	42	0	.364	17.5
Cincinnati Reds	64	21	43	0	.328	19.5

July 1, at Cincinnati
The Cards face off against the Reds in a doubleheader, taking the first game, 8-6. The marathon game lasts 18 innings, with Dizzy Dean pitching 17 of them and winning his 13th game. The teams combine for 39 hits. Joe Medwick goes deep to put St. Louis ahead in the top of the 17th, but the Reds tie it in the bottom of the inning. The Cardinals win it with two runs in the 18th. Frisch goes 4-for-8 with three RBIs. The second game is called on account of darkness after five innings, tied, 2-2.

July 2, at Chicago
The Cubs top the Cardinals, 7-1. Lon Warneke goes the distance for his 11th win. Woody English and Billy Herman drive in a pair of runs each. There was a successful protest, which caused the game to be resumed on July 31, with two outs in the bottom of the seventh inning and the score Chicago 5, St. Louis 1.

July 3, at Chicago
Bill Hallahan goes the distance for his third win, striking out seven in the 7-3 victory. Joe Medwick homers, Pepper Martin drives in two runs. Each team collects 13 hits.

July 4, at St. Louis
St. Louis and Chicago split an Independence Day doubleheader. The Cardinals take the opener, 6-2, for Tex Carleton's eighth win. The Cubs rebound in the nightcap, winning by the identical score as Jim Weaver wins his fourth game on the year.

July 6, at St. Louis
The Reds and Cardinals combine for 31 runs and 31 hits as Cincinnati comes out on top, 16-15. Wes Schulmerich, Gordon Slade, and Ernie Lombardi hit homers for the winners. Ripper Collins hits his 17th in a losing cause. A combined ten pitchers toe the rubber for both teams.

July 7, at St. Louis
Bill Hallahan goes the distance for his fourth win in the 10-4 Redbird victory. The Cardinals rap seven doubles — Burgess Whitehead (2), Spud Davis (2), Hallahan, Jack Rothrock, and Leo Durocher.

July 8, at St. Louis
St. Louis and Cincinnati split a doubleheader, with the Cardinals taking the opener, 6-1. Frank Frisch goes 3-for-4 and drives in four runs, and Dizzy Dean strikes out ten on his way to his 14th win. The Reds come back to take the second game, 8-4. Benny Frey goes the distance for his sixth win. Harlin Pool goes 3-for-5 and drives in five runs to lead the Cincinnati offense.

July 10, at New York
In the second annual All-Star Game, the American League comes away with a 9-7 win at the Polo Grounds. Frankie Frisch and Joe Medwick are elected starters, and each player hits a solo homer off Lefty Gomez. Pepper Martin is used as a pinch-hitter and Dizzy Dean pitches three innings of relief allowing one run on five hits.

July 11, at Philadelphia
Philadelphia starter Phil Collins pitches a shutout into the ninth inning, when Bill DeLancey hits a two-run homer, to make the final margin 5-2, Phillies. Collins raises his record to 9-8.

July 12, at Philadelphia
St. Louis and Philadelphia split a doubleheader. The Cards win the first game, 8-5, as Dizzy Dean wins his 15th game while pitching in relief. Ripper Collins goes 3-for-4, drives in two runs and scores three runs. Pepper Martin doubles twice. In the nightcap, but Curt Davis goes the distance for his 11th win, 8-3. The Phillies bang out 16 hits. Philadelphia's Lou Chiozza goes 4-for-5 with an RBI and Jimmie Wilson drives in three runs.

July 14, at Brooklyn
Dodgers' rookie pitcher John Babich gives up two runs on four hits and receives superior support from his offense in the 10-2 Dodgers win. Tony Cuccinello and Joe Stripp drive in three runs apiece. In the last 11 games against the three bottom teams in the league, the Cardinals' record is 4-7.

July 15, at Brooklyn
Dizzy Dean blanks the Dodgers on four hits for a 2-0 win in the first game of a doubleheader. It is Dean's 16th victory. He also hits a solo homer in the eighth inning to aid the cause. Tex Carleton wins his ninth in the nightcap, a 6-3 Cardinals victory. Joe Medwick hits two home runs and drives in five runs.

July 17, at Brooklyn
Len Koenecke's solo homer in the bottom of the seventh lifts the Dodgers to a 7-6 win over St. Louis. In relief, Dutch Leonard picks up his fifth win. St. Louis is in third place, five games behind first-place New York.

July 18, at Brooklyn
Joe Medwick homers in his third straight game and drives in two runs. Three of the Cardinal tallies in their 5-3 victory are unearned as Brooklyn commits four errors. Bill Walker strikes out eight to gain his third win.

July 19, at Boston
Dizzy Dean wins his 17th as the Cardinals defeat Boston, 4-2, at Braves Field. Four players each drive in a run for St. Louis.

July 20, at Boston
The Cardinals win, 5-1, over Boston as Tex Carleton wins his tenth game. Ripper Collins goes 2-for-4 with three RBIs

July 21, at Boston
The Cards topple the Braves again, 5-3. Jim Mooney is credited with the win in relief. Only one strikeout is recorded in the game (Jack Rothrock). Spud Davis is 3-for-4 with two RBIs and two runs scored.

July 22, at Boston
St. Louis sweeps Boston in a doubleheader. Bill Walker wins his fourth game, going the distance in the 5-4 win. Jack Rothrock is 3-for-5 with two RBIs. Dazzy Vance goes the distance to complete the sweep and earn his first win, 4-2. Pepper Martin goes 2-for-4 with two RBIs to lead the offense.

July 23, at New York
Dizzy Dean rings up seven K's on the way to his 18th win in the Cardinals' 6-5 victory over New York. Ripper Collins is 5-for-5 with two RBIs and his 21st home run. The win is the seventh in a row for the Redbirds. They trail the Giants by 2 1/2 games.

July 24, at New York
Roy Parmelee shuts out the Cardinals 5-0 on four hits and snaps their win streak. Parmelee strikes out seven in his third win. Mel Ott hits his 24th home run. None of the Giants outfielders makes a putout.

July 26, at New York
The Cardinals win the first game of a doubleheader against the Giants, 7-2. Paul Dean notches his 11th win. Jack Rothrock clubs a three-run homer and Spud Davis drives in two runs. The Giants come back to win the second game, 6-3, as Freddie Fitzsimmons wins his 14th game. Hank Leiber goes 3-for-4 with three RBIs and Hughie Critz drives in two runs.

July 27, at Pittsburgh
Pittsburgh pitcher Bill Swift is in complete command in the Pirates' 4-0 win. He strikes out seven and allows only one Cardinal to reach second base. Swift is one of four Pirates to collect an RBI.

July 28, at Pittsburgh
Waite Hoyt outpitches Dizzy Dean to guide the Pirates to a 5-4 win over the Cardinals, St. Louis's third straight loss. Paul Waner and Earl Grace homer to pace the Pirates' attack.

July 29, at Pittsburgh
St. Louis exacts some revenge on Swift and the Pirates with a 9-5 victory. Ripper Collins and Spud Davis hit two-run homers to help Tex Carleton capture his 11th win.

July 31, at Chicago
The two teams resume playing the July 2 game, which had been protested, and resumed in the seventh inning

with a 5-1 Cubs lead. Chicago scores two runs in the bottom of the eighth for a 7-1 victory.

In the regularly-scheduled game, Lon Warneke strikes out six on his way to his 14th win, a 7-2 Cubs victory. Charlie Grimm homers and drives in three runs. The Cardinals close out July in third place, five games behind the Giants and 2 1/2 games behind the Cubs.

National League standings at month's end

Team Name	G	W	L	T	PCT	GB
New York Giants	97	61	36	0	.515	-
Chicago Cubs	97	58	38	1	.604	2.5
St. Louis Cardinals	96	55	40	1	.579	5.0
Boston Braves	99	49	49	1	.500	12.5
Pittsburgh Pirates	94	45	48	1	.484	14.0
Philadelphia Phillies	97	42	55	0	.433	19.0
Brooklyn Dodgers	96	40	55	1	.421	20.0
Cincinnati Reds	96	33	62	1	.347	27.0

August 1, at Chicago
Paul Dean strikes out seven and shuts out Chicago 4-0 on five hits for his 12th win. All the runs score in the eighth inning as Jack Rothrock, Frank Frisch, and Joe Medwick all collect an RBI. The final tally crosses the plate on a wild pitch.

August 2, at Chicago
St. Louis commits four errors in a 6-2 loss to Chicago. Bill Lee wins his ninth game and Woody English drives in four runs, two of them coming on a home run.

August 3, at St. Louis
Dizzy Dean wins his 19th as he leads St. Louis to a 9-3 win over the Pirates. Dean, Jack Rothrock, Leo Durocher, and Ernie Orsatti knock in two runs each.

August 4, at St. Louis
St. Louis tops the Pirates, 6-4, bolstered by a four-run sixth inning. Chick Fullis is a perfect 4-for-4 and drives in two runs. Tex Carleton picks up his 12th win.

August 5, at St. Louis
The Pirates sweep a pair from the Cardinals by scores of 6-4 and 7-2. Larry French gets the win in the opener, pitching in relief. In the nightcap, Paul Waner goes 4-for-5 with three RBIs and two runs scored. Waite Hoyt wins his eighth game. The Giants' lead over the third-place Cardinals mounts to 6 1/2 games.

August 7, at Cincinnati
The Cardinals and Reds split a doubleheader with Dizzy Dean outdueling Si Johnson for his 20th win in a 2-0 shutout. Cincinnati salvages the day with a 9-2 pasting of St. Louis in game two. Adam Comorosky and Clyde Manion drive in a pair of runs each. Allyn Stout goes the distance for the win.

August 8, at Cincinnati
Dizzy Dean pitches three innings of relief to record his 21st victory. The game is tied, 4-4, after nine innings. The Cardinals score six times in the top of the 12th—the big blow being Joe Medwick's bases-loaded triple –to seal the 10-4 victory. Five of the Cardinals' ten runs are unearned.

August 10, at St. Louis
The temperature registers 120 degrees on the field. The Cardinals offense also heats up, belting 21 hits in their 17-3 victory over Chicago. Ripper Collins drives in five runs and hits his 24th home run. Frank Frisch is 4-for-4 and drives in three runs. Tex Carleton is the beneficiary of the offensive outburst and chalks up his 13th win.

August 11, at St. Louis
St. Louis spots the Cubs three runs and comes back to win the game, 6-4. Bill Walker wins his fifth game. Ripper Collins smashes his 25th homer.

August 12, at St. Louis
The visiting Cubs sent 36,000 unhappy customers home as they sweep a doubleheader from the Cardinals, besting the Dean boys in the process. Babe Herman hits two homers and Billy Herman also smashes a round-tripper as Jim Weaver get his eighth win, 7-2, in game one. In the nightcap, a 6-4 Cubs triumph, Pat Malone wins his 13th game and Kiki Cuyler is 4-for-4 at the plate. The Cardinals are looking up from third place, trailing New York by 7 1/2 games.

August 14, at St. Louis
Joe Medwick goes 2-for-4 and drives in two runs, and Bill DeLancey homers in the Cardinals' 5-1 win over Philadelphia. In relief, Jesse Haines wins his second game.

August 16, at St. Louis
St. Louis sweeps a doubleheader from the Phillies, winning the first game 4-3 in 11 innings and taking the nightcap, 7-2. Jesse Haines gains his third win in relief in the opener as Joe Medwick, Leo Durocher, and Chick Fullis double and collect an RBI each. In the second game, Jack Rothrock and Ripper Collins homer and drive in two runs each. Bill Walker strikes out six on the way to his sixth win.

August 17, at St. Louis
St. Louis completed a four-game sweep of Philadelphia with a lopsided 12-2 win. Paul Dean wins his 13th game. Ripper Collins socks his 28th home run. Jack Rothrock drives in three runs and Leo Durocher goes 3-for-4.

August 18, at St. Louis
Bill Hallahan is the beneficiary of offensive fireworks and gets his fifth victory as the Cardinals breeze to a 15-0 win over Boston. Jack Rothrock and Leo Durocher homer and the Cardinals smack seven doubles among their 20 hits.

August 19, at St. Louis
The Cardinals and Braves split a doubleheader, with Boston victorious in the first game by a 10-9 score and St. Louis coming out on top in the second game, 3-1. Huck Betts wins his 11th game in the opener as Buck Jordan homers and Wally Berger smashes his 26th round-tripper. Bill Walker wins his seventh in the nightcap as Joe Medwick, Ripper Collins, and Frank Frisch get an RBI each.

August 21, at St. Louis
Tex Carleton wins his 14th game and backs his performance with two RBIs. Leo Durocher and Ripper Collins also drive in two runs apiece in the 6-2 victory over the Braves.

August 23, at St. Louis
New York swaggered into St. Louis boasting a six-game lead over the third-place Cardinals. Apparently for good reason. Jo-Jo Moore's three-run shot in the top of the ninth is the difference as the Giants beat the Cardinals, 5-3.

August 24, at St. Louis
Dizzy Dean atones for the Cardinals' tough loss the day before by shutting out the Giants, 5-0. He strikes out six on the way to his 22nd win. Ripper Collins smashes his 30th home run and Jack Rothrock also homers.

August 25, at St. Louis
Travis Jackson's bases-loaded single scores the winning runs as the Giants come from five runs down to triumph, 7-6. After reliever Dizzy Dean gives Mel Ott an intentional walk, Jackson comes through. Bill DeLancey hits a three-run homer in the Cardinals' five-run fourth inning.

August 26, at St. Louis
St. Louis and Brooklyn split a doubleheader with the Dodgers winning the opener, 11-5, and the Cardinals taking a 7-2 win in the second contest. Brooklyn's Len Koenecke homers and drives in five runs, and Tony Cuccinello also hits a home run. Bill Hallahan chalks up his sixth victory in the nightcap as Chick Fullis and Joe Medwick drive in two runs apiece.

August 27, at St. Louis
The Dodgers bang out 16 hits on their way to a 10-1 thrashing of St. Louis. Brooklyn's Tom Zachary wins his fifth game. Buzz Boyle homers and drives in three runs, and Jimmy Jordan and Al Lopez collect two RBIs each.

August 28, at St. Louis
Paul Dean outduels Ray Benge for his 14th win as he shuts out the Dodgers, 2-0. Burgess Whitehead and Jack Rothrock each tally an RBI.

August 29, at St. Louis
Bill Walker earns his eighth win in a 4-1 St. Louis victory over Brooklyn. Walker backs his win with an RBI.

August 31, at Chicago
Dizzy Dean strikes out six on the way to his 23rd win, a 3-1 victory over Chicago. Frank Frisch, Ripper Collins, and Ernie Orsatti drive in a run apiece. St. Louis closes the month of August tied for second place with Chicago, 5 1/2 games behind the New York Giants.

National League standings at month's end

Team Name	G	W	L	T	PCT	GB
New York Giants	126	80	46	0	.635	-
Chicago Cubs	126	74	51	1	.592	5.5
St. Louis Cardinals	126	74	51	1	.592	5.5
Boston Braves	125	64	60	1	.516	15.0
Pittsburgh Pirates	124	59	64	1	.480	19.5
Brooklyn Dodgers	124	54	69	1	.439	24.5
Philadelphia Phillies	122	46	76	0	.377	32.0
Cincinnati Reds	125	45	79	1	.363	34.0

September 1, at Chicago
The Cardinals topple Chicago 7-1 to take over sole possession of second place. Ripper Collins smacks his 31st home run and Bill DeLancey also goes deep for his 11th round-tripper. Bill Hallahan gains his seventh win.

September 3, at Pittsburgh
St. Louis drops a Labor Day doubleheader to the Pirates at Forbes Field. In the opener the Pirates bang out 14 hits in a 12-2 triumph. A big chunk of the scoring comes in the third frame, when Pittsburgh crosses the plate eight times. Pie Traynor and Gus Suhr drive in three runs each. The second game is a bit tighter, but Pittsburgh scores three runs in the ninth inning to win, 6-5, and complete the sweep. Dizzy Dean takes the second-game loss in relief.

September 5, at Brooklyn
The Cardinals edge Brooklyn 2-1, as Dizzy Dean wins his 24th game of the season. The St. Louis runs come on solo home runs by Ripper Collins and Bill DeLancey.

September 6, at Brooklyn
Tex Carleton wins his 15th and Pepper Martin gets three hits and three RBIs to lead the Cardinals to a 7-5 win over Brooklyn.

September 9, at Philadelphia
Paul Dean strikes out ten and wins his 15th as the Cardinals top Philadelphia, 6-1, in the first game of their doubleheader sweep. Bill DeLancey collects two RBIs, St. Louis wins the second game, 7-3, as Bill Walker claims his ninth victory. Pepper Martin and Spud Davis drive in a pair of runs each.

September 10, at Philadelphia
St. Louis runs its win streak to five as Dizzy Dean wins his 25th. Pepper Martin, Jack Rothrock, Pat Crawford, and Ripper Collins tally an RBI each in the 4-1 victory. The Giants' lead is cut to four games.

September 11, at Philadelphia
The Cardinals and Phillies split a pair as Syl Johnson scatters five hits to blank St. Louis, 5-0, in the first game. Johnny Moore goes 3-for-4 and drives in three runs. The Cardinals turn the tables in the second game, outscoring the Phils, 6-4. Bill Hallahan wins his eighth game as Philadelphia strands ten baserunners.

September 12, at Philadelphia
The Phillies rallied with two outs in the eighth inning to get past the Cards by a 3-1 score as Ethan Allen drives in two runs for the home team. Losing pitcher Dazzy Vance goes deep for the Cardinals' lone tally.

September 13, at New York
The Cardinals trail the Giants by 5 1/2 games as they meet New York in a pivotal four-game series. The opener goes to St. Louis as they score twice in the top of the 12th inning to secure a 2-0 victory. Paul Dean pitches all 12 innings, striking out seven in his 16th win.

September 14, at New York
The Giants retaliate as Hal Schumacher fans six in winning his 22nd game of the year, 4-1. Hank Leiber, Travis Jackson, Gus Mancuso, and Schumacher all tally an RBI.

September 16, at New York
St. Louis sweeps a doubleheader from New York to close to within 3 1/2 games of first place. Dizzy Dean wins his 26th game and Frank Frisch drives in two runs to lead the Cardinals to a 5-3 win. The second game, an extra-inning affair, is decided when Pepper Martin socks a home run in the top of the 11th. Paul Dean pitches a complete game, striking out seven in his 17th win. The Giants announce the attendance at the Polo Grounds as 62,573, the largest crowd ever to attend a game in the National League.

September 20, at Boston
St. Louis sweeps the Braves in a doubleheader to mount a final charge for first place. Tex Carleton scatters three hits and adds an RBI to lead the Cardinals to a 4-1 triumph in the opener. In game two Bill Walker wins his tenth, 1-0. Leo Durocher bats in the only run with a fielder's choice. New York Giants manager Bill Terry names Carl Hubbell as the Giants' starting pitcher in Game One of the World Series, to begin in Detroit on October 3.

September 21, at Brooklyn
The Cardinals pull to within three games of first place as they sweep another doubleheader, shutting out the Dodgers twice. One of the whitewashes is a 3-0 no-hitter by Paul Dean in the second game. Dean walks just one batter and strikes out six. Ripper Collins collects two RBIs. The opener is a 13-0 laugher as Ripper Collins launches his 34th home run and knocks in six runs. Dizzy Dean strikes out seven for his 27th win.

September 23, at Cincinnati
In their final doubleheader of the season, the Cardinals split with the Reds. St. Louis extended its win streak to seven in the first game with a 9-7 victory. Joe Medwick and Ripper Collins drive in two runs each as the team bangs out 16 hits. Jesse Haines wins his fourth game in relief. The Cardinals pitchers fail to get a strikeout. The Cardinals streak is snapped in the second game as the Reds win 4-3, giving Paul Derringer his 15th win. The Cardinals make four errors in game two, leading to three unearned runs for the Reds.

September 24, at Chicago
Seven games are left on the schedule, and the Cardinals trail the Giants by 2 1/2 games. Bill Walker wins his 11th game and Pepper Martin slugs a two-run homer as the Redbirds win their final road game, 3-1, over the Cubs. The Cardinals go 47-29 in road games for the regular season.

September 25, at St. Louis
Joe Medwick, Spud Davis, and Ripper Collins each collect first-inning RBI's and Dizzy Dean wins his 28th game as the Cardinals win over Pittsburgh, 3-2. The Giants are shut out by the Phillies and their lead shrinks to one game.

September 26, at St. Louis
The Pirates' Waite Hoyt wins his 15th, shutting out the Cardinals, 3-0. Arky Vaughan strikes a two-run homer. The lowly Phillies open the door for St. Louis by beating the Giants again, but the margin stays at one game.

September 27, at St. Louis
The Cardinals open a season-ending four-game series with the Cincinnati Reds, and prevail, 8-5, as Bill Walker gets his 12th win. Cincinnati shortstop Gordon Slade commits three first-inning errors, leading to five unearned Cardinal runs. Leo Durocher and Pepper Martin knock in two runs each. The idle Giants see their lead shrink to a half-game.

September 28, at St. Louis
In the only major-league game played today, the Cardinals tie the idle Giants for first place as Dizzy Dean wins his 29th, shutting out Cincinnati 4-0. Leo Durocher and Joe Medwick drive in a pair of runs each. The Cardinals and Giants are deadlocked with 93-58 records. The Cardinals have not been in first place since June 5.

September 29, at St. Louis
Paul Dean gets his 19th victory, dominating the Reds, 6-1. Joe Medwick is 2-for-4 with three RBIs and two runs scored. Brooklyn beats New York 5-1, to give the Cardinals a one-game lead with one to play.

September 30, at St. Louis
The Cardinals finish the home portion of the regular season 48-29 and win the pennant by two games over New York as Dizzy Dean shuts out the Reds, 9-0, for his 30th win, and the Giants lose again to Brooklyn. Dean becomes the last pitcher to accomplish the 30-victory feat in the National League. Bill DeLancey and Ripper Collins (No. 35) hit home runs. DeLancey knocks in four runs.

National League standings at season's end

Team Name	G	W	L	T	PCT	GB
St. Louis Cardinals	154	95	58	1	.621	-
New York Giants	153	93	60	0	.608	2.0
Chicago Cubs	152	86	65	1	.570	8.0
Boston Braves	152	78	73	1	.517	16.0
Pittsburgh Pirates	151	74	76	1	.493	19.5
Brooklyn Dodgers	153	71	81	1	.467	23.5
Philadelphia Phillies	149	56	93	0	.376	37.0
Cincinnati Reds	152	52	99	1	.344	42.0

The 1934 Pennant Race

By Charles F. Faber

As spring training was winding down and it was nearly time for the 1934 season to get under way, the defending world champion New York Giants were slight favorites to repeat as National League champs. A poll of members of the Baseball Writers Association of America (BBWAA) gave the Giants a slight edge over the Chicago Cubs and Pittsburgh Pirates, with the St. Louis Cardinals ranked fourth. Boston, Brooklyn, Cincinnati, and Philadelphia made up the predicted second division. *The Sporting News* reported that "a neck-and-neck struggle among four clubs in the National League is presaged, with the Giants enjoying only slight favoritism over the Chicago Cubs, gaining 1,213 points to 1,194 for the Cubs, but being chosen for first place only 68 times against 62 times for Chicago."[1] Eight fearless forecasters among the 174 voters in the BBWAA poll picked the Cardinals to win the pennant.

Among the more prominent prognosticators not picking the Giants were Hugh Fullerton and Dick Farrington. Fullerton gave the nod to the Cubs, with the Pirates second, the Cardinals third, and the Giants dropping to fourth. His second division was ranked exactly the same as in the baseball writers' poll.[2] Farrington's prediction was identical to Fullerton's except he switched the Cubs and Pirates between the first two spots, placing the Pittsburghers first.[3]

The Cubs and Giants both got off to terrific starts, the Chicagoans winning their first seven games and the New Yorkers taking their first five. Both the Pirates and the Cardinals started slowly. By the end of April, the Cubs were in first place with a 10-2 record and the Giants were second at 8-3. The Pirates were 5-5 in April, and the Cardinals a mediocre 4-7.

In May Pittsburgh got hot, winning 11 of its first 15 games in the month. By May 24 the Pirates had overtaken the Cubs and moved into first place. However, the Giants swept the Pirates in a doubleheader on May 28, knocking Pittsburgh out of first place. The league lead was now taken over by the surprising St. Louis Cardinals. After their poor start the Cardinals had rebounded and posted the best record in the league for May, winning 21 out of 27 contests during that merry month. After the last games of the month, the Redbirds ruled the roost with a 25-13 record, the same number of wins as the Giants and Cubs, who were tied for second with 25-16 records. In the last few days of the month, three different clubs had occupied, albeit temporarily, first place, and the defending champion Giants were only 1 1/2 games out of the lead. Prospects for an exciting pennant race were promising.

A resurgence by the Giants in June threatened to change the outlook. The defending champions opened the month on a roll and remained strong. They took over first place on June 6 and held that lead for the next 114 days. The contenders hung tough, refusing to concede anything. After the games of July 4, the traditional midpoint of the season,[4] it was still a pennant race. New York was 20 games over .500 and in first place by three games over Chicago, four over St. Louis, and 6 1/2 over Pittsburgh. After the final games of July the Giants had not managed to pull away from the Cubs or the Cardinals. Their lead was 2 1/2 games over Chicago and five games over St. Louis. Pittsburgh, however, had failed to keep pace, falling below .500 at 45-48, and at 14 games back apparently was no longer in contention. It looked as though it was going to be a three-team race.

In early August the Giants maintained their lead, but neither the Cubs nor the Cardinals were going away. On Sunday, August 12, the Dean brothers lost a doubleheader to the Cubs. It was the first time all season that both Deans had lost on the same day. Gloom filled the Cardinals clubhouse. The Redbirds were now 7 1/2 games out of the lead. Roy Stockton of the *St. Louis Post-Dispatch* wrote that the Cardinals were "apparently hopelessly behind the Giants."[5] When the club boarded a train that night for a trip to Detroit for an exhibition game, neither Dean was aboard. Dizzy had decided that he and Paul would not participate in another game that didn't count in the standings. Manager Franie Frisch fined Dizzy $100 and Paul $50 for violating their contracts, which required a player to take part in all of his club's games. The Deans not only refused to pay the fines, but refused to take the field for an August 14 game against Philadelphia. When the brothers did not appear on the field, Frisch confronted them in the clubhouse, ordering them to get dressed and join their teammates. Dizzy was quoted as saying, "Nothing doing. We think the fine against us was unjust. We're quitting."[6] Upon hearing this, Frisch suspended them and ordered them to turn in their uniforms. Dizzy then ripped his uniform to shreds and made a great show for the news photographers, taking his road uniform out of his locker and destroying it also.

The amount of the fines was deducted from the pitchers' paychecks. An additional $36 was deducted from Dizzy's check as payment for the two ripped-up uniforms. As the game scheduled for August 15 was rained out, the brothers spent the afternoon in their apartment, listening to the radio. Sportscasters were reporting that the fans were highly critical of the Deans, calling them selfish, spoiled brats, and ungrateful.[7] Surprised by this rejection by the fans, the brothers decided to accept their fines and apply for reinstatement. Paul was reinstated immediately, but club officials believed that Dizzy was the ringleader of the rebellion and deserved further punishment. He was told he couldn't come back for another ten days. Dizzy appealed to Commissioner Kenesaw Mountain Landis, who upheld the suspension. After Dizzy issued a public apology, St. Louis owner Sam Breadon reduced the suspension to seven days.

What effect did the incident have on the pennant race? Stockton wrote that the rebellion of the brothers crystallized team spirit. The other players rallied around their manager and vowed to play harder so the Deans wouldn't be missed. Captain Leo Durocher, for example, was quoted as saying, "It isn't right for two players to think they are bigger than a ballclub. And you watch our smoke from now on. We'll show those two guys a thing or two."[8]

Stockton wrote that without the revolt by the Deans, "[I]t is unlikely that the Cardinals would have gone on to win the pennant. Before August, the team had ability in large measure. After the rebellion there was ability plus team spirit and team determination and two invincible Deans. It didn't take long for the boys to regain the good will of their comrades."[9]

In the last two weeks of August the Cardinals gained two games on the Giants. At the end of the month New York held a 5 1/2-game lead over the Cubs and Cardinals, who were tied for second place. With one month to go, the stage was set for an exciting stretch run. The final days of the 1934 pennant race were riveting enough that writers had no need to resort to hyperbole in reporting them. Nevertheless, Fred Lieb wrote: "There never was another major league race exactly like the National League Marathon of 1934, and it will be years before baseball sees anything just like it."[10] (Had he forgotten about the 1908 season when both major-league races went down to the final day of the season?) Lieb wrote that the no team ever blew a pennant as badly as the Giants did that year in blowing "a seemingly fool-proof early September lead."[11] Most baseball fans would probably recognize that a five-, six-, or seven-game lead in early September is not really safe. It certainly was not safe in 1934.

In September the Cubs were unable to keep up the pace and fell out of serious contention. It took a combination of St. Louis wins and New York losses to bring the season down to its thrilling conclusion. With exactly one week to play, the Cardinals were 2 1/2 games behind. They won six of their last seven. Meanwhile, the Giants lost five out of their last six. The Giants' victory over the Braves in the first game of a September 23 doubleheader was their 93rd and last win of the season. They lost the second game of the double bill. The Cardinals picked up a half-game in the standings by winning a game at Chicago on the 24th, while the Giants had the day off. On the 25th the Giants were shut out by the Phillies, and the Cardinals reduced the deficit to one game as Dizzy Dean defeated the Pirates for his 28th win of the season. New York and St. Louis both lost on the 26th, the Cardinals' final loss of the regular season. So the Giants maintained their one-game lead. The Giants were idle on September 27 and St. Louis gained another half-game by defeating Cincinnati in the first game of a four-game set.

The Giants had another day off on September 28. With Dizzy Dean pitching on two days of rest and throwing a shutout for his 29th victory of the season, the Cardinals moved into a tie for first place. With two games left, St. Louis and New York boasted identical 93-58 record. After 152 games, the two clubs were dead even. The league championship hinged on the outcome of the two remaining games. The Giants games were at the Polo Grounds against Brooklyn.[12] St. Louis was to close the season at home against Cincinnati. On September 29 Paul Dean put the Cardinals a game ahead by defeating the Reds, 6-1, while the Giants were losing to Brooklyn, 5-1. The Cardinals victory clinched at least a tie for the pennant. If St. Louis won on September 30, the pennant would be theirs. If the Cardinals were to lose and the Giants to win on the final day, there would be a best-of-three-games playoff for the league championship.

The Giants made a valiant attempt to create that tie. They led Brooklyn throughout the game until the Dodgers tied it in the eighth and then eliminated the Giants in ten innings, 8-5. Actually, it didn't matter what the Giants did on that final day of the season as long as St. Louis won. Dizzy Dean made sure the Cardinals were the 1934 National League champions by pitching with one day of rest and shutting out Cincinnati, 9-0, in the final game of the season, winning his 30th game of the year in doing so.

Sources

Gregory, Robert, *Diz: Dizzy Dean and Baseball During the Great Depression* (New York: Penguin Books, 1992).

Lieb, Frederick J., *The St. Louis Cardinals* (New York: G.P. Putnam's Sons, 1944).

Stockton, J. Roy, *The Gashouse Gang and a Couple of Other Guys* (New York: A.S. Barnes, 1945).

The Sporting News.

baseball-reference.com.

Notes

1. *The Sporting News*, April 5, 1934.
2. *The Sporting News*, April 19, 1934
3. *The Sporting News,*, April 26, 1934.
4. Tradition holds that the clubs holding first place on the Fourth of July will win the pennant. Of course, that is not always true. Other than its being Independence Day, there is nothing magical about July 4. Teams in first place on that date are no more likely to win titles than clubs in first place on any other date in the middle of the season.
5. J. Roy Stockton, *The Gashouse Gang and a Couple of Other Guys* (New York: A.S. Barnes, 1945), 53.
6. *The Sporting News,*, August 23, 1934.
7. Robert Gregory, *Diz: Dizzy Dean and Baseball During the Great Depression* (New York: Penguin Books, 1992), 171. Gregory's book gives the most complete account of the Deans' rebellion.
8. Gregory, 175.
9. Stockton, 53-54.
10. Frederick J. Lieb, *The St. Louis Cardinals* (New York: G.P. Putnam's Sons, 1944), 165.
11. Ibid.
12. Manager Bill Terry of the Giants had incurred the wrath of Dodger fans for allegedly asking, "Is Brooklyn still in the league?" Whether he actually said it or not is uncertain, but the Dodgers were fired up with the chance to prove they were still in the league by knocking Terry's club out of the pennant race.

The 1934 World Series

By Matthew Silverman

"*Me and Paul'll win two games apiece.*"[1] Jay Hanna "Dizzy" Dean was known for hyperbole, bragging, and flat out making up new words, but truer words were never spoken than his boast/prediction before the 1934 World Series. The 24-year-old pitcher led the league in strikeouts his first three seasons in the majors; in 1933 he pulled off the feat of leading the National League in both complete games and games pitched—and then did it again in 1936. (Dean was the only National League pitcher in the 20th century to twice lead in both categories in the same year.) In 1934 he won 30 games—the first time since Grover Cleveland Alexander in 1917 and the last time a National League pitcher has reached that big round number.

Old Diz could sling the bull as well as the ball, and having his rookie kid brother on the 1934 Cardinals made the braggart ever bolder. In spring training Dizzy said that he and Paul would win 50 games between them; the pair claimed 49 of the Cards' 95 wins. Seven of those victories came in the season's final ten days, including a doubleheader against the Dodgers with Dizzy hurling a shutout in the first game and Paul tossing a no-hitter in the second. The following weekend the Deans claimed wins in each of the last three games of the season to put the Cardinals in first place for the first time since June 5.

The Cards got plenty of help from Brooklyn, making New York Giants player-manager Bill Terry sorely pay for his snide preseason comment: "Is Brooklyn still in the league?" Though mired in sixth place, the Dodgers helped decide the pennant by beating the Giants twice at the Polo Grounds to end their year while the Cards swept four from the Reds to steal the pennant.

As the saying goes—and using the Diz's English—"It ain't bragging if you can back it up."[2] And in 1934, that is just what the Dean Brothers did.

Game One—Wednesday, October 3, 1934, at Navin Field

Cardinals 8, Tigers 3

The Detroit Tigers had a much easier time of reaching the World Series than the Cardinals—if you can call holding off the Yankees easy. New York, winner of seven pennants since 1921, started out hot. The Yankees held a 5 1/2-game lead over Detroit in mid-May of 1934, but from that point on the Tigers played .682 ball (90-42). Detroit won 101 times to claim the pennant by seven games over the Yankees in what was Babe Ruth's final season in pinstripes.

The Babe was among the 42,505 watching at Navin Field for the World Series opener on a cool Wednesday afternoon. Also on hand was renowned humorist Will Rogers, seated next to car moguls Henry Ford and his son Edsel, who'd signed a $100,000 deal for exclusive rights to sponsor the World Series on radio.[3] It was the first time Major League Baseball had sold radio rights.[4]

Both the Cardinals and Tigers were led by stars in their first full year as player-manager. Mickey Cochrane and St. Louis counterpart Frankie Frisch shook hands and exchanged pleasantries in front of the masses of cameras on the field before the game. But both teams would be out for blood in a long, tough World Series.

Cochrane's choice to start the Series was veteran Alvin "General" Crowder, who had been picked up in August off waivers from the defending American League champion Senators. Crowder had led the AL in wins the previous two years and started twice in the 1933 World Series, but after he went 4-10 with a 6.79 ERA in 1934, Washington gave up on him and the Tigers picked him up on waivers in August. The 35-year-old righty found new life in Detroit, winning five of six decisions, and Cochrane went with the veteran over his 20-something pitchers Schoolboy Rowe and Tommy Bridges, winners of 20-something games apiece in 1934.

Cochrane's former manager, Connie Mack of the Philadelphia Athletics, had shocked baseball in 1929 by sending little-used veteran Howard Ehmke to start the World Series opener against the Chicago Cubs. The 35-year-old Ehmke won that game and the A's took the '29 Series, with Cochrane batting .400 and catching every inning. Five years later was a different

Pepper Martin strokes a hit in Game One of the World Series. Detroit catcher Mickey Cochrane and Umpire Brick Owens look on.

story. The cash-strapped Mack had sent his star catcher to Detroit after the 1933 season, and now Cochrane was not only calling the shots in the Tigers' dugout, but he played well enough to be named the league's Most Valuable Player.

Neither Cochrane nor Crowder could have foreseen the miscues that cost Detroit the 1934 Series opener. The Tigers had committed the fewest errors (156) in the American League in 1934, but they were all thumbs in Game One. Detroit made five miscues with Crowder on the hill, resulting in three unearned runs. Joe Medwick's home run was the lone earned tally against Crowder in five innings.

Cochrane went to his top reliever, Firpo Marberry, in the sixth inning; Marberry's deficiencies could not be blamed on poor defense. The first batter he faced was opposing pitcher Dizzy Dean. Old Diz doubled and Pepper Martin singled him home. With a chance to get out of trouble—and with first base open—Medwick stroked his fourth hit of the day, scoring Martin. After a Ripper Collins hit sent Marberry to the showers, Bill DeLancey greeted reliever Chief Hogsett with a two-run double to make it 8-1.

Dean, who claimed National League MVP for 1934, was in control, as usual. He did allow a pair of late runs, including Hank Greenberg's first postseason home run, but it didn't fret Dean. Like several of his St. Louis teammates, he held Greenberg in contempt because of his Jewish heritage. "I was trying to keep my curveball outside on him, and I got it inside. Anybody could have hit that ball for a home run. Our clubhouse boy could have done it. I still don't think he's that bad to pitch to."[5] No matter how you sliced it, the Cards had stolen into the Tigers' den and taken the first game.

Game Two—Thursday, October 4, 1934, at Navin Field

Tigers 3, Cardinals 2

Comedian and avid baseball fan Joe E. Brown entertained fans with a pregame pantomime boxing sketch on the field.[6] Detroit and St. Louis would slug it long and hard.

The Cardinals started out fast once again with single runs in the second and third innings knocked in by Ernie Orsatti and Joe Medwick. After winning 24 games at age 24 in 1934—including 16 straight during the season—Lynwood "Schoolboy" Rowe seemed to only get stronger as the season of his life progressed. A superstitious and eccentric pitcher who was already besting professional ballplayers in his native Texas before he reached high school—hence the nickname—Schoolboy often talked to the ball while on the mound. In his World Series debut, Rowe had the Cardinals talking to themselves, retiring 22 straight batters after Joe Medwick was thrown out at the plate on a single to end the third inning. No pitcher retired more batters in a row in a World Series game until Don Larsen's perfect game in 1956.[7]

St. Louis starter Bill Hallahan was enjoying plenty of success himself. A seasoned vet who'd pitched for the Cards in the 1926, 1930, and 1931 World Series, Wild Bill kept the Tigers off balance. Even after doubles by Billy Rogell and Pete Fox cut the St. Louis lead to 2-1 in the fourth, he did not allow another Detroit hit—until the ninth inning.

Fox singled to start the ninth, just his club's fifth hit of the day. With the game on the line, Schoolboy Rowe batted for himself and bunted Fox to second. Then Mickey Cochrane sent up a pinch-hitter for leadoff hitter Jo-Jo White, hitless in six at bats in the Series so far. Gee Walker, a right-handed hitter, batted for the lefty-swinging White against the southpaw Hallahan. Gee singled home Fox and packed Navin Field went into hysterics. Bill Walker came on in relief, picking Gee Walker off first and fanning Cochrane to send the game into extra innings.

The Tigers had a chance to win it in the tenth inning, but Marv Owen's liner was hauled in by Ernie Orsatti in center field to strand two runners. Pepper Martin finally broke Rowe's string of seven innings without a baserunner when he doubled in the 11th. Rowe fanned Jack Rothrock and then induced manager Frisch to ground out to end the threat.

Bill Walker and Rowe followed with 1-2-3 innings as the game became the first World Series contest in a decade to reach 12 innings. The cause of the unraveling was by, as manager Frisch often lamented: "Oh, those bases on balls." In his third inning of relief, Bill Walker walked Charlie Gehringer and then issued a free pass to Hank Greenberg. Leon "Goose" Goslin climaxed the afternoon with a base hit to score Gehringer and even the Series.

With the complete-game win, Schoolboy Rowe became the last pitcher in history to toss 12 innings in a World Series game. Old-time Tiger Wild Bill Donovan had been the first pitcher in history to throw that many innings in a fall classic game, in 1907. (In his pre-slugger days, Babe Ruth set the record by pitching 14 innings for the Boston Red Sox in Game Two of the 1916 World Series.) Donovan's effort—in the first game of the 1907 World Series—had gone for naught as the contest against the Cubs had ended in a tie due to darkness. That World Series, like each of the three straight pennants won by Detroit between 1907 and 1909, ended with the Tigers on the losing end. Rowe had earned Detroit's first victory in a World Series game in 25 years. The Tigers were thrilled to leave town even.

Game Three—Friday, October 5, 1934, at Sportsman's Park

Cardinals 4, Tigers 1

There was no rest for the weary, as the clubs immediately boarded the train for St. Louis for a game the next afternoon. Offdays were rare in World Series schedules of the day, unless the distance traveled necessitated a break. The 550 miles from Detroit to St. Louis afforded no such luxury.

The Cardinals had just one baserunner over the final nine innings in Game Two, but back on home turf, they shook off the torpor quickly. Pepper Martin led off the game with a triple and trotted home on Jack Rothrock's long fly. Cards pitcher Paul Dean added another sacrifice fly as the home team went up 2-0 in the second.

The Tigers had a great chance against the younger Dean in the third inning, putting runners on second and third with one out. But Paul fanned Hank Greenberg, walked Goose Goslin intentionally to fill the bases, and then induced Billy Rogell to fly to center to end the threat. Detroit left the bases loaded again in the fourth and stranded a pair in the fifth.

In the home fifth, a single, double, and triple by the first three Cardinals in the order knocked out Tommy Bridges, a 22-game winner during the year. Handed a 4-0 lead, Paul Dean plowed through the Tigers, allowing just one baserunner through the next three innings. He was one out from a shutout when Greenberg finally got a hit with a runner on base after starting the Series 0-for-9 in such situations. The final score was 4-1, but the tally sheet might as well have read: Deans 2, Detroit 1.

Game Four—Saturday, October 6, 1934 at Sportsman's Park

Tigers 10, Cardinals 4

Though Hank Greenberg produced in his last at-bat in Game Three, manager Mickey Cochrane dropped

Game Four starters, Elden Auker of Detroit and Tex Carleton of St. Louis greet each other before the first pitch.

the slugger two spots in the order for Game Four. Greenberg, 23, had just completed his second full season in majors. He was not yet the 50-home-run slugger he is remembered for, but his 63 doubles in 1934 were a mere four shy of the all-time mark and he hit .339 for the year with 26 home runs and 139 RBIs. Cochrane left the top of the order the same with Jo-Jo White, himself, and Charlie Gehringer, but he installed Goose Goslin in the cleanup spot and Billy Rogell in the five-hole—with Greenberg hitting sixth, where he had batted more times (114) than any other Tiger during the year. Greenberg had not been shifted to cleanup until September.

Cardinals starter Tex Carleton breezed through the Tigers the first time through the order, but the revamped lineup responded enthusiastically when they saw him a second time. They even spotted Tex a 1-0 lead and the first two outs of the third inning. Then Cochrane doubled, Gehringer and Goslin walked, and Rogell singled home two runs to put Detroit up and knock out Carleton, just like that. Greenberg greeted Dazzy Vance with a single that gave Detroit a 3-1 lead.

Ripper Collins singled in a St. Louis run in the bottom of the inning and, after a wild pitch put Detroit back up by two runs in the top of the fourth, the Cardinals tied it in the home end of the frame. It was an odd way to tie a game, though.

After pinch-hitter Spud Davis singled in a run, manager Frankie Frisch sent Dizzy Dean to run for him. Though Dean was not terribly fast, Frisch chose his star pitcher for the role because "he always inspires the team."[8] What transpired next was less than inspired. Pepper Martin grounded to second and shortstop Rogell's return throw nailed Dean in the head. Eight Cardinals carried their star off the field and he was taken to a hospital, where the medical report became a fabled but apocryphal headline: "X-Rays of Dean's Head Show Nothing." Greenberg and most Detroit backers could have agreed with that without going near a hospital or picking up the *St. Louis Post Dispatch*, which had the real yet far less memorable headline of "X-Ray Photograph of Head Shows No Lasting Injury."[9] But the tying run had scored on the ball that hit Dean's head—the deadlock continued into the seventh.

Greenberg broke the tie with a single and was in the middle of the rally the next inning that put the game out of reach. Reliever Bill Walker's error on a bunt had set up a big inning as two walks, one of them an intentional pass to Goslin, brought up the newly installed fifth hitter, Rogell. He had his second two-run single of the afternoon and Greenberg followed with a ground-rule double for his fourth hit and third RBI of the day. Marv Owen singled in one run and helped steal another. Owen took off for second and when Cards catcher Bill DeLancey mishandled the pitch, Greenberg stole home to make it 10-4. The new lineup worked, to put it mildly.

Detroit sidewinder Elden Auker's ten-hitter was not a thing of beauty, but compared to the 13 hits and six walks issued by five Cardinals hurlers—especially the contributions of Bill Walker, who took his second loss of the Series—Auker looked like a Picasso painting.

Game Five—Sunday, October 7, 1934, at Sportsman's Park

Tigers 3, Cardinals 1

Showing no ill effects from getting clocked in the head with a throw the previous day, Dizzy Dean allowed three runs for the second time in as many World Series starts—only this time that wasn't good enough. Instead of Alvin Crowder, the surprise starter in Game One, Detroit's manager went with Tommy Bridges, who'd pitched well but lost to Dizzy's brother, Paul, in Game Three. Mickey Cochrane made the right call.

Bridges had been clipped for a couple of early runs in his first start against the Cards, but this time Detroit staked him to an early lead. Pete Fox's two-out double scored Hank Greenberg from first to put the Tigers on the board in the second inning. Bridges made the slim lead stand up, stranding leadoff baserunners in the first and third innings before retiring ten straight batters. Dean battled to keep the deficit at 1-0. Goose Goslin's double and Billy Rogell's bunt single put men on the corners with none out in the fourth, but Dizzy fanned Greenberg and then retired both Marv Owen and Pete Fox.

Charlie Gehringer took Dean deep to open the sixth. St. Louis center fielder Chuck Fullis then mishandled Rogell's single to put the Tiger on third with only one out. That brought up Greenberg in another RBI situation. Dean retired him again, but this time Hank got the bat on the ball and sent it deep enough for Rogell to tag up and score for a 3–0 lead.

Bill DeLancey put St. Louis on the board with a solo homer in the seventh. After Bridges survived a leadoff hit in the eighth, the Cards put the first batter on base in the ninth when Frankie Frisch singled. Joe Medwick came up as the tying run and flied out, but Ripper Collins singled to send Frisch to third and bring up DeLancey with the tying runs on base. Despite the lefty swinger against the right-handed pitcher — and a home run by DeLancey in their last confrontation — Cochrane stayed with his starter. This time Bridges caught the Cards catcher looking and then got pinch-hitter Ernie Orsatti to ground out and end the game.

On one day's rest, Tommy Bridges bested Dizzy Dean. Now the Tigers were in position to finish off the Cardinals and make them eat crow. That meal, however, was not available on the dining car on the train ride back to Michigan.

Game Six — Monday, October 8, 1934, at Navin Field

Cardinals 4, Tigers 3

Schoolboy Rowe had retired 27 of the last 28 batters he faced in his brilliant Game Two performance. In the rematch — and facing elimination — the Cards got their first hit two batters into the game and Joe Medwick's subsequent single put the Cards on the board first.

Detroit answered back in the third inning against Paul Dean, with the Tigers manager taking advantage of an error by the Cardinals skipper. Jo-Jo White should have been out stealing, but second baseman and skipper Frankie Frisch could not handle the throw and the runner went to third base. Detroit manager Mickey Cochrane, who had yet to drive in a run in the Series, singled home White to tie the game.

Cardinals shortstop Leo Durocher, unheard from in the Series — unless one counts his epithets hurled at Hank Greenberg — singled to start the sixth inning. Dean sacrificed Durocher to second and he scored on Pepper Martin's hit. Goose Goslin's errant throw sent Martin all the way to third, and Pepper dashed home on an infield out.

Paul Dean held the lead for an inning, but his error on a groundball allowed the Tigers to cut it to 3–2 in the sixth. Catcher Bill DeLancey then grabbed a bunt and fired to third, seemingly too late, but umpire Brick Owens punched out Cochrane. The Tigers and their manager voiced their displeasure, but the call was momentarily forgotten when Hank Greenberg tied it up with a two-out single.

Pepper Martin scores a run in Game Two of the 1934 World Series.

Dean's poor defensive play had led to the Tigers tying the game, but in the seventh he took matters into his own hands—with his bat. After Durocher doubled with one out, Dean singled the Lip home for the 4-3 lead. Dean's work was far from done, however.

The Tigers put runners on the corners with one out in the eighth. Rogell hit a fly to center that was too shallow to score slow-footed Charlie Gehringer. Dean still had to face Greenberg, whose hit had tied the game in their last confrontation. With the chance to tie—or even win—the World Series, Dean put a fastball right where Greenberg liked it… and the slugger watched it for a strike. He fouled out to end the threat. Dean set down the Tigers in the ninth, with pitcher Schoolboy Rowe—a .303 hitter during the season but hitless in the Series—flying out to center to end the game.

There were plenty of "shoulda's" and "coulda's" going around Detroit that night. What if Brick Owens had called Cochrane safe? (Photographs showed the ump's call to be wrong.) "I've been waiting 35 years to see Detroit win a championship here," Tigers owner Frank Navin lamented to Indians owner Billy Evans after the game, "and when we've got one in our grip, some guy blows it for us."[10] Greenberg felt that the guy who'd blown it might have been himself after taking that first fastball from Paul Dean. More than four decades later, Greenberg was quoted as saying, "I often wondered what might have happened if I'd jumped on that fastball."[11]

Game Seven—Tuesday, October 9, 1934 at Navin Field

Cardinals 11, Tigers 0

Frankie Frisch later admitted that his players rode the Tigers, especially Hank Greenberg, "something awful."[12] Dizzy Dean tormented the Tigers first baseman both on the mound and off it. He wandered over to the Tigers bench during warmups for Game Seven and spotted Greenberg. "It'll all be over in a few minutes," he said. "Old Diz is goin' to pitch and he's goin' to pin your ears back."[13]

It took 139 minutes, including several delays, for the game to be over, but Game Seven was decided long before that. Elden Auker, who'd won Game Four, took the mound against Old Diz and they matched zeroes for two innings. Then with one out in the third, Dean came to the plate. A ballplayer who could back up his words with his bat as well as his arm, Dean had batted .339 during his 30-win season. He doubled off Auker, beginning a barrage that saw the Cards amass seven runs on seven hits plus three walks against four Tigers pitchers in the inning. While Dean had two hits in the frame, the biggest blow was a line drive by Frankie Frisch that Greenberg mistimed; the ball bounced off his oustretched glove into right field to clear the bases.

Down 3-0, Auker was sent to the showers for Schoolboy Rowe, who'd pitched nine innings the day before. He got Joe Medwick out—an achievement given that Ducky, like Pepper and Ripper, had 11 hits for the Cardinals in the Series. Rowe was done two batters later. Chief Hogsett did not retire any of his four batters. Tommy Bridges had to be summoned to get the final out of the inning with the bases loaded and the score 7-0. The Tigers would use two more pitchers before the day was finally over.

Though the air went out of the 40,000 fans in Detroit, the crowd was far from lifeless. In the sixth inning Medwick tripled home Pepper Martin. Medwick knocked over Tiger Marv Owens and spiked him coming into third base. The two men nearly came to blows, but neither was ejected, and Medwick scored a few minutes later on a Ripper Collins single. When Medwick went out to left field in the bottom of the sixth, the crowd seethed hatred at the player who epitomized defeat of their club after it had waited a quarter-century just to get back to the World Series. Going from needing one win in two games to one loss and a 9-0 deficit in the deciding game, the fans turned on Medwick, hurling fruit, bottles, newspapers, and any garbage that was on hand. Tigers shortstop Billy Rogell said, "If somebody had an old Ford, they would have thrown that out at him."[14] Somebody apparently forgot that 71-year-old Henry Ford was in the stands.

Play was stopped three times to clean up the debris before Commissioner Kenesaw Mountain Landis made the unprecedented call to eject the Cardinals left fielder from the game. "For the safety of the crowd and the best interest of baseball, Landis removed Medwick from the game," a newsreel account told crowds in theaters all over the country. "An unusual but wise decision."[15] The wisdom and injustice of the decision can still be argued all these years later—especially without a similar incident in a deciding postseason game—but the 9-0 lead by St. Louis made the decision expedient and harmless to the outcome. Medwick did miss a chance to match a then-World Series record of 12 hits—ironically his replacement, Chuck Hollis, singled his only time up. But the point was moot. It was 11-0 in the bottom of the ninth when Owens grounded out to end the Series.

Dizzy Dean had lived up to his boasts and survived a frightening jolt to his noggin to be the star of the World Series. And he'd been right: Dizzy and Paul did win all four games against the Tigers. Just to show off a little more, the Deans won three of those four games on the road. The pair pitched 44 of their staff's 65 1/3 innings and sported an ERA of 1.43, compared with the rest of the club's mark of 4.23. Detroit's ERA was 3.74, though it went up by almost a full run because of the beating in Game Seven.

While St. Louis had its third world championship in eight years, along with two other pennants, Detroit would have to wait another season to get its first title in 1935. But after what might have been in the '34 World Series, it was a long, cold winter to endure.

Sources

Enders, Eric, *100 Years of the World Series: 1903-2004* (New York: Sterling, 2005).

Neft, David S., and Richard M. Cohen, *The World Series: Complete Play-by-Play of Every Game 1903-1989* (New York: St. Martin's Press, 1990).

Rosengren, Dan, *Hank Greenberg: The Hero of Heroes* (New York: New American Library, 2013).

Holmes, Dan, " 'Schoolboy' Rowe: The Most Superstitious Player in Detroit Baseball History," July 26, 2011. blog.detroitathletic.com/2011/07/26/schoolboy-rowe-the-most-superstitious-player-in-detroit-tigers-history/

McGowen, Roscoe, "This Day in Sports: Oh, Those Dizzy and Daffy Dean Boys," *New York Times*, September 21, 1934. nytimes.com/packages/html/sports/year_in_sports/09.21.html

1934 World Series newsreel and extended footage, youtube.com/watch?v=baWLXkoPeCQ

Baseball-reference.com

Dizzydean.com

Encyclopediaofarkansas.net

Notes

1. Roscoe McGowen, *New York Times*, September 21, 1934.
2. "Quotes," Dizzydean.com. dizzydean.com/quotes.htm.
3. 1934 World Series newsreel and extended footage, youtube.com/watch?v=baWLXkoPeCQ.
4. John Rosengren, *Hank Greenberg*, 94.
5. Rosengren, 98.
6. 1934 World Series newsreel.
7. Rosengren, 98.
8. Eric Enders, *100 Years of the World Series*, 83.
9. Rosengren, 99.
10. Rosengren, 101.
11. Rosengren, 100.
12. Ibid.
13. Rosengren, 101.
14. Rosengren, 102.
15. 1934 World Series newsreel.

Tex Carleton

By Gregory H. Wolf

WITH A GRACEFUL and deceptive side-arm delivery, Tex Carleton was a tough, no-nonsense right-handed pitcher who enjoyed an eight-year major-league career between 1932 and 1940. Notching exactly 100 career victories, Carleton was a member of the St. Louis Cardinals' Gas House Gang championship team in 1934, helped lead the Chicago Cubs to the World Series in 1935 and 1938, and pitched a no-hitter for the Brooklyn Dodgers in his final season, 1940.

As his nickname suggests, Carleton was a Texan. Born on August 19, 1906, in Comanche, a town southwest of the Dallas/Fort Worth complex, James Otto Carleton was the first of two children born to Ed Carleton, manager of a large ranch, and his wife, Annie. Otto, as his parents called him, and his younger brother, Scecil, grew up on the ranch. As a youngster Otto rode horses, herded cattle during the day, and milked cows in the morning and evening. When he was about 11 his family moved to Fort Worth, a fast-growing city of almost 100,000, where his father took a job in a rail yard. Otto played baseball in high school, seeing action as a catcher and infielder, then attended Texas Christian University in Fort Worth, where he played basketball, football, and baseball, and launched his career as a pitcher. Attracted to the pay and lifestyle while playing semipro baseball in Newport, Arkansas, Carleton quit college after two years to sign with the Texarkana Twins in the Class D East Texas League in 1925. However, after a contract dispute he switched teams, moving to the Marshall Indians in the same league.[1]

The tall (6-feet-1) and lanky (180 pounds) Carleton won three of five decisions for Marshall, but also had a stroke of luck:

Carleton posted a 100-76 record over an eight-year career. His 16 victories in 1934 were third-best on the Cardinals staff.

Legendary scout Jack Ryan spotted him and recommended him to the St. Louis Cardinals, who were in the initial stages of building the first modern farm system. Reporting to the Cardinals' spring-training site in San Antonio, Carleton was transferred to the Syracuse Stars in the International League, then was assigned to the Austin Senators in the Class D Texas Association to start the 1926 season. There the 19-year-old Carleton pitched his first full season in Organized Baseball, winning 11 of 20 decisions and logging 202 innings.

Carleton pitched for the Houston Buffaloes in the Class A Texas League in 1927 and 1928, winning ten games each season as a starter and occasional reliever. The 1928 Buffaloes, sporting one of the best pitching staffs in minor-league history, boasted four 20-game winners (Frank Barnes, Bill Hallahan, Jim Lindsey, and Ken Penner), won 104 games (lost 54), and defeated the Birmingham Barons in the Dixie Series. Carleton was promoted to the Cardinals' top minor-league affiliate, the Rochester Red Wings, in the International League, for the 1929 season.

At the Red Wings' spring training camp in Plant City, Florida, Carleton struggled and appeared to be overwhelmed by more seasoned competition. However, when the minor-league season commenced, he settled down and won 13 consecutive decisions, including a no-hitter against Toronto on September 14, wining 3-1 (the sole run was the product of a walk and two errors). He and fellow 22-year-old Paul Derringer, dubbed the "$100,000 Twins" because of their ability, led the team to the International League pennant.[2] Named to the league all-star team, Carleton finished with an 18-7 record and a 2.71 earned-run average in 262 innings. He won two more games as Rochester lost to the Kansas City Blues in the Junior World Series, 5 games to 4.

Anticipating an invitation to the Cardinals' spring-training camp in 1930 and an eventual spot on the team, Carleton was sorely disappointed when he was bypassed in favor of seasoned veterans from the team's deep farm system, which was stacked with pitchers. The success of 1929 was soon covered by his rocky performance for Rochester in 1930. Suffering through a series of arm and hand ailments, Carleton slipped to 13-13 and his ERA rose to 5.01, which earned him a demotion back to Houston for 1931.

Carleton's year with Houston was the turning point in his baseball career. The Buffaloes, powered by Carleton (20 wins and a 1.90 ERA) and 21-year-old phenom Dizzy Dean (26 wins, 1.57 ERA), won 108 games and the Texas League title before they were upset in the Dixie Series by Birmingham in seven games. From June 25 to August 13, Carleton won 13 consecutive starts before fracturing a finger on his pitching hand and missing the last five weeks of the season and the postseason. *The Sporting News* wrote before his injury that Carleton was "regarded by many as the equivalent of Dean" and on pace to win 30 games.[3] In light of his success the previous seasons, Carleton acquired the nickname Tex from the well-known sportswriter Ernest J. Lanigan, nephew of the founders of *The Sporting News*, and the moniker remained with him the rest of his life.[4] "Three New Cardinals Pitchers Won 66 Games. Dean, Carleton and Starr will Bolster Champs on Mound" read the headline in *The Sporting News* announcing St. Louis's purchase of Tex's contract for the 1932 season.[5]

Arriving at the Cardinals' spring-training site in Bradenton, Florida, Carleton baffled teammates and opponents with his smooth side-arm delivery. Deceptive and with a low release point, he generated unexpected speed and reminded some players of the Deadball Era side-arm hurler and strikeout artist Cy Falkenburg.[6] "He seems to have everything—speed, curves, poise, and self-confidence without being cocky," *The Sporting News* wrote.[7] On April 17 Carleton made his major-league debut by pitching six hitless innings against the Cubs, but issued a career-high nine walks in eight innings and lost the game, 4-1. Over the next two months he pitched mostly in relief, and didn't get his first victory until a start on June 19 when he shut out the New York Giants on two hits. Carleton hurled a ten-inning 8-7 victory over the Boston Braves on August 20 in St. Louis, followed by a 3-0 shutout of the Braves just two days later. He finished the season with a 10-13 record and 4.08 ERA in 196 1/3 innings for the Cardinals, World Series champions in 1931 but a disappointing 72-82 record for a sixth-place finish in 1932.

With a dark complexion, closely cropped black hair, and steely blue-gray eyes, Carleton brooded over losses. Moody, he could be filled with good humor at one moment and then be snippy to teammates in the next. He was especially belligerent to coaches who voiced any criticism of his pitching. A confident yet cantankerous pitcher, he became increasingly resentful of the attention Dizzy Dean received during their three seasons together on the Cardinals (1932-1934) and felt Dizzy and his brother, Paul, were coddled by the organization. Distrustful of the Deans and insulted by their braggadocio, Carleton didn't want to pitch in their shadow; consequently, he often feuded with teammates who questioned his ability. No doubt St. Louis fans were astonished when Carleton and teammate Joe Medwick got into a slugfest at home plate during batting practice on May 15, 1934, after an argument.[8]

Before the 1932 season Giants manager Bill Terry called Carleton one of the "hurling stars of the National League" and attempted to acquire him from the Cardinals, but St. Louis general manager Branch Rickey wasn't listening.[9] Carleton threw a two-hit shutout against the Cubs on April 22 to win his first start of the season, and won his first five decisions before losing to the Braves on May 23, 3-1, despite pitching a ten-inning complete game. He notched his league-leading 11th win on June 29 against the Giants, then, on two days' rest, squared off with Giants ace Carl Hubbell in an epic battle on July 2. In front of an estimated 50,000 fans at the Polo Grounds, Carleton and Hubbell pitched scoreless ball through 16 innings. Jesse Haines relieved Carleton to start the 17th and surrendered a walk-off single to Hughie Critz in the bottom of the 18th.

Hubbell went the distance, tossing an 18-inning, six-hit shutout. Carleton had held the Giants to eight hits (plus seven walks) in his 16 innings. Carleton went just 6-8 the rest of the season but finished with career highs in victories (17), innings pitched (277), games (44), and starts (33); he recorded a 3.38 ERA and tossed 15 complete games. Carleton finished third in the league in strikeouts (147) behind two future Hall of Fame hurlers, Dizzy Dean (199) and Hubbell (156).

At the age of 21 while still in the minor leagues, Carleton had married Fannie Francis Major of New Orleans. In the offseason they lived in Forth Worth, where Tex enjoyed hunting and fishing. He also played in exhibition games in Texas and throughout the South to earn extra income. Feisty and combative, Carleton took all games seriously. When he was on a barnstorming tour in Mexico City in the fall of 1934, he flattened the home-plate umpire after it was discovered that he had been betting on the games.

In an era when staff aces were expected to complete two-thirds of their starts, the high-strung Carleton had a reputation for lacking stamina, which may have been one of the reasons why Branch Rickey had been dilatory in promoting him to the major leagues. A worrier, Carleton reported to the Cardinals' 1934 spring-training camp 15 pounds under his normal playing weight of 180. (To solve the problem in 1933, Dr. Robert Hyland, the Cardinals' team physician, had recommended that Carleton have a few drinks to stimulate his appetite. "I used to get prescription whiskey—it still being Prohibition," Carleton said, "and carry it with me on the road."[10] The constitutional amendment ending Prohibition went into effect at the end of 1933, and Carleton no longer needed a prescription.)

Despite his "frail" appearance, Carleton got off to a fast start in 1934, completing eight of his first ten starts, but his record stood at just 6-5 in early June owing to weak run support in three of his losses (and one loss in relief).[11] After a poor June and media reports that he was "short winded," Carleton was maddeningly inconsistent for the rest of the year, winning nine games (seven of them complete games) but surrendering at least five runs in each of his five losses. Finishing with 16 wins (third on the team behind Dizzy's 30 and Paul's 19), 11 defeats, and 240 2/3 innings pitched, Carleton helped the Cardinals overcome a seven-game deficit on September 6 to win the pennant in dramatic fashion on the last weekend of the season.

The Gas House Gang, one of baseball's most memorable and enduring teams, beat the Detroit Tigers in seven games to win the 1934 World Series. Game Four pitted two side-arm hurlers against each other: Carleton and "Submarine" Elden Auker in his first full season. In his first start in almost two weeks, Carleton was chased in the third inning after surrendering four hits, two walks, and three runs, but was not charged with the loss. The following afternoon Carleton relieved Dizzy Dean and pitched a scoreless frame in a 3-2 loss. It proved to be his last game as a member of the St. Louis Cardinals. In a surprise move, Rickey dealt Carleton to the Chicago Cubs for pitchers Bud Tinning and Dick Ward plus cash on November 21, a day better remembered for the Yankees' acquisition of outfielder Joe DiMaggio from the San Francisco Seals.

Excited to leave St. Louis, Carleton joined a strong pitching staff in Chicago. "I just throw a little bit of everything when I'm out there on the mound and try to keep right on throwing," Tex, known for his stylish haberdashery and Sunday cowboy boots, told his new fans in the Windy City.[12] For most of the season, manager Charlie Grimm employed a five-man rotation headed by 20-game winners Lon Warneke and Bill Lee, and 17-game winner Larry French with the rest of the starts divided among Roy Henshaw (13 wins), 36-year-old Charlie Root (15 wins), and Carleton, who won 11. For the second consecutive year, Carleton was involved in a dramatic comeback. In third place and behind league-leading St. Louis by 2 1/2 games on September 2, the Cubs reeled off 21 consecutive victories to capture the pennant in convincing fashion. Tex started just once during the historic winning streak, tossing a complete game in the first game of a double-header against the Braves on September 9, triumphing 5-1. With the Cubs down two games to one in the World Series against the Tigers, Carleton was given the start in Game Four. Holding the vaunted Detroit offense to six hits, but walking seven in seven innings, Carleton surrendered just two runs (one earned);

however, the Tigers' General Crowder held the Cubs to one run in a complete-game victory. The Tigers finished off the Cubs two games later to capture the Series in six games.

The Cubs were picked by most to win their second consecutive pennant in 1936. The pitching staff was nearly intact from the previous season other than the late-May acquisition of pitcher Curt Davis replacing the aging Root as a spot starter. On his way to a league-leading four shutouts, Carleton blanked the Reds on four hits for his first victory of the season on April 26. As an encore he tossed an 11-inning complete game to defeat the Dodgers 2-1 on short rest four days later. It appeared as though the Cubs were on their way to another pennant when Carleton threw a masterful 11-inning 1-0 shutout against the Boston Bees on August 1, surrendering just five hits and giving Chicago a two-game lead over the Cardinals. However, it was the Cubs' last lead of the season as they lost their next five contests and played sub-.500 ball for the remainder of the season.

After an episode in late June when he tried to go into the stands in Boston to confront a heckler, Carleton was involved in a fight with his old nemesis Dizzy Dean on August 10 in St. Louis. Dean left the mound in the top of the first inning after continued taunts and barbs from Carleton (who was not pitching that day and thus in the dugout) and a brawl ensued near the first-base line. Neither player was injured, and plate umpire Larry Goetz ejected both. In an odd twist of events, Cubs manager Charlie Grimm persuaded Goetz in the name of sportsmanship to allow Dean to remain in the game. Dean pitched a complete game for his 19th victory.[13] For the season, Carleton had a 14-10 record and a 3.65 ERA in 197 1/3 innings as the Cubs finished five games behind for a disappointing second to the New York Giants.

After the Cubs' shocking four consecutive losses to the crosstown White Sox in the annual city series at the conclusion of the regular season, the 1936-37 off-season was a difficult one for Carleton. With rumors swirling that he'd be traded with Curt Davis to the Dodgers for starting pitcher Van Lingle Mungo, Carleton joined several teammates in a contract holdout when the Wrigley family, frustrated by the regular-season finish and embarrassed by the losses to the White Sox, vowed to cut salaries. The contract squabbles were resolved by mid-February. Bothered by elbow soreness in March and early April, Carleton was diagnosed with a chipped bone in his elbow, which required potentially career-threatening surgery. He opted for rest and a plaster cast, which sidelined him until he pitched in relief on May 11. On the 19th, with the season almost a month old, Carleton tossed a complete game against the Dodgers in his first start of the season, winning 3-1. Despite constant pain, Carleton enjoyed his best season, winning 16 games with 8 defeats, registering a career-low 3.15 ERA in 208 1/3 innings, notching a career-high 18 complete games in 27 starts and pitching four shutouts during a season for the third time in his career. On August 8 he threw a one-hitter to beat the Boston Bees 3-0 in Chicago. Finishing with seven complete games in his last ten starts, Tex took revenge against the Cardinals on September 10 when he struck out a career-high 11 batters in a six-hit shutout. Still, the Cubs squandered a seven-game lead in early August to finish in second place for the second consecutive year.

Forgoing elbow surgery again, Carleton was bothered by pain that worsened as the 1938 season progressed. After a complete-game 6-2 loss to Cincinnati in his first start, on April 21, he tossed a ten-inning complete game to defeat the Pittsburgh Pirates 5-3 on the 26th. Despite completing seven of his first 12 starts, Carleton was not able to pitch as often as he had in previous years and was surrendering more hits than he ever had. Consequently, when catcher Gabby Hartnett replaced Grimm to be a player-manager on July 20, he relegated Carleton (whose ERA was hovering around 6.00) to the role of spot starter and long reliever. While the Cubs rolled to the pennant by playing 44-27 ball for Hartnett, Carleton limped to a 10-9 record with a career-high 5.42 ERA in 167 2/3 innings. He was relegated to mop-up duty in the Cubs' four-game sweep by the New York Yankees in the World Series. Relieving Larry French with two outs in the eighth inning of Game Four with the Yankees leading 4-3 and two runners on base, Carleton faced three batters, walked two of them, uncorked two wild pitches, and surrendered a double before being relieved having given up two runs (on a double by Frank Crosetti off Carleton's successor, Dizzy Dean, as the Yankees took a commanding 8-3 lead and sewed up the Series. In December, citing Carleton's poor attitude and inadequate "zeal for work," the Cubs sent him outright to the Milwaukee Brewers, their affiliate in the American Association.[14]

The demotion was frustrating and disappointing for Carleton, who contemplated retiring. "I've been in the game 14 years and that is a long time," he said. "I just can't convince myself to keep on."[15] He finally reported, won 11 games, including a one-hitter on July 7 against the Louisville Colonels, and tossed a team-high 202 innings, but he was in pain all season.

Anticipating retirement in Fort Worth, Carleton was surprised when Brewers owner Henry Bendinger arranged a tryout with the Brooklyn Dodgers and sold his contract conditionally to Brooklyn. Carleton reported to the Dodgers' spring training in Clearwater and impressed manager Leo Durocher, who unexpectedly named him to the starting rotation. Carleton tossed a complete game in his Dodgers debut, beating the Boston Bees 8-3 on April 23. In his next start, on April 30, Carleton, considered washed up after the 1939 season, extended the fairytale motif by pitching a 3-0 no-hitter against the reigning World Series champion Reds in Cincinnati, striking out four and walking two. Carleton was in trouble in each of the first four innings because of three Dodger errors and two walks, but he retired the final 17 batters he faced.[16] Pitching on five or six days' rest, Carleton pushed his record to 4-1 by tossing a three-hit complete game to defeat the Phillies 4-1 on July 2. It was his last victory as a starting pitcher in the big leagues. As his arm pain worsened, his effectiveness waned and he was forced into the bullpen by the end of July. On September 23, in his last appearance in the major leagues, Carleton went out in a blaze of glory. He relieved Vito Tamulis with the score tied in the top of the ninth inning, intentionally walked the Giants' Joe Moore to load the bases, and then completed an unassisted double play by catching Johnny McCarthy's bunt attempt and racing to first base to retire Moore. The Dodgers scored a run in the bottom of the ninth to defeat New York 3-2 and give Carleton the victory, his sixth of the season and 100th and last in the major leagues.

With coaxing from Durocher, the 34-year-old Carleton unexpectedly agreed to report to the Dodgers' spring training in 1941 and made the Opening Day roster. But a week later, on April 23, he was optioned to the Montreal Royals. He won his debut, on May 4, but by midseason he was barely able to throw. He stayed on as an unofficial pitching coach, but before the end of the season he was released so he could pursue a career in radio in his hometown. Carleton retired with a 100-76 record and a 3.91 ERA in 1,607 1/3 innings in his eight-year major-league career. His statistics in nine seasons in the minor leagues are remarkably similar: 100 wins, 73 losses 1,625 innings, and a 3.00 ERA.

After retiring from baseball, Carleton engaged in various professions, working for Consolidated Aircraft in Fort Worth, operating sporting-goods stores, and owning an insurance agency. He died in Fort Worth on January 12, 1977, at the age of 70. He was buried at Oakwood Cemetery in Comanche.

Sources

Ancestry.com

Baseball-Almanac.com

BaseballLibrary.com

Baseball-Reference.com

NYTimes.com

Retrosheet.com

Golenbock, Peter, *The Spirit of St. Louis: A History of the St. Louis Cardinals and Browns* (New York: Harper, 2000).

The Sporting News

Notes

1 *The Sporting News,* March 28, 1935, 6.
2 *The Sporting News,* September 19, 1929, 1.
3 *The Sporting News,* August 20, 1931, 3.
4 *The Sporting News,* February 11, 1932, 3.
5 *The Sporting News,* October 22, 1931, 2.
6 *The Sporting News,* June 1, 1933, 1.
7 *The Sporting News,* March 17, 1932, 1.

8 *The Sporting News*, May 24, 1934, 1.

9 *The Sporting News*, January 26, 1933, 3.

10 Peter Golenbock, *The Spirit of St. Louis: A History of the St. Louis Cardinals and Browns,* 159.

11 *The Sporting News*, May 17, 1934, 2.

12 *The Sporting News*, March 28, 1935, 6.

13 *Milwaukee Journal*, August 11, 1936, 6.

14 *The Sporting News*, December 29, 1938, 1.

15 *The Sporting News*. February 16, 1939, 8.

16 *New York Times*, May 1, 1940, 33.

(The Ripper)
James Anthony Collins

By Cort Vitty

RUGGEDLY HANDSOME WITH dark wavy hair, an engaging smile and a boyish grin, the 1934 St. Louis Cardinals' first baseman was equally capable of leading the league in both home runs and pranks. General manager Branch Rickey suspiciously called him the instigator, to which James Anthony Collins remarked: "Rickey always accused me of being the ringleader; I never could understand why he picked on me—unless it could have been because there was considerable truth in his allegations."[1.]

Collins was born in Altoona, Pennsylvania, on March 30, 1904. His father, William Collins, was of Irish and Scottish descent, while his mother, Elizabeth, traced her heritage back to Germany. At the recording of the 1920 census, James was 15; sister, Arietta, was 12, and his brother, William, was 2. Both young James and his dad listed coal miner as their profession; Jimmy started working in the mines at 13.

The Collins family moved to Johnstown, Pennsylvania, where young Jimmy attended nearby Nanty Glo Elementary. His father played semipro baseball and the first time Jimmy saw him crush a fastball, it became his goal to follow in his dad's footsteps. During the cold, snowy Pennsylvania winters, Jimmy honed his skill, spending countless hours fielding grounders off a basement wall. When summer arrived he was on the ball field from sun-up to sundown.

The Cards' regular first baseman, Collins led the league in home runs with 35 and in slugging percentage (.615) in 1934. He hit .367 in the World Series.

Full-time school ended for Jimmy at the age of 14, when he took a job in the shipping department of the mine. Simultaneously, he attended night school—a common practice for boys his age in a coal-mining town. His dad, now a machinist, played ball on the company team. Jimmy joined the team and the father/son duo roamed left and center fields respectively. Jimmy originally threw left-handed and batted right-handed. The senior Collins, noting a short right-field fence at the company field, taught Jimmy to bat left and throw both left- and right-handed. Jimmy adapted to switch-hitting and continued to hit from both sides throughout his career.

The nickname Ripper developed during an on-field incident that occurred when Jimmy was a young player. A ball rocketed off his bat and struck a nail protruding from the outfield fence; it caused the cover to partially tear. When asked who hit the ball, the retrieving outfielder saw the ball hanging and said, "It was the ripper."[2]

In 1922 Jimmy married Helen Fasemeyer, also from Nanty Glo. At the time he was only 17 and couldn't legally get a marriage license in Pennsylvania. The couple decided to elope and drove to Cumberland, Maryland, to have the ceremony performed. As a young married man, Jimmy not only worked hard in the mines—he played ball even harder, hoping a scout would notice. Marriage immediately affected Collins's sense of responsibility:

"From that day on, I knew I had to make the grade in baseball. Handicapped by my lack of education, I realized that if I failed as an athlete, my life would be a dull, pitiful existence as a coal miner."[3] The couple had a son (also Jimmy) in 1923; a daughter, Betty, arrived in 1925 and another son, Warren, in 1930.

The lack of a paycheck during a mine strike in 1922 resulted in Ripper's signing his first professional contract, debuting in class C ball with York, Pennsylvania, of the New York-Penn League; he later shifted to Wilson, North Carolina, in the Virginia League, seeing only limited playing time at each stop before returning home to the mines.

In 1925 a lengthy strike put thousands of miners out work. Again with no paycheck and time on his hands, Collins approached the hometown Johnstown club of the Mid-Atlantic League for a tryout and impressed enough to be offered a $200 signing bonus — just about enough money to get the young family out of debt. Jimmy hit .327 in 99 games and suddenly scouts from higher classifications began to hover. George Stallings, then manager of the Rochester Red Wings and formerly a pretty fair minor-league ballplayer in his own right, saw Collins play and remarked: "I wouldn't give $5.00 for him."[4] A dejected Rip went back to the mines and his father recommended that he forget baseball.

In 1926 Johnstown was in a tough pennant fight. This time Ripper's .313 average in 102 games got him promoted to Double-A Rochester late in the season; the club was experiencing financial difficulties and players were not getting paid. Rip's performance suffered and he again returned to the mines.

Farmed out to Savannah in 1927, Collins was recalled by Rochester at the end of the season. Subsequently, the troubled franchise was sold to the St. Louis Cardinals and housecleaning started, with almost the entire squad placed on waivers. Collins survived, but was demoted back to Class B, making stops in Savannah and Jacksonville before returning to Rochester at the end of the season, where a lackluster .246 average got him demoted to Danville, Illinois, of the Three-I League. At this point, Collins's father wrote a long letter urging him to realize he wouldn't make it and recommended that he resume working in the mines. Despite his father's plea, Collins stayed in the Three-I league and ultimately led the loop with a .388 average in 1928, earning him a return trip to Rochester, where he posted an impressive .375 batting mark in 14 games. The Cardinals ordered Collins to report for spring training in 1929 with the parent club.

This time Collins's mother urged him to report, saying she had a feeling it was going to be his big break. Sure enough, Cardinals manager Billy Southworth was impressed and recommended that Collins learn to play first base. Despite not being a prototypical build (5-feet-9, 165 pounds) for the position, he had cat-like reflexes, plus an uncanny ability to pull down errant throws and scoop low tosses out of the dirt.

Thanks to a cash infusion from the parent Cardinals, Rochester opened a brand-new stadium in 1929 and Ripper christened the ballpark on May 2, hitting the first home run in the Red Wings' new home. All told, he hit .315 with 38 homers and 132 runs batted in. In 1930 he led the International League with a .376 average and an eyebrow-raising 40 home runs, while batting in a league record 180 runs. Collins was clearly instrumental in helping the Red Wings win pennants in 1928, 1929, and 1930 and blossomed into a definite major-league prospect.

Collins earned a promotion to the Cardinals and made his major-league debut in 1931, playing 89 games as a backup to Jim Bottomley. He posted a respectable .301 average, with 4 home runs and 59 RBIs, as a pinch-hitter and part-time first baseman/outfielder. Collins described to Arthur Daley of the *New York Times* how manager Frank Frisch once considered using him at third base when he was short an infielder; Collins was eager to play the position right-handed and said he regretted not having the opportunity.[5]

Collins's playing time increased to 149 games in 1932 and his home run total rose to a healthy 21; in 81 games at first base, he had a .999 fielding average. So promising was Collins that the Cardinals traded Bottomley to Cincinnati after the season.

In late July 1933, Gabby Street was replaced as the Cardinals' manager. Popular second baseman Frisch succeeded him. A fellow switch-hitter, Frisch worked with Collins and helped him become a more patient and disciplined hitter. He taught the stocky first baseman to choke the bat for better control and worked with him to improve his bunting skills from both sides of the plate. In general, Collins drove the ball for longer distances left-handed and stroked wicked line drives batting right-handed. According to author Rob Rains, Collins was "one (Cardinal) who knew how to play and when to be serious, Frisch's type of guy, was the versatile Collins."[6.] Collins contributed a .310 batting average with 10 home runs and 68 RBIs.

Collins enjoyed a breakout season in 1934, when his .333 average helped spark the Cardinals to the National League pennant and a World Series title. He became the first switch-hitter in the major leagues to hit 30 home runs in a season, winding up with 35 and tying for the league lead with the Giants' Mel Ott. (This became the single-season standard for switch-hitters until Mickey Mantle surpassed Collins with 37 homers in 1955.) All but four of Collins' home runs were hit left-handed; he had 200 hits, 40 doubles, 12 triples, 128 RBIs, and a league leading .615 slugging percentage. He led National League first basemen with 110 assists.

Along with Gas House Gang teammates Pepper Martin, Dizzy Dean, and Dazzy Vance, Collins sang on KMOX radio in St. Louis. They formed a washboard-style band called the Mississippi Mudcats and regularly performed in the team's clubhouse and hotel. At the Bellevue-Stratford in Philadelphia in 1936, fun loving Pepper Martin "noticed ladders, paint buckets, white overalls, and other painter's paraphernalia in a corner of a service area. He rounded up Collins, Dizzy Dean, Heinie Schuble, and Bill DeLancey. They donned the overalls, took the equipment into a busy dining room and began painting the walls and ceiling, splattering paint on the customers, shouting instructions to one another à la the Marx brothers and promoting general chaos."[7]

During the hard-fought 1934 pennant race, Collins was approached to author a series of daily newspaper articles in St. Louis and also for his hometown *Rochester Times Union*. He reported the baseball news and added commentary from roommate Pepper Martin. Two dictionaries accompanied Ripper on road trips, but neither did him any good: "I've pondered through both of them, but I've never run across any of Frankie Frisch's language. I now plan to write a ballplayers' dictionary. I'll gather all the pet words and answers from the players around the league. That book ought to be a best-seller." One day after striking out, Collins was taken to task when frustrated manager Frisch remarked: "Next time, swing your typewriter."[8]

The seventh and deciding game of the hard-fought 1934 World Series took place on October 9 at Navin Field in Detroit. The Cardinals supported winning pitcher Dizzy Dean with 11 runs to gain the victory. Batting fifth in the order, Collins led the offensive barrage with four hits. In the eighth inning he lost a potential fifth hit when his drive sent center fielder Jo-Jo White back to the 420-foot marker at the wall in right-center. White leaped, deflected the ball off his glove, and snagged it while lying on his back. Collins hit .367 for the Series.

On May 11, 1935, Collins took Philadelphia Phillies right-hander Euel Moore deep, hitting career home run 74, the major-league record at the time for switch-hitters. For the season Collins hit .313 with 23 round-trippers. On August 21 an unusual feat occurred when he played an entire game at first base without a putout. Collins placed in the top ten in several batting categories for the '35 season.

The efficient Cardinals farm system produced hard-hitting Johnny Mize, who appeared in 126 games (99 at first base) in 1936 and made Collins expendable. After the season he was traded to the Chicago Cubs with pitcher Roy Parmelee for pitcher Lon Warneke.

Wearing a Cubs uniform in 1937, Collins on June 29 again played an entire game at first base without recording a putout; this time also without an assist. He jokingly offered to pay the price of one admission ticket because "I was strictly a spectator."[9]

On August 9, 1937 the Cubs were leading the National League pennant race by six games when the team visited Cook County jail in Chicago. Collins thought it great fun to jokingly take a seat in the electric chair. Superstitious teammates chided him for doing what they considered to be an omen of bad luck. In the first inning the next day, Collins fractured his right ankle sliding into home plate. The Cubs lost the game to the Pittsburgh Pirates and nosedived to ultimately lose the National League flag to the New York Giants.[10]

Collins was never quite the same player, either at bat or in the field. All told in 1937, he appeared in 115 games, with 16 homers, 71 RBIs and a .274 batting average.

In 1938 Collins's playing time increased to 143 games. He hit .268 with 13 home runs and a league-leading fielding average of .996. Sparked by catcher-manager Gabby Hartnett's memorable Homer in the Gloamin', the Cubs edged the Pirates to win the National League flag. Prior to the start of the World Series, Collins and teammate Billy Jurges visited 14-year-old Johnny English at Mercy Hospital in Chicago. An ardent Cubs fan, young Johnny was ill with cancer and wasn't expected to live to the end of the season, let alone the World Series. Collins and Jurges brightened the boy's spirits with the visit, accompanied by autographed baseballs signed by every member of the team.[11] The Cubs were swept by a tough New York Yankees club. Commenting after being pummeled by the Bombers, the affable Collins remarked: "We came, we saw and we went home."[12]

Collins was sold to the Pacific Coast League Los Angeles Angels on March 30, 1939; the media speculated that Hartnett was seeking to protect his job from a potential rival. Settling in as the Angels first baseman, Collins responded nicely by hitting .334 with 26 home runs in 172 games. Back for an encore season with the Angels in 1940, he hit .327 with 18 homers in 174 games.

Collins was back in the major leagues when he was purchased by the Pirates on March 25, 1941; the move reunited him with his former St. Louis manager Frankie Frisch. His acquisition was intended to ease the workload of first baseman Elbie Fletcher. Collins played in 49 games, hitting .210, in what became his last hurrah as a major-league player. He was released after the season. The move gave him his first opportunity to manage in professional baseball when he was installed as player-manager of the Class A Albany Senators of the Eastern League, a Pirates farm team. Attendance in Albany had been lagging for years and Collins was viewed as a potential draw, since he was a fan favorite in New York.[13]

The Collins family had resided in Rochester since Rip's playing days; he managed a bowling alley in the city during the offseason. The Collins home was easily recognizable; Rip's collection of broken bats surrounded it as a makeshift fence. His house stored his league-leading (estimated at over 10,000 items) collection of signed baseballs and bats. Collins, with boyish grin and tongue in cheek, defended the size of his collection by mentioning how neighborhood kids and deliverymen "kept his collection from getting too big." A favorite bat in his collection was an ornate miniature given to Dizzy Dean by a Mexican fan to commemorate Dean's fine 1934 season. Collins admired the bat to the point of "borrowing" it for his collection. Suspecting that Dean might become suspicious, Ripper had the bat carved to read: "To James Rip Collins — from Dizzy." Collins estimated that he owned owning more than 3,000 autographed celebrity photos from many sports.[14]

A favorite glove in his collection was a "good luck" charm from the 1934 pennant race. Wild Bill Hallahan lost his glove during the stretch run and Rip loaned the lefty pitcher one of his well-worn four-fingered models. Hallahan proceeded to win every game he pitched wearing the borrowed glove. He asked Ripper if he could purchase the glove but Collins said no and the glove went back into his personal collection. Once asked how one man could collect so many baseball artifacts, Collins replied: "One man couldn't. Darn every guy in the game knows it's my hobby. When they see anything that looks good they pass it along."[15]

In addition to serving as Albany's skipper, Collins filled in at first base in 1942. He hit .276 in 118 games, but his home-run production fell to only 3 as the club finished first in the league but lost in the initial round of the playoffs. Remaining in Albany as player-manager in 1943, Collins batted .312 in 82 games with one home run as the club fell to 5th place. The wartime player shortage had Ripper back playing regularly at first base in 1944, seeing action in 100 games. At 40 years old he was named the outstanding minor-league player of 1944 by *The Sporting News*, hitting .396 for his second-place Albany Senators.

After five seasons, Collins resigned as Albany's manager on November 27, 1946, to become manager of the Pacific Coast League San Diego Padres, where he replaced Pepper Martin. Albany owner Tom McCaffrey commented: "Ripper has been a splendid manager and

I'm sorry to lose him. I have long known he deserves a promotion and I'm glad for his sake that he is going higher. He has been Albany's most popular manager."[16]

In 1947 San Diego finished dead last in the PCL. On August 3, 1948, after losing 13 of 17 games, Collins was ousted as manager. The move was unpopular with fans and the local media; Collins took the move in stride, citing player injuries as the source of his troubles. His next managerial slot was back in the Eastern League, with the Hartford (Connecticut) Chiefs for 1949 and 1950. Although he signed to run the club for a third year, he resigned to capitalize on an opportunity to go to Baltimore and become a color commentator in the new medium of television.

Still one to enjoy a laugh, Collins was up to his old tricks again when he couldn't resist entertaining the crowd at a 1950 old-timer's game in the Polo Grounds in New York with the old hidden-ball trick. The amused umpires investigated and found several baseballs in the pockets of many of the Cardinal players.[17]

Collins was elected to the International League Hall of Fame in 1951. He went to work for Wilson's Sporting Goods, for whom he authored a "how-to" manual for youngsters devoted to teaching proper baseball technique. He left Wilson to return to baseball as a roving minor-league instructor with the Chicago Cubs. During spring training 1961 Collins became a coach with the parent club and was part of the College of Coaches experiment initiated by owner Phil Wrigley. His last stint managing in the minor leagues was later in 1961 with San Antonio in the Texas League. Collins also worked in the Cubs' public-relations office and hosted the *Meet the Cubs* radio show.

A model athlete on and off the field, Collins was accessible and liked mixing with fans during personal appearances. He thoroughly enjoyed pleasing people and believed players should always be considerate and thoughtful. He never failed to answer a fan letter and especially enjoyed personally writing to youngsters. He was polite, affable, and a nonswearing type — who simply enjoyed a little good-natured fun. He said, "Left-handers are not screwballs.... We have color."[19]

Collins hit over .300 in four of his nine big-league seasons. His 135 home runs were tops among major-league switch-hitters until Mickey Mantle surpassed him. A clutch hitter, Collins referred to himself as "the All-American Louse," a moniker he chose after breaking up four no-hitters during his major-league career. He was elected to the Rochester Red Wings Hall of Fame in 1989.

In the spring of 1969 Collins, scouting for the Cardinals, was hospitalized in Oswego, New York, after suffering a serious heart attack. On April 15, 1970, at the age of 66, Ripper had a fatal attack in New Haven, New York. He is buried in Mexico Village Cemetery, Mexico New York.

Notes

1. Arthur Daley, "Sports of the Times," New York Times, January 20, 1957.
2. Robert E. Hood, The Gashouse Gang (New York: William Morrow & Co. 1976).
3. Harry T. Brundidge, The Sporting News, March 9, 1933.
4. Ibid.
5. Arthur Daley, "Sports of the Times," New York Times, January 20, 1957.
6. Rob Rains, The St. Louis Cardinals: 100th Anniversary History (New York: St. Martin's Press. 1992).
7. The Sporting News, May 2, 1970.
8. "Rip the Writer Consults Dictionaries," Raleigh Register (Beckley, West Virginia), June 25, 1936.
9. San Mateo (California) Times, March 9, 1959.
10. Life Magazine, September 9, 1937, 22.
11. "Boy Lives to See Cubs Win," Arizona Republic (Phoenix, Arizona), October 6, 1938.
12. Helena (Montana) Daily Independent, October 10, 1938.
13. The Sporting News, November 27, 1941.
14. "Rip Collins is No.1 Collector of Broken Bats," Oshkosh (Wisconsin) Northwestern, February 22, 1937.
15. (Ibid).
16. Dick Connors, "Collins Succeeds Old Roomie at San Diego," The Sporting News," November 27, 1946.
17. "Old Cards Pull Hidden Ball Trick on Giants," Washington Post, July 31, 1950.
19. Gene Henschel, "Rotarians Hear Collins Describe Career," Sheboygan (Wisconsin) Press, September 1, 1964.

Pat Crawford

By Gregory H. Wolf

PAT CRAWFORD WAS a reluctant professional baseball player. A devout Christian with a passion for baseball, Crawford objected to playing on Sundays. When he graduated from college in 1923 and accepted a position as teacher and coach at a high school in North Carolina, he anticipated that a career in baseball would be impossible to reconcile with his personal convictions and school-related responsibilities. But Crawford was a thinking man and found the perfect solution in the Class B South Atlantic (Sally) League: Start the season late and end early to accommodate his teaching schedule. Among the league's best hitters from 1924 to 1927, Crawford spurned offers from higher minor-league teams, refusing to change his principles. He ultimately compromised, signed with the New York Giants, and debuted with them in 1929. He abruptly retired after the 1930 season, but was lured by the St. Louis Cardinals to sign with them. After two seasons with the Columbus Red Birds (and an American Association MVP award in 1932), Crawford cemented his reputation as a versatile infielder and clutch pinch hitter in 1933 and 1934. His playing career came to a tragic halt when he developed a life-threatening blood infection in 1935, leaving him with a permanent limp.

Clifford Rankin "Pat" Crawford was born on January 28, 1902, in the bucolic town of Society Hill, Darlington County, in the northern part of South Carolina. His parents, James and Sallie (Ford) Crawford, were South Carolinians by birth and raised five children. Cliff, as his parents and friends called him, was followed by Alda, Lafon, Thomas, and William. His father, a salesman for a retail grocery company, moved the family to Dillon County and by 1915 to Sumter, a growing town of about 9,000 residents in the geographic central part of the state. An athletic youngster, Pat attended Sumter High School, where he excelled in the classroom and on the athletic fields, starring in baseball, basketball, and football. After graduating in 1919, he attended Davidson College, a prestigious liberal-arts college about 20 miles north of Charlotte, North Carolina. Guided by his faith, Crawford was active in his institution's YMCA and served as the vice president of his senior class. He forged an impressive athletic résumé, serving as captain of the basketball and baseball teams, and twice being named all-state as an infielder. He graduated with a B.A. in physical education.

Standing 5-feet-11 and weighing about 160 pounds in college, Crawford was quick and agile, and learned to play all infield positions. With his speed, natural instincts, and strong throwing arm, he was also an effective outfielder. Crawford's foray into professional baseball began in 1922, when he was signed by owner-manager and former big-league pitcher George Suggs to play left field for the Kinston (North Carolina) Highwaymen in the independent Eastern Carolina Baseball Association, which existed outside the jurisdiction of Organized Baseball.[1]

Crawford served as a reserve infielder in 1934, his last in the major leagues. He batted .271 in 61 games.

Despite Crawford's passion for baseball, he considered some aspects of professional ball distasteful, such as Sunday games, the hard living (drinking and carousing) of some players, and the time it took away from family. In the summer after he graduated from Davidson College, he returned to Kinston to serve as player-manager for a local semipro team in the Blue Ridge League. (The Highwaymen had disbanded after the 1922 season.) Not long after the season started, Crawford was offered a bonus of $150 by Dick Hoblitzell, manager of the Charlotte Hornets, to play in the Sally League; however, he had not yet decided if he wanted to a career in baseball.[2] He filed the contract at home and finished the season with a semipro team in Lenoir.

Crawford accepted a job as a teacher and coach at Gastonia High School, about 20 miles east of Charlotte, believing that his active baseball career was over. From the fall of 1923 through the end of May 1927, he established a reputation as a "mentor and idol of high-school athletes" and led the Green Wave to a football championship and baseball prominence.[3] During the spring baseball season in 1924, Crawford was surprised when Charlotte owner Felix Hayman inquired about his availability for the coming season. Crawford asked if he would be permitted to play for a semipro team in Abbeville, South Carolina. Hayman agreed with the stipulation that Crawford would report to the Hornets on a day's notice. "I packed up and went to Abbeville, arriving there on a Friday," Crawford said. "I worked out with the team Saturday and was all set to play Monday. Sunday I received a wire from Mr. Hayman telling me to report at once to take the place of the regular first baseman who had been injured. So without playing a single game with Abbeville, I boarded the train for Charlotte and began my professional baseball career on Monday at first base."[4] Crawford replaced injured future big leaguer Chick Tolson at first base and was later switched to third base. For the second-place Hornets, the 22-year-old left-handed hitting Crawford batted .303 (114-for-376).

Purchased after the season by the Louisville Colonels of the Double-A American Association, Crawford refused to report to the team, citing his objection to playing on Sundays. Further complicating matters was his insistence on finishing the baseball season as coach at Gastonia High School. Louisville loaned him to the Greenville (South Carolina) Spinners of the Sally League to start the 1925 season.[5] About three weeks after reporting to his new team, Crawford replaced player-manager Zinn Beck, who had unexpectedly resigned, and was charged with "pull[ing] the slumping team together."[6] In an offensively-minded league, Crawford batted .343 (20 players with a minimum of 300 at-bats batted at least .340) in 89 games. As he did in subsequent years, he left the team early to return to his teaching and coaching duties in high school.

Nicknamed Peppery Patrick and Captain Pat for his feisty personality and leadership abilities, Crawford was described by local papers as one of the "finest characters in baseball" for his unwavering commitment to his high-school athletic program, exemplary behavior, and excellent play on the field.[7] For the second consecutive season, he refused to report to his new, higher-level team (the Atlanta Crackers of the Class A Southern Association), which had acquired his contract in mid-season, and claimed that he would quit baseball before he would turn his back on his teaching career. In his second of three seasons with Greenville, Crawford batted .328 (146-for-445), developed a home-run stroke, belting 21, and knocked in 93 runs. Behind the pitching heroics of 30-game winner Wilcey Moore, the Spinners won the league title and then defeated the Richmond Colts of the Virginia League for the Southern Championship.[8]

By the beginning of the 1927 season, there seemed to be a consensus that the coming year with Greenville will "probably be [Crawford's] last in professional baseball" when Atlanta sold his contract to Greenville.[9] Fueling the rumors of his imminent retirement from baseball was his resignation from Gastonia High School to accept a position as head coach and faculty member at Guilford College in Greensboro, North Carolina. Crawford was considered "one of the best infielders of the Sally League" who might have already been in the majors had he been willingly to play baseball on Sunday.[10] Crawford reported to the Spinners in June, had his best season so far, and was named the league's most valuable player.[11] He hit .334 (148-for-443), knocked in 90 runs, and clubbed 24 home runs, the third most in the league, despite missing 30 games for player-manager (and owner) Frank Walker's second consecutive (league and Southern) championship team.

John "Little Napoleon" McGraw, manager of the New York Giants, was not someone who accepted no for an answer. On scout Dick Kinsella's advice, McGraw personally scouted Crawford in 1927. Making his best sales pitch to Crawford and Walker, McGraw persuaded Crawford to report to the Giants the following spring and purchased his contract for $10,000.[12] The news hit the printing press on August 3 and its publication met with a thundering ovation in Greenville and Gastonia. "A more popular ball player has never been in the South Atlantic Association," excitedly reported the *Gastonia Daily Gazette*.[13]

In Gastonia, Greenville, Charlotte, Sumter, and other areas where Crawford lived and worked, he was seen as more than just a ballplayer. He was humble, modest, and self-effacing, sincerely concerned about education, and seemed to harken back to another, less complicated era. He embodied the notion of sports as an ennobling undertaking. Newspapers predicted success in the major leagues because Crawford was a "natural, quick thinker" who "puts his whole soul" into baseball.[14] In a rapidly changing society in which individuality and egoism were commended, Crawford possessed the "mental and moral fitness to be a star."[15]

Crawford decided not to report to the Giants spring training in 1928, reiterating his commitment to Guilford College.[16] Frank Walker of the Spinners voiced his disapproval, and McGraw, frustrated with Crawford's obstinacy, claimed he didn't need a player who did not want to play for the Giants. "[McGraw] is interested in [Crawford] and proposes to use him this season," reported the *Gastonia Daily Gazette* near the end of the Giants' spring camp.[17] When the baseball season concluded at Guilford in late May, Crawford announced his resignation and willingness to play professional baseball on his terms.[18]

The Giants assigned Crawford to their top affiliate in the American Association, the Toledo Mud Hens, piloted by 37-year-old player-manager Casey Stengel. Crawford quickly adjusted to the jump from Class B to Double-A, then a notch below the big leagues. He batted .347 (tied for fifth) in the league among players with at least 400-at bats). He tailored his game to fit the large dimensions of Toledo's Swayne Field by becoming a slap hitter known for his good eye at the plate, striking out just 15 times in 481 plate appearances. His fielding at first base was as impressive as his hitting. By the end of the season, *The Sporting News* considered Crawford and Joe Kuhel of the Kansas City Blues "easily the best first base prospects" in the AA.[19] Crawford was a late-season call-up to the Giants when the rosters expanded in September, but he did not play.[20]

When Crawford reported to the Giants' camp in San Antonio in February, 1929, it was the first time in his professional career that he had participated in spring training. McGraw was determined to whip his team in shape, driven by the still-fresh memory of a disappointing second-place finish, two games behind the pennant-winning St. Louis Cardinals. The Giants were a young team with established major leaguers at the infield positions where Crawford could play. Hitting sensation Bill Terry was one of the best first basemen in the league, and the third sacker, 23-year-old Freddie Lindstrom, was just beginning his Hall of Fame career.

Crawford secured a spot on the Giants roster with his hustle, determination, versatility, and studious approach to the game. He made his major-league debut in the team's first game of the season, on April 18, when he unsuccessfully pinch-hit for Carl Hubbell in the Giants' 11-9 victory over the Phillies in the Baker Bowl. On April 27 Crawford pinch-hit for "King Carl" again, and connected for his first big-league hit, a home run into the right-field stands at the Polo Grounds, in the Giants' 5-4 loss to Boston. "Homer by Crawford Helps Giants Win," read a headline from the *New York Times* on May 27.[21] Crawford, pinch-hitting for reliever Dutch Henry in a slugfest with the Braves at the Polo Grounds, faced Socks Seibold with the bases full in the sixth inning. On a 3-1 count, Crawford launched an inside fastball over the right-field terrace for his first and only career grand slam to break the game open. Coincidentally, the Braves' Les Bell blasted a pinch-hit grand slam in the seventh inning to make it the first time in major-league history that two pinch-hit grand slams were hit in the same game. Crawford's third pinch-hit homer against the Phillies, on June 19, tied Ham Hyatt (1913) and Cy Williams (1928) for the most pinch-hit four-baggers in a season. (Brooklyn's Johnny Frederick broke that record with six in 1932.)

With little chance to displace Terry or Lindstrom, Crawford carved his niche as a clutch pinch-hitter. He saw action in the field just eight times, including three starts at first base. Two of those starts occurred at the end of the season, when he connected for four hits in seven at-bats and drove in three in runs during inconsequential wins for the third-place Giants. Crawford finished the season with a remarkable 24 runs batted in on just 17 hits (including three doubles and three home runs), scored 13 times, batted .298, and seemed to have a bright future.

Second base proved to be a problem for the Giants in 1929, when Andy Cohen and Andy Reese combined for 31 errors. Consequently, infield prospect Doc Marshall and Crawford, who had never played second base professionally, competed during 1930 spring training with the two veterans. Marshall won the job, but got off to a poor start, which paved the way for Crawford's first start at second base, on April 26 in the first game of a doubleheader at Philadelphia (he went hitless in five at-bats). In 13 subsequent starts, Crawford played steady if not spectacular baseball. In seven of his starts, he had at least two hits and twice knocked in four runs. On May 22 the Giants made a stunning trade sending their workhorse right-handed pitcher Larry Benton to the Cincinnati Reds for a slick-fielding second baseman, 29-year-old Hughie Critz, who had finished second and fourth in the MVP voting in 1926 and 1928 respectively. Overnight, Crawford lost his job and was relegated to pinch-hitting duties, despite a .270 batting average and 16 runs batted in from just 20 hits. Six days after the acquisition of Critz, the Giants made another deal with the Reds, exchanging Crawford for outfielder Ethan Allen and pitcher Pete Donohue.

Crawford reported to manager Dan Howley's Reds en route to a seventh-place finish. On a light-hitting team, he struggled in his first 33 games (which included five starts at first base and seven at second base), hitting just .243. After replacing Hod Ford at second base on August 16, Crawford proved his value by hitting safely in 13 of 14 games (.356 average). Crawford made a seamless transition to second base in 1930. His .968 fielding percentage was above the league average (.963) and just one percentage point lower than that of the Cardinals' Frankie Frisch. From August 16 through the end of the season, Crawford batted .312, the third-best on the team, trailing only Bob Meusel's .330 and rookie Tony Cuccinello's .350.

On December 1, in a "surprising development," the Reds traded Crawford and outfielder Marty Callaghan to the Hollywood Stars of the Pacific Coast League for first baseman Mickey Heath.[22] Howley desperately wanted a slugger and was willing to sacrifice Crawford to acquire Heath who had launched 75 round-trippers the previous two years with the Stars. Crawford was disappointed by the trade and in a letter addressed to Stars president William F. Lane wrote, "I am retiring. … Please consider this final. Salary increases are of no interest to me."[23]

The news of Crawford's retirement did not surprise the local media in North Carolina. During his playing days in Kinston, North Carolina, Pat met local resident Sarah Edwards, whom he later married. After living in Gastonia and Charlotte, the couple relocated to Kinston when Crawford began his big-league career. In the offseasons, Crawford taught physical education at local schools, coached basketball, and refereed games. With close ties to his community, Crawford considered the time away from his wife a necessary evil in order to play baseball. Just days after he was officially traded to the Stars, the Crawfords welcomed their first child, Patricia. Pat's perspective suddenly changed; he was not willing to live almost 2,700 miles away from his family.

Branch Rickey, general manager of the St. Louis Cardinals, sensed an opportunity to acquire a versatile player and orchestrated preliminary discussions among Crawford, Lane, and Larry MacPhail, president of the Columbus Red Birds of the American Association.[24] Less than a week before Opening Day, Columbus purchased Crawford's contract from Hollywood.[25]

Columbus was historically the weakest team in the American Association, had not enjoyed a winning record since the war-shortened season in 1918, and had finished in last place or next-to-last eight of the previous 12 years. But the team's history did not matter to Crawford. He was a one-man wrecking crew. Playing his natural position of first base, Crawford led the league in home runs (28) and runs batted in (154), ranked second in hits (237), fifth in batting (.374), fourth in doubles (41), and sixth in triples (13), easily led the league with 388 total bases, and finished third with a .613 slugging percentage.[26] Columbus finished in fourth place with an 84-82 record. Despite his phenomenal season, Crawford's ascendancy to the big-league club was blocked by 27-year-old rookie Ripper Collins, who gradually replaced longtime stalwart Jim Bottomley. Rickey bought Crawford's contract at the end of the season, but the acquisition could not squelch the rumors that he would trade Crawford at the winter meetings.[27]

Crawford participated in the Cardinals' spring training in Bradenton, Florida, but was optioned to Columbus for the start of the 1932 season. In leading the Red Birds to a second-place finish (88-77) and their most wins since 1913, the 30-year-old Crawford finished fourth in batting (.369) and second in home runs (30), runs batted in (140), and total bases (370), and was named *The Sporting News* Most Valuable Player of the league.

The Cardinals began spring training in 1933 coming off a disappointing sixth-place finish the previous season. Manager Gabby Street, under pressure from GM Rickey and club owner Sam Breadon to produce a winner, viewed Crawford as an ideal insurance policy to shore up an injury-prone infield from 1932. The 31-year-old Carolinian began the season as a pinch-hitter, but then had the opportunity at the end of April to be the regular first baseman when Collins suffered a knee injury. In his 17th consecutive start at first base, Crawford belted a bases-loaded, walk-off single in the tenth inning to defeat the Giants in Sportsman's Park, 8-7, on May 19. Despite the heroics, he ceded the first-base job to Collins the next day. There was a widespread belief that Crawford would be optioned to Columbus at some time during the season, but the tough veteran proved too valuable.[28] The "handy utility man" made 28 starts at first, nine at second base (spelling Frankie Frisch, who had injured his leg), and six at third base.[29] He finished the season with a .268 average (60-for-224), but with little pop in his bat (no home runs among his ten extra-base hits) and drove in 21 runs.

Player-manager Frisch, who replaced Street during the previous season, guided the St. Louis Cardinals' Gas House Gang to baseball immortality in 1934. The Cardinals benefited from an unusually healthy year from its starters (Collins, for example, played every inning of every game). "Crawford played an important part in the success of the Redbirds," wrote *The Sporting News* several years after the team's mythical season.[30] An unassuming role-player, Crawford made only five starts all season, but continued to manifest his uncanny ability to hit in clutch situations. Batting .271 in 70 at-bats, Crawford amassed 16 runs batted in on just 19 hits (all singles save for two doubles). He explained that as a pinch-hitter his goal was to make contact and avoid strikeouts (he struck out just 29 times in 651 big-league at-bats). He choked up on the bat in order to connect for a safe hit, and rarely took a full swing with all of his power.[31]

Crawford's educated disposition did not cloud his competitive nature. "One of the quietest, most gentlemanly members of our team was Pat Crawford," said the rough-and-tumble Pepper Martin. "It will probably be a surprise to hear that he turned out to be one of our great jockeys."[32] In the dugout Crawford acted like a coach, encouraging teammates and harassing opponents.

In the Cardinals' exciting World Series triumph over the Detroit Tigers, Crawford made two pinch-hit appearances. He grounded out to second in Game Four and was retired on a fly ball to right field in Game Five. After those two losses, the Gas House Gang won Games Six and Seven to capture the title. Upon Crawford's return home to North Carolina, he was feted as a celebrity.

Highly respected in the Cardinals organization, Crawford seemed prepared to transition into a coaching. When George "Specs" Toporcer because of failing eyesight abruptly quit as player-manager of the Rochester Red Wings, the Cardinals' affiliate in the Double-A International League, team president Warren

Giles selected Crawford over Burt Shotton and Ray Blades to lead the team.[33]

At almost the same time that Giles made the announcement of Crawford's hiring on January 25, 1935, the 33-year-old jack-of-all-trades was being rushed to the hospital in Kinston. Several weeks earlier Crawford had undergone a routine hemorrhoid operation. He had developed septicemia, a life-threatening blood infection that localized in his liver. He required six blood transfusions and his entire body was inflamed, leading his physician to proclaim that he had only a "slight" chance to survive.[34] Papers throughout the Carolinas reported daily on his illness and ultimate recovery. The *Charlotte Observer* wrote, "[Crawford] is a fine character, the sort that keeps baseball from degenerating to the low level it formerly occupied, [and an] upstanding, high-minded Christian gentleman."[35] Crawford spent weeks recuperating in Kinston Memorial Hospital, but as a result of the disease, he suffered a permanently stiff left hip and his career as a baseball player was tragically ended.[36]

In his four-year big-league career, Crawford batted .280 (182-for-651) and knocked in 104 runs. He batted .347 over 843 games in his seven-year minor-league career, including a phenomenal .365 average in three seasons in the American Association. Blessed with a positive outlook, Crawford never expressed bitterness or anger about his fate.

Crawford settled in Kinston with his wife, daughter, and son (Clifford, born in 1933) and dedicated the rest of his life to educating youngsters and coaching youth baseball. In 1936 he opened a baseball school and camp in Gastonia for the Cardinals. He scouted for the team and was credited with signing future Cardinals pitcher Ernie White. In Kinston Crawford helped found a recreation department, served as its director for many years, built public baseball diamonds, and organized local youth leagues. In 1937 he and his wife purchased a 20-acre site in Morehead City, North Carolina, about 70 miles southeast of Kinston on the southern edge of the Outer Banks. They established Camp Morehead by the Sea, a youth camp that they operated for many decades. Though he rarely spoke his accomplishments in the big leagues, Crawford proudly participated in reunions of the Gas House Gang. In 1983 he was an inaugural member of the Kinston Baseball Hall of Fame, along with George Suggs and Charlie Keller.

On January 25, 1994, three days shy of his 92nd birthday, Clifford Rankin "Pat" Crawford died in Morehead City and was buried in Westview Cemetery in Kinston. He was the last surviving player from the Gas House Gang. He was posthumously inducted into the Davidson College athletics hall of fame (1998) and the Kinston/Lenoir County Sports Hall of Fame (2012).

Sources

Newspapers

Gastonia News Gazette

New York Times

The Sporting News

Online sources

Ancestry.com

BaseballLibrary.com

Baseball-Reference.com

Retrosheet.com

Notes

1. Bryan C. Hanks, "Clifford was the city's first recreation director," Kinston.com, October 10, 2012. kinston.com/sports/local/crawford-was-city-s-first-recreation-director-1.27151

2. H.D. Osteen, "Pat Crawford: A New Type of Big Leaguer," *Sumter* (South Carolina) *Daily Item*, October 29, 1934.

3. "Pat Crawford Hits Homer in First game of Year," *Gastonia* (North Carolina) *Daily Gazette*, May 16, 1927, 2.

4. H.D. Osteen, "Pat Crawford: A New Type of Big Leaguer."

5. "Baseball Squibs," *Kingston* (New York) *Daily Freeman*, May 13, 1925, 18.

6. *The Sporting News*, June 25, 1925, 1.

7. "Pat Crawford New Property Atlanta Southern Outfit," *Gastonia News Gazette*, July 8, 1926, 2.

8. Marshall D. Wright, *The South Atlantic League, 1904-1963: A Year-by-Year Statistical History* (Jefferson, North Carolina: McFarland, 2009), 124-25.

9. "Pat Crawford to Guilford College as Head Coach," *Gastonia Daily Gazette*, May 28, 1927, 6.

10. "Pat Crawford Changes Mind About Playing Ball on Sundays," *Pittsburgh Press*, August 7, 1927, 1.

11 "Fear Pat Crawford's Playing Days Are Over" (Associated Press), *Gastonia Daily Gazette*, March 28, 1935, 6.

12 "Pat Crawford Sold to New York Giants for $10,000," *Gastonia Daily Gazette*, August 3, 1927, 6.

13 Ibid.

14 Ibid.

15 Ibid.

16 "McGraw Wants Pat Crawford," *Gastonia Daily Gazette* (Gastonia, North Carolina), April 5, 1928, 6.

17 Ibid.

18 "Pat Crawford to Join New York Giants," *Gastonia Daily Gazette*, May 24, 1918, 6.

19 *The Sporting News*, August 16, 1928, 4.

20 H.D. Osteen, "Pat Crawford: A New Type of Big Leaguer," *Sumter Daily Item,* October 29, 1934.

21 "Homer by Crawford Helps Giants Win," *New York Times*, May 27, 1929, 31.

22 Alan Gould, "Sports Slants" (Associated Press), *Havre* (Montana) *Daily News,* December 19, 1930, 6.

23 *The Sporting News*, February 19, 1931, 1.

24 *The Sporting News*, April 9, 1931, 5.

25 "Red Birds Offer Youthful Lineup and Not Done Yet," *Zanesville* (Ohio) *Sunday Times Signal,* April 12, 1931, 8.

26 Bill O'Neal, *The American Association. A Baseball History 1902-1991* (Austin, Texas: Eakin Press, 1991).

27 *The Sporting News, October* 22, 1931, 1.

28 "Columbus Ordered to Cut Its Payroll" (United Press), *Ames* (Iowa) *Daily Tribune-Times,* June 5, 1933, 6.

29 "The Lookout," *Lowell* (Massachusetts) *Sun,* July 19, 1933, 13.

30 *The Sporting News*, March 14, 1940, 3.

31 H.D. Osteen, "Pat Crawford: A New Type of Big Leaguer."

32 Richard Peterson, *The St. Louis Cardinals Baseball Reader* (Columbia, Missouri: University of Missouri Press, 2006), 27-28.

33 Jim Mandelaro and Scott Pitoniak, *Silver Season: The Story of the Rochester Red Wings* (Syracuse, New York: Syracuse University Press, 1996), 59.

34 "Pat Crawford Has Only Slight Chance to Recover," *Gastonia Daily Gazette*, January 26, 1935, 2.

35 "Pat Crawford," from the *Charlotte Observer*, reprinted in the *Gastonia Daily Gazette*, February 1, 1936, 4.

36 "Fear Pat Crawford's Playing Days Are Over" (Associated Press), *Gastonia Daily Gazette*, March 28, 1935, 6.

George 'Kiddo' Davis

By Don Harrison

IF THE FATES had been kinder to George "Kiddo" Davis, he would have had the opportunity to display his skills in five World Series during his eight major-league seasons.

In two Series with the New York Giants, 1933 and 1936, the center fielder complemented his outstanding defensive work with 8 hits in 21 at-bats, a robust .381 average—or 99 percentage points above his career regular-season average.

Davis also played for the 1934 St. Louis Cardinals and the 1937 Giants, both of whom went on to win National League pennants, and as a 24-year-old rookie he made one appearance with the pennant-bound 1926 New York Yankees. A winning ballplayer? One would say yes.

George Willis "Kiddo" Davis was born in Bridgeport, Connecticut, on February 12, 1902, the youngest of eight children of George E. and Bessie E. James Davis. All of his siblings were born in Nanticoke, Pennsylvania, where George's father worked in the coal mines, as did his father before him in Wales. His father's new and far less dangerous job, as a brakeman on the New Haven Railroad, prompted the family's move to the industrial city in southern Connecticut.

George was just a boy when he acquired the nickname that would forever be his trademark. As his son, 82-year-old George Jr., recalled in 2013: "He told me that when he was 9 or 10 years old, he was always playing with kids 11, 12, 13. When they'd choose up sides, they'd say, 'I'll take the kiddo.'"

George's mother died of Bright's disease when he was just 15, and his aunt, Edna Mary Waters, "kind of took over and watched over him," according to his 90-year-old niece, Edna Miller.

At Bridgeport High School, Kiddo quickly developed into a star third baseman and, as a sophomore sparked coach Fred Hunt's Hilltoppers to the 1918 state championship. The spring season was climaxed by Bridgeport's 3-2 victory over Evander Childs High School of New York City, a game billed as the Eastern championship. Bridgeport High captured the state title the next season as well.

For reasons lost in time, Davis left school in 1920 and went to work for a local biscuit company. Realizing that he would require a high-school diploma to obtain a college athletic scholarship, he met with Bridgeport High's principal and was allowed to re-enter the school. Because of his age, though, he was ineligible for baseball and worked part-time as a bookkeeper after school hours.

Eddie Reilly, the high school's three-sport coach, was well aware of Davis's baseball skills; he had coached the youngster in semipro competition. So he was able to place Davis in the lineup when Bridgeport High played a prep school or college freshman team.

Bill McCarthy, New York University's well-respected varsity coach, was an interested spectator on the day

Traded to the Phillies on June 15 for Chick Fullis, Kiddo Davis led the league in assists (14) and double plays (6) from his center-field position in 1934.

when Bridgeport High traveled to Manhattan and defeated the Violet freshmen, 6-5. Davis led the way defensively and at the plate with a 4-for-5 performance, including a home run. A baseball scholarship to NYU soon followed.

Davis went on to earn a bachelor's degree, with honors, in business administration. He also earned considerable accolades for his play on the baseball field, batting over .500 with the freshman squad and .501 and .486 as a member of the Violet varsity. As a senior he assembled a robust collection of extra-base hits (six home runs, seven triples, six doubles), and twice hit a pair of homers in a game.

The Yankees, mindful of other metropolitan colleges' contributions to the big leagues—Columbia sent Lou Gehrig to the Yankees and Eddie Collins to the Philadelphia Athletics; Fordham sent Frank Frisch to the Giants—took note of Davis's productivity at NYU, and scout Paul Krichell, who gained lasting fame for discovering Gehrig at Columbia, signed Davis to a Yankees contract after the Violets' season ended.

The Yankees team that Davis joined in June of 1926 was a powerhouse, featuring no fewer than seven future Hall of Famers: right fielder Babe Ruth, first baseman Lou Gehrig, center fielder Earle Combs, second baseman Tony Lazzeri, pitchers Waite Hoyt and Herb Pennock, and manager Miller Huggins. The left fielder, Bob Meusel, was a career .309 hitter who had led the American League with 33 home runs and 138 runs batted in the previous season. The 1926 club would win the first of three straight American League pennants.

Davis accompanied New York on a two-week Western trip, but he got into only one game. At Cleveland's Dunn Field, on June 5, he replaced Ruth in the bottom of the eighth inning in a game won by the Indians 15-3. The Babe had driven in all of the Yankees' runs, two coming on his 19th home run of the season. Davis recorded no putouts nor did he get an at-bat on that Saturday afternoon as he became the first NYU alumnus to play in the big leagues.

Shortly thereafter, Davis was optioned to Newark of the International League, where he played regularly in the second half of the season and finished with a .290 batting average in 78 games.

On December 18, 1926, Davis married his high-school sweetheart, Myrtle Prout, the daughter of a former Bridgeport police captain. Four years later they became the parents of George Jr.

On the baseball front, this was the beginning of a frustrating five-year period for Kiddo Davis. He distinguished himself at minor-league waystops yet was unable to return to the majors. In 1927 he failed to hit well with Nashville of the Southern Association (.220) and Reading of the International League (.267), and was shipped to Hartford of the Eastern League. Playing center field for the Senators, he won the EL batting title with a .349 average. Presto. His contract was sold to St. Paul of the American Association.

Davis, who stood 5-feet-11 and weighed 178 pounds, developed into a star during the next four summers with the Double-A Saints, hitting above .300 each year (.310, .315, .366, .343) and fielding superbly. In the latter season he reached career highs in hits (214), runs scored (134), home runs (26), triples (15), total bases (358), and stolen bases (24). Finally, the Philadelphia Phillies took notice and purchased his contract.

The 1932 Phillies, managed by Burt Shotton, proved surprisingly competitive, finishing in fourth place—their highest finish in 15 years—with a 78-76 record. Davis was a perfect complement to sluggers Chuck Klein (.348, 38 homers, 137 RBIs), Don Hurst (.339, 24 homers, 143 RBIs) and Pinky Whitney (.298, 13 homers, 124 RBIs).

As a 30-year-old rookie, Davis put forth the finest of his eight major-league seasons. After a slow start, he wound up batting a career-best .309, amassed 178 hits, including 39 doubles, scored 100 runs and drove in 57. His 16 stolen bases placed fifth in the league.

Davis hit the first of his 19 home runs off Brooklyn Dodgers relief pitcher Fred Heimach, a left-hander, at Baker Bowl on April 29, 1932. The Phillies won handily, 13-6.

In the field Davis ranked second among National League outfielders in putouts (411) and fourth in assists (15), and tied with Cincinnati's Babe Herman with six double plays. Veteran writers were labeling him the Phils' finest center fielder since Dode Paskert, who starred on the club's 1915 pennant winner.

On December 15, 1932, Davis was stunned to learn that he was a key component in a three-club, five-player deal that sent him to the Giants. New York parted with veteran outfielder Fred Lindstrom, who went to the Pittsburgh Pirates, and outfielder Chick Fullis, who became Phillies property.

The Giants' new manager, first baseman Bill Terry, was delighted to have Davis's defensive skills in center field; he was second among league outfielders with a .988 percentage. And although he batted just .258 (augmented by a personal-best seven homers) for the season, he was considered an important contributor as the club won the 1933 pennant.

The Chicago Cubs trailed the Giants by just 5 1/2 games on September 15 when New York arrived in Wrigley Field for a four-game series. With superb pitching from Hal Schumacher and Hi Bell, the latter working in relief of Roy Parmelee, the Giants swept the pair, 5-1 and 4-0.

In the opener Davis contributed a pair of hits and a run scored in four at-bats before being ejected for decking Cubs reliever Pat Malone, a husky 200-pounder, in a fight in the eighth inning.

The disturbance had its genesis in the fourth inning when Malone's high hard one sailed too close to Davis's head. "Davis yelled that he would come out after Pat if he sent up another bean ball," reported the next day's *New York Sun*. "Davis then singled, and he got another single in the sixth, and this incensed Malone, and he said he would take a punch at Davis the next chance he got.

"In the eighth Davis grounded out to Bill Herman and Malone swaggered over to the first-base line as Davis ran for the bag. 'Well, I got you that time,' said Pat, 'and I'll get you again, and right now.' And with that Malone threw down his glove at Davis' feet and swung a right that just grazed Davis' face. Davis feinted with his right and cleverly crossed his left to the button."

Two stitches were needed to close the cut on Malone's chin. Said Giants pitcher Fred Fitzsimmons: "I could hear Malone's teeth rattle where I was sitting in the dugout."[1]

New York Times columnist John Kieran, in praising Terry's managerial expertise, wrote: "Just what particular charm he used on Hughey Critz, George Davis or Joe Moore is still a mystery, but it brought results. If a great stop was needed to save the day, one of them would make it. If a hit was required to win a ball game, the weakest hitter on a weak-hitting team would rap a rousing blow to safe territory."[2]

In the Giants' World Series victory over the Washington Senators in five games, Davis elevated his batting to all-star level. Hitting safely in each of the five games, the 31-year-old center fielder went 7-for-19 at the plate, a .368 average. He outhit all of his better-known teammates save Mel Ott, who checked in with a .389 average (7-for-18) Terry, a lifetime .341 hitter, batted just .273 in the Series.

Davis appeared in another World Series with the Giants, in 1936, but not before he wore the uniform of two other teams. Seeking better hitting in 1934, the world champs dispatched him to the Cardinals for another outfielder, George Watkins, just as spring training was winding down.

Davis got off to a .303 start as a part-time outfielder with the Redbirds, the rollicking bunch known as the Gas House Gang. With Dizzy Dean, Joe Medwick, Pepper Martin, Rip Collins, Leo Durocher, and player-manager Frankie Frisch, among others, St. Louis was stocked with colorful, outspoken characters who played hard and well. They nosed out the Giants by two games for the pennant and defeated the Detroit Tigers in the World Series.

With an outfield of Medwick, Jack Rothrock, and Ernie Orsatti, though, Davis was deemed expendable and, on June 15, he was traded back to the Phillies for Chick Fullis. He played in 100 games for the seventh-place Phils and batted .293. For the second straight year, Davis ranked second among league outfielders with a .988 fielding percentage.

Bill Terry realized that he had erred in trading Kiddo Davis away and admitted as much. "Trading Davis for Watkins was the worst boner I pulled as manager of the Giants," he said.[3] In late December the club reacquired the outfielder from the Phillies in exchange for Joe Bowman, a second-year pitcher, and cash.

"Of course I am tickled to be back in New York, which is the ballplayers' paradise," Dan Daniel quoted

Davis as saying. "I'm in good shape right now. I work out nearly every day, never indoors. Right now I do a lot of ice skating. During the fall I played football — not the hard, tackling game but one suited for conditioning rather than injuries."[4]

The Giants had supplemented their outfield of Ott and Jo-Jo Moore with a hard-hitting newcomer, Hank Leiber. A rookie of promise, Jimmy Ripple, joined the squad in 1936. So Davis was relegated to backup duty the next two seasons, often as a defensive replacement in the late innings. He batted .264 in 47 games for a third-place Giants team in 1935, and just .239 in a like number of games the following year, when Terry's club held off charges from the Cardinals and Cubs and won the National League pennant by five games. Davis did, however, thump a pair of home runs as a pinch-hitter in 1935.

In the 1936 World Series, against the Yankees, Kiddo Davis made four appearances, twice as a pinch-hitter and twice as a pinch-runner. In Game Two he singled off Lefty Gomez and scored a run. But the Yanks won in a rout, 18-4. Davis entered the fourth game as a pinch-runner for Sam Leslie in the eighth inning and scored the Giants' second run in a 5-2 Yankee triumph.

In the Series finale — and what would be his World Series coda — Davis flied out to left against Yankee reliever Johnny Murphy in the eighth inning as the Bronx Bombers wrapped up the fall classic in six games with a 13-5 victory at the Polo Grounds. When the 1937 season opened, he was 35 years old and still the Giants' principal outfield backup behind Ott, Moore, and Ripple. The club would win yet another pennant, but Davis wasn't present for the celebration. He refused to accept a demotion to Jersey City (International League) in late July, and the Giants sold him to the Cincinnati Reds, a last-place outfit, on August 4. Combined, he batted .259 in 96 games. Still, there were moments with the Reds when Davis provided a glimpse of past glories. In a 4-1 triumph over the Dodgers at Crosley Field on August 7, he took away a pair of extra-base hits from Heinie Manush, a lifetime .330 hitter later elected to the Baseball Hall of Fame.

"The first time, he went back to the base of the centerfield wall which is far enough from the home plate to be in another county and caught a prodigious poke," Tommy Holmes wrote in the *Brooklyn Eagle*. "On the second occasion, he executed a spinning, diving catch of a line drive that Heinie seemed to have safely propelled down the left center alley."[5]

Davis began to have mixed feelings about continuing his baseball career; in fact, he announced — and then rescinded — his retirement during the Reds' 1938 spring training. "A few days ago I thought I had enough of baseball. I thought I could not do justice to myself or my club as a utility player, and I believed the honest thing to do was quit," he said an Associated Press dispatch. "It was just one big mistake."[6]

Davis eventually joined the Reds in early April, but appeared in just five games and batted .278. He concluded the summer with Jersey City, hitting just .202 against International League pitching before being released by Cincinnati on August 1.

"I was lucky to be allowed the privilege to play a game I loved and receive pay for it," he later told columnist Edward J. Shugrue of the *Bridgeport Sunday Post*.[7]

Unlike so many of his peers, Davis was prepared for post-baseball life. Already a partner in an accounting firm in his native Bridgeport before his playing days ended, he earned a comfortable living as a certified public accountant for many years.

Although out of the limelight, Davis was well-remembered by his home state's sports community. In 1962 he was presented the coveted Gold Key award at the Connecticut Sports Writers' Alliance's annual dinner. Former Yankees pitcher Frank "Spec" Shea (Naugatuck) and Maurice Podoloff (New Haven), the founding president of the National Basketball Association, were the other recipients.

A decade later, Davis was inducted into the New York University Sports Hall of Fame along with basketball All-American Sid Tanenbaum and Emil Von Elling, who coached the Violets track teams for more than 40 years. He later was joined in the NYU Hall of Fame by three other major leaguers of note, Ralph Branca, Eddie Yost, and Sam Mele.

Kiddo Davis died at the age of 81 on March 4, 1983. He was survived by his wife and son; two grandchildren, Ellen and James; and several nieces and nephews.

Sources

The author is indebted to George W. Davis, Jr. and Edna Miller, Kiddo Davis's niece, for sharing their memories of the late outfielder in interviews during the spring of 2013.

"A Great Player Leaves Our Midst," *Connecticut Elders,* April 1983.

Ancestry.com.

Associated Press, "Repairs Among Median Line Helped Giants to Win National Loop Flag," September 23, 1935.

The Baseball Encyclopedia, 10th Edition (New York: Macmillan, Edition, 1996).

Baseball-Reference.com.

Bielawa, Michael J., *Bridgeport Baseball* (Charleston, South Carolina: Arcadia Publishing, 2003).

Burr, Harold C., "Young George Davis Looks Like Fixture in Phillies' Garden," *New York Post,* undated.

Burr, Harold C., "Davis New King of Giant Corps," *New York Post,* April 4, 1936.

Cohen, Leonard, "Davis of N.Y.U. Batting Fame Joins Yankees," *New York Evening World,* June 4, 1926.

Daniel, Dan, "Terry Gives Joe Bowman and Cash for Outfielder," *New York World-Telegram,* December 13, 1934.

Daniel, Dan, "George Davis, Back with Giants, Hopes He's Now Off that Baseball Carousel," *New York World-Telegram,* January 5, 1935.

"Daniel's Dope," *New York World-Telegram,* April 9, 1932.

Davis, George "Kiddo," Obituary. *Bridgeport Post-Telegram,* March 5, 1983.

Davis, George "Kiddo," Obituary. *New York Times,* March 8, 1983.

"Davis Will Rejoin Reds; Decision to Quit 'Mistake,'" *New York Times,* April 10, 1938.

Drebinger, John, "Davis, Outfield 'Insurance Man,' Accepts Contract with Giants," *New York Times,* January 13, 1937.

"Frothy Facts," *New York World-Telegram,* July 3, 1934.

George "Kiddo" Davis's file at the National Baseball Hall of Fame library, Cooperstown, New York.

Graham, Frank, *Lou Gehrig: A Quiet Hero* (New York: G.P. Putnam's Sons, 1942).

Holmes, Tommy, "Flock Tumbled To 7th Place in 4 to 1 Setback," *Brooklyn Eagle,* August 8, 1937.

"Kiddo Davis Honored," *New York Times,* March 6, 1971.

"Kiddo Davis Too Tough for Chicago Pitcher in Personal Battle," *New York Sun,* September 16, 1933.

Kieran, John, "Sports of the Times: Black Magic," *New York Times,* September (date unavailable), 1933.

McConnell, Bob, and David Vincent, eds., *The Home Run Encyclopedia* (New York: Macmillan, 1996).

"N.Y.U. Swatsmith Will Make Tour of West with Yankees," *New York American,* June (date unavailable), 1926.

"N.Y.U. to Honor Tanenbaum, Davis and Von Elling," *New York Times,* April 23, 1972.

Parker, Charles E., "Davis Defends Bartell," *New York World-Telegram,* December 22, 1934.

Retrosheet.com.

Shugrue, Edward J., "Between Ourselves," *Bridgeport Sunday Post* (date unavailable), 1946.

Smith, Ken, "Giants Capture Two From Cubs, 5-1, 4-0," *New York Daily Mirror,* September 16, 1933.

Notes

1. *New York Sun,* September 16, 1933.
2. John Kieran, *New York Times,* September 1933. (Date unavailable)
3. Dan Daniel, *New York World-Telegram,* December 13, 1934.
4. Dan Daniel, *New York World-Telegram,* January 5, 1935.
5. Tommy Holmes, *Brooklyn Eagle,* August 8, 1937.
6. Associated Press, April 9, 1938.
7. Edward J. Shugrue, *Bridgeport Sunday Post,* 1946. (Date unavailable)

Spud Davis

by Andy Sturgill

SUGGESTING THAT A player was not good enough to make the 1927 New York Yankees is hardly an insult. The original Murderers Row is widely considered the greatest club ever to take the field. Spud Davis' first opportunity to break into the major leagues was with the '27 Yankees, and while he did not make that club he did go on to have a very good major-league career, including playing for a World Series winner with the St. Louis Cardinals.

Virgil Lawrence Davis was born December 20, 1904 in Birmingham, Alabama, the son of John and Kate Davis. According to the 1910 census, the Davis family lived in the household of Kate Davis' mother Zillah Schwinn in the Jefferson neighborhood of Birmingham. The household listed ten different people (including Spud's sister, Helen) with six different last names. By 1920 Virgil's family lived in a different household in Jefferson as the step-son of George Hanlin, who by this time was married to Virgil's mother. Whether John Davis passed away or was separated from Kate Davis is unknown.

Davis attended high school at Gulf Coast Military Academy in Gulfport, Mississippi, where he starred in the offensive backfield and defensive line for the football team that won the 1922 Mississippi state title. Davis broke into professional baseball in 1926, hitting .356 for the Gulfport Tarpons of the Class D Cotton States League. He split his time between catcher and third base. In September 1926 Davis' contract was purchased from Gulfport by the New York Yankees, setting up a chance for Spud to make an impact upon perhaps the greatest baseball team of all time. The exact dollar figure that Yankees paid for his rights was not reported, but the sum "was said to be large."[1]

Davis did not make the roster of the legendary team, but Commissioner Kenesaw Mountain Landis ruled that the Yankees had too many players out on option. Landis then subjected a few of the players, including Davis, to waivers where they could be claimed by another team, and Davis was snagged by the St. Louis Cardinals.

Spud played the 1927 season for the Reading (PA) Keystones of the Class AA International League, an affiliate of the Chicago Cubs. Catching almost every day, Davis hit .308 for the season, his last minor-league action for 20 years.

Davis made his major-league debut on April 30, 1928 as the Cardinals played host to the Reds. He started behind the dish for the Redbirds, opposite Bill Sherdel on the hill. Davis went 0-2 at the plate before Ray Blades pinch hit for him. Davis' next game on May 8 was a 15-4 shellacking of the Phillies in which Davis recorded his first hit, run, RBI, and walk in the major leagues.

After only those two games with the Cardinals, Davis was traded on May 11 to the Philadelphia Phillies with two other players for a package of

Acquired from the Phillies in the offseason, Spud Davis split time with Bill Delancey at catcher. He hit .308 for his career that lasted 16 seasons. After his playing days, Davis coached for ten years with the Pirates and Cubs.

three players highlighted by catcher Jimmie Wilson. While Davis left the pennant-winning Cardinals for the 43-109 Phillies, he didn't mind the switch, saying many years later that he was happy to go anywhere that he could get a chance to play.[2] Spud hit his first career home run on with the Phillies on June 8, taking Sheriff Blake of the Cubs deep for a game-winning three-run shot in the bottom of the eighth of the Phillies' 6-5 win. Davis finished his rookie season hitting .280 with three home runs and 19 RBIs for the last-place Phillies, who finished 51 games behind the Cardinals squad he had begun the season with. Davis split the catching duties for the Phillies with fellow rookie backstop Walt Lerian.

Lerian and Davis again split time behind the plate for the Phillies in 1929. Spud appeared in 98 games, hitting .342, his first of seven straight seasons at or above .300 and ten seasons overall throughout his career.

Davis became the Phillies' primary backstop in 1930, not so much because of his play but because of tragedy. Just weeks after the conclusion of the 1929 season, Walt Lerian was killed in Baltimore when a delivery truck jumped a curb at a trolley stop and caught him as it ran into a building.

From 1930-33, Davis was one of the best offensive catchers in baseball, averaging a .333 batting average with ten home runs and 63 RBIs. While the Phillies of this era struggled in the standings (finishing above .500 in 1932 for the only time between 1918 and 1948), the team routinely put up impressive offensive numbers, no doubt helped by playing their home games in the hitter-friendly confines of the Baker Bowl.

Davis had one of his best years in 1933. He hit .349 for the Phillies while playing in 141 of the team's 152 games. Davis' batting average was good enough for second in the National League and third in all of baseball, trailing only each league's batting champ, teammate Chuck Klein in the National League and Jimmie Foxx of Philadelphia's other major-league team. in the American League. Spud's .395 on-base percentage was also second in the NL, again trailing only Klein.

Despite his tremendous success with the bat, Davis was not seen as an exceptional defender. He struggled with weight issues, thus making catching more difficult, and routinely ranked among the league leaders in stolen bases allowed. Likely because of how many runners attempted to steal against him, Davis also routinely ranked among leaders in runners caught stealing. He did lead the league's catchers in fielding percentage with a .994 mark in 1931, committing only three errors and contributing 78 assists from behind the dish.

In November, the Phillies traded away the top two hitters in the National League, sending Chuck Klein to the Cubs and Davis back to the Cardinals, with Jimmie Wilson again serving as the primary player opposite Spud in a trade. Wilson became the Phillies' player-manager, and Davis became the Cardinals' primary catcher. In contrast to his excitement in joining the Phillies in 1928, Davis expressed greater joy in returning to the Cardinals, saying, "Who wouldn't throw his arm off for this bunch after getting away from the Phillies?"[3]

The 1930's era St. Louis Cardinals have gone down in history as the Gashouse Gang, the scrappy, unkempt squad known for its antics as much as its play. Colorful characters such as Pepper Martin, Dizzy Dean, and Leo Durocher filled the roster. The Gashouse Gang was not just colorful, however- it was really good. The Cardinals won the National League pennant in 1930, and won the World Series in 1931 and again in 1934.

In some respects, the 6-1 200 pound Alabaman did not fit in with the roughhouse image of the Gang. A contemporary writer referred to Spud as "the personification of the Southern Gentleman... He does not strut into hotel lobbies, on main thoroughfares, or on the ball field. The Spud does not poke his nose into an open conversation but is reserved and retiring. He does not hoard his money, dresses in the height of fashion, enjoys good shows and is fond of movies." Davis also spoke with a heavy southern drawl.[4]

On the other hand, doesn't a team like the Gashouse Gang need to have a catcher named Spud? The nickname was given to Davis by an uncle in his childhood. "I liked potatoes so much early in life that I was nicknamed Spud," Davis explained. "But I loved baseball more than potatoes, so I cut them out."[5]

Like many ballplayers, Davis was superstitious. For a few days in July of 1934 he asked pitcher Dazzy Vance to recite a Seminole prayer over his bat before going up to hit. One game when Vance was in the bullpen, Spud went hitless. For the next game, in Boston against the Braves, Vance performed the ritual for Davis before his at-bats in the second and fourth innings, and Davis got two hits. Vance was in the bullpen for Davis' fifth-inning at-bat, and Davis grounded out with two runners on. Seeing that he was likely to come to the plate in the seventh, David begged reserve infielder Pat Crawford to take his bat to the bullpen for Vance to perform the ritual. "Much against his better judgment, (Crawford) carried the Davis war club out to the bullpen for the Vance Seminole medicine. Vance willingly quit warming up for a minute, stroked the bat affectionately and muttered the words of the Seminole chiefs. Crawford, feeling very foolish, carried the bat back to the dugout and the happy Davis strode to the plate with the bases filled and whacked a single through the box. Two runs scored on the base hit of the Seminole medicine."[6] Davis had three hits, two RBIs, and scored two runs in the 5-3 Cardinals victory.

Davis caught 94 games for the Cardinals in 1934 but made only two appearances in the seven-game World Series victory over the Tigers, both as a pinch hitter. He singled in both at bats, and following his hit in Game Four was pinch run for by Dizzy Dean. Dean was subsequently knocked unconscious when he was hit in the head by a throw by Detroit shortstop Billy Rogell. Dean eventually came to and started on the mound for the Cardinals the next day.

After the 1934 World Series championship season, Davis played two more seasons for the Cardinals. 1935 was the last of Spud's seven consecutive seasons hitting above .300, notching a final tally of .317. While Davis may have been the perfect Southern gentleman, he wasn't above getting into an altercation with a teammate. Davis was catching for Dizzy Dean one game against the Reds, and Dean felt that Davis didn't try hard enough to catch a foul ball and requested of manager Frankie Frisch that Davis not catch Dean anymore. While teammates sided with Davis in the spat, Frisch bent to his star pitcher's wishes.[7]

In December of '36 he was sold to the Cincinnati Reds along with infielder Charlie Gelbert. He would never again appear in as many as 100 games in a single season. Davis struggled with the Reds, seeing his average drop to a career-low .268 in 1937. Late in the season when manager Chuck Dressen and his coaching staff were relieved of their duties, Davis added the role of assistant coach to his primary role as the team's backup catcher.[8] He played in only 12 games for the Reds in 1938 before again being traded to the Phillies, where he remained through the end of the 1939 season. Davis witnessed the first of Johnny Vander Meer's consecutive no-hitters, but his trade to the Phillies was completed between the two games.[9]

At the end of the 1939 season Davis was about to turn 35 years old and had not had a particularly successful season since the 1935 campaign in St. Louis. Around this time Frankie Frisch, Davis' old teammate and manager with the Cardinals, took over as the skipper of the Pittsburgh Pirates. Frisch's first move after taking the reins was to purchase Davis from the Phillies.

As a 12-year veteran of the major leagues, Davis had carved out a decent living for himself in Depression-Era America. His 1940 U.S. census record indicates that he earned greater than $5,000 for the year (around $85,000 in 2013 dollars) and that he had other sources of income than just playing baseball. Spud, his wife Helen, and son Virgil, also had a live-in housekeeper, another sign that the Depression was not as severe for the Davis clan as for many American families.

Davis spent two seasons with the Pirates, regaining his .300 form with (hitting for ; note-Davis hit .307 with the Phillies in 1939.) a .326 average in 99 games for Pittsburgh 1940. At the end of the 1941 season he was released from the active roster with the understanding that he would have a role in the organization, whether as a coach, minor-league manager, or scout.[10] Two months after his October release Spud was named a coach on Frankie Frisch's staff, a position he would hold through the 1943 season.

In 1944, with the U.S. involved in World War II across Europe and the Pacific, the supply of young men available to play major-league baseball was diminished. As such, the Pirates needed a catcher and found one on their own coaching staff, as Spud Davis strapped on the tools of ignorance once again and resumed his playing career at age 39 after a two-year absence. Appearing in 54 games as a backup to starting catcher Al Lopez, "Old Folks" (as Davis was referred to in the Pirate dugout) again hit over .300, logging a .301 average in 93 at-bats.[11] After one more season on the field during the similarly war-affected 1945, Davis retired back to coaching for the 1946 season. It proved to be his last with the Pirates, as Frisch was let go as manager late in the season and Davis served as the interim skipper for the Pirates' last three games.

Spud was offered the job as the manager of the Class AA Birmingham Barons for the 1947 season, but he declined, preferring to stay with the Pirates organization that had employed him since 1940. No longer a coach, Davis served as a scout in 1947 while also finding time to play 120 games for the Class D Alexander City (AL) Millers of the Georgia-Alabama League. Davis played for Alexander City again in 1948 as a 43-year-old, but had given up his job as a scout for the Pirates to devote more time to a sheet metal business he owned in Birmingham.[12]

Davis made one more foray into major-league baseball, joining his old pal Frankie Frisch as an assistant coach when Frisch took over as the permanent manager of the Chicago Cubs for the 1950 season. He remained with the Cubs until the conclusion of the 1953 season, two years after Frisch's departure.

After being let go by the Cubs, Davis retired to his hometown of Birmingham, living on his baseball pension and a bit of money he had saved from his career in the game.[13] He was inducted into the Alabama Hall of Fame in 1977. He remained in Birmingham from the time he retired until his death on August 14, 1984 at the age of 79, after which he was buried at Birmingham's Elmood Cemetery.

Sources

In addition to the sources listed, the author also consulted Ancestry.com and Baseball-Reference.com.

Notes

1. "Yanks Buy Third Baseman." *The New York Times*, September 7, 1926, 29.
2. Paul Green. *Forgotten Fields*. (Waupaca, WI: Parker Publications, 1987), 165.
3. John Heidenry. *The Gashouse Gang*. (New York: Public Affairs, 2007), 126.
4. G.H. Fleming. *The Dizziest Season*. (New York: William Morrow, 1984), 89.
5. Michael Eisenbath. *The Cardinals Encyclopedia*. (Philadelphia: Temple University Press, 1999), 165.
6. Fleming, 178.
7. Eisenbath, 165.
8. *Reading Eagle*, September 14, 1937.
9. Green, 167.
10. "Pirates Drop Catcher Davis." *The New York Times*, October 3, 1941, 33.
11. Chester Smith, "Davis Predicts Pirates Will Be Tough to Beat." *Pittsburgh Press*, March 24, 1945, 8.
12. "Davis Quits Bucs For His Business." *Pittsburgh Press*, January 20, 1948, 19.
13. "Gas Housers Best, Davis Claims." *Milwaukee Journal*, May 1, 1959, 33.

Dizzy Dean

By Joseph Wancho

Frankie Frisch may have been playing possum, or just being coy. But after the St. Louis Cardinals won Game Six of the 1934 World Series, the big question was which pitcher manager Frisch would send to the hill for the seventh and deciding game. His star pitcher, Dizzy Dean, was coming off a loss in Game Five just two days earlier. The loss put the Cards in a 3-2 hole as the Series headed back to Detroit. In Game Six Dizzy's brother Paul went the distance, giving up three runs, only one of them earned, in the 4-3 win. It was more than Paul's pitching that saved the season for the Cardinals. With the score tied, 3-3, in the top of the seventh inning; Leo Durocher hit a one-out double to center field, and Paul followed with a single to right to untie the game and eventually force a Game Seven.

To the surprise of many, Frisch named Bill Hallahan to take the ball in the deciding game. Hallahan had pitched well in Game Two, but had a no-decision for his effort. Durocher was stunned by the skipper's choice. "I don't want Hallahan. I want Dean," said the Lip. "I was still $6,000 in debt, which is just about what the winner's share is going to come to. The loser's share, I'm not interested in."[1]

Frisch let Dizzy in on the secret: Indeed Diz would be toeing the rubber in Game Seven, but he should keep it a secret to keep the Tigers off balance. Diz later recalled, "Frisch lets on that Hallahan is going to pitch, and the next day, when I come up through the Tigers dugout, which I have to do to get to ours, I set down, just for fun, and all the Detroit players holler at me to get out and go where I belong. So I laugh and start across the field and they holler after me, 'It's too bad you aren't going to pitch today! We'd just love to get another crack at you!'"[2]

Dean was never at a loss for words, nor did he lack confidence in his ability. He spotted Detroit slugger Hank Greenberg and said, "Hello Mose. What makes you so white? Boy, you're shakin' like a leaf. I get it; you done hear that Old Diz was goin' to pitch. Well, you're right. It'll all be over in a few minutes. Old Diz is goin' to pitch, and he's goin' to pin your ears back."[3]

Elden Auker was pitching for the Tigers in the third inning of a scoreless tie. With one away, Dizzy came to the plate. He hit a popup foul, to the back of home. Detroit catcher and manager Mickey Cochrane did not give chase, and the foul nestled into the first row of seats. Dean then hit a blooper over third base. Goose Goslin in left field was slow getting to the ball and Diz never let up, pulling into second base. Pepper Martin hit an infield single to first and Jack Rothrock followed with a walk to load the bases. Frisch doubled, clearing the bases. After Dean scored, he turned to Cochrane and said, "You're beat now, Mickey."[4] Indeed, the Cardinals scored seven runs in the frame on their way to an easy 11-0 win and the world championship. The Dean boys carried the Series, each winning two games. As it turned out, it may not have mattered whom Frisch chose to pitch on this day.

Dizzy Dean was the last pitcher in the National League to pitch a 30-win season in 1934. He followed that up with 28 victories in 1935. He led the senior circuit in strikeouts from 1932 to 1935 and was elected to the Hall of Fame in 1953.

Jay Hanna Dean was born on January 16, 1910, in Lucas, Arkansas, near the Arkansas Ozarks. He was the fourth child born to

Monroe and Alma Dean. The two oldest children, Charles and Sarah May, died in infancy. Jay had two brothers, Elmer and Paul. Monroe and Alma worked as sharecroppers, living rent-free and earning a share of the profits for tending to the crops of the landowner, Mrs. Hattie Blair.

Alma Dean was stricken with tuberculosis and died when Jay was 7 years old. Monroe remarried, taking the widowed Cora Parham as his new wife. She also had three children and the Dean household doubled in size. The clan moved to Chickalah, about 45 miles southeast of Lucas. Monroe continued there as a sharecropper.

The Dean family was on the move again in 1925, this time relocating to Spaulding, Oklahoma. During the harvest season, it was not uncommon for the family to look as far as southern Mississippi for work. Because of the Deans' picking up stakes, Jay and his siblings did not receive much of a formal education. Tales differ about how long they actually attended school, for even at a young age, Jay would accompany his father to work in the cotton fields.

Another tale that had varying assumptions was why Jay changed his name to Jerome Herman. The most accepted truth is that he had a childhood friend who had died, and in an effort to possibly lessen the pain of the child's mother, Jay took his friend's name. Monroe consented to the name change.

Dean, his brothers, and Monroe played sandlot ball around town, in less than adequate conditions. Makeshift equipment was all the players had at their disposal. Nonetheless, the younger Dean boys stood out as superior players, even in their early teen years.

As the Deans made their way through Texas looking for work, they came upon Fort Sam Houston, near San Antonio. Jerome remembered how his stepbrothers, Claude and Herman, preached about the good lifestyle the Army provided. He believed that the Army would offer a better standard of living that what he was accustomed to picking cotton and moving around the Southern states like a gypsy. But but he had not yet reached the required age of 18. Monroe consented to Jerome's wishes and vouched that his son was 18 years old and had an elementary-school education. Although it may have not seemed like the brightest idea at the time, Dean enlisted under his real name of Jay Hanna in 1926. He was assigned to the 3rd Wagon Company of the Quartermaster Corps as a private and for the most part was given menial tasks to complete around the camp.

It did not take Dean long to discover the base's baseball diamonds. He was given a tryout and quickly gained recognition as one of the better players. He eventually was assigned to the 12th Field Artillery and was promoted to private first class. The news of the hard-throwing youngster spread throughout San Antonio, with many semipro teams vying for his services. But Master Sergeant James K. Brought kept Dean under wraps, and was often a tough disciplinarian with him. After one outing in which Dean struck out 11 batters in a two-hit shutout, Brought sat him down for a chat. "You see, kid, there was a major-league scout out there today," said Brought. "A scout from the St. Louis Cardinals. He came all the way down here to see you pitch. I told this scout that you are the clumsiest kid I ever seen going into a windup, but you can throw hard and you have a good curve." After a pause, Brought added, "I also told him that you were the dizziest kid I ever had in my outfit."[5]

The appellation stuck, and Jay Hanna/Jerome Herman Dean would be known to the world as Dizzy Dean.

Although the bird-dog scout liked what he saw of Dean, the pitcher was the property of the United States Army. Over the next two years Dean pitched in barracks leagues on the base. Just after New Year's Day in 1929, he was approached about pitching for a semipro team in San Antonio. Since he had served just over two years, he could buy his way out of the Army for $100. Monroe, his father, helped raise the money and civilian Dean reported to work for the San Antonio Public Service Corp. His day job may have been that of reading gas meters, but his real function was to pitch on the company baseball team.

He was again spotted by a bird-dog scout, who contacted Don Curtis, a scout for the Cardinals. Curtis signed Dean to a contract to pitch for the Houston Buffaloes of the Texas League beginning in 1930. He was to be paid $100 a month. But as spring training camp broke, he was assigned to St. Joseph (Missouri), a Cardinals affiliate in the Class A Western League.

By this time Branch Rickey had built a stout farm system. He is credited with creating the idea, remarking, "I could find prospects to become the next Hornsbys and Frisches. I would find them young. I would develop them. Pick them from the sandlots and keep them until they were ready for the Cardinals. All I needed was the place to train them."[6] By the time Dean reported to St, Joseph, Rickey's farm empire stretched from Houston to Greensboro and up to Rochester, New York.

Dean pitched extremely well for the Saints, considering it was his first year in Organized Baseball. He went 17-8 with a 3.69 earned-run average. "He was better than the rest of us, "said teammate Mace Brown. "And to have control of his pitches like he did to go with all that speed and to be so young, well, that was rare for the time. You could tell that he was going to be great."[7]

The term "Good Ol' Country Boy" may have fit Dean, as he had a carefree, cavalier attitude about most matters. His first car was a Ford roadster that he drove off a "U-Drive It" rental lot. "I don't think he ever paid for that car or even turned it in," said teammate Peaches Davis. "When he got tired of it, he'd park it somewhere and go get another one from somebody else, just like they were free. We told him that's not the way you did things, but he'd say sure, and do what he felt like doing. That's the way he was."[8]

The Buffaloes were vying for the pennant in the Texas League, so Dean was sent to Houston to lend a hand. He went 8-2 in 14 games, but the team fell short of the mark. He earned a call-up to St. Louis in September.

When Dean and Houston teammate Tony Kaufman met the Cardinals, the team was at the Polo Grounds in New York in the midst of a pennant race of their own. St. Louis manager Gabby Street kept Dizzy idle until after the Redbirds clinched the flag, on September 26. Diz made his major-league debut on the 28th against Pittsburgh at Sportsman's Park. He went the distance, striking out five Pirates in the 3-1 victory. He singled and scored a run. "Dizzy and me were sitting side by side on the bench," said pitcher Burleigh Grimes, whose spikes Dean borrowed because he had lost his own. "He was as unconcerned as if he was tossing rocks at a mud turtle in the Meramec River."[9]

As spring training approached, the Cardinals front office was dealing with another matter, and that was the excessive bills that Dean racked up, charging the purchases to the ballclub. The figure was up to $2,700 and growing. Rickey eventually put him on a restricted pay allowance equal to a dollar a day. Dean was also getting on the nerves of Street, and his teammates. He was loud and incorrigible, broke team rules, and was generally viewed as a pest. Yet, wherever the club went, it was Dean whom the media and fans had the most interest in. This also grated on the veteran players.

Dean opened the 1931 season on the bench. It may have been a form of punishment for his actions, or because the starting rotation was pitching well. In any case he was sent to Houston, where he spent the rest of the season. Despite his grating personality, there was no denying his talent. Dean recorded a 26-10 record for Houston with 11 shutouts. He racked up 303 strikeouts in 304 innings pitched. The Buffaloes, who played a split-season schedule, won the second-half pennant and Dean was named the league's Most Valuable Player.

Despite Dean's achievements, Houston manager Joe Schultz thought it could have been even better. Dizzy would try to strike out all the good hitters, pitching to their strengths, and often letting up on the weaker hitters. Schultz believed this was a case of overconfidence, something Dean surely did not lack.

Schultz and Dean went to eat at a diner, each ordering scrambled eggs and bacon. By mistake the kitchen substituted calves' brains for the bacon. Dizzy, always a big eater, cleaned his plate. He asked the waitress what it was he had eaten and she informed him of the mistake. "What?" he said. "I didn't order no brains." Schultz replied, "Be quiet, she knows what you need."[10]

On June 15, 1931, Dean married Patricia Nash of Bond, Mississippi. She took control of Dizzy's wild spending, and was really like a mother to him in many ways, teaching him manners and picking out his clothes. She was also his business manager, his banker, and his bookkeeper. They were married for 43 years, and had no children.

Paul Dean had also signed with St. Louis and was making his way through the Cardinals' minor-league chain. He was not putting up the numbers Dizzy had, but was still a talented prospect.

In 1932 Dizzy reported to Bradenton, Florida, for spring training, looking for a spot on in the Cardinals rotation. The Redbirds were coming off back-to-back pennant-winning seasons under Street's leadership. Gabby's mound corps was stocked with talent, a nice blend of veterans and young arms. Dean was well aware that the Cardinals had won pennants without him. He was not to be the cure-all for a team that was already winning.

Pat Dean was ill back home in Mississippi during spring training and Dean made noise about leaving camp to tend to her. He made noise in the papers about how management frowned on young players having their wives accompany them to camp. He actually did leave the team for a while during the regular season, claiming the contract he signed with the Cardinals was invalid because he was underage at the time he signed it. He insisted that he was born in 1912, and that he was only 20 when he agreed to terms. It was Dean's way of trying to get more money out of the Cardinals. But a meeting in Commissioner Kenesaw M. Landis's office set the record straight, as the front office produced a copy of his wedding license, showing that his birth year was indeed 1910.

Despite his shenanigans, Dean won his last three starts of the season, including a five-hitter against the Reds, to finish the year at 18-15. He was a streaky pitcher, especially in the second half of the season. He lost four, won three, lost two, won four, lost three, and then won three to end the year. He was by far the team leader in wins, and his 3.50 ERA was second only to Bill Hallahan's 3.11. His 191 strikeouts led the league. But as a team St. Louis sank to near the bottom of the standings, tying the New York Giants for sixth place with 72-82 records.

The Cardinals were in the race in 1933, trailing league-leading New York by 5 1/2 games at the All-Star break. (It was the year of the first All-Star Game.) But they went on a losing skid, dropping nine of 12 games over the next two weeks. They were 46-45 when Street was shown the door. Rickey replaced him with second baseman Frankie Frisch, in spite of Street's having won two pennants and one world championship in his four years. Frisch, nicknamed the Fordham Flash from his days on the gridiron at Fordham University, had been acquired from the Giants for Rogers Hornsby after the 1926 season. The team played a bit better for Frisch but was never able to get back in the race and finished in fifth place.

Dean won 20 games and lost 18. It was the first of four straight seasons in which he won at least 20. He led the league in strikeouts again with 199. On July 30 against the Chicago Cubs, whiffed 17 batters and went 3-for-4 at the plate, doubling twice, driving in two runs, and scoring once.

Dizzy summed up his final strikeout this way: "With me havin' 16 strikeouts already, (Chicago manager) Charlie Grimm sends in Jim Mosolf as a pinch-hitter. As this Mosolf steps up to the plate (catcher Jimmie) Wilson gives him the needle. 'Jim, you sure are in a tough spot. Ol' Diz just hates pinch-hitters, and you better look out!' While Wilson is poundin' his fist in his big mitt right behind Mosolf's ear, I just breeze three right across the plate for Strikeout No. 17."[11]

Dizzy was a pitchman's delight, endorsing Grape-Nuts cereal and Lucky Strike cigarettes among many other products. He also took to barnstorming, joining a major-league team that included teammate Pepper Martin, Paul Waner, Forrest Jenkins, and Glenn Wright. J.L. Wilkinson, owner of the Negro Leagues' Kansas City Monarchs, created a series between the two teams through Nebraska and Kansas. Satchel Paige, Joe Rogan, and Buck O'Neil were the big stars for the Monarchs. Paige and Dean stole the show, whipping the crowds into a frenzy. It was an arrangement that would go on for years.

Powered by a 22-7 record at Columbus, Paul Dean was invited to spring training in 1934. "Me 'n Paul" became a favorite refrain of Dizzy's—especially when he was predicting how many games the two pitchers would win during the season. Paul was quiet in contrast to his older brother. Sportswriters had a difficult time finding the right nickname for Paul. At first they tried

Harpo because he rarely spoke. But they settled on Daffy, because they found it went better with Dizzy.

Dizzy was never short on making predictions, either about the Cardinals or about how many games he might win. Before the 1934 season he predicted a pennant for the Redbirds. "How are they going to stop us?" he said. "Paul's going to be a sensation. He'll win 18 or 20 games. I'll count 20 to 25 for myself. I won 20 last season and I know I'll pass that figure."[12] It may have surprised Dizzy how prophetic he was come October.

The 1934 Cardinals were basically the same team as the year before, except for the addition of Jack Rothrock in right field and Spud Davis at catcher. Frisch would be at the helm from the start of the year, giving fans optimism since the team had played close to .600 ball after he succeeded Street.

It was Paul who put together an 8-0 start to add stability to the rotation. Dizzy, who suffered through a miserable April, righted the ship with a 5-0 record and a 1.45 ERA in May. From May 5 through August 5 he posted an 18-2 record. In spite of the fine pitching by the Dean boys, the Cardinals found themselves in third place on August 25, seven games behind front-running New York.

The end of the season was not without drama. The Cardinals inched closer to the Giants, but with a week left in the season, they found themselves 2 1/2 games out of first place. During spring training, New York skipper Bill Terry, giving his view of the pennant race to the press, had remarked of the Dodgers, "Brooklyn? Are they still in the league?"[13] Now, with the pennant in their sights, the Giants closed the season against the rival Dodgers. Terry would have to eat his words, as his club dropped the last five games of the season, the final two to Brooklyn.

As the final week of the season commenced, shortstop Leo Durocher remembered the confidence that Dean was showing in a team meeting: "I'll pitch today, and if I get in trouble, Paul will relieve me. And he'll pitch tomorrow, and if he gets in trouble I'll relieve him. And I'll pitch the next day and Paul will pitch the day after that and I'll pitch the last one. Don't worry, we'll win five games straight."[14] St. Louis capitalized behind its star pitcher. In the final week of the season, Dean took the ball three times and won all three, going the distance each time. His last two starts were shutouts against Cincinnati. The last win gave him 30 victories; he remains as of 2014 the last pitcher to accomplish the feat in the National League. Paul Dean won the second-to-last game, a 6-1 triumph. The victory gave him 19 wins, for a total of 49 for the brothers. For the third straight year, Diz led the league in strikeouts (195). He had seven saves (retrospectively; saves were not a statistic in those days) and a 2.66 ERA. He was named the Most Valuable Player by both the Baseball Writers' Association of America and *The Sporting News*. He was named to *The Sporting News* Major League All-Star team for the first of three straight years. The Cardinals finished two games ahead of New York to claim their fifth pennant.

Facing the Detroit Tigers in the World Series, the Cardinals dispatched the American League champs in seven games. The two teams' Series rosters had eight future Hall of Famers.[15] It was the Cardinals' third world championship.

It was not until the next year that the team was given the name the Gas House Gang. There are varying versions of how and when the name came to be. The 1991 HBO documentary *When It Was a Game*, compiled largely from home movies taken by players and fans in the 1930s, described the Gas House Gang as "a collection of fast-talking, free-spirited players like Leo Durocher who never ducked a fight and always played hard," the best team of the era and its most colorful. "Entertaining came naturally to the Gas House Gang, keeping clean, however, was a different matter."[16] New York Yankee Tommy Henrich said, "I saw Frankie Frisch in New Orleans in '36 when they were the real Gas House Gang. They came around, most of them needed a shave, and every one of them had on a dirty uniform on. I said what a bunch of bums. Now these are the real Gas House Gang."[17] Cardinals infielder Burgess Whitehead said, "The Gas House Gang was the greatest baseball club I ever saw. They thought they could beat any ballclub and they just about could too. When they got on that ballfield, they played baseball, and they played it to the hilt too. When they slid, they slid hard. There was no good fellowship between them and the opposition. They were just good, tough ballplayers."[18]

Dean was never one to be short on antagonizing the opponent. He was in rare form after he pitched three innings of a spring-training game against the Giants in Miami. After his day's work he strolled by the Giants dugout, asking if any of them could cash a check for $5,300. Which was the winner's share from the 1934 World Series. Rubbing it in just a bit more, Dean remarked, "I wanna thank you fellas for collapsin' so we could make all that dough."[19]

As good as the Dean bothers were, they were also short-tempered. Paul followed Dizzy at every turn, and it seemed as though every year Dizzy would threaten to hold out and take Paul with him. There was little doubt they were the class of the pitching staff, but they also had massive egos, and often blamed others when the going got tough. In a game against the Phillies, Diz was getting shelled early and responded by "dusting" the Phillies batters. He threw at one's head and pelted another. His ex-batterymate in St. Louis, Jimmie Wilson, was now a backstop in Philadelphia and a close friend. "It's getting so you can't get a base hit off those Deans without getting beaned your next time up," said Wilson. "They think they can get away with anything, but by God, the Phils have declared war on them."[20]

Dizzy's response to Wilson's charge? "You can tell that Wilson he can kiss my ass. Them Phillies can't hurt anybody. None of 'em can hit a lick."[21]

The frustration felt by Dean's teammates toward him came to a head at Forbes Field in Pittsburgh on June 4, 1935. Staked to a 2-0 lead in the third inning, Dean was a victim of a lackluster defense as Pittsburgh answered back with four runs. All the runs were unearned and Dean was cursing his teammates on the mound. Reasoning that others were not trying, so why should he, Dean began to lob the baseball to the plate as if he were pitching batting practice. The Pirates showered the field with hard smashes to all corners. Dizzy started to spout off about the shoddy defense to his teammates in the fifth inning. A heated exchange ensued between Rip Collins and Dean, with Joe Medwick and Paul Dean joining the fray. Pepper Martin and others interceded and calmed everyone down.

St. Louis Post-Dispatch sportswriter J. Roy Stockton wrote that Dean's lobbing the ball to the Pirate hitters was "one of the most unusual and disgraceful exhibitions of childish temper that the writer had ever seen on a baseball diamond."[22]

"It was an unwarranted display of temper on Dean's part," said Frisch. "I told him if he ever failed again to give his best I'd fine him $5,000 and put him under suspension. That's all. It's a closed incident."[23] Dean was contrite but as usual had to throw in a comment. "The best thing the Cardinals can do is trade me. I'm not goin' to stand for this stuff. As for Medwick, I'll crack him on his Hungarian beezer."[24]

Word of the incident reached home, and when Dean made his next start, five days later, he took the mound with not so much as a cheer from the 14,000 in attendance at Sportsman's Park. He breezed through the first two innings and when he came to bat in the bottom of the second frame, a cascade of boos greeted him. A dozen or so lemons were thrown in his direction from the upper deck. Different accounts had Dean either crying or acting unfazed by the demonstration.

Nonetheless, Dean went on to have his second-best season with a record of 28-12 and a 3.04 ERA. Paul again was second on the team with 19 victories. But it was not enough this time, with St. Louis finishing second to Chicago by four games.

Dean had another great year in 1936, going 24-13. He was sailing along the next season, 1937, winning his first five games. At the All-Star break he was 12-7 and was given the starting assignment for the National League in the midsummer classic. In the third inning Cleveland's Earl Averill smashed a line drive back through the box. It hit Dean on the left foot and caromed to second base, where Billy Herman grabbed it and threw out Averill. The end result was a broken left toe that kept Dean out of the lineup for weeks.

On July 21 in Boston, Dean insisted that he was OK to pitch. Frisch relented, and Dean went out and pitched well, but lost 2-1. "I was unable to pivot my left foot because my toe hurt too much," said Dean, "with the result I was pitchin' entirely with my arm and puttin' all the pressure on it and I felt a soreness in the ol' flipper right away. I shouldn'ta been out there."[25]

It was diagnosed as bursitis, and the treatment prescribed was rest. Dean made sporadic starts the remainder of the year, his last outing coming on September 8.

The next year, Dean was traded to the rival Cubs on April 16, just before Opening Day. The Cardinals got pitchers Curt Smith and Clyde Shoun, outfielder Tuck Stainback, and $185,000. Dean was at a loss for words when he heard of the trade, after a Cardinals-Browns exhibition game at Sportsman's Park. "I'll hate to leave the fellas, but I am glad to go to Chicago," he said.[26] Rickey, who had been talking to the Cubs about a possible trade, did not follow his own advice: Trade a player a year too early rather than a year too late.

Dean was used as a spot starter by the Cubs, a role in which he flourished. His record was 7-1 with a 1.81 ERA, but he started only ten games. One of his early wins was against his old Cardinal mates, and he shut them out in a 5-0 victory. Chicago was in the midst of a dogfight for the flag with Pittsburgh. Manager Gabby Hartnett called on Dean to pitch a crucial game on September 27 against the Pirates at Wrigley Field. Dean got the win in a 2-1 victory, pulling the Cubs to within a half-game of first place. He went 8 2/3 innings, striking out none.

The victory was part of a ten-game winning streak for Chicago, which won the pennant by a slim two games. The Cubs met the New York Yankees in the World Series, and were swept in four games. Dean started the second game, losing to Lefty Gomez, 6-3.

Used similarly in 1939, Dean was 6-4 with a 3.36 ERA. He started the 1940 season in the Cubs' rotation, but did not have much success. At his request he was sent down to the Tulsa Oilers in early June so that he could work on a new side-arm delivery. He was 8-8 at Tulsa; his pitching ability brought mixed reviews. Dean returned to the mound for the Cubs on September 11 and won two of his four starts to finish at 3-3 for the season.

Diz toed the rubber on April 25, 1941 at Forbes Field. He was the starting pitcher and surrendered three runs to the Pirates (two of them earned) in one inning of work. The pain in his arm was too severe, and he lamented that perhaps he should have given up the game four years earlier. In a letter to Chicago general manager Jim Gallagher dated May 14; Dean asked to be placed on the voluntary retired list for the remainder of the season. The Cubs granted his request, but at the behest of Owner Philip K. Wrigley, Dean was offered a job as a first base coach, as well as to help out with the team's young hurlers. Dean jumped at the opportunity. He closed the book on his major-league career with a 150-83 record and a 3.02 ERA. He had 1,163 strikeouts. His number 17 was retired by the St. Louis Cardinals in 1974.

While Diz was coaching in Chicago, the Falstaff Brewery Corporation of St. Louis reached out to him to broadcast Cardinals and Browns games over the radio. Wrigley thought it was a wonderful idea and offered to help Dean with the financial details of the deal. On July 6, 1941, Dean's brief coaching career came to a halt. The sponsor wanted a person with drawing power to team with local announcer Johnny O'Hara. Where O'Hara was smooth, meticulous and had a command of proper grammar and pronunciation, Dean mangled it.

Many radio stations were reluctant to broadcast ballgames. They were difficult to program since the length of games was uncertain. At times other programming might be sacrificed. Because stations were hesitant to air baseball games, Dean and O'Hara only broadcast home games. Forking over money for travel expenses was out of the question. The games were split between WEW and WTMV radio stations.

Dean hit the airwaves on July 10, 1941, broadcasting a Yankees-Browns game in his debut. He was a fan favorite, even though he distorted the English language. Although some chalked it up to his lack of an education, others felt that he made mistakes on purpose to draw attention to himself. "Diz always knew what he was doing," said Mel Allen. "The things he came up with—a guy sludding into third—they were professional. I'll never forget: He said 'slid' correctly, by mistake, and he corrected himself. He *wanted* to goof up—it was a part of the vaudeville."[27] O'Hara was a perfect foil for Dean's antics. Wrote J.G. Taylor Spink, editor of *The Sporting News*, "Contrary to the thought of some, Dizzy is no clown over the air. True, he uses an informal, colorful style, establishing his own rules of grammar. But this only adds to the interest of his broadcasts, which give listeners an accurate picture of what is transpiring on the diamond."[28]

In 1947, Dean and O'Hara were relegated to broadcasting Browns' games exclusively. Diz, never one to hold back an opinion, criticized the St. Louis pitching staff. He asked what right they had to cash their paychecks when all they offered was shoddy pitching. He claimed that he could throw just as well or even better than those currently on the roster. The team's hitters were also taken to task. The Browns' organization signed Dean to a one-game contract, as he was to start the final game of the year. Undoubtedly their motive was to entice more folks through the turnstiles. The ploy worked as over 15,000 patrons attended the contest. On September 28, 1947 against the White Sox, Dean started and pitched four scoreless innings. He even managed a base hit in his only at bat.

Dean also called games for the Yankees and Boston Braves. Later he moved over to the television side, calling the Game of the Week, first for ABC and then CBS.

A movie about Dean's life, *The Pride of St. Louis* premiered in 1952. Dan Dailey was cast in the lead role.

On July 27, 1953, Dean was inducted into the National Baseball Hall of Fame. He called the enshrinement his "greatest honor" and ended his speech saying, "The Good Lord was good to me. He gave me a strong body, a good right arm and a weak mind."[29] Dizzy retired to Bond, Mississippi. He died on July 17, 1974, as the result of a heart attack in Reno, Nevada. He was survived by Pat, and brother Paul.

At the conclusion of the World Series in 1934, Tigers outfielder Goose Goslin, chatting with a reporter about the Series, said, "This Dizzy Dean they're all talking about told the boys what he's going to do to them, but after listening for a while I kind of liked the kid. There's no real harm in him."[30]

Right on, Goose.

Sources

(Other than those mentioned in the notes)

Fleming, G.H., *The Dizziest Season* (New York: Morrow, 1984).

Gay, Timothy M., *Satch, Dizzy & Rapid Robert* (New York: Simon & Schuster, 2010).

Golenbock, Peter, *The Spirit of St. Louis* (New York: Avon Books, 2000).

Peterson, Richard, *The St. Louis Baseball Reader* (Columbia: University of Missouri Press), 2006.

stlouis.cardinals.mlb.com/index.jsp?c_id=stl

baseball-reference.com/

retrosheet.org/

baseballhall.org/

Notes

1. Vince Staten, *Ol' Diz: A Biography of Dizzy Dean* (New York: Harper Collins, 1992), 147.
2. Staten, 148.
3. Ibid.
4. Staten, 150.
5. John Heidenry, *The Gashouse Gang* (New York: Perseus Books, 2007), 37.
6. Robert Gregory, *Diz: The Story of Dizzy Dean and Baseball During the Great Depression* (New York: Viking, 1992), 39.
7. Gregory, 43.
8. Gregory, 44.
9. Gregory, 50.
10. Gregory, 66.
11. Staten, 93.
12. Staten, 103
13. Gregory, 122.
14. Staten, 133.
15. National Baseball Hall of Fame (Hank Greenberg, Charlie Gehringer, Mickey Cochrane, Goose Goslin, Joe Medwick, Frankie Frisch, Leo Durocher, Dizzy Dean).
16. HBO Productions, *When It Was a Game*, 1991.
17. *When It Was a Game*.
18. *When It Was a Gamne*.
19. Gregory, 250.
20. Gregory, 256.
21. Ibid.
22. Staten, 165
23. Gregory, 257.
24. Ibid.
25. Gregory, 336.
26. Gregory, 343.
27. Curt Smith, *Voices of the Game,* (South Bend, Indiana: Diamond Communications, 1987), 102.
28. Gregory, 368.
29. Staten, 255.
30. Heidenry, 220.

Paul Dee Dean

by Paul Geisler

As a rookie in the season that he turned 21, Paul Dean threw a no-hitter and helped lead the St. Louis Cardinals to the 1934 National League pennant. He then won two games to help the Cardinals win the World Series that year.

The younger and less talkative brother of Dizzy Dean, Paul Dee "Daffy" Dean was born on August 14, 1913,[1] to sharecroppers Albert Monroe "Ab" Dean and Alma Nelson Dean in Lucas, Logan County, Arkansas. Albert and Alma had five children, two of whom, Charles and Sarah May, died in infancy. Paul had two older brothers, Elmer, born in 1908, and Jay Hanna—to be known later as Dizzy—in 1910. Alma contracted tuberculosis and died in 1918, leaving Ab with three young sons. He later remarried.

The Dean family moved to Chickalah, Arkansas, then to Spaulding, Oklahoma, migrating to where they could find work. Their best annual profit from cotton-picking and sharecropping came to $155 in 1923.[2]

The sons learned baseball from their father, once a semipro ballplayer, but most who knew Alma said that the Dean brothers inherited much of their athletic ability from their mother, known as a "superb girl athlete with natural ability."[3]

The Deans fashioned their baseballs out of yarn or socks wound around a rock, or tape around an apple core, and used an old broom or hoe handle for a bat. Not able to afford shoes, they played barefooted most of the time. They strengthened their arms and sharpened their aim by throwing at squirrels while working in the fields. Paul could usually pick about 500 pounds of cotton a day. Jay (Dizzy) never reached 400, and their dad usually did only 200 pounds, because he had to keep checking on Jay.[4]

The boys usually stayed home to work, and attended school sporadically. They made sure to go to class on Fridays, however, to play in the weekly baseball games, where Jay and Paul began to shine. At 12, Paul was the biggest boy in his class.

An often-told story relates a time when Elmer became separated from his father and brothers when they were driving in two vehicles. Driving the second vehicle, Elmer was cut off from the others by a long freight train. He was not reunited with his family until a couple of years later when he recognized his brothers in pictures in a Dallas newspaper.

At first Paul played shortstop and Dizzy pitched for a San Antonio semipro team, until Jay signed with the Cards. One day Paul came in to pitch when the regular pitcher was knocked out of the game. He stayed a pitcher from then on.[5]

At 16 Paul made a strong impression with an industrial team in San Antonio in 1930. After a tip from Jay, now called Dizzy, Don Curtis, a scout for the Cardinals, signed Paul to play for the Houston Buffs

Paul Dean won 19 games in his rookie season in 1934, second on the Cardinals staff to brother Dizzy. He also tossed a no-hitter against the Dodgers on September 21, 1934. But it was his work with the bat that was key to their World Series win. His RBI single in the seventh inning of Game Six tied the series at three wins apiece, and forced a Game Seven, won by the Cardinals.

in the Cardinal farm system. Paul showed similarities to his older brother, but soon distinguished himself as "a serious youngster and not at all given to the horseplay" that characterized his brother.[6]

Paul moved quickly on to Columbus of the American Association, then spent the majority of his first year with Springfield of the Western Association. Promoted to Columbus in 1931, he pitched a no-hit game and led the league with 169 strikeouts.

Now standing 6-feet-3 (an inch taller than Dizzy) and weighing 189 pounds, the right-hander began to dominate at Columbus in 1933, winning 22 games, including another no-hitter, while losing seven. He placed third in the MVP voting for the American Association.

Cardinal fans anxiously awaited "Dizzy the Younger."[7] Cardinals manager Frankie Frisch said Paul could throw the "damnedest, heaviest sinker you ever saw," adding, "When a batter hit one of those pitches, his hands stung as painfully in July as if he had swung an icicle in December."[8] The elder brother Dean made a famous brag at the beginning of the season that he and Paul would win a total of 45 games that year.[9]

At Dizzy's insistence, Paul held out for a better salary before ever pitching for the Cardinals: "If Paul don't get it, he's goin' back to Houston and work in a mill for some real money."[10] He said Paul would pitch for nothing until he won at least 15 games, then get $500 per win. General manager Branch Rickey threatened to charge Paul for postage if he continued to send back contracts. Afraid of being demoted back to the minors, Paul started the season on time.

Paul played in only three games in April, then got his first win on May 3, against the Philadelphia Phillies. In his next appearance, on May 11, he got a complete-game win against the New York Giants and Carl Hubbell.

Before his start against the Giants, while on a train back to St Louis from Pittsburgh, Paul shared a double porterhouse with Dizzy in the dining car. Frisch suspected that Paul was trying too hard to imitate his older brother. Frisch went through the Giants' lineup, striking pose after pose in the aisle, but never mentioned Dizzy's name. "I kept telling Paul he had the stuff to beat them. When I paid the check, he said his only words, 'Thanks, Mr. Frisch.'"[11]

Paul also had a temper. Once he got "considerably nettled" because the Giants club would not give him the free passes for a Polo Grounds game that he had requested for a fellow who had given him a harmonica.[12] Another time he got in a fight with Joe Medwick during a poker game on a train. Out of the hand, Paul took a quick look at Medwick's hole card. Medwick took offense and slugged Dean, who then jumped on the Cardinal outfielder. "Medwick and me made up," Paul said later. "We was good friends until the day he died."[13]

Dizzy continued to push for a raise for Paul. On June 1, though it was his turn to pitch, Dizzy sat in the stands in Pittsburgh in civilian clothes in protest, proclaiming that neither he nor Paul would pitch again until the team met their demands. Paul dressed in uniform that day but agreed with his brother, saying, "What Dizzy says is right."[14] No raise came, and Dizzy returned to the team the next day with a complete-game win against the Pirates.

Baseball columnist Joe Williams hailed the one-day strike as a true breakthrough for the players, with little guys taking on the great moguls, and called for more of the same. "The hired hands of baseball ought to start a labor department and put the pitching Deans in charge. Dizzy and Nutsey indeed!," Williams wrote.[15]

By mid-July Paul had fared well. His first 21 games included 13 starts. He won ten and lost four, and had one save. Then a sprained ankle on July 12 in Philadelphia caused him to miss nearly two weeks.

One time Casey Stengel asked Dizzy if he had any more brothers. Diz replied, "We got another brother named Elmer, and Casey, you ought to grab him. He's down at Houston, burnin' up the league." Stengel actually pursued the tip, until he learned that Elmer was a peanut vendor for the Texas League club.[16] Dizzy arranged for the Cardinals to hire Elmer at Sportsman's Park in St Louis, and the headline read "The Dean Brothers—Two Nuts and One Goober." Embarrassed, Dizzy's wife, Pat, insisted that Elmer go back to the minor leagues. When he got back to Houston, Elmer went on strike himself and asked for a raise.[17]

Both Deans lost on the same day in a doubleheader August 12 against the Chicago Cubs. The team had an exhibition game the next day in Detroit against the Tigers. Upset by their double loss, plus the burden of playing on a day off, the Dean boys rebelled. "I ain't going," insisted Dizzy. "Me, neither," added Paul.[18]

When the Cards returned, on August 14, Paul's 21st birthday, team owner Sam Breadon fined Dizzy $100 and Paul $50 for missing the game. Dizzy tore up his uniform in disgust and refused to pay the fines. "We're quitting this club and goin' to Florida to fish," he said.[19] Breadon suspended them both indefinitely, even though Dizzy had already won 21 games and Paul 12. The boys watched the game on August 15 from the grandstand.

In the midst of this brouhaha, Paul's nickname, Daffy, first appeared on August 15, in a story in the *Brooklyn Eagle*, with no byline. He never embraced the term, and asked writers not to use it. Neither his teammates nor family members ever used the term to refer to him.[20] Will Rogers even made a direct appeal on Paul's behalf at a baseball writers dinner for them not to use the term.[21] Yet scribes and fans alike seemed attached to the moniker, and the brothers were continually referred to as Dizzy and Daffy Dean. Sometimes his teammates called him Harpo, after the mute member of the Marx Brothers, due to Paul's very quiet yet sometimes mischievous personality.[22]

People interviewed on the street were not sympathetic, referring to the brothers as selfish, ungrateful, spoiled brats.[23] Paul relented and paid his $50 fine and $70 of lost salary. He returned to the team to earn his 13th win on August 17. Dizzy ended his revolt a few days later, after a hearing before Commissioner Kenesaw Mountain Landis.

On September 21 Dizzy pitched a three-hit shutout in Brooklyn in the first game of a doubleheader. In the second game, Paul pitched a no-hitter against the Dodgers, not allowing a baserunner after a first-inning two-out walk. Dizzy remarked, "Shucks, Paul, you shoulda told me you was gonna pitch a no-hitter, then I woulda pitched one, too!"[24] Paul later remembered that after the game, "Me 'n' Diz went out to get our supper, and he says I did so good, I wouldn't have to pay for his supper."[25]

The Cardinals won 24 of their last 31 games to capture the pennant from the Cubs and the Giants. Dizzy and Paul won 14 of those games, while losing only four. Paul finished his rookie year with 19 wins and 11 losses. Diz won 30, more than fulfilling his promise to win 45 games between them.

Dizzy won the first game of the World Series, in Detroit on October 3, but the Tigers prevailed the next day. Back in St Louis on October 5, Paul started the third game. Without sharp control—he walked five and gave up eight hits—he held the Tigers to one run, and the Cardinals won, 4-1.

Back in Detroit on October 8, Paul started Game Six, now an elimination game for the Cardinals, behind in the Series 3 games to 2. Schoolboy Rowe started for Detroit, in front of the 45,551 fans, the largest crowd of the Series. Paul's single in the seventh inning broke a 3-3 tie, scoring Leo Durocher. The Cards went on to win, 4-3, and Paul earned his second victory of the Series. The Cardinals took Game Seven easily, 11-0, behind Dizzy's shutout pitching, his second win of the series, making St Louis the 1934 world champions. The Dean boys were the stars of the Series, as they notched all four of the Cardinal victories, with Paul not suffering a loss. Two pitchers seldom dominate a World Series, and no two brothers ever have.

Reporters who covered the Cardinals often remarked on their rough style of baseball and their competitiveness in winning the championship. Dan Daniel, in the *New York World-Telegram* on October 9, described the outcome as the "gas house gang playing the nice boys from the right side of the tracks."[26]

After the World Series the Deans started a barnstorming tour of the country, organized by Ray Doan. They teamed with local white semipro players and played most of their games against Satchel Paige and other prominent black teams, such as the Kansas Monarchs and the Pittsburgh Crawfords. The games often drew big crowds, many times the biggest the towns had ever seen, but "wreaked havoc with Jim Crow customs."[27]

Every day for two weeks the tour carried the Deans to a different town, with stops in Oklahoma City, Kansas City, Wichita, Des Moines, Chicago, Milwaukee,

Philadelphia, Brooklyn, Baltimore, Cleveland, Columbus, and Pittsburgh.

In Des Moines, Paul left a game early, complaining of soreness in his throwing arm. He had slipped while warming up in the outfield, perhaps "the beginning of arm woes that would hasten the end of Paul's career at the too-young age of 27."[28]

The rough travel schedule left no room for a good night's rest and began to wear on Paul. Though the money began to roll in, he became very worried about his aching arm. He sat out some games, played outfield in others, and threw underhand if he had to pitch. Cardinals owner Breadon gave direct orders for Paul to stop the tour. Paul visited a doctor in Philadelphia, who prescribed rest.

More money came in as the boys moved on to vaudeville, from Broadway's Roxy Theater to points as far west as Milwaukee. They signed a monthlong contract with the theatrical producers Fanchon and Marco, bringing in $5,000 a week. On stage, Dizzy did the talking, and Paul played the quiet, straight man.

They became movie stars, in *Dizzy and Daffy*, with Shemp Howard, later of Three Stooges fame. The movie, filmed in a high-school stadium, featured the two brothers as rookie hurlers called up from the "Farmers," a minor-league team, to lead the Cardinals to the World Series. Howard got in lots of stunts as their half-blind pitching coach, and the film gave fans some actual footage of the Deans from the World Series. Dizzy's wife, Pat, estimated that after finishing the vaudeville tour, they had earned at least $35,000.[29]

The brothers also joined Ray Doan, one of the main promoters of their exhibition tour, in his baseball school in Hot Springs, Arkansas. The city built a new field and commissioned it Dean Field.

The tag "Dizzy and Daffy" marketed well, earning the Deans endorsements for such things as table baseball games, sweatshirts, and cigarettes. Twice they won court battles against corporations using their names without permission. One man tried to trademark "Dizzee and Daffee" sweatshirts, and another developed the "Dizzy and Daffy Bar, Dean of Candy Bars."[30]

Back home in Arkansas, Paul began dating Dorothy Sandusky, Miss Russellville of 1933. After a two-month courtship, they were married on December 21, 1934, beginning 47 years of married life. Asked what his older brother might think about his short courtship and wedding, Paul replied, "It's none of his business, anyhow."[31]

The 1935 season began with Paul again holding out for more pay, on Dizzy's initiative. Dizzy wanted $25,000 for himself and $15,000 for Paul;[32] he eventually signed for $18,500, still the highest for any National League pitcher. Still seeking as much as $10,000, Paul refused Cardinals offers that reached $8,500, but he finally settled for the $8,500, plus a $500 gift.

In early May, Paul got into a dispute over balls and strikes with umpire Dolly Stark. He threw a fit and stalked off the mound after walking three batters. "Gee whillikins, I wished I had a hun'red thousand dollars," he said. "I'd walk right up to Stark and punch him square on the nose. Then I'd do the same to [Cy] Rigler. But I ain't got the hun'red grand." "Okay, Paul," said Diz. "We'll save up our money, get the 100 grand, and then we'll both punch 'em on the nose."[33]

Dizzy and Paul disliked playing exhibition games during the season. On July 5, 1935, the Cardinals headed to Minnesota to play the St. Paul Saints. Fans anxiously awaited the famous pair, but they both sat in the dugout and refused to take a bow. Dizzy had pitched the day before in Chicago, and Paul would start soon in St Louis. The busy schedule had begun to wear them both down.

The Cincinnati Reds installed lights at Crosley field that year, and scheduled seven night games, one against each of the other National League teams. Nearly 30,000 fans piled in to see the Cardinals face the Reds under the lights on July 31, Paul's turn to pitch. The overflow crowd forced many of the spectators to find places on the playing field, mostly in foul territory. In the bottom of the eighth inning, Reds outfielder Babe Herman struggled his way through the mob to take his turn at the plate. Spectator Kitty Burke, a local nightclub entertainer wearing a pink dress, grabbed the bat from Herman and stepped into the batter's box. Paul bluffed a few exaggerated windups, then she hit his underhand pitch back to him. He easily tagged her out. Cards manager Frisch protested, to no avail, that the out should count. Kitty appeared for weeks afterward in clubs around Cincinnati, billing herself as "The Only Girl Who Ever Batted in the National League."[34]

Paul began to lose his focus on baseball by mid-August. According to Dick Farrington in *The Sporting News*, he was "not keenly interested in continuing his pitching career." With much more money than he could have ever imagined, he seemed ready to drop back to his life on the farm. "Paul would like to break away from the spotlight and be himself—an Arkansas, or if you prefer, an Oklahoma lad without the worry of the diamond," Farrington wrote.[35]

The Deans held the Cards in the 1935 pennant race almost by themselves. St Louis sat in first place from August 25 through September 13, but the Cubs won 21 games in a row and took the pennant from the Cardinals by four games. Together Paul and Dizzy logged 595 innings. Dizzy won 28 games and Paul won 19 again, repeating for the second year in a row the promise Diz had made in early 1934 that they would total 45 wins.

After the 1935 season, Paul bought a farm in Garland, Texas, just east of Dallas. He took some time out for more barnstorming, even with his arm bothering him again. He dropped out of the tour when his wife became hospitalized in St Louis with a serious illness. He later worked again with Dizzy and other pro ballplayers at Doan's baseball academy and played some golf.

One time umpire Lee Ballanfant joined Paul on the links at Tennison Park in Dallas. Paul shot a 99, after an 83 just two days before, and blamed his poor play on Ballanfant, saying, "How could I do anything with a 'tom' looking over my shoulder on every shot?" He later played another nine holes with Ballanfant, at a dime a hole.[36]

When contract time came, Paul threatened to stay on his farm all summer if he did not get the $15,000 he wanted. His contract came back with $8,500, a repeat of his pay for the last season, and he and Dizzy began to sit out spring training.

Dizzy got the sportswriter J. Roy Stockton to write a letter for him to Branch Rickey in which he extolled his family's loyalty to the club but also mentioned the many innings and wins that they had contributed the team. After a meeting with Rickey, Dizzy agreed to $22,800. Paul agreed to take $12,000[37] and reported to camp on the last day of spring training. "I weighed 235 pounds and that was about 50 over my regular weight. I had trouble getting into shape," he said.[38] He blamed playing golf in Bradenton, Florida, during the offseason for the extra poundage. "I think that was the thing that hurt my arm. I had no looseness in throwing. I was always tightened up."[39]

The 1936 season seemed like a split season, with a good start followed by horrible results. After missing a large part of camp, Paul started slowly with three starts in April, but had a solid May, with three complete-game victories and a 2.91 ERA.

On June 2, with only two days' rest, Paul pitched a shutout for eight innings against Brooklyn, but allowed four runs (three earned) in the ninth. Two days later he pitched two innings in relief against Brooklyn, gave up three runs, and took the loss. He remembered feeling a little twinge in his shoulder that did not bother him at the time, "but when I went out the next day to get in a pepper game, I couldn't hardly raise it." He did not realize that he had torn a piece of cartilage. He tried resting, and even blamed his pain on a sore tooth.[40] After X-rays ruled out a dental problem, Dr. Robert F. Hyland, the Cardinals' physician, diagnosed a pulled tendon and prescribed "easy throwing for a few days."[41] Paul again felt like leaving baseball and returning to his farm.

He never dominated hitters in the big leagues again. After the day he felt pain in his arm, he pitched in only five more games that season, giving up 28 hits in 13 1/3 innings, with a 13.50 ERA.

At the end of the 1936 season, Paul had won a total of 43 big-league games. He won only seven more. Although he attempted to come back several times, he posted only mediocre results the rest of his career. After 1936, he appeared in 54 games, with 13 starts, over parts of five seasons, and allowed 210 hits in 179 innings and a 4.32 ERA.

On August 25, 1936, Paul requested voluntary retirement status and retreated to his farm near Dallas to rest, hoping to return strong the next season. *The Sporting News* saw Paul's problems in 1936 as "the prime reason why the Cardinals are not in first place by a comfortable margin."[42] Branch Rickey commented that Paul "was a complete loss [this season]. We would have been stronger if he never had played this season."[43] Paul "simply pitched himself into a collapse," commented writer Kyle Crichton.[44]

Several factors contributed to Paul's arm failure: barnstorming for two tours, the lack of immediate and proper care for his ailment, missing most of the spring work in 1936 and reporting several pounds heavier than usual, and the extra heavy work his first two years with the Cardinals, especially pitching without adequate rest between appearances. Yet Dizzy downplayed the seriousness of Paul's ailment, saying, "There ain't nothin' wrong with Paul. It's all in his head." Replied Paul, "But my shoulder's where it's hurtin', Diz."[45]

Paul sought reinstatement in January 1937, and signed a contract that could potentially equal the previous year's salary if he could repeat some of his earlier success. He assured Rickey that his arm felt as good as ever. His spring work, however, did not look promising, as he did not show the same zip on his fastball, and he again reported to camp overweight. He reported a "relapse of the arm trouble" and visited Lee Jensen, a Southern Association trainer, when the Cardinals were in Chattanooga, wrapping up their exhibition season. After some quick work with "muscle manipulator" Jensen, Paul returned to his team.[46]

The Cardinals used Paul in relief against the Cubs on April 24, but he gave up a hit and two walks without retiring a batter. He returned to Dr. Hyland for surgery to remove a piece of torn and ossified cartilage in his right shoulder.[47] Several weeks later Hyland told him to go out and throw as hard as he could. Paul replied, "Doc, was I to do that, the arm would open up and everything would fall out."[48] Nevertheless, Paul did try to work out but never got his arm stretched into playing shape. The Cardinals asked waivers on him in midseason, but he did not pitch again that year.

Well rested after an offseason spent on the farm and playing golf in Florida, Paul returned to spring training in 1938, hoping for a new start. Wayne K. Otto of the *Chicago Herald and Examiner* predicted, "Few arms that were as bad as Daffy's ever recover their normal strength."[49] The Cardinals re-assigned Paul to Houston, hoping he could regain some strength pitching for the Buffs. In an unusual move, Dean moved to another team in the same league, the Dallas Steers, owned by the Chicago White Sox but closer to his farm. He relied mostly on a side-arm curveball, throwing his true fastball only a few times each game.

The Cardinals recalled the rejuvenated Dean in September for five games, including four starts. He won three games and posted a 2.61 ERA in 31 innings. Paul pleaded with owner Breadon not to send him on trips to the north, thinking the cold weather would further hinder his arm's recovery. "This sore-arm business has become an obsession with Paul," commented sportswriter Dick Farrington.[50]

As spring training started in 1939, Paul continued with the Cardinals but began to distance himself from his older pitching brother. "Dizzy meant all right, but he's responsible for my arm trouble," he told Sid Keener of the *St. Louis Star-Times*. "He made me hold out in the spring of 1936." Paul said he had a rare confrontation with his brother and told him "to go his way and I'd go my way. I wished him all the luck in the world, but from now on I was attending to my own affairs."[51]

By mid-August Paul had appeared in only 16 games for 43 innings and a 6.07 ERA. The Cards sent him to Columbus of the American Association. After the season, the New York Giants claimed Paul in the Rule 5 draft, but he announced in February that he was retiring. He said he preferred not to go through another training season. (Paul's wife, meanwhile, said he would be out only for the 1940 season.)

Then in March, Paul changed his mind and asked Giants manager Bill Terry to assign him to Dallas of the Texas League. In the end, he played for the Giants and had a fairly respectable season, pitching 99 1/3 innings, with four wins and four losses and an ERA of 3.90.

Dean returned to the Giants in 1941 but pitched in only five early-season games, all in relief, with a 3.18 ERA, allowing five hits in 5 2/3 innings. On May 14 the Giants sold him to the Sacramento Solons of the Pacific Coast League (property of the Cardinals, with Pepper Martin as manager). Paul never reported to Sacramento, however, claiming he would not play that far away from his home in Texas. Consequently, he found himself suspended from baseball.

In April 1942 Sacramento sent Paul to the Houston Buffs, where he successfully re-established his pitching skills. He won 19 games and lost 8, allowing 182 hits in 219 innings and posting a 2.05 ERA. Impressed, the Washington Senators arranged on October 1 to purchase his contract from the Cardinals.

Paul seriously contemplated skipping his assignment with the Senators in favor of staying with his defense job as a guard in an aircraft company plant near Dallas. The Senators meanwhile traded him to the St. Louis Browns for pitcher Elden Auker. When Auker decided to quit baseball and do defense work, the Browns bought Dean outright from the Senators.

Paul entered the 1943 season with excitement about his prospects to return to form. He had worked during the winter in Arkansas, operating a barrel-stave mill with his father-in-law, sawing and chopping though not a lot of throwing, and felt in prime physical condition. He pitched his final three major league games in May for the Browns, with 3.38 ERA in 13 1/3 innings, then decided to return to the barrel-stave factory.

On the Browns' retired list now, Paul passed an Army physical on February 25, 1944. As he awaited his call-up to military service, the Browns released him to play for Little Rock of the Southern Association. He worked an agreement with the team to play only in home games, to remain close to home and supervise at the stave mill. The Browns recalled him in August, simply to protect him from the baseball draft.

In October 1944 the 31-year-old father of three reported to Camp Chaffee, Arkansas, for induction into the Army. When he finished basic training at Fort Riley, Kansas, he was sent to the Fairfield-Suisun Army Air Base in California as a staff sergeant and managed the Air Transport Command's baseball nine in a 50-game season.

After his discharge from the Army, Paul began workouts at his Texas farm in December 1945. For a while he had thoughts of pitching in the major leagues, but he did not want to pitch in day games, because "my trouble, they told me, was bursitis—and I can't pitch effectively under a hot, humid sun."[52] He changed his mind and waived his protection under the GI Bill to return to his major-league job. He requested a transfer back to Little Rock and played briefly in the summer of 1946 for Sherman, Texas, in the Class C East Texas League.

Looking for a "name player," the Ottawa Nationals of the Class C Border League grabbed Paul as their manager for the 1947 season. He even pitched a few innings. After winning the league championship, Paul abandoned the team amid local controversy. Editorials in the local sports pages protested that professional baseball did not fit in their stadium. Paul took offense. "You-all can't run a ballclub with opposition like that on the editorial page," he said as he vowed not to return the next year.[53]

The next several years, Paul spent most of his time in Little Rock. He operated the Purple Cow restaurant, contributed to Little Rock Junior College, and re-created major-league games from wire reports on a local radio station. He also traveled some as a scout for the Browns across Texas, Oklahoma, Louisiana, and Arkansas. He re-entered the baseball world in 1949 when he purchased the Clovis, New Mexico, team in the Class C West Texas-New Mexico League. In 1950 he served as president and manager of the team. In 1951 he shifted to operating the Lubbock Hubbers in the same league. The team fared well, with higher attendance than in any of the previous four years. Dizzy joined Paul as a silent partner in the Lubbock venture, each of them investing money they would make from Hollywood.

Controversy swirled around Paul when Twentieth Century-Fox decided to make a movie about Dizzy's life. He first balked at the $15,000 offered by the producers for the use of his name. He wanted $25,000. He also insisted on approving the script. He feared that the movie would include "a lot of love stuff" instead of the true Dean family story[54]—which he claimed would surely bring in much bigger crowds than any fictionalized accounts. "Tell a true story based on our lives, and if the public doesn't come out in larger numbers the second night than the first, I'll do it for nothing," he said.[55]

The younger Dean perceived the elder Dizzy and his wife, Pat, attempting to twist his arm to get him to follow their plans. He was especially unhappy about a *Saturday Evening Post* article, "Dizzy Dean: He's Not So Dumb," by a *Dallas News* sportswriter, Frank X. Tolbert. Paul felt Tolbert used Dizzy's words to denigrate their modest upbringing and their limited educational experiences. For example, Tolbert had written, "J.H. Dean [Dizzy] was easily the most backward and ornery scholar in the one-room schoolhouse at Chickalah, Arkansas," and that he was "figured least likely to succeed."[56]

Tolbert retorted that he had spent a full morning going over the article with Dizzy before it was published.[57] Paul preferred to stay in the background, despite Dizzy's talkative tendencies. "My wife Dorothy and I have three children, and we want them to lead a quiet, normal life," he said. "If Diz doesn't mind zany stories about himself, that's okay by me. But because of my children, I wish he would leave me and all the rest of the Deans out of his stories."[58]

Eventually Paul made peace with Dizzy and Pat and signed the movie contract. *The Pride of St. Louis — the Story of Dizzy Dean* premiered on April 11, 1952, with Dan Dailey as Dizzy and Joanne Dru as his wife, Pat. Richard Crenna moved up from radio to take the role of Paul.

In February 1953 Paul moved his family — now with four children — to El Paso to become general manager of the El Paso Texans of the Arizona-Texas League. He planned to step on the field as manager, too, if needed, and he intended to promote attendance by having Dizzy make personal appearances, as he had for the Lubbock team. He left the El Paso job in April 1953, but returned to baseball for the 1954 season as president, general and business manager, and field manager with Hot Springs of the Class C Cotton States League.

In 1955 Paul's son, Paul Jr., impressive as a high-school pitcher in El Paso and Little Rodk, signed to play baseball for Southern Methodist University in Dallas. He registered for premedical studies, heading for a degree in dentistry.[59] In his freshman season, however, he lacked control on the mound, as well as his share of self-confidence, surrendering a large number of home runs. Some felt he was trying too hard, striving to match the reputation of his famous pitching family.[60] In 1957 the 18-year-old left baseball at SMU and signed with the Milwaukee Braves, who assigned him to Syracuse in the American Association. He also played with Lawton of the Sooner State League that season. He developed arm trouble of his own the next year, and left professional baseball in midseason of 1959.

Paul spent several years in various business ventures, including managing several service stations in the Dallas area and running Dizzy's carpet business in Phoenix. He accepted a new challenge in April 1966 as baseball coach and athletic director at the new University of Plano, just north of Dallas. Now a grandfather of six, Paul began to set up programs for football and track and field, as well as for baseball. "I don't know much about coaching football, but I know conditioning and fundamentals are important in any sport," he said. Remembering his recent experience with minor-league teams, he remarked, "I was president, groundskeeper, clubhouse boy, and manager. I did it all. Yeah, I know I can coach baseball."

In his later years Paul used his playing skills in several old-timer's games, including reunions of the old Buffs teams in Houston, in which he and Dizzy were hailed as "the two most popular players in the entire Houston baseball history."[61] In 1973, at nearly 60 years old, he matched up once again with Satchel Paige, 67 years old himself, in an old-timer's exhibition.[62]

Dizzy had heart problems in the summer of 1974, beginning with a heart attack on July 11. He had another severe one four days later. Paul joined his sister-in-law Pat at Dizzy's side in Reno, Nevada, where his brother on died July 17.

On March 17, 1981, Paul died of a heart attack in Springdale, Arkansas. He is buried in Oakland Cemetery in Clarksville, Arkansas.

In their two healthy years together, the Dean brothers combined for a 96-42 won-loss record, with an ERA slightly over 3.00. They had similar pitching motions, and looked and talked alike. They enjoyed many of the same things: Jean Harlow and Mae West movies, hillbilly music, Lucky Strike cigarettes, FDR, golf in

Florida, quail hunting, peanuts, cold milk, and beating the New York Giants. They lived in the same hotel on the same floor, and used the same barber, shoeshine boy, grocer, and mechanic. Each also believed his arm would last forever.[63]

As J. Roy Stockton told it, "Dizzy talked. Paul listened. Dizzy wisecracked. Paul laughed. Dizzy was a great comedian. Paul was his best audience. Each was the other's hero."[64]

Yet they had very different, if not opposite, personalities. After his first year with the Cardinals, reporters recognized that, as *The Sporting News* put it, Paul "does not have the color or the swaggering egotism of his older brother, nor the latter's ready tongue or unconscious braggadocio that the public likes. Reticent, unassuming, and retiring, Paul is not the kind that the fan can slap on the back, or bandy wisecracks with, but Dizzy glories in all that. Paul never will fit into the showmanship role that Dizzy occupies, thought he younger Dean gives promise of equaling and even surpassing his older brother as a pitcher.[65]

Paul saw the world through the eyes of his simple country upbringing. After the 1934 World Series victory, Dizzy bought an airplane to celebrate. Paul bought a farm. He once remarked, when he heard what Bill Walker, the fashion plate of the Cardinals, had paid for a suit, that that was more than he had ever spent for all the clothes he had ever owned.[66]

He said it best in his own words: "Gee, we're just a couple a natural pitchers and ordinary fellas, but God gave us perfect pitchin' builds—long and loose like houn' dogs. We never ate no special vittles or nothin' like that to put speed in our soupbones, just lucky fellas to be born great pitchers."[67]

Notes

1. Sources vary as to Paul's actual birth year. His school enumeration in Spaulding, Oklahoma, said 1911. His Social Security records as well as baseball-reference.com list 1912. His marriage-license records, his Army enlistment records, his grave index, and various biographers of Dizzy Dean all say 1913.
2. Robert Gregory, *Diz—Dizzy Dean and Baseball During the Great Depression* (New York: Viking, 1992), 25. (Hereafter cited as *Diz*).
3. Vince Staten, *Ol' Diz—A Biography of Dizzy Dean* (New York: Harper Collins, 1992), 13. (Hereafter cited as *Ol' Diz*).
4. *Ol' Diz*, 24.
5. *Ol' Diz*, 105.
6. "Introducing Paul Dean, Dizzy's Kid Brother," *The Sporting News*, March 26, 1931, 5.
7. "Paul Dean Just Another 'Dizzy,'" *Massillon* (Ohio) *Evening Independent*, October 26, 1933, 8.
8. "Milestones." *Time,* March 30, 1981, 86.
9. Dizzy claimed the prediction, but some sources credit it to the Cardinals' public-relations man, Gene Karst, (See *Ol' Diz*, 103).
10. *Diz*, 125.
11. *Diz*, 135.
12. Dick Farrington, "Fanning with Farrington," *The Sporting News*, December 10, 1936, 4.
13. John Heidenry, *The Gashouse Gang*, (New York: Public Affairs, 2007), 118. (Hereafter cited as *The Gashouse Gang*).
14. *The Gashouse Gang*, 134.
15. *Diz*, 152.
16. J. Roy Stockton, *The Gashouse Gang and a Couple of Other Guys.* (New York: A.S. Barnes, 1945), 31.
17. *Diz*, 167.
18. Milton Shapiro, *The Dizzy Dean Story* (New York: Julian Messner. 1963), 92.
19. *The Gashouse Gang*, 165.
20. *Diz*, 171.
21. J. Taylor Spink, "Three and One—Looking Them Over," *THE SPORTING NEWS.* October 3, 1935, p. 4.
22. Timothy M. Gay, *Satch, Dizzy, and Rapid Robert* (New York: Simon and Schuster, 2010), 77.(Hereafter cited as Gay).
23. *Diz*, 171.
24. Shapiro, *The Dizzy Dean Story,* 99.
25. *Diz*, 195.
26. *Diz*, 237. (Joe Williams of the *World Telegram* actually introduced the idea five days earlier when he wrote of the Cardinals, "They looked like a bunch of boys from the gas house district who had crossed the railroad tracks for a game of ball with the nice kids," *Diz*, 213).
27. Gay, 81.
28. Gay, 85..
29. "Deans Still Dazzle 'Em," *The Sporting News*, October 18, 1034, 1.
30. *Ol' Diz*, 158-159.
31. Heidenry, *The Gashouse Gang,* 283.
32. Shapiro, *The Dizzy Dean Story,*122.
33. "A Hundred Grand Orgy." *The Sporting News,* May 16, 1935, 5.
34. John McDonald, "Night in Cincy When McDonald Wished for a Farm," *The Sporting News.* December 30, 1943, 8. "Crosley

Field—First Lighted Big League Park—Always Packed Opening Day." *The Sporting News.* February 26, 1947, 15; Dick Kaegel, "Inside Corner—Swinging Blonde 'Pinch-Hit' for Babe," *The Sporting News,* November 26, 1966, 4.

35 Dick Farrington, *The Sporting News.* August 29, 1935, 1.

36 "Daffy Dean Makes His Debut as Tournament Golfer Under Handicap—Against an Umpire," *Corsicana* (Texas) *Daily Sun,* February 11, 1936, 8.

37 Reports of Paul's 1936 salary vary from $10,000 to $12,000.

38 "Obituary," *The Sporting News.* April 4, 1981, 54.

39 Grantland Rice, "The Sportlight," *Syracuse Herald,.* March 27, 1939, 14.

40 *Diz,* 288.

41 "Pitching Puts Two Strikes on Cards," *The Sporting News.* July 16, 1936, 1.

42 "Vulnerable Cards Spoil Pennant Hand," *The Sporting News.* September 3, 1936, 3.

43 Edgar G. Brands, "Cards Turn Down $100,000 Bid for Minor Star, Rickey Reveals," *The Sporting News,* September 17, 1936, 5.

44 Kyle Crichton, "All Pitched Out," *Collier's,* April 1, 1939, 20.

45 *Diz,* 289.

46 "Browns in the Pink as Barrier Goes Up," *The Sporting News.* April 22, 1937, 3.

47 Red Byrd, "Hit-and-Miss Pace Jars Hornsbymen," *The Sporting News.* May 13, 1937, 2.

48 J.G. Taylor Spink, "Three and One," *The Sporting News.* June 24, 1937, 4.

49 "Scribbled by Scribes," *The Sporting News,* March 31, 1938, 4.

50 Dick Farrington, "Cards Look Better to Owner Than Fans," *The Sporting News,* April 13, 1939, 6.

51 "Scribbled by Scribes," *The Sporting News,* March 23, 1939, 4.

52 "Paul Dean Says He Can Pitch Night Games in Majors," *San Jose News,* July 21, 1945, 35.

53 Austin F. Cross, "Dean's Run-Out During Playoffs at Ottawa Laid to Editorial Rap," *The Sporting News,* October 22, 1947, 25.

54 Choc Hutcheson, "Paul Says He'll Tell True Story of 'Me and Diz,'" *The Sporting News.* July 18, 1951, 23.

55 "Refused Peek at Script, Paul Snubs Dizzy's Film," *The Sporting News,* January 24, 1951, 16.

56 Frank X. Tolbert, "Dizzy Dean: He's Not So Dumb!" "Saturday Evening Post," July 14, 1951, 25.

57 Bill Rives, " 'Diz' Boswell Suggest Commission to Sift Dean History," *The Sporting News,* August 8, 1951, 16.

58 Choc Hutcheson, "He's Writing Book Called 'Me an' Diz,'" *The Sporting News,* August 1, 1951, 6.

59 Charles Burton, "Paul Dean Jr to Pitch for Mustangs Next Season," *Dallas Morning News,* June 29, 1955, 15.

60 Charles Burton, "Young Paul Dean Trying Too Hard," *Dallas Morning News,* April 20, 1956, 19.

61 John F. Lyons, "9,828 See Former Buffs, Hallahan and Diz, Pitch," *The Sporting News.* July 16, 1952, 34.

62 Gay, 283.

63 *Diz,* 4-5.

64 Stockton, 29.

65 "The Dean Brothers," *The Sporting News,* October 18, 1934, 4.

66 J.G. Taylor Spink, *The Sporting News,* June 11, 1936, 4.

67 *Diz,* 202.

William "Bill" Delancey

By Thomas Ayers

As a 22-year-old Bill DeLancey caught every inning of the 1934 World Series for the St. Louis Cardinals as the club won its third championship. Later, he was named by Branch Rickey as one of the best three catchers he had ever seen, alongside Roy Campanella and Mickey Cochrane. However, DeLancey accumulated only 686 plate appearances in his major-league career, as he soon fell ill with serious lung problems that effectively ended his playing days. Although DeLancey spent several years as a minor-league manager and returned to the majors briefly, he was never at full health again and died on his 35th birthday.

Born on November 28, 1911, in Greensboro, North Carolina, William Pinkney DeLancey was part of a large family of Irish background; he had seven brothers and six sisters. His father, William Pinkney DeLancey, was born in Guilford County, North Carolina.[1] His mother, Rosa Ann Brame, was born in Rockingham County, North Carolina. He had at least two older brothers, Frank and James.

DeLancey played baseball as a child and starred in the sport for Bessemer High School in Greensboro before briefly playing as a semipro in the city.[2] He began his professional career in 1930 when he signed with the Shawnee Robins of the Class C Western Association. The 18-year-old stood 5-feet-11 and weighed 185 pounds. A left-handed batter, he hit .297 in 192 at-bats for Shawnee.

After the season the Cardinals signed DeLancey and assigned him to the Danville Veterans of the Class B Illinois-Indiana-Iowa (Three-I) League.[3] There he hit .260 in 97 games and showed extra-base power by hitting 13 doubles, 12 triples, and 7 home runs. He finished the year by playing 11 games for the Columbus Red Birds of the Double-A American Association.

With several catchers vying for playing time in Columbus in 1932, DeLancey was sent to Springfield of the Class C Western Association. He became the club's primary backstop and one of the key offensive contributors as the team won the Western Association title. He led the team with a .329 batting average and .414 slugging percentage, hit 20 triples and swatted 18 home runs. He had 110 runs batted in and led the league with 108 runs scored. Recalled to Columbus after the Western Association season ended, DeLancey while driving from Springfield to Columbus stopped in St. Louis to visit Branch Rickey, who told him not to continue to Columbus but to head to New York to join the major-league club for the rest of the season.[4]

DeLancey made his major-league debut on September 11, 1932, as the starting catcher against the New York Giants at the Polo Grounds. DeLancey went 1-for-3 and got his first major-league hit off a future Hall of Famer when he singled off Carl Hubbell.

After the season DeLancey and Frances Yasaitis, a nursing student whom he had met while playing at Danville, were

DeLancey hit .316 in 1934 while sharing catching duties with Spud Davis. His home run in Game Five of the World Series accounted for the Cardinals' only tally.

married. For the 1933 season the Cardinals sent him to Columbus, where he hit .285 with 21 home runs. Perhaps his finest game of the year came on August 27 against the Minneapolis Millers, when he went 4-for-6 with two doubles and two homers.[5]

For the 1934 season Branch Rickey pondered whether to bring DeLancey to the major leagues on a permanent basis. St. Louis had a new catcher, Spud Davis, but Rickey wasn't sure if Davis was strong enough defensively to be an everyday catcher and he was worried about the club asking a rookie catcher, DeLancey, to do too much. Rickey ultimately decided that the club would indeed go with Davis and DeLancey.[6]

Manager Frankie Frisch was initially hesitant to play DeLancey, and by May 29 he had only 12 at-bats. On May 30 he got his first start of the season, against Cincinnati, and had one of the best games of his career, going 4-for-5 with a triple, a home run, and four RBIs. From that point on, DeLancey split the catching duties with Davis. He started 63 more games over the course of the season and the Cardinals had a .641 winning percentage when he started. DeLancey had a good batting eye and reached base four times in a game on several occasions.

The Cardinals won the National League pennant, finishing two games ahead of the Giants. DeLancey made several important contributions when the Cardinals played the Giants. On June 27 in St. Louis the Giants and Cardinals were tied in the ninth inning when DeLancey hit a home run off Dolf Luque to give St. Louis an 8-7 victory and a split of the four-game series, which kept the Cardinals two games behind New York.

When the Cardinals went to the Polo Grounds for a key series in mid-September, DeLancey figured in two St. Louis victories. On September 13 he drove in Joe Medwick in the 12th inning for the go-ahead run, and on the 16th his single sparked a four-run rally and a 5-3 St. Louis victory.[7] On September 30 DeLancey went 3-for-4 and caught a Dizzy Dean shutout as St. Louis clinched a berth in the World Series.

The 22-year-old DeLancey posted a .316 batting average with a .414 on-base percentage and a .565 slugging percentage in 253 at-bats with 18 doubles and 13 home runs. He had his finest season defensively, throwing out 14 of 30 attempted basestealers, for a 47 percent caught-stealing mark, which was above league average.

The 1934 season was a happy time for DeLancey off the field. He and Frances became parents when Doris Ann DeLancey was born on August 29. On the diamond, though, DeLancey was a prickly and hard-nosed player who often complained at and swore at umpires.[8] One sportswriter described him as a "spirited, fighting athlete who gives no ground at the plate and has more color than the average catcher."[9]

An example of DeLancey's feisty attitude came when Frisch told him to lay off the rising fastball during one game; DeLancey had been struggling to hit that pitch, always getting under the ball and popping it up. The next time he came to bat, DeLancey hit a high fastball onto the roof of Sportsman's Park for a homer. When he got back to the dugout he snapped at Frisch, "That's how much you know, you dumb Dutchman."[10]

Although he was only 22, DeLancey assumed a leadership role on the field and in the clubhouse. Once he saw Dizzy Dean goofing around on the mound and went out to the pitcher and sternly said, "[I]f you ever make a joke of it again when I'm catching, I'll knock your damned block off." Reportedly, this display of fortitude impressed Dean so much that he asked Frisch if DeLancey could catch him regularly.[11]

By the end of the season the Cardinals were so impressed by DeLancey that he caught every single inning of the World Series. He hit only .172, but that included three doubles and a home run. DeLancey's round-tripper accounted for St. Louis's only run in Game Five. DeLancey became the second rookie catcher to hit a home run in the World Series; the first was Wally Schang of the 1913 Philadelphia Athletics.[12] DeLancey contributed an RBI double during the key seven-run third inning in the Cardinals' Game Seven victory. During the Series DeLancey was fined $50 by Commissioner Kenesaw Mountain Landis for swearing at home-plate umpire Brick Owens.[13]

In 1935 DeLancey ended up splitting time with Davis behind the plate. The young catcher suffered from a nagging cough throughout the year and wasn't able to claim the starting job on a permanent basis.

DeLancey was a chain-smoker, but that didn't seem to be the cause of his cough.[14] He didn't equal his rookie year at the plate, but still posted a strong .279 batting average, and the Cardinals were 52-25 in the games he started. The team finished second, four games behind the Chicago Cubs. For DeLancey the most memorable stretch of the season occurred over seven games between July 13 and 21, when he went 11-for-24 with four doubles, a triple, a home run, and nine RBIs as the Cardinals won six of the seven contests.

Although he often gained more attention for his offense, DeLancey was a strong defensive catcher and an intelligent student of the game. He possessed a strong throwing arm. He was respected by other ballplayers for his fearless nature. He didn't back down to veterans and demonstrated his leadership with a stern gaze or a streak of curse words. Branch Rickey would call him "a master with his pitchers," regardless of their age, and pitchers recognized this immediately.[15] Still, away from the diamond DeLancey was one of the club's best pranksters. Branch Rickey described him as "the most hardened practical joker in baseball that I ever knew, worse than Johnny Evers."[16]

DeLancey's health problems persisted throughout the season. A few days after the season ended he had a cyst removed from his right eye at St. Elizabeth's Hospital in Danville. Two weeks later he was readmitted to the hospital with a lung infection. DeLancey was transferred to St. John's Hospital in St. Louis, where the Cardinals team physician, Dr. Robert F. Hyland, diagnosed him with pleurisy with effusions.[17]

Dr. Hyland kept DeLancey in the hospital until he had regained his strength,[18] then recommended that DeLancey go to the Southwest because the region's dry air would assist his recovery, so Bill and Frances decided to move to Phoenix.[19] Upon his release from the hospital, DeLancey was reportedly still so weak he had to be carried to the train on a stretcher. After arriving in Phoenix he was confined to bed rest for a further eight months, during the first four of which he was so weak that he could only sit upright for 30 minutes a day.[20] Realizing he couldn't play baseball in the immediate future, DeLancey voluntarily retired on February 12, 1936.

Initially DeLancey was depressed at the possible end of his baseball career, saying, "If I can't play ball again, what's the use?"[21] However, his old friend Branch Rickey played an essential role in helping DeLancey recover through both his finances and his presence. Bill's lungs had to be drained every 48 hours and the Cardinals paid the cost for specialized medical courses so Frances could learn how to perform this task.[22] Rickey also came by the DeLanceys' residence during the spring of 1936 and spent about five hours with Bill. His wife later described Rickey's visit as a huge boost to her husband and recalled that he gained confidence and "no longer looked ahead despairingly."[23] Aside from their friendship, Rickey may have taken a particular interest in DeLancey's health because he himself had also been a young catcher who had had to give up his playing career because of an injury and because he had managed two players on the 1922 Cardinals club, Bill "Pickles" Dillhoefer and Austin McHenry, who both died in their 20s during the season.[24]

Rickey's visit helped improve DeLancey's mood, but the key to lifting his spirits may have been the addition to the family of some four-legged friends. While he was recovering, Frances bought Bill a bulldog to keep him busy. The dog seemed to lift Bill right out of his depression and Frances said the dog, as well as her efforts to train it, got him smiling and laughing again.[25] Soon the DeLanceys were the owners of two more dogs and Bill spent a great deal of time teaching the dogs tricks and, once he was no longer on bed rest, taking them on small walks.[26]

DeLancey's recovery went so well that he returned to baseball in 1937. He hadn't recovered enough to play, so the Cardinals made him the manager of their new Albuquerque farm club in the Class-D Arizona-Texas League. A primary reason behind the birth of the Albuquerque Cardinals was to give DeLancey a team to manage.[27]

Rickey said, "I believe DeLancey is going to make a wonderful manager. He's a keen student of the game. … It was a tough blow to the Cardinals when we lost him as a catcher, just when he was reaching his peak, but I know he's going to prove valuable to the organization as a manager. He knows baseball and he knows players as well."²⁸ He was proved right as DeLancey, despite being only 25 and having no managerial or coaching experience, managed Albuquerque to the league title.

DeLancey managed Albuquerque again in 1938, and took his first small steps toward resuming his playing career. He inserted himself into nine games as a pinch-hitter and got two hits. His first at-bat came during a 10-8 victory over El Paso on August 7. During Albuquerque's five-run ninth inning DeLancey smacked the ball over the center fielder's head to drive in two runs. It would have been a triple, but DeLancey was not at full health and stopped at first before lifting himself for a pinch-runner.²⁹

Meanwhile, the DeLanceys were adapting well to life in Arizona. They owned a small ranch house and 2 1/2 acres of land near Phoenix. They did a lot of riding in the desert.³⁰ Doris Ann went to live with her maternal grandmother during the season and Frances split her time between returning to Westville when the Cardinals were on the road and staying with Bill when the club was back in Albuquerque.³¹

DeLancey managed Albuquerque for a third season in 1939 and made further small steps toward restarting his playing career, going 3-for-14 with two doubles. He led the team to its second title in three seasons, overcoming losses in the first two games of the playoffs.³² In late September it had been decided that DeLancey wouldn't return to the club to manage the next season. The early speculation was that he would become a coach for St. Louis.³³

DeLancey's brief returns to the diamond hadn't been a rousing success statistically, but they suggested to the catcher that he might be able to play major-league baseball again, even if he couldn't return to his old heights. In 1940 DeLancey attended spring training with the parent club. At the end of spring training, he went to St. Louis for a physical examination, was declared fit to play for the Cardinals, and was signed by the club on March 20, 1940.³⁴

The Cardinals planned to use DeLancey as a reserve catcher, pinch-hitter, and tutor for young Cardinals pitchers and catchers. One of his primary duties was to teach Mickey Owen (who was only four years younger than DeLancey) about being a major-league catcher. DeLancey was given a lot of credit for helping to turn Owen into a fine defensive catcher for the Cardinals and Dodgers.³⁵

DeLancey played in only 15 games during the season, starting two of them. He got four singles in 18 at-bats and drove in two runs. It was clear that he wasn't the player he used to be and that his health problems had had a permanent impact on his talents.³⁶ DeLancey's final major-league game came on September 8, 1940, against the Pittsburgh Pirates at Sportsman's Park. He came into the game as a defensive replacement and didn't register a plate appearance. His final major-league hit came as a pinch-hitter against the Brooklyn Dodgers. On September 11, 1940, eight years to the day after he made his major-league debut, DeLancey was released as a player. He signed as a coach the next day. After the season he was released³⁷ and was named manager of the Pocatello Cardinals of the Class C Pioneer League. He played in 49 games, batting .277. DeLancey also made his only professional appearances as a pitcher, hurling ten innings over two games. He never played professional baseball again.

In 1942 DeLancey began the season as manager of the Asheville Tourists of the Class B Piedmont League. During the season he was succeeded by Ollie Vanek, and he left professional baseball. Whatever the reason—whether it was health-related, whether he had given up on playing in the majors again, or whether he was tired of managing and wanted to do something else—DeLancey retired to Arizona.

The following year, DeLancey worked as a sporting-goods salesman in Phoenix and served as commissioner of the Arizona Servicemen's Baseball League. He watched semipro baseball when he had the time, hoping to unearth talent that he could recommend to his good friend Branch Rickey.³⁸ Thoughts of playing again hadn't left him completely and he entertained the idea of playing independent league baseball in Phoenix, although he never did, as he knew it was best not to for his health.³⁹

After suffering only periodic sick spells for several years, DeLancey's health worsened a few years after his retirement and he was forced to leave his sales job.⁴⁰

His last public appearance in the baseball world came when he umpired an exhibition contest in Phoenix between the Chicago Cubs and St. Louis Browns.[41] The effects of his tuberculosis often kept him on bed rest during the final year of his life and he spent his last six months almost entirely in bed.[42]

DeLancey died of pleurisy on November 28, 1946, his 35th birthday.[43] He was survived by Frances; their two daughters, Doris, 12, and Mary Jane, 1; his father; four brothers; and six sisters.[44] After a funeral at St. Frances Xavier Parish, he was buried in St. Francis Cemetery in Phoenix on December 2.[45]

Rickey later paid glowing tribute to DeLancey in his seminal work, *The American Diamond*. He said DeLancey and Roy Campanella were the two best catchers he had ever signed and named the two of them and Mickey Cochrane on his "All-Time Team" of 30 players.[46] The only member of the team who wasn't an established star, DeLancey was selected ahead of such luminaries as Bill Dickey, Yogi Berra, and Gabby Hartnett.

Writing about why he chose DeLancey for his squad, Rickey explained that many of the catcher's best attributes weren't apparent from looking at a box score or his statistics. Rickey wrote, "On the field, he knew everything. He knew movements of the baserunners backwards and forwards and learned hitting traits of batsmen overnight. He anticipated managerial tactics and acted on his judgment. He had a remarkable pitching sense."[47]

Rickey described DeLancey as a master at reading a hitter's mood and mindset. "He knew there's a lingering hold on the consciousness of the last pitch that hasn't passed by yet with the hitter. He's still seeing it, he's still thinking about it. It may be that you should throw that next pitch within five seconds," while for other batters it might be better to let them stew about the past pitch and let self-doubt surface in their mind. Rickey noted that DeLancey also "knew the time to delay an anxious power hitter who could hardly wait for the next pitch. Let him exercise, let him exercise a lot. ..."[48]

Rickey described DeLancey as an effective player of mind games, describing him as a great psychologist on the diamond with an innate talent for reading people.[49] "He knew how to talk to a batter—and when to do it and when not to do it."[50]

Rickey perhaps best summarized DeLancey in one short passage in the book when he wrote, "He was a natural student of what, how and when. And he could hit! And throw! And run! He was unafraid physically and morally. He was a hell raiser, but he was victory bound."[51] If it wasn't for a terrible illness ending his career and then his life so prematurely, perhaps Rickey wouldn't have needed to explain DeLancey's virtues to his readers, as they would be much more widely recognized.

Notes

1 The catcher's full name in the 1934 World Series program is listed as William P. DeLancey, Jr. However, all other sources encountered, including his gravestone, refer to him as simply William DeLancey, and both his father and grandfather were also named William Pinkney.

2 Baseball Hall of Fame Library, player file for Bill DeLancey.

3 A clipping from the 1934 World Series program lists DeLancey as having spent time in Greensboro, presumably playing for the Greensboro Patriots, the Piedmont League affiliate of the Cardinals. There is no other source that lists him having played for Greensboro.

4 DeLancey player file. .

5 DeLancey player file. .

6 Lee Lowenfish, *Branch Rickey: Baseball's Ferocious Gentleman* (Lincoln, Nebraska: University of Nebraska Press, 2009), 237.

7 Robert E. Hood, *The Gashouse Gang: The Incredible, Madcap St. Louis Cardinals of 1934* (New York: Morrow, 1976), 114-115.

8 DeLancey player file.

9 DeLancey player file.

10 Hood,, 151. Bob Broeg related a similar anecdote regarding DeLancey hitting a home run in Cincinnati shortly after Frisch told him to lay off the low changeup. Frisch would reportedly relate for years that DeLancey sat in the dugout and said loudly, "I wonder how that old Dutch so-and-so liked that one?" It's unclear if this is the same incident with details mixed up or if this was a habit of DeLancey's. See Bob Broeg, "DeLancey—So Great, So Young," *St Louis Post-Dispatch*, December 9, 1978.

11 Bob Broeg, "DeLancey—So Great, So Young."

12 Schang and DeLancey have since been joined by Rod Barajas of the 2001 Arizona Diamondbacks and Buster Posey of the 2010 San Francisco Giants.

13 Hood, 132. Brick Owens umpired at home plate in Games One and Five, and the incident most likely occurred in the latter game.

14 Hood, 78.

15 Branch Rickey with Robert Riger, *American Diamond: A Documentary History of the Game of Baseball* (New York: Simon and Schuster, 1965), 47.

16 Ibid.

17 DeLancey player file.

18 DeLancey player file.

19 Lowenfish, , 267.

20 DeLancey player file.

21 DeLancey player file.

22 Lowenfish, 267.

23 DeLancey player file.

24 Lowenfish,. 267; DeLancey player file.

25 DeLancey player file.

26 DeLancey player file..

27 Lowenfish, 237.

28 DeLancey player file.

29 DeLancey player file.

30 DeLancey player file.

31 DeLancey player file.

32 DeLancey player file.

33 DeLancey player file..

34 DeLancey player file.

35 George Fossum, "Bill DeLancey, Former Card Catcher, Dies" *Arizona Republic,* Phoenix, November 29, 1946.

36 Ibid.

37 DeLancey player file.

38 Bob Allison, "DeLancey 'Out At Home' In Hard-Fought Death Battle," *Phoenix Gazette,* November 29, 1946.

39 Fossum, "Bill DeLancey, Former Card Catcher, Dies."

40 Ibid.

41 Allison, "DeLancey 'Out at Home.'"

42 Fossum, "Bill DeLancey, Former Card Catcher, Dies."

43 DeLancey player file. The exact cause of death on his Arizona State Department of Health death certificate was not decipherable to the author.

44 Allison, "DeLancey 'Out at Home.'" One source in the Baseball Hall of Fame Library player file for Bill DeLancey lists of all DeLancey's siblings as having survived him, but that is contradicted by other sources.

45 Allison, "DeLancey 'Out at Home.'"

46 Rickey with Riger, 157.

47 Rickey with Riger, 47.

48 Ibid.

49 Rickey with Riger, 48.

50 Rickey with Riger, 47.

51 Rickey with Riger, 48.

Leo Durocher

By Jeffrey Martlett

From his birth in 1905, in West Springfield, Massachusetts, to his death in 1991, in Palm Springs, California, Leo Durocher witnessed a great deal of social, political, and international change, some of which he helped bring about. Durocher played an important supporting role in the integration of major-league baseball. His frank assessment of African American baseball talent remains a simple, if coarse, endorsement of the American belief in meritocracy. He stood in the third-base coach's box for one of baseball's most memorable home runs, Bobby Thomson's 1951 "Shot Heard 'Round the World" off Ralph Branca. He led the New York Giants to a surprising World Series victory in 1954.

More than a decade later he piloted the Chicago Cubs through six and a half frustrating seasons, always falling short of the postseason. Along the way Durocher kept company with movie stars, entertainers, and an entire retinue of shady underworld characters. He had legal difficulties, four divorces, and fights with fans, jilted women, and angered husbands, fathers, and boyfriends. Through it all he maintained the utmost confidence in his own ability to come out ahead. Then as now, many have seen Durocher's competitiveness as an excuse for playing dirty.

Durocher found success in both playing and managing, winning World Series titles while playing shortstop for the 1928 Yankees and 1934 Cardinals and then as the manager of the 1954 Giants. He won National League pennants but no world championships with the 1941 Brooklyn Dodgers and the 1951 Giants. Finally, the famous phrase "nice guys finish last," attributed to him, has achieved recognition throughout American culture.

Leo Ernest Durocher was born on July 27, 1905, to George and Clarinda Durocher (nee Provost) in West Springfield, Massachusetts. He was the youngest of four sons, but at five feet ten grew to be the tallest. His French-Canadian parents often spoke French at home. Like his older brothers, Leo served Mass at the local Quebecois parish, St. Louis.

He also became quite adept at playing pool, and soon frequented the local pool halls to hustle money. His athletic abilities also became evident. While playing several sports, Leo became a local baseball prodigy. Company teams offered him increasingly lucrative and easy jobs if he would play for them and not for competing companies.

The fast-talking, hard-playing Durocher was an integral part of the Gashouse Gang. After his playing days, he won over 2,000 games, three pennants, and one World Series in his 24 years as a manager. He was elected to the Hall of Fame in 1994.

Discovered by a Yankees scout, he broke into professional baseball with Hartford of the Eastern League in 1925, and earned a call-up to the Yankees that season. He got into two games and had one at-bat. Durocher spent the next two seasons in the minor leagues, at Atlanta of the Southern Association (1926) and St. Paul of the American Association (1927). He came back to the Yankees in 1928 and never completely left the major leagues until his retirement in 1973.

Durocher's time with the Yankees was volcanic. Protected by manager Miller Huggins, he quickly made enemies with his incessant yapping, extravagant living, and antagonizing Yankees stars like Babe Ruth and Lou Gehrig. Ruth nicknamed Durocher the "All-American Out" for his diminutive batting average. Ruth also accused him of stealing his watch, a charge Durocher denied vehemently.

Durocher lost his protective mantle when Huggins died in 1929, and he was waived to the Cincinnati Reds before the 1930 season. In Cincinnati he found his gambling appetite even more easily indulged than in New York. He married Ruby Hartley in 1930 and fathered a child. The marriage quickly fell apart, and the couple divorced in 1934. Durocher omitted this first marriage—and his only biological child—in his 1975 autobiography. Midway through the 1933 season, mired in debt and a dissolving marriage, Durocher was traded to the St. Louis Cardinals. He became captain of the famous Gashouse Gang, the 1934 Cardinals team that fought with one another as much as with the opposition and won the World Series against Detroit in seven games.

On September 27 Durocher took time to remarry, this time to Grace Dozier, a prominent St. Louis businesswoman and fashion designer who paid off Leo's substantial debts. After the 1937 season friction between Leo and the Cardinals' player-manager, Frankie Frisch, led to a trade to the Brooklyn Dodgers. After the 1938 season, Dodger general manager Larry MacPhail named Durocher became the Dodgers' player-manager.

Leo received his nicknames "The Lip" or "Lippy" during his first full year in the majors, 1928. The roots for these names, and the behavior that spawned them, reached back to his boyhood days in West Springfield. Durocher dutifully idolized Walter "Rabbit" Maranville, the Boston Braves diminutive shortstop who hailed from nearby Springfield. Maranville, only five feet five and weighing 155 pounds, recognized that smaller players needed a mental edge to compensate for their lack of size.

Maranville came to know of the neighborhood's emerging star. He once told the young Leo, "Never back up," because "the first backward step a little man takes is the one that's going to kill him."[1] Maranville obviously meant this advice to apply to fielding the ball, but one might wonder if Leo took Maranville a bit too literally. George Durocher and his other sons exhibited the rock-ribbed but nonetheless quiet stoicism French-Canadian immigrants were known for in the Northeast. Maranville's words could also be understood as "don't back down from a fight," advice Leo often took to heart.

The tutorials in baseball's mental game continued as Leo progressed through the minor leagues. Miller Huggins completed Leo's apprenticeship when he reached New York. During the 1928 season with the Yankees Durocher became a full-blown, loudmouth bench jockey. The verbal assaults continued through his managing years. Boyhood friends who visited Durocher for games would note that almost every one of Leo's sentences included several obscenities. Branch Rickey once remarked of Durocher, when pushed into a corner, "He's still that kid from West Springfield with a pool cue butt in his hand."

From the earliest days of his playing career to the end of his managing days, Durocher loved to yap. Miller Huggins had encouraged the 160-pound youngster to compensate for his weak bat with hustle. Huggins, Leo said, "kept telling me I'd stick around for a long time if I kept my cockiness and my scrappiness and that fierce desire to do anything to win."[2] Durocher willingly obliged his mentor. First as a player then as a manager, he never shied away from verbal combat. As of 2010, Durocher ranked third all-time for the most times ejected from a major-league game as a player or a manager. Strictly as a manager, Durocher ranks fourth.

As a player, Durocher also distinguished himself with quick fielding. Throughout his managerial career he often reverted to his boyhood games, playing pepper with players several decades younger than himself. Even when he managed the Cubs in his sixties, Durocher surprised two of his stars, Ernie Banks and Ron Santo, with his ability to keep up with the younger players.

Durocher was certainly not a threat with the bat. He was a career .247-hitter, with just twenty-four home runs. His highest batting average came in 1936, when he hit .286 for the Cardinals. Overall, though, he performed better the preceding year, hitting .265 in 143 games. That season (1935) included career highs in home runs (8), slugging percentage (.376), and RBIs (78).

Durocher's already limited productivity tailed off significantly in the 1940s. In 1940 he played in little more than half the games (62) he had the year before, and came to bat only 175 times. In 1939, Durocher came in eighth in the MVP voting, and he was second among shortstops. In 1941, 1943, and 1945, his last three years playing, he appeared in only 26 games total, batting just 67 times. (He managed, but did not play for, the Dodgers in 1942 and 1944.) In 1941 Brooklyn won its first pennant since 1920, but lost the World Series to the Yankees, four games to one. The next year, the Dodgers won 104 games but lost the pennant to the Cardinals. Brooklyn finished third in 1943, the same year Durocher and Grace Dozier divorced.

With the players who had been in the military returning in 1946, Leo shifted over to managing full time. It was in that season that he made a statement that was later simplified to "nice guys finish last." Aimed at the last-place Giants and their manager, Mel Ott, the phrase quickly took on a life of its own, appearing in all sorts of publications, popular and scholarly, ever since.

The groundbreaking 1947 season was noticeable for Durocher's absence. He had been present during spring training in Havana, Cuba, playing along with Branch Rickey's orchestration of Jackie Robinson's promotion to Brooklyn. Throughout the winter, Rickey had planted stories that Durocher was "pressuring" him to add Robinson to the Dodgers' roster. However, just when Rickey was ready to announce that Robinson would in fact start on Opening Day, Durocher's past threw Rickey and the Dodgers an exploding curveball.

On the very day Robinson was to be introduced, Commissioner Albert B. "Happy" Chandler suspended Durocher from baseball for a year. Chandler claimed that Durocher had once again associated with known gamblers. Prior to a 1947 spring training game in Havana, Durocher noticed two such men sitting with Yankees owner Larry MacPhail. Rickey and Durocher complained to Chandler about double standards. MacPhail responded by decrying the charges as slanderous. Chandler fined both owners and suspended Durocher, a move that astonished Rickey, Durocher, and Brooklyn's fans.

This latest fiasco concerning Durocher only added to Rickey's headaches. In January, Leo had been in the papers again—this time for his marriage to Laraine Day, whom he had met in 1945. The Utah-born Day was already married to Ray Hendricks, but in January 1947, Day divorced Hendricks in Mexico, then married Durocher the next day in El Paso, Texas. Back in California, Durocher and Day, who still had a year to wait before her California divorce from Hendricks was final, had to plead before a judge so she could avoid conviction for bigamy.

Compounding the scandal's impact was a boycott of the Dodgers by the local chapter of the Catholic Youth Organization. The director of the Brooklyn CYO, Rev. Vincent Powell, removed CYO support for the "Knothole Gang" and published a letter in the newspapers on March 1, 1947 charging that Durocher was "undermining the moral training of Brooklyn's Roman Catholic youth." The CYO contributed both youths and money to the Brooklyn Knothole Gang, the team's adolescent fan base. Supported by U.S. Supreme Court Justice Frank Murphy, the Brooklyn Diocese had presented Rickey with the ultimatum: fire Durocher for his moral turpitude or face a boycott.

Durocher's suspension solved the boycott issue; nevertheless, with the beginning of the 1947 season a week away, Rickey had no manager for his new team. Eventually he named Burt Shotton as interim manager. Shotton promptly led the team to the National League pennant.

Before he left, Leo did manage to contribute significantly to the Dodgers' 1947 season. In Havana, the Dodgers learned of Rickey's plan to integrate the team with Robinson. Some players circulated a petition protesting Rickey's move. As soon as he heard of it, Durocher called a team meeting—at midnight. Surrounded by sleepy and cross players, Durocher flatly told them to "wipe your ass" with the petition. Finally, Leo concluded, many black players shared his own fierce desire to win. They were hungry, and unless the Dodgers and the other white players themselves played harder, they would find themselves replaced. Leo cared about winning, and if that meant starting black players, he had no problem doing so. He went public with his support for Robinson: "I don't care if he is yellow or black or has stripes like a fucking zebra. I'm his manager and I say he plays."

Underneath his coarse language, Leo believed in meritocracy. Those who are most able are the ones who start, regardless of appearance or background. This managerial approach led him to start three African Americans in the 1951 World Series (Monte Irvin, Willie Mays, and Hank Thompson). When he arrived at the Giants' spring training camp, Hank Thompson recalled Durocher's introduction: "I'm only going to say one thing about color: You can be green or be pink on this team. If you can play baseball and help this team you're welcome to play." Thompson concluded: "And it was true."[3]

Throughout the 1947 season, Rickey assured Durocher that he would get his manager's job back. Shotton's performance—winning the pennant and pushing the Yankees to seven games in the World Series—made Rickey reconsider his promise, but in the end, he kept it. When Leo arrived at spring training in 1948, he did seem changed. Reporters, players, and even Rickey himself noticed that the marriage (and perhaps the suspension) had mellowed him. The old Leo resurfaced briefly when Jackie Robinson reported to camp. Over the winter Robinson had gained significant weight. Durocher reverted to his older hectoring self, badgering Robinson incessantly. Robinson lost the weight and regained his playing form.

Rickey, though, remained unsatisfied. Wishing perhaps for a managerial change himself, Rickey often mused aloud that the team needed shaking up. The season's start bore out Rickey's worries as the Dodgers stumbled to a 35-37 record. When Horace Stoneham, owner of the cross-town archrival Giants inquired about Burt Shotton's availability as a replacement for Mel Ott, Rickey had his chance. With Durocher away in Montreal on a scouting trip, Rickey and Stoneham met. While Rickey did not offer Durocher's services, he also did not refuse when Stoneham asked for Durocher instead of Shotton.

Thus, the Dodgers' irascible manager switched in midseason to manage their hated rivals. Fans of both teams were stunned, as was Leo, who did not learn of the managerial transfer until he returned. The night the deal was completed Stoneham visited Laraine Day at the couple's Manhattan apartment. When she learned the news, she switched off the radio broadcast of that night's Dodgers game, saying, "Then why am I listening to this?"

Many of Ott's players were slow-footed veterans, and Durocher's aggressive, gambling style did not sit well. He did manage the team to a .519 record (41-38) for the rest of the season. That was only good enough for fifth place in the National League. The next season, 1949, was Durocher's worst with the Giants; the team finished fifth again, but this time with a 73-81 record. From 1950 through 1955, though, the Giants and Durocher enjoyed four winning seasons, only once finishing lower than third. During that span the Giants won two National League pennants and the 1954 World Series. In 1951, they made up a thirteen-game deficit in August against the Dodgers and forced a three-game playoff for the pennant.

The Giants won the third game, 5–4, on Bobby Thomson's famed home run. According to author Joshua Prager, Leo did more than just watch; his rudimentary telescope-and-bell system rigged in the Polo Grounds offices 483 feet away from home plate had tipped Durocher, Thomson, and the Giants that Branca was about to throw a fast ball. The Giants then lost a hard-fought World Series to the Yankees, four games to two. In 1954, the Giants swept the heavily favored Cleveland Indians in four games. The next year they finished third, a distant eighteen and a half games behind the Dodgers. After that 1955 season, Stoneham replaced Durocher with Bill Rigney.

Durocher's stint with the Giants ranked second only to his time with the Dodgers. He managed the Giants for almost seven and a half seasons and finished with a .549 winning percentage (637-523). He managed the Dodgers for eight and a half seasons and finished only slightly better (738-565). After the Giants replaced him, Durocher pursued his long-desired goal of shifting careers to show business. However, despite his several celebrity friends, most endeavors quickly fell through. His attempt to host a variety show on NBC flopped. Durocher appeared on several television shows, but he made more money doing baseball broadcasts on radio and television. Day divorced him in 1960. Durocher served as a coach for Los Angeles Dodgers from 1961 to 1964. True to form, he often criticized manager Walter Alston for indecisiveness and tentative leadership.

In 1966 the Chicago Cubs named the sixty-year-old Durocher manager. That season Leo suffered through his worst year as a manager, going 59-103. But much like his stint with the Giants, Durocher then led his team through several winning seasons. From 1967 to 1971, the Cubs enjoyed five straight winning seasons.

The club stood at 46-44 when owner Phil Wrigley fired Durocher midway through the 1972 season. Durocher's time with the Cubs is remembered mostly for what did not happen. For several years the talent-laden club finished below expectations. The 1969 season was the best example. The Cubs led the National League East division for over 100 days, and were nine and a half games ahead of the Mets in August. However, the team faltered badly.

As the season wore on, he misused his pitchers, and his tendency to berate players often backfired. Once again Durocher's hard-driving style had begun to wear thin. During two weeks in September, the Cubs fell from five games ahead of the Mets to four and a half games behind them, and eventually finished eight games back. The Cubs finished second again in 1970, albeit without the spectacular meltdown. In 1971 they wound up third. That year the locker room finally boiled over with fights between Durocher and the players. Unlike previous stints with the Dodgers and Giants, Leo never related well with the Cubs' African American players.

One of his most common managerial tactics was to belittle and enrage players so that they played better. He had picked up this technique from Miller Huggins, and it worked quite well with stars like Jackie Robinson and Sal Maglie. With the Cubs, it backfired. Pitcher Ken Holtzman took offense at Durocher's repeated use of anti-Semitic remarks. In the years after Curt Flood's legal challenge to the reserve clause, Durocher's well-known hostility to union organizing appeared shockingly retrograde. Halfway through the 1972 season, owner Phil Wrigley had enough and replaced Durocher with Whitey Lockman. Leo did not remain idle for long. The Houston Astros made him skipper for the last thirty-one games of 1972. As before, he wrangled with the team's established stars, in this case pitcher Larry Dierker. Durocher managed the entire 1973 season, going 82-80, before retiring for good.

Leo moved back to California and waited for the Hall of Fame recognition he felt he was due. He and fourth wife, Lynne Walker Goldbatt, divorced in 1981, but the couple had already separated years earlier. Durocher had married the Chicago socialite in 1969.

As the years went by, Leo rediscovered his Catholic faith. He served faithfully as an usher at the Saturday evening Mass at his local parish. He also became increasingly bitter over his perceived slight by the Hall of Fame. He died on October 7, 1991, and was buried in Hollywood Hills Cemetery in Los Angeles. The Hall of Fame recognition finally came in 1994. On Induction Day, Laraine Day accepted the award.

Durocher's posthumous election to the Baseball Hall of Fame rested exclusively on his managerial career. In twenty-four seasons, Durocher amassed 2,008 victories and 1,709 losses, a .540 winning percentage. However, Durocher's effectiveness as a manager exceeded the raw numbers. Throughout his managerial career, he took a tough, scrappy, take-no-prisoners approach to the game. Only at the end of his managerial career did Durocher encounter significant player resistance to his style. When he retired, he seemed a relic from an earlier baseball age.

This essay was originally published in Lyle Spatz, ed. *The Team That Forever Changed Baseball and America* (Linoln: University of Nebraska Press, 2012).

Sources

Claerbaut, David. *Durocher's Cubs: The Greatest Team That Didn't Win*. Dallas, Texas: Taylor Publishing, 2000.

Day, Laraine. *Day with the Giants*. Edited by Kyle Crichton. Garden City, New York: Doubleday & Co., 1952.

Durocher, Leo. *The Dodgers and Me: The Inside Story*. Chicago: Ziff-Davis, 1948.

_____. *Nice Guys Finish Last*. With Ed Linn. New York: Simon & Schuster, 1975.

Eskenazi, Gerald. *The Lip: A Biography of Leo Durocher*. New York: Quill, William Morrow & Co., 1993.

Feldmann, Doug. *Miracle Collapse: The 1969 Cubs*. Lincoln: University of Nebraska Press, 2006.

Prager, Joshua. *The Echoing Green: The Untold Story of Bobby Thomson, Ralph Branca, and the Shot Heard Round the World*. New York: Pantheon, 2006.

Tygiel, Jules. *Baseball's Great Experiment: Jackie Robinson and His Legacy*. 25th Anniversary Edition. New York: Oxford University Press, 2008.

Hazucha, Andrew. "Leo Durocher's Last Stand: Anti-Semitism, Racism, and the Cubs Player Rebellion of 1971." *NINE: A Journal of Baseball History and Culture* 15 (#1, Fall 2006): 1-12.

Heidenry, John. *The Gashouse Gang: How Dizzy Dean, Leo Durocher, Branch Rickey, Pepper Martin, and Their Colorful, Come-From-Behind Ball Club Won the World Series and America's Heart During the Great Depression*. New York: Public Affairs, 2007.

Mandell, David. "The Suspension of Leo Durocher." *The National Pastime: A Review of Baseball History* #27 Cleveland, Ohio: Society for American Baseball Research, 2007: 101-4.

Mann, Arthur. *Baseball Confidential: Secret History of the War Among Chandler, Durocher, MacPhail, and Rickey*. New York: David McKay Company, 1951.

Marlett, Jeffrey. "Durocher as Machiavelli: Bad Catholic, Good American." *The Cooperstown Symposium on Baseball and American Culture, 2007-2008*, edited by Bill Simons. Forthcoming, McFarland Press, 2009.

Shaplen, Robert. "The Nine Lives of Leo Durocher." *Sports Illustrated*. June 6, 1955.

Treder, Steve. "A Legacy of What-Ifs: Horace Stoneham and the Integration of the Giants." *NINE: A Journal of Baseball History and Culture* 10 (#2, 2002): 71-101.

Williams, Peter. "You *Can* Blame the Media: The Role of the Press in Creating Baseball Villains." *Cooperstown Symposium on Baseball and American Culture (1989)*. Edited by Alvin L. Hall. Westport, Connecticut: Meckler Publishing and State University of New York College at Oneonta, 1991: 343-60.

Woodward, Stanley. "That Guy Durocher!" *Saturday Evening Post*, June 3, 1950: 25-27.

Notes

1 Leo Durocher, *Nice Guys Finish Last*, p. 34.

2 Leo Durocher, *Nice Guys Finish Last*, p. 46.

3 Gerald Eskenazai, *The Lip*, p. 248.

Frankie Frisch

By Fred Stein*

Frankie Frisch, the 35-year-old manager and second baseman of the 1934 St. Louis Cardinals, was an infielder for 19 years, spent 16 years managing NL teams, and put in some time as a broadcaster, all in the National League. His playing and managing exploits won him election to the Hall of Fame.

Frank Francis Frisch was born in the Bronx, New York, on September 9, 1898,[1] to Franz and Katherine (Stahl) Frisch. Franz Frisch was a prosperous lace-linen manufacturer who assumed that his son would enter the business after completing his college education. The elder Frisch apparently never imagined that his athletic son would find a completely different means of earning a living. But the independent-minded young man had other ideas.

Frisch displayed his natural athleticism at Fordham Prep School and Fordham University, where he majored in chemistry. He was a track star (gaining the lifelong nickname Fordham Flash) and captained the football, basketball, and baseball teams. In 1918 Frisch was named a halfback on an All-American football team. The following year he signed with the New York Giants baseball club, and never played in the minor leagues.

Frisch worked out with the Giants in the spring of 1919 and joined the club after his college graduation in June. Manager John McGraw wanted to send him out for minor-league schooling, but Frisch talked McGraw into keeping him, citing pressure from his father to join the family firm if he was farmed out. So McGraw worked intensively with the aggressive Frisch on all aspects of his game. Frisch was a switch-hitter, who batted cross-handed from the right side; that is, when he hit right-handed, he kept his left hand above his right hand. McGraw worked with him each morning, teaching him fielding and sliding techniques and how to hold the bat properly.

Frisch made his major-league debut on June 14, 1919, in Pittsburgh, taking three called strikes in his first time at bat. In September Frisch impressed McGraw in his first start at third base when, in a crucial game, a hard smash took a bad hop and bounced off Frisch's chest. The 5-foot-9, 175-pound rookie pursued the ball and threw the runner out. As McGraw said, "That was all I had to see. The average youngster, nervous anyway at starting his first game in a pennant situation like that, would have lost the ball. Frisch proved right there that he is going to be a great ballplayer."[2]

Frisch hit .226 while playing second base, third base, and shortstop during his first season, and improved to .280 as a third baseman in 1920. (He had played shortstop as a collegian, but McGraw decided that he did not have the sure hands or range to excel there.) His breakthrough season came in 1921, when he had 211 hits, hit .341, and stole a league-leading 49 bases while splitting the year between second and third. He became a Giants stalwart as

The second baseman/manager for the Cardinals batted .305 in 1934. He hit .290 or higher in 15 of his 19 major-league seasons. The "Fordham Flash" stole 419 bases, leading the league for three seasons. He was inducted into the Hall of Fame in 1947.

McGraw's club won the first of four consecutive NL pennants. As Bob Broeg described his play: "Frisch was tremendous, a whirling dervish of the diamond, knocking down hot smashes with his chest, diving for others that seemed out of his reach, ranging far and wide for pop flies, pawing at the dirt to get a long lead and then stealing bases."[3] Frisch gave a solid performance as the Giants beat the Yankees in the 1921 World Series. He was the key player, averaging .335 and 196 hits over the next three years while playing almost exclusively at second base.

The energetic Frisch was a slashing switch-hitter, who made up for his lack of home-run power with a steady barrage of clutch hits and stolen bases. He was a more consistent hitter when batting left-handed although he had more power right-handed. Hitting from the left side, he was an adroit bunter and with his speed when he was young, he often drag-bunted for a base hit. He was especially skilled at punching outside pitches to left field.

The extremely competitive Frisch became a favorite of McGraw, who saw in him a kindred soul, and Frisch was appointed team captain early in his playing career. There were no problems between the two while the Giants won pennants in the early '20s, despite the very rough McGraw, who traditionally was especially hard on the Giants' captains. But as the Giants' performance deteriorated and McGraw became more irritable and frustrated, he singled out his captain and verbally abused him in the clubhouse after difficult losses with words meant not so much for him as for other members of the team. Frisch bridled at the abuse but took it for the good of the team.

Frisch took a lot of verbal punishment when the Giants lost the pennant to the Pirates in 1925 and to the Cardinals the following year. By late in the 1926 season he could no longer stand it. After an especially tough loss in St. Louis on August 20 and an especially cruel postgame McGraw diatribe, Frisch left the team the next morning and returned home to New York. He came back in early September to finish the season, but his relations with McGraw were beyond healing. He was traded to the Cardinals on December 20, 1926. It was a blockbuster deal, as the Giants gave up Frisch and pitcher Jimmy Ring for St. Louis manager-second baseman Rogers Hornsby. Hornsby, considered by many as the greatest right-handed hitter ever, had just played and managed the Cardinals to a World Series championship over the Yankees. The Cardinals made the trade because of owner Sam Breadon's irreconcilable differences with Hornsby.

Hornsby, having just brought a championship to St. Louis, was a fan favorite. But Frisch, who called his new team the "Cawd'nals" in his New York accent, won over the fans with a brilliant season, hitting .337 with a league-leading 48 stolen bases, and setting a still-standing (as of 2013) major-league record for second basemen of 641 assists. Frisch was the one indispensable sparkplug as St. Louis narrowly missed winning the pennant, and he was the field leader as the Cardinals won pennants in three of the next four seasons. Frisch was voted the National League Most Valuable Player in 1931 as the Cardinals won the pennant and then defeated the favored Philadelphia Athletics in the World Series.

Frisch became the Cardinals' player-manager midway through the 1933 season, his team finishing in fifth place. Shortly before taking over as manager, he played in the first All-Star Game, at Comiskey Park in Chicago. Batting right-handed in his first at-bat, Frisch grounded out. In the sixth inning, hitting left-handed, he became the first National Leaguer to hit a home run in the classic. (He also homered off Lefty Gomez on the first pitch he saw in the 1934 All-Star Game.)

Frisch's colorful 1934 club was a smashing success. It included such unforgettable characters as pitchers Dizzy and Paul Dean, the inimitable Pepper Martin at third base, Leo Durocher at shortstop, and slugging outfielder Joe "Ducky" Medwick. The loud but talented Dizzy Dean's unpredictable antics kept Frisch on constant edge. Martin, like Dizzy, was an uninhibited country boy whose zany activities did not detract from his spirited play. Medwick was a tough New Jersey native with an extremely potent bat and an unusually low boiling point. A writer dubbed Frisch's club the Gas House Gang when they appeared in badly soiled uniforms before a game, not having had time to have the uniforms cleaned. For much of the season the Cardinals were barely within striking distance of the NL lead, but they came on strong in the last month to edge out the Giants for the pennant. They topped off the season with a tumultuous World Series win over the Detroit Tigers in seven games.

The 1935 club had a virtually identical won-lost record as in the previous year, but the Cubs surpassed the Cards with 21 consecutive wins late in the season. Frisch became recognized as a manager as intense as McGraw. The Cardinals finished second in 1936, losing to the Giants, and slipped to fourth place the following year. The colorful Gas House Gang years were largely over and Frisch's managerial years in St. Louis ended after the 1938 season.

Frisch had ended his playing career after playing infrequently in 1937. Early in that season, he reached second base with the fleet-footed Terry Moore the runner at first base. Joe Medwick laced a drive off the right-field wall. By the time Frisch reached third, Moore was well past second. As Frisch touched home plate, Moore slid in under him. The embarrassed Frisch told a writer after the game, "Any time they can run down the Flash, it's time to quit."[4]

Frisch left the playing field in 1939 for the radio booth, doing play-by-play broadcasts for the Boston Bees. He returned to the field the following year and managed the Pirates for seven seasons. His Pittsburgh clubs finished in the first division five times, but were never a serious threat to capture a pennant. The Pirates finished in second place only in 1944, but even then by a distant 14 1/2 games behind the Cardinals. Frisch's years with the Pirates were remembered for his antics, mostly his umpire-baiting. He was thrown out of one rainy game for going out to home plate carrying an umbrella to protest the umpire's failure to call the game. On another occasion he was photographed giving an umpire a sweeping bow in sarcastic protest after the umpire cleared the Pirates bench.

There was the time when Frisch was coaching third base for his Pirates. Cubs third baseman Eddie Stanky interfered with one of Frisch's players by giving him the hip as he tried to score a run on the following hitter's extra-base hit. The lead Pirates runner was knocked sprawling and was awarded the run because of Stanky's obstruction. As the hitter ran out a triple, he slid into third base from one side, and Frisch, determined to react to Stanky personally, slid into the bag from the coach's box. Umpire Jocko Conlan called the runner safe and immediately ejected Frisch.

Frisch left the Pirates after the 1946 season and spent the next two years living in his beloved home in New Rochelle, tending to his garden when not doing the radio play-by-play of Giants home games. Frisch was a hit on the radio despite his high-pitched voice and lack of training as a broadcaster. Fans encouraging Frisch loved to imitate his radio style, especially his longtime managerial lament, "Oh, those bases on balls." He returned to the field in 1948, coaching for the Giants.

In 1949 Frisch coached for Leo Durocher's Giants until June 10, when the Cubs hired him to replace manager Charlie Grimm. Frisch returned to managing against the advice of his wife and many of his friends. He admitted later that he took the job because he loved being a manager, although he realized that the Cubs were a last-place club with no immediate hope of improving. They finished last in 1949, in seventh place the next year, and were last again in 1951 when Frisch was fired on July 21. According to first baseman Phil Cavarretta, who replaced Frisch, the firing was triggered when general manager Wid Matthews saw the disinterested Frisch sitting in the dugout reading a book during a game.

As a player, Frisch had a lifetime average of .316 in 2,311 games with 2,880 hits and 1,244 RBIs. He led the National League in stolen bases in 1921, 1927, and 1931 for a career total of 419, an excellent number for the era in which he played. Frisch set several fielding records for NL second basemen and various hitting and fielding marks in his 50 World Series games. He was elected to the National Baseball Hall of Fame in 1947.

Frisch compiled a 1138-1078 (.514) career managerial record. In his *New Bill James Historical Abstract*, Bill James wrote, "Frisch was an effective field leader because he had tremendous energy and a forceful personality. But once he could no longer play he began to romanticize the past, to deride his own players, and to launch into long (but apparently entertaining) monologues."[5]

Frisch was a popular figure over and above his prowess as a player. He had a robust sense of humor and constantly exchanged jokes and ribald stories with fellow baseball men, umpires, and sportswriters. He maintained his home in Westchester County, New York, for many years after he left the Giants in 1927, and he was often accused jokingly of attempting to get thrown out of games so he could spend more time at home. Frisch carried on a series of practical jokes with other managers. When Casey Stengel was hit by a car in 1943 while managing the woeful Boston Braves, Frisch wired Casey that he understood the reason for the attempted suicide and expressed his sympathy that it was unsuccessful.

Despite his rugged persona, Frisch had genteel interests off the field. He enjoyed frequenting fine restaurants and reading good literature. He was an enthusiastic gardener, whose roses were a source of pride. He was a devotee of classical music. As he grew older, he was often a gruff old-school observer of the playing styles of a later generation of ballplayers. For example, he referred to spring training as "a country club without dues."[6] It is not difficult to imagine Frisch's reaction to the changing baseball strategies and the players' on- and off-field customs and mores that he did not live to see.

Frisch was able to honor the memories of some of his teammates when he joined the Hall of Fame Veterans Committee in 1967. The outspoken, persuasive Frisch became a leader on the committee, and sponsored six old Giants and Cardinals into the Hall. They included his double-play partner Dave Bancroft, Giants first baseman George Kelly, and St. Louis pitcher Jesse Haines. Some baseball historians have judged them to be among the least deserving players ever selected.

Frisch married Ada A. Lucy in 1923. The couple had no children. After Ada died in 1971, Frisch married Augusta Kass the following year. He also moved to Quonochontaug, a beach community in the town of Westerly, Rhode Island. He died in Wilmington, Delaware, on March 12, 1973, after an automobile accident while he was returning from a Veterans Committee meeting in Florida.

*This biography was written by the late Fred Stein. Notes were added and minor modifications in the text were made by Charles F. Faber.

Sources

Broeg, Bob, *Super Stars of Baseball* (St. Louis: The Sporting News, 1971).

Golenbock, Peter, *Wrigleyville: A Magical History Tour of the Chicago Cubs* (New York: St. Martin's Press, 1996).

Graham, Frank, *McGraw of the Giants* (New York: G.P. Putnam's Sons, 1944).

James, Bill, *The New Bill James Historical Baseball Abstract* (New York: Free Press, 2001).

Notes

1. Although Frisch used 1898 as the year of his birth, New York City birth records, Social Security death records, and US Census records indicate that he was born in 1897.
2. John McGraw, quoted in Bob Broeg, *Super Stars of Baseball* (St. Louis: The Sporting News, 1971), 89.
3. Broeg, 89.
4. Broeg, 92.
5. Bill James, *The New Bill James Historical Baseball Abstract* (New York: Free Press, 2001), 493.
6. Broeg, 88.

Chick Fullis

By Jack Morris

There may have been no one more surprised to find Chick Fullis playing for the St. Louis Cardinals in Game Seven of the 1934 World Series than Fullis himself.

In his only start in the World Series (in Game Five), Fullis had misplayed two balls in center field that directly led to two runs in the Cardinals' 3-1 loss to the Detroit Tigers and gave the Tigers a three-games-to-two lead. Writing in the *Brooklyn Eagle* the next day, sportswriter Tommy Holmes opined, "Fullis made an admirable bid for the long curved horns of the goat of this World Series."[1]

Fullis, who had been brought to the Cardinals in mid-June in a trade with the Philadelphia Phillies, had primarily played as a platoon right-handed hitter and defensive replacement with the Cardinals. But after the two miscues in Game Five, Cardinals manager Frankie Frisch clearly lost any confidence he had in Fullis. It seemed doubtful that Fullis would see any playing time in the remaining two games.

However, the Cardinals roared back with a win in Game Six. In Game Seven St. Louis took a 9-0 lead going into the bottom of the sixth when Tigers fans, incensed by a hard slide into third base by the Cardinals' Ducky Medwick in the top of the sixth, pelted Medwick with anything they could throw when he took his position in left field in the bottom of the inning. Baseball Commissioner Kenesaw Mountain Landis ordered Medwick off the field for his safety.

Fullis was acquired from the Phillies in midseason, providing the Cardinals with depth and experience in the outfield.

To replace Medwick, Fullis entered the game, undoubtedly surprised and relieved. He acquitted himself well, playing errorless ball and singling in his only at-bat as the Cardinals beat the Tigers, 11-0, to win the World Series. And while he didn't exactly become the hero of the Series, thanks to his Gas House Gang teammates he definitely was able to shed the goat horns.

Charles Philip "Chick" Fullis was born on February 27, 1901, in Girardville, Pennsylvania, in the coal-mining region northwest of Reading. He was the youngest of five children of Barbara (Schaefer) and Charles W. Fullis. His father, a miner, was the son of German immigrants and his mother was born in Germany.

Chick followed his father into the mines, working nine years in total even in the offseason when he was in the minors. He attended Girardville High School, where he got his start in baseball, playing shortstop. After high school, when he wasn't in the mines he played on town teams around Girardville.[2]

In 1923 Fullis hooked up with the semipro Shenandoah Braves of the Pennsylvania Anthracite League, where he batted close to .400. Years later, Fullis credited coal mining with helping him with baseball. "Mining is hard work," he told F.C. Lane, "but it is toughening. Playing baseball is easy in comparison."[3]

Fullis stood only 5-feet-9 but was powerfully built with broad shoulders. He was listed at 170 pounds. He was a speedster on the basepaths. It's no wonder he caught the eye of the

Frederick (Maryland) Hustlers of the Class D Blue Ridge League, who signed him for the 1924 season.

Fullis took the league by storm, "a sensation all over the circuit," batting .450 into late June and trailing only one other player in stolen bases. But in the middle of July Fullis left the team unexpectedly. Sometime before coming to Frederick, he had married a hometown resident, Mary Boxer. Now his young bride was calling him home. It would become a yearly ritual for the next few years: Fullis would leave his team sometime during the season to head home for one reason or another. But the teams he played for couldn't afford to lose his bat from the lineup for too long and put up with it.[4]

Also, sometime during this period, Fullis changed the year of his birth from 1901 to 1904, so instead of being a 23-year-old professional baseball rookie, he was listed as 20 years old. He claimed the 1904 birth year for the rest of his career.

Fullis came back to the team on July 22 but by the middle of August was back home again, this time with the team's permission, as he tried to heal from some nagging injuries that had him in a bad batting slump. Still, he ended the season batting .353 in 60 games.[5]

After the season Fullis was sold to Portsmouth of the Class B Virginia League. He refused to report, demanding more money. Portsmouth may have also been too far from home for Fullis. Finally, in April 1925, Portsmouth gave up on Fullis and returned him to Frederick.

Fullis again had a great season for the Hustlers. In early August he was leading the Blue Ridge League in batting with a .386 average and led the league in triples as well. He again slumped late in the season but still finished the season with a .338 batting in 95 games. Of course, he unexpectedly left the team in June, this time for a "sickness in the family." After the season, the *Frederick Post* noted that Fullis was one of the first to leave town when the season ended. His first child, a daughter named May, was born in 1925 so that may have hastened his departure.[6]

Frederick again sold Fullis after the season, this time to Columbus of the Double-A American Association for $4,000. And again Fullis refused to report, again saying the contract amount was too small. Clearly, Fullis impeded his own route to the major leagues by refusing assignments, especially with Columbus, which was just one rung below the majors.

Columbus returned Fullis rather than try to force him to play and in March Frederick sold him to Macon of the South Atlantic League for $1,000. This time, Macon made it worth his while so Fullis reported to camp.[7]

Fullis, however, played poorly with Macon, batting only .263 in 23 games, and was returned to Frederick on May 18. Again he tore up the Blue Ridge League, having his best season ever. Playing in 88 games, he batted .364. He also moved his wife and child to Frederick for the season, precluding any need for him to head home.[8]

Immediately after the 1926 season, Fullis joined the Blue Ridge League champion Hagerstown (Maryland) Hubs in the Five States Series against the Eastern Shore League champion, the Crisfield Crabbers. (Hagerstown was allowed to draft two non-Hagerstown players from its league for the series.) Fullis acquitted himself well, batting .333 in the series and helping lead Hagerstown to the championship.[9]

Fullis was sent to Macon for the 1927 season. This time he stuck. He hit Sally League pitching to the tune of .336 in 148 games. He also showed his versatility by moving from the outfield to shortstop for part of the season. But it was in the outfield where Fullis really shined. *The Sporting News* wrote that he was "pronounced by everyone as the best judge of a fly ball they have seen in the Sally League in years." And it was while playing center field for Macon that Fullis got his big break.[10]

In July New York Giants manager John McGraw traveled to Charlotte to scout Charlotte pitcher Jake Levy in a game against Macon. While there McGraw noticed Fullis's work in the outfield and wound up signing both Levy and Fullis to contracts. McGraw paid Macon $15,000 for Fullis, the highest price paid for a prospect to that point.[11]

Fullis reported to the Giants on September 15 after Macon's season was over. He didn't get into any games,[12] but didn't waste any time impressing at Giants spring training in 1928. He was dubbed the Macon Flash and was described as a "young, promising player with lots of ability." The Giants were beset by injuries so Fullis got plenty of playing time. He made the squad and traveled north with the Giants. But during the regular season, McGraw hardly used the rookie. He played in 11 games, nine as a pinch-runner and twice as a pinch-hitter. Mostly he sat on the bench. The *New York Sun* wrote that Fullis "never go much of a chance to show after the season opened" and that he "visibly pined on the bench at this inaction."[13]

Finally, on July 6, McGraw released Fullis to Toledo of the American Association. In his place, McGraw signed left-handed pitcher Garland Buckeye.[14]

After Fullis finished out the season with Toledo, the Giants recalled him. Again he had a very good spring in 1929 and made a name for himself despite a crowded Giants outfield that included Mel Ott, Fred Leach, Ed Roush, and Jim Welch. As the Giants barnstormed from the South back to New York, Fullis was moved to a starting job.[15]

But when the season started, Fullis was back on the bench. McGraw did play him more though he started only one game in April. But in May, Fullis started four straight games. In the first of those games, on May 6, he got his first major-league hit, a home run off Clarence Mitchell of the Cardinals.[16]

But on May 10, after his fourth straight start, Fullis left the Giants to go home to be with his dying father. Charles died on May 19, after Chick returned to the team. He left for the funeral, then when he finally returned for good, Fullis caught fire. By the end of June he was hitting .327. McGraw couldn't keep his hot bat out of the lineup. Roush got hurt, making it easier for McGraw to find time for Fullis. Fullis maintained his torrid batting until a late-season slump dropped his final batting average to .288 in 88 games. During this time, on July 27, Chick and Mary's second child, Charles W., named after his father, was born.[17]

Fullis experienced what could be deemed a lost season in 1930. Beset by injuries and illness starting in spring training, he played in only 13 games the entire season, none as a starter. He failed to get even one hit.[18]

It was no surprise that McGraw looked to trade Fullis in the offseason but he wasn't able to move the outfielder. At the beginning of the 1931 season, Fullis saw time for the Giants at second base, playing for the ailing Hughie Critz. He also was catcher Shanty Hogan's designated runner in late-inning situations. Playing every day in Critz's spot, Fullis was hitting .400 on the Fourth of July. When McGraw traded for second baseman Bill Hunnefield, he moved Fullis into a starting outfield position. *The Sporting News* wrote, "The development of Chick Fullis into a first-class outfielder and hitter has convinced McGraw that it would be a mistake to take him off the [starting] team."[19]

Fullis continued his torrid hitting for the rest of the season, finishing the year with a .328 batting average in 89 games. After the season Fullis barnstormed with teammate Johnny Vergez and many other Giants players.[20]

In December McGraw was quoted as saying that Fullis would be a fixture in the Giants outfield in 1932. But at the end of the month, McGraw purchased outfielder Len Koenecke from Indianapolis for $75,000. Fullis was again in a battle for a starting spot.[21]

The situation eased when halfway through spring training the Giants sold outfielder Fred Leach to the Boston Braves. Still, Fullis was the odd man out. By season's end, he had started in only 55 games and found that new manager Bill Terry preferred Jo-Jo Moore and Freddie Lindstrom to round out the outfield with Mel Ott. But Fullis had another good season at the bat, hitting .298 in 96 games.[22]

After the season Fullis barnstormed with a team called the Major League All-Stars which played a seven-game series against the Negro League Pittsburgh Crawfords. Included on Fullis's team were Brooklyn Dodgers Hack Wilson and Danny Taylor, the Pirates' Tom Padden, the Braves' Fred Frankhouse, and the retired Philadelphia Athletic Howard Ehmke. The Crawfords beat the All-Stars in the series, five games to two.[23]

After the tour, on December 13, Fullis was traded to the Philadelphia Phillies in a three-team deal. Along with Fullis, the Phillies received outfielder Gus Dugas and cash. The Giants got pitcher Glenn Spencer and outfielder George "Kiddo" Davis. The third team, the

Pittsburgh Pirates, received outfielder Freddie Lindstrom.[24]

In 1933, for the first time in his career, Fullis was given a starting job in the outfield out of spring training. He responded with a great season. He led the National League in plate appearances (698), at-bats (647), and singles (162); was second in hits (200), tied for second in stolen bases (18) and was sixth in the league in runs scored (91). On June 24 he went 5-for-5 in a game against St. Louis. By late July he was in third place in the NL in batting average behind teammates Chuck Klein and Spud Davis. He slumped toward the end of the season and finished the season batting .309. Fullis had a fine defensive year as well in center field. He led all center fielders in putouts (410) and assists (15). He missed only three games all season, leaving the team to attend his sister's funeral. The promise of the talent Fullis had shown in previous seasons finally came to fruition.[25]

As a member of the Phillies, especially if you played well, it was not unusual for trade rumors to be swirling. During the 1933 season it had been reported that the Brooklyn Dodgers were interested in Fullis. In the offseason the Chicago Cubs had expressed interest. But the Phillies, for a change, held onto a good player and kept Fullis for the 1934 season.[26]

Unfortunately, Fullis started the season in a bad slump. He was 2 for his first 26 at-bats and was benched with an .077 average after just seven games. It didn't help that the Phillies lost all seven games. Fullis was returned to the starting lineup about a week later and promptly started hitting. He raised his batting average to .263 by May 18 before an injury forced him out of the lineup for nearly three weeks. When he got back, he again slumped. This time the Phillies had enough. On June 16, in a swap of outfielders, Fullis was traded to the Cardinals for Kiddo Davis, the second time the two were involved in a trade together.

While the trade meant that Fullis was back on the bench, going from the seventh-place Phillies to the second-place Cardinals put him squarely in the middle of a pennant race. Late in the season he often platooned with left-handed center fielder Ernie Orsatti. He also was used as a defensive substitute for Ducky Medwick.[27]

Eventually, the Cardinals outbattled the Giants and Cubs for the pennant. Fullis saw action in Game One of the World Series as an eighth-inning defensive replacement for Orsatti. He got an at-bat, singling in the top of the ninth in the Cardinals' 8-3 win.

Fullis didn't play again until he was inserted into the starting lineup for the ailing Orsatti in the fateful Game Five. In the second inning, he misplayed a Pete Fox single into a double, allowing Hank Greenberg to score from first, putting the Tigers up 1-0. He wasn't charged with an error on the play, however. Then in the sixth, a groundball single went through his legs for a two-base error, allowing Billy Rogell to get to third base. Rogell scored on a sacrifice fly by Greenberg, putting the Tigers up 3-0. The Tigers won the game, 3-1, their third victory of the Series.

Without Fullis in the lineup the Cardinals won Game Six, 4-3, and then helped Fullis shed the goat horns by winning Game Seven, 11-0. Fullis played in that game only because Landis had ordered Medwick off the field for his own safety. For the Series, Fullis was 2-for-5 in three games.

In the offseason, the Cardinals purchased youngster Terry Moore, making Fullis expendable. On January 1, 1935, St. Louis sold him to Columbus of the American Association. Fullis spent the entire 1935 season in Columbus, batting .301 in 125 games.[28]

Fullis started the 1936 season with Columbus but after 19 games, batting .333, he was purchased by St. Louis on May 10. Fullis managed to stay with the Cardinals for the rest of the season though he saw little playing time. He started 15 games, mostly in center field, and ended the season batting .281 in 47 games. His last major-league game came on September 26, when he got into a game as a pinch-hitter. Years later, Fullis claimed that eye trouble hastened the end of his career, but he was 35 years old (though the press continued to say that he was three years younger).[29]

On December 7, 1936, the Cardinals sent Fullis, pitcher Ed Heusser, outfielder Lynn King, and cash to Columbus for catcher Mickey Owen. Fullis played only 44 games for Columbus in 1937, batting .268. In the offseason Columbus sold him to Memphis. But Fullis was through with baseball. Earlier in his career, he had bought a bar in Girardville. He planned to work full-time at the bar with his career over. Fullis never even bothered to inform Memphis of his decision to retire. In April 1938 Memphis finally returned Fullis's rights to the Columbus club, which released him.[30]

Fullis wasn't finished playing baseball, however. In 1939 he played center field and managed the Tremont (Pennsylvania) Miners of the semipro Lebanon Valley League. The team also had future major leaguer Joe Buzas playing for it. The team was so good that in 1940, it arranged games against the semipro powerhouse Bushwicks and another fine semipro team in the New York area, the Bay Parkways.[31]

When Fullis wasn't playing baseball, you could find him at his bar, where you could "eat soft-shelled crabs, clams, oysters, crab cakes, drink all the beer you wanted, and listen to Chick tell of the big leagues." He also purchased a hotel in Girardville.[32]

But Fullis's retirement from baseball was short-lived. In 1946, just nine years after his last game in Organized Baseball, he died of uremia, an illness accompanying kidney failure, in a hospital in Ashland, Pennsylvania, at the age of 45. He was survived by his wife, Mary, and his children, May and Charles. He was buried in the Odd Fellows Cemetery in Tamaqua, Pennsylvania. In 1976 Fullis was inducted into the Pennsylvania Sports Hall of Fame.[33]

Notes

1 *Brooklyn Eagle*, October 8, 1934.

2 The 1940 US Census lists Fullis as going to school only until the eighth grade. He may have played for the high-school team yet not attended school. *The Sporting News*, April 4, 1946; Lane, "He Lost Out With the Champions," *Baseball Magazine, August 1934,* 300; *Frederick* (Maryland) *Daily News*, June 27, 1924.

3 *Lebanon* (Pennsylvania) *Daily News*, March 29, 1946; Lane, "He Lost Out," 300.

4 *Frederick Daily News*, June 27 and July 17, 1924;

5 *Frederick Daily News*, July 22 and August 25, 1924

6 *Frederick Daily News*, September 16, 1924; *Frederick* (Maryland) *Post*, March 26, April 29, June 2, August 4, and September 9, 1925.

7 *Frederick Post*, October 11, 1925, and April 1, 1926; *Hagerstown* (Maryland) *Daily Mail*, February 26, 1926.

8 *Frederick Post*, May 19, 1926.

9 *Frederick Daily News*, September 13, 1926; *Frederick Post*, September 21, 1926.

10 *Frederick Post*, June 3, 1927; *The Sporting News*, August 11, 1927.

11 *The Sporting News*, April 4, 1946; *Rockford* (Illinois) *Republic*, August 2, 1927; *Augusta* (Georgia) *Chronicle*, June 1, 1929; Doug Feldman, *Dizzy and the Gas House Gang* (Jefferson, North Carolina: McFarland, 2000), 54. Unlike Fullis, Jake Levy never played in the major leagues.

12 *Frederick Daily News*, August 6, 1927.

13 *Augusta Chronicle*, March 6, 1928; *Berkeley* (California) *Daily Gazette*, March 15, 1928; *Winnipeg* (Manitoba) *Free Press*, March 16, 1928; *New York Sun*, January 10, 1929.

14 *Greensboro* (North Carolina) *Daily Record*, July 7, 1928. Buckeye pitched one game for the Giants and was shelled. It was the last game of his major-league career.

15 *Seattle Daily Times*, December 19, 1928, and January 10, 1929; *Aberdeen* (South Dakota) *Evening News*, April 1, 1919.

16 Bob McConnell and David Vincent, *SABR Presents the Home Run Encyclopedia* (New York: Macmillan, 1996), 536; *New York Times*, May 7, 1929.

17 *Brooklyn Standard Union*, May 10, 1929; *Richmond* (Virginia) *Times-Dispatch*, June 30, 1929; *Cleveland Plain Dealer*, August 11, 1929; *The Sporting News*, August 22, 1929.

18 *Oregonian* (Portland, Oregon), March 2, 1931.

19 *San Diego Tribune*, December 10, 1930; *Boston Herald*, July 7, 1931; *Yonkers* (New York) *Statesman*, July 22, 1931; *The Sporting News*, July 2, 1931.

20 Thomas Bathell, *Baseball Barnstorming and Exhibition Games, 1901-1962* (Jefferson, North Carolina: McFarland, 2007), 219

21 *Seattle Times*, December 3, 1931; *Rockford* (Illinois) *Register-Republic*, December 19, 1931.

22 *Aberdeen* (South Dakota) *American-News*, March 20, 1932

23 William McNeil, *Black Baseball Out of Season* (Jefferson, North Carolina: McFarland, 2007), 100; Barthel, *Baseball Barnstorming*, 134, 219.

24 *Cleveland Plain Dealer*, December 13, 1932.

25 F.C. Lane, "He Lost Out."

26 *New York Sun*, June 14, 1933; *Oregonian*, March 17, 1934.

27 Feldman, *Dizzy and the Gas House Gang,* 53-54.

28 *Boston Herald*, March 20, 1935; *Baton Rouge State Times*, January 1, 1935.

29 *Omaha World-Herald*, May 11, 1936; *Lebanon Daily News*, March 29, 1946.

30 *Greenville* (Mississippi) *Delta Star*, February 1, 1938; *The Sporting News*, February 3, 1938; *Rockford Register-Republic*, April 14, 1938; *Greensboro Daily News*, April 17, 1938.

31 *Lebanon Daily News*, June 9, 1939; *Jamaica* (New York) *Daily Press*, July 1940; *Brooklyn Daily Eagle*, August 17, 1940.

32 Harry Humes, "The Girard Theater," *Now and Then,* Winter 1997, 19; *Lebanon Daily News*, March 29, 1946.

33 Pennsylvania Death Certificate for Charles P. Fullis; *Lebanon Daily News*, March 29, 1946.

Burleigh Grimes

By Charles F. Faber

Burleigh Arland Grimes, who pitched in four games for the St. Louis Cardinals at the beginning of the 1934 season, was born on August 18, 1893, on his parents' dairy farm about halfway between the towns of Emerald and Clear Lake in northwestern Wisconsin. (Wisconsin records indicate he was born in Emerald, but he always regarded Clear Lake as his hometown.) He was the oldest child of Ruth Tuttle and Cecil "Nick" Grimes. Soon after his birth the family moved to nearby Black Brook. His father died when the lad was quite young, and his mother struggled to support the family. When Burleigh got old enough, he went to work in a lumber camp, toiling from 4:30 in the morning until 9:00 at night for one dollar a day. Later he earned a raise to $36 a month. For four winters he worked in that camp. It was hard, dangerous work. Once a heavy load of logs tipped over on him, but fortunately, he lived to tell about it. Years later he related the story to a sportswriter: "I can remember that little episode as though it happened yesterday. I was driving the sled. There were seven tiers of logs, two footers at the butt, sixteen feet long. The load was fourteen feet wide. There were four horses, and I was guiding them down a steep grade through the snow. We struck a stump and the load pitched forward. The thought flashed through my mind to jump clear of the load, but I hadn't time. The upper logs slid right over me. Every log on the sled pitched off except one. That was the one I had my back braced against. For some unknown reason it caught on something and held. There was just enough space for me to lie there while the logs pitched and rolled over me. It took a crowd of husky lumber jacks several minutes to dig me out. It was a close shave."[1]

When Burleigh was 13 years old, he attended a baseball game in St. Paul, Minnesota, and was so impressed by the spitball offerings of Minneapolis Millers pitcher Hank Gehring that he went home and practiced the damp delivery until he mastered the pitch. In 1912, at the age of 18, he began his professional career with the Eau Claire Commissioners of the Class D Minnesota-Wisconsin League, but the circuit folded in midseason. He started the 1913 season with the Ottumwa (Iowa) Packers of the Central Association, where he was so effective that the Detroit Tigers purchased his contract for $400. After a week the Tigers shipped Grimes to Class A Chattanooga without his ever having put on a Detroit uniform. He had only moderate success with the Lookouts. In 1914 he was the property of the Class A Birmingham Barons, who loaned him to Richmond in the Class C Virginia League, where he won 23 games. The Barons recalled Grimes on September 12. During the offseason he broke his leg, but was ready to pitch in 1915 and had a fine season with the Birmingham club. By August 1916 Grimes had a 23-11 record with the

Grimes, one of the last of the legal spitball pitchers, was released in May by the Cardinals. But his five seasons of over 20 victories and 270 career wins in 19 years earned him a permanent home in Cooperstown in 1964.

Barons when the Pittsburgh Pirates bought his contract and called him up to the majors. One report asserts that over a six-game stretch in July and August, Grimes five times lost a no-hitter with two outs in the ninth inning. Another account gives a slightly different version of this story: "Burleigh never pitched a no-hit game in the majors, but five times he went into the ninth without having allowed a safety. Once, against the Phillies in 1918, there were two out in the ninth when Fred Luderus connected for the first hit."[2]

By the time Grimes reached the majors, he chewed slippery elm in order to better load up the ball. He sliced the bark right off the tree, and put the fiber from inside on the ball. However, he said the juice from the wood irritated his sensitive skin, so he refrained from shaving on the mornings of the days he was scheduled to pitch (and perhaps on the day before as well). The dark growth of stubble on his face gave rise to his nickname Ol' Stubblebeard. It also added to Grimes's menacing appearance. The *New York Times* reported that he was a pitcher who frightened the hitters. "When he pitched," the *Times* reporter wrote, "he always had a two-day black stubble on his face. He walked with a swagger that infuriated batters, and when he measured a hitter from the mound he would peel back his lips to show yellow teeth in a snarl. He often threw at the batters' heads without the slightest hesitation."[3] Someone once said that Burleigh's idea of an intentional walk was to throw four straight fastballs at the batter's head. He had first earned his reputation as an ornery battler at Chattanooga and his actions throughout his career served to magnify that perception.

Years later Grimes explained his willingness to brush back hitters as an economic necessity. "When I was a teenager, I decided that the best I could make back home was thirty-five dollars a week driving horses in a lumber camp. Baseball was my answer. ... There was only one man standing between me and more money, and that was the guy with the bat. I knew I'd always have to fight that man with the bat as if he were trying to rob me in a dark alley."[4]

On good days his spitter would break six to eight inches, four or five when he was not so effective. Unlike other spitball pitchers, who gripped the ball loosely, Grimes habitually held it tight and once he broke his thumbnail when he released the ball. Burleigh wet the ball more than most spitballers did. Fielders complained that a sloppy wet ball was hard to handle and could cause a wild throw. Babe Ruth told of the time in 1927 that Heinie Mueller was playing outfield for the Giants when Grimes was pitching for that club. Heinie had been warned about the sloppy ball and he was taking no chances. When a line drive was hit to him, he deliberately wiped the ball dry on his shirt while the runner scored from third base. Ruth said the blunder cost Mueller his job with the Giants, and the next year Heinie was back in the minors as he was sold to the Class AA Toledo Mud Hens before being purchased by the Boston Braves late in the 1928 season.

One account of how Grimes pitched reads as follows: "All eyes were on the man on the mound. Stocky and muscular, he had a day's growth of stubble and a scowl on his face. He brought the fingers of his right hand to his mouth and covered them with his gloved hand, so the batter could not see whether he wetted them or not. Then he delivered the pitch, a high hard one, up and in. The batsman hit the dirt to avoid being struck by the pitch. Then came an assortment of pitches, another brush back, a fast ball on the outside corner, a spitter in the dirt. Next the batter thought he saw a fast ball coming right down the middle of the plate. When the ball reached its destination, the bottom fell out of the pitch. The batter swung, topping the ball, causing it to roll harmlessly back to the mound where the hurler picked it up and threw it to first base, easily retiring the batter. This sequence, or something like it, was repeated hundreds of times in the pitcher's career. The brushback was an important part of his arsenal, and he never hesitated to use it. Was it a crucial game in a World Series or a mid-season contest between two second-division clubs with no bearing on the pennant race? It mattered not. For the man on the mound was Burleigh Grimes, as fierce a competitor as any who ever played the game, a battler who gave it his all every time he toed the rubber."[5]

Grimes made his major-league debut with the Pirates on September 10, 1916, and picked up the victory over the Chicago Cubs in relief. In his first major-league start, four days later, he pitched well but was the victim of some poor fielding by his teammates. Through five innings the rookie held the Brooklyn Robins scoreless on only three hits. With one out in the top of the sixth of a scoreless game, Jake Daubert was on first base and Casey Stengel was at the plate. Honus Wagner came to the mound to settle the young pitcher down. "Make him hit it to me, Kid," the great shortstop said. Sure enough, Stengel hit a hard grounder right to short—a made-to-order double-play ball. Grimes was proud of himself and figured old Honus would be impressed. Horrors, the ball bounced off Wagner's foot into the outfield. Wagner came over to Grimes with his head down and said. "Those damn big feet of mine have always been in the way."[6] Before the inning was over Daubert had scored on a hit by Zack Wheat, and Stengel tallied when left fielder Bill Hinchman was unable to catch a fly hit by George Cutshaw, giving Brooklyn a 2-0 lead. The Pirates tied it up in the seventh. With the score tied 2-2 and two out in the ninth, it appeared the game was headed for extra innings. Brooklyn's Ivy Olson was on second base and pitcher Larry Cheney was at the plate. The Pittsburgh management motioned for the outfielders to move way in toward the infield with the weak-hitting pitcher at bat. Cheney lifted a high fly to left field that Hinchman could have caught easily had he been playing in his usual position. The ball bounced to the fence and Olson scored the winning run. Once again the Pirate defense had let the rookie pitcher down.

Baseball lore abounds with stories about Burleigh Grimes. Some of these tales are true; others are questionable; and still others are demonstrably untrue. One of the latter ilk refers to the spitballer's rookie season. According to this yarn, Grimes reported to the Pirates for his first big-league trial while the club was in Cincinnati. He found his assigned hotel room occupied by Larry Doyle of the New York Giants, who were just preparing to leave town. Doyle treated the rookie with such kindness that when Grimes first faced Laughing Larry in a game, he grooved one and Doyle hit it out of the park for a home run. As Lee Allen pointed out, Grimes was hardly the type to groove one for anybody, but the clincher was that Allen checked the record books. He found that the first time Grimes faced Doyle was in 1917. Doyle hit six home runs that season, none of them off Grimes. In 1916 Grimes won two games and lost three for the Pirates. The next season was worse. He lost 13 straight during a 3-16 campaign. By the end of his sophomore year, Grimes had won five games and lost 19 in the major leagues. Despite his minor-league success there was some question about whether the burly right-hander could survive in the majors. In the midst of the 13-game losing streak, manager Hugo Bezdek passed over Grimes's turn and started someone else in his place. As the Pirates were returning by train to Pittsburgh after the game, Grimes protested to the manager. In his reply Bezdek implied that the pitcher's problem might be that his competitive spirit was not strong enough. Wrong thing to say. As writer Steve Gelman related the story: "He hardly had the words out of his mouth before Grimes was on him like a wildcat. Up and down the aisle of the Pullman the two battled for the better part of an hour. It wasn't in the Marquis of Queensbury tradition, but strictly lumberjack style. The combatants each had the same fundamental idea—to choke the life out of the other. And neither was above biting when a bite would help. Eventually the other players … pried them apart."[7]

In January 1918 the Pirates traded their brilliant but erratic young pitching star Al Mamaux to the Brooklyn Dodgers for the popular outfielder Casey Stengel and aging second baseman George Cutshaw. Pittsburgh also gave up Burleigh Grimes, described as another pitcher, and Chuck Ward, an infielder, but Mamaux was clearly the headliner in the deal. During the remainder of his major-league career the main man Mamaux won a total of 27 games. In contrast, the throw-in Grimes won 265 additional decisions during his long career in "The Show."

With Brooklyn, Grimes became an instant success. Reversing his 1917 stats, he won nine starts in a row at one stretch in 1918. He won 19 and lost only 9 for the Dodgers (or the Robins as they were frequently called during Wilbert Robinson's reign as their manager from 1914 through 1931.) Although Grimes and teammate Rube Marquard both enlisted in the Navy during the season (the US was by then in World War I), they were assigned to a recruiting station in Chicago and allowed to continue pitching for Brooklyn. In an arrangement that defies explanation, Grimes's naval duties cost him almost no playing time, as he led National League pitchers in game appearances with 40 in 1918. He tied for third in wins, ranked fifth in winning percentage, fourth in baserunners per nine innings, fourth in innings pitched, second in opponents' batting average, third in opponents' on-base average, and fifth in ERA.

In 1919 Grimes came out of the Navy and won 10 games, despite having a sore arm. It was in this season that his memorable feud with Frankie Frisch began. The Fordham Flash bunted and apparently spiked Grimes on a close play at first base. A verbal battle escalated to fisticuffs and the feud was on. "For the next ten years I aimed at least two balls at Frankie every time I pitched to him," Grimes said. "He was equally tough with me every time we came in contact on the base paths."[8] "He only gets three shots at me, and then the so-and-so must pitch," Frisch would growl. But once Grimes really crossed up his rival. He threw *four* dusters at Frisch, and the fourth really took the batter by surprise. He dropped to the ground so quickly that he literally fell from under his cap, which drifted slowly to the ground after him. "It was one of the few times in baseball that I was really scared," said Frankie, "and Burleigh just stood there and laughed at me."[9]

On February 9, 1920, the joint rules committee of the major leagues outlawed the spitter. Twenty-two pitchers were exempted for the 1920 season; after that no one was to be allowed to use the pitch. Bill Doak spearheaded a campaign to modify the rule so established spitball pitchers could continue using the pitch. Burleigh Grimes became one of the more eloquent spokesmen for the proposed modification. He maintained that it took him ten to 15 years to develop a big-league-caliber spitter. The muscles in a pitcher's arms develop according to the way the arm is used, Burleigh claimed, and it is physiologically impossible for a mature adult to change from his customary style of delivery. "If all spitball pitchers, including myself, are called upon to discard the moist ball next spring, I am sure that in the spring of 1923 there will be a large number of ex-major-league pitchers pounding the pavements in seeking an honest living. When a man has given his whole life to developing himself in a particular baseball specialty it is impossible for him to give up that specialty in his prime and yet retain his effectiveness and his drawing power. Nor is it fair to expect him to change."[10] The pleas of Doak, Grimes, and others prevailed and the rule was modified. Seventeen pitchers, including Grimes, were granted lifetime exemptions from the ban.

In 1920 Grimes pitched Brooklyn to the National League pennant. He led the league's pitchers in winning percentage, held opponents to the second lowest batting average and second lowest on-base percentage, tied for second in strikeouts, ranked third in wins, earned-run average, and innings pitched; tied for third in complete games, and allowed the fifth fewest baserunners per nine innings among all the circuit's hurlers.

After Cleveland's spitballer Stan Coveleski defeated Rube Marquard 3-1 in the World Series opener, both teams started their aces in the second game. It was 31-game winner Jim Bagby against 23-game winner Burleigh Grimes. Both hurlers pitched well, but Grimes was more effective in the clutch and shut out the Indians, 3-0. The first two games of the Series had each been won by a spitball pitcher. Cleveland started spitballers in the third and fourth games, Ray Caldwell losing the third to Sherry Smith of the Dodgers, 2-1, and Coveleski defeating Leon Cadore in the fourth, 5-1.

With the Series tied two games each, the Robins started Grimes against Bagby in the fifth contest, one of the most memorable games ever played in World Series history. The first two Cleveland batters led off with singles, and when Grimes fell down while attempting to field Tris Speaker's intended sacrifice, the bases were loaded. Up to the plate stepped Elmer Smith, who then hit the first grand slam in World Series history. In the fourth inning the Indians hit another historic home run. Jim Bagby hit the first fall classic round-tripper by a pitcher, this one with two runners on base. With the bases loaded in the Brooklyn half of the fifth inning, spitballer Clarence Mitchell, who had entered the game in relief of Grimes, was at the plate and hit a line drive that Bill Wambsganss speared and turned into the first triple play in World Series history.

It remains as of 2013 the only unassisted triple play ever accomplished in the World Series. Cleveland won the game, 8-1, and the next, 1-0, as Duster Mails pitched a masterful three-hit shutout to victimize Sherry Smith. Cleveland now led the best-of-nine series four games to two.

The seventh game was spitballer versus spitballer—Grimes against Coveleski. Burleigh pitched well, but Stan outdueled him, tossing a five-hit shutout for his third win of the Series and Cleveland's first-ever World Series championship. Grimes blamed his loss on everyone but himself. He told an interviewer that three or four of the team's key players had violated curfew and did not show up in the best of shape to play ball. He also found out later that Pete Kilduff, the Brooklyn second baseman, had been giving his pitches away. Grimes used the spitball as a decoy, faking it on almost every pitch. Kilduff would pick up a little handful of dust and put it in his glove every time the catcher called for a spitball. This was so the ball would not be slippery when it was hit to him and he had to throw it. Burleigh said that wasn't too bright. None of the other fielders thought it was necessary. But Kilduff did it and the Indians knew when the spitter was coming and laid off it because they knew it was his best pitch. Grimes blamed Detroit scout Jack Coombs for giving him bad advice that enabled Elmer Smith to hit the grand slam. As the Dodgers had not scouted the Indians, Grimes relied on Coombs, who told him to give Smith high fastballs. So Burleigh threw a high, hard one and Elmer gained immortality. When he was 90 years old, Grimes still waxed emotional about the 1920 World Series.

Even though the Dodgers had lost the World Series, Grimes had fashioned a great season and he expected to be paid accordingly. When his 1921 contract came from Brooklyn owner Charles Ebbets, Burleigh sent it back unsigned. Ebbets fired back a letter, demanding that the pitcher sign. Grimes wrote back that he would stay home all season rather than pitch for the money that was offered. The owner responded with a telegram: VERY WELL. STAY THERE. The Dodgers went to spring training without Grimes. The day before the season opened, Grimes still had not reported, and no one in the Brooklyn organization had heard from him in months. Manager Wilbert Robinson went to Ebbets and said, "I don't care how you get him. All I say is get him."[11] The owner yielded to Uncle Robbie's plea and agreed to Grimes's terms, which were not announced publicly.

In 1921 the burly spitballer won 22 games, tied for the most by any National League moundsman. He led the league in complete games and in strikeouts. He ranked third in innings pitched and fifth in earned-run average. Nevertheless, the Robins fell to fifth place and were not to win another pennant for two decades. Only once in Burleigh's remaining six seasons with the club did they finish in the first division.

Despite pitching for a poor team, Grimes had a good year by most standards in 1922. He won 17 games and lost 14, but he did not like to lose any. With the Dodgers entering their Daffiness phase, Burleigh was too fierce a competitor to accept lax play behind him. In an August 6 game against the Cincinnati Reds, he was hit hard. Convinced that some of the groundballs hit off his spitter should have been fielded and turned into inning-ending double plays, burly Burleigh boiled over. Disgusted, he threw a pitch right down the middle of the plate to Jake Daubert, who promptly drove the pitch to deep center for a two-run inside-the-park home run to climax a six-run inning. After being relieved by Mamaux, Grimes stomped to the dugout, and Robinson was waiting for him. The two laced into each other verbally. Robbie's biographers wrote that the manager had learned his cuss words with the old Baltimore Orioles, but Grimes invented his own. Ebbets fined Grimes $200 and issued a public reprimand. He instructed the pitcher to apologize to the manager and to refrain from future swearing.

In 1923 Grimes again won 21 games, but his 18 losses were hard for the spitballer to stomach. He led the league in complete games and in innings pitched, ranked third in strikeouts, and tied for fourth in wins. During the 1922 season, Grimes had extreme difficulty with the Philadelphia Phillies, one of the weaker teams in the league. In four appearances against them, he was 0-3 with an 8.06 ERA, The Phillies were laying off Burleigh's spitter and zeroing in on his fastball and curve. At first Robbie thought Philadelphia was stealing the signs from Brooklyn's new catcher, Hank DeBerry. From the bench and the field, the Robins watched their catcher and pitcher carefully to see if they could discover the tipoff. They even suspected a spy with binoculars had been planted in the scoreboard at Baker Bowl. However, even when DeBerry's sign delivery to Grines was altered, the Phillies continued hitting him hard. Philadelphia's veteran shortstop, Art Fletcher, had noticed a trend by Grimes and passed it on to his teammates. Fletcher observed that the spitballer's cap was tight-fitting. When Grimes faked the spitter, the peak of his cap never moved. When he actually moistened the ball, however, the peak wiggled slightly. Early in 1923, the Brooklyn batboy finally solved the mystery. Burleigh got a cap a half size larger, and the Phillies were no problem that season as Grimes went 6-0 against them.

In 1924 the Dodgers rebounded and found themselves in a pennant race for the first time since their championship year of 1920. With Dazzy Vance coming into his own, the Dazzler and Grimes won 50 games between them. The Daffiness Boys that year were a hard-drinking, hard-fighting, high-living crew, but they combined good baseball with their highjinks. Grimes did not live as high or drink as much as some of the others, because he always kept himself in top-notch physical shape. Of course, he fought as hard as anyone and occasionally he shared in their extracurricular fun.

But when crunch time came, Burleigh was all business. In September the Robins were in danger of falling out of the chase for the pennant. On the 24th, when Grimes was scheduled to take the mound against the Chicago Cubs, who had defeated Brooklyn the previous day, the sturdy pitcher addressed his teammates in the clubhouse. "This is what I have to say to you, fellas. This will be the toughest game you ever played in. Anybody who can't take it can get out now. Is that clear? You'll be thrown at, you'll be knocked down and they'll try to spike you. It's up to you to be ready."[12]

Brooklyn catcher Zack Taylor said it was the most harrowing day he spent in baseball. "I had a hunch what was coming, but I never thought it was going to be that rough. I figured Burleigh might throw at Grantham and at Hartnett because of the homers they had hit the day before, but I wasn't prepared when Grimes cut loose with the first pitch at the first Chicago hitter, a kid named Art Weis, who was just up from the Texas League. ... Bam! The first pitch sails past the kid's ears and he's in the dirt. ... I felt sorry for him. I didn't dare sympathize with him or Grimes might have come charging at me."[13] Weis was not the only Cub to hit the dirt that afternoon; they all did. Burleigh threw behind them and at their feet. When the opposing pitcher Grover Alexander came to the plate, Burleigh's pitch came in right behind Alexander's neck. "When Alex got up," Taylor said, "he had the strangest look on his face, like a person who finds himself locked in a room with a madman."[14]

Grimes won the game, 6-5. In the fifth inning he made one of the strangest plays ever seen at Ebbets Field. Weis was on third base when one of Burleigh's spitters broke into the dirt in front of home plate and caromed off Taylor's shin guards. Seeing the ball get past the catcher, the speedy Weis headed for home. Grimes was quickly off the mound. The ball rebounded in front of the plate and the spitballer scooped it up, dived for the plate, and tagged Weis just before he could score. Thus, Grimes made an unassisted putout on his own wild pitch.

Brooklyn did not win the pennant in 1924 but their second-place finish was the closest they would come for many years. Grimes led the league in innings pitched, tied his teammate Vance for the lead in complete games, and was second to Vance in both wins and strikeouts.

Grimes failed to win as many games as he lost during either of the next two years. The most memorable event of the 1925 season was one he would have preferred to forget. On September 22 in a 12-inning, 3-2 loss to the Chicago Cubs, Grimes pitched well enough but was woeful at the bat. In his first three trips to the plate he brought about seven outs, which matched the record for futility (responsibility for seven outs in three times at bat) set by Clarence Mitchell during Game Five of the 1920 World Series. Burleigh ended the third and sixth innings by hitting into double plays, and outdid that by hitting into a triple play in the eighth. With runners on first and third, Grimes grounded to the shortstop, who tossed to the second baseman, who rifled the ball to the first baseman, who heaved the ball home to catch the runner trying to score from third. That game was not indicative of the Wisconsin native's ability with the bat. The burly one was a good batter and was used occasionally as a pinch-hitter. Pinch-hitting one day, Grimes hit a double and moved to third on a groundout. The next batter hit a routine fly to the outfield. Grimes did not tag up and attempt to score. The next batter made the final out of the inning. Robbie raged at the pitcher, "Why didn't you tag up and score on that fly ball?" Heatedly, Grimes answered his manager, "Because I'm not a fast baserunner. You should have put in a pinch-runner for me. When you asked me to bat, I did and I got a hit. You should have replaced me then."[15] Robbie's biographers wrote that the battle raged on, down the clubhouse steps and into the locker room, each man cursing the other violently.

In 1926 Burleigh won 12 games and lost 13. On September 9 at Baker Bowl in Philadelphia, his teammates came off the bench in an amazing display of pinch-hitting to save Grimes another loss. Grimes had given up ten hits and was trailing, 5-1, after the sixth inning ended. In the seventh inning after Johnny Butler's double, three straight pinch-hitters—Zack Wheat, Jack Fournier, and Jerry Standaert—each singled to drive in two runs. The Phillies added another run in the bottom of the inning and went into the ninth leading 6-3. In the top of the final inning Butler led off with a double, and Dick Cox pinch-hit safely, driving in Butler. After Hank DeBerry popped out, Moose Clabaugh collected a pinch double. Then came three hits and two bases on balls, along with a groundout, and Cox came to bat for the second time in the inning. He hit another single, his second pinch hit of the inning and Brooklyn's sixth pinch hit of the game. Before the carnage was over the Dodgers had won the game 12-6, getting Grimes off the hook. (Under present rules Cox would be credited with only one pinch hit, as he would be considered batting for himself the second time around and would no longer be a pinch-hitter.)

Brooklyn's management thought that perhaps at the age of 33, Burleigh was losing his effectiveness. Besides, they were tired of constantly bickering over his salary. In a complicated deal that was consummated on January 9-10, 1927, the New York Giants obtained outfielder George Harper and catcher Walter "Butch" Henline from the Phillies in exchange for second baseman Fresco Thompson and pitcher Jack Scott. Henline was then traded to Brooklyn for Grimes. Before Philadelphia would give up Henline they insisted on getting pitcher Alex Ferguson from the Buffalo Bisons of the International League. The Phillies sent two players to Buffalo, the Giants agreed to option two players to the Bisons and the Robins agreed to do the same with a pitcher, these players to be named at the conclusion of spring training. Sportswriter James B. Harrison wrote that baseball men were inclined to agree that the Giants got the better of the deal.

Events proved the baseball men right. The spitballer signed a contract with the Giants for $15,000 a year, considered a rather good salary at the time. Grimes won 19 games, including 13 wins in a row, and lost only 8 during the 1927 season. He had the third best winning percentage of all National League pitchers and ranked fourth in strikeouts. He continued to ask and give no quarter. He snapped and snarled at his teammates if they failed to give their best. Once he came to blows with Rogers Hornsby in the clubhouse after a game, charging that the Rajah was bungling things in relaying McGraw's signals from the bench. But Ol' Stubblebeard rubbed McGraw the wrong way. The Little Napoleon's dictatorial methods and the fierce independence of the man from lumberjack country very likely were incompatible. At any rate the Giants benefited from Burleigh's spitball tosses for only one season.

On February 11, 1928, the Giants traded Grimes to Pittsburgh for pitcher Vic Aldridge in a straight player transaction, no cash or convoluted deals with other players involved. The newspapers said that the Pirates got the better of the deal. Once again the newspapers were right. The trade turned out to be much more lopsided than the scribes had predicted. In the remainder of his major-league career Aldridge was to win only four games while losing seven. On the other hand Grimes, at the age of 34, still had some of his best years ahead of him.

In 1928 Grimes won 25 games for Pittsburgh, leading the league in innings pitched and tying for the lead in wins. He also tied for first in complete games, had the second lowest opponents' on-base percentage in the circuit, and ranked fourth in strikeouts and in baserunners permitted per game.

In a July 20, 1929, game against the Giants, Grimes fired a fastball toward the plate. Bill Terry lined it back to the mound like a bullet. The smash was too hot to handle, but Grimes instinctively put up his hands. The ball struck the thumb of his pitching hand, then caromed off. Grimes picked up the ball and threw to first, then walked off the field. With 16 victories already under his belt, he had hoped to win 30 that year for the first time in his career. Those hopes were gone; he won only one more game in 1929. He finished the year with a record of 17-7 for a winning percentage of .708, third best in the league, and his earned-run average of 3.13 was second best in the NL. He had the fifth lowest opponents' batting average. Even so, it was not as good a year it would have been had Grimes avoided Terry's line drive.

In his early years Burleigh had relied so much on his spitter that Billy Evans feared he would not be nearly so effective if he was not allowed to continue using it after 1920.[16] As years went by Grimes developed a wide repertoire of pitches, all thrown with an almost straight overhand motion. He still faked a spitter on every pitch, of course, and threw a lot of spitters, but Burleigh had a live fastball for most of his career, developed a good curve, and had excellent control. He said, "The spitter, which has always been an ace in the hole for me, is supposed to be one reason for my success. No doubt it is. But the spitter has its drawbacks. When I'm pitching, I chew slippery elm all the time. I don't like it, but it's the only thing that I can chew that gives me satisfaction."[17] Most pitchers of that era had three pitches in their arsenal—fastball, curve, and change-up, called a slow ball in those days. The slider was thrown by only a few, among whom Burleigh Grimes was the most successful. Thus, Ol' Stubblebeard had five pitches in his assortment, even though he was starting to lose a little off his fastball by 1929. In addition, he had many years of experience. As he put it, "I haven't as much stuff as I used to have, but I'm a better pitcher. I know the batters. I know myself. I understand better what I can do myself and what the opposition is likely to do. A pitcher is like a good oak log. He needs seasoning. I work hard. I bear down all the time. ... I've hurt my arm more than once by exerting it. I've hurt it by throwing a fast ball. I've hurt it several times by throwing a spitter. Any ball will hurt your arm if you put everything you have behind it. But, after all, spitters and fast balls are easy deliveries compared with curve pitching."[18]

Responding to statement that at 36 he was growing old for a ballplayer, Grimes said: "They call me an old pitcher. Why should I be old? One of these physical culture experts told me that a man reached his prime, in physical strength, at thirty, but declined very little until he was forty or older. That's my schedule. ... I weigh 190 pounds, in condition. During the season I lose perhaps ten pounds. ... At season's end I'm a little stale, a little tired. So I go to a camp I have up in Wisconsin, where I spend the winter. I tramp miles every day in the snow with my gun. I breathe crisp, frosty air many hours out of the twenty-four. I eat a lot of wholesome, well-cooked food. I go to bed early and sleep like a badger in a burrow. And next season I'm fit for whatever deviltry the batters can invent."[19]

For two years with Pittsburgh, Grimes was arguably the best pitcher in the league, but after the thumb injury he was not quite the same again. He still had a few good years left, however, even if they did not match his seasons of greatness. Grimes and the Pirates were unable to agree on terms for a 1930 contract. The pitcher demanded a two-year contract at $20,000 per year. Club president Barney Dreyfuss announced that club policy was against giving more than a one-year contract to any player. Grimes replied that unless Dreyfuss gave him the salary he wanted, he would ask to be traded or sold. "If he turns me down I will spend this year hunting and fishing in Wisconsin."[20] On April 9, 1930, the Pirates traded Grimes to the Boston Braves for pitcher Percy Jones and an undisclosed amount of cash. The left-handed Jones won nary a game for Pittsburgh and disappeared from the major-league scene. Grimes did not fare well in Beantown. Although he won his first game for the Braves by a 13-4 score over Philadelphia on April 27, he won only two more games for Boston. He was hit on the ankle by a line drive and was placed on the invalid list for a while. On June 16 the Braves sent Lord Burleigh to St. Louis in return for hurlers Fred Frankhouse and Bill Sherdel, a former spitball pitcher who had long since given up the moist delivery. This trade worked wonders for Grimes, as he compiled a 13-6 record with the Cardinals, giving him a total of 16 wins for the year.

Best of all, the trade to the Cardinals gave him another shot at the World Series, an opportunity he had devoutly wished for. As he had told F.C. Lane in his lengthy interview the previous year. "I hope before I hang up my uniform for the last time, that I can pitch at least one more World Series game. I got a taste of the Big Series back there in 1920. But they told me afterwards that the Cleveland coaches tipped off the batters (about when the spitball was coming) when I was in the box. At that, I pitched at least one pretty good game against them, but I didn't cover myself with any glory. Now I'm older and a bit wiser and I think I'd make a better record. At least I'd like the chance to try."[21]

Grimes got his chance for glory in the 1930 World Series. According to Grantland Rice, Gabby Street, the Cardinals manager, picked Lord Burleigh to pitch the opening game against Philadelphia "[B]ecause the Athletics don't see much spitball pitching during the season and Faber of the White Sox always gives them trouble.... The A's are more concerned about Burleigh Grimes than anyone else. Grimes is a strong money pitcher, and he is a spitball pitcher when few are left."[22]

In the opener, Grimes held the hard-hitting Athletics to only five safeties, but two of their hits were home runs. Al Simmons and Mickey Cochrane each connected for a round-tripper and the Mackmen, behind Lefty Grove, prevailed, 5-2. Grimes had another chance in the Game Five. This time he matched up with George Earnshaw in one of the great pitching duels of all time. Inning after inning the two fought in a scoreless deadlock. According to John Drebinger, writing in the *New York Times*, "Throughout the struggle, Grimes tormented the A's unmercifully. Every time Mickey Cochrane came up, Burleigh would stick his thumbs in his ears and wiggle his fingers, admittedly a rather inelegant thing to do to a man whose ears protruded slightly. When Simmons came up he mimicked Al's mannerism of flecking dust from his shirt and trousers. For Foxx he saved the gesture of a man feeling his throat in a moment of great fright. Cochrane was furious, but the more good-natured Foxx gave his comrades the last laugh. In the ninth inning, with Mickey on base, Jimmy blasted a tremendous home run into the left-field bleachers."[23] Grimes lost the game, 2-0. In his two World Series starts (1920 and 1930) Ol' Stubblebeard had pitched two complete games, giving up five hits in each game, and had two losses to show for it.

Few men ever hated to lose more than Grimes did, yet Drebinger wrote: "But no sooner had he hopped into his street clothes than Grimes confounded the Athletics by jauntily breezing into their dressing room to make his peace with them. He assured them that now the battle was over he had meant nothing personal by his tactics and even offered to go on a vaudeville tour with Cochrane, Simmons, and Foxx."[24]

In 1931 Lord Burleigh won 17 games and lost only seven as he helped the Cardinals win another flag. The Redbirds again faced the mighty Philadelphia Athletics in the World Series. Connie Mack's team of powerful sluggers were favored to win their third straight fall classic, something that had not yet been accomplished since the Series was inaugurated in 1903. Lefty Grove, the dominant pitcher of the times, defeated the Cardinals in the first game, but Bill Hallahan evened the series by shutting out the Athletics, 2-0, in the second game. Burleigh was Gabby Street's choice to start the third game and he went up against Grove, a 31-game winner who had led the American League in wins, winning percentage, earned-run average, strikeouts, and almost every other pitching category. Grimes pitched a two-hit masterpiece, giving up two runs in the ninth inning on a home run by Al Simmons, and winning the game, 5-2. He even contributed two runs batted in to the cause. Earnshaw came back with a two-hit shutout in the fourth game to even the Series at two games apiece. Hallahan won his second game for the Cardinals, 5-1, and Grove won his second, 8-1, to give each team three victories. The world championship was riding on the seventh game.

In the deciding game of the Series, Grimes was again matched up with Earnshaw and turned in one of the gutsiest performances in the history of baseball. During the final weeks of the season, the ex-lumberjack's appendix had become inflamed, but he refused to take time off for an operation. As Game Seven of the 1931 World Series progressed, the appendix began acting up. He took more and more time between pitches. Ice packs were applied between innings. He was obviously pitching in great pain, but he was pitching brilliantly. He shut out the Athletics for eight innings. Going into the ninth, the Cardinals had a 4-0 lead. Grimes lost the first batter, Al Simmons, with a base on balls. Then Foxx fouled out, and Bing Miller forced Simmons at second base. Ol' Stubblebeard had to get only one more out to register a five-hit shutout and bring the world's championship to the banks of the Mississippi. Pitching in intense pain and showing it in every gesture, Grimes could not finish the job. A walk and two hits plated two runs and left the tying runs on base. Street brought in Hallahan, Wild Bill induced Max Bishop to lift a fly to center fielder Pepper Martin for the final out, and the championship belonged to the Cardinals. Grimes shared with Hallahan and Martin the role of star of the series. The veteran spitballer's two wins avenged his unfortunate losses in previous classics.

Despite Burleigh's heroism, he was expendable. The Cardinals were overstocked with pitchers and needed to make room for Dizzy Dean, the sensational young pitcher who had been burning up the Texas League. On December 11, 1931, St. Louis dealt Grimes to the Chicago Cubs for outfielder Hack Wilson and pitcher Bud Teachout. According to the Associated Press, in acquiring Grimes the Cubs obtained the one pitcher who had ruined more games for them than any other two pitchers combined in the National League.

Grantland Rice wrote: "When Burleigh Grimes rounds into form and begins pitching his spitter across the plate with all the fire and pugnacity of a veteran gamester, the Chicagoans will have still more to rave about. Grimes has always been an eyeful. He pleases the new men in the game because he has the stuff, and he's a favorite of the oldsters because he still sees a baseball game as a hard, zestful fight. He's been all over the circuit, but once the game starts he pitches to win, no matter what team he happens to be boosting. Incidentally, while Grimes has been pictured as passing into the shadows every year for the last half-dozen, it is true that of the four exponents of the famous spitball delivery, which was scotched some time ago, Grimes is the youngest. Clarence Mitchell, Red Faber, and Jack Quinn, all still active, are older than Grimes."[25]

Grimes won his first start for the Cubs, 12-5, on May 8, 1932, but never had a winning season in Chicago, posting a 6-11 record in 1932 and a 3-6 mark in a portion of the 1933 season. On July 30, 1933, the veteran spitballer was released by the Cubs and signed the next day by the Cardinals. He lost his first start on this, his second tour with St. Louis, on August 9. He lasted only one-third of an inning, giving up five runs (four earned) to the Cubs in the brief stint. Hampered by injuries, he pitched in only 13 2/3 innings for the Cardinals in 1933 and was involved in no more decisions.

By the spring of 1934 it was clear that the major-league career of one Burleigh Grimes was winding down. But the old spitballer was not yet ready to hang up his spikes. Nor were all clubs ready to give up on him quite yet. The Cardinals released him on May 15, Two weeks later he signed with the New York Yankees for his first venture into the American League. He appeared in only ten games for the Bronx Bombers, winning one and losing two. The Yankees released him on August 8. Three days later Grimes was signed by Pittsburgh for his third tour of duty with the Pirates. He pitched for the last time in the major leagues on September 20, 1934, in relief of Waite Hoyt in a 2-1 loss to the Dodgers at Ebbets Field. Grimes was 41 years old when he threw his last pitch in the majors. Available records do not show whether it was a spitball.

After his major-league playing career ended, Grimes remained active in baseball for another 35 years.

In 1935 Branch Rickey wanted Grimes to be the playing manager of the Cardinals' farm team at Bloomington, Illinois, in the Class B Three-I League. A problem developed as Rickey and the Bloomington officials wanted Grimes to pitch, using his spitball, as well as manage. John Butler, manager of the Decatur club, withheld his consent to use of the spitball until April 1. As soon as Butler relented, Grimes was appointed manager. As a pitcher Grimes had a record of ten wins and five losses, while as a manager he led the Bloomers to the league championship.

His success in the Three-I League earned Grimes a promotion to the Cardinals' top farm club, Louisville of the American Association. The Colonels finished seventh in 1936, Burleigh's only year with the club. On October 2, 1936, he was in the Polo Grounds watching Game Two of the World Series between the Yankees and Giants when Tony Lazzeri hammered a Dick Coffman fastball for a home run with the bases loaded. Ol' Stubblebeard no longer held the unenviable distinction of being the only pitcher to yield a World Series grand slam. On that same day, Grimes was approached by officers of the Brooklyn club to see if he would be interested in managing the Dodgers.

Grimes accepted the job. He was back in the major leagues, back in Brooklyn. The Dodgers were no longer the Daffiness Boys of the 1920s, but they had much less natural talent. They had finished in seventh place in 1936 under Casey Stengel, who was fired at the end of the season. They showed little improvement under their new manager, finishing in sixth place in 1937 and seventh in 1938. If they did not win, it was not for lack of trying by the manager. Grimes fought with the umpires, with his coaches, and with his players. The Dodger ownership brought in Babe Ruth, ostensibly as a coach, in reality as a box-office attraction. The Bambino entertained the crowds with hitting mammoth home runs in batting practice, but Grimes thought the Babe was derelict in his duties as a first-base coach. Tom Meany told a story about Burleigh's encounter with a young pitcher who had a great fastball but had not achieved much success with the Dodgers. Grimes decided the reason for the kid's failures was that he tended to give up on himself whenever he was in a jam. When Burleigh shared his opinion with the hurler, the young man became indignant. He started to say to the 43-year-old manager, "Why, if you weren't such an old man…"[26] He never finished the sentence as Burleigh's fist connected with his mouth. Grimes lasted two years with the Dodgers.

In 1939 Grimes was back in Double-A ball, managing the Montreal Royals of the International League. Another season, another seventh-place finish.

Grimes stepped down a few rungs on the ladder of Organized Baseball in 1940, clear down to the Class C Michigan State League where he took the helm of the Grand Rapids Dodgers. While in this league, his natural combativeness got the best of him on one occasion when the old spitballer apparently spat in the wrong place. On July 31 he became engaged in a shouting match with home-plate umpire Robert Williams over a close call. According to Williams, Grimes spat in the umpire's face. Burleigh was ejected from the game and suspended by the league for a full season. After several months of testimony and investigation by the National Association of Professional Baseball Leagues and some intervention by Commissioner Kenesaw M. Landis, Grimes's penalty was reduced to the remainder of the 1940 season.

The problems in the Michigan State League did not end Grimes's managerial career. From 1942 through 1946 he was back in the International League—with Toronto from 1942 through 1945 and with Rochester in 1945 and 1946, before finishing that season with Triple-A Kansas City. His Maple Leafs won the pennant in 1943 and finished third in 1944. All of his other International League clubs of the 1940s ended up in the second division. In 1948 Grimes managed the Independence Yankees in the Class D KOM (Kansas, Oklahoma, Missouri) League for part of the season. In 1952 and 1953 he again managed the Toronto Maple Leafs. This was his third time in the International League, and it met with moderate success, the Leafs posting identical 78-76 records in the two seasons he held the managerial reins.

From 1947 to 1952 Grimes scouted for the New York Yankees. In 1955 he was a coach with the Kansas City Athletics. He scouted for the A's in 1956 and 1957. From 1960 to 1971 he scouted for the Baltimore Orioles, relinquishing this assignment at the age of 77.

Even before Grimes retired from baseball, he spent some of his offseason time farming.. He had invested his savings from his baseball salary in farmland, first in Ohio and then in Missouri. Grimes was a hard-nosed negotiator with his baseball employers, which sometimes led to his being traded away, but also led to his making a higher salary than most players of his era. As a rookie, he earned $2,600. By the time of his retirement he was reported to be making $25,000 a year, among the highest salaries in baseball.

Grantland Rice wrote that Grimes had given midwinter interviews at his flourishing farm near New Haven, Missouri, just west of St. Louis in Franklin County, where members of the Corps of Discovery had received land grants after completing the Lewis and Clark Expedition. According to Rice, Burleigh's Oriental rugs and grand piano were not what one would find in a typical farmhouse parlor.[27] His 230-acre stock farm was operated by six farmhands. For recreation, there were sleek saddle horses, a pony for the children of the farm workers, and a trained horse, Crystal Lady, that could waltz, march, and do other circus tricks. Later Grimes raised horses, mules, and prize hogs, and farmed 545 rich acres near Trenton, in north central Missouri, where he lived with his third wife, Inez, in a large ranch-type house with one room devoted to his baseball souvenirs. He built his house facing away from the blacktop road and looking down across the fields to the Thompson Fork of the Grand River. Although his neighbors were aware of his reputation from his baseball days as a rough and tough character, they found him to be a very nice man, and he was well liked in the neighborhood. One neighbor said she never heard an unkind word said about him.[28] In the 1940s the local high school built a new baseball field and named it Burleigh Grimes Field in honor of the old spitballer.

When Grimes returned to northwestern Wisconsin, his hometown honored him by naming an athletic field in his honor and placing a sign at city limits proudly proclaiming Clear Lake to be the home of Burleigh Grimes. Best of all he shares with statesman Gaylord Nelson the distinction of having a special room in the village's historical museum. Among the many items on display in the room is a letter from Richard Nixon on White House stationery informing Grimes that the president had included him on his all-time team.

In 1964 Burleigh Grimes and Red Faber became the first two grandfathered spitballers to be elected to the National Baseball Hall of Fame in Cooperstown, New York. As Faber was the best exempted spitballer in the American League and Grimes the best in the National, it seems altogether fitting that they were the first of their ilk to be enshrined in the Hall and that both were inducted in the same year. In contrast to Faber, who pitched every one of his 4,086 2/3 major-league innings for the Chicago White Sox, Grimes toiled for seven different teams during his 19 years in "The Show."

Ol' Stubblebeard was married five times. In 1913 he married Florence Ruth van Patten in Memphis. They were divorced in 1930, following a series of court battles. Grimes filed suit for divorce on Christmas Eve 1929 in Canton, Ohio, charging that Florence interfered with his profession by accompanying him to spring-training camps in violation of league rules. The judge ordered Grimes to pay temporary alimony of $200 per month until a hearing on the divorce petition was held. After a long trial the divorce was denied in the spring of 1930. In October Florence sued Burleigh for divorce, claiming that he was cruel, displayed no affection, and received endearing and passionate letters from other women. This time the divorce was granted. In 1931 Grimes married Laura Virginia (surname unknown). This marriage lasted until 1939. In 1940 he wed Inez Margarete Martin, who died in 1964 after 24 years of wedlock. In 1965 Grimes married Zerita Brickell, widow of his former Pirate teammate Fred Brickell. She died in 1974. On October 17, 1974, the 81-year-old Grimes married 48-year-old Lillian Gosselin Meyer. There were no children from any of these marriages.

On December 6, 1985, at the age of 92, Grimes died at Clear Lake, Wisconsin, after a long struggle with cancer. His survivors included his wife, Lillian, and a brother. Memorial services were held in St. Barnabas Episcopal Church in Clear Lake. Grimes is buried in a cemetery in Clear Lake under a stone that includes a small Hall of Fame symbol.

Sources

This account is adapted from the chapter on Burleigh Grimes in Charles F. Faber and Richard B. Faber, *Spitballers: The Last Legal Hurlers of the Wet One* (Jefferson, North Carolina: McFarland, 2006).

In addition to the sources cited in the text and endnotes, the following friends of Burleigh Grimes were helpful to the writer through personal correspondence or interviews: Loma Hurst, John Rice, and Evelyn Trinkle.

Also useful were:

Faber, Charles F., *Baseball Ratings: The All-Time Best Players at each Position 1876 to the Present* (Jefferson, North Carolina: McFarland, 2006).

Palmer, Pete, and Gary Gillette, *The Baseball Encyclopedia*, (Mew York: Barnes and Noble, 2004).

Milwaukee Journal Sentinel

ancestry.com

baseball-reference.com

Notes

1. F.C. Lane, "The Ace of National League Hurlers," *Baseball Magazine,* October 1929, 76.
2. Lee Allen and Tom Meany, *Kings of the Diamond: The Immortals in the Hall of Fame* (New York: Putnam, 1965), 72.
3. *New York Times,* December 10, 1985.
4. Steve Gelman, *The Greatest Dodgers of Them All* (New York: Penguin Books, 1992), 60.
5. Charles F. Faber and Richard B. Faber, *Spitballers: The Last Legal Hurlers of the Wet One* (Jefferson, North Carolina: McFarland, 2006), 35.
6. Anthony J. Connor, *Baseball for the Love of It* (New York: Macmillan, 1982), 54.
7. Gelman, Op. cit.
8. Gelman, 81.
9. Ibid.
10. *The Sporting News*, February 3, 1921.
11. Gelman, 61.
12. Tom Meany, B*aseball's Greatest Pitchers* (New York: Barnes, 1951), 75-76.
13. Meany, 76.
14. Meany, 76.
15. Jack Kavanagh and Norman Macht, *Uncle Robbie* (Cleveland: Society for American Baseball Research, 1999), 159-160.
16. *The Sporting News*, February 3, 1921.
17. Lane.
18. Ibid.
19. Ibid.
20. *Chicago Tribune*, March 23, 1930.
21. Lane..
22. *Los Angeles Times*, September 30, 1930.
23. *New York Times,* December 10, 1931.
24. Ibid.
25. *Los Angeles Times*, May 19, 1932.
26. Meany, 84.
27. *New York Times,* December 22, 1933.
28. Evelyn Trimble, personal interview with Charles F. Faber, July 2, 2004.

Jesse Haines

By Gregory H. Wolf

The only St. Louis Cardinal to play on the first five National League pennant winners in franchise history (1926, 1928, 1930, 1931, 1934), Jesse "Pop" Haines was a 26-year-old "rookie" when he debuted for the Redbirds in 1920. He was a three-time 20-game winner and pitched for the Cardinals for 18 consecutive seasons before retiring at the end of the 1937 season at the age of 44 as the big leagues' oldest player. With 210 wins, he was elected by the Veterans Committee to the Baseball Hall of Fame in 1970.

Jesse Joseph Haines was born on July 22, 1893, in Clayton, Ohio, near Dayton, the youngest of the five children of Elias and Althea Haines. Five years later his father, an auctioneer and carpenter, moved the family to a farm in Phillipsburg, five miles from Clayton. For the remainder of his life, Jesse called the small Midwestern town home. "I played baseball from the time I can remember," Haines said. "[We] played with a hard rubber ball, a dime bat, and a quarter glove."[1] Haines pitched on his grammar school team, quit school after the eighth grade in 1907 to become a well driller with his oldest brother, and started to pitch for the town team in Phillipsburg, the All-Stars. "I had ambitions to become a professional," said Haines."[2] All big leaguers were heroes. We collected those little cards with pictures of ballplayers on them," he recalled. "Those cards were about the only way we ever got to see what a player looked like."[3] Raised by "honest, wholesome, God-fearing" parents who objected to playing baseball on the Sabbath, Jesse hid his uniform in a neighbor's corncrib to pursue his passion.[4] In Dayton, about 20 miles southeast of Phillipsburg, the fair-skinned, blond-haired Haines played semiprofessionally for Standard and later National Cash Register in 1912, and then for Lily Brew in 1913 when he was invited to pitch one game (a ten-inning, complete-game loss) for the Dayton Veterans of the Class B Central League.

In his first full season of professional baseball in 1914, the 21-year-old Jess, as he was known during his playing career, embarked on a grueling and frustrating six-year odyssey which included injuries and league closings with stops at at least eight minor-league teams, tryouts with major-league clubs, and a return to semipro ball before securing a permanent spot on the St. Louis Cardinals in 1920.

Used mostly as a reliever in 1934, Haines won 20 games three times earlier in his career and pitched a no-hitter in 1924. He was elected to the Hall of Fame in 1970.

Signed by player-manager Harry Martin of the Fort Wayne Railroaders in the Class B Central League for a salary of $135 per month in 1914, Haines pitched just twice before breaking his finger in batting practice.[5] Shunted off to the Saginaw Ducks in the Class C Southern Michigan League, Jess won 17 games, logged 258 innings and led the Ducks to the league title by pitching a ten-inning complete game in the final of the championship series.[6] "In the minor leagues you were lucky to get paid at all," said Haines, whose salary dropped to $115 per month with the Ducks.[7] "But I wanted to play so badly that the salary meant but little to me."⁸ Back with Saginaw in 1915, Haines got off to a good start and tossed a no-hitter against the Flint Vehicles in June.⁹ When the league disbanded on June 29, Haines was signed by the Detroit Tigers. On the Tigers roster for two months but not seeing action in an official game, Haines was strictly a batting-practice pitcher and may have suffered from diphtheria, causing weakness.¹⁰ Frustrated by his lack of playing time, Haines often credited Ty Cobb with giving him inspiration to forge ahead with his career. "Say, kid, you've got something on that fastball. It's hard to follow and some day they're going to reading about you," the Georgia Peach reportedly told him.¹¹

Expecting an invitation to the Tigers' spring training in 1916, Haines was disappointed to be assigned to the Springfield (Illinois) Reapers in the Central League. He won 23 games for Springfield, prompting rumors that he'd be called up to the Tigers. In the offseason he was sent to the Denver Bears of the Class A Western League, but was unexpectedly returned to Springfield to start the 1917 season.¹² Described as a "star pitcher" by *Sporting Life*, Haines notched 19 wins in 1917, but found himself in limbo again when the league folded at the end of the season.

Haines may have experienced his most taxing season in professional baseball in 1918. Signing with the Topeka Kaw-nees of the Class A Western League (the team relocated during the season 170 miles to the southwest in Hutchinson, Kansas, and was known as the Salt Packers), Haines pitched for Johnny Nee, his former manager during his one-game career with Dayton in 1913. With a 12-4 record in midseason, Haines was purchased by the Cincinnati Reds. He reported to manager Christy Mathewson's team and made his major-league debut against the Boston Braves on July 20 at Redland Field. In relief of Pete Schneider with bases loaded and no outs in the fifth inning, Haines put out the fire and surrendered five hits and one run over five innings in an 8-3 defeat.

Released by the Reds shortly after his promising debut, Haines returned to Phillipsburg and contemplated quitting baseball. George Textor, player-manager of Agathon Central Steel, a semipro team in Massillon, Ohio, persuaded Haines to join his team.¹³ An "unconquerable twirler" for Agathon, Haines parlayed his success into a contract with the Tulsa Oilers in the Class A Western League. With an unsightly 5-9 record and 4.19 ERA, he was sold by Tulsa in midseason to the Kansas City Blues of the Double-A American Association. Haines won 21 of 26 decisions in a remarkable turnaround to his season, indeed his career. The "best pitcher" in the league,¹⁴ Haines drew the interest of a number of big-league teams despite breaking his ankle against Indianapolis on September 4.¹⁵

"St. Louis Put Over the Real Big Deals," reported *The Sporting News* about the Cardinals acquisition of Haines.¹⁶ The perpetually cash-strapped Redbirds, who had enjoyed just three winning seasons since 1900, were a team in transition at that time. Branch Rickey took over as manager of the club in 1919 and borrowed $10,000 from local banks to take a chance on Haines. Stepping down as team president in 1920 when Sam Breadon purchased majority ownership in the team, Rickey remained at the helm but realized that the Cardinals could never compete financially with the richer teams. Consequently, he developed baseball's first farm system, and Jess Haines was the last player he ever bought.

Though Haines is remembered as a knuckleball pitcher, he began his career as a fastball-curveball pitcher. In his first start with the Cardinals, on April 17, 1920, the 26-year-old rookie held the Pittsburgh Pirates scoreless for 12 innings at Robison Field in St. Louis before giving up three runs in the 13th inning and losing the game, 3-0. He won the first of his 210 games for the Cardinals on May 6 when he shut out the Reds in St. Louis. (The Cardinals moved to Sportsman's Park on July 1, 1920.) Durable, the big, 6-foot, 190-pound Haines, started 37 games, completed 19, and led the NL with 47 appearances. "Hard-luck Haines" concluded the season with his career-high 20th loss in an epic duel with Pete Alexander at Cubs Park in Chicago on October 1. After surrendering two runs in the first five innings, Haines tossed 9 2/3 consecutive no-hit innings (from the seventh to the 16th) before giving up a one-out run in the 17th to lose, 3-2. Alexander pitched a career-best 17-inning complete-game to earn the victory. Haines finished the season with a career-high 301 2/3 innings for the 75-79 Cardinals.

"I soon found out I would have to have something [besides a fastball and curve], if I wanted to stick around long," said Haines, who followed up his promising rookie year by going 18-12 in 1921 and 11-9 in 1922 with an ERA slightly above league average each season.[17] With his fastball losing effectiveness and his hits per nine innings steadily rising, Haines began working on a knuckle ball. He credited Philadelphia A's pitcher, Eddie Rommel, the first big leaguer to use the knuckleball extensively, for teaching him the pitch. Unlike Rommel, who gripped the pitch with tips of his index and middle fingers, Haines gripped the ball with the first knuckles on his index and middle fingers with the ball resting against the inside of his ring finger.[18] The result was a hard knuckler that came straight down and did not flutter like Rommel's. "[My knuckler] acted like a spitball," said Haines. "I had very good control of it and threw it from different positions."[19] Even though Haines developed calluses on his knuckles because of the friction the ball caused, his knuckles had a tendency to bleed.

Adding the knuckleball to his pitching arsenal in 1923, Haines had his best season to that point. After finishing in third place in 1921 and tied for third in 1922, the Cardinals slipped to fifth at 79-74 in '23, but it was no fault of Haines. He led the team in wins (20), innings (266), complete games (23), and ERA (3.11). He celebrated his 30th birthday by shutting out the Reds on four hits en route to completing 11 of his next 16 starts and winning ten of them.

The Cardinals and Haines took sudden and unexpected steps backward in 1924. Despite a potent offense with Jim Bottomley and Rogers Hornsby (who batted .424), the Redbirds limped to a sixth-place, 65-89 record primarily due to poor pitching. In 31 starts Haines won just 8 games, lost 19, and notched a 4.41 ERA, well over the league average. Teams batted .309 against him. The following season, on a better Cardinals team, Haines won 13 of 27 decisions but his ERA rose to 4.57, and he started just 25 times.

Ironically, Haines pitched his only big-league no-hitter during his worst season. On July 17, 1924, he held the Boston Braves hitless at Sportsman's Park in a 5-0 win. It was the first no-hitter in St. Louis baseball history since George Washington Bradley pitched the first one for the St. Louis Brown Stockings in 1876, the inaugural season of the National League. "I had almost perfect control," said Haines of his game. "There was nothing special about my speed. I started as I always do — trying the corners with my curve on the outside to right-handed hitters and keeping the fast one close to the handle of the bat."[20]

A quiet, conscientious, humble, and serious person, Haines neither smoked nor drank, and eschewed the night life. He preferred life in the small town to the hustle and bustle of the big city. During the offseason, he lived with his wife, Carrie (Weidner) Haines, a Phillipsburg resident whom he married in 1915. They had one child, a daughter, Juetta Lou, born in 1925. For many years, Haines operated an auto garage with one of his brothers.

Easygoing off the field, Haines was described as a "clean sportsman, who has never taken advantage of a rival batter with an intimidating cranial shot."[21] But he was also a fiery and fierce competitor who took losing hard. Throughout his career, he was known for chewing out teammates for mental lapses, careless throwing errors, or a perceived lackadaisical approach to the game. Haines's hard-nosed attitude, his dedication to the game, and his desire to win impressed the equally competitive Hornsby, who took over the helm of the Cardinals in 1925 when Rickey was replaced as the field manager after 38 games.

By 1926 sportswriters and fans began to wonder whether the 32-year-old Haines had lost it. His fastball lacked zip, his knuckleball vanished, and he was no longer considered the staff ace.[22] But Hornsby was committed to Haines and named him to start the second game of the season, at home against the Pirates on April 14. When Pirates catcher Earl Smith hit a liner back to the mound leading off the third inning, it hit Haines on the instep near his right ankle. Haines fell to the ground, was removed from the game, and the team feared his ankle was broken. X-rays proved negative, but Haines pitched sporadically over the next nine weeks with only one start and 11 relief appearances. Led by Flint Rhem and Bill Sherdel, the Cardinals remained in the pennant race and were tied with the Pirates a half-game behind the Reds when Haines rejoined the starting rotation on June 19. In a dramatic return, Haines shut out the Braves on seven hits. Over the next three months he anchored the Cardinals' staff and was arguably the hottest pitcher in the NL, posting 10 wins and completing 13 of 18 starts with three shutouts in one of the best stretches of his career. After a nerve-racking race with the Pirates and Reds, the Cardinals, who played their final 24 games on the road, captured their first pennant despite losing five of their last seven games.

Haines attributed his new-found success and rebirth in 1926 to two pitches. "Thought I had [the knuckler] in 1923, but it eluded me the next years. Not until midsummer 1926 did the mystery of it come back to me," he said. "And then I started to throw a slow ball. That helped me as much as the knuckler."[23]

Haines's pitching in the 1926 World Series against the overwhelming favorite New York Yankees has been overshadowed by Babe Ruth's baserunning blunder (he was caught stealing in the ninth inning of Game Seven of a 3-2 game to end the Series) and by Pete Alexander's dominating performance (two complete-game victories, and his famous save in Game Seven). After pitching an inning of scoreless relief in Game One, Haines limited the Bronx Bombers, blanked only three times during the regular season, to just five singles in a dominating shutout in Game Three, wining 4-0. In the fourth inning, Haines belted a two-out, two-run homer, his first since 1920, and one of four in his career. Given the start in Game Seven, Haines held the Yankees to two runs over 6 2/3 innings. With his knuckles bleeding so profusely that he had a difficult time gripping the ball, Haines surrendered eight hits and issued five walks before giving way (with the bases full) to Alexander, who preserved Haines's victory for the Cardinals' first World Series championship.

With a cerebral approach to pitching, Haines altered his pitching motion and delivery as he aged. When he pitched semipro ball in Massillon, his delivery was described a "deceptive" and his pitches were faster than they seemed.[24] "I was wild for years," said Haines, "wilder than Bill Hallahan ever was" (referring to his Cardinals teammate nicknamed Wild Bill[25]). Haines was a strict overhand pitcher when he arrived in St. Louis, but Rickey suggested he alter his motion to overcome bouts of wildness.[26] Consequently, he began to pitch side-arm to three-quarters. His short, rhythmic delivery put little stress on his shoulder and arm, and undoubtedly helped him play until after his 44th birthday.

The world champions experienced a tumultuous offseason. Hornsby, involved in a contract dispute, was traded in late December to the New York Giants for second baseman Frankie Frisch and pitcher Jimmy Ring. Haines held out, demanding a "substantial increase in salary," reportedly a $5,000 increase to $12,500.[27] After signing in time to participate in spring training in Avon Park, Florida, the 33-year-old began the season by tossing a two-hit shutout against the Cubs in Chicago, and won his first five starts, all complete games. Haines led the league with 25 complete games and six shutouts (both career bests), and was used only twice in relief all season. On three occasions he tossed extra-inning complete-game victories (13 innings against the Cubs on June 21 and the Reds on September 26, and 11 innings against the Pirates on August 12) en route to 300 2/3 innings. He also set personal bests with 24 wins and a 2.72 ERA. With the 40-year-old Alexander (21-10), Haines formed the most formidable pitching duo in the NL, but it was not enough to overcome the Pirates, who won the pennant by 1 1/2 games over the Redbirds.

Under new manager, Bill McKechnie (the team's fourth different Opening Day skipper in as many years), the Cardinals got off to a slow start (10-11) in 1928 before the offense, led by MVP Bottomley (31 HRs, 136 RBIs, .325 BA) and Chick Hafey (27, 111, .337), woke up. Continuing his success from 1927, Haines hurled ten complete games in his first 12 starts. By the end of July it appeared as though the Redbirds would run away with the pennant, but after a poor August (14-13) they were in a tight race with the New York Giants, who went 25-8 during September. At his best when the Cardinals needed him the most, Haines pitched complete games to win his last eight starts and help lead the Cardinals to their second pennant. Completing 20 of 28 starts, Haines won 20 games and notched a 3.18

ERA. In a rematch of the 1926 World Series, the Yankees swept the Cardinals, defeating 21-game-winner Bill Sherdel in Games One and Four, Alexander in Game Two, and Haines in Game Three. Given a two-run lead after one frame, Haines surrendered a towering solo home run to Lou Gehrig in the second inning and then a two-run inside-the-park home run to him in the fourth. Haines was undone by two errors by his catcher that led to three unearned runs in the sixth inning, and departed after six innings having surrendered six hits and three walks during a 7-3 defeat.

Haines's 1929 season was a study in contrasts. A complete-game win against the Reds on May 20 gave him his 14th consecutive win over two seasons. Notching his ninth victory of the season on June 22, Haines appeared headed to a third consecutive 20-win season, but then encountered the worst slump of his career. He won just four more times, posted an unfathomable 8.00 ERA over his final 84 1/3 innings, lost control of his knuckleball and his spot in the rotation. The Cardinals pitching staff, the oldest in the major leagues, fell apart. Sherdel (10-15, 5.93), Haines (13-10, 5.71), and Alexander (9-8, 3.89) seemed to be on their last legs. In disarray all season, with three different skippers, the reigning pennant winner finished in fourth place.

By the start of the 1930 season, newspapers began making more references to Haines's age. "[Haines] has gone rapidly downhill" said an Associated Press report;[28] "[Haines] slip[s] out of star class," announced another headline.[29] Gabby Street, the Cardinals' fifth different Opening Day skipper in the last six years, still had confidence in his 36-year-old starter. Given five or more days of rest in 15 of his 24 starts, Haines rebounded to post 13 wins (tied with 36-year-old spitballer Burleigh Grimes, a newcomer to the Cardinals and his roommate, for second on the team) and led the team with 14 complete games. Sluggish almost the entire season, the Cardinals caught fire, going 44-13 the last two months of the season. In fourth place on Labor Day, 6 1/2 games out of first, they overtook the Cubs, Brooklyn Robins, and Giants in the final two weeks of the season in an exciting four-team race. Reminiscent of 1928, Haines pitched his best at the most crucial time of the season, winning his last six decisions (in seven starts). Haines enjoyed his final dramatic moment on the national stage against Connie Mack's heavily favored Philadelphia Athletics in Game Four of the World Series in St. Louis. Facing Lefty Grove, the era's best pitcher, with the Cardinals down two games to one, the big right-hander tossed a complete-game four-hitter (all singles). In the third inning Haines tied the game with an RBI single in the remarkable 3-1 victory. However, three days later, the A's won Game Six to claim their second consecutive championship.

Throughout his career, Haines was a fast worker on the mound. His victories over Grove and the A's and his shutout of the Yankees in 1926 lasted just 1:41. "You get the heebie-jeebies if you are out on the mound too long," said Haines, who rarely had discussions with his catcher during a game. "When you take too long pitching, you think about pitching one way and then change your mind. And then you end up not doing it either way you planned."[30]

Three weeks in the thermal waters at Hot Springs, Arkansas, prior to camp must have worked wonders on Haines's creaking body. He began the 1931 season by winning five of his first six starts with four complete games. But when he was hit in the right wrist on June 9 by a line drive from the Robins' Babe Herman, he missed a month. Returning to the starting rotation on July 10, he won six of eight starts, including two shutouts and four complete games, and notched an impressive 1.65 ERA in 60 innings, enabling the Cardinals to run away with the pennant. He won 12 of 15 decisions, but his season, indeed his career, took a drastic turn when he injured his right shoulder on September 5 against the Pirates. Out for the remainder of the season and missing the Cardinals' stunning upset of the heavily favored A's in the World Series, Haines was never the same after the injury. It was his last season as predominantly a starter.

Haines's shoulder injury appeared to signal the end of his career. He logged just 85 1/3 innings in 1932 in 20 appearances (10 starts) and struggled. But he returned in 1933 and transformed himself into a valuable reliever and occasional starter for the remainder of his career. From 1933 to 1936, he averaged 31 appearances (9 starts) and 105 innings per year, but his importance to the

Cardinals extended far beyond his pitching. He was like a stern father-figure to a cast of new young players, among them hurlers Dizzy and Paul Dean, and Tex Carleton, and sluggers Joe Medwick and Johnny Mize. Teammates began calling him "Pop" because of his age, and papers often referred to him as "Papa Jess." Above all, Haines had the respect of his teammates. He harkened back to a time before Rickey and Breadon had transformed the Cardinals into the National League's most consistent team.

The Cardinals won their fifth pennant in nine years in 1934. The Gas House Gang, one of baseball's most enduring teams, was led by player-manager Frankie Frisch and a host of scrappy, rough, hard-nosed players like Medwick, Ripper Collins, Leo Durocher, Pepper Martin, and the Dean brothers. The team's brash personality was in stark contrast to Pop's more austere and staid approach to baseball. Haines led the team with 31 relief appearances (he started six times) and provided veteran leadership. In the Cardinals' exciting World Series championship over the Detroit Tigers, Haines pitched just once, two-thirds of an inning of mop-up duty in Game Four loss. In his World Series career, Haines won three of four decisions and posted a minuscule 1.67 ERA.

The Cardinals under Rickey and Breadon had a reputation of getting rid of their star players at the first sign of age or slippage, but they kept Haines well past his peak years. "I could have earned $4,000 or $5,000 more with the Giants or Cubs in my best years," said the intensely loyal Haines, "but then I don't think I would have lasted as long as I have."[31] Haines returned for his 18th consecutive season with the Cardinals in 1937, at the time an NL record for longest continuous service with one club. In a gesture of respect and recognition of Haines's career, Bill Terry, manager of the NL All-Star squad, named him an honorary coach of the team. Haines was pressed into the starting rotation after the All-Star Game and tossed a complete-game six-hitter to defeat Brooklyn on July 23, one day after his 44th birthday. In his next start he hurled another complete-game victory against the Dodgers. They were the final two wins in his career. "It's not my arm that's given up on me. It's my legs," he said. "After four or five innings they start wobbling."[32] By mutual agreement, the Cardinals released Haines at the end of the season.

"Old Jess" retired with 210 wins, 158 losses, 208 completes games, and 3208 2/3 innings pitched in his 19-year big-league career. He won 107 games in his seven-year minor-league career.

In 1938 Haines was the pitching coach for the Brooklyn Dodgers, skippered by Burleigh Grimes. He returned to Phillipsburg the following year and served as the Montgomery County auditor for 28 years before retiring.[33] A country gentleman and farmer at heart, Haines did not miss the bright lights of the city or excitement of the stadium. "They'd never get my name on a baseball contract (today)," Haines said in retirement. "As much as I loved the game—loved to walk out there and challenge the hitters—I just couldn't take all that big-city noise."[34]

Haines received baseball's highest honor in 1970 when he was elected by the Veterans Committee to the Baseball Hall of Fame. However, his election is now seen as controversial. Frankie Frisch was the chair and major voice of the Veterans Committee during a notorious period in the early 1970s. Supported by Bill Terry and two sportswriters, Fred Lieb and J. Roy Stockton, Frisch successfully led efforts to have former teammates (Dave Bancroft, George Kelly, Haines, Chick Hafey, and Ross Youngs) enshrined. Historians have since then questioned the credentials and Hall-worthiness of these players.

After a long bout with cancer, Jesse Joseph Haines died at the age of 85 on August 5, 1978, in Dayton. He was buried at Bethel Cemetery in his hometown of Phillipsburg. Once asked to explain his longevity, Haines had a simple answer: "Get eight hours of sleep every night, watch what you eat, lay off the alcohol, and throw the ball where you're looking."[35]

Sources

Jesse Haines player file at the National Baseball Hall of Fame, Cooperstown, New York

Ancestry.com

BaseballLibrary.com

Baseball-Reference.com

New York Times

Retrosheet.com

The Sporting News

Notes

1. Harry Brundidge, "Jesse Haines, Cardinal Pitcher, Used to Hide His Ball Suit in Corncrib," *St. Louis Star*, June 12, 1926, 3.
2. Ibid.
3. Ed Rumill, "They never get Jesse Haines to sign today," *Christian Science Monitor*, September 13, 1972 [no page number]. Jesse Haines player file at the National Baseball Hall of Fame.
4. Ibid.
5. "The Central League," *Sporting Life*, December 20, 1913, 15; Ernest Lanigan "Baseball Beginnings. Jesse Joseph Haines" (Associated Press), unnamed, undated publication, Jesse Haines player file at the National Baseball Hall of Fame.

    Ibid.
6. *Sporting Life*, October 31, 1914, 15.
7. Rumill.
8. Eugene F. Karst, director of information, "Jess Haines Had Another Great Year," St. Louis Cardinals press release, January 15, 1928. Jesse Haines player file at the National Baseball Hall of Fame.
9. *Sporting Life*, July 17, 1915, 63.
10. Unnamed article with no date and page, Jesse Haines player file at the National Baseball Hall of Fame.
11. Ibid.
12. John H. Farrell, "Official Notice of Players Signed, Released, and Suspended in All Leagues of the National Association," *Sporting Life*, November 11, 1916, 9.
13. *Massillon* (Ohio) *Evening Independent,* August 10, 1918, 10.
14. *The Sporting News*, February 19, 1920, 2.
15. *Hutchinson* (Kansas) *News*, September 4, 1919, 3.
16. *The Sporting News*, February 19, 1920, 2
17. Eugene F. Karst, director of information, St. Louis Cardinals Press Release. 1929. Jesse Haines player file at the National Baseball Hall of Fame.
18. Neil Russo, "Batters Knuckled Under to Haines and Schultz," September 6, 1964, Jesse Haines player file at the National Baseball Hall of Fame.
19. Ibid.
20. Billy Evans, "Hitless Hero Says Good Control Gave Him Record Game," *Olean* (New York) *Times,* September 17, 1924, 7.
21. *The Sporting News*, January 18, 1934, 6.
22. The Old Scout, "Pitcher Haines Runs Up Record in Long Service," November 6, 1936. Jesse Haines player file at the National Baseball Hall of Fame.
23. Eugene F. Karst, director of information, St. Louis Cardinals Press release, 1928. Jesse Haines player file at the National Baseball Hall of Fame.
24. *Massillon Evening Independent,* August 19, 1918, 7.
25. Brundidge.
26. Ibid.
27. World Series Pitching Star Hold Out for Redbirds," (Associated Press), unnamed, undated publication. Jesse Haines player file at the National Baseball Hall of Fame.
28. "Chances of St. Louis Cards for Pennant Are Not so Hot," *Burlington* (North Carolina) *Daily News,* March 13, 1930, 10.
29. Philip Martin, "In the World of Sports," *McIntosh County Democrat* (Checotah, Oklahoma), January 13, 1930, 10.
30. *The Sporting News*, February, 1968, 31.
31. Paul Thomas Dix, " 'Pop' Haines Satisfied with 25-Years' Work" (United Press), November 6, 1936. Jesse Haines player file at the National Baseball Hall of Fame.
32. Bill Corum, "Jesse Joseph Haines Come Up to Forty-four and Looks Back 18 Years," *New York Journal-American*, July 19, 1937, Jesse Haines player file at the National Baseball Hall of Fame.
33. *The Sporting News*, February, 19, 1977, 38.
34. Rumill.
35. Mike Eisenbath, *The Cardinals Encyclopedia* (Philadelphia: Temple University Press, 1999), 201.

Bill Hallahan

By Gregory H. Wolf

Considered one of the hardest throwers of his era, two-time National League strikeout king Wild Bill Hallahan lived up to his name by leading the league in walks and wild pitches three times each in the early 1930s. The left-hander, who had a reputation as a big-game pitcher during his best years with the St. Louis Cardinals (1930-1935), tossed two shutouts in the World Series and won 102 games in his 12-year big-league career, most of it with the Cardinals. "When Hallahan is in control," said Charlie Grimm of the Cubs, "he is a mighty hard man to beat. He puts more stuff on the ball than (Lefty) Grove."[1] Hallahan was also the NL's starting (and losing) pitcher in the inaugural All-Star game in 1933.

William Anthony Hallahan was born on August 4, 1902, in Binghamton, New York, the fourth of seven children born to John and Alice (Kane) Hallahan. Binghamton, at the confluence of the Susquehanna and Chenango Rivers in New York near the Pennsylvania border, was a developing manufacturing center and transportation hub affording families like the Hallahans a middle-class lifestyle. John Hallahan, whose parents were from Ireland, was born in New York and worked as an inspector for the Delaware & Lackawanna Railroad. Alice came from Pennsylvania. By the time Bill was 18 months old, his parents were concerned that he was left-handed. His mother tried everything to break that habit, from tying his arm behind his back to putting his arm in a sling, but nothing helped. In his adulthood Hallahan said he had few pleasant memories of childhood other than playing baseball. At school he was chided for his big ears and small stature. "I muffed most of my studies," he admitted, and failed several grades.[2] Young Bill dreamed of baseball, started pitching for his grammar school by the age of 11, and looked forward to the day he could quit school, which he did after the eighth grade.

After years of playing sandlot ball, Hallahan approached Bill Fischer, manager of the prosperous and successful semipro team for the Endicott-Johnson shoe factory in the highly competitive industrial leagues in Binghamton, for a tryout. Though Fischer turned the 19-year-old Hallahan away because of his youth and small size (just 130 pounds), he suggested that he contact John Haddock, a former minor-league catcher and the manager of the Corona Typewriter semipro team in Groton, New York, about 50 miles northwest of Binghamton.[3] Hallahan reported to Haddock, got a job in the factory, and secured a spot as a pitcher on the team, earning about $35 per week. A "sensation in semipro circles,"[4] Hallahan was a strikeout artist and was known as the hardest thrower around. Other semipro teams actively recruited him, but he stayed loyal to Corona and continued to pitch for them until after the 1923 season. Legend has that he struck out 55 batters in his last three games while surrendering just six hits. Drawing

Hallahan tied Jumbo Elliott and Heinie Meine for the league lead in wins with 19 in 1931. He also posted a 2-0 record in the World Series, as St. Louis topped the Philadelphia Athletics in seven games.

the attention of professional scouts, Hallahan signed a contract with the Syracuse Stars of the International League after the 1923 season.

Branch Rickey, general manager and manager of the Cardinals, had acquired a half-interest in the Stars in 1921, and was in the process of building the first modern farm system. In 1924, the 21-year-old Hallahan reported to Bradenton, Florida, where the Cardinals and Stars conducted spring training together. "He's so wild, he can hardly hit the backstop, but there's a pitcher who someday will pitch and win a World Series game," Rickey supposedly said of Hallahan during his first spring training.[5] The legend of "Wild Bill" was under way. Hallahan began the season with manager Shag Shaughnessy's Stars but after he had made eight appearances, the Cardinals purchased his contract in mid-June and put him on the fast track to the majors. Hallahan was optioned to Fort Smith in the Class C Western Association, where he made five starts and pitched 43 innings, then was promoted to Kalamazoo in the Class B Michigan-Ontario League. In two months with Kalamazoo, Hallahan won eight games, surrendered a league-low 6.7 hits per nine innings, and tied for the third-best ERA (2.80); but true to Rickey's assessment of his wildness, he issued 79 walks in 106 innings (6.7 per nine innings). In September, Hallahan was called up by the Cardinals. "[I] was permitted to sit in the dugout, in uniform, and watch the big-league ballgames," he said.[6]

Hallahan's speed was as tantalizing as his lack of control was frustrating. During spring training in Stockton, California, in 1925, he was praised for his "speed and curves."[7] Rickey predicted that "that boy will make good if he can keep control of his stuff."[8] Hallahan made the team and debuted on April 16 at Redland Field in Cincinnati when he took over for Bill Sherdel to start the fourth inning. He pitched scoreless two-hit ball the rest of the way, striking out two and walking three in a 7-3 loss. On May 7 Hallahan earned his first big-league win by pitching two hitless innings of relief against the Pirates at Forbes Field. "I thought I was going to make the grade," he said, but after two ineffective outings (five earned runs in 5 1/3 innings), he was optioned to Syracuse to work on his control.[9]

"I was disappointed," said Hallahan, who struggled with the Stars, winning eight, losing 15, and walking 114 in 178 innings.

"Hallahan—Big Show," read a headline about the hard thrower's third spring training with the Cardinals.[10] Playing for Rogers Hornsby, who had replaced Rickey as manager in 1925, Hallahan joined a strong staff with veteran starters Sherdel and Jesse Haines as well as Flint Rhem and Hallahan's boyhood hero, Grover Cleveland Alexander, who have come on waivers from the Cubs in June. Described as a "quiet mannered" and "soft spoken" man,[11] Hallahan roomed with 19-year-old pitcher Ed Clough (they were dubbed the "silent twins"[12]), and Hallahan bristled under the authoritarian rule of Hornsby, who liked his players to be as vocal and fiery as he was.

During the Cardinals' exciting march to the first pennant in their history, Hallahan was used sparingly. In 16 relief appearances, he pitched well (3.03 ERA with 14 walks in 38 2/3 innings), but struggled in three starts (5.00 ERA with 18 walks in 18 innings). With only two appearances after August 9, Hallahan was no doubt surprised and a bit rusty when he relieved Hi Bell in Game Four of the World Series against the New York Yankees in Sportsman's Park. In his only appearance in the Cardinals' dramatic and unexpected Series victory, Hallahan pitched two innings, surrendering one run and two hits, and walked three. It was his last major-league game for more than two years.

Optioned to Syracuse to start the 1927 season, Hallahan was subject to recall on one day's notice, but remained with the Stars the entire season. "Hallahan, when he is locating the plate," said Syracuse manager Burt Shotton, "can win in any league."[13] He posted a team-high 19 wins, but had a tendency to tire early in games because he threw so hard. He led the International League with 195 strikeouts (a team record) and 135 walks in 229 innings.

Wild Bill enjoyed a breakthrough year with the Houston Buffaloes of the Class A Texas League in 1928. Described as "one of the greatest sensations the league has ever seen," he won 23 games, and led the league with 244 strikeouts, 149 walks, a sparkling 2.25 ERA, and 276 innings pitched.[14] Associated Press reports in August claiming that Hallahan would soon join the Cardinals in their pennant race with New York Giants and Chicago Cubs proved to be wrong. Wild Bill remained with the Buffaloes and led them to their first league title in 16 years by winning three games in the championship series. He capped the season by winning one game in the Buffaloes' Dixie Series championship over the Birmingham Barons. The Gunslinger of the West, Wild Bill had finally lived up to his name. "Hallahan is such a great natural pitcher that he doesn't have to bother to pitch to the batter's weakness," said Cardinal scout Charley Barrett, who charted Hallahan's progress all season. "All he has to do is get the ball over the plate."[15]

Arriving at Avon Park, Florida, for his sixth consecutive spring straining with the Cardinals after offseason surgery on his big toe (the result of pushing off the pitching rubber), Hallahan competed for a spot on the NL's oldest staff (averaging 32.2 years). "There will probably be a lot of shuffling around the batter's box when Bill Hallahan takes the mound," read one report about the excitement around Wild Bill.[16] Named to the Opening Day roster, Hallahan was quick to credit catcher-manager Frank Snyder at Houston for his transformation, "I had been living up to the name of 'Wild Bill' for a long time until Snyder got hold of me," he said. "He was the first one who ever had confidence on me."[17]

That confidence did not transfer to manager Billy Southworth who used Hallahan just eight times before he was replaced as skipper in late July. While the reigning pennant winners struggled to play .500 ball, Hallahan labored to throw strikes. Through August, Wild Bill issued 35 free passes in 30 innings (including a career-high ten in his first complete game, an 8-2 loss to Brooklyn on July 31). New manager Bill McKechnie, renowned for his handling of pitchers, gave Hallahan a chance to prove himself in September. Hallahan responded by winning four of seven starts, tossing four complete games, and posting a stellar 3.20 ERA over 59 innings. Even more promising was his improved command.

The Cardinals' sixth different Opening Day manager in the last six seasons, Gabby "Old Sarge" Street, a former big-league catcher, took Hallahan under his wing in 1930. He thought Wild Bill's problems resulted from a lack of concentration, so he decided to scrap Branch Rickey's complicated (some said convoluted) signal-calling system which involved the pitcher adding and subtracting from the catcher's signs, so that the pitcher could think exclusively about pitching.[18] Hallahan had a tendency to stare at the ground and then look up in his delivery, thereby losing his sense of direction. "Keep your eyes on the plate and the batter," Street told him. "Don't turn you head away or look down when you deliver the ball."[19]

Hallahan responded in his first start of the season by tossing a complete game, striking out 11 in an 11-1 shellacking of the Cubs. His season-high nine walks were tempered by just two hits (both singles). Street was patient with Hallahan whose record (8-7) and ERA (5.47) were as unimpressive as the Cardinals' 48-49 record at the end of July. On August 10 Hallahan tossed his first big-league shutout, a two-hitter, striking out 12 while issuing just two walks to reduce the NL-leading Brooklyn Robins' lead over fourth-place St. Louis to nine games. "St. Louis players insist that Hallahan is as fast as (Dazzy) Vance and faster than Robert Moses Grove," said the Associated Press.[20] With every game seemingly a must-win contest, the Cardinals reeled off 23 wins in 32 games in August and started September by winning 11 of 13 games to find themselves just a half-game behind Brooklyn on the eve of a possible pennant-deciding three-game series at Ebbets Field.

The most important game of the Cardinals' 1930 season comes across like a soap opera. Flint Rhem, a 20-game winner in 1926 but whose career and behavior since then had been affected by alcoholism, was scheduled to take the mound against Vance, the seven-time NL strikeout king, in the opening game. When Street discovered that Rhem had been out drinking all night and was nowhere to be found, he turned to Rhem's roommate, none other than Hallahan, and named him starter. Hallahan had injured his hand hours before when he smashed a cab door on his fingers returning from a Broadway performance. "There was never any doubt in my mind that I was going to pitch," said Hallahan, who hid the injury from Street. "It was an important game and I wanted to be in it. Two fingers on my right hand were packed in some sort of black salve and I had to cut my glove so that they could protrude on the outside."[21] Hallahan pitched a no-hitter through seven innings and battled Vance for nine scoreless innings before center fielder Taylor Douthit scored the only run of the game on Andy High's pinch-hit double in the tenth. Hallahan pitched another scoreless frame in the tenth to secure the win. More importantly it ended Brooklyn's 11-game winning streak, moved the Cardinals into a dead heat with the Robins, and established Hallahan's reputation as a big-game pitcher. The Cardinals swept the series, went 21-4 in September, and won their third pennant in five seasons. In the "Year of the Hitter," Hallahan notched 15 wins (with 9 losses), started a career-high 32 times, posted an above-average 4.68 ERA, and led the league with 126 walks and 177 strikeouts. In an era when strikeouts were rare, NL pitchers struck out ten or more batters in a game nine times; Hallahan notched three of them.

The Cardinals faced the Philadelphia Athletics, the overwhelming favorites, in the World Series. Down two games to none, Hallahan tossed a seven-hitter, shutting out the slugging A's while striking out six and walking five. In Game Six, with the Cardinals facing elimination, Hallahan lacked command of his pitches and surrendered two runs in the first inning on two hits and two walks. After pitching a scoreless second inning, but walking a batter and hitting another, he was lifted for a pinch-hitter in the third inning of the 7-1 loss.

Hallahan's shutout in the World Series brought him increased attention, but he was not one to search for headlines. Preferring to spend his free time at a concert, play, or especially the movies, Hallahan was a modest, studious type. He was an avid reader, especially Wild West stories, and also enjoyed golfing. Throughout most of his career with the Cardinals, he lived with his parents in Binghamton and worked in the offseason at the Corona typewriter factory.

Lee Allen, former historian at the Baseball Hall of Fame, likened Hallahan to a left-handed version of Burleigh Grimes, and suggested that the lines at the side of his mouth gave him the impression of a bulldog.[22]

Always conscious of his appearance, the 5-foot-10 Hallahan was considered small for a power pitcher, and weighed just 170 pounds, but gave the impression of being smaller. Among teammates he was known as Moon, a nickname catcher Earl Smith gave him because of his round face accentuated by closely cropped blond hair, blue eyes, and pronounced ears. Other appellations were Pug and Lefty, but sportswriters preferred Wild Bill, or Sweet William when Hallahan pitched well.[23]

With a classic overhand delivery, Hallahan was primarily a fastball pitcher, but possessed a devastating hard curveball, and developed a deceptive slow curve as a change of pace which undoubtedly contributed to his success in 1930. "I simply threw the ball in there," Hallahan said of his early career. "When I was in the hole, I had the impression that the soundest way to fool a batter was to cut loose with everything. I discovered that the slowballs are pretty effective when they aren't expected."[24] Though Hallahan never overcame his wildness, he managed to control it enough to have a good run of success from 1930 through 1935, when he won a total of 85 games and averaged more than 200 innings pitched per year. "Bill Hallahan certainly has great speed," said Ray Kremer, a standout pitcher for the Pirates in the late 1920s and early 1930s, but noted that his success resulted from the movement on his pitches. "[He] has a lot of stuff on the ball. The old ball certainly hops and shoots when Bill is having a good day."[25]

In 1931 Hallahan reported early to camp in Bradenton in the best shape of his life and boldly predicted that the Cardinals would win the World Series.[26] Before it was commonplace to train year-round, Hallahan was described as a "demon for condition" and was said to be "in the gym every day."[27] "Condition is 50 percent of a pitcher's stock in trade," he said. "All through spring training I chase fungoes to strengthen my legs, and after the season starts I'm always running."[28] Brimming with confidence and acknowledging manager Street's patience in helping him develop into a staff ace, Hallahan overcame early-season control problems (22 walks in his first three starts) to have a dominating June. He tossed five complete games in six starts, won four of five decisions, and posted a 2.28 ERA in 51 1/3 innings while issuing just 18 walks. He hurled consecutive shutouts when he held Brooklyn to six hits on June 7 and the Boston Braves to eight hits on June 13. On August 30 he struck out a career-high 13 in a convincing complete-game 4-1 victory against the Pirates. Concluding the season winning four of five starts, each victory a complete game, Hallahan finished with a career-high 19 wins to tie for the lead in the NL. Logging a career-high 248 2/3 innings, Wild Bill led the NL in walks (112) and strikeouts (159) for a second straight year, and in wild pitches (11) for the first of three times.

St. Louis ran away with the pennant behind a scrappy, hard-nosed team led by MVP Frankie Frisch, 5-foot-8 rookie Pepper Martin, and veterans Chick Hafey and Jim Bottomley. Though they hit just 60 home runs, they scored the second most runs (815) in the league. The pitching staff was a model of consistency and ranked second in ERA. Hallahan led the team with 30 starts and innings; Burleigh Grimes, Paul Derringer, Rhem, and Syl Johnson each started at least 23 games, and Jesse "Pop" Haines started 17; all six won at least 11 games to help the Cardinals set a franchise record with 101 wins.

Overwhelming underdogs in a World Series rematch with the Athletics, the Cardinals pulled off one of the great upsets in baseball history by defeating the A's in seven games behind Hallahan's masterful pitching and Martin's legendary hitting and basestealing. In Game Two, Wild Bill issued seven walks, but limited the A's to just three singles while striking out eight in a commanding 2-0 shutout in St. Louis. With the Series tied at two games apiece, Hallahan pitched another complete-game gem, limiting the A's to one run on nine hits and one walk, and won 5-1 in Philadelphia. In the seventh game, evoking memories of Alexander's relief of Haines in Game Seven of the 1926 World Series, Hallahan relieved the fading Burleigh Grimes in the ninth inning with St. Louis leading 4-2. Needing just one out and facing the go-ahead run at the plate, Hallahan induced a deep fly ball to center field from Max Bishop for the final out of the game and clinched the Cardinals' second championship in five years. George Talbot of the Associated Press wrote, "[Hallahan has pitched] two of the greatest games in World Series history," yet noted that Martin's hitting and running (12-for-24 with five stolen bases) "have virtually overshadowed Hallahan's Homeric hurling."[29]

After a disastrous sixth-place finish in 1932, Street was replaced by player-manager Frankie Frisch after 91 games in 1933. The Redbirds were in transition with a crop of young players (pitchers Tex Carleton and Dizzy Dean, and fielders Ripper Collins, Leo Durocher, and Joe Medwick) gradually replacing veterans. Hallahan bounced back from an injury-plagued season in 1932 (though he posted a 12-7 record and a team-best 3.11 ERA), and hurled three consecutive complete-game victories to begin the 1933 campaign. Behind the pitching of Hallahan and Dean, the Cardinals battled the Giants for the lead through late June before slumping and playing inconsistently in the second half of the season. On July 4 Hallahan improved his record to 10-4 with a complete-game win over the Pirates in the Cardinals' 72nd game, and appeared headed for a 20-win season. Often a victim of poor run support, Hallahan notched just six more victories and lost nine games (in which the Redbirds scored a total of 19 runs) to finish with a 16-13 record and a 3.50 ERA while matching career highs with 32 starts and 16 complete games for the fifth-place Cardinals.

Hallahan's participation in one of the most historic games in baseball history, the inaugural All-Star Game played in Chicago's Comiskey Park on July 6, 1933, is often overlooked. National League manager John McGraw, the newly retired boss of the New York Giants, named four pitchers to his staff: Carl Hubbell (11-5 at the All-Star break), Hal Schumacher (9-5), Lon Warneke (9-7), and Hallahan. In a surprise decision, he chose Hallahan to start the game to counter the left-handed sluggers on the AL squad. Hallahan was lifted in the third inning after walking Charlie Gehringer, surrendering a towering home run to Babe Ruth (whom he had struck out in the first inning) and walking Lou Gehrig. Charged with the loss, Wild Bill lived up to his name, issuing five bases on balls and surrendering three runs in two innings.

At 31, Hallahan was the veteran among the Cardinals' five primary starting pitchers (Dizzy and Paul Dean,

Carleton, and Bill Walker) for the legendary Gas House Gang in 1934. He struggled for most of the season, and his record dropped to an unsightly 4-12 with an ERA of 5.05 after a 9-2 loss to the Reds on August 7. In his next start, 11 days later, Hallahan pitched his best game of the year, a six-hit shutout of the Braves, to resurrect his season. Taking a back seat to the Dean brothers and Carleton, Hallahan pitched his best during the Redbirds' exciting rush to the pennant, winning his last four decisions and posting a stellar 1.82 ERA. He finished the season with an 8-12 record and a slightly below league-average ERA (4.26). Called to rekindle his magic, Hallahan started Game Two of the World Series against the Detroit Tigers. He limited Mickey Cochrane's sluggers to six hits, four walks, and two runs over 8 1/3 innings before being replaced by Walker in a tie game that the Tigers eventually won 3-2 in 12 innings. Hallahan did not pitch again in the Gas House Gang's exciting seven-game Series victory. Nonetheless, he proved to be one of the best World Series pitchers in Cardinals history. With a 3-1 record, including two shutouts, Hallahan posted a 1.36 ERA in 39 2/3 innings for four pennant winners.

The 1935 season started off horribly for Hallahan. Shelled in his first two starts, he lost his spot in the rotation and was used sparingly through June, posting a dismal 6.52 ERA in 13 appearances for the inconsistent Cardinals. Beginning with a three-hit shutout over the Pirates on July 2, Hallahan commenced a streak of five consecutive complete-game victories helping propel the Cardinals from 9 1/2 games back to just a half-game behind the Giants on July 22. Pitching more often than at any other time of his career, Hallahan made 27 appearances (19 starts) in the last three months of the season. (Only Dizzy Dean pitched more often.) During that stretch Hallahan won 12 of 16 decisions and posted a 2.57 ERA, but the Cardinals could not match the red-hot Cubs who won a major-league record 21 consecutive games in September to overtake the Cardinals and Giants and win the pennant. In his last year as an effective major leaguer, the 32-year-old Hallahan pitched in a career-high 40 games (23 starts), and posted an above-average 3.42 ERA for the second-place Cardinals.

Hallahan's contract dispute and holdout prior to the 1936 season preceded another ineffective start to the season. Cardinals owner San Breadon, renowned for jettisoning his players before they lost value, did not make an exception for Wild Bill. With a 2-2 record and an unsightly 6.38 ERA, Hallahan was sold to the Cincinnati Reds on May 31. The remaining 2 1/2 years of his career were occasionally highlighted by reminders of his once powerful fastball, but were more often filled with frustratingly ineffective outings. In a season and a half with the second-division Reds, Hallahan won just 8 times, lost 18, and posted a 4.91 ERA. Relegated to a rarely used reliever and occasional starter with a 6.14 ERA in 1937, Hallahan was released by the Reds on February 3, 1938.

Former Cardinals catcher Jimmie Wilson, in his fifth season as player-manager for the woeful Philadelphia Phillies, was instrumental in his team's decisions to sign the 35-year-old Hallahan. After all the success with the Cardinals, Hallahan endured his second consecutive last-place finish as the Phillies won only 45 times the entire season. With ten starts among his 21 appearances, Hallahan seemingly turned back the hands of time on August 25. He pitched all 11 innings to defeat the Pittsburgh Pirates, 2-1, his only victory of the season and the last game of his big-league career. Before 3,093 fans at Forbes Field, Hallahan needed just 2 hours and 25 minutes to pitch his last complete game. At the end of the season, the 36-year-old veteran was released.

Hallahan signed with the Minneapolis Millers of the American Association, but was released after an abbreviated tenure (five games), bringing his 16-year career in the majors and minors to an end. He won 102 games and posted an above-league-average 4.03 ERA in his 12-year big-league career. He won 62 games in the minor leagues. For all of his unsettling wildness, Wild Bill hit only eight batters in the majors. He was a fiercely competitive pitcher who wanted to pitch the big game. "[Hallahan] was a truculent guy who used to stalk onto the field with his glove jammed into his hip pocket and a big wad of tobacco in his cheek," reminisced Hall of Fame historian Lee Allen.[30]

In retirement, Hallahan returned to Binghamton with his wife, Marion Teresa (Forbes) Hallahan, and their daughter, Mary. In 1942 he was inducted into the Army and was stationed at Fort Niagara, New York. For more than 20 years he worked as a supervisor for General Aniline and Film Company (GAF) in Binghamton. Always ready to talk about baseball to anyone interested, Hallahan regularly participated in Cardinals reunions and occasional old-timers games. For decades after Hallahan's playing career was over, his name was invoked to describe hard throwers in the Cardinals organization, like Max Lanier, Johnny Grodzicki, and Bob Gibson, and also those who fought to control their stuff.

After a battle with cancer, Bill Hallahan died on July 8, 1981, at the age of 78. He was buried at Calvary Cemetery in Johnson City, New York, just a few miles from his hometown. "One nice thing about baseball," Hallahan once said matter-of-factly, "you're remembered for the successes you've had rather than the failures."[31] Wild Bill had his share of successes.

Sources

Bill Hallahan player file at the National Baseball Hall of Fame, Cooperstown, New York

Ancestry.com

BaseballLibrary.com

Baseball-Reference.com

New York Times

Retrosheet.org

The Sporting News

Notes

1 Clifford Bloodgood, " 'Wild Bill' Becomes 'Sweet William,' " *Baseball Magazine*, July 1932, 297.

2 *The Sporting News*, January 1, 1931, 7.

3 "Hallahan Proves a Great Pitcher," undated article in Hallahan's file at the National Baseball Hall of Fame.

4 *The Sporting News*, May 25, 1933, 2.

5 "Talent That Is Complicated," *Monitor-Index and Democrat* (Moberly, Missouri), June 6, 1940, 6.

6 *The Sporting News*, January 1, 1931, 7.

7 "Young Southpaw Shows Rickey Stuff," *San Antonio Light*, March 4, 1925, 12.

8 "Young Southpaw."

9 *The Sporting News*, January 1, 1931, 7.

10 "Hallahan Big Show" (Associated Press), *Kingsport* (Tennessee) *Times*, March 12, 1926, 12.

11 *The Sporting News*, May 25, 1933, 2.

12 Paul W. White, "New York Carping Critics Claim Cardinals Exceedingly Nervous," *Portsmouth* (Ohio) *Daily Times*, October 1, 1926, 28.

13 "Haid and Morrow, Star Battery in First Game," *Syracuse Herald*, April 12, 127, 19.

14 *The Sporting News*, November 1, 1928, 7.

15 "Cardinal Scout Is Quite Enthusiastic," *Akron Register Tribune*, December 20, 1928, 2.

16 "Bill Hallahan. Cardinals," *Waterloo* (Iowa) *Evening News*, March 15, 1929, 18.

17 "Ready to Thank Pancho Snyder for His Success," (NEA Service), *Lima* (Ohio) *News*, April 5, 1929, 27.

18 John Kieran, "Sports of the Times," *New York Times*, October 1, 1930, 40.

19 *The Sporting News*, May 25, 1933, 2.

20 "Cards Fans Flock to Wild Bill Hallahan," (AP), *Meriden* (Connecticut) *Daily Journal*, October 4, 1930, 4.

21 Richard Peterson, *St Louis Baseball Reader* (Columbia, Missouri: University of Missouri Press, 2006), 161.

22 *The Sporting News*, October 12, 1968, 68.

23 *The Sporting News*, May 25, 1933, 2.

24 Clifford Bloodgood, " 'Wild Bill' Becomes 'Sweet William,' " *Baseball Magazine*, July 1932, 298.

25 Ray Kremer, "Pitching From a Veteran's Viewpoint. Comprising an interview with Ray Kremer," *Baseball Magazine*, July 1932, 347.

26 Sam Murphy, "Hallahan Sees Cards as Champs," *Appleton* (Wisconsin) *Post-Crescent*, January 8, 1931, 12.

27 "Hallahan Sees."

28 Clifford Bloodgood, "'Wild Bill' Becomes 'Sweet William'," *Baseball Magazine*, July 1932, 298.

29 George Talbot, "Bill Hallahan's Wonderful Pitching gets Sidetracked," (AP), *Lewiston Evening Journal* (Lewiston, Maine), October 8, 1931, 10.

30 *The Sporting News*, October 12, 1968, 68.

31 Richard Peterson, *St. Louis Baseball Reader*, 159.

Francis Healy

By Greg Erion

OVER THE YEARS, there has been no shortage of adjectives to describe the 1934 St. Louis Cardinals. Raucous, rambunctious, and rowdy have been just a few of the terms used to portray the Deans, Durochers, Martins, and Medwicks of the club. Yet not everyone on the team fit the public's perception of this hell-raising, pennant-winning contingent. For instance, Francis Healy, the bullpen and reserve catcher, was by all accounts quiet and a devout Catholic. His demeanor was such that Dizzy Dean came to call him "Father" Healy.

Francis Paul Healy was born on July 29, 1910, in Holyoke, Massachusetts to Catherine and Jeremiah Healy, the fifth of seven children.[1] His parents had come from Ireland around the turn of the century and married a few years later; some sources say in 1902. Jeremiah worked for the city.

Healy reminisced that as a child he spent a great deal of time on the playground watching the older boys play, and eventually was asked to join in their games. Early on, he showed athletic potential playing baseball and football.[2] Healy went to school in the local parochial system, eventually attending St. Jerome High School.

There Smiling Mickey Welch, a resident of Holyoke and a former major league pitcher who was elected to the Hall of Fame in 1973, spotted Healy. Welch's 307 major-league victories came predominantly with the New York Giants, and he maintained a strong affinity for the Giants and a good relationship with manager John McGraw. So when Welch sized up Healy's potential as a player during the summer of 1929, he contacted the Giants skipper.

McGraw thought he saw in Healy the same potential he had seen five years earlier in Mel Ott. Like Ott, Healy was to be kept with the Giants so that McGraw could personally coach him in the ways of the game, not wishing to risk his being ruined through inadequate or incorrect tutelage on a minor-league team. That path had worked for Ott. McGraw was supremely confident it would work for Healy who, McGraw observed, had "natural abilities" and was "the find of the year." He went on to describe Healy's talents in effusive terms.[3]

While McGraw's comments were impressive, he often described newcomers similarly. Several years earlier, he spoke of a rookie named Fay Thomas as having "more stuff than any young pitcher I have seen since Mathewson." He touted Jimmy Ring, obtained in a trade, as "one of the best pitchers in the League and a glutton for work." Neither pitcher left much of an impression on Giants fans.[4]

Healy joined the Giants for spring training in 1930 having never played ball beyond local contests in Holyoke. He was out of his element. While his talent was a potential, his naïveté was a certainty. The same article that spoke of his ability described him as "a green, freckled faced boy, the most gullible in the

Healy appeared in only 15 games for the Cardinals in 1934. He was a valuable utility player, filling in at catcher, third base, and the outfield. His nephew Fran was a catcher in the 1970's, primarily with the Royals and Yankees.

camp. He's a sucker for a pail of steam, and if you tell him to fetch a left-handed bat, he'll go look for it." Tom Clarke, a Giants coach, took Healy under his guidance, sharing a room and arranging for them to eat their meals together. Of Healy, Clarke observed, "Healy is young and hasn't been around much."[5]

Healy stayed with the Giants through the first few months of 1930 until he was sent to the Bridgeport Bears in the Class A Eastern League. Appearing in 31 games, he hit .269 before returning to the Giants for a single pinch-running appearance during the last week of the season. For the year, Healy appeared in seven games, mostly as a pinch-runner. He had two unsuccessful at-bats pinch-hitting.[6]

In 1931 Healy stayed with the Giants the entire year, appearing in six games and getting one hit in seven at-bats, his first major-league hit. He collected that hit the last week of the season, a single in a 15-7 slugfest victory over the Chicago Cubs at Wrigley Field. Healy also had two passed balls after replacing Bob O'Farrell in the fifth inning

Healy's quest to crack into the Giants' starting lineup was stymied because there were two accomplished receivers ahead of him. Shanty Hogan, a solid .300 hitter, and backup O'Farrell, then a 16-year veteran, had ability as well as experience that a young man off the sandlots of Holyoke with just and a handful of minor-league games could not come close to matching.

McGraw, who had championed Healy's abilities, was not the same man who had adroitly transformed Ott five years before from raw rookie to accomplished outfielder. He was frequently ill and absent from the club, and his hold on the Giants by the end of 1931 had become tenuous.[7] In early June 1932, McGraw resigned and was succeeded by first baseman Bill Terry.

By then Healy was in the minors. He was assigned to the Double-A Columbus Red Birds after a single appearance with the Giants in late April. There, under manager Billy Southworth, Healy hit .347 in 44 games. They were the most games he had played in during any professional season. Although the Red Birds were a Cardinals affiliate, there is no record of Healy being dealt to them by the Giants.

The Giants recalled Healy in early September. After three seasons of almost total nonuse, the Giants decided to test his potential. He appeared in 13 games, catching in 11 and batting .250.

How Healy stood with the Giants organization became quickly obvious. Before the 1933 season they let Hogan go to the Boston Braves and traded O'Farrell to the Cardinals. In the latter transaction, receiver Gus Mancuso came to the Giants. Youngsters Harry Danning and Paul Richards joined the team to back up Mancuso. Healy went to the minors, splitting time between Columbus and Toledo in the American Association and hitting .272 for the season in 73 games. Mancuso, then Danning eventually became the Giants' main receivers for the rest of the decade. Healy was expendable.

St. Louis, familiar with Healy's ability through his play at Columbus, purchased his contract from the Giants on May 5, 1934. To make room for Healy on the roster, the Cardinals released 40-year-old Burleigh Grimes, the last major-league spitball pitcher. Grimes had pitched in the majors in 1933 and had hoped to stick with St. Louis, but Healy's purchase made him odd man out.[8]

Healy's role with the Cardinals was to serve as a utilityman and bullpen catcher. During the season he played in 15 games as a catcher, third baseman, or outfielder, pinch-hitter or pinch-runner, hitting .308 in 13 at-bats. None of his appearances proved consequential. He did not play in the World Series against the Detroit Tigers; but got a Series share worth $5,306 for being on the world champion Cardinals' roster.[9] The season was his last in the major leagues. Healy appeared in 42 games over four seasons with the Giants and Cardinals, hitting .241 with three doubles. He caught in only 18 of his 42 games; in the rest he was mostly a pinch-hitter or pinch-runner.

In 1935 Healy was assigned to the Rochester Red Wings in the Double-A International League. There he played in 61 games and hit .271. In 1936 he was sent down to the Columbus (Georgia) Red Birds in the Class B South Atlantic League, where he hit .316 in 122 games, the most games he played in during a season. His play drew favorable attention. The July 30 issue of

The Sporting News ran an article about a poll among Columbus fans on who they though would be the most likely Red Bird to reach the big leagues. Healy was among those mentioned. It was not to be. He played a handful of games in 1937 and finished his career with the Houston Buffaloes of the Texas League in 1938 alongside fellow catcher Walker Cooper, who was two years away from his debut with the Cardinals. Healy hit .269 in his final year. He was 28 and his professional career was over. That same year also marked the end of an abbreviated career for his younger brother, Bernie, who made appearances for the Cambridge (Maryland) Cardinals of the Class D Eastern Shore League.

After leaving professional baseball, Francis Healy was virtually forgotten, but he was remembered in the early 1970s when his nephew Fran, Bernie's son, caught for the Kansas City Royals, San Francisco Giants, and New York Yankees.

Some references in Francis Healy's Hall of Fame player file indicate he had been ill for a number of years after his professional career had ended. An article in the *Springfield* (Massachusetts) *Union-News & Sunday Republican* after his death said that after being "shuffled off to the minors … (i)t was then, with the advice and consent of his brother Bernie, that he finally gave up the game and came home to Holyoke."[10] Whether this advice was triggered by the onset of Healy's illness is subject to conjecture, but it appears Healy was incapacitated for several years.[11] Healy alluded to illness himself in describing the end of his career: "The Cards shipped me to Houston and soon afterwards I was taken ill, ending my career."[12]

Healy went to work for the local Department of Public Works in the mid-1940s and was employed for about 25 years before retiring in 1971. He lived quietly with a brother and sister in an apartment in Holyoke. Never married and highly religious, he belonged to the Passionist Retreat League and was a communicant of Holy Cross Church. He did not own a car and stayed close to home except when his brother Bernie took him to see young Fran play for the Royals in Boston or New York.

Described as a reticent conversationalist by his interviewer, Healy opened up when the subject was baseball. Of his years with the Giants, Healy recalled that while the Chicago Cubs were interested in him, he signed with the Giants on the advice of his father. Healy said he had pleasant experiences with most of those he came into contact with, although for a while he was mad at Bill Terry for shipping him off to the Cardinals until "I learned that Branch Rickey had arranged a deal to get me."[13]

Despite competing with Shanty Hogan for the catcher's job, Healy considered the fellow Irishman his best friend on the Giants. "We liked to eat out together, going to restaurants where they served corned beef and cabbage," he said. "(Hogan) helped me tremendously, how to work back of the plate."

Healy had the experience of catching two of the game's pitching greats of the era, Dizzy Dean and Carl Hubbell. Comparing them, he said, "I believe Hubbell was a better pitcher. Further, I always felt Dizzy Dean's side-arm pitch was faster than Diz threw. But I also felt Wild Bill Hallahan was faster than either one."

Of the Gas House Gang, he recalled their wild behavior:

"Sure, they were a fun-loving and hell-raising group but not as bad as they have been painted. Dizzy Dean was more or less the ringleader. I vividly recall being in a Boston hotel and Dizzy, from his fourth-floor window, poured a pitcher of water on Frank Frisch, then manager, and Leo Durocher who were standing in front of the hotel. Honestly, I never saw a fistfight between two of the players on this club.

"Diz was forever cutting up and it was always in pure fun. There wasn't a dull moment all the time we were together. It was sure great to play baseball with the Deans, Pepper Martin, Bill DeLancey, Medwick, Durocher, and the others. There was something doing all the time in the clubhouse and in the dugout, but don't get any idea they weren't out there to play baseball and to win. They gave 100 percent. I'm happy to have been a small part of the Gang. They were a great bunch."

Healy felt Frisch was the brains on the club. "He was a good guy and a tough guy; so was Leo Durocher in my book." Healy was grateful for his time in the big leagues: "I felt lucky to be playing baseball at that time because of the Depression and jobs were so hard to find." Having had a ringside seat for Joe Medwick's slide into Marv Owen in the seventh game of the 1934 World Series, Healy was asked for his opinion on the incident that led to a riot. "I have read and heard stories about Joe Medwick and Marty (Marv) Owen, in the series and a fistfight. Honestly, I think Medwick accidentally kicked him and Marty thought otherwise."

Years after he left baseball, Healy's interest remained strong. "I missed the game terribly; I missed those I played with. … My interests today are as high today in baseball as they were in my playing days, no doubt even higher now that my nephew is up there with Kansas City."

Healy and Dizzy Dean remained friends over the years. The incongruous duo met up at the 1973 Hall of Fame celebration and there Healy even got together with Bill Terry, his former teammate, manager, and, for a while, nemesis.

Healy died on February 12, 1997, at the age of 86. He was buried at St. Jerome Cemetery alongside his brother Daniel and sisters, Anne and Mary.

Healy's obituary said he was the last surviving player from the 1934 Cardinals championship team. That was incorrect; in May 1999 Clarence Heise, a pitcher who appeared in one game for the team, died at 91 in Winter Park, Florida. They were the last of the team whose year of glory fascinates latter-day fans of the game.[14]

Notes

1. Some sources list Healy's full name as Francis Xavier Paul Healy. Neither Ancestry.com nor his obituary in the local paper reflect this.
2. Healy's player file at the National Baseball Hall of Fame.
3. "McGraw Believes He Has Another Melvin Ott in 17-Year Old Francis Healy," *New York Graphic*, April 3, 1930.
4. Charles C. Alexander, *John McGraw* (New York: Penguin Group, 1988), 270-271.
5. "He Who Runs Away," unnamed newspaper in Healy's Hall of Fame file, April 17, 1930.
6. Statistics for this article from either Baseball-reference.com or Retrosheet.org.
7. Alexander, *John McGraw*, 304-308.
8. "Grimes Released," *Moberly* (Missouri) *Monitor-Index and Democrat*, May 15, 1934.
9. "Series Checks Mailed Out," *The Sporting News*, November 1, 1934, 6.
10. "Quiet Man Francie Healy one of Holyoke's Greats," *Springfield* (Massachusetts) *Union-News & Sunday Republican*, March 13, 1997. The author thanks Mathew Jaquith of the Springfield City Library for providing articles from the *Union-News & Sunday Republican*.
11. Comments in Healy's Hall of Fame player file suggest some sort of mental incapacity, perhaps brought on by the stress of playing ball.
12. Hall of Fame player file.
13. All quotes by Healy are from his player file at the Hall of Fame.
14. Baseball-reference.com.

Clarence Heise

By J.G. Preston

CLARENCE "LEFTY" HEISE had an extremely brief major-league career. He opened the 1934 season with the Cardinals but was released to their Columbus farm team on May 1 when major-league rosters had to be cut to 25 players. He pitched in just one major-league game, and he was the only man who played in a game for St. Louis in '34 who did not have a plate appearance. Heise developed a sore arm after returning to the minors and never won a professional game after the 1934 season.

But while Heise has a scant major-league record, he had been a 20-game winner in the minors and led the American Association in winning percentage in 1933 as a member of one of the greatest teams in that league's history. Just 5-feet-10 and described at various times in newspaper accounts as "stocky" or "rotund" (although based on photos that seems to be an exaggeration), he was a hard thrower who twice led his league in strikeouts. And he is the only member of the Gas House Gang who had a son who played in the major leagues.

Clarence Edward Heise (rhymes with "rice") was born on August 7, 1907, in Topeka, Kansas, the only child of Henry F. and Pearl Black Heise. Henry was the Kansas-born son of German immigrants and worked as a railroad machinist.[1] It's not known when the Heise family moved to Springfield, Missouri, but they were there by the time of the 1920 US census, and Clarence graduated from Springfield High School in 1925.[2] He was a standout high-school pitcher who reportedly struck out 24 batters in a game.[3] By the 1930 census, Henry and Pearl Heise lived in Sedalia, Missouri; it's not known when they moved, but in the summer of 1925 Clarence was pitching for the Missouri Pacific (Railroad) Boosters team of Sedalia, and his mound appearances were advertised to help promote attendance.[4]

Clarence signed his first professional contract, with the Cardinals' Danville, Illinois, farm club, in the summer of 1927 for the 1928 season.[5] He later said he made a mistake signing with a team that had such an extensive farm system with so many players under control. "I could have signed with the Giants," Heise said in a 1985 interview. "In 1928 they didn't have a farm system; they had no minor-league teams. I'd have gone to the majors with the Giants, no question about it."[6]

Heise sent a letter home from spring training in Danville on April 11, 1928, telling his parents he had pitched two innings that day at the request of Cardinals general manager Branch Rickey, who wanted to see him in action. Heise held his opponent scoreless, and afterward Rickey shook his hand.[7]

In 1928 Heise had a 6-5 record in 15 games with Laurel (Mississippi) of the Class D Cotton States League and a 3-4 mark in 13 games with Topeka of the Class C Western Association. He began spring training in 1929 with the Cardinals so team officials could get a closer look at him.[8] At the request of the Cardinals, he went to St. Louis on his way to spring training so that he and another minor-league pitcher, Harold Brown, could drive team owner Sam Breadon's car to Florida.[9]

Heise was one of three Cardinals rookies who combined to shut out the Philadelphia Athletics in the

Heise compiled a 90-68 record in a minor-league career that spanned nine years. He made one appearance for the Cardinals, surrendering a home run to Gabby Hartnett of the Cubs on April 22, 1934.

team's first exhibition game, on March 7.[10] He was assigned to their Class B farm team at Danville on April 10,[11] but before the season started he was sent to the Cardinals' Class C farm club at Scottdale, Pennsylvania.

It was a memorable year for the young left-hander. On the field he led the Middle Atlantic League in strikeouts, fanning 154 batters in 184 innings. Off the field, he met and fell in love with a young woman who worked at a local shop, Hazel Reese, and they were married before year's end.[12] Scottdale was Heise's home for the next 40 years.

Aside from the strikeouts, Heise's 1929 pitching record was undistinguished (a 7-13 record with a 4.59 ERA), so the Cardinals sent him back for another season at Scottdale in 1930. While his ERA was about the same (4.67), Heise improved his record to 16-12 and was second in the league in strikeouts with 174. Only three pitchers in the league won more games.

The Cardinals' Texas League farm club at Houston purchased Heise at the end of the 1930 season, and he went to spring training with the Buffaloes in 1931. But before the season started he was assigned to Danville, where he finished second in the Class B Illinois-Indiana-Iowa (Three-I) League with 167 strikeouts in 176 innings. Again Heise's ERA was unimpressive (4.50), but he managed a 10-10 record for a last-place team that finished 28 games under .500.

Just before the Three-I League season ended, the Cardinals promoted Heise to the highest level of the minor leagues (then known as Class AA, or Double-A), with Columbus of the American Association. The Red Birds' schedule extended through September (the Three-I season ended on Labor Day) and Heise made four appearances for them during that final month, starting three games and winning two: a 14-3 decision over Toledo in his Columbus debut, and a 4-1 win at Louisville in a game called after six innings because of darkness as the second game of a doubleheader on September 22. Heise went the distance in both games and also contributed with the bat, hitting a double in the win over Toledo and a triple in the game at Louisville.

On April 2, 1932, Columbus traded Heise to the Cardinals' other Double-A farm club, Rochester of the International League,[13] and he started the season with the Red Wings, but it did not go well. In six appearances he walked 13 batters in 13 innings, striking out only four. On May 10 Heise was returned to Class B, this time with Elmira of the New York-Pennsylvania League.[14] There he had his best season to date. Pitching for another last-place team (despite the presence of 19-year-old future Hall of Famer Johnny Mize in the outfield), Heise posted a 20-8 record, led the league with 187 strikeouts, and finished second in ERA among pitchers who worked at least 140 innings with a 3.08 mark. He was chosen as the league's top left-handed pitcher.

Heise got his 20th win with a little help from his manager. He told the story to an Elmira newspaper reporter in 1967: "I was getting my last start in the first game of a Saturday doubleheader against Scranton. [Actually, box scores in *The Sporting News* show the games in question were on Thursday, September 8.] I didn't last long [knocked out in the second inning]. … I was in the clubhouse relaxing when [Jack] Bentley came in and asked me if I'd like to start the second game. He knew it would be my last chance for 20 victories—and he was going to the wire with me. I grabbed at the chance and felt even stronger than when I started the first game."[15] Elmira won the second game, 5-2, and Heise had reached his milestone.

(Heise appears to have misremembered, unless the interviewer filled in the name of his manager; Jack Bentley had started the season as Elmira's skipper but was replaced by Clay Hopper, who started the season in Mobile before being out of a job when the Southeastern League folded in May.)

Heise suffered a broken nose in a game on July 12 when he was hit by an errant throw to the plate by center fielder Buster Mills, also a member of the 1934 Cardinals. Heise had struck out 12 Hazleton batters in 7 1/3 innings but had to come out of the game after the injury. He missed one turn in the rotation before returning to action and needed surgery at the end of the season to repair the damage.[16]

His performance at Elmira earned Heise another shot at Double-A, this time with Columbus after Rochester traded him back to the Red Birds on January 5, 1933.[17] And this time he was ready to shine at that level.

The 1933 Columbus Red Birds were selected as the 43rd best minor-league team of all time, and fifth best ever in the American Association, by minor-league historians Bill Weiss and Marshall Wright in 2001.[18] The Red Birds won 101 games, the most of any Columbus team ever, and finished 15 1/2 games ahead of second-place Minneapolis in the regular season, then defeated Minneapolis in the league championship series and knocked off American Association playoff champion Buffalo in the Junior World Series.

Catcher Bill DeLancey, outfielder Jack Rothrock, and second baseman Burgess Whitehead all went on to play important roles for the 1934 Cardinals after starring in Columbus in 1933. But the key to the Red Birds' success was a pitching staff that allowed the fewest runs in the league. Paul Dean, the 20-year-old younger brother of Cardinals star Dizzy, led the American Association in wins (22), strikeouts, and ERA. Bill Lee, a 23-year-old right-hander, was right behind Dean in wins with 21, his second straight 20-win season at Columbus.

Heise finished with a 17-5 record for the best winning percentage in the league (.773) and ranked fifth in the league in strikeouts. He was also the starting and winning pitcher in Game Four of the Junior World Series. And he played a crucial role in relief in the Red Birds' clinching win over Minneapolis in the American Association playoff. In the bottom of the ninth inning he was called on to face Millers slugger Joe Hauser, a left-handed hitter, with runners on second and third in a tie game. Hauser had set a professional record (since surpassed) with 69 homers during the regular season and had already homered off Dean in that game. Hauser was especially dangerous at Minneapolis's Nicollet Park, which measured just 279 feet down the right-field line; he had hit 47 of his regular-season homers in his home park.[19] Heise struck out Hauser, then was removed; Columbus scored three runs in the top of the tenth to win the game and take the series.

Perhaps the most memorable game of Heise's career came on August 27, 1933, at Minneapolis, and it was even more notable for his bat than his arm. He delivered a home run, two doubles, and a single, driving in five runs, and pitched a complete game. Heise was cruising along with a 17-1 lead when he let up and allowed the Millers to score four runs in the bottom of the eighth; the final score was 17-5. A left-handed hitter, Heise was far from an automatic out at the plate, with five career home runs and a lifetime minor-league batting average estimated at .242. (A handful of at-bats for teams with which he played just a few games are missing from his record.)

On September 5, as the American Association's regular season was winding down, the Cardinals traded Lee to the Chicago Cubs for delivery in 1934. Cardinals general manager Branch Rickey made the deal with Cubs president Bill Veeck, Sr., whose son Bill Jr. wrote about the transaction in his 1965 book with Ed Linn, *The Hustler's Handbook*. The younger Veeck discussed the trade as part of a point he was trying to make that he thought Rickey would often give trading partners a choice of players but would set up the offer in a way that the other team would be inclined to take the player he actually wanted to part with, allowing Rickey to retain the player he preferred to keep.

"You take risks when you play that game, of course," Veeck wrote. "I know that Branch got caught early in the game when he offered my daddy the choice between Big Bill Lee, a right-hander, and Clarence Heise, a lefty. The Cubs were solid in right-handers … and they had only one lefty, Larry French."[20] (Actually, every Cubs game in 1933 was started by a right-handed pitcher, and French didn't join the team until 1935.)

While he didn't say so explicitly, Veeck implied that Rickey believed the Cubs would be inclined to take the lefty instead of the righty, allowing Rickey to keep Lee. Instead, Veeck Sr. selected Lee, and the trade may well have cost the Cardinals a second straight pennant in 1935, as they finished four games behind the Cubs and Lee posted a 20-6 record.

Hindsight shows that the elder Veeck made the correct choice, as Lee went on to win 169 games in a 14-year major-league career and was runner-up in the

Most Valuable Player voting in 1938. But Veeck Jr.'s contention that Rickey outsmarted himself by giving the Cubs a choice between Lee and Heise may be overstating the case. Even though Lee was right-handed, Rickey couldn't have been shocked that he was the pitcher the Cubs chose. Not only was Lee two years younger than Heise, he had moved through the Cardinal farm system faster and more successfully. He had twice won 20 games at the Double-A level (Heise had not done so once), and in 1931 he had won 22 games at Scottdale, where Heise had won 16 the year before.

Most likely Rickey was happy to part with either player, as one of the goals of the Cardinals' extensive farm system was to provide surplus for sale or trade, and Rickey benefited directly by receiving a percentage of any cash the Cardinals received. As Bill Dooly of the *Philadelphia Record* put it in the winter after the trade: "The reply to why the Cardinals let [Lee] go, if he was any good, seems to run to the effect that the Cards had more pitchers than they needed, but not more cash."[21]

Rickey also sold the top pitcher at his other top farm club, Fritz Ostermueller of Rochester, who led the International League in ERA in 1933 and had a 16-7 record before having his appendix removed. But Rickey didn't part with all his top prospects. He reportedly turned down "something like $50,000 cash" from the Boston Red Sox for Paul Dean,[22] and an item in *The Sporting News* of September 14, 1933, said Heise was "not offered for sale."[23] However, in 1985 Heise told an interviewer that Rickey had turned down an offer of $25,000 for him from the Tigers in the fall of 1933.[24] (He told a 1967 interviewer Cleveland had also made an offer.[25])

At any rate, on September 7 the Cardinals purchased Heise and Jack Rothrock from Columbus, with the players to join St. Louis for spring training in 1934.[26]

The Cardinals had plenty of pitchers in training camp, and Heise appears to have been a long shot to make the team; in fact, a note in *The Sporting News* in January said Heise was expected to return to Columbus.[27] Cardinals player-manager Frankie Frisch, conducting his first spring training after being appointed manager during the 1933 season, didn't give Heise much of a look. But his only start was impressive enough; on March 24 at Lakeland, Florida, facing a Tigers team that had most of its regulars in the lineup, Heise pitched four shutout innings, allowing just two singles and striking out four.

Heise said that after the game, to his surprise, he was asked by Columbus manager Ray Blades whether he wanted to return to Columbus in 1934 or go to Rochester. "The Tiger game was the last game Frisch put me in that spring," Heise recalled in 1985.[28]

That wasn't quite true, but it was close. On March 30 he pitched a scoreless ninth inning in relief against the Yankees and got credit for a win when the Cardinals scored in the bottom of the inning. And he did make one relief appearance in the Cardinals' four-game exhibition series against their crosstown rivals, the American League's Browns, in St. Louis just before the regular season began.

Although he had seen little action in spring training, Heise started the regular season with the Cardinals, and on April 22 at Sportsman's Park he got into what would turn out to be the only game of his major-league career, in the fifth game of the season. After the Cubs had knocked around both Dean brothers and Jim Winford (who had been a Columbus teammate of Heise), Frisch brought Heise in to pitch in the eighth inning with St. Louis trailing 12-2. In the eighth inning, Cubs second baseman Billy Herman singled, advanced to second on a groundout, and then scored after Heise threw two wild pitches. Catcher Gabby Hartnett pulled a two-run homer to left field in the ninth inning; both runs were unearned after Billy Jurges had reached base on an error.[29]

Heise later recalled that Rickey called him into his office after the game. "He told me to go to Columbus. I said I wouldn't. He told me I'd be suspended. Leo Durocher, then the Cardinal shortstop, told me to go home and wait. He said they'd never suspend me, not after the offers teams had made for me. But I was foolish. I didn't listen to Durocher. I had a wife and a 3-year-old son, so I went back to Rickey. He said he'd known for several years that I had major-league talent, but Columbus was drawing way better than the

Cardinals. 'Columbus is keeping us out of the red,' he told me. 'I need you there.'"[30]

Whether Heise's meeting with Rickey came right after his April 22 appearance or sometime shortly thereafter, he stayed with the Cardinals until May 1, when under major-league rules rosters had to be reduced to 25 players. On cutdown day he was released on option to Columbus along with fellow pitcher Bob Klinger, who had not appeared in a game with St. Louis.[31]

At Columbus Heise was part of another championship team, as the Red Birds again won the American Association playoff and Junior World Series. But Heise was not as effective as he had been the previous season, going 9-7 with a 4.78 ERA; for the first time since his first professional season he was not among the league leaders in strikeouts. By the end of the year his arm had gone bad and he did not start any of the Red Birds' postseason games, although he was the winning pitcher in relief in Game Two of the Junior World Series in Toronto when Columbus rallied with six runs in the ninth inning for a 7-4 victory.

That would be Heise's last win as a professional pitcher. His daughter Judy said her father told her he had "an infection in his tonsils that went into his shoulder."[32] Assigned to Rochester in 1935, he had a sore arm all spring[33] and visited a surgeon in Miami who "found that several nerves were crossed in the left-hander's pitching arm."[34] In May the Cardinals sent him to Dallas of the Class A Texas League, where he pitched in one game, on May 23, and lasted just two innings.[35] Heise was returned to Rochester the next day, as Dallas manager Alex Gaston "explained he had seen Heise when he was at his best and that he was only a shadow of his former self."[36]

Heise got back on the mound for Rochester on June 13 but would pitch in just three more games that season.[37] In 1936 he was in spring training with Knoxville of the Class A Southern Association but was returned to Rochester and then dropped to the Class B Piedmont League and appeared in just three games for Asheville.

In 1937 Heise went to spring training at his own expense in an attempt to catch on with the Cleveland Indians' organization[38] and was assigned to their New Orleans farm club in the Southern Association.[39] He was released by the Pelicans on May 8,[40] later going to Chattanooga of the Southern Association and Charlotte of the Piedmont League before retiring as a player.[41]

After his baseball career ended, Heise went back to Scottdale and sold life insurance for Prudential, which he did for 30 years, retiring in April 1968.[42] He stayed involved with baseball, as an American Legion coach and as a player in local leagues.

Clarence and Hazel Heise had three children: Jim, born in 1930; Judy, born in 1937; and Carole, born in 1941.[43] Jim Heise followed in his father's footsteps as a major-league pitcher after a stellar career at West Virginia University that resulted in his being selected for the WVU Hall of Fame in 2011. A right-handed pitcher, Jim Heise was a three-time all-Southern Conference selection (1953, 1955, and 1956) and signed with the Washington Senators after graduating. He pitched in eight games for the Senators in 1957. After his playing career he worked as a high-school science teacher, baseball coach, and school administrator for 32 years and died in 2011.

Hazel Heise died in July 1969,[44] and the following year Clarence married a woman who had also recently lost a spouse, Eunice Chaffee Hall. They moved to Apopka, Florida, outside Orlando, in 1970. Jim and Carole already lived in the area, and Judy moved there as well when her father did. Clarence Heise worked as an usher at Orlando's Tinker Field during the Minnesota Twins' spring training and for the Orlando Twins of the Southern League from 1971 through 1990. After that the Twins stopped holding spring training in Orlando and Heise retired from ushering.

"My biggest problem is that I'm up in the stands now and when I look at the players on the field I get to fidgeting," Heise said in a 1990 interview. "This is screwy, but I feel I could go out there and pitch batting practice. I know I can't, but I sure want to."[45] He was 82 years old.

Heise had never missed a day of work as an insurance agent[46] and missed only three days of work as an usher.[47] "He always stayed in shape and was still doing his own yard work when he was in his late 80s," his daughter Carole remembered. "We all tried to convince him to get someone to do it for him because it is so darn hot down here in the summer, but he was a little stubborn about keeping himself in shape and being independent."[48] He never smoked or drank, according to his daughter Judy.[49]

Clarence Heise died at the age of 91 on May 30, 1999, at the Manor Care Nursing and Rehab Center in Winter Park, Florida, and was buried at Highland Memory Gardens in Apopka.[50] His second wife, Eunice, had preceded him in death in 1996.

"He really was a good ballplayer in his day and he sure loved playing," Carole Heise Clelland said. "I just remember him as a great dad with a great belly laugh, and everyone loved him."[51]

Sources

Thanks to Clarence Heise's daughter Carole Clelland for sharing copies of items about her father in a family scrapbook; Bill Francis of the National Baseball Hall of Fame Library for sharing Heise's file there; and SABR member Stew Thornley for sharing copies of articles in the *Minneapolis Journal* and *Minneapolis Tribune* as well as information about the 1933 American Association playoff. Minor-league statistics are taken from the appropriate Spalding's or Reach annual baseball guides, or, in the case of his 1932 Rochester statistics, from the Hall of Fame file.

Notes

1. 1920 US census accessed via Ancestry.com.
2. Email message from Carole Heise Clelland, July 26, 2013.
3. "Heise Stars For Elmira," undated 1932 clipping in the Heise family scrapbook from an unidentified source.
4. The Heise family scrapbook includes some of the advertising placards, including the phrases, "See 'Lefty' Heise, the Boy Pitcher, in Action" and "See Lefty Heise, 17-Year-Old Booster Pitcher in Action." No other players were mentioned by name.
5. The Heise scrapbook has a letter from Harry Johnson, president of the Cedar Rapids, Iowa, club of the Mississippi Valley League, dated August 30, 1927, in which Johnson writes, "glad to know that you have signed a contract for next year with Danville." He goes on to tell Heise that if Danville has too many pitchers and releases him, "we will be glad to bring you back here." It's not clear what relationship Heise had with the Cedar Rapids club prior to that.
6. Philip Singerman, "This Baseball Season, These Three Men Share Life In The Minor Leagues, But Their Sights Are Set Higher," *Orlando Sentinel*, August 11, 1985.
7. Letter from Clarence Heise to Henry and Pearl Heise, April 11, 1928, in the Heise family scrapbook.
8. The Heise scrapbook has a letter on Danville team letterhead (signature unreadable) dated January 16, 1929, saying, "Arrangements have been made for you to train with the Cardinals at Avon Park, Florida. This will give you an excellent opportunity to receive higher class training and get into condition early." The letter accompanied his 1929 contract with Danville at a salary of $250 per month, but the letter added that he would be cut to $200 per month if he had to be sent to a team in a lower classification.
9. The Heise scrapbook has letters from Cardinals secretary Clarence Lloyd. A letter dated January 29, 1929, includes: "Do you know how to drive an automobile and, if so, would you be interested in helping to drive Mr. Breadon's new Ford from St. Louis to Avon Park? Mr. Breadon plans to arrive in Avon Park on or about February 27th and would like to have this car there on his arrival. We would allow you your railroad fare and berth from here [St. Louis] to Avon Park but your expenses in driving would not amount to that much thus enabling you to make a little spending money enroute." A follow-up letter on February 9 included a check for $9.78 to cover Heise's transportation from Sedalia to St. Louis.
10. Associated Press, "Macks Need Practice," *Canton Repository*, March 8, 1929.
11. United Press, "Training Camp Notes," *Sandusky Star-Journal*, April 10, 1929.
12. Telephone interview with Judy Heise Keller, June 28, 2013.
13. Associated Press, "Red Birds Get Pair Of Rochester Pitchers," *Lima (Ohio) Sunday News*, April 3, 1932.
14. "Heise Sold To Elmira," *Rochester (New York) Journal*, May 10, 1932.
15. Al Mallette, "Lefty Heise Has Fond Memories of Elmira Playing Days," undated clipping from an unknown source in the Heise family scrapbook; Mallette was sports editor of the *Elmira Star-Gazette*, and from the text of the article it clearly seems to have been published in January 1967.
16. Ibid.; *The Sporting News*, July 21, 1932.
17. "Columbus Club Gets Cullop and Teachout," *Cleveland Plain Dealer*, January 6, 1933.
18. milb.com/milb/history/top100.jsp?idx=43.
19. Halsey Hall, "Millers Enter Association Play-Off With High Respect for Birds' Staff," *The Sporting News*, September 14, 1933.
20. Bill Veeck with Ed Linn, *The Hustler's Handbook* (New York: G.P. Putnam's Sons, 1965), 127. The story is also told in *Rob Neyer's Big Book of Baseball Blunders* (New York: Fireside, 2006), 82-83.
21. Bill Dooly, "Cubs Have 'Everything' on Paper," *The Sporting News*, February 1, 1934.
22. Dick Farrington, "Cards Snub $50,000 and Keep Paul Dean," *The Sporting News*, September 7, 1933.
23. J.G. Taylor Spink, "Three And One," *The Sporting News*, September 14, 1933.
24. Philip Singerman, "This Baseball Season."
25. Al Mallette, "Lefty Heise"; see note 15.
26. "Birds Go Up," *Zanesville (Ohio) Signal*, September 7, 1933.

27 Irven Scheibeck, "Columbus Club Seeks Help From Cleveland," *The Sporting News*, January 18, 1934.

28 Philip Singerman, "This Baseball Season."

29 Irving Vaughan, "Cubs Beat Cards, 15-2; One Hit Off Warneke," *Chicago Tribune*, April 23, 1934.

30 Philip Singerman, "This Baseball Season."

31 Associated Press, "Cards Cut Squad to 25 Players," *Moberly (Missouri) Monitor-Index*, May 1, 1934.

32 Telephone interview with Judy Heise Keller, June 28, 2013.

33 From a newspaper clipping in a scrapbook that is part of the collection at the Monroe County (New York) Library, available online at libraryweb.org/~digitized/scrapbooks/Red_Wings/vol_2_07_29_1934.pdf.

34 John Burns, "Sports," *Rochester (New York) Evening Journal*, April 3, 1935.

35 "Indians make Few Hits Count To Beat Herd Again, 6-1," *Dallas Morning News*, May 24, 1935.

36 "Steers Dispose Of Four Players, Reducing Roster," *Dallas Morning News*, May 25, 1935.

37 "Red Wings Moaning Over Condition of Pitching Staff," *Rochester (New York) Evening Journal*, June 15, 1935.

38 "O'Neill To Cut Hurling Staff," *Sandusky (Ohio) Star-Journal*, March 31, 1937.

39 Val J. Flanagan, "Drake's Return as Pelican Puts Mound Staff in Order," *The Sporting News*, April 22, 1937.

40 *New Orleans Times-Picayune*, May 9, 1937, sect. 4, 7

41 The number of games Heise played for each team is not known, but it was not enough to be listed in the 1938 Spalding's Official Baseball Guide, which required a minimum of ten games for both leagues to have full statistics listed. Heise did pitch in at least two games for New Orleans, starting a game on April 25 (Wm. McG. Keefe., "Pelicans Drop Both Ends of Doubleheader to Little Rock Travelers," *New Orleans Times-Picayune*, April 26, 1937) and pitching in relief on May 4 ("Four Pitchers, One Outfielder Fail to Stop Crackers, Pels Lose, 11-4," *New Orleans Times-Picayune*, May 5, 1937).

42 "George Hunt Retires As Insurance Agent," *Uniontown Morning Herald*, April 8, 1968.

43 Email message from Carole Heise Clelland, July 26, 2013.

44 Email message from Carole Heise Clelland, July 26, 2013.

45 Jim Caple, "Twins Have Fond Memories of Orlando's Tinker Field," *St. Paul Pioneer Press*, April 1, 1990.

46 Philip Singerman, "This Baseball Season."

47 Jim Caple, "Twins Have Fond Memories."

48 Email message from Carole Heise Clelland, August 2, 2013.

49 Telephone interview with Judy Heise Keller, June 28, 2013.

50 Death certificate on file at the Baseball Hall of Fame.

51 Email message from Carole Heise Clelland, August 2, 2013.

Jim Lindsey

By Alan Cohen

Jim Lindsey made a name for himself pitching for semipro teams in his native Louisiana. Signed first by the Cleveland Indians, he eventually landed with the Cardinals, and pitched for six seasons as a starter and reliever before being released midway through the 1934 season.

James Kendrick Lindsey was born in Greensburg, Louisiana, on January 24, 1899.[1] One of eight children, he had four sisters and three brothers. His father, Hollis Womack Lindsey, Sr., was a farmer and cattleman and a sheriff, who later became a state game conservation agent for St. Helena Parish. His mother was the former Margaret Minerva Thompson. His sister, Doris Lindsey Holland, was the first woman to serve in the Louisiana legislature.[2]

Lindsey's first mound success came at the Chamberlain-Hunt Academy in Port Gibson, Mississippi, where he pitched for two years. He was later with Cleveland, Mississippi, in the semipro Delta League. By 1919 Plantation Jim, as he was then called, was working as a crude-oil stillman and pitching for the the Standard Oil Company of Louisiana refinery, called Stanocola.[3]

In May 1920 Lindsey and Carlotta Matthews were married. They remained married for 43 years, until Lindsey's death, and had one daughter and three grandchildren.[4]

Lindsey signed his first professional contract with the Cleveland Indians in 1920, but although he trained with the team and pitched briefly for the New Orleans Pelicans of the Southern Association, he spent 1920 and 1921 with Stanocola.[5] He also pitched in the New Orleans semipro Dixie League for a team known as the Peppermints. In fact, after returning home from most of his minor-league seasons, he would pitch for a semipro team. One such outing took place on September 19, 1926, when his Stanocola team defeated Placquemine 8-0 as Lindsey limited the opposition to two hits and went 3-for-4 at the plate.[6]

In 1922 Lindsey was among 18 pitchers who reported to Dallas for spring training with Tris Speaker's Indians.[7] On March 27, in an intrasquad game, he virtually assured himself of a roster spot by limiting a squad of Indians regulars to two hits over five innings in a 3-2 win. His control in that game set him apart. In his first two springs with the Indians, he had been the "wildest thing in pitching," but his efforts that day were universally praised. Smoky Joe Wood, who had won 34 games as a pitcher with the 1912 Boston Red Sox, was finishing his career as an outfielder with the Indians and was also working with Cleveland's pitchers during spring training. He said, "I never saw Jim look as good as he did today. He could throw the ball where he wanted to. In other years, he has lacked control."[8]

The Indians brought Lindsey north. It was his first time out of the South. Upon arriving in Chicago for the first time, Plantation Jim observed, "She's some village."[9] He was one of 46

Acquired from St. Paul of the American Association in June, Lindsey appeared in 11 games in 1934. Previously, he pitched on both of the Cardinals pennant winners in 1930 and 1931.

players on the Cleveland revolving-door team of 1922. He appeared in 29 games, all but five as a reliever.

Lindsey was pressed into service as a starter for the first time on May 11, pitching the first six innings in a game against the Philadelphia Athletics that Cleveland won, 5-4. His first win came a month later, on June 11 against Philadelphia. He came on in relief and pitched four shutout innings as the Indians, down 8-4 at one point, came back to win, 9-8.

Lindsey's prowess at the plate was not particularly exceptional. His first major-league hit, a single, came on June 17, 1922, in a 14-inning marathon against Boston. Lindsey put out the fire in the fourth inning and pitched 2 2/3 scoreless innings in relief. After singling in the sixth, he injured himself sliding, and came out of the game. His only RBI of the 1922 season came in an 11-3 loss to the Yankees on July 6.

Facing the Yankees on July 9, Lindsey had his best outing of 1922. He came into the game in the bottom of the eighth inning with New York leading. Lindsey allowed an unearned run in the eighth, the Indians tied the score in the ninth, and the game went into extra innings. The Indians scored a pair in the 13th to go out in front and Lindsey held off the likes of Babe Ruth and Bob Meusel, going six innings to earn his third win of the season. Four days later, against the Red Sox, he was almost as good. He came in with runners on first and third and none out in the sixth and allowed but one hit in the last four innings as the Indians came back to win, 4-2. It was Lindsey's fourth and last win of the season.[10]

Despite these flashes of brilliance, Lindsey's overall performance in his rookie season was not superlative. For the season, he went 4-5 and posted an ERA of 5.92. He was sent back to the minors in 1923, and spent most of the next seven seasons in the minor leagues. In 1923 he was with Milwaukee in the American Association and went 8-12. The Indians brought him back for the start of the 1924 season, but he got into only three games, allowing seven runs in three innings, before being sold to Kansas City of the American Association at the end of June. During the balance of the season, he went 3-4 with the Blues before developing neuritis in his pitching arm that lingered into the following season.[11]

The next five seasons were spent in the Texas League. Lindsey began the 1925 season with Dallas and was released on May 3. He signed on with San Antonio, where an examination determined that he had three bad teeth that were causing his problems. The teeth were removed and his arm came around.[12] With the two teams he was 9-10.

Over the next two seasons, Lindsey went a combined 28-24 for San Antonio. The National League champion Pittsburgh Pirates drafted him, but he wound up back in the Texas League, this time with the Houston Buffaloes.[13] His two years with Houston, under the tutelage of former minor-league catcher Frank Snyder were exceptional, and he went 46-20. In 1928 he led the circuit with 25 wins as Houston won the league championship, then won the Dixie Series against Birmingham of the Southern Association, taking four straight games after losing the first two. Lindsey pitched Houston to its first win in Game Three.

Lindsey resumed his march back to the major leagues in 1929 by winning six of his first seven starts, including four shutouts. (One of the shutouts was observed by Cardinals general manager Branch Rickey.)[14] In all, Lindsey had a league-leading eight shutouts in his 20 wins with Houston that season. At one point, he pitched a league-record 30 straight shutout innings, and he allowed five hits or less in nine games, including a one-hitter. Lindsey was sold to the Cardinals at the end of August.[15] In his first start for St. Louis, on September 15, he pitched a complete game as the Cardinals beat the New York Giants 6-4 at Sportsman's Park. A week later he pitched six innings of one-hit ball against the Brooklyn Robins (the only hit was by pitcher Dazzy Vance), but ran into problems in the seventh and eighth, surrendering six runs as Brooklyn won, 7-2.[16]

Lindsey had a poor spring training in 1930, and was on the verge of being sent back to the minor leagues.[17] But he stayed with St. Louis and had a 7-5 record. On May 13 against the Giants, he entered the game with the bases loaded and none out in the sixth inning and was in command the rest of the way as the Cardinals came from behind to win, 6-4.[18] Lindsey was used as both a starter and reliever, and his versatility was apparent in the month of August. On August 6 he preserved a victory over the Cubs, pitching the final two innings in a 4-3 win and striking out Charley Grimm and Gabby Hartnett in the ninth inning.[19] In addition to five relief appearances, Lindsey started five games in August. In his starts, he went 3-2. He pitched three complete games in those starts.

On a very deep pitching staff, led by Wild Bill Hallahan and Burleigh Grimes, Lindsey didn't get noticed much, but he showed his mettle as the Cardinals won the pennant and went on to face the Philadelphia A's in the World Series. Lindsey got into two games that the Cardinals lost, pitching 4 2/3 innings and allowing one run. In Game Two he relieved Flint Rhem, and pitched 2 2/3 scoreless innings. In his one at-bat, he singled off George Earnshaw, and in characteristic Lindsey style, he said that he "stretched a triple into a single."[20] Lindsey was effective in the decisive sixth game, pitching two innings, but once again he entered the game too late to make a difference as the Cardinals fell to the Athletics.

Lindsey had one of his best seasons in 1931, primarily as a reliever when relieving was not a role many pitchers aspired to. In his first eight appearances, he pitched 14 innings and allowed but one run. Observed a sportswriter, "No matter how gloomy the outlook, when manager Gabby Street gives him the nod, Big Jim strolls to the hill with the nonchalance of a bride making her fifth trip to the altar. They say, in St. Louis, that his attitude upsets the mental poise of the enemy batters. Regardless of whether there is anything to the theory, he usually gets them out with undue delay."[21]

As the Cardinals headed toward a pennant, Lindsey came out of the bullpen for a spot start on September 15, and came through with a 5-0 shutout to bring the Cards to within a game of clinching the pennant.[22] It was his sixth win of the season, against four losses. Out of the bullpen, he had seven saves, good for second in the league (the saves are retrospective; the statistic didn't exist when Lindsey was pitching), and his ERA for the season was 2.77.

The Cardinals once again faced the Philadelphia Athletics in the World Series. They lost both of the games in which Lindsey appeared in relief, but won the Series in seven games. In two World Series, Lindsey pitched eight innings in relief with no decisions, giving up five runs (three earned) for a 3.38 ERA.

It was common for Lindsey to eat up innings coming out of the bullpen, and this was very much the case on July 20, 1932. He came in when starter Tex Carleton faltered in the second inning, stopped the bleeding, and pitched the remainder of the game, securing his third win of the season, as the Cardinals won, 16-5. For the season Lindsey went 3-3 with a 4.94 ERA as the Cardinals dropped to a sixth-place finish.

Lindsey started 1933 with St. Louis but appeared in only one game before being sent to Columbus at the end of April. Later, when his record was 7-2, he was moved to Rochester, another Cardinals affiliate, in an eight-player transaction. One of the reasons for the deal was that Columbus was over the American Association salary limit. League officials had suspended Lindsey and three other players and fined Lindsey $200. The fine was later rescinded.[23] With Rochester Lindsey was only 3-9, but pitched well in the playoffs.

Before the 1934 season the Cincinnati Reds purchased Lindsey's contract, and he began the season with the Reds.[24] On May 23 of that year, after appearing in four games, he was sold to St. Paul of the American Association, and he was back with the Cardinals on June 5. Between June 6 and July 8, he appeared in 11 games, all in relief.

One game in particular was memorable. On July 1 Dizzy Dean was matched up against Tony Freitas of Cincinnati. Although neither pitcher was particularly effective, they were still pitching and the score was 5-5 after nine innings. There was no further scoring, with Dean and Freitas pitching, until the 17th inning. Ducky Medwick put St. Louis in the lead with a homer, but the Reds tied the score in the bottom of the inning. The Cardinals then took the lead in the 18th with a pair of runs off Paul Derringer, who had come in to relieve Freitas in the 17th inning. Lindsey pitched the bottom of the 17th, holding the Reds scoreless. It was Lindsey's last hurrah with St. Louis. There were two more appearances, neither notable, and he was released on July 10 after going 0-1 with a 6.43 ERA. He may not have been around to see the Cardinals win the pennant over the New York Giants, but that last save, on July 1, made him part of the story.

Lindsey's next stop was in Atlanta. For four seasons, beginning at age 35, he hurled with success for the Crackers, going 36-25. Used mostly as a reliever, he continued to excel, as he had in his major-league days when given an occasional spot start. His curveball was still effective as he pitched the Crackers to a 9-2 win over Oklahoma City in the second game of the 1935 Dixie Series.[25]

Released by Atlanta late in the 1937 season, Lindsey signed with the Brooklyn Dodgers, who were short of pitchers.[26] In 20 games with the Dodgers, the 38-year-old Lindsey went 0-1 with two saves, with a 3.52 ERA. His last major-league appearance came on September 27, 1937.

In nine major-league seasons, Lindsey won 21 games and lost 20 with a 4.68 ERA. Although the save statistic wasn't used at the time, he had 19 saves using current the save definition.

In 1938 Lindsey worked out with the New York Giants, who were training in Baton Rouge, so as to be in shape for the Southern Association season, or maybe even another crack at the big leagues. He spent the year in the Southern Association, playing with Chattanooga and Arkansas. There was still something left in the 39-year-old arm. In his last outing of consequence, he pitched a seven-inning shutout as Chattanooga defeated Atlanta 5-0 in the second game of a doubleheader on May 29.[27] But the writing was on the wall. For the season Lindsey went 3-8, and his professional baseball career was over.

After he retired from baseball at the end of the 1938 season, Lindsey operated a dairy farm in Baton Rouge. Governor Earl Long appointed him farm manager at the East Louisiana State Hospital in Jackson, and he sold the farm. His daughter Colleen kept Lindsey's herd, bought another farm, and eventually bred prize-winning Holstein cattle

Lindsey, a member of the Jackson Methodist Church, continued in his position as farm manager until he died on October 25, 1963, at the age of 64.

Sources

The following databases and files were used:

Ancsestry.com

Baseball-Reference.com

Paper of Record

GenealogyBank.com

NewspaperArchive.com

Jim Lindsey file at the National Baseball Hall of Fame and Museum Library

The following newspapers were used:

Cleveland Plain Dealer

Dallas Morning News

New Orleans Item

Rochester Democrat and Chronicle

Springfield (Massachusetts) *Republican*

State Times Advocate (Baton Rouge, Louisiana)

Times-Picayune (New Orleans, Louisiana)

Newspaper Articles:

Bell, Stuart M., "Jim Lindsey is Big Noise as Cleveland Yannigans Hang it on to the Regulars," *Cleveland Plain Dealer,* March 28, 1922, 13.

Dixon, Margaret, "Two Big League Baseball Players Consider Retirement," *Morning Advocate* (Baton Rouge, Louisiana), December 4, 1938, 7-B.

Holmes, Tommy, "Robins Lost Golden Opportunity by Failing to Sweep St. Louis Series," *Brooklyn Daily Eagle*, September 23, 1929, 22.

Keyerleber, Kyle, "Laughs in Sports," *Cleveland Plain Dealer,* January 17, 1939, 16.

Powers, Francis J., "Red Sox Miscalculate on Joe Sewell's Ability and Indians win again 4-2," *Cleveland Plain Dealer,* July 14, 1922, 18.

Singleton, W.B., "Familiar Faces in the Big Show," *Dallas Morning News,* December 21, 1930, sports section, 2.

Whitman, Burt, "Close Decision Is Given Against Sox, Who Lose," *Boston Herald,* July 14, 1922, 15.

Notes

1. There is some question about his actual birth date and year, with sources listing years from 1896 through 1900. Baseball-Reference.com shows January 24, 1896. According to his draft card, the date is January 24, 1899. The Louisiana Marriage Records Index reflects that Lindsey was born "about 1899." The 1900, 1910, and 1940 census

records also reflect the 1899 birth year, but the 1920 and 1930 census records showed him being born in 1897, and his death certificate lists his date of birth as January 24, 1898. Papers in his file at the Baseball Hall of Fame Library give dates in 1900. One date, from a release titled "Major League Newcomers," shows February 23, 1900.

2. *Baton Rouge State Times Advocate,* March 24, 1936.
3. *Baton Rouge State Times Advocate,* March 5, 1920, 2
4. *New Orleans Times-Picayune*, May 5, 1920.
5. *New Orleans Item*, October 26, 1922, 18.
6. *Baton Rouge State Times Advocate,* September 20, 1926.
7. *Dallas Morning News*, March 6, 1922, 10.
8. Stuart M. Bell, "Jim Lindsey is Big Noise as Cleveland Yannigans Hang it on to the Regulars," *Cleveland Plain Dealer,* March 28, 1922, 13.
9. Bell, *Cleveland Plain Dealer,* April 8 1922, 16.
10. Francis J. Powers, "Red Sox Miscalculate on Joe Sewell's Ability and Indians win again 4-2," *Cleveland Plain Dealer*, July 14, 1922, 18; Burt Whitman, "Close Decision Is Given Against Sox, Who Lose," *Boston Herald*, July 14, 1922, 15.
11. W.B. Singleton, "Familiar Faces in the Big Show," *Dallas Morning News,* December 21, 1930, sports section, 2.
12. *Springfield Republican*, December 21, 1930, 18.
13. Baton Rouge Advocate, October 13, 1927, 10.
14. *Boston Herald*, May 26, 1929, 21.
15. *Dallas Morning News*, September 1, 1929, sports section, 2
16. Tommy Holmes, "Robins Lost Golden Opportunity by Failing to Sweep St. Louis Series," *Brooklyn Daily Eagle*, September 23, 1929, 22.
17. *Sarasota Herald Tribune*, March 27, 1930, 10.
18. *New Orleans Times-Picayune*, May 14, 1930, 15.
19. *Pittsburgh Post-Gazette*, August 7, 1930, 16.
20. Lindsey Obituary on file in the Baseball Hall of Fame Library.
21. *Sarasota Herald Tribune,* June 1, 1931, 6
22. *Baltimore Sun*, September 6, 1931, 15.
23. *Milwaukee Journal*, November 17, 1933, D-7.
24. *Montreal Gazette*, February 20, 1934, 12.
25. Kenneth Gregory (Associated Press), "Jim Lindsey Hurls great 9-2 victory, in the *Baton Rouge Advocate,* October 1, 1935, 8.
26. *Miami News*, August 4, 1937, 7
27. *Augusta* (Georgia) *Chronicle*, May 30, 1938, 6

Pepper Martin

By Norm King

THE ONLY THING a team with players named Dizzy, Ducky, and Daffy needed to become truly legendary was a dash of Pepper. And that's exactly what the famed Gas House Gang St. Louis Cardinals got in their sparkplug extraordinaire, Pepper Martin.

Johnny Leonard Roosevelt Martin was a leap-year baby, born February 29, 1904, in Temple, Oklahoma, 120 miles south of Oklahoma City. He was the youngest of seven children born to Celia Spears Martin and George Washington Martin. The Martins struggled to make ends meet as cotton farmers, forcing Johnny to learn very early on that everything he got in life would come only through hard work. Even as a boy he worked with his brothers and sisters tending the family livestock. Despite the presence of animals on the farm, meals often didn't offer much variety.

"In lean times the family ate cornmeal mush and fried mush, too," wrote Martin biographer Thomas Bartel. "Beans and cabbage, bought by the hundred-pound sack, supplied much of the family diet."[1]

The family moved to Oklahoma City in 1910 after the farm was ruined by a drought. Their financial circumstances didn't improve very much, and in those days this meant that Martin often had to leave school and work to contribute to the family income. He delivered newspapers, getting up at 3:30 in the morning to deliver the *Daily Oklahoman*, but before beginning his appointed rounds, he caught up on major-league box scores during the summer, and read about offseason goings on in the winter. In the afternoon he delivered another paper, *The News*. Eventually, he saved up to buy what became one of his prized possessions, his first baseball glove.

"Not so many kids in my neighborhood had gloves and owning that mitten gave me almost as much happiness as would a couple of home runs in a World's Series game," Martin said.[2]

Pride in ownership aside, Martin's frequent absences from elementary school delayed his graduation until he was 15 years old, in 1919. He went to high school in the next year, but quit again to make deliveries for the Mistletoe Shoe Company at $12 per week. After a brief return in 1921, he quit school for good, "to earn money instead of fiddling around and getting an education."[3]

Most of Martin's early experience as a ballplayer was in the Oklahoma City sandlots with various club and company teams. He first played organized ball for the Second Presbyterian Church (Martin was a Baptist) in 1921 as a pitcher. Over the next few years he also played for the Brooks Hardware Company, Kelley Jewelry, the Oklahoma Gas and Electric Company, and even the Oklahoma National Guard (the latter arrangement ended when Martin didn't join the outfit).

Martin's athletic endeavors weren't restricted to the baseball diamond. In the early 1920s (accounts differ as to which years), he played halfback for the Hominy

Martin spent all of his 13 major-league seasons wearing a Cardinals uniform, owning a career .298 batting average. He batted .418 in three World Series. Martin led the league in steals in 1934 with 23.

Indians, a popular and often powerful team during the Jazz Age that was backed by members of the Osage Native American tribe that had gotten wealthy due to the Oklahoma oil boom.[4]

But baseball was Martin's first love and he finally got into the professional ranks in 1924, when a friend named Cliff Campbell put in a word for him with the Guthrie team in the Oklahoma State League, a circuit that was teetering on the edge of extinction. The Guthrie franchise moved twice before the league finally disbanded in July of that year. The league's demise was a blessing in disguise for Martin, because he went to a Cardinals tryout camp in Greenville, Texas, where St. Louis had a team in the Class D East Texas League. The Cardinals signed him on July 10, 1924, and paid Guthrie $300 for him. Martin appeared in 27 games as a pitcher and center fielder for the Greenville Hunters. He hit a respectable .274 and had a 1-1 record.

Martin started the 1925 season in Greenville and while he continued to pitch and play the outfield, his primary position was second base. He pasted the ball at a .340 clip in 98 games, with 18 home runs and 38 stolen bases, and the Cardinals promoted him to Fort Smith (Arkansas), their team in the Class C Western Association. There he showed he could handle higher-level pitching, batting .344 the rest of the season. Fielding was another issue. Playing shortstop, Martin committed 21 errors in 203 chances for an .897 fielding percentage.

It was in Fort Smith that John Martin became "Pepper" Martin, although the exact origin is not clear. He is quoted as saying that team owner Blake Harper began calling him Pepper after watching him run the bases and "listening to my line of chatter."[5] In another version, Martin arrived in Fort Smith and saw the headline "Pepper Martin to Join Twins." Angry at the headline, Martin stormed down to the newspaper office to complain, only to see Harper there and be told that Harper had picked out the name.[6] Harper may have borrowed the nickname from Vincent "Pepper" Martin, a prominent featherweight and junior lightweight boxer of the time. Whatever the origin, the moniker stuck.

Despite his adventures in fielding, Martin's hitting earned him a spot with the Syracuse Stars of the Double-A International League (there was no Triple-A designation at that time). When it came time to go to from Oklahoma to spring training in Greenwood, South Carolina, he cashed the check that was supposed to pay for his train ticket and rode the rails like a hobo to his destination.

After not bathing for several days while en route, Martin was rather stinky when he arrived in camp. That was somehow appropriate because the Syracuse club's play that season could be described much the same way, as its 70-91 record will attest. Martin duplicated his good-hit, no-field results from the previous season; he batted .300, but he committed 35 errors in 88 games at second base. Cardinals management evidently felt the leap from Class C to Double-A was too much for Martin and demoted him to the Houston Buffaloes of the Class A Texas League in 1927 for more seasoning and to learn how to play the outfield.

Offensively, Martin continued peppering the ball to the tune of a .306 average and eight home runs, and had a .963 fielding percentage as an outfielder. His numbers impressed Cardinals brass enough to win him a spot on their major league roster for the 1928 season.

Once Martin got to the big leagues, however, it seemed the Cardinals didn't know what to do with him. He appeared in only 39 games all season, including just 16 plate appearances, with all but one being pinch-hit appearances. He played only four games in the field, and was used as a pinch-runner 21 times. He did get his first taste of World Series action that year as a pinch-runner in Game Four against the New York Yankees. He scored a ninth-inning run, but it was of little use; it was in the game in which Babe Ruth hit three home runs in leading the Yankees juggernaut to a 7-3 victory and a sweep of the Redbirds.

Since Martin wasn't getting playing time in the major leagues, he was better off returning to the minors, and that's exactly what he did, being sent to Houston in 1929. He played a full season there, batted .298, and captured the fans' fancy.

"The fans of Houston voted Johnny the most popular player on the team," said his wife, Ruby. "He was given a Chevrolet coupe for a prize."[7]

As popular as Martin may have been with the Houston fans, the Cardinals still didn't think he was ready to rejoin the big club. They did, however, promote him to Rochester for the 1930 season. Unlike his previous sojourn in Double-A, he left no doubt this time about his abilities by hitting .363, with 20 home runs and 304 total bases. The major-league career, and the legend, of Pepper Martin were about to begin in 1931.

Martin was essentially a 27-year-old rookie when he donned a Cardinals uniform during the spring of 1931. The Cardinals won the National League pennant going away that year; they won 101 games and were 13 games ahead of the second-place New York Giants by season's end. Martin made a substantial contribution with a .300 batting average, 75 RBIs, 68 runs scored, and 16 stolen bases, but it was in that year's World Series that he really shone.

The Cardinals' opponent in the fall classic was the two-time defending champion Philadelphia Athletics, the last great team Connie Mack ever had. The Cardinals knew how formidable the A's were, having lost to them in the previous year's Series in six games. The 1931 Series was a back-and-forth affair, as neither team held more than a one-game advantage at any time. Martin proved the difference between winning and losing for the Cardinals when he tied a Series record (since broken) with 12 hits, and batted .500 with one home run, five RBIs, and five stolen bases. If they had a World Series MVP in those days, Martin would have won it hands down.

Martin's outstanding World Series performance made him a household name and after the Series was over he embarked on a vaudeville tour at $1,500 per week, an outstanding salary in Depression-era America. The great salary notwithstanding, he quit the gig after just four weeks, saying, "I ain't no actor, I'm a ballplayer."[8]

Before the 1932 season, Martin had this to say about baseball fans' expectations: "One day they holler for you to take off your cap; the next say they yell at you to take off your uniform."[9] All the Cardinals probably heard a lot of yelling that season season as an injury-plagued Martin appeared in only 85 games and batted .238 with only 34 RBIs, both career lows, and the team plummeted to sixth place with a 72-82 record.

Still, the season was significant for Martin in two respects. First, manager Gabby Street decided to experiment by moving Martin from center field to third base in early September once it became apparent that the Cardinals weren't going to win the pennant. It ended up being his primary position for the next three seasons. Second, a young pitcher named Jay Hanna Dean, or Jerome Herman Dean (depending on which day of the week you asked him), known to all as Dizzy, joined the team. Dean's arrival gave Martin a partner in crime for stunts considered humorous among players of that era. Their teammate Leo Durocher related a story about how Dean and Martin pulled a gag involving a society women's luncheon at Philadelphia's elegant Bellevue-Stratford hotel, where the team was staying:

What Pepper did first was to go to a trick store for a handful of smoke bombs. What he did next was to go down to Wanamaker's (department store) with a couple of the others to buy firemen's uniforms. The lunch hour ended, the dowagers filed out into their cars and from there it was nothing except explosions and smoke and jumping hoods. The women went running back into the dining room in panic to mix with the women who were trying to leave and a whole new group that was trying to get in. In the middle of all this pandemonium, Pepper and his crew arrived in their firemen's uniforms to enforce the fire regulations. Well, they had women moving from one table to the other, they had three women standing up here and five others sitting down there. They had the manager and the captains running all over the place.[10]

Durocher gives us other insights into Martin that may fall into the "too much information" category, such as that he never wore underwear or a "protective cup" when playing.

"God apparently watches over drunks and third basemen who play without any protective gear," wrote Durocher. "Pepper must have been hit in every other portion of his body at one time or another except the crucial one."[11]

When Martin wasn't causing chaos in fancy hotels, he was having a string of some pretty productive years at his new position, beginning in 1933. He hit .316 and led the league in runs scored (122) and stolen bases (26), which he pilfered using a head-first slide that Durocher claimed he invented.[12] Martin was also the very first batter in the very first All-Star Game, at Comiskey Park in Chicago. Gabby Street's experiment of having Martin play third base was unsuccessful from a defensive standpoint, as Martin was second in the league in errors by a third baseman with 25. But overall, his improved productivity helped the Cardinals rebound from their bad 1932 season, and although they finished fifth, their 82-71 record set the table for the famous 1934 season.

The Gas House Gang, as the Cardinals were nicknamed in 1934, were seven games behind the New York Giants on September 6, but roared back to win the pennant by two games. They went on to defeat the Detroit Tigers in seven games in the World Series. Injuries limited Martin to 110 games that season, but he nonetheless repeated as stolen-base champion (23) and as an All-Star, even though his average dipped to .289. His performance in the fall classic didn't quite measure up to the standard he had set three years earlier, but it was still impressive: 11 hits, a .355 batting average, 4 RBIs, and 8 runs scored.

Martin made his third consecutive trip to the All-Star game in 1935, and his average improved to .299, although he lost his stolen-base crown to Augie Galan of the Chicago Cubs (Galan had 22, Martin had 20). He was second on the team in runs scored with 121, 11 behind team leader Joe "Ducky" Medwick.

Martin regained the stolen-base title in 1936 in what turned out to be has last complete season in the major leagues. He pilfered 23 bags, drove in a career-high 76 runs, batted .309 and scored 121 runs for the second year in a row, yet he was not chosen for the All-Star team. It is possible that his switch to right field from third base may have been the reason because the right fielders on the National League All-Star team were Frank Demaree of the Cubs and Mel Ott of the Giants. Both those players had superior power numbers: Demaree hit 16 home runs and drove in 96 runs, while Ott led the league with 33 homers and 135 RBIs.

The 1937 season got off to a good start for Martin. He was hitting .317 around the time of the All-Star Game, and regained a berth on the National League team.[13] Then he suffered a serious knee injury in August and ended up playing in only 98 games for the season.[14]

Martin, in fact, never appeared in that many games again. Between 1937 and 1940, he averaged 91 games per season and never did appear again in the World Series.

While injury reduced his playing time, Martin found other ways to stay productive. One of them was the formation of his Mississippi Mudcats band, with teammates Lon Warneke (guitar), Bill McGee (violin), Lefty Weiland (jug), outfielder Frenchy Bordagaray (washboard, auto horns). The band played real ol' down-home country music, and was even good enough to appear on radio.[15] Their repertoire included such classics as "They Buried My Sweetie Under an Old Pine Tree."

Martin retired after the 1940 season to become manager of the Sacramento Solons, the Cardinals' affiliate in the Pacific Coast League. He managed in the minors for 13 seasons with several teams from as low as Class B all the way up to Triple-A. He interrupted his managerial career in 1944 to play 40 games in the outfield for the Cardinals in the manpower-depleted World War II season. After that he returned to managing in the minor leagues, except for a stint as a coach with the Cubs in 1956.

Martin's managerial career reached a low point in 1949 when he choked an umpire while piloting the Miami Sun Sox of the Class B Florida International League, and was suspended for the remainder of the season. The Sun Sox were playing the Havana Cubans in Havana on August 26 when a rhubarb erupted after a decision by base umpire W.E. Williams on a close play. In the ensuing argument, Williams ejected Sun Sox second baseman Knobby Rosa and when Rosa refused to leave, chief umpire Clem Camia declared the game forfeited. Martin became a manager gone wild, went after Camia and started choking him until police pulled Martin off.

The suspension was handed down on September 1, with less than a week to go in the season, causing Martin to miss only five games. He was back in the manager's chair in 1950.[16]

Martin's high point came in 1953 when he led the Fort Lauderdale Lions to a first-place finish, with a 92-46 record, 14 games ahead of the St. Petersburg

Saints. The Lions went on to win the league championship in six games over St. Petersburg.

Martin was a Renaissance Man of sorts, and not just for his ability playing what he called the "gittar." He was in the fight game as co-manager of a boxer, played basketball for the House of David basketball team, served briefly as a placekicker for the National Football League's Brooklyn Dodgers, and was an avid outdoorsman.

In 1961, after he had left Organized Baseball, Martin worked as the athletic director for the Oklahoma State Penitentiary, where he coached the prison's baseball team, and, presumably, taught his players how to steal.

Martin died on March 5, 1965, at the age of 61 in McAlester, Oklahoma, from a heart attack he had suffered the night before at his ranch in Blocker. His wife, Ruby, and three daughters, Alyne, Jennie and Alice, survived him.

Sources

Barthel, Thomas, *Pepper Martin: A Baseball Biography* (Jefferson, North Carolina: McFarland and Company, Inc., 2003).

Durocher, Leo, with Ed Linn, *Nice Guys Finish Last* (Chicago: University of Chicago Press, 1975).

Pittsburgh Press, March 3, 1932

Milwaukee Journal, October 22, 1938

The Independent, (St. Petersburg, Florida), September 2, 1949

The Sporting News, March 20, 1965

baseball-reference.com

baseball-almanac.com

nndb.com

Notes

1. Thomas Barthel, *Pepper Martin: A Baseball Biography* (Jefferson, North Carolina: McFarland and Company, Inc., 2003) 5-6.

2. Barthel, 7.

3. Barthel, 10.

4. The inscription on a bust of Martin at Redhawk Ballpark in Oklahoma City attributes the nickname "Wild Horse of the Osage" to his time as a football player for the Hominy Indians (waymarking.com/waymarks/WMAYAC_John_LR_Pepper_Martin_Oklahoma_City_OK). An article in the *Miami News*, April 9, 1959, credits the nickname to the Cardinals' trainer, who thought it up during the 1931 World Series.

5. Barthel, 19.

6. Ibid.

7. Walter W. Smith, "'Pepper' Martin Hero to his Wife," *Pittsburgh Post-Gazette*, October 10, 1931.

8. Joe Reichler and Ben Olan (Associated Press), "Pepper Gallops to National Fame," *Tuscaloosa News*, January 26, 1961.

9. "Pepper Martin Unspoiled by World Series Fame," *Pittsburgh Press*, March 3, 1932.

10. Leo Durocher with Ed Linn, *Nice Guys Finish Last*, (Chicago: University of Chicago Press, 1975), 91.

11. Durocher, 89.

12. Durocher, 82.

13. Edgar G. Brands, "All-Star Tilt to Test N.L. Hurling Against A.L. Bats," *The Sporting News*, July 1, 1937.

14. Red Byrd, "Cards' Bubble Pops on Dizzy's 'Bursitis,'" *The Sporting News*, September 2, 1937.

15. "Radio: Programs Previewed: September 5, 1938," *Time*, September 5, 1938.

16. Associated Press, "Pepper Martin Suspended Rest of Season for Choking Umpire," *The Independent* (St. Petersburg, Florida), September 2, 1949.

Joe Medwick

By Charles F. Faber

TEN TIMES HE was named to the National League All-Star team; he won the circuit's Most Valuable Player Award in 1937; and in that same year he became the league's last batter (as of 2013) to win the Triple Crown by leading the loop in batting average, home runs, and runs batted in during the same season. Yet perhaps Joe Medwick is better remembered for being banished from a World Series game by Commissioner Kenesaw Mountain Landis than for his exploits on the field.

It was the seventh and deciding game of the 1934 World Series in Detroit between the St. Louis Cardinals and the hometown Tigers. Behind the stellar pitching of Dizzy Dean, who with some justification proclaimed himself the greatest pitcher in the world, the Gas House Gang were leading 7-0 in the sixth inning. But they wanted more. Pepper Martin led off the top of the frame with a single to left and made it to second on Goose Goslin's misplay of the ball. Jack Rothrock and Frankie Frisch both flied out. Up came Medwick with Martin on second and two out. Joe slashed a long hit against the right-field bleachers, knocking in Martin. As Medwick slid into third base, Marvin Owen, the Tiger third sacker, dug his foot into Joe's leg. The hot-tempered Cardinal, still lying on the ground after the slide, retaliated by kicking Owen in the stomach with both spiked shoes. For a moment it appeared that a fight would break out, but players and umpires quickly separated the potential combatants and the game continued. Ripper Collins batted Medwick home with a single to make the score 9-0. The half-inning ended when Bill DeLancey was thrown out at first base after he and the catcher both missed strike three.

Medwick was a .324 lifetime hitter over a 17-year career. He led the league in triples with 18 in 1934, and batted .379 in the World Series. He was inducted into the Hall of Fame in 1968.

When Medwick took the field in the bottom of the sixth, Detroit fandom greeted him with resounding boos and a barrage of missiles hurled into left field. Mostly apples, oranges, and grapefruit, but also a few pop bottles were thrown onto the playing field. No bottles hit a player, and Medwick and fellow outfielders Ernie Orsatti and Rothrock started playing catch with some of the fruit on the field, further incensing the crowd. That Medwick seemed to be not at all intimidated by the barrage made the crowd even more upset. The umpires halted play, and sent workers out with burlap bags to pick up the debris. Three times the umpires and Detroit manager Mickey Cochrane called for order, to no effect. Each time Medwick attempted to take the field, the assault began anew. When it appeared that all the fruit and vegetables in the stands had already been thrown, someone discovered that hot-dog buns and folded-up newspapers could be used as missiles and the assault began anew. The booing had continued unabated the whole while. After a delay of 17 minutes, Commissioner Landis called Owen, Medwick, and the two managers to his box and held court. The potentate asked Medwick if he had any reason to kick Owen. When Medwick replied in the negative, Landis asked why he had done it. Joe replied, "It was just one of those things that happen in a ballgame."[1]

Landis immediately thumbed him out, and Medwick was escorted from the field by five policemen. The commissioner defended his actions: "I saw what Medwick did and I couldn't blame the Detroit crowd for what it did. I did the proper thing." He said he took the action "to protect the player from injury and permit the game to proceed."[2] To some it seemed that Landis had set a dangerous precedent. What could prevent a future crowd from rioting against the star of a visiting club and having him removed? However, that has not happened. A more just decision might have been to forfeit the game if Detroit management could not maintain order and protect the safety of the players. The problem is that such a decision might have provoked a full-scale riot. As it was, Chick Fullis replaced Medwick in left field and the game continued to its conclusion, with the Cardinals posting an 11-0 victory and winning the world championship.

Joseph Michael Medwick was born November 24, 1911, in Carteret, New Jersey, the fourth child of Elizabeth and John Medwick, a carpenter. Joe was of Hungarian descent, both of his parents having been born in the Austro-Hungarian monarchy and having immigrated to the United States in 1893. According to his obituary, Joe was a four-sport star at Carteret High School, participating in track, football, basketball, and baseball. He won all-state honors as a high-school halfback and had many offers of college scholarships to play football. However, he preferred baseball. As a teenager, Joe was signed off the New Jersey sandlots by the St. Louis Cardinals organization.

In 1930 the 18-year-old outfielder made his professional baseball debut for the Scottdale, Pennsylvania, Scotties, an affiliate of the Cardinals in the Class C Middle Atlantic League, playing under the name Mickey King in order to protect his amateur status. Stockily built at 5-feet-10 and 187 pounds, the youngster hit and threw right-handed. And how he hit! In 75 games he clubbed 22 home runs and led the league with a .419 batting average and a .750 slugging percentage. Many observers declared that he was the best young ballplayer ever to come into the Middle Atlantic League. This stellar performance earned Medwick a promotion to the Houston Buffaloes club in the Class A Texas League, skipping Class B ball entirely. In 1931 Medwick led the league in total bases, but he really starred in 1932, when he led the circuit in slugging at .611 and was second in batting average with .354. His 342 total bases were only two fewer than Hank Greenberg's league-leading output. In addition he had a strong and accurate throwing arm and was considered the best all-around outfielder in the Texas League.

While playing with Houston, Medwick acquired the nickname Ducky. Some say it was because he waddled like a duck when he walked. His teammates picked up on it and started calling him Ducky or even worse Ducky Wucky. Joe detested the name, but it caught on and for years sportswriters routinely referred to him as Ducky. Medwick much preferred to be called Muscles and induced some of his teammates to use that appellation.

With three years of minor-league experience behind him, Joe made his major-league debut with the parent St. Louis Cardinals on September 2, 1932. He went hitless in his first game, but had a run batted in on a sacrifice fly, and scored once himself after getting on base with a force out. Despite this inauspicious beginning, Medwick had an outstanding month. In 26 games that September, Medwick hit .349, slugged .538, and had an on-base-plus-slugging percentage (OPS) of .905. He was well on his way to stardom.

During the next four seasons, Medwick twice led he league in total bases, and once each in hits, doubles, triples, and runs batted in. In 1936 he set a National League record with 64 doubles, a mark that has not been matched as of 2013. The year 1936 also saw his marriage on August 24 in St. Louis to 19-year-old Isabelle Heutel. Then came that magical season of 1937, when he led in hits, doubles, home runs, batting average, slugging percentage, on-base plus slugging, runs scored, and runs batted in — all in the same year. Naturally, he won the National League's Most Valuable Player Award in 1937. In eight full seasons and two partials from 1932 to 1940, Joe never hit less than .300 for the Cardinals.

At that time the Cardinals were notorious for penurious treatment of players. In Joe's opinion he was the best player in the league and deserved more pay. Contract negotiations were strenuous, but with the reserve clause in effect Medwick had little leverage. In 1938 the outfielder had received $20,000. Despite leading the league in runs batted in that season, Medwick was forced to accept a cut to $18,000 for 1939. Relations between the club and its star became strained. To Joe Medwick, baseball was all about "Base hits and Buckerinoes." He delivered with base hits, and he expected the club to deliver big bucks. Joe did not have an engaging personality, to say the least. Even some of his teammates did not like him. Cardinals owner Sam Breadon had little patience for impudent hired hands. Eventually, he convinced general ganager Branch Rickey that the slugger was expendable. On June 12, 1940, Rickey traded Medwick along with pitcher Curt Davis to the Brooklyn Dodgers for four players and a sum variously reported as $125,000 or $200,000.

On June 19 in his sixth game for the Dodgers, Medwick faced his former team. Once again Joe became the central figure in a contentious ball field incident that threatened to become even more serious than the event in the 1934 World Series. Batting cleanup for the Dodgers, Medwick faced his former teammate Bob Bowman in the first inning, with two runs already in and a runner on base. Bowman's first pitch was a high, hard one on the inside. It struck Medwick in the head, knocking him unconscious. The Dodgers rushed out of their dugout, intent on wreaking vengeance on Bowman, who they believed had beaned the outfielder deliberately. Some tried to punch him. Even Larry McPhail, the Dodgers president, got in a swing, knocking off the pitcher's hat. Medwick was carried off the field on a stretcher and taken to the Caledonian Hospital, where it was discovered that he had a concussion but no fracture. He tried to get out of his hospital bed and go after his assailant. Meanwhile, Bowman was removed from the game and escorted by policemen back to his hotel.

One reason the Dodgers were so irate about this incident is that Bowman had been in a verbal confrontation with Medwick and Dodgers manager Leo Durocher in the hotel the previous morning. The pitcher had shouted, "I'll take care of you! I'll take care of both of you."[3] Bowman said he meant that he would hold them hitless in the game. The Dodgers' version was that the pitcher had threatened them with beanballs. Acting on this belief, McPhail appealed fruitlessly to National League President Ford Frick to ban Bowman from baseball for life. Further he attempted to have Bowman arrested for assault. The Brooklyn district attorney investigated and found no evidence of criminal intent on the pitcher's part.

Medwick was out of the hospital in four days and quickly back in the lineup, missing far less than the three weeks he was expected to be on the shelf. He was named to the National League All-Star team for the seventh consecutive season. Starting the game in left field, he was hitless in two times at bat before departing in favor of Jo-Jo Moore in the NL's 4-0 victory. One result of the beaning was a renewed interest in the use of batting helmets. Many players were opposed to the use of helmets, fearing that such would make them seem less daring than they wished to appear. Furthermore, the fans liked their baseball rough and reckless. But some fans realized they can't cheer the exploits of a player who lies in a hospital bed. In July Spalding Sporting Goods began advertising a batting helmet with ear flaps. However, it was not until 1971 that it became mandatory for all new major leaguers to wear helmets, and even then veterans were exempted through a grandfather clause.

After the beaning, Medwick played eight more years in the major leagues, not hitting with quite the power he had shown previously, but still topping the .300 mark several times, including .337 in 1944. During these years he played variously with Brooklyn, the New York Giants, and the Boston Braves, before closing out his major-league playing career with the Cardinals on July 25, 1948, at the age of 36. But he was not done with baseball. He finished the 1948 season with Houston in the Texas League. From 1949 through 1951 he was a minor-league player-manager, with such clubs as the Miami Beach Flamingoes and the Tampa Smokers of the Florida International League and the Raleigh Capitals of the Carolina League.

After waiting impatiently for 20 years, Medwick was elected to the National Baseball Hall of Fame in Cooperstown in 1968. His long wait may have been caused by the antagonism felt toward him by many baseball writers, whom he often dismissed rudely when they approached him for interviews. By 1968 this animosity had been largely forgotten and he received votes from 84.8 percent of the writers casting ballots.

On March 21, 1975, Joseph Medwick died at St. Petersburg, Florida, of a heart attack. He had been working as a batting instructor in the Cardinals' spring-training camp. He was 63 years old. The great player was survived by his widow, Isabelle; a son Joe Medwick, Jr. of Key Largo, Florida; and a daughter, Susan Medwick George of St. Louis. His body was taken back to Missouri and he was buried in St. Lucas Cemetery in Sunset Hills, a suburb of St. Louis.

Many honors came to Medwick posthumously. It's too bad the fiercely proud competitor could not have lived to relish them. At the turn of the century, several groups published lists of the country's most outstanding players. In 1999, Joe was ranked 79th on *The Sporting News* list of Baseball's Greatest Players. A poll of members of the Society for American Baseball Research ranked Medwick 100th. *Sports Illustrated* named him the second-best baseball player of the century from New Jersey and the seventh-greatest overall from the Garden State.

Sources

Graham, Frank, *The Brooklyn Dodgers: An Informal History* (New York: G.P. Putnam's Sons, 1945).

Lieb, Frederick G., *The St. Louis Cardinals: The Story of a Great Ball Club* (New York: G.P. Putnam's Sons, 1945).

Stockton, J. Roy, *The Gashouse Gang and a Couple of Other Guys* (New York: A.S. Barnes & Company, 1945).

Notes

1. J. Roy Stockton, *The Gashouse Gang and a Couple of Other Guys* (New York: A.S. Barnes, 1945), 131.

2. Frederick G. Lieb, *The St. Louis Cardinals: The Story of a Great Ball Club* (New York: G.P. Putnam's Sons, 1945), 174.

3. Frank Graham, *The Brooklyn Dodgers: An Informal History* (New York: G.P. Putnam's Sons, 1945), 185.

Buster Mills

By Bill Nowlin

BORN AS COLONEL Buster Mills, this outfielder-turned-soldier during World War II got a little extra kick out of going up to ranking officers and introducing himself as Colonel Mills.

His father was Elvis, a merchant who owned a general store in Ranger, Texas, about 65 miles east of Abilene in the west central part of the state. Elvis was born of parents from Tennessee. Buster's mother, Lucy, was from Arkansas, born of parents from Mississippi. Elvis and Lucy started off giving familiar names to their children. Their first-born was named Charles and the second was William. Then they had a daughter and named her Merkel. And when their fourth child was born, on September 16, 1908, they gave him the first name of Colonel and the middle name of Buster. Whether they had other children later on is not known. Buster described himself in his Hall of Fame questionnaire as "Scotch, Irish, Dutch, English, and Indian." He got his unusual first name because his father's best friend was an Army colonel—or because of a great-uncle who was a colonel during the Civil War, as he himself wrote in a letter to J. Roy Stockton of the *St. Louis Post-Dispatch*.[1] He often went by the nickname Bus.

The 5-foot-11 1/2-inch, 195-pound right-hander, who spent the first half of the 1934 season with the Cardinals, was a football star at the University of Oklahoma, named all-Big Six quarterback in 1930. He capped off the year playing right halfback and scoring all the points by kicking a field goal in the last four minutes of play for a 3-0 final before 60,000 fans in the sixth annual Shrine Game, the East-West All-Star Game. Listening to his son on the radio at home in Ranger, Elvis Mills leapt up and in his excitement kicked a vase and fractured his foot. The *Chicago Tribune* was more restrained but placed a headline reading, "Mills in Hero Role" above its box score and game story.[2] Mills lettered in football, basketball, track, and baseball. In the spring of 1931, while he was playing baseball, the track coach beckoned him over from an adjacent field. Asked to throw the javelin to see if he could help the track team, he did—for 180 feet, enough to give Oklahoma sufficient points to win its track meet. Then, presumably still wearing his baseball uniform, he returned to the ballgame.[3]

Mills was a rookie outfielder in 1934. He was a much-traveled player in his career, suiting up for six teams in seven years. He also coached in the major leagues for seven years.

Mills could have tried to pursue a career in football. His father was on the board of trustees of the Ranger school system and hired Blair Cherry as coach for the team. It was under Cherry—now honored by the Texas Sports Hall of Fame for his work coaching Texas Longhorn football—that Bus played halfback and went to the state interscholastic finals.[4]

But it was in baseball that Buster pursued a pro career, one that had an unusual twist. St. Louis Cardinals scout Charley Barrett saw him playing center field in a game between Oklahoma and Washington University in St. Louis. He hit for the cycle and more, banging out a single, two doubles, a triple, and a home run.

The saying goes that you can't tell the players without a scorecard, and there were no printed scorecards for the game. When Barrett asked one of the players for the hitter's name, he didn't get the most knowledgeable student and was told it was Wahl — there was a Tilford Wahl on the team, who also had the nickname Bus. Barrett had to rush off to cover another event, but sent a message to a colleague in Oklahoma and asked him to sign Wahl to a Cardinals contract. Wahl was perhaps a bit surprised, but signed on the dotted line.

In the meantime, Cleveland signed the other "Bus" — Buster Mills — and sent him to Decatur (Three-I League) and then to New Orleans (Southern Association), which quickly swapped him to Mobile of the Southeastern League, a Cardinals farm club.[5] Mills wound up playing with three teams: 32 games with Class B Mobile (he batted .367); 109 games with the Elmira Red Wings in the Class B New York-Penn League (his .337 mark was second in the league); and, to finish his year, with the Rochester Red Wings in the Double-A International League. He hit .360 with one home run in the 15 games he played for Rochester. The January 5, 1933, *Sporting News* looked ahead to the season to come for Rochester and pronounced, "Mills, because of his showing at the end of last year, won himself the right to have the outfield built around him. He is a certainty to land a regular job and what's more, predictions are made that he will advance at the end of the season."

Rochester manager Specs Toporcer had already conceded Mills the center-field job before spring training got under way; another look back at 1932 called him "sensational" and said, "He showed fighting spirit and defensive skill."[6]

With the proper Bus under contract, the Cardinals were pleased to see him bat .309 in 405 at-bats for Rochester in 1933; "Colonel Fence Buster" hit 7 home runs, 28 doubles, and 8 triples. He led the league in getting hit by pitches, with 15. By the end of the year, St. Louis had already determined he'd be with the big-league team in the spring of 1934. Team VP Branch Rickey enthused over three recruits for his outfield: Gene Moore, Jack Rothrock, and Mills. "If somebody said to me, 'Go out and buy the three best outfielders you can buy,' these three would have been among the first four that I would have considered," he told the Associated Press.[7]

Mills made his Cardinals debut in the second game of the year, on April 18, 1934, against the Pittsburgh Pirates. (The 18th was also the debut date for pitcher Paul Dean, younger brother of Dizzy Dean. Diz had started and won the Opening Day game, 7-1. Paul didn't fare as well, giving up a couple of home runs early on and making it through only two innings. In the fifth inning Mills batted for Bill Walker, the second pitcher of the game. He was retired uneventfully.

It wasn't a good start for St. Louis, which won the Opening Day game but then lost five in a row. The AP said that when manager Frankie Frisch stuck Mills in the lineup on April 26, it was to try to "shake the jinx" — Mills made an out his first time up, but then hit two singles, a double, and a triple in his final four at-bats. On the 27th Mills hit three singles his first three times up before finally being retired. Two days later he hit his first major-league homer, off Pat Malone of the Chicago Cubs at Wrigley Field.

It was a very nice start, but by July 5 Mills, batting .236, was released back to Rochester. He had time to get into 63 games, but hit a disappointing .269 and Red Wings fans were also down when Toronto beat Rochester in the playoffs. Nonetheless, the October 4 *Sporting News* predicted that Mills might be one of the three players most likely to be selected by another major-league club in that fall's player draft. He was not, and played a fairly full season with Rochester in 1935, hitting .313 in 549 at-bats, with eight homers.

The Red Wings didn't even make the first division in 1935, and both Gene Moore and Mills were sent to the Brooklyn Dodgers for two unnamed players and cash. Given a shot with Brooklyn in September, the "fast, sturdy right-handed hitter" pounded the first pitch he saw for a double in his debut, drove in a run, and was one of four cited for some "brilliant fielding" in a game game against the Cubs on September 13. The next day he hit a three-run homer off Charlie Root, also at Wrigley. Still, Bus ended the year with a .214 average over the 56 at-bats that constituted his year as a Dodger. It hadn't taken long for opposing pitchers to realize that he could be fooled with the curveball. They had him "swinging for low curves outside and the rangy young Texan went fishing with a vengeance."[8]

It was Mills's speed that caught a lot of eyes, along with the hope that he could discipline himself at the plate. A couple of impromptu races saw him beat Bill Werber both times, and Werber was highly regarded for his speed.

Mills didn't make the Dodgers in 1936. It would have cost the team $10,000 to keep him, but Rochester said it was glad to have him back, and that it believed it could sell him for $25,000 by the fall.[9] Mills spent 1936 with Rochester once again, hitting .331 with 18 home runs and a league-leading 134 runs batted in. The Cubs scouted him and the Yankees made an offer during the latter part of the campaign, but the Red Wings didn't want to give him up while still competing. In November the Boston Red Sox sent a "bundle of cash" and, later, infielder Dib Williams to Rochester to complete their purchase of Mills for 1937.[10]

The Red Sox had added both Mills and Fabian Gaffke to their outfield crew, and both were expected to contend with Dom Dallessandro to see who would join Doc Cramer in the Boston outfield in 1937. It was considered to be a "comeback" year for Buster, and he came back all right—with the best year of his career, playing a full major-league season for the Red Sox and batting .295 in 505 at-bats, driving in 58 runs and scoring 85. He hit seven homers.

Breaking in on the same April 20 date as two other Red Sox, second baseman Bobby Doerr and third baseman Mike "Pinky" Higgins, Mills played right field and was 2-for-4 with a triple as Boston beat Philadelphia, 11-5. It wasn't all clear sailing, though. With the bases loaded and two outs in the first inning on August 14 in Washington, Mills camped under an "ordinary fly"—and dropped it. Three runs scored and the Red Sox never recovered in that game.[11]

Mills was named to *The Sporting News* All-Star team as the best rookie left fielder in the majors. Though he did have his best year, the Red Sox sought improvement with Joe Vosmik, who'd had an even better one. On December 2, Mills, pitcher Bobo Newsom, and infielder Red Kress—and, in a separate deal, coach Oscar Melillo—were traded to the St. Louis Browns to secure Vosmik. New York sportswriter Dan Daniel said that the Red Sox "salted their tender with $35,000 in addition."[12] They'd been trying to land Vosmik for two years, and now felt they would have (with Vosmik, Cramer, and Ben Chapman) their best outfield since the days of Duffy Lewis, Tris Speaker, and Harry Hooper.

The Browns would be Mills's fourth major-league team. Sportswriter Paul Shannon declared that he "has a world of speed and is a pretty fair batsman, but does not rank so highly as a ball hawk. Yet he has youth and ambition on his side and [Browns manager] Gabby Street may develop him into a star."[13] Newsom and Kress were the keys to the trade, though, and for the two of them, and Melillo, it was a return home to a club where they'd all previously worked.

Mills had a very good 1938 for his second St. Louis team. Though laid up for a while with a sprained ankle suffered on Opening Day, he still appeared in 123 games, earned 466 at-bats, drove in 46 runs and scored 66, while batting .285. In late October, the Yankees traded outfielder Myril Hoag and catcher Joe Glenn to the Browns for pitcher Oral Hildebrand and Mills. It was Hildebrand they wanted and in early January 1939, New York assigned Mills to its Double-A Newark Bears farm team.

Mills turned 31 years old by the end of the season, spent entirely in Newark. He hit .305 in 149 games but got his photograph in the newspapers for another reason. A *New York Daily News* photo showed him wearing a "safety cap" which, the caption in the August 3 *Sporting News* said, "fits snugly over the regular uniform cap … made of hard fiber with sponge-rubber knobs to protect the temples." The caps became optional protective gear in the International League and Mills was reportedly the first to wear one.

Mills began 1940 with Newark as well, but with outfielders Jake Powell and Joe DiMaggio both disabled, the Yankees brought him up on May 3. He was hitting only .222 at the time, but the Yankees needed him. *Washington Post* sports editor Shirley Povich was unkind, decrying the paucity of talent in the Yankees farm system and writing, "When they needed an outfielder a couple of months ago, the best man they could bring up was Buster Mills, a two-time failure in the majors."[14] It was one of several disparaging references to Mills by Povich. Two days earlier, he'd written that Mills had been sent from Boston to the Browns and from there to the minors "because he couldn't hit. Mills is wearing a Yankee uniform, but he doesn't strike the enemy pitchers as a proverbial Yankee, if we are not being too subtle."

When he did hit for the Yankees, he hit well, batting .397 for the season—but in just 63 at-bats. When the Yankees tried to send him back to Newark, three clubs put in waiver claims. Bus spent most of 1940 not playing at all, though after the Yankees farmed him back out to Kansas City of the American Association on August 15, he hit .348 in 132 at-bats for the Blues. Then Mills hit .307 for the Blues in 1941, with 63 RBIs.

The Cleveland Indians took another crack at Buster in early April 1942, taking him in trade for outfielder Larry Rosenthal and some money. They'd seen his play against them in spring training and were impressed, and planned to have him play outfield in place of Gee Walker, who had been sold to Cincinnati. Mills wasn't quite as impressive over the next couple of weeks and was slated for a backup role and platooning against left-handers—though in his first crack, on April 18, he singled three times, one of which helped beat the White Sox, 1-0. He drove in half the runs in a 6-1 win against the Athletics on the last day of April, including the game-winner. As seemed to often be the case, Mills started off exceptionally well (10-for-18 for the Tribe through early May), but then softened. Three singles, a triple, four RBIs, and a steal of home helped him do in Washington, 7-1, on July 26. Not swinging the bat at all helped him win the September 17 game; he walked to plate the winning run in the bottom of the 11th inning against the Senators. For the season, Mills hit .277 in 195 at-bats.

Except for military service, Mills stayed in the Indians system throughout the World War II years. He joined the Army Air Force in mid-November of 1942, departing the Indians on the same day as Bob Lemon. Mills was initially stationed in Waco, Texas, recruited there by Birdie Tebbetts, who pulled together quite a group of ballplayers—Hoot Evers, Sid Hudson, and more. Hank Greenberg became the assistant director of physical training at Waco. Mills was commissioned a second lieutenant in April 1943—but still had a little fun since now he had officially become Lieutenant Colonel Buster Mills.

Oddly enough, another baseball playing Buster Mills made his appearance around this time, a catcher for Holy Cross. His name was William H. Mills, and had been given the nickname Buster with Colonel Buster Mills in mind. This Mills, who went by Bill, played in five games for the Athletics in 1944.

Baseball, by the way, had another ballplayer who could honestly introduce himself as an officer, at least in name: Major Kerby Farrell.

Our man Mills was transferred to the Aloe Army Air Field in Victoria, Texas, in July 1944, but not before he helped the Waco Wolves win their 14th game in a row with a tenth-inning homer against a semipro team from Dallas. He did continue to play some for Waco, though Tebbetts had to give up a gold case that Mills had been eyeing in order to land him for the semipro tournament.[15]

In 1945, now a first lieutenant, Mills was sent to Hawaii, where he managed the 73rd Wing Bombers in a series of exhibition games for the troops in the Marianas. Buster's Bombers beat Birdie Tebbetts' 58th Wing team, 4-3, on Tinian on July 27, with Ferris Fain's home run in the bottom of the ninth making the difference. Tex Hughson was Buster's starter. The Bombers beat the 313th Flyers the next day, 5-4.

Buster's Bombers beat Birdie's crew in the Tinian series, but both Mills and Tebbetts were on the American League all-star team when it came to playing a Pacific all-stars series on Iwo Jima. On August 26 the Americans beat the Nationals on Tinian, 3-2, but lost to the Nationals at Higashi Field on Iwo Jima, 5-1, on September 2. Mills played left field in that game and was 0-for-4.

There was at the same time an ongoing round-robin series on Iwo Jima. Mills' Bombers had won nine of 11 games in the Marianas series, and took the first game on Iwo Jima as the 73rd Bombers beat the 313th Flyers on August 29, 3-2. Joe Gordon's three-run homer for Tebbetts' 58th Wingmen helped beat the Flyers in the second game, 5-4, on August 30. The Flyers came back to tie it, but Enos Slaughter's seventh-inning homer won it for the 58th and reliever Rugger Ardizoia bore the defeat. Tebbetts' team won the series when 23-year-old White Sox rookie Nick Popovich shut out Mills' Bombers on three singles, 3-0, in the August 31 final game.

After being mustered out of the service and coming off the National Defense List in February 1946, Mills joined those competing for a slot with the Indians. Early in spring training, manager Lou Boudreau announced that Mills would be hired as first-base coach but kept on the active roster so that he could be used as a pinch-hitter as occasions arose.[16] Melillo became the third-base coach.

Mills appeared in nine games in 1946, until he was formally released from the active list on July 3, and he coached full time all season for Cleveland. There was one downside to the job that year; the Indians—now under Bill Veeck's leadership—typically had baseball comedian Max Patkin "coach" road games for the first inning or two. Mills had the unenviable job of replacing Patkin in the box as the game got under way. Fans immediately noticed the change and would shout at Mills, "What are you doing out there? Go into your act, you dope. We want Patkin."[17] When the Browns picked Cleveland baserunner Ray Mack off first while Patkin was doing his jitterbugging, Boudreau called a halt to the levity.

After the season Mills joined a touring group of American League all-stars put together by Paul Richards, then catching for Detroit. His grand slam helped win a 10-2 game against the Sherman club of the East Texas League. The Indians offered to give Mills a job managing in the minors, but he took his time to look around for a position that would keep him "in the Big Time" and by December was offered a job coaching with the White Sox under manager Ted Lyons.

In his second career as a coach, Mills coached for the White Sox from 1947 to 1950 under Lyons, Paul Richards, and Jack Onslow. Onslow let Mills go after the 1950 season because of his "conservatism in sending runners home."[18]

The day he was officially released, Mills was managing in a night game in Memphis. Just as he had in leading the 73rd Wing Bombers in the war, Mills led a tour of barnstorming all-stars after the season. A 33-game schedule running from October 10 in Montreal to November 5, with a day game in Oakland and a night game in San Francisco, kept him busy as the "American League" manager. Players including Early Wynn, Jerry Coleman, Mike Garcia, Al Rosen, and others toured, with Duke Snider, Red Schoendienst, Alvin Dark, Gil Hodges, Ralph Kiner, Sam Jethroe, and others on the NL team.

In January 1951 Mills was hired to skipper the Superior Blues of the Northern League. The Wisconsin team was one with which the White Sox had a working agreement. The Blues came in third. In the playoffs, it was Eau Claire and Superior with one win apiece when five games in a row were called off because of rain, and Superior canceled the series. Eau Claire won by default but lost the best-of-three finals in two games to Grand Forks. Early in the season, Mills had been ejected from a game for allegedly pushing umpire Don Spillman. While sitting out the game, he reportedly came up with the idea of managing from his car via walkie-talkie while a player on the bench filled him in on what was happening. The league president shot down the idea.[19]

It's not clear what Mills did during the 1952 season, but in October he was hired as a coach for the Cincinnati Reds, under manager Rogers Hornsby. Near the end of the 1953 season, Hornsby quit the sixth-place team with eight games remaining. Mills became acting manager, but the team made it clear that it would not be considering him for the position on a permanent basis and was looking for an experienced skipper for the year to come. The team played 4-4 under Mills.

Two days after Cincinnati's season ended, Mills was hired by the Boston Red Sox to coach under manager Lou Boudreau in 1954. Before reporting to Sarasota for Red Sox spring training, he went to Venezuela. Cincinnati had asked him to manage the Pastora club in the Venezuelan league, with which the Reds had placed some players. The team was based at Maracaibo, and won the league by a 7 1/2-game margin with a record of 48-30. He was asked to return to the post for another winter in 1959, but had to decline for unspecified personal reasons.

When Pinky Higgins was named to skipper the Red Sox for 1955, he dropped Mills, "blamed for several bad decisions" in handling third-base traffic, according to the *Hartford Courant*.20 The respected Ed Rumill of the *Christian Science Monitor* agreed with the common perception: "Important runs were constantly eliminated because of Buster's judgment. Catchers would be waiting with the ball when green-lighted Bostonians raced innocently homeward."21

Mills maintained a residence in Waco and for a number of summers starting in 1955 helped coach at the Big State Boys Baseball Summer Camp, with Sid Hudson, Monty Stratton, and Joe Moore among the other staff.

Buster took up scouting for Kansas City, and was a determined one—actually signing one prospect on Christmas Day itself, in Abilene. But he was part of a revolt in September 1961. After owner Charlie Finley had fired farm director Hank Peters, manager Joe Gordon, and GM Frank Lane, the director of player personnel (George Selkirk) also quit, and then so did a group of six scouts, one of whom was Mills. Within a month, he was snapped up and signed to scout for the Yankees.

Mills died on December 1, 1991, at Arlington, Texas, and was buried in Waco. He had lived in Ranger, Texas, much of his life, moving to Waco for a short time and then Arlington. He had been a member of First Methodist Church of Ranger, on the board of directors of Ranger Savings and Loan, a member of Masonic Lodge in Ranger, and a member of the American Legion. Survivors at the time of his death included his wife, Madge Mills of Arlington; and a sister, Myrtle Watson of Grants Pass, Oregon.

Sources

All consulted sources are mentioned in the text. Baseball-Reference.com and Retrosheet.org were the sources for baseball statistics.

Notes

1. *The Sporting News*, January 18, 1934.
2. *Chicago Tribune*, December 28, 1930. The vase kicking was told by sportswriter Shirley Povich, among others. See the April 1, 1937, *Washington Post*.
3. *The Sporting News*, November 7, 1935.
4. *Chicago Tribune*, July 21, 1948.
5. *The Sporting News*, May 11, 1933, and January 18, 1934.
6. *The Sporting News*, March 9, 1933.
7. *Hartford Courant*, November 27, 1933.
8. *The Sporting News*, September 19 and 26, 1935.
9. *Hartford Courant*, May 3, 1936.
10. *The Sporting News*, December 3, 1936.
11. *Washington Post*, August 15, 1937.
12. *The Sporting News*, December 9, 1937.
13. *The Sporting News*, December 9, 1937.
14. *Washington Post*, May 24, 1940.
15. *Christian Science Monitor*, October 17, 1944.
16. *The Sporting News*, March 21, 1946.
17. *The Sporting News*, September 11, 1946.
18. *The Sporting News*, April 19, 1950.
19. *The Sporting News*, June 13, 1951.
20. October 14, 1954. See also *The Sporting News*, October 27, 1954.
21. *Christian Science Monitor*, September 13, 1955.

Jim Mooney

By Charlie Weatherby and Gregory Wolf

ALTHOUGH HE RECORDED a surprising six straight victories (and a 7-1 record) as a New York Giants rookie after his August 1931 debut, and was later a member of the 1934 St. Louis Cardinals' champion Gas House Gang, Jim Mooney was much more than a professional baseball player.

He was also a scholar, teacher, university professor, baseball coach, naval officer and war hero, and veterans' adviser. A great believer in education, Mooney wanted to prepare his players and students for life after baseball and the college campus.

A quiet, patient, and easygoing gentleman with a nonjudgmental demeanor and a good sense of humor, the 5-foot-11, 168-pound left-handed hurler played four years (1931-1934) with the Giants and Cardinals, posting a 17-20 record and a 4.25 earned-run average in 92 games. He also had a 16-season minor-league career, which included two feats that rated a mention in *Ripley's Believe It Or Not*. According to Mooney's daughter Jeanne, "He truly loved the game and was proud of the doors it had opened for him."[1] From Jim's perspective, baseball "was a rugged and tough life but just putting on a major-league uniform was the greatest thing in the world."[2]

James Irving Mooney was born on September 4, 1906, in Mooresburg, a rural hamlet in the hills of northeastern Tennessee. He was the youngest of four children born to Robert C. and Rebecca A. (Isenberg) Mooney, having a brother, Charles, and a sister, Love, who were five and two years older. Tragedy struck the family twice shortly after Jim's birth. His father, a sawmill worker, died in 1907 at the age of 36 from a cerebral hemorrhage. Eula, his oldest sister, died in 1908 at the age of 6. His mother, Rebecca, an Ohio native, married J. Coleman Hicks a year later; he was a neighbor and 29 years her senior.

Jim grew up on Hicks' Snow Flake farm on the outskirts of Mooresburg. According to his nephews, he learned to pitch there; as he walked down the road and through the fields, he would throw stones, apples, or corncobs at fence posts, knotholes, bottles, and other targets instead of doing his chores. In the opinion of Mooney's daughter, these tales "sound very much like one of his 'I grew up in the country' stories that he loved to tell as long as he had a gullible listener."[3]

Mooney first played sports at Mooresburg High School. In 1924 his mother, a strong-willed woman who stressed education, sent him to East Tennessee State Normal School in Johnson City for his last year of high school. Though technically still a high-school student, Mooney turned out for college coach Jim Luck's spring baseball tryout. Faced with a shortage of players and impressed by the 17-year-old's strong left arm, Luck gave him a uniform and named him the starting pitcher for the first game, against the Emory and Henry College Wasps, an 11-0 win. It was the first of 13 wins that gave East

Jim Mooney pitched four years in the major leagues, mostly as a reliever with the Giants and Cardinals.

Tennessee its only undefeated season; Mooney pitched every game.

A fastball pitcher, Mooney specialized in strikeouts. According to *The Sporting News*, "Mooney started early to establish a reputation for shutouts, whiffing 116 batters in eight games while at Eastern [*sic*] Tennessee Teachers College."[4] Another publication said he averaged 11 strikeouts per game during his four-year college career. In 1927, his final season, he continued to torment Emory and Henry College, striking out 24 batters in an 11-inning 1-0 win over another future major leaguer, Monte Weaver, who fanned 19. On May 3, in a 4-3 win over the Wasps, Mooney struck out 17 and allowed only four hits.

An all-around athlete, Mooney was also a star halfback for the East Tennessee football team and a standout basketball player, although both teams were less successful than the baseball club.

During his college years, Mooney earned expense money by working summer jobs for coal-field companies in Virginia, Tennessee, and Kentucky, pitching for their baseball teams on weekends. According to author L.M. Sutter, "Dorchester's reputation for hiring ringers was as notorious as its field [in Virginia]. In [1924] operators at the camp hired a young southpaw ... named Jim Mooney before he was snagged by the Sally League." "[He] shone as a Dorchester Cardinal," and teams "repeatedly suffered at the hands of [the] future New York Giants pitcher."[5] In 1925 and 1926, Mooney played at Mascot, Tennessee, and Secco, Kentucky.

On June 10, 1927, Mooney signed a contract with the Chattanooga Lookouts of the Class A Southern Association and made his first professional appearance in the sixth inning of an 11-5 loss to the Mobile Bears, surrendering two runs in three-plus innings. Three days later he made his first start and, in the opinion of the *Augusta Chronicle*, "showed promise" in a 5-0 loss.[6] Mooney's first victory came on June 26, a 10-5 verdict over Atlanta. Although he gave up 14 hits, the *New Orleans Times-Picayune* said, "Mooney ... pitched good ball but was handicapped by [the] listless fielding of his mates."[7] Mooney pitched in 21 games for the Lookouts (59-94, seventh place), posting a 4-4 record and a 6.63 earned-run average in 76 innings.

Mooney returned to Chattanooga in 1928, had a loss and a win in his first two games, and after two weeks was sent to Columbus (Georgia) of the Class B Southeastern League. A 4-3 win in relief against Tampa on May 18 was an early highlight, but a 6-0 loss to Tampa on July 2 found him wild and ineffective, a result that typified his 6-13 record and 4.20 ERA in 30 games. Nevertheless, he was returned to Chattanooga in August and finished his 3-3 season (11 games, 4.34 ERA) on a high note with a 6-1 six-hitter against Nashville.

Back in Chattanooga in 1929, Mooney pitched five innings of one-hit ball against Grover Cleveland Alexander and the St. Louis Cardinals in an exhibition game on April 7 in Chattanooga and earned the win.[8] "Jim Mooney," raved the *Times-Picayune*, "has been casting joy, refined and unrefined, into Manager Jimmy (Johnston's) heart. This youngster stood the lordly Cards on their heads last Sunday, allowing them one hit and a string of goose eggs in five innings."[9]

A 10-0 loser in his first start against Atlanta, Mooney rebounded to win three straight by May 7. Thereafter, six consecutive losses prompted Johnston to use him in relief. Control was Mooney's biggest problem; by mid-July, he had a 3-9 record (5.10 ERA), led the league in wild pitches, and was among the league leaders in walks. Another demotion followed, this time to Spartanburg, South Carolina, to play for the Spartans of the Class B South Atlantic (Sally) League. Mooney's performance was only marginally better for the last-place (59-84) Spartans; he was 6-10 on the mound with a 4.86 ERA.

Meanwhile, Mooney took offseason classes at East Tennessee State Teachers College and received his bachelor's degree in industrial arts in 1929. He then moved to Erwin, Tennessee, where he lived at the YMCA, taught industrial arts, and coached girls' basketball at Unicoi High School. He continued to teach during the winter and play baseball during the summer for most of the next 18 years.

Mooney trained with Chattanooga in 1930 but lacked control and was released. Signed by the Sally League's Charlotte Hornets in early June, he showed good command of his pitches during early starts; on July 16 he set down the Asheville Tourists 2-1 on four hits.

With attendance in ballparks lagging throughout the US due to the effects of the Depression, night games were introduced to generate more fan interest. Two and a half months after the first night game in professional baseball (at Western League Park in Des Moines, Iowa), Mooney pitched the game of his life, striking out 23 batters and giving up only five hits in a 7-3 Charlotte win in the first night game played at Municipal Stadium in Augusta, Georgia, on July 19, 1930. His performance caught the attention of major-league scouts for the first time in his life (and a mention in *Ripley's Believe It or Not*).

Mooney's mound dominance led Charlotte manager Dick Hoblitzell to recommend that New York Giants manager John McGraw travel south to see him in action. Though Mooney's 11-11 record and 3.95 ERA in 189 innings for the Hornets may not have been eye-catching, McGraw was impressed with the hurler's potential. "Giants Buy Southpaw. Mooney, Promising Charlotte Youngster to Report in Fall," read a headline in the *New York Times* on August 7, 1930.[10] The Giants reportedly paid between $7,000 and $10,000 for Mooney's contract. With the Giants in a tight pennant race at the time, rumors that the Sally League All-Star would join the team proved incorrect.

On February 22, 1931, Mooney reported to the Giants' spring-training camp at San Antonio, Texas. He pitched three innings in a 3-1 exhibition loss to the Texas League's Dallas Steers on March 15, and the *Dallas Morning News* said that he "showed some good southpaw stuff."[11] On April 12, pitching for the Giants' second team, Mooney defeated the Eastern League's Bridgeport Bears 3-1, giving up six hits and striking out seven. After the game he was one of eight Giants players who were assigned to the Bears. In the opinion of *The Sporting News*, Mooney "appears to need some polishing to fit him for major league duty."[12]

At Bridgeport the "sure-fire prospect" was developed by McGraw's former player and trusted coach, Hans Lobert.[13] "It seems like fate has been against me this spring," Mooney wrote dejectedly to his brother, Charles, about his demotion to the minors." Acknowledging stiff competition from the Giants staff, he vowed to make it to the big leagues. "There are these old timers on the Giants club so I do not have much chance with them, however, I am still going to give somebody a battle."[14] With the Bears, Mooney blossomed into the league's best pitcher, winning 17 contests, losing just four (all to eventual champion Hartford), and posting a microscopic 1.69 ERA.

"My dream has come true or perhaps not a dream but hard work," Mooney wrote Charles on August 8, 1931. "I am reporting to the Giants tomorrow and boy I sure hope I can stay with them."[15] Upon his arrival, McGraw placed him under the tutelage of former pitching great, future Hall of Famer, and then Giants coach Chief Bender. On August 14 against the Pittsburgh Pirates at the Polo Grounds, Mooney debuted with a sparkling nine-hit complete-game victory, surrendering just one run. "Mooney Recalled from Bridgeport. Fans Seven in Auspicious Big League Debut," reported the *New York Times* the following day.[16] Dan Daniel of the *New York World-Telegram* called it "one of the most impressive debuts by a New York recruit in ten years" and stamped Mooney as "a slinger of more than interesting possibilities, adding, "The manner of his entry on the stage was quite dramatic."[17] After two relief appearances (winning one of them), Mooney tossed his first career shutout in his second start, blanking the Cincinnati Reds on four hits while striking out six on August 22. "This youngster seems to have given the club's staff just what is needed to settle into a winning stride," reported *The Sporting News*.[18]

With his great curveball and fastball with "burning speed," Mooney was making a name for himself as a strikeout artist and was called the modern version of Rube Waddell.[19] The *Wisconsin State Journal* reported that opponents taunted Mooney during games by yelling that they "didn't have to teach school in the winter" to earn a living.[20] Despite the taunts, Mooney kept winning. After his triumph over the Cubs on August 26, he pitched for the first time in an opponent's ballpark and shut out the Boston Braves at Braves Field on September 1, surrendering eight hits. "Mooney of Giants Quells Braves 4-0. Young Southpaw Breezes to an Easy Victory," read the New York Times subheading about his accomplishments.[21] When he beat

Brooklyn 10-1 in his next start (the only run the Dodgers scored was unearned), Mooney ran his record to 5-0 and lowered his ERA to 0.77 with just four earned runs in 46 2/3 innings. "Mooney Scores Sixth Straight Triumph for McGrawmen in Nightcap," ran yet another subhead in the *New York Times* about the 24-year-old's dreamlike season.[22] Accompanying the article was a picture of Mooney with his cap slightly cocked to the side in a style common at the time. In that game the notoriously bad-hitting Mooney (11-for-105 for a .105 major-league batting average) registered one of his six career RBIs.

Mooney finished the season with a 7-1 record, including six complete games, two shutouts, and a 2.01 ERA in 71 2/3 innings. "I have never seen a newcomer pitch with more confidence and skill," a delighted McGraw commented on Mooney's success.[23] Celebrated around the city, the "sensational southpaw" capitalized on his notoriety and went on a barnstorming tour after the season with some other members of the Giants, including Ethan Allen, Chick Fullis, Doc Marshall, and Johnny Vergez.[24] In late February 1932 *The Sporting News* reported on his successful duck hunt in the Mooresburg Valley, showing him with three of the six mallards he bagged.

The 1932 Giants were counting on improved pitching to help them contend for the pennant. John McGraw had returning starters Bill Walker, Freddie Fitzsimmons, and Carl Hubbell to anchor the rotation, and much was expected of Mooney, who received a "substantial increase in salary" enabling him to resign his high-school teaching position.[25] After a few weeks of training in Los Angeles, the press wasn't sure that optimism was warranted. When Mooney endured a 10-5 exhibition loss to the Seals in San Francisco, the *New York Times* said that he "still appears behind in his home work. … [He] ran full tilt into trouble as early as the second inning," giving up five hits and four runs.[26] Off to a rough start to begin the season, Mooney wrote his brother, "Perhaps you are wondering why I have not been winning any ball games. It seems that I am unable to keep off of the injured list. I stepped on a base ball bat two weeks ago and I sprained my ankle pretty bad and I am not over it yet."[27] Unable to generate the power he needed to throw strikes, Mooney struggled, lost velocity, and was wild "like a jack rabbit."[28] He lost his first four decisions and struck out just nine batters in 22 innings, but most concerning to McGraw was his 9.00 ERA at the end of May. Mooney revealed 45 years later that the injury caused him to change his stride, and arm problems developed that he never overcame.

With the Giants struggling at 17-23, McGraw announced his retirement on June 2 and was succeeded by player-manager Bill Terry. Mooney registered victories in his first two starts under Terry, including a complete-game 3-2 triumph over the Reds on June 9. After starting on an irregular basis and pitching in long relief for most of June and July, Mooney made eight consecutive starts from July 31 to September 9, but could not replicate the consistent magic from the previous season. Nonetheless, his masterful four-hit shutout over the cellar-dwelling Reds on August 17 suggested that the 25-year-old still had the potential to be a bona-fide major-league pitcher. He finished his first full season in the majors with a disappointing 6-10 record and 5.05 ERA in 124 2/3 innings.

On October 10, 1932, the Giants traded Mooney, outfielder Ethan Allen, catcher Bob O'Farrell, and pitcher Bill Walker to the St. Louis Cardinals for catcher Gus Mancuso and pitcher Ray Starr. Cardinals manager Gabby Street thought that Mooney's pitching woes resulted from the Giants' attempt to transform him from a high-fastball pitcher into a low-ball pitcher. "Don't forget this Jim Mooney we got from the Giants," bragged Cardinals owner Sam Breadon. "Street and [Branch] Rickey like him."[29] When asked about the trade, Mooney said he wasn't surprised; "I will give Gabby Street everything I have and will try to make a good man for his club. I think I will like to play for St. Louis, for they are the one team in the National League that has a pennant-winning fever. And I will do all in my power to help bring the pennant to St. Louis next year."[30] Before Mooney played in his first regular-season game with the Cardinals, rumors swirled that he'd be traded along with Pepper Martin to the Chicago Cubs for Mark Koenig and cash; however, the deal fell through.[31]

On October 17, 1932, Mooney married Maude Elizabeth "Sweetie" Wilkinson, an Erwin, Tennessee, native, in Sylva, North Carolina, their new offseason home. They had three daughters, Jeanne, Susanne, and Judith.

Mooney's 1933 season started with promise. He was effective (three hits, one run, seven innings) in relief of loser Dazzy Vance in a 4-0 loss to Pittsburgh on April 23. He started, went seven innings, and lost a 2-0 four-hitter at Pittsburgh on April 28. In his next outing, on May 4, he tossed a six-hitter, beating the Phillies 5-2 at Baker Bowl for his first victory of the season. By mid-May his ERA was 2.10 in 34 1/3 innings. Mooney's season soured on May 18 in a Sportsman's Park start against Brooklyn. In two-thirds of an inning, he faced eight batters and surrendered four hits, two walks, and six runs in a 14-5 loss. He won his next start, on May 28, a 5-3 victory over Philadelphia despite giving up 11 hits and four walks. The Phillies helped by leaving ten runners stranded. Thereafter, Mooney started only two more games, pitching four innings or less in his last 13 appearances; he seldom saw action after his ERA ballooned to 4.06 in early July. His last appearance of the season came on July 26 when he preserved a 3-2 win over the Reds for Bill Hallahan with three innings of one-hit, scoreless relief. In August the Cardinals were losing ground to first-place New York and were behind by six games in midmonth. According to *The Sporting News*, "Gabby [Street] would not be having his troubles today if Bill Walker and Jim Mooney … had come up to expectations."[32]

It came as no surprise, then, when Mooney, who had come down with tonsillitis, was sent to Rochester of the International league to recuperate. In a disastrous first start, he gave up two home runs (and six RBIs) to Baltimore's Moose Solters, the league batting champion, during an eight-run fourth inning in a 12-3 loss on August 18. Mooney was 2-3 in seven appearances for the Red Wings, two of which were against Buffalo in the playoffs. Recalled by St. Louis in mid-September, he did not see action.

Invited to the Cardinals' 1934 spring-training camp in Bradenton, Florida, Mooney arrived without fanfare, but his erratic performances continued. Making the team as the left-handed relief specialist, Mooney was part of one of the most cherished and fabled World Series championship teams, the Gas House Gang, so named because of their unkempt, shabby appearance and scrappy play. "Mooney is Star as St. Louis Gains 11th Victory in 12 Starts," read the *New York Times* subhead after he pitched six innings of relief on May 10 to earn his first win of the season.[33] With a career-high 32 appearances, including seven spot starts spread out over the season, Mooney won two and lost four (all four losses were in games he started), and posted a 5.47 ERA in 82 1/3 innings, but did not pitch in September when the Cardinals overcame a seven-game deficit to the New York Giants to win the pennant in dramatic fashion on the last weekend of the season.

A game against the Giants was notable: On June 27 Dizzy Dean held a 7-6 lead going into the top of the ninth inning. With two outs, the Giants tied the score and Mooney was brought in and got the third out. St. Louis then won the game in the bottom of the ninth, 8-7, and because Mooney was the pitcher of record when the score was tied, the official scorer gave him credit for the victory. However, in a reversal reminiscent of a decision made on a June 23 Cardinals' win against the Dodgers, National League President John Heydler again invalidated an official scorer's decision and gave the win to Dean. Both decisions gave Dean an even 30 wins. Mooney got one less win out of the decision but recorded his second major-league save (the save is retrospective; the statistic was not created until three decades later).

The Gas House Gang won the World Series by winning Games Six and Seven (the latter was Dean's dominating shutout) over the Detroit Tigers and securing their place in baseball lore. Pitching for the first time since August 27, Mooney saw mop-up duty in the Cardinals' Game Four 10-4 loss. Allowing one hit in one inning, he pitched for the last time in the major leagues and finished as a champion

With the press reporting that he'd lost some zip from his fastball, the Cardinals sold Mooney's contract to the Columbus (Ohio) Red Birds of the Double-A American Association on January 2, 1935. Posting a 17-20 record and a 4.25 ERA in 356 innings in a four-year big-league career, Mooney never made it back to the majors; however, he continued to pitch in professional baseball until 1948 and remained involved in the sport for the rest of his life.

Keeping in shape by playing basketball for the Erwin team in the Appalachian Independent Basketball Conference during the winter, Mooney reported to the Red Birds' spring training in 1935 hoping to jump-start his career. After eight appearances and 37 innings of work, he was the league's top pitcher at the end of May with a 3-0 record. Thereafter, he was 1-4, finishing with a 4-5 mark and a 6.17 ERA in 29 games, mostly in relief. By mid-August he was optioned to the International League's Baltimore Orioles. Mooney pitched well in his debut against Rochester on August 18, but lost 1-0 on a run-scoring wild pitch. Four days later, he triumphed over Syracuse, 8-3, fanning nine. After three more losses, his final Baltimore record was 1-4.

Ineffective in three stints at the highest minor-league level, Mooney was optioned by the Cardinals to the Memphis Chicks of the Class A1 Southern Association in 1936, and was 2-0 in three games. In mid-May he was transferred to the Knoxville Smokies of the same circuit, where he struggled, finishing with a 3-12 record. In a combined 41 games for both teams, his record was 5-14 with a 5.21 ERA in 186 2/3 innings.

Taking yet another step down the minor-league ladder, Mooney was with the Southeastern League's Mobile Shippers in 1937 and 1938. The Shippers won the league championship and the Little Dixie Series (Class B championship of the South) both years. In 1937 Mooney (16-11, 2.90 ERA) won four straight games in the playoffs, completing one of his most successful minor-league seasons.

During the fall Mooney took a faculty position at Tennessee High School in Bristol, Tennessee, where he taught industrial arts. During the winter he refereed basketball games; in the spring, he was a track and field official for the Big Six Conference.

In the spring of 1938, Mooney pitched for the amateur Saltville Alkalies in Virginia's newly organized Burley Belt League. He then returned to Mobile. Mooney (10-7, 2.65 ERA) didn't play in Mobile's Little Dixie Series triumph over Macon, instead returning to Bristol to teach.

Still in the Cardinals' chain, but now closer to home, Mooney was assigned to Asheville of the Class B Piedmont League in 1939. With four 12-win pitchers, a speedy infield that turned a league-record 165 double plays, and an abundance of clutch hitting, manager Hal Anderson's youthful Tourists (89-55) sprinted to the regular-season championship by a league-record 14-game margin over Durham.

Mooney (14-7) was one of the team's three (past and future) major-league hurlers, along with Red Munger (16-13) and Hersh Lyons (12-1). Moose Fralick (12-1) was equally as good, and catcher Walker Cooper was a year away from starting his 18-year major-league career. "Mooney," Anderson told the *Richmond Times-Dispatch*, "has helped our young pitchers a lot by correcting glaring faults in the way they throw curves and other pitches."[34] His most important victory came on September 18, when he pitched a 4-2 six-hitter against Rocky Mount to clinch the playoff championship.

Mooney's second *Ripley's Believe It Or Not* moment came during one of his Asheville relief appearances. He entered the game with one out and runners on first and third, and retired the side without throwing a pitch. His pickoff attempt to first resulted in a rundown; the runner was tagged out and a throw to Cooper got the runner from third trying to score.

After enrolling in graduate school at the University of Tennessee in the fall of 1935, Mooney spent four offseasons attending classes before receiving his master's degree in industrial education in August 1939. Shortly thereafter, East Tennessee State President C.C. Sherrod hired him as a professor and baseball coach.

Mooney was out of Organized Baseball in 1940 but hadn't lost his desire to play. In May 1941 he pitched for the Johnson City Soldiers semipro team. By late July Mooney was purchased from Asheville by his hometown Johnson City Cardinals of the Appalachian League. It was an ideal setup for him. Once college was in session, he could teach classes during the day and play ball in the evening. On July 27 Mooney saved a game against Newport; his first win was in relief on July 29, a 5-4 victory over Kingsport. The *Kingsport*

Times noted that "he had plenty of steam on his fast one," but "was not in the best of shape."³⁵ On August 27 Mooney (8-2, 2.44 ERA) gained his eighth straight triumph by scattering ten hits and fanning 17 Greeneville batters in a 5-1 Johnson City win. The fourth-place Cardinals (63-57) lost the league playoff finals to Elizabethton, three games to one.

The 35-year-old Mooney (15-11, 2.11 ERA) was a workhorse for Johnson City in 1942, leading the league with 192 innings pitched; two sources noted that he was never relieved and didn't issue a single walk all year. (Baseball-reference.com says he gave up 25 walks.) On July 26 Mooney took over as interim manager when Mercer Harris was indefinitely suspended after a run-in with an umpire.

In November 1942 Mooney resigned from East Tennessee State, reported for duty in the US Navy and was commissioned as a lieutenant junior grade. After training in Boston and New Orleans, he was sent to San Francisco in February 1943 and by May he was at sea, just "floating around from place to place."³⁶

In April 1944 Mooney returned to the States for more training and to pick up his new crew of five officers, 104 enlisted men, and a landing ship tank, LST-555, in Chicago. They were soon deployed in the South Pacific, where they participated in eight major landings as the US forces drew ever so close to Japan. Their last major operation was the assault and occupation of the Okinawa island group from April through June of 1945, a dangerous time given that they served as an ammunition ship that could be targeted by kamikazes.

LST-555 endured four typhoons during these operations. During the final (and worst) typhoon, the vessel grounded off Wakayama, Japan, and was rendered unsalvageable. The ship earned four battle stars. Mooney, who was mustered out as a lieutenant commander, was cited for "personal courage and leadership in performing duties and accomplishing designated assignments under regulated enemy air attack."

Mooney returned to Johnson City in January 1946 after 25 months at sea. Shortly thereafter, he resumed his duties as a professor and coach at East Tennessee State, with an added role—veterans' adviser. He also returned to the diamond. On June 21 he pitched the Bristol State Liners to a 12-3 win over Cavalier Grill in a semipro Burley Belt League game. Ten days later he signed with the Johnson City Cardinals and posted an 8-7 record and a 3.05 ERA in 18 games. He returned in 1947 at the age of 40, won his first start on May 11, compiled an 8-2 record by early July, was named to the Appalachian League All-Star team, and was the winning pitcher in the all-star game. Mooney (13-7, 2.92 ERA) was the Cardinals' best pitcher in 1947, walking only 16 men in 22 games. Despite his fine work, the Cardinals released him after the season. "I still feel like I've got some pitching days left," he told the *Kingsport News*. "I don't have any plans now, and next summer is still a long way off. If I don't pitch in professional ball, I may hook up with a semipro team."³⁷

On October 19, 1947, a team of barnstorming major leaguers stopped in Johnson City to play a team managed by Mooney. The major leaguers prevailed, 7-1.

In 1948 Mooney pitched on summer weekends for the Class D Blue Ridge League's Abingdon (Virginia) Triplets. (The club started the season in Leaksville-Draper-Spray but the franchise was forfeited when the team owner became embroiled in a game-fixing scandal in mid-May, and new owners moved it to Abingdon.) Abingdon (43-81) finished the season in last place. Mooney appeared in 12 games, posting a 7-5 record (and 3.32 ERA) in his last professional season. One of his better efforts was an 8-0 six-hit shutout of Radford on August 21.

In 16 minor-league seasons, Mooney's record was 153-137 (3.39 ERA). He continued to play semipro baseball for several more years; in July 1950, he pitched a 6-0 shutout for Saltville in the Burley Belt League, giving up five hits and fanning 12 Gate City Moccasins. In 1953 the *Kingsport Times-News* mentioned that he was still active in semipro circles.

In his second stint (1946-1965) as East Tennessee State's baseball coach, Mooney's record was 142-147-1. His best teams were in 1946-48 when they were a combined 24-10. Mooney often took a few of his players to Burley Belt games so they could earn extra expense money before NCAA rules prohibited such activity. One of Mooney's players, infielder Ernie Bowman, went on to play in the major leagues (San Francisco Giants, 1961-1963).

Mooney rose to the position of assistant to the dean during his last 28 years at East Tennessee State. Besides coaching baseball and teaching engineering drawing and other industrial arts, he helped thousands of veterans in his role as veterans' adviser. By the time he retired in June 1974, he was regarded as one of the foremost authorities on veterans' affairs in Tennessee.

Baseball was always Mooney's main interest. If a World Series game was on TV, he could be found in his office with a group of students watching the game. According to his daughter, when he was at home he could listen to two games on the radio and watch one on TV. In his spare time, he was a Little League coach for many years and made sure that every boy got to play, sometimes to the chagrin of some of the parents. Mooney was also a popular speaker at banquets and other community gatherings. When asked, he would share baseball stories, often relating funny incidents about Dizzy Dean and others from the Gas House Gang. He enjoyed traveling to St. Louis for a Gas House reunion in June 1959.

Mooney kept busy during his retirement. He had a woodworking shop in his basement and enjoyed making gifts and toys. He planted a garden every spring and produced enough vegetables to share. Family gatherings and reunions were favorite pastimes; each new grandchild was warmly welcomed into the family.

Mooney was inducted into the East Tennessee State University Athletics Hall of Fame in 1977. He died at 72 from heart failure on April 27, 1979, in Johnson City, and was survived by his wife, Elizabeth, and three daughters. He is buried at Evergreen Cemetery in Erwin, Tennessee. In 1980 ETSU's new on-campus baseball facility was named Mooney Field.

Sources

Singletary, Wes, *Florida's First Big League Baseball Players: A Narrative History* (Charleston, South Carolina: History Press, 2006).

Stone, George, *Muscle, a Minor League Legend* (Haverford, Pennsylvania: Infinity Pub., 2003).

Sutter, L.M., *Ball, Bat, and Bitumen: A History of Coalfield Baseball in the Appalachian South* (Jefferson, North Carolina: McFarland, 2009).

Barger, Melvin D., "Large Slow Target: A History of Landing Ships (LSTs) and the Men Who Sailed Them," Volume II (Oregon, Ohio: U.S. LST Association, 1989).

Green, Allen, "Baseball No Fun Anymore, Old Jim Mooney Asserts," *Bridgeport* (Connecticut) *Sunday Post*, April 3, 1960, C13.

"Half Century at State," *Alumni Quarterly — East Tennessee State University* 38.3 (Spring 1974), 8-9.

Mooney, Jack, "Jim Mooney," *Hawkins County Historical Society* (n.d.), 387-89.

Moore, Richard, "ETSC's Jim Mooney Holds Several Titles at School." *Kingsport Times-News*, June 3, 1962, 39.

Stone, George, "Jim Mooney Made Hit with 1931 New York Giants," *Johnson City Press-Chronicle*, April 10, 1977, 36.

Ancestry.com

Baseball-reference.com

Retrosheet.org

Baseball Hall of Fame Library, Jim Mooney player file

The Sporting News

Richmond (Virginia) *Times-Dispatch*

Kingsport (Tennessee) *Times, Kingsport News*

New York Evening Graphic

Chattanooga Times

Morning Advocate (Baton Rouge)

Augusta (Georgia) *Chronicle*

Times Picayune (New Orleans)

Tampa Tribune

Salt Lake Tribune

Hartford Courant

Washington Post

New York Times

Omaha World Herald

Boston Herald

Trenton (New Jersey) *Evening Times*

Olean (New York) *Times Evening Herald*

Dunkirk (New York) *Evening Observer*

Salamanca (New York) *Republican Press*

Dallas Morning News

National Labor Tribune (Pittsburgh)

Panama City (Florida) *News-Herald*

Biloxi (Mississippi) *Daily Herald*

Greensboro (North Carolina) *Record*

Johnson City (Tennessee) *Press-Chronicle*

Wisconsin State Journal (Madison)

Jim Mooney Letters, 1931-1946, Archives of Appalachia, East Tennessee State University.

Notes

1. Letter to Charlie Weatherby from Jeanne Mooney Smith, June 2012.
2. George Stone, "Jim Mooney Made Hit with 1931 New York Giants," *Johnson City Press-Chronicle*, April 10, 1977, 36.
3. Jeanne Mooney Smith letter.
4. "His Speed Burns Them Up," *The Sporting News*, September 10, 1931, 1.
5. L.M. Sutter, *Ball, Bat, and Bitumen: A History of Coalfield Baseball in the Appalachian South* (Jefferson, North Carolina: McFarland, 2009), 33, 55.
6. "Vols 5, Lookouts 0," *Augusta Chronicle*, June 14, 1927, 6.
7. "Eight-Run Rally Wins for Lookouts, 10-6," *Times-Picayune*, New Orleans, June 27, 1927, 16.
8. "Training Camp News. Cardinals are Defeated," *Pittsburgh Press*, April 8, 1929, 17.
9. "Outfielders Main Worry of Lookouts," *New Orleans Times-Picayune*, April 14, 1929, 81.
10. "Giants Buy Southpaw," *New York Times*, August 7, 1930, 29.
11. George White, "Garland and Erickson Tame Giants as Steers Win Third Straight," *Dallas Morning News*, March 16, 1931, 12.
12. "Caught On The Fly," *The Sporting News*, April 16, 1931, 6.
13. Ibid.
14. Letter from Jim Mooney to his brother Charles, undated [1931]. Jim Mooney Letters, 1931-1946, Archives of Appalachia, East Tennessee State University (hereafter cited as Jim Mooney letters).
15. Jim Mooney letters.
16. John Drebinger, "Giants Rookie Stops Pirates by 2-1," *New York Times*, August 15, 1931, 11.
17. Dan Daniel, "Giants Gloat Over Mooney Despite Cardinal Invasion," *New York World-Telegram*, August 15, 1931.
18. Joe Vila, "Rookie Gives Giants Fresh Lease of Life," *The Sporting News*, August 27, 1931, 1.
19. Joe Vila, "Sterling Pitching Puts Giants Back in National Pennant Race," *The Sporting News*, September 10, 1931, 1.
20. Roundy Coughlin, "Roundy Says," *Wisconsin State Journal* (Madison), October 24, 1931, 2.
21. "Mooney of Giants Quells Braves 4-0," *New York Times*, September 2, 1931, 25.
22. "Mooney Scores Sixth Straight Triumph for McGrawmen in Nightcap 4-3," *New York Times*, September 9, 1931, 32.
23. "Both New York Teams Gather Timber Early For Next Year," *The Sporting News*, August 20, 1931, 1.
24. Ralph S. Davis, "Bucs Want Neither Malone Nor Davis," *The Sporting News*, September 17, 1931, 3.
25. John Drebinger, "Lindstrom Joins Giants' Hold-Outs," *New York Times*, January 19, 1932, 27.
26. John Drebinger, "Giants Are Beaten By Seals, 10-5," *New York Times*, April 3, 1932, 5J.
27. Jim Mooney letters.
28. Jim Mooney letters.
29. John Kieran, "Sports of the Times," *New York Times*, February 7, 1933, 24.
30. "Mooney Glad He's Card," Mooney Hall of Fame Clipping File, November 3, 1932.
31. Edward Burns, "Hazen Cuyler Lost to Cubs Until June," *The Sporting News*, April 6, 1933, 1.
32. "Hornsby Looms Up In King Row As Next Leader of the Browns, "*The Sporting News*, July 20, 1933, 1.
33. John Drebinger, "Cardinals Conquer Giants 5-4," *New York Times*, May 11, 1934, 28.
34. "Tourists Seek to Establish New League Winning Record," *Richmond Times-Dispatch*, August 30, 1939, 9.
35. "Jim Mooney Halts Final Attempt Of Frank Massimo," *Kingsport Times*, July 30, 1941, 6.
36. Jim Mooney letters.
37. "Jim Mooney Given Outright Release From Johnson City," *Kingsport News*, October 2, 1947, 12.

Gene Moore

By Greg Erion

THE OBITUARY PUBLISHED in *The Sporting News* when Gene Moore died centered on his having made his only World Series appearance because of "a weird circumstance."[1] Although accurate, the article overlooked the fact that Moore was a player of All-Star caliber, the type of player any manager would want on his team. Statistics did not reflect the intensity Moore brought to baseball.

The "weird circumstance" *The Sporting News* cited was a trade of catchers between the Washington Senators and the St. Louis Browns in March 1944, Washington's Tony Giuliani for the Browns' Rick Ferrell. Giuliani refused to go to the lowly Browns and instead retired. Moore was substituted for Giuliani. He too was reluctant to go to St. Louis for whom little success was forecast in 1944, and did so only after receiving a cash inducement from the Senators. So it was Moore rather than Giuliani who earned a World Series check that season.

Eugene Moore, Jr. was born in Lancaster, Texas, on August 26, 1909, to Eugene and Sarah Moore, the fifth of ten children. Like many of his era, Moore shaved a year off his birth — the player file at Baseball's Hall of Fame shows his birth date as August 26, 1910.[2] Eugene Sr. was a pitcher who spent nine years in the Texas League with brief major-league appearances in three seasons. Almost simultaneously with his son's birth, Moore was called up to the Pittsburgh Pirates, making one appearance late in September 1909. He also pitched briefly for the Pirates in 1910 and for Cincinnati in 1912, compiling a career record of 2-2.

After retiring from the game, Moore Sr. returned to farming in Lancaster, near Dallas. Three of his sons showed enough talent to rate consideration as professionals. Neither Collins nor Hal Moore ever made it past tryouts, but Eugene Jr. went on to play ball in all or part of 14 major-league seasons.

Moore first came to prominence playing for Waxahachie High School, which at one point won 65 games in a row and featured two other future major leaguers, Paul Richards and Art Shires.[3] After graduating and playing semipro ball for a year, Moore signed for $600 to pitch with Midland of the West Texas League in 1929.[4] It quickly became apparent that his skills were better suited to playing the outfield than pitching.

A reserve in 1934. Moore played for six teams over a 14-year career. His father pitched briefly for the Pirates and Reds in the Deadball Era.

Appearing with five different clubs in his first three seasons, he hit over .300 at each stop, climbing rapidly from Class D to Double-A (then the highest minor-league classification.[5] In September 1931 he played in four games for the Cincinnati Reds, itting .143 in 14 at-bats.

On December 24, 1931, Moore married Gladys Bryan in Dallas. The marriage produced two children, Robert Gene, born in 1933, and Donald Bryan, born in 1936.[6]

In 1932 Moore was back in the minors, playing for three Class B teams, Peoria of the Three-I League and Harrisburg and Elmira, both of the New York-Pennsylvania League.

Transferred to the vast St. Louis Cardinal organization in 1933, he played well at Houston, Columbus, and Rochester, but, except for brief appearances was unable to crack a St. Louis outfield containing players like Joe Medwick, Terry Moore (no relation), and Jack Rothrock. He was with the world championship 1934 team in April and May before being sent back to the minors.

In September 1935 Moore was sold to Brooklyn after a solid season with Rochester. The Dodgers had plans to call him up for the final few games of the season, but word did not reach him until he arrived home in Texas.[7] Moore was not destined to play for Brooklyn—yet. He was traded to the woeful Boston Bees (Braves) with pitcher Johnny Babich for Bees pitcher Fred Frankhouse.

Freedom from the vast Cardinal minor-league system was a gift, and joining the worst team in baseball was a great opportunity. Bert Keane in describing 1936's rookie crop for the *Hartford Courant* wrote of Moore, "He can throw with accuracy and power. He hits for distance and when under way scurries around the bases like a scared rabbit."[8] Moore wasted no time showing the Bees the wisdom of their trade, hitting an opposite-field homer on his first at-bat in an exhibition game against the crosstown rival Red Sox—a particular skill at which the left-handed hitting Moore became quite proficient.[9]

Given the chance, Moore did not disappoint. He had an outstanding rookie season. Playing right field and appearing in 151 games, Moore hit .290, placing in the top ten in the National League in hits, doubles, triples, and home runs. Keane's description of Moore's throwing ability ("with accuracy and power") was dead on. Moore's 32 outfield assists led the majors.

Moore gave evidence of his opposite-field power early on. Playing at Forbes Field in Pittsburgh on May 1, the left-handed batter hammered two home runs, the second over the left-field fence. The *New York Times* noted, "Old-timers said this was the first time a left-handed batter performed that feat."[10] Less than two weeks later Moore showed a streak of independence not looked upon kindly by his manager, Bill McKechnie. Playing against Pittsburgh, he was ordered to bunt. Disregarding the sign, he swung away and tripled. McKechnie raked Moore over the coals—and watched him slam another triple later in the game.[11] McKechnie must not have been too hard on Moore; he played the next day.

On August 25 Moore hit two doubles in the first inning of a game against St. Louis, tying the record for the most doubles by a player in an inning. His teammates hit five more doubles in the inning and the seven two-baggers were a record for the most by a team in an inning. (It was tied by the Cardinals in 2012.[12])

Moore finished the 1936 season with a .290 batting average and 13 home runs. Thanks to his play and that of two other newcomers, Tony Cuccinello and Al Lopez, the Bees climbed from eighth place to sixth. Moore had another productive season in 1937. His average fell to .283 but his home runs rose to 16, a good number for that era. His assists dropped from 32 to 21, no doubt because baserunners no longer desired to challenge his arm, but he still led the league. The team improved again finishing over .500 in fifth place just behind the Cardinals. Moore was named to the National League's squad for the All-Star Game. He didn't start (the NL's starting outfield was Paul Waner, Joe Medwick, and Frank Demaree), and grounded into a force play as a pinch-hitter.

Moore went back home to farming after the season. His father was ill, and Gene was helping to support his brothers, sisters, and mother as well as his wife and children. Eventually Moore bought a farm near Lancaster, Texas, raising cotton, corn, and wheat as well as pigs. His farm adjoined that of Dizzy Dean, whose career had taken an abrupt turn for the worse in 1937 after the All-Star Game.[13] Earl Averill's line drive broke the big toe on Dean's left foot. Dean came back before the injury properly healed, hurt his arm in the process, and lost his effectiveness as a premier pitcher. That a player's career could be changed by injury was part of the game. It happened to Moore the next season.

Moore played for a new manager in 1938, Casey Stengel having replaced McKechnie, who left to manage Cincinnati. Moore welcomed the opportunity to play for Stengel. "I know Manager Casey Stengel is a good man to play for, and I will do my best for him and for the club," he wrote to general manager Bob Quinn.

Stengel for his part believed Moore could use his speed to advantage by bunting more often.[14] Although Moore honed his bunting skills, it did not mean he neglected other aspects of his offense. In the second game of the season, with the Bees down 4-2, he hit a grand slam to win the game.[15] Ten days later Moore hit another grand slam to help win a 16-11 slugfest against the Phillies. The Bees were off to a good start; in late May they were in third place, close behind the Giants and Cubs.

On May 19 the *Boston Globe* reported that Moore was playing with neuralgia and an injured ankle.[16] The next day the *Globe* reported that Moore was "badly handicapped by an injured ankle and would have to take a few days off to rest it.[17] Moore was out of the lineup for a few days but came back going all-out; within a few weeks he injured a foot and elbow when he ran into the grandstand wall attempting to catch a foul ball.[18]

On June 11 the Bees were victimized by Cincinnati's Johnny Vander Meer, who shut them down with the first of what would be two consecutive no-hitters. Moore, who drew one of Vander Meer's three walks, was picked off first after catcher Ernie Lombardi caught a pop foul. Moore twisted his ankle trying to get back to the base and went out of the lineup for a week.[19] In late June he was reported to have locked cartilage in his left knee and began playing with a knee brace.[20] He continued to play, in one game crashing into Cuccinello as both went for a ball.[21] On July 18 Moore collapsed chasing after a hit, and took himself out of the game. His season was over.[22] He would never again perform as well as he had with Boston.

Moore had surgery to have cartilage removed from his knee. According to the practice of the time, he was placed on the voluntarily retired list.[23] Meanwhile, on August 30 his father died from the lingering effects of a brain tumor.

In December Stengel visited the convalescing Moore to see how he was faring. If Moore could come back, it would be a boon to Boston; his loss was considered the main reason the Bees had finished out of the first division.[24] Stengel must have been less than impressed; Moore was traded to the Dodgers. Brooklyn had sent scout Ted McGrew to Moore's farm and after "hitting a flock of fungoes to Gene" determined it was worth the chance to obtain his services.[25]

It was a bad trade from the Dodgers' perspective. Although Moore looked healthy in spring training, he had lost his stroke. He played in 107 games for the Dodgers in 1939 and hit just .225 with only three home runs. Brooklyn sold him back to Boston six weeks into the 1940 season. Although Moore's batting average rebounded to a respectable .290, his loss of power proved permanent. After posting slugging averages in the range of .450 in his first two seasons with the Bees, Moore never topped .400 after 1940.

In February 1942 Moore was traded to the New York Yankees for Tommy Holmes. Overjoyed at being traded to a pennant contender, he was disappointed when he was sold less than three weeks later to Brooklyn's top minor-league team, the Montreal Royals. Moore felt this was a setback; Montreal was glad to gain his services. Manager Clyde Sukeforth was said he was a "tailor-made player for the dimensions of the Montreal Park."[26] Sukeforth was correct. Moore had a solid year, hitting .315 and leading the league in triples, runs scored, and total bases. He led the Royals' outfielders in assists with 13—no mean feat considering he was playing alongside future Dodgers star Carl Furillo, who became renowned for having one of the best outfield arms in the game.

Normally a 32-year-old former major-league outfielder with bad legs could expect no higher level of play, but these were not ordinary times. Though World War II manpower requirements were high, Moore's bad knees exempted him from the draft. It also made him attractive to major-league teams trying to fill their rosters. At season's end Moore was purchased by the Washington Senators.

He joined a team that had finished in either sixth or seventh the previous four years. By 1943 teams experienced fluctuating rosters because of increasing draft demands. The Senators, in dealing with this challenge, amassed a mixture of players who had yet to be drafted or were exempt from the draft. They jumped to second place in 1943; Moore batted .268 as a backup outfielder and .400 as a pinch-hitter.

During the offseason Moore was on the trading block. Rumors had him going to the Yankees.[27] That did not take place, but in March 1944 Moore was traded again. It was anything but a routine transaction. The Senators and St. Louis Browns traded catchers. Rick Ferrell went to Washington in exchange for Tony Giuliani.[28] Giuliani balked at going to the Browns and retired. Browns owner Donald Barnes demanded cancellation of the transaction. Washington needed Ferrell. Commissioner Kenesaw M. Landis backed Barnes, who then demanded Moore as Giuliani's replacement.[29] Moore was reluctant to report, but Senators owner Clark Griffith reportedly gave him a bonus to go.[30] Giuliani's perception of the situation proved amiss. Washington finished last in 1944 and the Browns won the pennant.

Barnes knew what he was about prying Moore from the Senators. He and general manager Bill DeWitt approached the game during the war by stocking the roster with "drunks, rogues cast off as troublemakers by others … worn and frayed strands of playing talent. …"[31] Moore was unfit for military service because he had no cartilage in either knee. At 34, he was one of the older players on the St. Louis roster. The Browns, like Washington, experienced ups and downs during the war, finishing third in 1942, sixth in 1943, and were not expected to do well in 1944.

What sort of person were the Browns getting? By all accounts, Moore was a quiet individual, not given to brag. In Harold Kaese's history of the Boston Braves, Moore, while with Boston, was described as spending evenings as an inveterate "hotel lobby sitter." Of his lobby sitting, the laconic Moore commented, "I went to High School like Art Shires (a very colorful and eccentric personality), and I just want to show we turn out all types there, quiet as well as noisy."[32]

His habits did not change with the Browns. David Heller in his book on the 1944 Browns, described Moore's demeanor and penchant for lobby-sitting; "He wasn't vocal, and didn't drink, usually hanging out with (first baseman George McQuinn) in hotel lobbies, both players relaxing by smoking cigars and watching the traffic of people around them." Heller wrote that Moore's nickname, Rowdy, was bestowed on him as one might call a tall person Shorty.[33]

Moore may have been devoid of color, but on a team of "drunks, rogues, and troublemakers," his steady demeanor and serious approach to the game gave the team needed stability. Bill Borst, author of *The Best of Seasons*, portrayed Moore as a "steady presence," invaluable during the pennant drive.[34] These were intangibles, hard to measure. By standard measures, Moore did not do well in 1944, hitting .238 with six home runs. Yet he came through at crucial times.

The Browns won their first nine games of the season, boosting the team's confidence. Moore started hot, hitting .421 in the first five games of that streak. Leading the team in RBIs in May, he finished the month with a game-winning single against Washington on May 31. The victory put the Browns back in first place. Several days later, after St. Louis had lost three straight games to Cleveland and were losing a fourth, Moore was called on to pinch-hit, and hit the first pitch he saw for a game-winning grand slam.[35] His hits were few, but when he hit they counted. On the last weekend of the season with the Browns trying to hold onto first place over Detroit, they played the Yankees. With St. Louis holding a 1-0 lead, Moore homered in the sixth inning for an insurance run in the Browns' 2-0 victory. They clinched the pennant the next day, the last game of the season, and went into the World Series against the heavily favored Cardinals.

The Browns shocked the Cardinals, winning two of the first three games. However, the National Leaguers roared back to take the Series in six games. Cardinal pitching proved the difference, holding the Browns to a .183 average. Moore hit well at the beginning of the series, but went hitless in the last three games, and ended batting .182 for the Series. In Game One he singled with two outs in the fourth inning, and when McQuinn followed with a drive over the right-field pavilion at Sportsman's Park, Moore became the first Brownie to score a run in a World Series. McQuinn's homer proved enough to win the game 2-1 as the back-to-back hits were the only two safeties that day by the Browns. In the first inning of Game Four, with the Browns down 2-0 and a man on base, Moore drove the ball to deep center, but it was caught on a brilliant play by Johnny Hopp. It was one of the crucial plays of the Series. Moore and the Browns had nothing to be ashamed of; they played tough against the finest team of the era. The Browns' losing share of the World Series receipts, $2,743.79 per full share, was the lowest received by players on a losing team since 1920.

As the 1945 season opened, World War II was nearing an end. Many regulars were coming back from the service, replacing those who had filled in. The Browns played well, finishing third behind Detroit. Moore hit creditably well, finishing at .260. The last game of the season Detroit needed a win to clinch the pennant. The Tigers won it in the top of the ninth at St. Louis thanks to Hank Greenberg's grand slam. Moore had a run-scoring double. It was his last major-league game.

Moore finished his major-league career with a .270 average and a .400 slugging percentage. Although he signed to play in 1946, it was not to be.[36] Gladys became ill and Moore left the game to take care of her. In early 1947 he was reactivated, and the Browns sold his contract to Toledo in the American Association.[37] Moore refused to report, and soon word came out that he was in the scrap business at Laurel, Mississippi.[38]

According to Moore's grandson Bryan, Gladys's father, Selma Bryan, who operated junkyard businesses at several locations in Mississippi, offered Moore management of Laurel Steelworks. This, coupled with his wife's illness and the ever-present pain in Moore's knees, made retirement the feasible choice.[39] Mrs. Moore's illness continued for several years. In 1948 she had surgery for a ruptured disc and spinal fusion.[40] (She recovered and lived until 1999, when she died at the age of 88.) Moore continued in the junk business until he retired and passed ownership of the business to his son Robert.

Over the years Moore made appearances at old-timer's games, including reunions of the 1937 All Stars and the 1944 Browns. He hunted, fished, and started Little League in Laurel. He enjoyed his grandchildren, allowing them to play with several of his autographed baseballs. Moore spoke very little of his playing days, once telling grandson Bryan that if he spoke of his experiences, folks might think he was bragging. This was in keeping with how his daughter-in-law, Martha, Robert's wife, and grandson Bryan remembered him: A mild, soft-spoken person.[41]

Moore died on March 12, 1978, in Jackson, Mississippi. He was 68. Mild and soft-spoken he might have been, but he was a fierce competitor. He fought off injuries, even when his legs gave way, showing no fear in crashing a wall, going into the stands, or risking collision with another player chasing a ball. The Browns saw his determination in 1944. But what else might one expect of the slim outfielder who grandson Bryan recalled having written, "I'll never give up on baseball."

Notes

1 *The Sporting News,* April 1, 1978, 61.

2 Moore's file in the Baseball Hall of Fame, no date.

3 "Looping the Loops," *The Sporting News,* October 25, 1950, 4; "Lane Talks of Trades, Richards Adds Coach," *The Sporting News,* December 13, 1950, 20.

4 Phone conversation with Bryan Moore, February 27, 2013.

5 All statistical data from either Baseball-reference.com or Retrosheet-org.

6 http://msgw.org/hinds/bible_anderson_askew.html (Family Bible of William Henry Anderson and Mary Ann Askew which records their births and the marriage of Gladys Maree Bryan).

7 "He Gets Around," *The Sporting News,* February 27, 1936, 1.

8 "Cards Have Greatest Number of Outstanding Rookies in Major League Camps," *Hartford Courant,* March 29, 1936, C3.

9 Harold Kaese, *The Boston Braves, 1871-1953* (Boston: Northeastern University Press, 2004), 236-237.

10 "Moore's 2 Homers Help Bees Triumph," *New York Times,* May 2, 1936, 19.

11 Moore's Hall of Fame file, May 21, 1936, no attribution available.

12 "Bees Topple Cards in Double-Header, *New York Times,* August 26, 1936, 24.

13 Phone conversation with Bryan Moore, February 27, 2013.

14 "Gene Moore Signs His Bees Contract," *Boston Globe,* February 16, 1938, 22.

15 "Moore's Home Run With Bases Full Defeats Giants," *Hartford Courant,* April 21, 1938, 14.

16 "Bees Beat the Pirates and Take Third Place" and "Diamond Dots," *Boston Globe,* May 20, 1938, 27.

17 "MacFayden Is to Pitch Today," *Boston Globe,* May 21, 1938, 5.

18 "Bill Lee to Try for 5th in Row Against Bees," *Chicago Daily Tribune*, 28.

19 "Vander Meer Joins the Hall of Fame, *Boston Globe*, June 12, 1938, C25.

20 "Bees May Lose Moore, Operation Seems Likely," *Boston Globe*, June 27, 1938, 7.

21 "Hutchinson Wins His First Starting Game," *Boston Globe*, July 3, 1938, B5.

22 "Cubs Sweep Bees' Series: Win in Ninth, 7-6, *Chicago Daily Tribune*, July 19, 1938, 15.

23 "Bees Lose Gene Moore for Balance of Season," *Boston Globe*, July 26, 1938, 7.

24 "Big Boston Sox Deal Said to be "in the Bag," *The Sporting News*, October 20, 1938, 10.

25 "Dodgers Get More Power in Moore," *The Sporting News*, December 22, 1938, 2.

26 "Gene Moore News Welcome, Montreal Wants More Like It," *The Sporting News*, March 5, 1942, 3.

27 "McCarthy Applies Skids to Snuffy Stirnweiss Bids," *The Sporting News*, December 9, 1943, 18.

28 "Senators Need Knuckler Receiver; Get Ferrell Back," *Boston Globe*, March 2, 1944, 9.

29 "Nat Outfield Crippled by Forced Deal," *The Washington Post*, March 29, 1944, 12.

30 "Obituaries," *The Sporting News*, April 1, 1978, 61.

31 William Mead, *Even the Browns, the Zany, True Story of Baseball in the Early Forties*, (Chicago: Contemporary Books, 1978), 19.

32 Kaese, *The Boston Braves*, 237.

33 David Alan Heller, *As Good As It Got: The 1944 St. Louis Browns*, (Charleston, South Carolina: Arcadia Publishing, 2003), 53.

34 Bill Borst, *The Best of Seasons: The 1944 St. Louis Cardinals and St. Louis Browns*, (Jefferson, North Carolina: McFarland), 1995.

35 Borst, 99.

36 "St. Louis Shortstop Aces Demand Hike in Antes," *The Sporting News,* February 21, 1946, 16.

37 "Gene Moore Is Sold to Toledo Ball Club," *Hartford Courant*, January 1, 1947, 13.

38 "Major flashes," *The Sporting News*, March 26, 1947," 20.

39 Phone conversation with Bryan Moore, February 27, 2013.

40 "Caught on the Fly," *The Sporting News*, June 30, 1948, 29; phone conversation with Bryan Moore, February 27, 2013.

41 Phone conversations with Martha Moore, February 26, 2013, and Bryan Moore, February 27 and March 21, 2013.

Ernie Orsatti

By Lawrence Baldassaro

Few people have the talent and good fortune to have successful careers in two such diverse fields as professional sports and the film industry. Ernie Orsatti was one of those lucky few.

In his nine-year career with the Cardinals (1927-1935), Orsatti hit .300 or better in six seasons, twice hit over .330, and finished with a lifetime average of .306. The Los Angeles native's colorful wardrobe also lent a touch of Hollywood glamor to the notoriously unkempt Gas House Gang. As successful as it was, Orsatti's baseball career was really an interlude in a more extensive career in Hollywood. Before he became a professional ballplayer, he was a movie stuntman, prop man and bit player. Then, when his major-league career ended, he and his brothers ran one of the most influential talent agencies in Los Angeles.

Ernest Ralph Orsatti was born in Los Angeles on September 8, 1902. He was the sixth of seven children born to Maurizio and Maria (Manze) Orsatti, Italian immigrants whose names were anglicized to Morris and Mary in the US. Employed as a tailor when the couple were living in Philadelphia, after moving to Los Angeles Morris became the owner of the International Steamship and Railroad Ticket Agency.

Orsatti's path to professional baseball was anything but typical. In fact, he had no childhood aspirations of playing baseball. Growing up in Los Angeles, he dreamed of a career in the movies and spent his spare time hanging around the studios and doing odd jobs.

Orsatti, a fine-fielding center fielder, played all nine years of his major-league career with the Cardinals. He batted 300 or better in six of those seasons and appeared in four World Series.

"My interest, as a boy, was in motion pictures and not in baseball," he told *The Sporting News*. "I wanted to be an actor, a director, a cameraman, anything that would identify me with motion pictures. In 1920, I decided to quit school and devote all my time to the picture business."[1] He went to work full-time at the studios, first as a "gofer," then as a stunt man. He walked on the wings of airplanes, dived off cliffs, and did automobile and boat stunts.

In 1922 Orsatti went to work as a prop man and bit player at the studio of the great silent film comedian Buster Keaton. Though he never doubled as a stuntman for Keaton (who did his own stunts), he did double for the actor in a scene in the 1924 film *Sherlock, Jr.* At 5-feet-7 and 150 pounds, Orsatti was a good physical match for the 5-foot-6, 140-pound Keaton.

A lifelong baseball fan and a decent player, Keaton had an indoor baseball team and was also part-owner of the Vernon (California) Tigers in the Pacific Coast League. Orsatti played first base and caught for Keaton's team from 1922 to 1925. When Turkey Mike Donlin, a former major leaguer turned Hollywood supporting actor, saw Orsatti play, he told Keaton that the young man could make more money playing baseball than by working in the studio. In the spring of 1925, Keaton walked onto the movie set where Orsatti was working and handed him a contract to play for Vernon.

After appearing in six games for Vernon, Orsatti was sent to Cedar Rapids (Iowa) in the Class D

Mississippi Valley League, where he hit .347. It was while Orsatti was at Cedar Rapids that Branch Rickey saw him play and made him part of the Cardinals organization by purchasing his contract.[2] Orsatti moved up the Cardinals' minor-league ranks quickly, hitting .386 at Omaha of the Class A Western League in 1926 and .330 with Houston of the Double-A Texas League in 1927. The 24-year-old, left-handed-hitting outfielder made his major-league debut on September 4, 1927.

Though he showed he could hit major-league pitching (.315 in 92 at-bats), Orsatti was less adept at playing the outfield (five errors in 26 games) and was sent Minneapolis Millers of the Double-A American Association in 1928. After hitting .381 with a career-high 15 homers, he was recalled by the Cardinals on August 18.

On August 24 Orsatti's first-inning home run gave the Cardinals a 1-0 win over the Philadelphia Phillies, keeping the team in first place, where it remained for the rest of the season. In his first six games, Orsatti hit three home runs, the only homers he would hit in 69 times at bat that season. (That brief power surge notwithstanding, in 2,165 career at-bats with the Cardinals, Orsatti hit only ten home runs.)

In 1929, appearing in more than 100 games for the first time, Orsatti hit .332 while playing all three outfield positions. He did not play in 100 games again until 1932, when he had his best season, hitting .336 (sixth best in the NL) and driving in a career-high 44 runs.

After the 1932 season Orsatti was sent a contract offering the same $4,500 he received in 1932. He met with Branch Rickey, hoping to convince him that his performance merited a raise. No sooner did Orsatti raise the issue than Rickey received a phone call he said was from the general manager of one of the Cardinals' minor-league clubs. Rickey purportedly said, "You need an outfielder? I'll call you back in a few minutes. I think I'll have one available for you."

When Orsatti again tried to discuss the contract after Rickey hung up, the phone rang again. This time it was the GM of another farm team asking Rickey for an outfielder. To this request Rickey replied, "I'm sure I've got the guy for you." When Rickey hung up and asked Orsatti what it was he wanted, Orsatti replied,

"I just wanted to ask you for a pen, Mr. Rickey, so I can sign my contract." According to William Veeck, Sr., the Chicago Cubs executive (and father of the more famous Bill Veeck), the phone calls were fake. Rickey could set off the telephone bell by stepping on a foot pedal under his desk.[3]

After hitting under .300 (.298) for the first time in 1933, Orsatti hit an even .300 in 1934, then slumped to .240 in 1935. Before the 1936 season the Cardinals planned to send him to Rochester, but Orsatti refused and left baseball.

Orsatti's first four seasons with the Cardinals (1927-1930) came at a time when batting averages were among the highest in history. In fact, three of the top ten National League averages were recorded in those four years. Still, Orsatti hit well above the league average in every one but the last of his nine seasons. In 1930, when the NL batting average of .303 was the second highest in history, Orsatti beat it by 18 points. And in 1932, his career-high average of .336 was 60 points above the league average.

Orsatti played in four World Series (1928, 1930, 1931, and 1934). In the 1934 win over the Tigers, he appeared in all seven games and hit .318 with a .423 on-base percentage. According to player-manager Frankie Frisch, Detroit fans were so bitter about losing the 1934 Series to St. Louis that when Orsatti was in Detroit on a business trip 25 years later and tried to check into the Sheraton-Cadillac Hotel, where the Cardinals stayed during the '34 Series, the desk clerk refused to give Orsatti a room. "Ernie had to go over the clerk's head to get a room at the hotel," said Frisch.[4]

For a consistent .300 hitter, Orsatti had a hard time cracking the starting lineup. In only four of his nine seasons did he play in more than 100 games. (An ankle injury limited him to 48 games in 1930.) A 1931 preseason article in *The Sporting News* speculating on who might start in left field concluded that Orsatti "seems to be the outstanding candidate for the job" since he was "an athlete with plenty of color and a fine competitive spirit. He is fast and able to cover a large outfield, and with a better-than-average throwing arm."[5]

However, Orsatti played in only 70 games that season, 32 as a starting outfielder. Chick Hafey replaced him in left field (even though "Orsatti was pounding the ball hard") because left field was the only position Hafey could play. As for a possible trade, "the little Italian probably would not object to a transfer, if it meant he could play regularly. No ball player hates the bench more than Ernie."[6]

Orsatti himself attributed his limited playing time to the abundance of good outfielders in the Cardinals organization. "In one way, I came along at the wrong time," he said. "The Cardinals were loaded with outfielders. Every year I'd go to camp thinking I finally had a regular job locked up when some phenom would come along. In 1934, I finally thought I had a regular job in right field. But Branch Rickey drafted an American League retread, Jack Rothrock, who had the best year of his career."[7] Rothrock started nearly every game in right field, while Orsatti started 90 in center.

It was during that 1934 season that Orsatti made a brief return as an actor. On June 26, before a game against the Giants, a scene from a murder mystery, *Death on the Diamond*, was filmed at Sportsman's Park. In the movie a number of Cardinals players are murdered as part of a plot to keep the team from making it to the World Series. The scene takes place late in the season, when the fictional Cardinals are fighting for the pennant. Orsatti played the role of a player who was shot to death while running the bases.[8] A *New York Times* movie critic wrote that in the film the "hitherto unsuspected hazards of ball playing are described with an entertaining combination of humor and grim melancholy."[9]

Having risked his life as a Hollywood stuntman, Orsatti brought that same daredevil mentality to the baseball diamond. Leo Durocher, who joined the Cardinals in 1933, described baseball in that era as "a rough-and-tumble no-holds-barred game played predominantly by farm boys. Generally unschooled, generally unspoiled, generally unsophisticated. Right off the farm or down from the hills."[10]

According to Durocher, Orsatti fit right in with the scrappy Gas House Gang. Along with Pepper Martin and Frisch, who were called the "diving seals" because of their penchant for sliding head-first, Orsatti, a speedy baserunner, also liked to slide head-first. "The uniforms were so filthy that we could have thrown them in the corner and they'd have stood up by themselves," said Durocher. "The bills of our caps were all bent and creased and twisted. We looked horrible, we knew it and we gloried in it."[11]

Teammate Jim Mooney noted that Orsatti was also a regular part of the famous pepper game the Cardinals put on to amuse the fans during warmups. "Orsatti was a great little ol' outfielder," recalled Mooney. "One time we were playing in Chicago, and someone hit a line drive out into center field, and he went out there and caught it and turned two or three somersaults. He was a great little fellow. Orsatti was a showman."[12]

But if Orsatti's aggressive style and soiled uniform made him a bona fide member of the Gas House Gang on the field, he did not glory in looking horrible off the field. Once the uniform came off and he put on his civilian clothes, he stood apart from his teammates. In addition to his impressively consistent hitting, Orsatti brought a splash of Hollywood style to the happily disheveled Cardinals. A photo above a 1932 *Sporting News* story shows him wearing fashionable golf knickers and looking for all the world like golf legend Bobby Jones. In the accompanying story, Harry T. Brundidge described Orsatti's look: "He never wears a hat, and his thick growth of well-oiled black hair is pushed back from his forehead. His flashy sweaters, golf hose, knickers and sports suits are Hollywood importations, and his wardrobe is the envy of most of the younger players."[13] In its obituary of Orsatti *The Sporting News* wrote that "Ernie's ensembles made him stand out like a peacock in the ranks of the Gashouse Gang."[14]

At a time when ethnic terminology now considered offensive was commonplace, in the same 1932 *Sporting News* story Brundidge referred to Orsatti as the Dashing Dago, and added that the player, "affectionately known as The Wop in the Cardinals baseball clubhouse, is one of the most popular players on the team."[15]

When Orsatti's major-league career ended in 1935, he returned to Los Angeles and joined his brothers, Frank, Vic, and Al, in the Orsatti Talent Agency.[16] According to Orsatti's son, Ernest F. Orsatti, it was the largest agency in Hollywood.[17] Among its clients were such stars as Sonja Henie, Margaret O'Brien, Betty Grable, Judy Garland, and Edward G. Robinson.

In 1939 Orsatti returned to the minor leagues for one season, appearing in 37 games for Hollywood in the Pacific Coast League and in 31 games for Columbus in the American Association. At the time of his signing with the Hollywood Stars, the *New York Times* reported that Orsatti, "now an actors' agent, is expected to prove a strong drawing card in the film colony."[8]

While still working with his brothers in the talent agency, at some point in the mid-1940s he opened Ernie Orsatti's Oddity Shop and Florist on Sunset Boulevard in Hollywood. His business cards were decorated with a replica of the Cardinals redbirds perched on a bat. According to *The Sporting News*, at that time Orsatti also held a patent on a candy-vending machine and "collects the royalties on the candy bars found in the lobbies of most theaters throughout southern California."[9]

For Orsatti, who spent most of his career in the film industry, the Hollywood lifestyle carried over into his nonprofessional life. In January 1929 he married Martha Von Estey, a San Antonio newspaper writer he met while playing for Houston. In February 1934 Orsatti sued for divorce from Von Estey, charging her with "impairing his baseball efficiency by her 'constant nagging and quarrelsome nature.'"[10]

Orsatti wed for a second time in September 1934, marrying opera singer Inez Gorman in Beverly Hills. The couple had two sons, Ernest F. and Frank. While Orsatti's own career as a stunt performer was short-lived, his two sons continued a tradition that as of 2013 included four generations of Orsattis.

Both sons had long and distinguished careers, each appearing in dozens of films and TV series. In *The Poseidon Adventure* (1972), Ernie, known as "The Legend," performed the death-defying stunt of falling from an upside-down table through what had been the ballroom's ornate glass ceiling. Frank, who died in 2004, worked as Arnold Schwarzenegger's stunt double in *The Terminator* and doubled for Burt Reynolds for nine years.[11] Young Ernie's son, Noon, has also appeared in dozens of films and TV series since beginning his career in 1983. Noon's son, Rowbie, and his daughter, Allie, continue to maintain the Orsatti legacy as stunt performers.

Orsatti's marriage to Gorman ended in 1952. His son, Ernie, who was 12 years old when his parents divorced, described his father as a great athlete and a talented chef. "One of the biggest parties was held on Christmas Eve," he recalled, "when he cooked for dozens of people from show business and the opera world."[2]

In 1960 Orsatti married Canadian native Alice Joyce Ritchie. He and Ritchie operated Orsatti Bail Bonds in Van Nuys, California, until his death at the age of 65 of a heart attack on September 4, 1968. He is buried in San Fernando Mission Cemetery, Mission Hills, California.

Sources

Durocher, Leo, and Ed Linn, "That Old Gang Of Mine," *Sports Illustrated*, April 7, 1975, 78-94.

Frisch, Frank, as told to J. Roy Stockton, *Frisch: The Fordham Flash* (Garden City, New York: Doubleday, 1962).

Golenbock, Peter, *The Spirit of St. Louis: A History of the Cardinals and Browns* (New York: Avon Books, 2000).

Snyder, John. *Cardinals Journal: Year by Year & Day by Day with the St. Louis Cardinals Since 1882 (*Cincinnati: Clerisy Press, 2010).

Los Angeles City Directory, 1908

New York Times

San Antonio Express

San Antonio Light

The Sporting News

Toledo Blade

Ernie F. Orsatti, telephone interview, March 7, 2013.

Scott Orsatti, telephone interview, May 31, 2013.

Notes

1. *The Sporting News*, February 4, 1932, 5.
2. Ibid.
3. *Toledo Blade*, April 1, 1972, 16.
4. Frank Frisch, as told to J. Roy Stockton, *Frisch: The Fordham Flash* (Garden City, New York: Doubleday, 1962), 177.
5. *The Sporting News*, April 9, 1931, 1.
6. Ibid.
7. *The Sporting News*, September 21, 1968, x.

8. John Snyder, *Cardinals Journal: Year by Year & Day by Day with the St. Louis Cardinals Since 1882* (Cincinnati: Clerisy Press, 2010), 264.

9. *New York Times*, September 24, 1934.

10. Leo Durocher and Ed Linn, "That Old Gang Of Mine," *Sports Illustrated*, April 7, 1975, 84.

11. Ibid.

12. Peter Golenbock, *The Spirit of St. Louis: A History of the Cardinals and Browns* (New York: Avon Books, 2000), 186.

13. *The Sporting News*, February 4, 1932, 5.

14. *The Sporting News*, September 21, 1968, 36.

15. *The Sporting News*, February 4, 1932, 5.

16. Vic, who starred in football and baseball in high school, was honored as the best all-around athlete in Los Angeles in 1923 and went on to play quarterback at the University of Southern California. As the prize for winning a home run-hitting contest while in high school, he received the bat used by Babe Ruth to hit the first homer in Yankee Stadium, on April 18, 1923. Ruth had donated the bat to the *Los Angeles Evening Herald*.

17. Ernest F. Orsatti, telephone interview, March 7, 2013.

18. *New York Times*, March 29, 1939.

19. *The Sporting News*, February 5, 1947, 7.

20. *San Antonio Light*, February 8, 1934, 17.

21. Frank, who aspired to follow in his father's footsteps as a ballplayer, appeared in 12 games with the Cardinals' affiliate Brunswick in the Georgia-Florida League in 1963, but his career was cut short by an injury.

22. Ernest F. Orsatti, telephone interview, March 7, 2013.

Flint Rhem

By Nancy Snell Griffith

PITCHER CHARLES FLINT "Shad" Rhem is part of a notorious baseball species. While he put together 12 seasons in the majors, and had a 20-win season in 1926, most of the stories told about him revolve around alcohol. Some sportswriters, like Bob Broeg, go so far as to say that Rhem "boozed away the greatness expected of him."[1]

Whatever the case, the various legends certainly make for fascinating reading. Broeg remembered a time when manager Gabby Street scolded Rhem for drinking, and Flint replied, "Well, Sawge, ah was with Alex, and ah figured he was mo' potent to the club than me, so ah drunk the fastest and the mostest."[2] Alex was probably Grover Cleveland Alexander, a fellow pitcher with the St. Louis Cardinals and Rhem's drinking companion. Apparently on another occasion, Rhem fell asleep in the bullpen after a long night of drinking, and woke up with adhesive tape over his eyes, making him think he'd gone blind.[3] During one game, perhaps not prompted by drink, he asked the groundskeeper for a trowel and stopped the game to do some landscaping on the pitching mound. There were many other such stories, including the famous "kidnapping," which we'll get to a little later.

Rhem had three separate stints with the Cardinals, being traded three times and bought back twice. He pitched in five games for the 1934 team before being traded away in June.

Charles Flint Rhem was born in Rhems, South Carolina, not far from the coastal town of Georgetown, on January 24, 1901. Rhems, an unincorporated area near Black Mingo Creek, was named for the Rhem family after Flint's ancestor, Furnifold Rhem, Sr., settled there in 1846. Flint was one of nine children born to Durward Dudley Rhem and his second wife, Margaret Esther (Essie) Durant, whom he married in 1893. In 1900 the Rhems were living in Mingo, Williamsburg County, South Carolina. Living with them were daughter Lauria, the child of Durward's first marriage, and Laura, Durward, Durant, and Furnifold, offspring of the second marriage.

Flint was named after New York shipbuilder Charles Flint, who was a lifelong friend of his father's. Durward Rhem worked in the family business, F. Rhem & Sons, which was extensive and included the production and sale of cotton, naval stores, turpentine, real estate, timber, land, shingles, and the Black River and Mingo Steamboat Company. Durward died in July of 1922 of complications from diabetes.

Rhem studied engineering at Clemson University from 1920 to 1924, but apparently did not graduate. According to *The Cardinals Encyclopedia,* Flint was bashful and gawky when he arrived at Clemson. Although he had been playing baseball since he was 9 years old, he did not intend to play in college. Indeed, he said later that his father disapproved of the sport, thinking it too rough-and-tumble. Flint said later, "I'd have to sneak off and play baseball when I was a kid. …My parents thought only cutthroats and roughnecks

Rhem led the league with 20 wins in 1926, leading the Cardinals to the pennant. He pitched in four World Series for St. Louis, but was sold to the Boston Braves in June, 1934.

played baseball. Maybe they were right."[4] Someone brought him to the attention of the coach, however, and he played from 1922 to 1924, averaging 15 strikeouts per game. His nickname while at Clemson was not Shad, but Big Smoky. In an undated clipping provided by East Carolina University, Rhem is called "the leading college pitcher of South Carolina. ... [He] is a wonderful strikeout pitcher, probably the leader of the South in this respect."

Along the way Rhem also played for some teams in the South Carolina textile leagues. In 1922 he played for Westminster of the Oconee County League, and the following season he played for Belton of the Saluda Textile League, a team that also included future major leaguer Leroy Mahaffey. W.A. (Willie) Hawkins, a former player with the Oconee Mills Mountaineers, remembered that Flint could hold five baseballs in one hand, and called him the "most talented baseball player and athlete I can recall seeing play the game."[5]

In 1922 Flint actually tried to bring himself to the attention of Frank Navin, owner of the Detroit Tigers. His letter to Navin came to the attention of player-manager Ty Cobb. In his autobiography, Cobb called this "one more on a long list of my bitter memories. In 1922 I received a letter from Rhem. ... His spelling didn't indicate that he was about to graduate magna cum laude, but young Flint cited a flock of one- and two-hitters he'd pitched and asked for a tryout in Detroit."[6] In May 1923 Cobb wrote back to Rhem, and his reply is preserved in the collection of East Carolina University. He encouraged Flint to join the Tigers, saying that the team sported a number of Southern boys, many of them college-educated. He went on to say, "If you have the ability, you can expect the Detroit Baseball Club, through myself and Mr. Navin, the owner, to look out for your best interests. ... Now, if you haven't the goods, then you do not want to be in baseball, but if you have, then when you have shown your ability, I can absolutely assure you that Mr. Navin will pay you as much or more in salary than any other man in baseball. I say this as a ball player, a Southern boy, and one who is interested in a man from my section of the country. We would like to have you with us."[7]

Cobb's assurances proved to be hollow, however. Frank Navin was not interested, and according to Cobb, Rhem "turned out to be a regular Frank Merriwell at the college level" and then turned into a real star for St. Louis several years later. Flint actually signed with the Cardinals in 1924 and joined them for spring training. In a letter to his mother, he mentioned that his arm had been bothering him since his arrival in camp, and that he had "asked Mr. Rickey to send me out to a small League for two or three months so I could get some more experience. He said he thought it was best too for me."[8]

Rhem was assigned to the Fort Smith (Arkansas) Twins of the Class C Western Association on April 16. He had a 22-15 record with Fort Smith that year, leading the league with 282 strikeouts. On August 21 he pitched a no-hitter against the Hutchinson Wheat Shockers, and Rickey brought him back up to the big leagues, where he debuted with the Cardinals on September 6. He pitched six games for the Cardinals that year, finishing with a record of 2-2 and an earned-run average of 4.45. The nickname Smokey followed him from Clemson to St. Louis, where he was listed that way on the Cardinals' roster. It was apparently only later that he received the nickname Shad because of all the fish stories he told.

After the 1924 season ended, Rhem managed to make yet another appearance with a textile mill team, this time on October 11 with Brandon Mill. Brandon was playing Judson for the league championship, and both teams had brought in players to beef up their ranks. Judson had recruited infielder Walt Barbare, who had last played for the Pirates. Brandon had Rhem and future major leaguer Pel Ballenger. Brandon came away with the championship.

By May 1925 the *Atlanta Constitution* was predicting great things for Rhem. Observing that he took the engineering course at Clemson "with fair success" and "the baseball course with wonderful results," the paper noted that he had averaged 16 strikeouts per game at Clemson while allowing only one to three hits in most of his games. On a more personal level, the *Constitution* portrayed Flint as "a southerner through and through ... a tall, husky, supple boy, earnest, [with] a lot of unction, a pronounced southern drawl and a lot of courage, confidence and good sense." According to the *Constitution*, Rhem had kept a tabulation of his strikeouts with Fort Smith and maintained that he had over 300, the difference coming because his records on the road were not kept carefully. As for his playing style, "Rhem has a rifle shot fast ball, sharp curves ... an old fashioned 'drop,' and he has the physique and the natural turn to make a great pitcher. Rickey regards him as the most wonderful prospect of recent years if he will only concentrate his entire effort and thought on the game."[9]

Rhem remained with the Cardinals through the 1928 season, compiling a record of 49-40. In 1925 he appeared in 30 games, 24 of which he started. He pitched 170 innings, and had a record of 8-13 and an ERA of 4.92. On May 9, in a game against the New York Giants at the Polo Grounds, he struck out ten batters while hurling a complete-game shutout

The 1926 season was the best of Rhem's career. He and three other pitchers tied for the NL lead in wins, with 20. He started all of the 34 games he appeared in, and pitched 20 complete games. From May 6 to July 1, he had an eight-game winning streak. In a career-high 258 innings Rhem had an ERA of 3.21. The Cardinals were in a close race with the Cincinnati Reds, and on September 16 Rhem pitched in the first game of a doubleheader with the Philadelphia Phillies, leading the Cardinals to a 23-3 win. Thirty-six players were used in the course of the marathon game, 22 by the Phillies.

The Cardinals won both the pennant and the World Series that year. This was the first pennant for St. Louis in 38 years. Flint started Game Four of the Series against the Yankees, but was removed in the bottom of the fourth for a pinch-hitter after giving up two home runs to Babe Ruth. Rhem was part of baseball history, however, since this was the game in which Ruth fulfilled his promise to a bedridden boy, Johnny Sylvester, by hitting three home runs. While Rhem tied for the league lead with his 20 wins, and was third with a won-lost percentage of .741, he was also third in the league in the number of hits given up per nine innings pitched, 8.407.

The next year did not produce a stellar season for Rhem. He refused to sign his contract at first, and missed spring training. In an interesting telegram from Branch Rickey to Flint dated April 2, 1927, Rickey said, "Mr. Breadon's [Cardinals owner Sam Breadon] position on salary unchanged and terms in his last wire to you are definite and final. However I think you and I can make some adjustment on basis of conditional clause in contract previously referred to in our correspondence." This conditional clause was apparently that Rhem would receive a total of $2,500 in bonus money if he refrained from drinking during the season.

Although he had pitched two two-hitters and one three-hitter by early June, Rhem's frequent drinking was beginning to cause problems. In July Breadon fined him $2,000 for violating training rules. This fine was the remainder of his $2,500 conditional bonus, of which $500 had already been paid for good behavior. Flint actually threatened to quit baseball because of the incident, but was back with the team within a few days.

Rhem was a holdout again in 1928, but rejoined the Cardinals after they threatened to trade him. That year his record was 11-8, and the Cardinals won another pennant. In May Jesse Haines wrote in *Baseball Magazine* that "Flint Rhem has a knuckle ball that would make your hair stand on end. But catchers don't like to have him use it for neither they, nor he, nor anyone else knows just where it's going when he cuts loose with it."[10] According to *The Cardinals Encyclopedia*, manager Bill McKechnie wanted Rhem to start the third game of the 1928 World Series against the Yankees, but his mother didn't want him to pitch on a Sunday. He ended up pitching two innings in relief, anyway.

By December of 1928, Rhem had been banished to the Minneapolis Millers of the Double-A American Association. Manager McKechnie, quoted by the Associated Press in the *Milwaukee Journal* on December 16, said "Rhem did not fit into our club. ... He thought more about doing as he pleased than he did about helping out the club. Furthermore, in his infractions of club rules he took others with him. ... (T)he fact that the other major league clubs passed him along indicates that Rhem has been pretty well sized up by the managers of both leagues."[11] Rhem appeared in 23 games for the Millers that year, compiling a 5-11 record.

Later in the season he played for the Houston Buffaloes of the Class A Texas League, where he went 7-2.

On April 10, 1930, Flint married schoolteacher Lula Dillard, a graduate of Anderson College in Indiana. Gabby Street, the new manager of the Cardinals, decided to give Rhem a second chance. The St. Louis correspondent of *The Sporting News*, quoted in an unidentified newspaper called the *Sunday Record*, said, "Rhem has been a wayward boy and for this reason he was removed from major league environs last season and sent to Minneapolis. He did not stay the season, however, but moved on to the Cardinals' farm at Houston. He pitched some mighty good ball there, but got into difficulty toward the close of the season and found himself suspended. Reinstated over the Winter, he was placed on the Cardinal reserve list and Skipper Street believes he can help him. At least he wants to try and if he succeeds, the Cardinal pitching staff will have a big asset."[12] Rhem posted a 12-8 record and a 4.45 ERA with the pennant-winning Cardinals that year. St. Louis lost the World Series to the Philadelphia Athletics in six games. Rhem started Game Three and was the losing pitcher.

Undoubtedly the most amazing thing about that 1930 season for Flint was the famous "kidnapping," which has gone down in baseball history. Apparently Gabby Street was not as successful as he hoped in helping Rhem. A wire-service story, published in the *Atlanta Constitution* on September 19, 1930, tells the tale. "Rhem, who through his diamond career has never been celebrated as an ardent prohibitionist, failed to appear at the Cardinals' local headquarters [before a game in Brooklyn] on Monday night. Last night, however, he returned and faced 'Gabby' Street, the manager. 'Yes?' said Street coldly. 'Yes,' mumbled Rhem. 'Bandits. Guns. Kidnapping. They made me drink the awful stuff.'" Rhem's claim was that two thugs had kidnapped him and taken him to a remote roadhouse. They were armed, and forced him to drink a large quantity of hard liquor. "'And I am sorry to say that I got drunk. Imagine that happening to me! Of all people, me! ... I was helpless, always in fear of my life.'"[13]

Apparently even the Cardinals management didn't believe the story at the time, and Rhem later admitted to being drunk, but said that he had never left the hotel, and that Gabby Street had made up the story about the kidnapping.[14] In any case, it was a media sensation, and was forever after everyone's chief memory of Flint Rhem.

Rhem was back with the Cardinals in 1931, starting 26 of the 33 games in which he appeared. He ended the season with an 11-10 record and a 3.56 ERA. He also, however, gave up 17 home runs, the most in the NL. He went four innings in game two of a doubleheader against the Cubs on July 12 which broke all records for the number of doubles hit in a game and in a doubleheader. It seems that Sportsman's Park in St. Louis, designed to hold around 30,000 fans, was crowded with almost 46,000, of whom 8,000 were actually on the ballfield. Balls continually dropped into the overflow crowd, and were ground-rule doubles. There were 32 doubles hit in the two games, 21 of which came in the second game, which Rhem pitched. The Cardinals won that contest 17-13. Rhem fired a three-hit shutout against the Reds on September 6 to set the stage for a doubleheader sweep and push the St. Louis lead to seven games over the Giants. The Cardinals won both the pennant and the World Series. Rhem pitched just one inning in the Series.

Flint started out the 1932 season with the Cardinals. He went 4-2 before he and infielder Eddie Delker were sold to the Philadelphia Phillies in a cash deal on June 4.

Rhem's drinking remained a problem. In his history of the Phillies, David Jordan quoted shortstop Dick Bartell as saying, "If he'd ever stayed sober, what a pitcher he could have been. He was the nicest guy in the world, never mean or nasty, never bothered nobody."[15] Despite his problems, Rhem posted an 11-7 record with the Phillies and had a 15-9 record for the year with a 3.58 ERA. This was the second of two seasons in which he would have 15 wins or more. By early August, Herbert Barker of the Associated Press was reporting that the "erstwhile play-boy of the St. Louis Cardinals" was having "the year's greatest baseball comeback."[16]

The comeback wasn't to last, however. Flint was with the Phillies again in 1933, and had a record of 5-14 and an ERA of 6.62. Sometime during his tenure with the Phillies he managed to return to his South Carolina roots, striking out ten batters in six innings while pitching for Kingstree in an October game against Florence. To the delight of local fans, two other major-league pitchers, Van Lingle Mungo and Clise Dudley, also appeared in the game.

Before the 1934 season Philadelphia sold Rhem back to St. Louis. He appeared in only five games for the Cardinals, starting one and winning one. On June 23 the Cardinals sold him to the Boston Braves. On July 29 he pitched a one-hit shutout against Brooklyn. He appeared in 25 games for the Braves, 20 of which he started, but he was credited with only eight wins. Rhem's combined record for the season was 9-8, with an ERA of 3.69.

Rhem was with the Braves again in early 1935, pitching in six games and posting a record of 0-5. On June 2 he was sent to Syracuse of the International League in exchange for pitcher Bob Brown. He appeared in 21 games for the Chiefs that year, with a record of 8-6. In December 1935 the Braves sold Rhem to the Cincinnati Reds, who put him on their Nashville farm team. He appeared in 13 games for Class A-1 Nashville in 1936, posting a record of 4-3. In mid-June, the Cardinals bought him from the Reds, and he pitched in ten games for St. Louis, starting four and winning two. His ERA was 6.75.

Rhem's final appearance in the major leagues came on August 26, 1936. He was released by the Cardinals the next day. Over his 12 seasons in the major leagues, he pitched 1,725 1/3 innings, and had a record of 105-97 and an ERA of 4.20. During his four different stints in the minors over the years, he pitched 655 2/3 innings, with a record of 46-37 and an ERA of 3.91. He later said of his career, "I loved to travel…. Until I got into baseball, the biggest places I'd ever seen were Greenville and Columbia. Boy, New York floored me."[17] In March of 1936, Flint and Lula had their first and only child, Charles Flint Rhem, Jr.

Flint apparently tried to get back into baseball several times after that. In 1937 he attempted a comeback with the Lyman Pacifics of the Eastern Carolina League, and also appeared for the Kannapolis (North Carolina) Towelers. The *Calgary Herald* reported in June 1941 that he was trying to make a comeback with a South Carolina semipro team. Rhem signed up for the military draft in Georgetown, South Carolina, in 1942, but ended up pitching for the Bell bomber plant in Marietta, Georgia, during World War II.

Apparently that was Rhem's last experience with baseball. He and his family settled in Greer, South Carolina, where his wife had a long career as a teacher. Flint had inherited a large tract of land in Williamsburg County, South Carolina, which he leased for farming and hunting. He routinely went there during hunting season to visit his brothers and sisters and to hunt and fish. He died in Columbia, South Carolina, on July 30, 1969, and was buried in Wood Memorial Park in Duncan. In 1993 he was posthumously inducted into the Greater Greenville Baseball Hall of Fame. Lula Rhem died in Greer, South Carolina, in 2001.

Sources

Eisenbath, Mike, and Stan Musial, *The Cardinals Encyclopedia* (Philadelphia: Temple University Press, 1999).

Perry, Thomas K. *Textile League Baseball: South Carolina's Mill Teams, 1880-1955*. (Jefferson, North Carolina: McFarland, 2004).

Baseball-Reference.com

Retrosheet.org

Some correspondence and newspaper clippings were provided by Special Collections at East Carolina University.

Notes

1 Bob Broeg, *Memories of a Hall of Fame Sportswriter* (Champaign, Illinois: Sagamore Publishing, 1995), 47.

2 Broeg, 47.

3 *Spokesman-Review* (Spokane, Washington), May 15, 1962.

4 "Charles Flint Rhem," *The Sporting News*, August 16, 1969, 44.

5 Jack L. Hunt, "Remember When? Baseball Memories Abound." *Westminster News*, February 9, 1994.

6 Ty Cobb and Al Stump, *My Life in Baseball: The True Record* (Garden City, New York: Doubleday, 1961), 212.

7 Letter from Ty Cobb to C.F. Rhem, Clemson University, dated May 10, 1923. Courtesy of Archives and Special Collections at East Carolina University.

8 Letter from Flint Rhem to Mrs. D.D. Rhem, dated only Sunday (1924). From the collection of East Carolina University.

9 "Flint Rhem Shows Promise of a Great Major Career," *Atlanta Constitution*, May 24, 1925, B3.

10 Quoted in *The Neyer/James Guide to Pitchers: An Historical Compendium of Pitching* (New York: Simon and Schuster, 2004), 357.

11 "St. Louis Cards Send Flint Rhem to Millers," (Associated Press) *Milwaukee Journal*, December 16, 1928, 14.

12 Unidentified clipping from the collection of East Carolina University.

13 "Imagine Me, of All People, Wails Flint Rhem as He Tells of Booze Seduction," *Atlanta Constitution*, September 19, 1930, 17.

14 Neal Russo of the *St. Louis Post Dispatch*, quoted in "Rhem Kidnaped? A Hoax, he Confesses," *Baseball Digest*, October, 1960, 16.

15 David Jordan, *Occasional Glory: The History of the Philadelphia Phillies* (Jefferson, North Carolina: McFarland, 2002), 75.

16 *Evening Independent* (St. Petersburg, Florida), August 2, 1932, 5.

17 *The Sporting News*, August 16, 1969, 44.

Lew Riggs

By Bob Webster

Lew Riggs played parts of ten seasons in the major leagues, debuting with the St. Louis Cardinals in 1934 at the age of 24. Riggs appeared in only two games with the Cardinals that year and on November 3 he was sold to the Cincinnati Reds for $30,000. Cincinnati was where Riggs played his best baseball; he was named to the 1936 All-Star Game as a third baseman and played in the 1940 World Series for the Reds.

Lewis Sidney Riggs was born on April 22, 1910, in Caswell County, North Carolina, to Sidney Cainer and Annie Warren Riggs.[1] His large family (Lew was one of ten children) moved to nearby Mebane, North Carolina, when Lew was 4 years old.[2] Lew enjoyed sports and played baseball, football, and basketball in high school. He went on to the University of North Carolina, where he played baseball for two seasons (1928 and 1929) before St. Louis Cardinals scout Frank Rickey, brother of Branch Rickey, offered him a $2,000 signing bonus.[3] Riggs left Mebane with one thought in mind—to make it to the big leagues. In a newspaper interview in 1962, Riggs said, "It was pretty hard for me to make myself believe that I would ever make the big time, but without a purpose there is no sense in striving for anything. So I told myself I was good enough to make it."[4]

Riggs reported to the Shawnee (Oklahoma) Robins of the Class C Western Association in 1930 at the age of 20, and hit .356 with 52 hits in 36 games, which earned him a promotion to the St. Joseph (Missouri) Saints of the Class A Western League. He had signed as a shortstop but the Cardinals wanted him to play third base. Riggs spent the next three seasons and most of a fourth playing for the Columbus (Ohio) Red Birds of the Double-A American Association, where he was pretty consistent, hitting between .277 and .293 in his four seasons there. In 1931 and 1932 Riggs showed some power, hitting 18 and 20 home runs, respectively. In St. Joseph he roomed with Dizzy Dean for a couple of weeks before Dean was promoted to Houston of the Texas League. In 1931 Riggs set an American Association record, hitting six home runs in six days.[5]

Riggs made his major-league debut for the Gas House Gang Cardinals on April 28, 1934, in Wrigley Field against the Chicago Cubs, striking out as a pinch-hitter for Dizzy Dean. His only other appearance was as a pinch-runner. The Cardinals planned to move Pepper Martin to center field to make room for Riggs at third base. "They told me the job was mine," Riggs said 30 years later. "This put me up on cloud nine. But I trained wrong and came up with a sore arm, so they shipped me back to Columbus for another season."[6]

After being sold to Cincinnati, Riggs played in 142 games in 1935. He hit .278 with 26 doubles and 73 runs scored.

Riggs hit .257 in 141 games and made the NL All-Star team in 1936. As an eighth-inning pinch-hitter facing Cleveland's Mel Harder, he was called out on strikes and finished at third base alongside shortstop Leo Durocher in the game at Braves Field.

After playing two more full seasons, Riggs appeared in only 22 games in 1939 (Billy Werber

Riggs appeared in only two games for the Cards in 1934, but started at third base for Cincinnati from 1935-1938. He was selected to the All-Star team in 1936.

was acquired in mid-March and played the bulk of the games at third base) and batted just .158. The Reds won the pennant but Riggs did not appear in any of the four games as the team was swept by the New York Yankees. He played in 41 games in 1940, hitting .292, as the Bill McKechnie-led Reds repeated as pennant winners, this time winning the World Series in seven games over the Detroit Tigers. Riggs appeared in three games — as it happened, the three the team lost. He was 0-for-3, but scored a run in Game Three after reaching base on a forceout as a pinch-hitter.

On December 9, 1940, Riggs was traded to the Brooklyn Dodgers for infielder Pep Young. In his 1941 season for Brooklyn, now playing for manager Leo Durocher, Riggs hit .305 in 77 games and led the National League with 10 pinch hits in 29 at-bats. For the third year in a row he was with a pennant-winner. He appeared in three games of the 1941 World Series against the Yankees. Riggs was 2-for-8 with an RBI single in a pinch-hitting role as the Yankees won the Series in Five Games.

In 1942 Riggs again played in about half of Brooklyn's games. In his first nine pinch-hitting appearances, through May 12, he hit two home runs and two doubles, walked once, drove in seven runs, and had two game-winning hits. One timely pinch hit broke up a no-hitter by the Cincinnati Reds' Gene Thompson. Durocher said, "Riggs is the best pinch-hitter I have ever seen." Riggs said, "The fans and players realize mine is a tough job and that I can't be expected to come through too often. For that reason I can be relaxed, wait for a good pitch and cut at it real hard."[7] Riggs ended the season hitting .278 in 70 games.

After the season Riggs enlisted in the US Army Air Corps and served in the Pacific as player-manager of the 313th Bombardment Wing Flyers team that played in the Mariana Islands as part of the 20th Air Force Tour.[8]

Discharged in late 1945, Riggs was nearly 36 when he reported to the Dodgers' training site at Daytona Beach, Florida, in the spring of 1946.[9] After not getting the ball out of the infield while going 0-for-4 on Opening Day, he was released and spent the rest of the season with Montreal of the International League. That one game, on April 16, 1946, was his final one in the major leagues. Riggs spent the remainder of his professional baseball career (1946-1950) playing on Triple-A rosters in the Brooklyn, Cleveland, Yankees, and St. Louis Browns organizations.

At Montreal Riggs hit .303 with 15 home runs and 73 RBIs. With St. Paul in 1947 he hit .315, but after that season, his batting average dropped each year, and significantly so.

After playing 13 games for Baltimore in 1950, Riggs ended his playing days. Near the end of his career in Baltimore he was beaned by a pitch that fractured his skull.[10]

Riggs had a knack for being on first-place teams. In 1934 the Cardinals won the World Series while his Columbus team came in first place in the American Association for the second consecutive year, and they won the Little World Series both years. The Cincinnati Reds won the NL pennant in 1939 and the World Series in 1940, while the Brooklyn Dodgers captured the league flag in 1941. In 1946 the Montreal Royals finished the season in first place and won the Little World Series.

Riggs returned to Mebane for good after his playing days. He and his brother Hurley opened Riggs' Shoe Store. Ron Oakley, president of the Mebane Historical Society, delivered the *Greensboro Daily News* to Riggs's home in the early 1950s. Oakley, who was a Dodgers fan, said he visited Riggs at the shoe store and Riggs always enjoyed talking baseball, even though he was very modest when asked about his own career. Oakley said of Riggs, "Lew was always good natured, friendly, civic-minded, a businessman, a pillar of his church, and a real gentleman, the nicest man I ever met." Oakley said that on his teams' long train trips, "while the other guys played poker and drank beer, Lew would play bridge or read books. No four-letter words ever passed his lips." In addition to running Riggs' Shoe Store, Lew also worked as a clothing salesman at Malone and Crawford.[11]

Riggs said that the New York Giants' Carl Hubbell and Hal Schumacher were the toughest pitchers he ever faced. "One of the easiest pitchers for me to hit off was Dizzy. That is something I will never be able to understand," Riggs said with a grin.[12]

On May 8, 1943, Riggs married Nellie Dace Hornaday. She died on November 2, 1999. They had no children.

Riggs died of cancer at the age of 65 on August 12, 1975, at the Veterans Hospital in Durham, North Carolina, and was buried at the Rock Creek United Methodist Church Cemetery in Snow Camp, North Carolina. Riggs was a member of the Kiwanis Club and the Mebane Methodist Church. In 1996 he was honored by being inducted into the first Mebane Sports Hall of Fame class.

Notes

1. rootsweb.ancestry.com/cgi-bin/igm.cgi?op=GET&db=caswellcounty&id=I45002.
2. Email from Ron Oakley, July 31, 2013.
3. Ibid.
4. Walt Riddle, *Burlington* (North Carolina) *Daily Times-News*, April 16, 1962.
5. *Chillicothe* (Missouri) *Tribune,* September 16, 1931.
6. *Burlington* (North Carolina) *Daily Times-News,* April 16, 1962.
7. *Ottawa* (Ontario) *Journal*, May 18, 1942.
8. baseballinwartime.com/player_biographies/riggs_lew.htm.
9. baseball-almanac.com/teams/springtrainingsites-nl.shtml.
10. *Burlington* (North Carolina) *Times-News*, April 21, 2010.
11. Ibid.
12. *Burlington* (North Carolina) *Daily Times-News,* April 16, 1962.

Jack Rothrock

By Bill Nowlin

JACK ROTHROCK, A solid outfielder for the 1934 Cardinals, played every position there was for the Boston Red Sox in 1928, a year in the middle of a good long run (1925-1932) for a really bad team. The versatile outfielder played 639 games in the outer garden in his eight major-league seasons, and more than 200 games in the infield between 1925 and 1930 (78 games at shortstop, 63 at second base, 48 at third base, and 38 at first). And in 1928 he caught in one game and pitched in one.

Statistically, pitching is where Rothrock excelled —though with a tiny sample size. Motor City fans who came to the game on September 24, 1928, saw the Red Sox' Sam Gibson throw a five-hit, 8-0 shutout for the Tigers. Rothrock played the outfield (left field) then the infield (shortstop), and pitched in the bottom of the eighth inning (without letting a runner reach base). He fielded his position well, credited with assists on two of the three outs. He's in the record books, with a perfect 0.00 ERA, having retired all three batters he faced, and a 1.000 fielding percentage. His lifetime major-league batting average was a more pedestrian but still good .276.

Five days after his inning on the mound, Rothrock strapped on the "tools of ignorance" and caught the first inning on September 29 at League Park in Cleveland, playing his ninth field position of the season. Pitcher Danny MacFayden played left field in the bottom of the first (no Indians scored), and then left the game with Rothrock retreating to left field and Johnnie Heving moving in behind the plate. Slim Harriss got credit for Boston's 6-5 comeback win. Rothrock committed an error while playing in left. He had no fielding chances in his inning serving as the catcher for starter Merle Settlemire. A versatile player indeed.

Jack Houston Rothrock was born in Long Beach, California, on March 14, 1905. "A lot of the newspapers called him John, but he was christened Jack," said his son, Jack Jr. Jack Sr.'s father, Ray, was a motorman on the street railroad, a position he held for many years. Ray had come to California from Indiana, where his father had been a blacksmith. Ray was a schoolteacher at first, living with his aunt and uncle, but progressed to the possibly better-paying job of motorman. Apparently, Ray was also a competitive bicyclist at one point.[1] Clara Law Rothrock, Jack's mother, was either a Canadian or a Nebraskan depending on which United States Census one believes; Nebraska beat out Canada two to one. Her first-born was Ralph, four years older than Jack. Ralph found work as a mechanic.

Rothrock spent the majority of his career as an outfielder with the Red Sox. He led the league with 647 at-bats in 1934. His triple and subsequent run scored proved to be the difference in the Cardinals' 4-3 victory in Game Three of the World Series. He led St. Louis in RBIs with six in the Series.

Jack was a switch-hitter, the last one the Red Sox had from his April 1932 trade to the White Sox until Pumpsie Green joined the team in 1959. He threw right-handed — from the mound, from behind the plate, from all seven other positions. He was a half-inch shorter than an even 6 feet tall and is listed with a playing weight of 165 pounds. His first major-league game was on July 28, 1925. "I'd rather play ball than eat," he told writers on his first day with the Red Sox. He'd begun his career in Organized Baseball just the year before.

Jack had played for Long Beach Polytechnic High School, but he'd also played semipro ball in the area and that cost him eligibility for his senior year of baseball for high school and all of college—forcing him to turn down scholarships from four colleges. He kept busy, playing shortstop for Bellflower over the winters of 1923-24 and 1924-25, before and after his first year in Organized Baseball (1924), playing in the Class D Southwestern League for the Arkansas City (Kansas) Osages. Rothrock was 19 and played in 120 games, batting .314. He played shortstop and had three homers, 19 doubles, and six triples.

He may have played one year earlier, in 1923. According to a lengthy feature on Rothrock, he initially signed with the Hutchinson Wheat Shockers of the Southwestern League. Manager Marty Purtell was the shortstop as well, and was hurt and on the bench when Jack arrived. He played a few games at short but when Purtell got better, it was Jack riding the bench. Later in the season, he was sent to the Topeka Kaws in the same league but wasn't needed at all there. Hutchinson sold him to Arkansas City.[2]

In 1925 Rothrock reprised with Arkansas City and boosted his average to .337, upping his extra-base totals across the board. In mid-June, Boston Red Sox president Bob Quinn couldn't know what his end-of-year totals would be; in fact, when he announced that he'd signed Rothrock to report at the close of the minor-league season in September, the *Boston Globe* reported that his average wasn't known at the Red Sox headquarters, "but reports received there were to the effect that he is hitting better this year than he did last."[3] He'd been recommended to Quinn by Steve O'Rourke of St. Marys, Kansas, who had earlier recommended infielder Billy Rogell to the Red Sox. Scouts from three or four teams had their eyes on Rothrock, and one just missed. Walter McCredie of the Detroit Tigers turned up just after Jack had signed; had he been just a bit earlier, bird dog Ed Teck would have earned a $500 bonus. It had been Teck who had landed Rothrock the job with Arkansas City.[4] Bob Broeg of the *St. Louis Post-Dispatch* wrote an appreciation of Rothrock after his death, and said he'd been signed "out of a softball game in which he'd shown aggressive base running and sliding—on concrete."[5]

The Red Sox decided not to wait until September, and Rothrock joined the team in Chicago on July 21, assigned to be pitcher Red Ruffing's roommate. He played in his first game on July 25, and it was a blowout of a game in Boston, with Tris Speaker's Cleveland Indians winning, 16-7. Rothrock came into the game late at shortstop, and in his only at-bat he rolled out to pitcher Sherrod Smith, but impressed fans with how quickly he made it down the line. He'd done well in the 100-yard dash at Long Beach, and was exceptionally fast—widely considered the fastest man in baseball at the time. More than one article dubbed him Baseball's Charley Paddock—a reference to the world record holder in the 100-meter race (who held the record for more than 30 years). A newspaper clipping in his son's possession told of when Paddock and Rothrock ran against each other from left field to home plate. Paddock crossed the plate perhaps eight inches ahead. Paddock reportedly told Jack that if he'd trained as a runner instead of playing baseball, Paddock might well have lost. Grantland Rice ran a letter from a reader who told about Paddock giving Rothrock a five-yard handicap during a race in Los Angeles and the two of them running even.[6]

Rothrock had an exceptionally good first year, filling in when he could, getting into 22 games and batting .345 in 55 at-bats. His first hit, a double, came in his third game, when he pinch-hit and took over at shortstop. His first start was the next day, August 4, and he collected his first run batted in. The 1925 Red Sox were so bad that it was only in Rothrock's tenth game that he enjoyed the pleasure of seeing the team win a game that he'd played in. It was a 5-1 win over the New York Yankees at Fenway Park on September 7, some six weeks after his debut. His top batting performance that year was his last, a 3-for-5 day with a three-run triple on October 2 against the visiting Washington Senators. He was shaky in the field his first year, committing nine errors, all at shortstop, for an .893 fielding percentage.

It was around this time that Jack married his high-school sweetheart and high-school classmate, Vivian Viola Anspach. Jack Jr. was born in 1930 and daughter

DeAun came later. Some years later, Jack and Vivian divorced.

New Orleans hosted Red Sox spring training in 1926, Rothrock's first with the club. He made the team as a utilityman and stuck with Boston the first month and a half of the season, pinch-hitting and doubling in a run against the Yankees on Opening Day. In June he was placed with the Rochester (New York) Tribe of the International League, subject to 48-hour recall. He played 84 games, mostly at second base, batting .302, and was called back just in time to get into one last Red Sox game. He hoped to become a regular in 1927 and hoped to play shortstop.

A full year of work saw Rothrock as a sort of super-utility player in '27; he appeared in 117 games somewhat evenly spread among all four infield positions. For whatever reason, his average plummeted from .294 to .259, precisely the team average for the season. He scored 61 runs and drove in 36.

In 1928 Rothrock broadened his palette, playing all nine positions, three of them in the one September 24 game. To fit all the information into the AP box score as it appeared in the *Washington Post*, a radical contraction of Jack's last name was in order: R'k lf, ss, p. His average nudged up slightly (.267), in exactly the same number of games. He was again second fiddle at every position, an invaluable utility player.

For 1929, Rothrock finally became a regular. He was the team's center fielder, the better to take advantage of his speed and his strong arm, and he played in 143 games. But manager Bill Carrigan didn't hesitate to move him around as the situation dictated. An example would be a July 2 game against the Yankees. With Babe Ruth up, Rothrock replaced Elliot Bigelow in right field and made a running catch of Ruth's long fly ball. Then he was moved to center, switching positions with Ken Williams, and he pulled in Tony Lazzeri's fly after a good long run. He hit an even .300, the highest average among any of the Red Sox regulars, and stole 24 bases. Both were career highs.

Rothrock entered 1930 full of hope for the year to come, looking to build on his 1929 season. Just as it seemed that he had arrived, he broke his leg in the season's fourth game sliding into second base in the seventh inning. He didn't return until July 9, and when he did, he was almost exclusively used for pinch-hitting duties. (He didn't start another game until September 25.) He hit .277.

In 1931 Rothrock appeared in 133 games, starting most of them as the left fielder, but was also brilliant as a pinch-hitter, reaching base nearly 50 percent of the time: 9-for-20 and one base on balls. His batting average was essentially the same as in 1930, one point higher. In his years with the Red Sox, he pinch-hit safely 27 times.

The Red Sox did two deals with the White Sox on April 29, 1932. They traded catcher Charlie Berry to Chicago for outfielders Smead Jolley and Johnny Watwood and catcher Bennie Tate. In a separate deal, Rothrock was moved to the White Sox for the waiver price of $7,500. He'd been in 12 games for the Red Sox before the trade, batting .208. Oddly, he started the season with a nine-game hitting streak; only in his 10th and 12th games did he fail to collect a hit. For the White Sox, there was an adjustment period. In his first 28 games, Rothrock managed only three hits, though he didn't have as many opportunities since much of his work was in pinch-hitting. After June 11, batting .088, he was sent to Toronto, where he recovered, batting .327 in 79 games. He came back to Chicago on September 5 and hit well enough to add an even 100 points to his average.

A month after the season, on November 2, Rothrock and infielder Carey Selph were sent to St. Louis to complete a deal with the Cardinals made on September 11 when they sent outfielder Evar Swanson to the White Sox.

Rothrock spent all of 1933 in the American Association, playing for the Columbus (Ohio) Red Birds, and he had an excellent year that *The Sporting News* called a "stirring comeback" (even though the article got the year wrong). He was named to the league's All-Star team.[7] He hit .357 with 11 home runs, and then was a big factor in Columbus's defeating Minneapolis in the American Association playoffs and then Buffalo in the Little World Series.

Rothrock's play earned him a trip back to the majors with the Cardinals in 1934—and he had a terrific season. Not a great deal was expected of Jack. He was one of the contenders to take over right field from George Watkins, traded to the Giants near the end of March. The Cardinals were always pretty strong in those days, but they had finished sixth in 1932 and fifth in 1933. Second baseman Frankie Frisch had taken over as player-manager in mid-'33. Some saw the Cardinals as having an "outside chance" to grab the 1934 NL flag, but the reigning world champion Giants and the Cubs were probably better bets.

The Cardinals did have pitching, though, and three of the first five batters in the batting order were switch-hitters. After a 2-7 start, the team won 12 of 13 in early May and advanced from seventh place to within a half-game of the league lead. The last of the 12 wins was the third in a row taken from the Giants, won in the bottom of the tenth by Rothrock's bases-loaded single.

Rothrock became a big part of the St. Louis Gas House Gang as the team made it into, and won, the World Series. He generally batted second and played in every single game—the team carried only 21 players that year. "I had to play every day," he told Robert L. Burnes of the *St. Louis Globe-Democrat*. "There wasn't anybody to take my place."[8]

Rothrock posted personal bests in runs scored (106), RBIs (72), and home runs (11), and hit .284. His average was a bit below the team's .288 mark and he wasn't tops on the team during the regular season in anything other than games played, at-bats, and plate appearances, but he was a solid contributor. Forty-nine of the team's 95 wins were due to the pitching Deans. Dizzy Dean's 30-7 record on the mound and Ripper Collins' 128 RBIs were the key individual stats. Diz's younger brother Paul had started off his rookie year 10-1, and finished 19-11. In the World Series against Detroit, Jack hit only .233 but it was a very productive .233—he accounted for three of the team's four runs in Game Three's 4-1 win. Rothrock tied for the team lead in doubles and extra-base hits, and (most importantly) led in runs batted in, with six. His fielding was "steady to the point of brilliance," in the words of J. Roy Stockton of the *St. Louis Post-Dispatch*.[9] Jack played every inning of every game in the Series, too.

As the Cardinals were celebrating their lopsided 11-0 win over the Tigers in Game Seven, Miss Jackie Coogan ("a show girl") filed a lawsuit in Boston demanding that Rothrock return to her a $500 diamond ring she claimed she had entrusted to him at a party two years earlier. Rothrock's counterclaim said that the ring wasn't hers.

The 1935 season was a good one, too, though it got off to a very slow start. It was Jack's 12th year in Organized Baseball. He hit .273 with three homers and 56 RBIs, a bit of a decline. The Cardinals finished in second place, four games behind the Cubs. The team was ready to turn right field over to Pepper Martin. Rothrock had now turned 30 and after the season was over he passed through waivers—not one team claimed him—and was released to Rochester, back again in the minor leagues. It was with a bit of tongue in cheek that New York sports scribe Tom Meany wrote that Rothrock "is being overcome with the infirmities of senility."[10] Jack was studying civil engineering in the offseason and contemplated quitting the game. He relented and played for the Red Wings in 1936. Maybe he was getting old; his .299 batting average was the first time he'd come in under .300 in a minor-league season.

In August 1936, Jack changed affiliations once more. He was traded to the Cincinnati Reds for outfielder Sammy Byrd, but Byrd elected to retire to become a golf pro. That left the Reds needing to either make a fresh deal to keep Jack or return him to Rochester. They returned him, and Rochester turned around and sold him for an undisclosed sum to the Philadelphia Athletics on April 16, three days before the season began.[11]

It was Jack's last season in the majors, back where he began, in the American League. He was still only 32, but at least one article included him in a list of "aging ballplayers" looking to make a comeback.[12] Rothrock played in 88 games, hitting .267 as a utility outfielder. In his 11 seasons of major-league ball, he'd hit safely 27.6 percent of the time, driven in 327 runs, and scored 498 times. As soon as the season was over, he was purchased by Indianapolis of the American Association, but he refused to report. He wanted to play on the West Coast, and the Los Angeles Angels worked out a deal in March 1938 to buy his contract from Indianapolis.

Jack spent the next three seasons in the Pacific Coast League. The first two-plus were for the Angels in 1938 and 1939; a knee injury the first year and a lame leg the next limited his playing time a bit. It's too bad when facts get in the way of a good story. *Los Angeles Times* columnist Bob Ray wrote on September 30, 1939, that Jack had a $10 bet with teammate Lee Stine that he'd hit .300. As Ray told it, there were two outs when Jack came up to bat in the ninth inning of the final game of the season. Stine was on second base at the time—and got picked off. Game over. The trouble with the story is that Rothrock's final average was .292. That December, Stine purchased the house next door to Rothrock's Lakewood Village home.[13]

Before the end of 1939, Rothrock asked the Angels for his release so he could play for the Hollywood Stars, managed by his old Red Sox teammate Bill Sweeney. No dice, at first. He opened the 1940 season with the Angels, but was released on April 30 when the team needed to cut down to the player limit. He signed on with the Stars in mid-July, and finished the year with them.

In 1941 Rothrock turned to managing, handling the San Bernardino Stars, a New York Giants team in the Class C California League. The team disbanded on June 29. Before they did, he got in his last ten games as a player, hitting .444 in 18 at-bats, but going 0-2 when he tried his hand at pitching a couple of final times. During the war years, he performed "government engineering work in the Los Angeles Harbor area, after he was obliged to close his profitable café, which was in a vital defense zone."[14] "He owned a restaurant down on the Navy landing in Long Beach," said his son. "And he had two cabin cruisers. Dad had an offer to go in the Coast Guard because of the fact that he had these cabin cruisers and been familiar with navigation in the area, but he had to get my mother's permission to go and she wouldn't give it to him. He went into the Army Engineers and helped build some of the gun emplacements along the West Coast here. He came home almost crying one day because they put one on the 15th green of a very beautiful golf course."[15]

From 1947 through 1950, Rothrock managed again—first with the Sunset League's Anaheim Valencias, where he saw the team leading the league but was fired because the owners wanted to economize by having a playing manager. Two days later, he was hired by the Riverside Dons, who wound up finishing ahead of Anaheim by one game. (Anaheim got its revenge in the playoff finals, defeating Riverside four games to one.) He skippered the Tallahassee Pirates in the 1948 Georgia-Florida League, and then San Bernardino again in 1949. His last season as a manager—and in baseball—was in Virginia with the Big Stone Gap Rebels of the Class D Mountain States League. "Big Stone Gap is coal-mining country, and these coal miners would come out of the mines and they just went wild," said Jack Jr. "The ballpark was set up by scraping the top of a mountain and flattening it out. The clubhouses were down on the side. One of the guys struck out with the tying run on third and the winning run on second, and he went down to take a shower and heard a couple of plunks. They were up on the mountainside shooting down through the opening in the clubhouse."[16] It was time for other pursuits.

Rothrock was versatile in his choice of offseason and post-baseball occupations, too. Though originally involved in insurance, he'd been working as a necktie salesman during the offseason in Columbus before his 1934 season with the Cardinals. After the 1935 season, he joined a barnstorming tour in California. In 1937 he worked in real estate and built a house for Red Ruffing. He played winter ball, and even ran a basketball team in Long Beach for a couple of winters. In February 1940, a news clipping reported that he had "branched out from a Long Beach, Cal. restaurateur to a hotel man," taking a five-year lease on the Pickwick Hotel in Anaheim.[17]

For many years Rothrock worked with the city of San Bernardino Parks Department until retirement. Jack Jr. explained, "He was in the firefighting area. Dad was not a firefighter per se. He worked in the office. The only thing Dad did as far as athletics go was to work in Little League."

Rothrock died of a heart attack on February 2, 1980, in San Bernardino. He left behind his wife, Ardith; Jack Jr. (a 28-year Marine Corps veteran who served both in Korea and Vietnam); a daughter (DeAun Pyka); and a stepdaughter (Norma Casper).

Sources

Interview with DeAun Pyka on December 29, 2009, and with Jack Rothrock, Jr. on December 30, 2009.

In addition to the sources cited in the Notes, the author consulted the online SABR Encyclopedia, retrosheet.org, and Baseball-Reference.com.

Notes

1 *Los Angeles Times*, April 17, 1940.
2 *Christian Science Monitor*, August 22, 1935.
3 *Boston Globe*, June 23, 1925.
4 *Los Angeles Times*, July 26, 1925.
5 February 1980 clipping in Rothrock's Hall of Fame player file.
6 *Atlanta Constitution*, May 16, 1929.
7 *The Sporting News,* February 22, 1934.
8 1980 clipping in Rothrock's Hall of Fame player file.
9 *The Sporting News*, December 19, 1935.
10 *New York World-Telegram*, December 5, 1935.
11 *The Sporting News*, April 22, 1937.
12 *Los Angeles Times*, February 26, 1937.
13 *Los Angeles Times*, December 19, 1939.
14 Unattributed February 26, 1942, clipping in Rothrock's Hall of Fame player file.
15 Interview with Jack Rothrock, Jr. on December 30, 2009.
16 Jack Rothrock, Jr. interview.
17 *Los Angeles Times*, February 12, 1940.

Dazzy Vance

By Charles F. Faber

COULD A FRIENDLY poker game among minor-league teammates lead to a Hall of Fame career for a 29-year-old who had been pitching in professional baseball for nine years, never had won a major-league game, and seldom had put together two good years back to back in the minors? Perhaps. Arthur Vance had earned the nickname Dazzy for the dazzling fastball he had shown as a teenage semipro in rural Nebraska. He even had two shots at the major leagues, but nary a victory there as his total big-league record consisted of zero wins and four losses. In the minors he showed occasional flashes of brilliance, but his best performances were usually followed by a sore arm and a disappointing next season. He was with the New Orleans Pelicans in the Southern League that evening when the fateful poker game occurred.

Arthur Charles Vance,[1] who spent the second half of the 1934 season with the St. Louis Cardinals after a Hall of Fame career with the Brooklyn Robins/Dodgers, was born near the village of Orient in Adair County, in southwestern Iowa, on March 4, 1891, the fifth child of Sarah Elizabeth (Ritchey) and Albert Theophilus Vance, a farmer. While Arthur was still a small child the family moved to a farm in Pleasant Hill Township in Webster County, Nebraska, near the Kansas state line. The youngster attended Hardy High School, but made his baseball reputation by pitching for a semipro club in nearby Hastings. He married Edythe Carmony, daughter of Thomas Carmony, a railroad employee in Hastings, and his wife, Martha. The newlyweds established their home in Hastings and maintained a residence there until 1925. Their son, Bob, was born there in 1918 and a daughter came along a few years later.

The fireballing right-hander, who stood 6-feet-2 and weighed 200 pounds, broke into professional baseball in 1912 at the age of 21 with the York Prohibitionists in the Class D Nebraska State League. For a few years he advanced up the minor-league ladder. In 1914 he split the season between the Nebraska State League and St. Joseph, Missouri, of the Class A Western League, winning 26 games. But he strained his arm by pitching four games in six days. After that his arm usually gave out soon after the season began and he moved on to another team. "Something went wrong with my right arm," he said. "I no longer could throw hard, and it hurt like the dickens every time I threw."[2] In the spring of 1915 his contract was purchased by the Pittsburgh Pirates. He lost his major-league debut on April 16 and was promptly dealt to the New York Yankees, where he lost all of his three decisions. The Dazzler had failed to dazzle big-league hitters. The Yankees sent him back to St. Joseph. In 1916 he was promoted to Columbus, Ohio, of the Double-A American Association, but he developed arm trouble and bounced back and forth between A and Double-A clubs for the next several years. The Yankees gave Vance medical treatment and sent him to various minor-league clubs on option over the next several years. The Yankees gave him

Vance won 20 or more games in a season three times with Brooklyn in the 1920's. He was selected as Most Valuable Player in 1924 and pitched a no-hitter in 1925. He was elected to the Hall of Fame in 1955.

another major-league trial in 1918, but he failed miserably (with an ERA of 15.43 in two games). After two years in Memphis, Rochester, and Sacramento, the sore-armed hurler found himself in New Orleans in 1920.

It was in the Big Easy that the career-changing poker game occurred. According to Jack Kavanagh and Norman Macht,[3] Vance banged his arm on the edge of the table while raking in a pot. He immediately felt intense pain. When the arm still hurt the next morning, Vance went to a doctor, who diagnosed an underlying injury that had not been discovered by all the medicos who had examined him previously. Exactly what the doctor did is unknown. Bill James[4] speculated that the surgeon probably removed bone chips and debris from the elbow. That guess seems as good as any. At any rate, the operation was a success and the patient not only survived, but he thrived. After receiving this treatment, Dazzy was able to pitch again painlessly. The Dazzler rebounded to win 21 games for the Pelicans in 1921, his first 20-win season since 1914. He made it to the majors to stay the very next year. "It was an odd thing," Dazzy later recalled. "My arm came back just as quickly as it went sore on me in 1915. I awoke one morning and learned I could throw without pain again."[5]

One of Vance's teammates in New Orleans was a highly regarded young catcher named Hank DeBerry. The Brooklyn Robins were in need of a catcher and attempted to recruit DeBerry. Frank Graham[6] wrote about the signing of DeBerry and Vance. Charley Ebbets, president and principal owner of the Robins sent Larry Sutton, his top scout, to New Orleans to inquire about acquiring DeBerry. Sutton replied that DeBerry looked like a good prospect, and he could be had for a fair price, but there was a catch to it. The Pelicans wanted them to take a pitcher, too. When he found out that the pitcher in question was Vance, Ebbets rebelled. "Oh, no," he said. "I could have drafted him long ago if I wanted him. You go back and tell them if we have to take Vance the deal is off."

Soon Sutton called his boss back. "They say, no Vance, no DeBerry."

"In that case, "Ebbets replied, "tell them they can …" Sutton interrupted: "Wait a minute, Mr. Ebbets. I just talked to DeBerry. He wants to go to Brooklyn, naturally, but he says he don't want to go without Vance. He says to tell you that if he looks good down here, it's because Vance makes him look good. And, really, Daz is hot. He's knocked around a long time and he's learned how to pitch. And he has a fastball. A real good fastball. He's the best pitcher in the league."

According to Graham that is how Dazzy Vance at the age of 31, after ten years in the minors and 133 minor-league wins, finally made it to the majors to stay. At an age when some pitchers are beginning to slow down, the Dazzler was just getting started on the road to the Hall of Fame. Vance made an impressive showing during the Robins' spring training and won a spot in the starting rotation. He made his 1922 debut on April 13, pitching a complete game to batterymate DeBerry but losing to the New York Giants, 4-3. He achieved his first major-league victory on April 26 at Braves Field, defeating Boston's spitballer Dana Fillingim, 10-1. Daz pitched a complete game, allowing seven hits, walking five, and striking out four. He helped his own cause by collecting three hits at the plate, including a double, and driving in two runs. Vance hurled a league-leading five shutouts that year. He won 18 games in each of his first two seasons in Brooklyn and led the NL in strikeouts both years, starting a string of seven straight strikeout championships. Although Vance is remembered primarily as a fastball pitcher, he also had a devastating curve, with which he finished off many batters. Kavanagh and Macht wrote: "Dazzy's pitching style was simple. He reared back, kicked his left foot high and catapulted the ball overhand. It exploded past the batter or swerved away. Although his speed excited the fans, it was his control of the curve that delighted his manager."[7]

Dazzy had his best season in 1924. He won the mythical Triple Crown Award for pitchers by leading the league in wins (28), ERA (2.16), and strikeouts (262). At one stretch he won 15 straight games. He also led the circuit with 30 complete games en route to winning the league's Most Valuable Player Award, the only NL pitcher to cop that trophy until Carl Hubbell did it in 1933. Instead of awarding a trophy for the MVP Award, the National League presented Vance with $1,000 in gold coins. Vance set a league record for strikeouts in a nine-inning game by fanning 15 Chicago Cubs on August 23. One month later he came back against the Cubs and struck out the side on nine pitches. Vance and Burleigh Grimes became the only teammates to rank one-two in strikeouts in the NL between 1905 (Mathewson and Ames) and 1960 (Drysdale and Koufax). On July 20, 1925, Vance struck out 17 St. Louis Cardinals in a ten-inning game.

They were quite a pair—Vance and Grimes. The two were both great pitchers, but they had little else in common. Dazzy was a fun-loving flake; Burleigh was grim, dour, and dead serious on the mound and in the clubhouse. Uncharacteristically, Grimes joined Vance and two or three teammates in one after-midnight episode, not out on the town, but in a Pullman car. After a series against the Giants in Flatbush, the Robins took a midnight train for Boston and found that the Braves, who had just finished a series in Philadelphia, were on the same train. The miscreants cut eyeholes in pillowcases, pulled them over their heads, and invaded the Braves' sleeping car. Announcing that they were the Ku Klux Klan, the miscreants awakened the Boston players and dragged some of them out of bed. When they found catcher Mickey O'Neil they demanded to know what his signs were, and the terrified backstop eventually told them.

By the mid-1920s the Brooklyn club was being referred to less as the Robins and more as the Dodgers. One contingent of the team was being called the Daffiness Boys. During the first game of a doubleheader on August 15, 1926, against the Boston Braves that nickname was firmly established by the famous three men on third base misadventure. Although he was not to blame for the incident, Vance was right in the middle of the mixup. He was on second base and Chick Fewster was on first when rookie first baseman Babe Herman hit a long drive to the outfield. As the Babe rounded second, the third base coach yelled at him to go back as Fewster had not yet reached passed third. Vance had already rounded third and was heading for home, but he thought the coach was yelling at him and headed back to third. About this time Fewster reached third, and Herman ignored instructions and also chugged into the bag. To the everlasting hilarity of baseball fans, the Dodgers had three men on third base at the same time. (The third baseman tagged Fewster and Herman for two outs, but Vance was ruled safe because by arriving first he had a legitimate claim to the base.) Herman had doubled into a double play.

Babe Herman had a reputation as the daffiest of the Daffiness Boys, but Dazzy Vance was undoubtedly their leader. He even had a title—president of the "4 for 0 Club," so named for their penchant of getting no hits in four at-bats. According to Graham, Vance carried the farce to the extent of drawing up bylaws for the club, including "Raise all the hell you want but don't get caught." Pitcher Jesse Petty violated that rule. He got caught by manager Wilbert Robinson coming into the hotel after a late-night party. Robbie fined him. Worse yet, Vance expelled him from the club. When Petty asked teammates to intercede for him, they refused. Jesse took his woes to baseball writer Joe Gordon. The scribe composed a letter of apology pleading for the hurler's reinstatement. Petty copied the letter, signed it, and left it in Vance's mailbox. That night Jesse was summoned to Vance's room for a hearing.

"Did you write this letter," Dazzy asked.

"Yes."

"You are not only a big dope to be caught by Robbie, but you are deceitful as well. There are words in this letter that you can't spell and don't know the meaning of."

Petty's expulsion from the club was made permanent.[8]

While pitching, Vance wore a tattered, sweat-stained shirt. Opposing players accused him of using a razor blade to slit the right sleeve of his sweatshirt from the forearm to the wrist in narrow strips. The effect of the fastball coming out of waving strips of flannel was disconcerting to batters, to say the least. When rival hitters claimed that he had cut the shirt on purpose, Dazzy denied the charge. He said it got that way only because it was wearing out. If so, one opponent said, Vance should buy a new shirt. "Oh, no!" Dazzy responded. "This is my lucky shirt. I've had it since I was in New Orleans, and I ain't even washed it."[9]

John McGraw, feisty manager of the New York Giants, complained to John Heydler, president of the National League. The prexy could find nothing in the rulebook against tattered shirts, so Vance continued wearing the offending garment. And he continued winning. During the first game of a doubleheader on September 13, 1925, he pitched a no-hitter against the Phillies. Dazzy pitched well for the Dodgers throughout the 1920s, although he never again matched that fabulous 1924 season. In 1925 he led the league in wins, shutouts, and strikeouts. He had a down year in 1926, but still led the circuit in punchouts. In 1927 he was tops in complete games and strikeouts. His last 20-win season came in 1928, when he won the ERA title, as well as leading in shutouts and strikeouts for the seventh consecutive season. The last year in which he was a league leader was 1930, when he topped the circuit in ERA and shutouts. In 1932, the 41-year-old Vance won 12 games, the 10th time in 11 years in Flatbush that he had posted double-digit wins.)

To the chagrin of many of his Brooklyn fans, the Dodgers traded Vance to the St. Louis Cardinals before the start of the 1933 season. At the age of 42 the Dazzler was not quite so dazzling as in days of yore, and he managed to win only six games for the Redbirds. During the offseason he was claimed off waivers by the Cincinnati Reds, but was used sparingly in the Queen City, posting no victories before returning to St. Louis via the waiver route in midseason. The Gas House Gang won the 1934 pennant, giving the Dazzler his first shot at October glory. For the first time in his long and distinguished career, Vance appeared in a World Series that fall. He got into one game, pitched 1 1/3 innings, allowed two hits and no earned runs, and struck out three Detroit Tigers.

The Cardinals released Vance in the spring of 1935. The veteran was signed as a free agent by his erstwhile longtime employer, the Brooklyn Dodgers. Used exclusively in relief by the Dodgers, Dazzy posted a three-win, two-loss record in his farewell season. Fittingly, he ended his career with the team with which he had enjoyed his finest years. The right-hander made his final appearance at Ebbets Field on August 14, 1935, in the second game of a Sunday doubleheader against the Chicago Cubs, replacing knuckleballer Dutch Leonard in the lineup. After Brooklyn had taken a 3-2 lead in the bottom of the seventh, Leonard was lifted for a pinch-hitter. Vance came in to begin the top of the eighth and nearly blew the lead. He faced only two batters and put both of them on base. Gabby Hartnett led off the top of the inning with a pinch-hit single. Augie Galan was up next, and Dazzy hit him with a pitch. That was the last hurrah for Vance. Bobby Reis came in and put out the fire, saving the game for Leonard and the Dodgers. Under the peculiar scoring system in use today, Vance would have received credit for a hold. Although he put two men on base, neither of them scored, and the Dodgers held the lead; thus, a hold.

Dazzy Vance retired at the age of 44 with 197 major-league wins. Including 133 victories in the minors, he had won 330 professional games in 26 years.

In the mid-1920s Vance had moved his family to Homosassa Springs, Florida, on the Gulf Coast about 100 miles north of the Dodgers' spring training camp in Clearwater. The family loved the area, and Dazzy spent his offseasons hunting and fishing in the vicinity. Immediately upon retirement he opened a hunting and fishing camp nearby. Later he operated a Homosassa Springs hotel for sportsmen. He spent his latter years boosting tourism for the area and guiding visitors on hunting and fishing trips.

In 1955 Dazzy Vance received baseball's highest honor, election to the National Baseball Hall of Fame in Cooperstown. Vance learned of the honor in a telephone call from Walter O'Malley, president of the Dodgers, but he suspected he had been selected when a Florida highway patrolman flagged down his car and told him a photographer was waiting at his house.[10] He was very appreciative of the honor. Later he said, "It's a great thing to happen to you, but I still can't believe it's true."[11] Appropriately, his plaque depicted him wearing a Brooklyn cap. The wording on the plaque summarized his career nicely: "Arthur Charles (Dazzy) Vance. First pitcher in N.L. to lead in strikeouts for 7 straight years, 1922 to 1928. Led league with 28 victories in 1924; 22 in 1925. Won 15 straight in 1924. Pitched no-hit game against Phillies, 1925. Most Valuable Player N.L. 1924." Those words describe Dazzy the ballplayer, but no plaque can capture the essence of the man.

Dazzy Vance died of a heart attack in Homosassa Springs on February 16, 1961, just two weeks before his

70th birthday. His death was a surprise. An outdoorsman, he had remained physically active and seemingly fit to the very end. Although complaining of occasional tiredness, he had been in reasonably good health and actually had played in an old-timer's baseball game in St. Petersburg just a month before his death.

When informed of the pitcher's demise, Hall of Fame manager Casey Stengel said: "I hit against Dazzy when I was with the Giants from 1921 to 1923 and I can say he was a great one. I recall a four-game series between the Giants and the Dodgers when Vance struck out 11 men in one game and 14 in another. I'll always remember his getting out there on the mound with his shirt flapping. It used to bother the opposing hitters, but it wasn't the undershirt that made them swing and miss like they claimed, but the stuff he had on the ball." He added that Vance was "a pleasant man with a good disposition, a fellow you liked to be with and have around."[12] The Ol' Perfessor may have misremembered some of the details, but he got one thing right. Vance was a great one.

Charles Arthur Vance was survived by his wife, Edythe. He was buried in Stage Stand Cemetery, in Citrus County, just outside Homosassa Springs.

Sources

Graham, Frank, *The Brooklyn Dodgers: An Informal History* (New York: G.P. Putnam's Sons, 1945).

James, Bill, *The New Bill James Historical Baseball Abstract* (New York: Free Press, 2001).

Kavanagh, Jack, and Norman Macht, *Uncle Robbie* (Cleveland: Society for American Baseball Research, 1999).

ancestry.com

baseball-research.com

newspaperarchive.com

TheDeadballEra.com

Notes

1. There is disagreement about the order of Vance's given names. The US Censuses for both 1900 and 1910 list him as Charles A. Vance. When he registered for the World War I draft in 1917 he gave his name as Arthur Charles Vance. It is listed that way in the 1920 census and in the Florida death index. Modern references are almost evenly divided between Charles Arthur and Arthur Charles. At least two sources inexplicably identify him as Clarence Arthur Vance. The most likely explanation seems to be that he was named Charles Arthur, but as a teenager preferred the name Arthur, so changed the order of the names.

2. Fred Lieb, "Dazzy Vance, Hall of Fame Pitching Star, Dies at 69," in thedeadballera.com.

3. Kavanagh and Macht, 132.

4. James, 869.

5. Lieb.

6. Graham, 87.

7. Graham, 102-03.

8. Graham, 98.

9. Kavanagh and Macht, 133

10. Associated Press account printed in many newspapers; including *The Bee* (Danville, Virginia), January 27, 1955. Retrieved from newspaperarchive.com.

11. *Sheboygan Press,* February 18, 1961.

12. Ibid.

Bill Walker

By Gregory H. Wolf

LEFT-HANDER BILL WALKER overcame two life-threatening heart attacks by the age of 15 to become a big-league pitcher. He debuted with the New York Giants in 1927 after a mentally taxing seven-year journey in the minor leagues. With two National League ERA titles in three years (1929 and 1931), it appeared that Walker was headed for stardom, but arm miseries led to his trade to the St. Louis Cardinals after the 1932 season. Often overlooked by history and overshadowed by the more gregarious members of the Gas House Gang, Walker with a 12-4 record in 1934, including eight wins in the last seven weeks of the season, helped propel the Redbirds to the World Series.

William Henry Walker was born on October 7, 1903, in East St. Louis, Illinois, the last of six children of John Henry and Ann (Anderson) Walker. John and Ann were born in England, as were their first three children, Frank, Nellie, and George. The family immigrated to the United States in the early 1880s and settled in East St. Louis, where John's brothers were pawnbrokers. The family welcomed three more children, Maude, Mary, and finally Bill, in their new homeland. John left his brothers' business and held several jobs before finding steady and permanent employment as a night watchman. Bill was a frail, weak boy, and at the age of 7 suffered what physicians at the time considered a heart attack. His physicians at St. Louis Children's Hospital diagnosed a valvular deficiency (commonly called a leaking heart) and suggested that Bill refrain from physical activity the rest of his life. Bill's parents were understandably shocked. Ann, whose father, George Anderson, was a well-known cricket player in England in the 1850s and 1860s, doted on her young child. "I was interested in athletics," said Bill, "but because of my weak heart, sat on the sidelines, and watched other boys (playing)."[1] While attending Emerson and then Hawthorne grammar school in East St. Louis, Bill took a chance and started playing ball. "I regarded the pitcher as the big shot in any ballgame," he said. "I wanted to be a big shot instead of a sickly kid."[2] After playing a few years with no ill effects, Bill thought his problems were behind him. An articulate youngster with flair, he quit school at the age of 14 and began working as a messenger for the Morris Packing Company. But tragedy struck again, when Bill had another heart attack at the age of 15. Physicians feared for his life.

Unexpectedly, Bill recovered and resumed his job. To his parents' astonishment, he returned to the local sandlots and began pitching. After working for Armour Meats and playing for the company team in 1919, Bill learned a trade at a local steel plant and pitched in the semiprofessional St. Louis Trolley League in 1921. He caught the attention of area resident Benny Meyer, a former big-league player, who invited him to try out at Sportsman's Park for a minor-league team he was putting together to compete in the newly created Class D Southwestern League. Walker made the team and

Walker posted a 12-4 record and a 3.12 ERA in 1934. In 1929 and 1931, he led the league in ERA.

reported to Miami, Oklahoma, to play for the Indians. Just 17 years old when the season began, Walker notched 11 wins, lost 16, and logged 202 innings.

Walker showed potential in his first year of professional baseball, but it took him another six years, filled with frustration, an overwhelming sense of failure, and a desire to quit, before he finally made it to the big leagues. Walker was farmed out to the Duncan (Oklahoma) Oilers in the Class D Oklahoma State League and to the Independence (Kansas) Producers in the Southwestern League in 1922, but struggled. "I was a failure," Walker said. "And while my weak heart long since had apparently mended, I felt discouraged. So I packed up and went home."[3] Walker moved back to his parents' house and pitched once again for the East St. Louis team in the Trolley League.

"My 'stuff' came back," said Walker about pitching in the Trolley League in the summer 1922.[4] Benny Meyer invited him to Salina, Kansas, for another tryout, this time with the Millers, a team Meyer personally skippered in the Southwestern League, which had been elevated to Class C after its inaugural season. More mature physically and emotionally, Walker led the team in wins (15) and innings (251); his team-high 18 losses placed him in a three-way tie for the most in the league.

Walker began the 1924 season back with Salina but was sold to the Kansas City Blues in the Double-A American Association in June. The jump from Class C to the American Association, just one step below the major leagues, was overwhelming for Walker. Against seasoned professionals, most of whom had had or later did have major-league experience, Walker struggled, lost all four decisions, and logged just 42 innings. Plagued by wildness with Miami and Salina (averaging almost six walks per nine innings), he fared even worse with the Blues, issuing 6.6 walks and surrendering 11.6 hits per nine innings. The team consequently sold him to the Springfield (Illinois) Senators in the Illinois-Indiana-Iowa League. Splitting the season with Springfield and the Evansville (Indiana) Pocketeers, Walker rebounded in the Class B Three-I League in 1925. He notched nine wins, and importantly issued fewer walks per nine innings, though his 115 bases on balls and his 16 losses tied for third most in the league.

Just 22 years old, but starting his sixth season in professional baseball in 1926, Walker began doubting his future as a big leaguer. Kansas City optioned him to the Omaha Buffaloes in the Class A Western League to start the season. "I was a failure there," said Walker.[5] Suffering from a spinal-column injury and possessing a miserable 2-4 record,[6] he reached the breaking point: "I finally said to myself, 'Bill, you're through. You'll never be a pitcher.' "[7] When he approached manager Barney Burch of the Buffaloes about his desire to quit, he was surprised to learn that he had been released, and subsequently purchased by the Denver Bears in the same league.[8] Reporting to manager Joe Berger in July, Walker resurrected his season and his career and finished with 14 combined wins for the Buffaloes and Bears.

Walker enjoyed a breakout year on a mediocre, 77-75 Bears team in 1927. With a team-high 19 wins (tied for fourth-most in the league), he was the league's most unhittable pitcher, surrendering just 8.2 hits per nine innings. "[Walker] attracted attention of many major league scouts," reported the *New York Times* in mid-season.[9] The Pirates and Yankees seemed like probable destinations for Walker, but Charles Stoneham, owner of the New York Giants, dispatched scout Dick Kinsella to Denver authorized to sign the "strike-out artist" at all costs.[10] Kinsella, who had previously inked Giants standouts Frankie Frisch and Freddie Fitzsimmons to contracts, signed Walker for a reported $25,000.

Reporting to New York in September 1927, Walker joined the Giants in a tight four-team pennant race with the Pirates, Cubs, and Cardinals. He debuted in the first game of a doubleheader on September 13 against St. Louis at Sportsman's Park, the site of his first professional tryout. In relief of starter Larry Benton, Walker pitched the last two frames in a 5-2 loss, surrendering two hits and a run while striking out three. He made two more appearances for new Giants manager Rogers Hornsby, who had replaced John McGraw for the final 32 games of the season.

Walker reported to his first big-league spring training, in Augusta, Georgia, as one of the game's most heralded rookies. "He's the best left-hand pitcher who has entered baseball for three or four seasons," reported George Chadwick.[11] Less than two years removed from wanting to quit baseball, Walker seemed to possess everything needed for stardom. His delivery was described as "graceful and smooth," his curveball was considered "as elusive as an oil bond in a senate investigation," and his pickoff move to first base was deceptive.[12] In camp he battled late-season call-ups Ben Cantwell, Jim "Lefty" Faulkner, and Art Johnson, as well as Dutch Henry for a starting job. McGraw, who returned to pilot the Giants in 1928, named Walker to start the fourth game of the season. He struggled with control (six walks in 7 1/3 innings) in a loss to the Phillies and was relegated to the bullpen. The highlight of Walker's season was his first big-league victory, a six-hit complete game against the Phillies on June 25 at Baker Bowl. With eight starts among his 22 appearances, Walker's inconsistencies and penchant for surrendering the long ball (nine home runs in just 76 1/3 innings) ultimately led to his option in midseason to the Toledo Mud Hens of the American Association to work on his control. He returned to the parent club, won three of nine decisions and posted a 4.72 ERA for the season, but did not pitch after August 16. George Kirksey of the United Press reported that Walker was "handicapped by illness" at the end of the 1928 season. Throughout his life, Walker claimed that after his second heart attack at 15, he never again experienced heart problems, suggesting that the "illness" was some other physical ailment.[13]

The Giants convened spring training in San Antonio in 1929 with arguably the best pitching staff in the National League. Larry Benton and Freddie Fitzsimmons, coming off 20-win seasons in 1928, were joined by left-handers Carl Hubbell (a midseason callup who notched ten wins in the last two months of 1928) and Walker. "McGraw's two young southpaws … are on the verge of stardom," wrote George Kirksey of the United Press."[14] Hubbell and Walker were roommates, became good friends, and constantly talked pitching. While the 25-year-old Hubbell seemed polished and had excellent control (thanks to his screwball), Walker had not yet harnessed his fastball and his curve was inconsistent. For the first four months of the season as starter and reliever, he failed to impress with a 5-7 record and 3.97 ERA.

Lost deep in the bullpen, Walker took the mound on August 6 at Pittsburgh for the first time in ten days and tossed a complete-game victory over the Pirates. But a shoulder injury in his next start, nine days later, sidelined him for two additional weeks, and it appeared as if his season might be over. He returned on August 29 and proceeded to have the best five-week stretch in his big-league career. He pitched eight consecutive complete-game victories and posted an impressive 2.13 ERA. On September 15 he hurled his first major-league shutout, a six-hitter against the Cardinals at St. Louis. While the *New York Times* raved about Walker's "baffling curves,"[15] the lefty's success resulted from a new-found control as he issued only 13 walks during his 72-innng streak. Walker credited submariner Carl Mays, whom the Giants acquired prior to the 1929 season, for his seemingly sudden transformation. "[Mays] told me to keep my mind on pitching to a certain spot and not to put everything I had on every pitch," Walker said. "His advice helped a lot."[16] Walker finished the season with 14 wins and logged 177 2/3 innings. His 3.09 ERA led the NL. Through the 2013 season, it still ranked as the highest league-leading mark in the National League; only Early Wynn of the Indians in 1950 led the American League with a higher ERA (3.20).

Once described by Washington Senators owner Clark Griffith as a "natural," Walker tossed a complete-game victory over the Boston Braves on Opening Day in 1930.[17] With his second complete-game victory of the season on April 21 (over the Phillies), Walker extended his career-longest winning streak to 11 games, including complete-game victories in his previous ten starts. Not renowned for his hitting (a career .127 batting average in 489 at-bats), Walker whacked his only big-league grand slam among his career-high three hits in a complete-game victory on May 5 against the Pirates at Forbes Field. A streaky pitcher, Walker finished June with a stellar 10-3 record and it appeared as if he would notch 20 wins for the first time. However, he slumped in July, losing five of six starts. On August 2 at Ebbets Field he tossed a ten-inning complete game to defeat the league-leading Robins and pull the Giants to within four games of the Robins. While the Robins faded in August and September, the Giants plodded along, winning 32 of 55, but were no match for the streaking Cardinals, who won 44 of 57 in the last two months of the season. Clearly suffering from the effects of overwork in September, Walker started eight times in 28 days, but completed just two starts (including a masterful two-hit shutout over Cincinnati at the Polo Grounds) on September 19. For the third-place Giants, Walker led the team with a career-high 34 starts and 245 1/3 innings. His 17 victories tied with Hubbell for second-most on the club behind Fitzsimmons' 19. Contextualized within the batting exploits in a "Year of the Hitter," Walker's season is more impressive. His 3.93 ERA was third-best in the NL; he held batters to a .268 average, well under the league average of .303; and he ranked sixth in the NL by allowing less than 9.5 hits per nine innings.

An infected left hand delayed Walker's arrival at the Giants' 1931 spring training in San Antonio and bothered him throughout camp. After tossing three innings of scoreless relief on Opening Day, he hurled a five-hit complete-game victory four days later over the Phillies at the Baker Bowl in his first start of the season. With just two starts through April, Walker got on track in May, shutting out the Braves twice in four starts. Walker was arguably the most effective pitcher in baseball beginning with his four-hit shutout over the Reds at the Polo Grounds on June 26 and extending through the end of the season. He completed 14 of 18 starts, winning 11 of them, saved three games, posted a 1.79 ERA over 165 2/3 innings, and limited batters to a .216 average. Though the Giants led the NL in home runs, ranked second in batting, led the league in ERA, and tied for the lead in fielding, they were no match for the rough-and-tumble Cardinals, who streaked away with the pennant. Walker finished with 16 wins (second-most on the club behind Fitzsimmons' 18), completed a career-high 19 of 28 starts, and led the league for the second time with a 2.26 ERA. He also led the league with a career-best six shutouts. In a year without a 20-game winner for the first time in the history of the National League, *The Sporting News* noted that Walker was an "incredibly hard luck" pitcher for having lost seven times when the Giants scored three runs or less.[18]

Described as "soft-spoken" and "well-mannered," Walker shied away from the media attention his success with the Giants brought him.[19] With his sandy blond hair, light-colored eyes, light complexion, and chiseled facial features, Walker was considered one of the most eligible bachelors in baseball. "[He] looks like a movie actor," wrote *The Sporting News*.[20] Sportswriters enjoyed playing on Walker's English background and detectable English accent, and referred to him as the "Prince of Wales."[21] Despite the hard times of the Depression, Walker was known for his "thirty suits of tailor-made clothes" which gave rise to the moniker the "Beau Brummel" of baseball, a description lost on contemporary readers but a well-known reference in Walker's time to a 19th-century fashion icon in England.[22]

In 1932 the Giants suffered through their worst season since 1915 and fell to sixth place. The ailing McGraw was replaced in early June by the hitting sensation Bill Terry after 40 games, but the offense and pitching continued to slump. After surrendering just six home runs in 239 1/3 innings in 1931, Walker was pounded for a league-high 23 round-trippers in just 163 innings. With 22 starts among his 31 appearances, Walker managed just eight wins in 20 decisions and his ERA almost doubled, to 4.14. "I nursed a sore arm all season," he said. "I didn't feel like myself until the end of the season."[23] A week after the season the Giants sent him, outfielder Ethan Allen, pitcher Jim Mooney, and catcher Bob O'Farrell to the Cardinals for catcher Gus Mancuso and pitcher Ray Starr. "The first thing I knew about the trade was when I read it in the newspapers," Walker said. "I wasn't really surprised because I had a bum year."[24]

Even before Walker arrived at the Cardinals' spring training, *The Sporting News* reported rumors that he would soon be traded to the Cubs, doubting that the St. Louis would carry three left-handers (Bill Hallahan, Mooney, and Walker). Walker's stock had dropped so precipitously that Mooney (6-10 with a 5.05 ERA in 1932) seemed more desirable. The United Press reported that Walker "lacks clutch" and can't win the big game.[25] However, *The Sporting News* cautioned, "[Walker] is not built for heavy criticism or riding. Let him alone and he will come through. Worry him and he will worry with you and get worse."²⁶ The Cardinals ultimately kept all three lefties for the 1933 season.

Walker's return to his hometown area was anything but a homecoming. After he lost his first two starts, Walker's success in May (he won all four decisions, including three complete games and a ten-inning shutout against the Braves) proved illusory. Competing for the fourth starter's position with grizzled veterans Jesse Haines and Dazzy Vance, Walker battled inconsistency all season. "A big disappointment," reported *The Sporting News*. "Had [Walker] come through as reported, there probably would be a different story to tell about the Cardinals."²⁷ For the fifth-place Redbirds, Walker started just 20 times, made nine appearances in relief, and logged 158 innings while posting his second consecutive losing record at 9-10.

The Gas House Gang and Walker seemed to be an odd match. While player-manager Frankie Frisch and his players like Pepper Martin, Leo Durocher, and Dizzy Dean were hard-nosed scramblers full of braggadocio, Walker was a laid-back, shy player who still lived at home with his folks in East St. Louis. Slated as the team's fourth starter for 1934, Walker notched two complete-game victories to inaugurate the season before suffering a freak injury on May 6 during batting practice. Joe Medwick smashed a line drive that hit Walker on the left arm near his wrist. The result was a fractured bone, sidelining him for seven weeks. He returned to the starting rotation after the All-Star Game, but struggled, winning two of five decisions and posting an ERA of close to 5.00 for the month.

The Cardinals concluded a dramatic campaign in 1934 by going 40-18 in the last two months to win the pennant on the last weekend of the season. History rightly focuses on the amazing accomplishments of Dizzy Dean during those exciting two months; however, Walker's dependability deserves more attention. Beginning on August 11, when he tossed a complete game to defeat the Cubs at Sportsman's Park, Walker began one of his hot streaks at the most important time of his career. He completed seven of 11 starts, won eight of nine decisions, and posted a 2.62 ERA. (For the purpose of comparison, Dizzy Dean won nine of 12 with a 1.55 ERA and Paul Dean won seven of 13 with a 2.16 ERA during that same span.)

Despite Walker's impressive 12-4 record and 3.12 ERA in 153 innings, Frisch opted for a starting rotation of Dizzy Dean, Bill Hallahan, Paul Dean, and Tex Carleton in the World Series against the slugging Detroit Tigers. With Game Two tied 2-2 and one out in the ninth inning, Walker relieved Hallahan and pitched three hitless innings before encountering trouble in the 12th. After issuing one-out walks to Charlie Gehringer and Hank Greenberg, Walker surrendered a walk-off single to Goose Goslin to lose the game, 3-2. Taking the mound to start the fifth inning in Game Four, tied, 4-4, Walker experienced the hitherto most ineffective game in his tenure with the Redbirds. He surrendered five hits and six runs (four earned) and walked three in 3 1/3 innings. Charged with losses in two of the first four games, Walker did not pitch again in the Series. The Cardinals surged back to win Games Six and Seven, capture one of the most exciting World Series, and etch their names in sports history.

Walker teamed with the Dean brothers and Hallahan to form a formidable starting rotation in 1935. A strong push in August catapulted the team into first place to begin the last month of the season; however, the Redbirds were no match for the streaking Cubs, who went 23-3 in September, including 21 consecutive wins, to capture the pennant. A study in inconsistency, Walker posted a 2.12 ERA in his 13 wins but a 4.14 ERA in his eight losses, which led to his demotion to the bullpen in September with the Cardinals attempting to hold off the Cubs.

Walker made the trip to Cleveland for the third annual All-Star Game under curious circumstances. "I had the dubious honor to be the batting practice pitcher," he said.²⁸ Cardinals manager Frisch piloted the NL squad and named Walker to the pitching staff. "Lefty Grove was going to be one of the pitchers for the AL team and my delivery was similar to his. So that was my reason for being there," he said.²⁹ Unexpectedly, Walker started the game and surrendered two hits and three runs, including a home run to Jimmie Foxx, and was collared with the loss. As it turned out,

Lefty Grove did not pitch, but another Lefty did. Lefty Gomez limited the NL to three hits over six innings to win the game.

Walker's promising start to the last season in his ten-year big-league career (three complete-game victories in his first three starts) gave way to a pattern of inconsistency, wildness, and hittable pitches in 1936. After he surrendered ten hits and four runs in just 4 2/3 innings in his first start after the All-Star Game, Walker's career in St. Louis was at a crossroads. He made three relief appearances before being sent in August to the Toronto Maple Leafs in a waiver transaction for pitcher Si Johnson. Walker notched four wins in the Double-A International League, was waived, and then re-signed with the Cardinals in September. His major-league career came to an unceremonious end with two disastrous starts in which he yielded six hits and seven runs in six innings. In the offseason, he was released to the Rochester Red Wings, the Cardinals' affiliate in the International League.

Initially reluctant to play in the minors after ten years in the big leagues, Walker agreed to terms with Rochester in March 1937. Though he won 12 games, it was apparent that his days in the major leagues were behind him. The following season he played with the Sacramento Solons and experienced a rejuvenation of sorts in the warm climate and long season of the Double-A Pacific Coast League. As the grizzled veteran on the staff, Walker won 17 games while logging 226 innings for skipper Bill Killefer, former manager of the Cubs and Browns. Walker remained in the PCL for his final two years in professional baseball and posted records of 16-18 and 12-14 for the unaffiliated Seattle Rainiers while pitching more than 200 innings each year. In his final season, Walker claimed he had finally mastered the screwball which he supposedly learned from his former teammate and screwball aficionado, Carl Hubbell.[30]

At the age of 36, Walker retired after a 20-year professional baseball career. The two-time National League ERA leader won 97 games and posted a 3.59 ERA (114 ERA+) in 1,489 2/3 innings. He won 132 games and pitched more than 2,100 innings in his 13-year minor-league career.

A resident of East St. Louis and St. Clair County, Illinois, his entire life, Walker married Bernadine Parish in 1941. They had two children, Ann and Bill. A lifelong baseball fan, Walker regularly attended games at Sportsman's Park and participated in occasional reunion games for the Gas House Gang. He supported local American Legion baseball and coached during the years his son played. Walker enjoyed a distinguished and varied career as an elected and appointed public servant in East St. Louis in his post-playing days. Even before retiring, he was elected trustee of the East Side Levee and Sanitation District in 1939, and subsequently was elected treasurer of St. Clair County, and later Probate Court clerk in Belleville.[31] A reservist in the US Navy during World War II, Walker served in the Illinois state auditor's office and was also appointed chief deputy sheriff in East St. Louis.[32]

William Henry Walker died of cancer at Christian Welfare Hospital in East St. Louis on June 14, 1966, at the age of 62. Praised for his "indomitable spirit" for overcoming his childhood health problems, Walker was buried in the Valhalla Garden of Memory in Belleville, Illinois.[33]

Sources

Ancestry.com

BaseballLibrary.com

Baseball-Reference.com

New York Times

Retrosheet.com

The Sporting News

Notes

1. *The Sporting News*, November 17, 1932, 5.
2. Ibid.
3. Ibid.
4. Ibid.
5. Ibid.
6. "Walker, Whom Burch Released, Sold for $25,000 to Giants," *Sunday World-Herald* (Omaha), July 17, 1927, 1.
7. *The Sporting News*, November 17, 1932, 5.
8. Walker, Whom Burch Released."
9. "Giants Buy Pitcher," *New York Times*, July 17, 1927, 53.

10 George Kirksey, "Giant Problem As Training Starts is Loss of Hornsby" (United Press), *Denton* (Texas) *Record Chronicle,* February, 17, 1928, 3.

11 George Chadwick, "Majors' Rookie Crop Unusually Good This Year," *Miami News*, April 1, 1928, 15.

12 Ibid.

13 George Kirksey, "New York Giants Look Dangerous" (United Press), *Oelwein* (Iowa) *Daily Register,* February, 9, 1929, 4.

14 George Kirksey, "Yanks, Browns, Cubs, Giants Look Strong in Majors" (United Press), *Salt Lake Tribune*, March 25, 1929, 13.

15 Roscoe McGowen, "Walker of Giants Checks Robins, 6-2," *New York Times*, August 30, 1929, 25.

16 *The Sporting News*, June 25, 1966, 50.

17 George Chadwick, "Majors' Rookie Crop."

18 *The Sporting News*, April 7, 1932, 1.

19 *The Sporting News*, November 17, 1932, 3.

20 *The Sporting News*, February 2, 1933, 4.

21 *The Sporting News*, November 17, 1932, 3.

22 Ibid.

23 *The Sporting News*, October 20, 1932, 5.

24 Ibid.

25 Henry McLemore, "Yankees Like Earnshaw But Not $50,000 Worth" (United Press), *El Paso Herald-News*, October 13, 1932, 13.

26 *The Sporting News*, November 17, 1932, 3.

27 *The Sporting News*, August 17, 1933, 3.

28 *The Sporting News*, July 9, 1958, 10.

29 Ibid.

30 *The Sporting News*, June 20, 1940, 3.

31 *The Sporting News*, December 6, 1961, 15.

32 *The Sporting News*, February 11, 1953, 30.

33 *The Sporting News*, November 17, 1932, 5.

Burgess Whitehead

By C. Paul Rogers, III

BURGESS URQUHART WHITEHEAD was a solid contributor to the success of the Gas House Gang in 1934, appearing in 100 games while spelling Leo Durocher at shortstop, Pepper Martin at third base, and Frankie Frisch at second. In his first full year in the big leagues, Whitehead had 332 official at-bats and hit a solid .277. He was relegated to the bench, however, in the epic seven-game World Series against the Detroit Tigers, appearing in only a single game as a late-inning pinch-runner and replacement at shortstop.

Whitehead was born on June 29, 1910, in Tarboro, North Carolina. His father was a dentist and tobacco farmer and shortly moved the family to Lewiston, North Carolina. Burgess, who was called Whitey, first attended Lewiston High School and then the Augusta Military Academy in Virginia, where he graduated in 1927 with the highest academic record of anyone who had attended the school in 75 years. He also batted .484 and .523 in his two years on the baseball team.[1]

He was a hot prospect but wanted a college education and enrolled at the University of North Carolina. After a season starring on the freshman team, he spent three weeks in the summer of 1928 working out with the New York Giants under the watchful eye of John McGraw and then two weeks with the Detroit Tigers. Both teams offered him contracts, but Whitehead opted to return to the University of North Carolina, where he became the varsity shortstop, playing alongside future big leaguer Lew Riggs.[2]

While at North Carolina Whitehead played semipro ball in Emporia, Virginia, for $35 a week and during the school year sold football tickets and worked in a dormitory laundry to earn spending money.[3] Along the way, he continued to excel in the classroom, earning Phi Beta Kappa honors.

Burgess was named team captain before his senior year but was ruled ineligible when it was learned that he had signed a professional contract with the St. Louis Cardinals. He was assigned by the Cardinals to the Columbus (Ohio) Red Birds in the Double-A American Association. (At the time Double-A was the highest rung in the minor leagues.)[4] Whitehead got off to a rough start in Columbus, however, and manager Nemo Leibold told him the club was going to release him. Whitehead then went to club president Larry MacPhail to receive his paperwork and travel money. MacPhail, however, noticed Burgess's Phi Beta Kappa key hanging from his vest chain and decided a ballplayer with that kind of smarts deserved a longer look. So MacPhail explained to Leibold the significance of the key and further suggested that Whitehead might be more suited to second base than shortstop.[5]

A utility infielder for St. Louis in 1934, Whitehead moved on to New York and became the Giants' starting second baseman for several years. He was named to the N.L. All-Star team in 1935 and 1937.

It turned out to be a great move. Whitehead proceeded to hit .328 in 135 games for the fourth-place Red Birds. During a doubleheader against the

Louisville Colonels he knocked out eight hits in nine at-bats[6] and was later named to the American Association All-Star team.

The Cardinals had future Hall of Famer Frankie Frisch ensconced at second base so Whitehead was back with Columbus in 1932. Playing in 162 games with 675 official at-bats, he totaled 211 hits and batted .313 for the Red Birds, who rose to second place. The Cardinals invited Burgess to spring training in 1933 and he stuck with the club, beginning the season as a utility infielder, but after seeing sparse playing time was shipped back to Columbus.

There he became an integral part of one of the best minor-league teams of all time. The Red Birds swept to the American Association pennant by 15 1/2 games, finishing with a 101-51 won-loss record.[7] Whitehead played in 89 games and hit a resounding .346 to lead the team, before a late-season call back to the Cardinals.[8] In limited action as a late-inning defensive replacement for the fifth-place Cardinals, Burgess appeared in 12 games with two hits in seven at-bats.

He made the team for good, however, in 1934, although still only 23 years old. Whitehead, who had befriended Paul Dean at Columbus, quickly became pals with Dizzy Dean and often stayed out late with the Diz. When Whitehead would express concern about missing manager Frankie Frisch's curfew, Dizzy Dean would say, "Look, if they ship you out, I'll go, too."[9]

Frisch was enamored with Whitehead's fielding prowess and made sure he got plenty of playing time. For the year, Whitehead appeared in 100 games, 48 at second base, 29 at shortstop, and 28 at third, with one pinch-hit at-bat. (In a half-dozen games he played more than one position.) Although he played in only one game of the World Series, he was able to put his World Series money to good use, helping his parents save their tobacco farm back in North Carolina.[10]

Whitehead was unable to crack the Cardinals' starting infield again in 1935, and spent another season as a semi-regular. In 107 games and 338 official at-bats, he hit .263. He frequently spelled the 36-year-old Frisch, appearing in 80 games at second base. Whitehead was named to the National League All-Star team and appeared as a pinch-runner during the contest in Cleveland.

The way was paved for Whitehead to become a starter after the 1935 regular season, only it would not be for the Cardinals. On December 9 St. Louis shipped him to the New York Giants for starting pitcher Roy Parmelee, as outfielder Phil Weintraub, relief pitcher Allyn Stout, and infielder Al Cuccinello.[11] The Giants, who in 1935 had finished in third place, 8 1/3 games behind the pennant-winning Cubs, had long been in need of a second baseman, but many thought they had given up too much for Whitehead, who had never played regularly and who many considered too frail to play every day.[12] (He is listed at 5-10 1/2 and 160 pounds.) Dizzy Dean, however, knew what the Cardinals had lost, telling a reporter that the Giants had picked up "the best second baseman in the business, or the next best, anyhow, outside of Billy Herman."[13]

Whitehead raised some eyebrows when he showed up to the Giants' spring training with a tennis racket.[14] But the trade turned out to be a stroke of genius by Giants manager Bill Terry. With Whitehead's addition the only significant lineup change, the 1936 Giants won the pennant by five games over the Cubs and Cardinals.[15] Burgess played all 154 games, teaming with shortstop Dick Bartell to form a stellar keystone combination. He batted a solid .278 in 632 at-bats and led the team with 14 stolen bases to prove his doubters wrong.

In the first game of the World Series against the powerful Yankees, Whitehead made a memorable play to preserve a 2-1 eighth-inning lead for Carl Hubbell. With runners at first and third, he raced to his left to spear a low line drive off the bat of Joe DiMaggio, then wheeled and threw to Bill Terry at first to double off Red Rolfe.[16] Whitehead struggled mightily at bat in the World Series, however, going 1-for-21 as the Giants eventually lost to the across-the-Harlem River Yankees in six games.

On July 11, 1936, the Giants played a memorable game against the Cardinals in Sportsman's Park in St. Louis. Dizzy Dean was on the mound and was known to groove one occasionally to his pals on other teams. Whether he did or not to Whitehead in the sixth inning is a matter of speculation, but in any event Whitehead smashed a line drive off Dean's forehead, knocking him unconscious for about seven minutes.[17] The ball bounded into the left-field corner for a double; Whitehead, however, was distraught over the incident.[18]

Whitehead later denied that Dean ever took it easy on him, saying that those Giants-Cardinals games were too important. In a 1975 interview he said, "I can remember more than once passing Diz on the field at the Polo Grounds after I'd been traded and he would say, 'Sorry, Whitey, Ol' Diz is pitching. So be ready to go down.' And down I'd go."[19]

Whitehead had an even better year in 1937 as the Giants won their second consecutive pennant, this time by three games over the Cubs. He again played in every game at second base, and increased his batting average to .286. His fielding was spectacular as he led all second basemen in putouts (394), double plays (106), and fielding percentage (.974), while finishing second in assists (514) and total chances per game (6.1). He made the National League All-Star team for the second time, although he again appeared in the game only as a pinch-runner. The Giants lost again to the Yankees in the 1937 World Series, this time in five games. This time around Burgess hit a more respectable .250, with four hits in 16 at-bats.

On May 19 that season, the Giants had another dust-up with Dean and the Cardinals. Dizzy, trailing 3-1, was being subjected to ugly bench-jockeying from the Giants dugout and had been called for a balk when he decided to take matters into his own hands. He proceeded to low-bridge every player in the Giants lineup except his buddy Whitehead and his respected opposite, Carl Hubbell.[20]

Whitehead's slick fielding led Ethan Allen to nickname him "The Gazelle."[21] He also reputedly had the largest hands in baseball and although soft-spoken and "courteous to a fault," would "jump for joy when he made a good play."[22] He also had a reputation, at least in the press, as being something of a Renaissance man. One sportswriter wrote that "[he] could probably answer every question you asked on philosophy, psychology, and astronomy and then tie you in knots with a few of his own. If you seated him at a banquet table he probably would not make one mistake if they put seven different forks in front of him."[23] Still, Whitehead, although a brilliant student and obviously exceedingly bright, was apparently a man without airs, as attested by his close friendship with fourth-grade dropout Dizzy Dean.

Although Whitehead seemed to be riding on top of the world after two pennant-winning seasons with the Giants, his world was about to come crashing down. He came down with appendicitis in February 1938 which was so severe that gangrene had set in.[24] He was operated on immediately in Rocky Mount, North Carolina, and barely survived. The ordeal scared the daylights out of him and his convalescence at home was slow. When he finally reported to the Giants just before they broke camp in Hot Springs, Arkansas, he was still in a weakened condition and very concerned that he would do something to reopen his incision.[25]

Whitehead continued to lose weight, was unable to play once the season opened, and was finally admitted to a New York hospital on April 23 with what was described as colitis.[26] There an attending physician announced that Whitehead's concern over his physical condition had induced a nervous breakdown.[27] As a result, Whitehead returned home to rest and missed the entire 1938 season.

He recovered enough to play in about 40 semipro games around his home in the late summer and early fall[28] and traveled to New York to accompany the Giants for the last six games of the season, although he was not activated.[29] He had recovered enough after the season to marry Ruth Lyon of Windsor, North Carolina, on December 26, 1938. The two had met ten years earlier when Burgess was in college at Chapel Hill and Ruth was attending St. Mary's, a girls school about 25 miles away. Whitehead had left college without graduating to play professional baseball and so the two had planned on attending Duke University so that they both could work on obtaining their degrees.[30]

Whitehead's 1939 return to the Giants, who had slipped to third in 1938, was anything but smooth. He had played in 305 consecutive games in 1936 and 1937 and was convinced that manager Bill Terry had overused him, contributing to if not causing his mental and physical breakdown.[31] He was late reporting to spring training in Baton Rouge, and after a slow start there, seemed to play himself into shape. He was in the Giants' Opening Day lineup, a win over the Brooklyn Dodgers.

On June 6 in the Polo Grounds, Whitehead participated in a record-breaking inning as the Giants hit five home runs in the fourth inning against the Cincinnati Reds in a 17-3 Giants win.[32] It was one of two home runs Burgess would hit for the season, and one of only 17 that he had for his career.

As the season wore on, Whitehead again began behaving erratically, sometimes saying he was too tired to play and often arriving at the ballpark just before game time. Finally, manager Terry suspended Burgess on August 16 for violation of team rules. Whitehead reacted to the suspension by appearing the next day at Yankee Stadium in his full uniform, seeking permission to work out with the Yankees. Not surprisingly, Yankees manager Joe McCarthy turned him away.[33]

Terry reinstated Whitehead after five days, but on September 9 he left the team and was suspended for the rest of the season.[34] For the season he batted a career-low .239 in 95 games and 335 at-bats. Although he was only 29 years old, his future with the Giants and indeed in baseball was very much in doubt.[35] When later asked about Whitehead during this period, Bill Terry said simply, "He was crazy."[36]

Although Whitehead had a difficult year in 1939, he did manage to gain a famous admirer. Actress Tallulah Bankhead wrote that in 1939 she "swooned over Burgess Whitehead because he moved like a ballet dancer. He was Phi Beta Kappa, a brilliant fielder but he couldn't hit his way out of a paper bag."[37]

Amazingly, after his trouble-filled 1939 season on and off the field,[38] Whitehead came back strong in 1940 and hit .282 in 133 games and 568 at-bats, with only 17 strikeouts. Manager Terry shifted him to third base to begin the season and he ended up playing 74 games at third, 57 games at second, and four games at shortstop. As one writer noted late in the season, "[t]his is indeed a reconstructed Whitehead; there is no suggestion of the flighty, uncertain Whitey of 1939."[39] But even with Whitehead's resurgence, the Giants limped to a sixth-place finish, eight games under .500.

On July 31 Whitehead was inadvertently involved in one of baseball greatest tragedies. With the Giants trailing the Reds 4-1 in the bottom of the ninth in the Polo Grounds and a runner on with two outs, Whitehead worked an 0-and-2 count to 3-and-2 before lofting a fly ball just into the stands in right field to bring the score to 4-3. Mel Ott then coaxed a walk off the Reds' Bucky Walters to bring Harry Danning to the plate as the winning run. Danning responded by hitting an 0-and-2 fastball deep into the left-field stands for a home run and a dramatic 5-4 Giants comeback win.

The Reds catcher that day was Willard Hershberger, filling in for Ernie Lombardi, who was out with an injury to his leg. The 30-year-old Hershberger had a lifelong battle with depression and blamed himself for the defeat for not calling the right pitches. Two days later in Boston, he was again the catcher in a 12-inning, 4-3 loss to the Bees, going 0-for-5 and failing to field a ball topped in front of the plate. The following day, August 3, Hershberger did not show up at the ballpark and was found dead in his hotel room, a suicide victim.[40]

On the heels of his strong comeback in 1940, the Giants welcomed Burgess back for the 1941 season. Manager Terry moved him back to second base, where he played in 104 of his 116 appearances. Whitehead battled injuries and slumped to a .228 average, the lowest of his career, as the Giants could climb only to fifth place, five games under .500 and 25 1/2 games out of first place.

After the season Mel Ott took over as manager and the Giants proceeded to clean house, selling Whitehead to the Toronto Maple Leafs of the International League on December 11. As a result, Burgess spent the 1942 season playing second base in Toronto, where hit .259 and stole 26 bases in 148 games for the sixth-place Maple Leafs. He played well enough to attract the attention of the Pittsburgh Pirates, who purchased his contract at the end of the International League season. Although he reported to the Pirates, a hand injury kept him from appearing in any major-league games at the end of the season.

Although the complete circumstances are lost to history, after the season Whitehead and Frank Rickey, a scout who was Branch Rickey's brother, paid the way for a black man from North Carolina named Octavius to watch the World Series in New York.[41]

With World War II in full swing, the 32-year-old Whitehead was inducted into the Army Air Corps later that fall and reported to Fort Bragg, North Carolina, on December 7. He rose to become a staff sergeant, serving as a physical-fitness instructor at Daniel Field, Georgia, and then Miami Beach, Florida. In 1945 he was transferred to Buckley Field in Denver and served as player-coach for the Second Air Force Falcons, playing with former major-league pitcher Lee Grissom among others.[42] Whitehead was discharged in October 1945, after missing three full seasons of professional baseball.[43]

At age 35, Whitehead reported to spring training with the Pirates, who were managed by his old Gas House Gang teammate Frankie Frisch. He made the team and it was hoped that he would be a steadying influence on Billy Cox, the team's youthful shortstop. Whether or not he was is questionable; Whitehead ran afoul of Frisch during spring training and was suspended on March 13 and reinstated over a month later on April 19.[44] Once active, Burgess was slowed by injuries and did not hit much, so the younger Frank Gustine received most of the playing time at second base. For the year, Whitehead batted just .220 in 55 games for seventh-place Pittsburgh.

Not surprisingly, the Pirates gave Whitehead his unconditional release in January 1947, effectively ending his big-league career. In his nine major-league seasons, Whitehead had compiled a .266 batting average. One of the best contact hitters of his era, in 3,563 plate appearances he had struck out only 138 times. Even more amazing is that he was caught stealing only one time in 52 career stolen-base attempts.

Whitehead was not out of work long, however, and signed with the Jersey City Giants of the International League. There he helped the team to the pennant in a very tight race with the Montreal Royals. The Giants prevailed by a half-game and finished with a 94-60 record before being swept in four games in the playoffs by the Buffalo Bisons. Whitehead played in 141 of the 154 games and hit .257 in 508 plate appearances, striking out only 23 times. For his efforts, he was named the second baseman on the International League All-Star team.[45]

Whitehead was back with Jersey City in 1948 but injuries slowed him to only 79 games for a team that slid all the way to seventh place. Still, at 38 years old, he hit a solid .284 in 316 plate appearances with only 16 strikeouts.

Whitehead called it quits after 1948 and returned to his native North Carolina. He went into the feed mill and livestock business with two brothers in Windsor, North Carolina, where he "had some good years and some rugged ones."[46] He had no formal association with baseball although he did enjoy watching Gaylord Perry pitch when he was a high-school phenom at a nearby town and arranged for him to try out with the crack semipro Alpine Cowboys in far west Texas.[47]

Whitehead retired from the feed mill business in 1974 and afterward helped out as an assistant golf pro at the Cashie Golf and Country Club.[48]

He was elected into the North Carolina Sports Hall of Fame in 1981 and was the last surviving member of the Gas House Gang when he died from a heart attack on November 25, 1993, at the age of 83. He was survived by Ruth, his wife of almost 55 years; a son, Charles Lyon Whitehead; a daughter, Susan Whitehead Harrell, and four grandchildren.

Sources

Alexander, Charles, *Breaking the Slump — Baseball and the Depression Era* (New York: Columbia University Press, 2002).

Bartell, Dick, with Norman L. Macht, *Rowdy Richard — A Firsthand Account of the National League Baseball Wars of the 1930s and the Men Who Fought Them* (Berkeley, California: North Atlantic Books, 1987).

Barthel, Thomas. *The Fierce Fun of Ducky Medwick* (Lanham, Maryland: The Scarecrow Press, Inc., 2003).

Barthel, Thomas. *Pepper Martin — A Baseball Biography* (Jefferson, North Carolina: McFarland & Co., Inc., 2003).

Blaisdell, Lowell L. *Carl Hubbell — A Biography of the Screwball King* (Jefferson, North Carolina: McFarland & Co., Inc., 2011).

Bloodgood, Clifford, "The Giants Get a Second Baseman," *Baseball Magazine*, February 1936.

Broeg, Bob, *The Pilot Light and the Gas House Gang* (St. Louis: The Bethany Press, 1980).

Daley, Arthur, *Times At Bat — A Half-Century of Baseball* (New York: Random House, 1950).

Einstein, Charles, ed., *The Fireside Book of Baseball* (New York: Simon & Schuster, 1956).

Farrington, Dick, "The Man Who Found Himself After Boss Gave Him Up," *The Sporting News*, June 6, 1940.

Feldman, Doug, *Dizzy and the Gashouse Gang—The 1934 St. Louis Cardinals and Depression-Era Baseball* (Jefferson, North Carolina: McFarland & Co., Inc., 2000).

Fleming, G.H., *The Dizziest Season—The Gashouse Gang Chases the Pennant* (New York: William Morrow & Co., Inc., 1984).

Frisch, Frank, as told to J. Roy Stockton, *Frank Frisch: The Fordham Flash* (New York: Doubleday & Co., 1962).

Golenbock, Peter, *The Spirit of St. Louis—A History of the St. Louis Cardinals and Browns* (New York: Avon Books, Inc., 2000).

Graham, Frank, *The New York Giants* (New York: G.P. Putnam's Sons, 1952).

Gregory, Robert. *Diz—The Story of Dizzy Dean and Baseball During the Great Depression* (New York: Viking, 1992).

Grosshandler, Stan, "Burgess Whitehead: Last of the Old Gas House Gang," *Baseball Digest*, June 1992.

Heidenry, John, *The Gashouse Gang* (New York: Public Affairs, 2007).

Hood, Robert E., *The Gashouse Gang* (New York: William Morrow & Co., Inc., 1976).

Hynd, Noel, *The Giants of the Polo Grounds—The Glorious Times of Baseball's New York Giants* (New York: Doubleday, 1988).

Johnson, Lloyd, and Miles Wolff, eds. *The Encyclopedia of Minor League Baseball* (Durham, North Carolina: Baseball America, Inc., 2nd ed., 1997).

Kelley, Brent. *The Early All-Stars* (Jefferson, North Carolina: McFarland & Co., Inc., 1997).

Lanctot, Neil, *Negro League Baseball—the Rise and Ruin of a Black Institution* (Philadelphia: Univ. of Pennsylvania Press, 2004).

Lieb, Frederick G., *The St. Louis Cardinals* (New York: G.P. Putnam's Sons, 1945).

Lowenfish, Lee, *Branch Rickey—Baseball's Ferocious Gentleman* (Lincoln, Nebraska: University of Nebraska Press, 2007).

Martin, Alfred H. *Mel Ott—The Gentle Giant* (Lanham, Maryland: The Scarecrow Press, Inc., 2003).

McKelvey, G. Richard, *The MacPhails—Baseball's First Family of the Front Office* (Jefferson, North Carolina: McFarland & Co., Inc., 2000).

Neft, David S., Lee Allen, and Robert Markel, eds., *The Baseball Encyclopedia* (New York: The Macmillan Co., 1969).

Reichler, Joe, and Ben Olan, *Baseball's Unforgettable Games* (New York: The Ronald Press Co., 1960).

Smith, Curt, *America's Dizzy Dean* (St. Louis: The Bethany Press, 1978).

Stein, Fred, *Mel Ott—The Little Giant of Baseball* (Jefferson, North Carolina: McFarland & Co., Inc., 1999).

Stein, Fred, *Under Coogan's Bluff—A Fan's Recollection of the New York Giants Under Terry and Ott* (Glenshaw, Pennsylvania, Chapter & Cask, 1981).

Stein, Fred, and Nick Peters, *Giants Diary—A Century of Giants Baseball in New York and San Francisco*, (Berkeley, California: North Atlantic Books, 1987).

Stockton, J. Roy, *The Gashouse Gang and a Couple of Other Guys* (New York: A.S. Barnes & Co., 1945).

Tiede, Joe, "Brushbacks, 2 hands, and day (games) gone by," unidentified Raleigh newspaper, June 1981, in National Baseball Library clippings file on Burgess Whitehead.

Van Blair, Rick, *Dugout to Foxhole—Interviews With Baseball Players Whose Careers Were Affected by World War II* (Jefferson, North Carolina: McFarland & Co., Inc., 1994).

Werber, Bill, and C. Paul Rogers, III, *Memories of a Ballplayer: Bill Werber and Baseball in the 1930s* (Cleveland: Society for American Baseball Research, 2001).

Williams, Peter, *When the Giants Were Giants—Bill Terry and the Golden Age of New York Baseball* (Chapel Hill, North Carolina: Algonquin Books of Chapel Hill, 1994).

Clippings file on Burgess Whitehead, National Baseball Library.

baseballinwartime.com.

retrosheet.org.

Notes

1 Clipping dated February 2, 1936, from the National Baseball Library clippings file on Burgess Whitehead.

2 Clifford Bloodgood, "The Giants Get a Second Baseman," *Baseball Magazine*, February 1936.

3 Joe Tiede, "Brushbacks, 2 hands, and day (games) gone by," unidentified Raleigh newspaper, June 1981, in National Baseball Library clippings file on Burgess Whitehead.

4 Whitehead was originally slated to go to the Rochester Red Wings in the International League but was assigned to Columbus instead.

5 Joe Williams, "Patience of MacPhail Made Whitehead a Keystone Star," undated column from National Baseball Library clippings file on Burgess Whitehead.

6 Whitehead later said that going 8-for-9 in a doubleheader was his biggest thrill in baseball. Brent Kelley, *The Early All-Stars*, 177.

7 Columbus then defeated the Minneapolis Millers four games to two in the league playoffs to advance to the Little World Series, where they defeated the Buffalo Bison of the International League five games to three.

8 Columbus was loaded with future major leaguers including Whitehead's college teammate Lew Riggs, Nick Cullop, Jack Rothrock, Bill DeLancy, and pitchers Bill Lee (21-9), and Paul Dean (22-7).

9 Bob Broeg, "Whitehead a Keystone Gazelle." August, 30, 1975, unidentified column from National Baseball Library clippings file on Burgess Whitehead.

10 Charles C. Alexander, *Breaking the Slump - Baseball in the Depression Era,* 198.

11 John Drebinger, "Whitehead Traded to Giants by Cards," *New York Times,* December 10, 1935.

12 Dick "Rowdy Richard" Bartell with Norman L. Macht, *Rowdy Richard*, 162; J. Roy Stockton, *The Gashouse Gang and a Couple of Other Guys*, 106-07.

13 Peter Williams, *When the Giants Were Giants—Bill Terry and the Golden Age of New York Baseball*, 189.

14 Fred Stein, *Mel Ott—The Little Giant of Baseball*, 70-71.

15 Brent Kelley, 177.

16 Noel Hynd, *The Giants of the Polo Grounds*, 303-04; Joe Reichler and Ben Olan, *Baseball's Unforgettable Games,* 347. The Giants scored four more runs in the top of the ninth and went on to win Game One 6-1, breaking the Yankees' 12-game World Series win streak. In a statistical oddity, the Giants outfielders had no fielding chances for the entire game.

17 Robert Gregory, *Diz—The Story of Dizzy Dean and Baseball During the Great Depression,* 293; Doug Feldman, *Dizzy and the Gashouse Gang,* 55; Arthur Daly, *Times At Bat—A Half-Century of Baseball,* 94; Frank Frisch as told to J. Roy Stockton, *Frank Frisch: The Fordham Flash,* 100; Thomas Barthel, *Pepper Martin—A Baseball Biography,* 132.

18 Robert Gregory, 293.

19 Bob Broeg, "Whitehead a Keystone Gazelle."

20 Dick Bartell, 245-47; Dean's beanballs apparently drew no warning from the umpires. Not surprisingly, a bench-clearing brawl ensued in the ninth inning after a drag bunt by Jimmy Ripple with Dean covering first. Robert Gregory, 322-24; Noel Hynd, 307-08; Fred Stein, 85-86; Rick Van Blair, *Dugout to Foxhole,* 67-68.

21 Bob Broeg, "Gas House Gang: Tag Later Than Burgess Whitehead," *St. Louis Post-Dispatch*, August 5, 1975, 2C.

22 Robert Gregory, 143-44. His speech was described as a "smooth, syrupy southern voice." Bob Broeg, "Whitehead a Keystone Gazelle."

23 Doug Feldman, 55.

24 Clipping dated February 20, 1938, from National Baseball Library clippings file on Burgess Whitehead.

25 Peter Williams, 251.

26 Clipping dated April, 27, 1938, from National Baseball Library clippings file on Burgess Whitehead.

27 Tom Meany, "Chiozza to Carry on at Giant Keystone," *New York World-Telegram,* May 3, 1938.

28 Clipping dated December 21, 1938, from National Baseball Library clippings file on Burgess Whitehead.

29 Clippings dated September 16, 1938, and September 27, 1938, from the National Baseball Library clippings file on Burgess Whitehead. Even though he missed the entire year, Whitehead's teammates voted him a full share of their third-place money. Clipping dated September 27, 1938, from National Baseball Library clippings file on Burgess Whitehead.

30 Dick Farrington, "The Man Who Found Himself After Boss Gave Him Up," *The Sporting News*, June 6, 1940. It does not appear that they ever did attend Duke, however.

31 Bob Broeg, "Whitehead a Keystone Gazelle."

32 The other Giants hitting home runs in the inning were Harry Danning, Frank Demaree, Manny Salvo, and Joe Moore. It was the only home run of pitcher Salvo's big-league career. The record was later tied by the 1949 Philadelphia Phillies and the 1961 San Francisco Giants. C. Paul Rogers, III, "June 2, 1949, the Day the Phillies Came of Age," 19, *The National Pastime* 31 (1999).

33 Clipping dated August 17, 1939, from the National Baseball Library clippings file on Burgess Whitehead. Another account had Whitehead not reporting for the Giants' game in Ebbets Field against the Dodgers but instead showing up in full uniform in Yankee Stadium. Fred Stein, 101.

34 Fred Stein and Nick Peters, *Giants Diary*, 84.

35 Harold C. Burr, "Giants to Drop Burgess in '40," clipping dated August 17, 1939, from the National Baseball Library clipping file on Burgess Whitehead; Fred Stein, *Under Coogan's Bluff*, 74.

36 Peter Williams, 259.

37 Charles Einstein, ed., *The Fireside Book of Baseball*, 23.

38 According to one unsubstantiated source, Whitehead was involved in both an assault of a woman and a nightclub incident in 1939. Neil Lanctot, *Negro League Baseball—the Rise and Ruin of a Black Institution*, 224.

39 Joe King, "Whitehead's Comeback Is a Success," unidentified clipping from the National Baseball Library file on Burgess Whitehead dated September 19, 1940.

40 Joe Reichler and Ben Olan, 124-27; Charles C. Alexander, 255-57; Dick Bartell with Norman L. Macht, 293-94; Bill Werber and C. Paul Rogers, III, *Memories of a Ballplayer—Bill Werber and Baseball in the 1930s,* 175-77.

41 Lee Lowenfish, *Branch Rickey—Baseball's Ferocious Gentleman*, 355.

42 baseballinwartime.com/player_biographies/whitehead_burgess.htm.

43 Brent Kelley, 175; Joe Tiede.

44 Undated clipping from the National Baseball Library clippings file on Burgess Whitehead.

45 Lloyd Johnson and Miles Wolff, eds., *The Encyclopedia of Minor League Baseball,* 357.

46 Brent Kelley, 177.

47 One report has Whitehead helping the Giants sign Perry to a bonus contract (Joe Tiede, "Brushbacks, 2 hands, and day (games) gone by," unidentified Raleigh newspaper, June 1981, in National Baseball Library clippings file on Burgess Whitehead), but Perry's recollection is different. According to Perry, based on Whitehead's recommendation, he and his father flew to Alpine for a tryout in 1957. Perry made the team and was the first high-school player ever to make the Cowboys. Telephone interview with Gaylord Perry, June 7, 2013.

48 Joe Tiede.

Jim Winford

By Clayton J. Trutor

JIM WINFORD PITCHED professionally for 14 years (1929-1942). The lanky, 6-foot-1 right-hander spent parts of six seasons in the major leagues with the St Louis Cardinals (1932, 1934-1937) and the Brooklyn Dodgers (1938). He was a knuckleballer who could be counted on as both a starter and a long reliever. Nicknamed Cowboy for his Oklahoma upbringing and his long and lean physique, Winford pitched in 14 different cities over the course of a 12-year minor-league baseball career, which began in 1929 with the Scottdale (Pennsylvania) Scotties of the Class C Mid-Atlantic League and ended in 1942 with the Oklahoma City Indians of the Texas League.[1]

Cowboy Winford spent 12 of his 14 years in professional baseball with the Cardinals organization. At 24 he pitched in five early-season games for the 1934 Gas House Gang Cardinals, his second stint with club. In 1932 he pitched in four September games for the Cardinals, garnering a 1-1 record with an earned-run average of 6.48. In 1934 he went 0-2 with a 7.82 ERA for the Cardinals before being sent in June to the Rochester Red Wings of the International League for the remainder of the season.[2]

A study of Winford's career reveals the texture of an increasingly distant yet not forgotten America. He was idiosyncratically craftsmanlike and journeymanlike in an era laden with craftsmen and journeymen. Winford was a mechanic of the mound beginning in his teens, relying not on power pitching to advance through the Cardinals' system but on his skill as a knuckleballer. Despite his brief tenure in the major leagues, *The Sporting News* described him in 1937 as a "master of the knuckleball."[3] Winford was a journeyman in the romantic age of American travel, the decades between the World Wars when trains and automobiles passed right through the middle of the nation's cities and towns as peers. He moved from one club to another a total of 24 times, including multiple stops in St Louis, Rochester, and Columbus. Winford lived in the Branch Rickey farm system as fully as anyone, experiencing success and failure in big league metropolises, Double-A industrial cities, and Class D small towns. He made his home in Northern California, Piedmont North Carolina, Central Oklahoma, Eastern Texas, Ozark Arkansas, Appalachian Pennsylvania, and Brooklyn, New York, in a career that spanned the Great Depression and the early years of World War II.

James Head Winford was born in Shelbyville, Tennessee, on October 9, 1909. During his childhood, his family settled in Meeker, Oklahoma, a town of less than 1,000 residents in the center of the newly-admitted state. Winford excelled as a pitcher at Meeker High School, where several years earlier Hall of Fame left-hander Carl Hubbell had starred for the Meeker Bulldogs.[4] Winford grew up in the Cardinals' expansive scouting territory, which radiated out from the franchise's industrial Midwestern base into the mid-South, across the

Jim Winford was a relief pitcher for the Cardinals in 1934. In his lone year as a starter in 1936, he posted a 11-10 record and a 3.80 ERA.

Plains, and the Old Southwest. The Cardinals assigned Winford to Scottdale in the Class C Mid-Atlantic League, bypassing Class D ball for the young knuckleballer.

After a 10-15 campaign in Scottdale, Winford was assigned to the Shawnee (Oklahoma) Robins of the Class C Western Association for 1930. He excelled for the Robins, earning a 14-10 record before being elevated to Houston of the Class A Texas League late in the season. During the 1931 season, Winford pitched in five cities for the Cardinals organization: Scottdale, Columbus (Ohio), Greensboro (North Carolina), Springfield (Missouri), and Bartlesville (Oklahoma). He compiled a 15-8 record with a 2.00 ERA.[5]

During the 1932 season, Winford went 8-10 with a 3.64 ERA for the Rochester Red Wings of the International League, and earned a September call-up by the Cardinals. He had finished strongly for the Red Wings, striking out 13 in his final International League appearance, an 8-2 victory over the Buffalo Bisons on September 8.[6]

Winford appeared in four games for the Cardinals in September 1932, earning a 1-1 record with a 6.48 ERA. The Cardinals finished the season tied for sixth place, 18 games off the pennant-winning pace set by the Chicago Cubs, enabling St Louis to give a half-dozen promising pitchers in their farm system National League experience in the season's final weeks. Winford debuted for the Cardinals in a two-inning relief appearance against the New York Giants at the Polo Grounds on September 10, two days after his final start with Rochester.[7] He allowed two hits and one unearned run and got a no-decision in an 11-7 defeat. Winford earned his first major league win in a scoreless 4 2/3-inning relief appearance against Cincinnati on September 22 at Sportsman's Park. Two days later, he made his first major-league start, against Pittsburgh. Winford lasted two-thirds of an inning, allowing six earned runs and taking the loss in a 7-4 defeat. The shellacking by the Pirates raised his ERA from zero to 6.48 to finish the season.[8]

Splitting the 1933 season between Rochester and Columbus, Winford compiled a 16-9 record with a 3.72 ERA. Pitching alongside future National League aces Paul "Daffy" Dean and Bill Lee, Winford and the Columbus Red Birds won the 1933 American Association championship. He returned to the Cardinals in the spring of 1934, appearing in five games for the eventual world champions before being sent back to Rochester in June.[9] His 1934 campaign, both at the major- and minor-league levels, proved unsuccessful. Winford went 0-2 with the Cardinals, posting a 7.82 ERA. At Rochester, he finished 2-7 with a 5.96 ERA. Winford returned to form in 1935 with the Columbus Red Birds. He went 14-11 with a 3.65 ERA. Winford appeared in two late-September games for the St Louis Cardinals, not earning a decision in either game, but pitching for 11 1/3 innings with a 3.97 ERA.

The 1936 season proved to be Winford's most successful in the major leagues and the only season in which he spent most of the season in the majors. He became the Cardinals' fourth starter, filling in for Paul Dean, who missed much of the season with arm trouble. Winford finished the season with an 11-10 record and a 3.80 ERA. His 11 wins were good for second on the Cardinals' roster behind Dizzy Dean.[10] Winford pitched ten complete games, including a 15-inning, 3-1 victory over the Boston Braves on September 9. He threw a four-hit shutout against the Brooklyn Dodgers in the second game of a July 30 doubleheader after Dizzy Dean shut out the Dodgers in the first game.[11]

Winford's 1936 season earned him a reputation as a talented young pitcher. *The Sporting News* took particular note of his crafty work on the mound, describing him as a "master of the knuckle ball" in its preview of the Cardinals' season.[12] The paper projected Winford as the club's number four starter behind the Dean brothers and Bob Weiland.[13] But Winford pitched poorly, going 2-4 with a 5.83 ERA in 16 appearances. He lost all four games he started. Additionally, Winford suffered from appendicitis during the season, missing 2 1/2 months of action. Over the course of the season, Si Johnson, Lon Warneke, and Mike Ryba performed well as starters and in long relief, relegating Winford to the back burner.[14]

The following spring, Winford pitched for the Houston Buffaloes, the Cardinals' affiliate in the Class A Texas League. Winford won a career-high 17 games.

On September 10 the Brooklyn Dodgers purchased Winford's contract and brought him up for the rest of the season. Winford pitched in two games for the Dodgers, taking the loss in a September 16 start against his former team, the Cardinals, and allowing three earned runs in 1 2/3 innings of relief against Pittsburgh on September 22.[15]

Winford's two appearances for the Dodgers proved to be his final major-league games. Still the property of Brooklyn, he pitched for their Montreal and Nashville farm teams in 1939 before being released and subsequently signed off waivers by the Cardinals for the 1940 season.[16] Winford bounced around the Cardinals' minor-league system in 1940 before taking on the position of player-manager of the Batesville Pilots of the Class D Northeast Arkansas League in 1941. The veteran right-hander went 8-3 on the mound for the Pilots in 13 starts.[17] In 1942 Winford, then a resident of McCloud, Oklahoma, pitched his final season in Organized Baseball, for the Oklahoma City Indians, the New York Giants' affiliate in the Texas League. Winford appeared in 11 games for Oklahoma City as a relief pitcher.[18]

After the 1942 season, Winford enlisted in the US Navy. In 1943 he was stationed at the Norman (Oklahoma) Naval Air Station, where he was a naval fireman and played on the base's baseball team, the Norman Zoomers.[19] After his discharge from the Navy, Winford became a firefighter in Oklahoma City.

Winford married Magdalena Kohler on November 18, 1932. The couple divorced in 1937. They had one child, a daughter, Sara.[20] Winford died at age 61 on December 16, 1970, in Miami, Oklahoma. He was buried in his hometown of Meeker, at the New Hope Cemetery.[21]

Sources

Milwaukee Journal

New York Times

The Sporting News

Baseball-Reference.com

The Encyclopedia of Oklahoma History and Culture: digital.library.okstate.edu/encyclopedia/

Ancestry.com

The Baseball Necrology: thebbnlive.com

Notes

1. "Minors Coming Up to Majors in '33," *Sporting News*, November 3, 1932, 5; "Minors Coming Up to Majors in '35," *Sporting News* December 27, 1934, 8.

2. "Winford Sent to Columbus," *New York Times*, January 1, 1935, 35; "Minors Coming Up to Majors in '35," 8.

3. "Cards Still Rated in Terms of 'Ifs,'" *The Sporting News*, April 15, 1937, 1.

4. Frankie Fair Burchette, "Meeker," *Encyclopedia of Oklahoma History and Culture*, accessed on July 5, 2013: digital.library.okstate.edu/encyclopedia/entries/M/ME009.html

5. "Minors Coming Up to Majors in '35," 8.

6. "Rochester Wins 8-2; Winford, Soon to Join Cardinals, Sets Back Buffalo," *New York Times*, September 9, 1932, 26.

7. "Minors Coming up to Majors in '33," 5.

8. Ibid.

9. "Winford Sent to Columbus," 35; *The Sporting News*; "Santa Makes Early Gallop to Cullop, Delivering Brewer Pilot Job to Nick," *The Sporting News*, December 21, 1944, 2.

10. "Young Bob Can't Be Discounted," *The Sporting News* October 22, 1936, 3; "Cards Still Rated in Terms of 'Ifs,'" 1.

11. "Winford Gives Dodgers Four Hits as the Cardinals Breeze to 7-0 Victory," *New York Times*, July 31, 1936, 12.

12. *The Sporting News*, April 15, 1937.

13. "Cards Still Rated in Terms of 'Ifs,'" 1.

14. "Cardinal Collapse Muffles Flag Talk," *The Sporting News*, July 15, 1937, 3.

15. "Lights Shed Bright Ray on 700,000 Dodger Gate," *The Sporting News*, September 15, 1938, 2.

16. "Columbus Buys Winford," *New York Times*, June 23, 1940, S6.

17. "Hershel Martin, Jim Winford Add Class to Oklahoma City," *The Sporting News*, March 19, 1942, 11.

18. Ibid.

19. "In the Service," *The Sporting News*, May 6, 1943, 7.

20. "Jim Winford Sued for Divorce by Wife," *Milwaukee Journal*, October 5, 1937, 19; "Sara L. Winford: 1940 Census," Ancestry.com: accessed on July 5, 2013: interactive.ancestry.com/2442/m-t0627-03294-00830/89418026?backurl=http%3a%2f%2fwww.ancestry.com%2f1940-census%2fusa%2fOklahoma%2fMagdalena-W-Winford_33thvg&ssrc=&backlabel=Return

21. "Jim Winford," The Baseball Necrology, accessed on July 5, 2013: thebbnlive.com/PlayerInfo.aspx?FullName=Winford%2c+Jim-09%2f10%2f1932

Red Worthington

By Jimmy Keenan

CALIFORNIA NATIVE RED Worthington was a hard-hitting outfielder with a powerful throwing arm. A top prospect in the St. Louis Cardinals organization, Red, who threw and batted right-handed, appeared to be on the fast track to major-league stardom. Before his ascent to the major leagues, a sportswriter wrote of Worthington, "This young man from the Pacific Coast does many things well but his hitting and throwing are the accomplishments that gave observers their biggest thrill during training games in Florida. Too, he owns that indefinable quality called COLOR or personality. He makes friends with the kids and the grown ups. He's the sort that can breeze into town in the morning and know everybody in the afternoon. Red, if he doesn't break an ankle, will be in the majors next year or the year after that anyhow."[1]

Brought up through the Cardinals farm system, Worthington was unable to break into the Cardinals' talented outfield ranks, and was sold to the Boston Braves. Four years later, he returned to the Cardinals in a waiver deal, and in his only at-bat with the 1934 pennant winners, he struck out.

Robert Lee "Red" Worthington was born on April 24, 1906, in San Gabriel, California. He was the second youngest of seven children born to Jerry Worthington, a laborer, and Hannah (McNamara) Worthington. Hannah and Jerry were Irish Catholics from Illinois. The Worthingtons were married in 1891 and left Illinois around the turn of the 20th century. They lived briefly in Iowa and Kansas before moving California. The family first lived in San Gabriel before settling in nearby Alhambra.

Red, who derived his nickname from the color of his hair, played baseball on the local lots of Alhambra. According to *San Gabriel Valley Tribune* sportswriter Jim McConnell, Worthington briefly attended Alhambra High School in the early 1920s but did not graduate.[2] The Los Angeles area was noted for its year-round amateur and semipro baseball leagues during the early and mid-20th century. There is little information available on Worthington's amateur days on the diamond, but by the summer of 1925 the 19-year-old outfielder was traveling the country with a semipro team from Los Angeles. While playing at Eldora, Iowa, he caught the attention of a scout for the Waterloo Hawks of the Class D Mississippi Valley League, who signed him on the spot. Joining the Hawks in the middle of July, he hit .273 in 57 games. In 1926 he had a breakout year, leading the league with a .389 batting average. His 185 hits that season were the most in Mississippi Valley League history.[3]

A starting outfielder for the Braves in 1931 and 1932, Worthington was claimed on waivers by St. Louis in September 1934. He appeared in only one game.

The St. Louis Cardinals purchased Worthington's contract from Waterloo at the end of the 1926 season. Cardinals general manager Branch Rickey wanted to see how the youngster would fare in the high minors so he sent Worthington to the Syracuse Stars in the Double-A International League. Never short on confidence, Worthington wrote in a letter to the Stars' president of baseball operations, Warren Giles, "I hope Mr. Shotton (Syracuse manager Burt Shotton) isn't one of those strawberry pickers that picks out his lineup in the middle of the winter because if he is I'm afraid I'll have to spoil some of his plans. I am going to break into that Syracuse outfield. I have looked up the records of the others on the payroll and I am convinced that I will be banging the ball all over the lot for you. I'll be one of the first men to training camp and I am confident when I leave Syracuse it will be to go up to the majors and not to slip down."[4]

True to his word, Worthington earned a spot on the Syracuse roster. Shotton used him as a reserve outfielder and pinch-hitter. Worthington had a respectable year moving up from Class D to the highest level of the minors, hitting .261 in 73 games. In the outfield, he recorded eight assists while committing only three errors.

In January 1928, the Syracuse franchise was sold and the players were transferred to Rochester.[5] In early March, Branch Rickey traded Worthington to Danville of the Class B Three-I League for outfielder Frank Murphy. Commenting on the deal, *The Sporting News* wrote, "Worthington was with Syracuse last season and several games were pulled out of the fire by his timely blows which came when hits meant runs and the ball game."[6]

Scarcely had Worthington settled in with Danville than Houston Buffaloes outfielder Homer Peel, a highly touted St. Louis prospect, ran into an outfield fence and broke his leg. Rickey sent Worthington to the Texas League club to help fill the void. While Worthington, a dead pull hitter, was in Houston, manager Frank Snyder taught him the art of hitting the ball to all fields.

The Texas League played a split schedule in 1928 and Worthington's hot bat helped the Buffaloes win the first half of the season. He finished the season with a .353 batting average, 47 doubles, 11 triples, 7 home runs, and 12 stolen bases. His 211 hits topped the circuit and he struck out just 16 times in 599 at-bats. In the outfield, his strong arm accounted for 19 assists. Houston defeated Wichita Falls, the second-half winner, in the league playoff, then defeated the Southern Association champion Birmingham Barons in the Dixie Championship. Worthington and four other Houston players were selected to the Texas League all-star team.

A few weeks before the start of spring training in 1929, Worthington informed Rochester president Warren Giles that he would not report to the team until he received a higher salary. Meanwhile, Hillerich & Bradsby, maker of the Louisville Slugger, informed Giles that Worthington's bats would be shipped to the team in time for the start of spring training. Giles wrote back to Worhington, "What kind of holdout are you, anyway? You tell me you are not going to report but you tell the bat company to get your bats to camp before opening day practice. "It only costs three cents to try," Worthington replied, enclosing his signed contract with the letter.[7]

Red put together a big year for the Red Wings in 1929. The 5-foot-10, 170-pound outfielder, who swung a 42-ounce bat, batted .327, with 202 hits, 34 doubles, 15 triples, 8 home runs, and 113 RBIs. He had 21 outfield assists. Rochester won 103 games and captured the International League crown for the second year in a row, but lost to the Kansas City Blues of the American Association in a hard fought Junior World Series, five games to four.

The Cardinals' roster was loaded with talented outfielders, so Worthington was back with Rochester for the start of the 1930 season. On April 13 the Red Wings played an exhibition game against the Washington Senators. Washington pitcher Carlos Moore took a swing and the bat flew across the diamond and struck Worthington on the elbow of his throwing arm. The Cardinals' team physician, Dr. Robert F. Hyland, reported that there was a torn ligament but no fractured bones. The severity of the tear forced Worthington to miss six weeks of the season. The injury was so bad that he considered learning how to throw left-handed.

During this time, the Red Wings were hit with a number of injuries and they began to drop in the standings. The loss of Worthington along with player-manager and star center fielder Billy Southworth had the most impact on the team.[8]

In late May, cleared by Dr. Hyland to play, Worthington rejoined the Red Wings and resumed his hot hitting. On June 20 he reinjured his elbow crashing into the outfield wall in the first game of a doubleheader against Reading. But he returned to the lineup in the nightcap, banging out two hits and throwing a runner out at the plate.

Worthington went on to have a fine season, hitting .375 with 25 doubles and 12 triples in 123 games. His arm gave him trouble for most of the season but he still finished with 11 outfield assists. Winning 105 games, Rochester again took the International League pennant, and defeated the Louisville Colonels in the Junior World Series.

Rickey, having an abundance of talent in his farm system, sold Worthington and utilityman Charlie Wilson to the Boston Braves on September 17, 1930, for a reported $60,000. In his first spring training with the Braves, Worthington got off to an amazing start. By April 7, he had compiled 47 hits in 67 spring-training at-bats against major-league pitching for a .701 batting average. Babe Ruth and Wilbert Robinson spoke glowingly about his prowess with the bat. Ruth told a reporter for *The Sporting News* that Red was a natural hitter who would do well in the big leagues. Robinson in an interview with the Associated Press said that in his opinion, Worthington was the best batter on the Braves roster. The Associated Press also reported that Branch Rickey was following Worthington's hitting exploits and considering a deal with the Braves to reacquire the slugging outfielder.

Red's good showing in spring training earned him a spot in the Braves' starting outfield, replacing Lance Richbourg, who was moved to the infield. On April 20 Worthington was hit in the mouth by a foul ball that caromed off the netting behind home plate. The injury forced him to sit out the next three games. When he returned, Red did not miss a beat, lashing a triple in his first game back in the lineup. He continued to hit well so the Braves moved him to the cleanup spot in the batting order. *The Sporting News* observed, "Bob is one of the best of the Brave hitters and does very well in the pinches. He bats right-handed but does not seem to care if a right-hander is pitching."[9]

By the end of June, Worthington had been shifted from right field to left and was clubbing the ball at a .333 clip. He and fellow outfielders Wes Schulmerich (another rookie) and second-year man Wally Berger were the backbone of the Braves' offensive attack. A late-season swoon brought Worthington's average down to .297 but it was a solid year for the rookie. He was not a basestealing threat but he ran well enough to leg out 25 doubles and 10 triples. Defensively, he was sure-handed in the field and covered a lot of ground. In 1931 he led National League outfielders with a .988 fielding percentage and finished second with 8 outfield assists.

Worthington shook off any type of sophomore jinx and after 17 games in 1932 he was hitting .360 with four home runs. He cooled off a bit as the campaign wore on but he was still batting over .300 when a broken ankle, suffered sliding into third base in a game against Pittsburgh, ended his season on August 7. The Braves were in third place when Worthington was injured. He was hitting .303 with 35 doubles, 8 triples, 8 home runs and 61 RBIs. Without him the club faltered, ending up in fifth place.

When spring training began in early March 1933 at St. Petersburg, Florida, neither Worthington nor shortstop Billy Urbanski, was in camp on time. Braves manager Bill McKechnie was not happy, telling an Associated Press reporter, "If Urbanski and Worthington know what side their bread is buttered on, they won't do much quibbling this season."[10]

As it turned out, Red had gotten married in the offseason to his high-school sweetheart, Bernice Brown, and he was a few days late reporting to camp. His ankle had healed sufficiently over the winter and he appeared to be back in form. But when the season started he began suffering from debilitating dizzy spells, possibly vertigo, and was sent home after playing in only 17 games. In late June, Worthington had his tonsils and adenoids removed. Recuperating from these maladies, he missed the rest of the season. Once the 1934 season started, he was mainly used as a pinch-hitter and by late June his batting average was round .300. His bat cooled off during the next few months and Boston put him on waivers on September 11. The Cardinals, who were attempting to gain ground on the first-place New York Giants and trying to hold off the hard-charging Chicago Cubs, claimed Worthington.

On September 14 the Cardinals lost to the Giants 4-1 at the Polo Grounds. Worthington was sent up to pinch-hit for pitcher Bill Walker in the sixth inning and the Giants' Hal Shumacher struck him out. St. Louis went 13-2 down the stretch, edging out the Giants by two games for the pennant. Cardinals manager Frankie Frisch did not play Red in any other regular-season games or in the World Series. Sportswriter Jim McConnell suggested that the main reason Rickey signed Worthington was to keep the Cubs or Giants from picking him up during the tight pennant race.

Still under contract with the Cardinals in 1935, Worthington reported to spring training in Bradenton, Florida. Frisch informed the players that he would carry only five outfielders on his roster. Veterans Jack Rothrock and Ducky Medwick were guaranteed to make the team. That left Ernie Orsatti, Gene Moore, Johnny Winslett, Terry Moore, and Worthington to fight it out for the remaining three outfield spots.

Red pinch-hit and played the outfield in spring training and from all accounts, it appeared that he had a good chance of making the team. That all changed in early April when Worthington, Dizzy Dean, and Charlie Gelbert missed the team train at Dublin, Georgia. The three hastily rented a car and sped off to the team's next stop, Macon. When they arrived the next morning, Frisch was furious. He fined Dean $100 and Gelbert $50 and sent Worthington and Charlie Wilson, who had started trouble on the train, back to St Louis.

A few days later, the New York Yankees worked out a deal to acquire Worthington while allowing the Cardinals to retain the rights to his contract. The Yankees optioned Red to their Pacific Coast League team in Oakland. In July he was sent to the Mission Reds, who played in San Francisco. For the season, he slumped to .247.

In the offseason Rickey transferred Worthington to Houston. On March 26, 1936, he was traded from Houston to Sacramento of the Pacific Coast League for catcher Harold Doerr. Worthington seemed to rediscover his batting stroke with the Solons, hitting .306 in 127 games. Defensively, he played well, committing only three errors in the outfield. He also filled in as the manager when Bill Killefer was called home late in the season.

Worthington stayed on with Sacramento as a player and coach in 1937 but injuries limited him to 30 games in the outfield. Including pinch-hitting appearances, he finished what would be his last season in Organized Baseball with a respectable .304 batting average.

Worthington was released by the Solons in March 1938. He went on to work at a variety of jobs after baseball, including gardener and machinist, before serving as an Army warrant officer during World War II. After the war, he was employed at the Lucky Lager Brewing Company in Azusa, California.

In the fall of 1963 Worthington underwent surgery for a duodenal ulcer. Complications arose and he contracted pneumonia. He never recovered and died at the age of 57 on December 8, 1963, at Sawtelle Veterans Hospital in Los Angeles. His obituary in the *Los Angeles Times* noted that he was survived by a sister and two brothers.[11] Worthington's funeral Mass was held at All Souls Church in Alhambra and he was buried in San Gabriel Mission Cemetery.

Sources

Berkeley (California) *Daily Gazette*

Helena *(Montana)* Independent

Lawrence *(Kansas)* Journal World

Los Angeles Times

Pittsburgh Press

Rochester (New York) *Evening Journal and The Post Express*

The Sporting News

Sunday Morning Star (Wilmington, Delaware)

Syracuse Herald

Telegraph and Times Journal (Dubuque, Iowa)

Wikipedia.com

Baseball-reference.com

Retrosheet

San Gabriel Valley Tribune sports writer Jim McConnell, telephone interview, June 26, 2013.

Special Thanks:

Alhambra High School librarian Cathy Doran

Alhambra Historical Society

Sister Kathleen Callaway, Ramona convent secondary school

Bill Thomas, Loyola High School alumni relations director

San Gabriel Valley Tribune sports writer Jim McConnell

Notes

1 Cray L. Remington, "Red Worthington Is Young But He Knows Plenty About the Gentle Art of Filling an Outfield Position," *Rochester* (New York) *Evening Journal and The Post Express,* April 8, 1929, 17.

2 The 1940 US Census lists Worthington as a high-school graduate, but his draft registration card in 1942 lists his education as one year of high school. An article by *San Gabriel Valley Tribune* sportswriter Jim McConnell, published on July 6, 2010, called Worthington an alumnus of Alhambra High School. School librarian Cathy Doran went through every yearbook from 1921 through 1926 and found no record of Worthington ever attending the school. She checked the yearbooks' baseball team pictures and he was not present in any of them. McConnell told the author in a telephone interview that his research along with an interview with Max West (a former major leaguer and Alhambra resident) points to Worthington briefly attending Alhambra High School. Sister Kathleen Callaway, a Catholic historian, assisted me in tracking down possible Catholic schools in the Alhambra area that Worthington might have attended. Loyola High School in Los Angeles seemed a viable choice, but alumni relations director Bill Thomas reported that Worthington is not listed in the school's records. Further research throughout the Los Angeles school system yielded no information on Worthington's educational background.

3 The Mississippi Valley League was a Class D league that operated from 1922 through 1932. In 1933 the circuit upgraded to Class B status in its final year of existence.

4 *Syracuse Herald,* January 23, 1927, 47.

5 Syracuse's refusal to build a new ballpark led the Cardinals to sever ties with the city. St. Louis sold the Syracuse franchise to Frank Donnelly and a group of investors from Jersey City. The Cardinals then purchased the International League team in Rochester for a reported $130,000. The Syracuse players were transferred to Rochester and the Rochester team's roster from the previous year was sent to Jersey City. Rochester changed its name from the Tribe to the Red Wings in honor of its new ownership.

6 *The Sporting News,* March 8, 1928, 2.

7 *Helena* (Montana) *Independent,* March 17, 1929, 8.

8 Southworth missed a number of games with a broken finger. In addition, he was called home during the season after his wife lost twins during childbirth.

9 *The Sporting News,* May 7, 1931.

10 "McKechnie Warns Red Worthington to Watch His Step," *Rochester Evening Journal and The Post Express,* March 7, 1933, 12.

11 Worthington's wife, Bernice, was not mentioned in the *Los Angeles Times* death notice or obituary, nor were any children mentioned. I contacted the San Gabriel Mission Cemetery, the San Gabriel Cemetery and a number of other Los Angeles cemeteries in search of Bernice Worthington's grave but I was unable to find any information regarding her interment. The last mention of Bernice Worthington was in the 1942 Alhambra City directory.

Sam Breadon

By Mark Armour

IN THE LONG and successful history of the St. Louis Cardinals baseball club, few people have been more important than Sam Breadon, who owned the team for 27 years and presided over nine league pennants and six World Series titles. Much of the club's success has been attributed to Branch Rickey, the team's genius general manager, who built baseball's first and largest farm system, revolutionizing the relationship between the major leagues and minor leagues and turning the Cardinals organization into a model of player development and instruction. But Breadon and Rickey worked together, and it was Breadon who funded Rickey's farm system and lobbied for its legality. Breadon sold the Cardinals in 1947, and there have been very few baseball owners who left such a legacy of success.

Samuel Breadon (pronounced BRAY-din), one of eight children, was born on July 26, 1876, to William and Jane (Wilson) Breadon. "I was born in New York and grew up in the old Ninth Ward in old Greenwich Village," recalled Sam. "Near the docks. Nothing fancy, a tough neighborhood. You had to be able to handle yourself, or you did not do so well."[1] His mother was Scottish, and his father an Irish drayman who died when Sam was a young boy. After finishing grammar school Sam dropped out to help his mother, and as a young adult he held a steady job as a bank clerk on Wall Street, earning $125 a month. In his youth he played basketball and football and boxed.

About 1902 Breadon moved to St. Louis to join two New York friends, brothers, who had gone west to open an automobile dealership and garage. It was somewhat of a risk, but young Breadon was attracted by the possibilities of the new industry. Within a year or two the brothers got wind that Breadon was looking to open his own shop, and they fired him. Some fast talking got him a concession to sell popcorn at the 1904 World's Fair, held in St. Louis. This earned him enough money to open up his own garage. A wealthy customer, impressed with his work and honesty, offered him an executive position in the Western Automobile Company, and Breadon worked his way up to the very top, buying the business himself. By 1917 Breadon and a partner owned a distributorship of Pierce-Arrow automobiles, which he held for the next 20 years.[2]

Meanwhile, Breadon had become a rabid fan of the St. Louis Cardinals, a generally struggling club in the National League. He bought into the club in the mid-1910s, and gradually increased his stake to help the struggling ownership group. In early 1919 he was on the board of directors, and that fall he was named president. As a condition of accepting this position, he worked on his partners until he was able to purchase enough stock to get 51 percent of the club. He planned to run the team, not just the board. The Cardinals had joined the National League in 1892, but had finished as high as third place just twice in their first 29 years in the league. They were also heavily in debt. At the time of Breadon's ascension, Rickey was the club's president, while serving the club

The Cardinals' majority owner from 1920-1947, the franchise flourished under Breadon's leadership, winning nine pennants and six world championships.

as both field manager and business manager, essentially also acting as what we now call a general manager. Breadon left Rickey in the latter two positions, while also offering him a piece of the club and naming him a vice president. After the club finished sixth in 1924 and started the next year 13-25, Breadon removed Rickey as manager, leaving him to run the club off the field. "In time, Branch, you will see that I am doing you a great favor," Breadon told a disappointed Rickey. "You can now devote yourself fully to player development and scouting."[3]

The two men worked together for more than two decades, turning a struggling club into one of the more successful in the game. Their relationship grew more contentious over the years, but there can be little doubt that they needed each other. As historian Lee Lowenfish wrote, "Under their arrangement, there was no doubt that Breadon was the boss who controlled the purse strings and Rickey was the employee who engineered the baseball transactions. However, unlike many baseball owners who get so intoxicated with their power that they think they understand the mechanics of the game itself, Breadon deferred completely to Branch Rickey on the nuts and bolts of player development."[4]

Breadon's first important decision after taking control in 1920 was to sign a lease to play in Sportsman's Park, as a tenant of Phil Ball's St. Louis Browns. Cardinals Park, formerly Robison Park, had been the Cardinals' home since 1893 but was both a firetrap and in danger of collapsing. "The building inspector, who was a friend of mine, said he was afraid he couldn't let us go another season with those stands. I couldn't blame him," Breadon said.[5] He dismantled the ballpark, and sold the property and land for $275,000, which got the club out of debt and provided operating capital for the years ahead. "It was the most important move I ever made on the Cardinals," Breadon later said. "It gave us money to clean up our debts, and something more to work with. Without it, we never could have purchased the minor-league clubs, which were the beginning of our farm system."[6]

As the new Cardinals manager, Breadon named 29-year-old Rogers Hornsby, their great second baseman, who had been the best player in the National League for several years. Hornsby made Breadon look smart right away, as he rallied the club to a more respectable fourth-place showing, all the while hitting .403 and winning his second Triple Crown. The next year Hornsby led the club to a first-place showing, and a seven-game triumph over the Yankees in the World Series. It was the first championship for the Cardinals since their days in the American Association in the 1880s.

Late in the 1926 season, Breadon and Hornsby got into an argument about a series of in-season exhibition games Breadon had arranged, which Hornsby thought was more than his tired players needed. During a heated disagreement, Hornsby apparently used choice words to insult his boss. Not forgetting the slight, after the season Breadon traded his pennant-winning hero-manager to the New York Giants for star second baseman Frankie Frisch and pitcher Jimmy Ring. Though Cardinals fans were livid, they soon learned that Breadon and Rickey were generally willing to trade the team's most popular players if they thought they were nearing the end of their peak years. After Hornsby, the Cardinals later dealt Dizzy Dean, Joe Medwick, Jim Bottomley, Chick Hafey, Johnny Mize, Mort Cooper, Walker Cooper, and many others. Rickey was able to find young replacements with their careers ahead of them, and the pennants piled up.

Though Breadon gave Rickey a fair amount of authority, he followed the team closely on a daily basis, and often left to himself the decision to hire and fire the Cardinals manager. In fact, he had a quick trigger in this area. Besides Hornsby, he replaced Bill McKechnie just a half season after he had won a pennant, and then Gabby Street a year and a half after Street's team had won two more pennants. Not counting interim managers, Breadon presided over nine managerial changes in 27 years despite tremendous on-field success.

It was Rickey who first conceived of the idea of operating a farm system, but it was Breadon who paid for it. Rickey convinced his boss that the club could save money by signing and developing its own players on its own minor-league clubs rather than paying the high prices demanded from independent minor-league teams. And it was Breadon who had to fight for the right to operate the farm system in the major-league boardrooms, a fight that occasionally grew contentious since Commissioner Kenesaw Mountain Landis was adamantly opposed to the idea.

By 1940 the Cardinals owned or had working agreements with 32 minor-league teams, controlling more than 600 players. One of the brilliant side effects of this extensive system was that Rickey could both sell the developed players the Cardinals did not need, and also sell Cardinals stars once they hit their early 30s, knowing he had other players ready to step in. Breadon and Rickey traded the 28-year-old Dean to the Cubs in 1938 for $185,000 and three players—Dean had hurt his arm the previous year after altering his pitching motion due to the foot injury he had suffered during the 1937 All-Star Game, and Rickey thought he might not return to his old self. Most importantly, Rickey had convinced Breadon that the system could produce new players. It always had, and it would again. During their long run of success from 1926 to 1949, when they finished first or second 18 times, the Cardinals never purchased a player from another organization.[7]

Rickey generally got all the credit for the moves that worked out well, but he also developed a reputation from his players and the press for being cheap or heartless. But Breadon, who gave little indication that he desired more attention for himself, deserves to share both the credit and the reputation—he set the salary budgets and approved the ballplayer sales Rickey was praised or derided for. "There was never a decision made in which I didn't have the final say," Breadon later said. "Many of Rickey's moves I approved, others I rejected."[8]

By the late 1930s, Breadon had sold his auto business, making the Cardinals his sole business interest. Coincidentally, after winning five pennants in nine years, in 1935 the Cardinals began a seven-year pennant drought. During this period Breadon began to meddle a bit more in the affairs of the team, including the firing of a few Rickey protégés in the farm system, causing a gradual deterioration of their relationship. In 1938 Commissioner Landis freed more than 70 Cardinals farmhands, claiming that the Cardinals controlled players on more than one team in some minor leagues, allowing the Cardinals to affect their pennant races. Breadon was apparently embarrassed by this decision, while Rickey was upset that Breadon did not fight it. In 1939 Breadon, who prided himself on maintaining great health and physical appearance, suffered a severe spinal injury when he was thrown from a horse. His recovery was difficult and slow, and Lowenfish opined that Breadon never completely recovered physically or emotionally from the accident.[9]

In February 1941, Breadon informed the board of directors, which included Rickey, that he would not be renewing Rickey's contract after the 1942 season. His stated reason was that the current economic climate, including America's possible entrance into a world war, made Rickey's large salary ($50,000, plus large bonuses for his share of player sales) an unwanted burden. This was likely part of Breadon's reasoning, but the two men's deteriorating relationship and the club's failure to win pennants for the previous six years were surely factors as well. The Cardinals lost a tough pennant race to the Dodgers in 1941, and then won the World Series in 1942, with Rickey still running the team. Rickey moved to Brooklyn to run the Dodgers, with more historic accomplishments ahead of him. In their remaining years as rival executives, the two men always spoke kindly of each other, at least publicly.

While the Cardinals were having another great year in 1943, Breadon fended off any attempts to mitigate Rickey's previous contributions. "I don't want to be placed in a position of 'crowing' about the way things are going in the wake of Rickey's departure," Breadon said. "After all, we had a good foundation built. But I've seen all angles of the game for the last quarter of a century and if I didn't know something about running a ballclub now, I'd be pretty damned dumb."[10]

Breadon's reputation as a tight-fisted owner only grew once he became more the public face of the team. Brothers Mort (pitcher) and Walker (catcher) Cooper held out in 1945 before capitulating just before Opening Day. Walker was soon in the armed forces, but Breadon traded Mort to the Boston Braves in late May. When Jorge Pasquel of the Mexican League plucked several major-league players in 1946, in defiance of the long-held reserve clause, it was the disgruntled Cardinals who suffered the biggest losses—star pitcher Max Lanier, pitcher Fred Martin, and infielder Lou Klein.

The Cardinals finished the 1946 regular season tied with the Dodgers, forcing a three-game pennant playoff. At a banquet held after the final regular season game, Breadon was chided from the lectern by writer Roy Stockton. "It looks, Sam," said Stockton, "as if you sliced the baloney too thin this time."[11] Breadon shrugged it off, and the Cardinals went on to beat the Dodgers and then the Red Sox in the World Series. It was Breadon's sixth championship.

In November 1947 Breadon sold his majority share (75 percent) of the Cardinals to a group headed by his longtime friend Robert F. Hannegan and Fred Saigh, Jr., a prominent St. Louis attorney. The price for Breadon's shares was reported to be $3 million, the highest such figure in baseball history, and a pretty fair return on his initial $2,000 investment. "This is not a pleasant day for me," Breadon said, "but every year I am less sufficient and at my age it is time to quit."[12] He later told Dan Daniel, "I am seventy years of age [actually 71]. I am in fine condition. As far as I know I might live to be ninety. But I felt that, in justice to my family, I should put my estate in order. This meant selling my stock in the Cardinals."[13]

Despite his reputation as a tight-fisted owner, Breadon could be very generous. One of the stars of his first World Series team was the great pitcher Pete Alexander, whom the Cardinals got off waivers in June 1926 only to see him return to stardom for a few more years. Alexander had a difficult life after his career was over, and at the time of his death in 1950 it was revealed that the Cardinals (under Breadon) had for many years paid him $50 per month, which Alex thought was a pension, to allow him to live a little better.[14] In 1948 Mort Cooper, having washed out of baseball soon after Breadon discarded him, was arrested for passing three bad checks. Breadon, who was retired, paid his bond, and later talked the Cubs' Phil Wrigley into signing Cooper and giving him one last shot.[15]

Breadon's marriage to Josephine in 1905 yielded a daughter, Frances. He married Rachel (Ray) Wilson in 1912, and the couple adopted their own daughter, Janet. Breadon was said to be the life of many parties in his younger days, and he earned the nickname "Singing Sam" because he often sang in barbershop quartets. Before his accident on his horse in 1939, he was an avid swimmer and horseman, and worked out by taking groundballs during the Cardinals' spring-training season. By the time he reached middle age he was more interested in golf and retiring early so he could read in bed.[16]

Breadon succumbed to cancer on May 8, 1949, at age 72. He had been a patient at St. Joseph's Hospital in St. Louis for several weeks. He was survived by his wife and daughters. At his request, there was no funeral service, and his ashes were dropped from a plane over the Mississippi River. Branch Rickey, who worked for Breadon for two decades, said he was "deeply grieved over the passing of one of the game's finest sportsmen and outstanding businessmen. We always got along splendidly, even after I returned to Brooklyn."[17]

In the ensuing decades, Breadon's role as the head of one of baseball's best organizations has been often overlooked. The most recent attempt to rectify this came in 2012 when Breadon was on the ballot considered by the Hall of Fame's Veteran's Committee, though he was not elected. The Cardinals have had much success in their history, and their 11 World Series victories are topped only by the New York Yankees. But it is worth remembering that their success began when Sam Breadon bought the club, and that six of the 11 titles came during his reign.

Notes

1   Daniel M. Daniel, "Sam Breadon Left Indelible Imprint on Baseball Operation," *Baseball*, July 1949, 261.

2   Lee Lowenfish, *Branch Rickey—Baseball's Ferocious Gentleman* (Lincoln: University of Nebraska Press, 2009), 120.

3   Lowenfish, *Branch Rickey*, 150.

4   Lowenfish, *Branch Rickey*, 122.

5   John Kieran, "How to Buy a Ball Club," *New York Times*, undated clipping in Breadon's file at the National Baseball Library.

6   Mark Tomasik, "Top 5 reasons why Sam Breadon should be in Hall," retrosimba.com, November 15, 2012.

7   Warren Corbett, "Eddie Dyer," SABR's Baseball Biography Project, sabr.org/bioproject.

8   Fred Lieb, "Flashbacks—Sam Breadon," *The Sporting News*, November 18, 1943.

9   Lowenfish, *Branch Rickey*, 298.

10 Dick Farrington, "Breadon Nixes 'Mr. Brain' Idea as Birds Soar Without Rickey," *The Sporting News*, June 24, 1943.

11 Bob Broeg, *Memories of a Hall of Fame Sportswriter* (Champaign, Illinois: Sports Publishing LLC, 1995), 157.

12 Associated Press, "Not Pleasant, But It Is Time to Quit," *New York World Telegram*, November 24, 1947

13 Daniel M. Daniel, "Sam Breadon Left Indelible Imprint On Baseball Operation," *Baseball*, July 1949, 261.

14 Jan Finkel, "Pete Alexander," SABR's Baseball Biography Project, sabr.org/bioproject.

15 Gregory H. Wolf, "Mort Cooper," SABR's Baseball Biography Project, sabr.org/bioproject.

16 J. Roy Stockton, "Singing Sam, the Cut-Rate Man," *The Saturday Evening Post*, February 22, 1947, 140.

17 "Baseball Mourns Breadon," *New York World Telegram*, May 11, 1949, page unknown.

Bill DeWitt

By Dwayne Isgrig

(The sound of knocking on an office door)
"Come in."
"Sir, you asked me keep an eye out for a boy in the ranks who looked like he had the makings of someone you could use around the office; a boy who can be trusted."
"Yes."
"Well, sir, I think I've found one. He's a hard worker. Very ambitious, reliable, has a good head for math."
"Yes, yes. Go on."
"This boy is a real go-getter and he wants to work all summer. It can't hurt that he's a big baseball fan."
"Well, Judas Priest! Send the boy in."

BACK IN 1916 a teenager was working at Sportsman's Park in St. Louis as a soda vendor to bring in extra money to help support his family. The concessions manager at the ballpark found the teenager to be a good worker and recommended him to the business manager of the St. Louis Browns. The teenager had a meeting with the business manager and he made a good impression on the executive. This good impression served as a steppingstone for the young man to move from the ranks of the concession workers at the ballpark and into a new job as an errand boy and switchboard operator in the front office of the Browns. This change in station for the ambitious young man led to lifelong employment in the business of baseball, a change that eventually led to the ownership of two major-league baseball teams.

The young soda vendor promoted to office boy in this real-life Horatio Alger story was William Orville DeWitt, Sr. and the business manager of the Browns was Branch Rickey.

DeWitt was born in St. Louis on August 3, 1902. His parents were William J. DeWitt, a butcher or grocer, and Lulu (Sowash) DeWitt. Young Bill had a brother, Charles (Charley), who was also a baseball fan. Charley and Bill grew up on the north side of the city and they were never far from the city's two main ballparks (Robison Field and Sportsman's Park). The brothers loved to play baseball growing up but as they got older their family needed the income two teenage boys could earn, so they went to work at the ballpark in order to be close the game they loved.[1]

It didn't take Rickey long to see that Bill had "the right kind of fiber for development" as an office worker for the Browns. The Mahatma encouraged DeWitt to better himself through education. "There is no future in any business for a boy who lacks education," Rickey told the young DeWitt. And so DeWitt, who did not complete high school because of his job, went to night school to further himself.[2]

In 1917, when Rickey had a falling-out with Browns' owner Philip de Catesby Ball, he left the Browns to take a position with Sam

A protégé of Branch Rickey's, Dewitt rose within the ranks of the front office. Eventually, he became general manager of the Browns and Tigers and the Reds. He became owner of the Reds shortly thereafter. His son William Dewitt Jr. is the current principal owner and managing partner of the St. Louis Cardinals.

Breadon in the Cardinals' front office. The young DeWitt followed his mentor to the Cardinals.[3]

World War I was a time of uncertainty in professional baseball with many players being drafted by the military or enlisting. Rickey left to serve in the Army. While Rickey was away in the service, DeWitt found a job as an assistant cashier and stenographer for the J.I. Case Threshing Machine Company in St. Louis.[4]

After the war Rickey returned to the Cardinals and DeWitt went back to work with his mentor. With Rickey's encouragement, he furthered his education, first at St. Louis University, then at Washington University, then back to St. Louis University Law School. In his final year at St. Louis University, DeWitt was elected president of the Student Conclave and was appointed to Alpha Sigma Nu, a Jesuit honor society, even though he was not a Catholic.[5] (He passed the bar exam in 1931.)

In 1926 Sam Breadon, owner of the Cardinals, promoted Rickey's "boy" to the post of treasurer. The Cardinals were coming into one of the most successful periods in the history of the team. Rickey's farm system was beginning to pay big dividends and DeWitt had grown up with the system from the earliest days of its inception. The team won its first pennant in 1926 and defeated Babe Ruth and the New York Yankees in the World Series. The Cardinals won the pennant again in 1928, 1930, 1931, and 1934, with World Series wins in 1931 and 1934 — a very successful run with DeWitt in charge of the team's wallet.

Looking back to his duties in the Cardinals' first fall classic, DeWitt remembered in 1944, "Making arrangements and handling tickets in that Series was quite a job. The Cardinals have been in eight now and have a well-oiled machine. But in 1926, everything was new; we were new to World's Series, and had a crazy town to deal with. But somehow we got by without disappointing too many persons."[6]

In 1934 the Cardinals won the World Series in seven games over the Detroit Tigers with the colorful hurler Dizzy Dean emerging as a national celebrity on the famed Gas House Gang. His celebrity status turned into many lucrative product endorsements for Dean, a young man from humble beginnings in rural Arkansas.

By this time DeWitt was well-established in the ways of law and business and he served as a booking agent for Dean's postseason ventures, among them a barnstorming tour, product advertisements and a Hollywood contract for a B movie featuring Dizzy and his brother Paul (*Dizzy and Daffy*, Vitaphone Corporation, 1934). These ventures netted an estimated $13,000 for Dean during 1933 and 1934. (His salary from the Cardinals for the 1934 season was $7,500.) As Dean's agent, DeWitt was supposed to receive 33 percent of the earnings. At some point there developed some ill feelings or bad blood over the business arrangement. DeWitt sued Dean to recover his fees. Commissioner Kenesaw Mountain Landis became involved in the dispute. Dean complained to Commissioner Landis that 33 percent was too high. Landis agreed and cut DeWitt's proceeds to 10 percent.[7]

In 1936, after the death of longtime Browns owner Philip de Catesby Ball, Rickey helped Ball's estate find a buyer for the team, an ownership group headed by St. Louis financier Donald Barnes. Barnes hired DeWitt as his general manager. (For his help in putting the deal together, Rickey received a $25,000 fee.[8]) To help shore up revenues for the Browns, the new owners finalized a deal to install lights at Sportsman's Park. DeWitt and the front office also worked to build a farm system.[9]

The Browns lived on a shoestring and struggled through the years. In 1941 DeWitt and Barnes hired Luke Sewell as manager, and the Browns began a long climb toward respectability that culminated in 1944 with the team's first pennant. In an all-St. Louis World Series, the Browns lost to the Cardinals in six games. The Browns also suffered financially because Commissioner Landis decreed that half of the World Series receipts would go to the Army and Navy Relief Fund. It "really was a jolt to us financially, because … we needed that money," Barnes said.[10]

DeWitt was named Executive of the Year by *The Sporting News*.[11]

The Browns were unable to repeat their success in 1945, finishing in third place. One of the Browns' players in 1945 was Pete Gray, a one-armed outfielder. Some critics of the signing believed DeWitt intended Gray to serve as a drawing card. Gray appeared in 77 games for the Browns, batting only .218, and was released after the season.[12]

But the major development for the team that year was Donald Barnes's sale of his interest in the team. DeWitt remained as vice president and general manager for the new majority owner, Richard "Dick" Muckerman, who owned ice and coal businesses.[13]

In 1946, with World War II over and front-line players returned from the service, the Browns fell to seventh place. Sewell resigned shortly before the season ended. He was succeeded by Muddy Ruel, a former catcher and pitching coach who was a special assistant to Commissioner A.B. "Happy" Chandler.[14] DeWitt had dealt away most of the stars from the 1944 pennant winners so Ruel was working with a new crop of players in 1947. Initially things appeared promising for Ruel and the Browns in 1947. By the end of the first half of the season, the Browns were mired in the American League cellar.

In July 1947 Bill Veeck and the Cleveland Indians signed Larry Doby to integrate the American League. Less than two weeks later, DeWitt followed in the footsteps of his mentor, Brooklyn GM Branch Rickey, and signed two players from the Negro Leagues, Henry "Hank" Thompson and Willard "Home Run" Brown, both from the Kansas City Monarchs. The Browns also took a 30-day option to purchase Lorenzo "Piper" Davis from the Birmingham Black Barons. (A fourth African American player, Charles "Chuck" Harmon, was also signed by the Browns and assigned to the team's Class C farm team in Gloversville-Johnstown, New York.) The event was newsworthy in a city with traditional ties to the South. The *St. Louis Globe-Democrat* reported the news at the very top of the front page with the bold headline: "Browns Sign 3 Negro Ballplayers."[15]

By late August DeWitt's bold move was not going well. Thompson and Brown got off to a slow start with the Browns. The clubhouse environment was not as welcoming as it could have been. One of the Browns' regulars, Paul Lehner, a native of Alabama, skipped the team briefly and bristled at the prospects of playing on an integrated team.[16] Thompson (batting .256) and Brown (.179) were released. The Browns finished the season in last place with a record of 59 wins and 95 losses and Ruel was fired.[17]

In 1948, under new manager Zack Taylor, the results were much the same as they were in 1947, 59 wins and 94 losses, though, thanks to the ineptitude of the White Sox and Senators, the Browns were able to move up to sixth place. The harsh economic reality of the expenses involved with being the majority owner of a losing team was setting in for Richard Muckerman, the ice and coal baron.

In early February 1949, Muckerman sold his interest in the Browns (56 percent of the stock in the team) and DeWitt and his brother Charley became the principal owners of the team. The deal cost the brothers about $1 million. The brothers who once sold soda and peanuts at Sportsman's Park now owned the team and the ballpark.[18]

No matter the ownership, with the exceptional bright spot of the 1944 World Series year, the Browns' troubles always seemed to follow a cycle of poor attendance, a poor finish in the league standings, and the trade or sale of good players during the offseason. During a time when a team's revenue relied heavily on attendance, the Browns were always in a downward financial cycle. Of his many trades, DeWitt once said, "I always had someone knocking at my door to make a deal, which is fun, but when you're forced to make a deal, that takes all the fun out of it."[19]

The DeWitt brothers struggled as owners in a city that no longer had a population large enough (or willing enough) to support two baseball teams. In the early years of the 20th century, St. Louis had been the fourth largest US city in population. By 1950 it was the eighth largest. Under Rickey's guidance the Cardinals had become the dominant team with the St. Louis fan base. The Cardinals won nine pennants in 20 years while the Browns won the pennant only once. It was only natural that the team with the most success on the field would have the most success in attracting fans to the ballpark. The Browns owned Sportsman's Park and the Cardinals were tenants, beneficiaries of a low-rent lease dating back to Rickey's days with the Cardinals in the early 1920s. The DeWitts went as far as trying to evict the Cardinals from Sportsman's Park before the 1949 season, or to force a new, more beneficial lease. In the end, the Browns were unsuccessful.[20]

The brothers were forced to look for other ways to improve the Browns. Bill DeWitt was an early proponent of increasing the number of night games teams were allowed to play. He felt more night games league-wide would boost the Browns' home attendance and earn them more of a share of road-game revenue. DeWitt also attempted to work out deals for regulating television rights to baseball games in two-team cities in a way that could benefit the Browns.[21]

During spring training in 1950, the team made headlines by hiring Dr. David Tracy to use hypnosis on the players to help them relax and become better ballplayers. Hypnosis was supposed to help players on a losing team feel like winners and lift the team out of the cellar. Though it is not clear to what extent Dr. Tracy and his techniques of hypnosis helped the team, the Browns finished in seventh place in 1950.[22]

Unable to turn the Browns around in their two years as owners, in June 1951 the DeWitts sold their interest in the team to an ownership group headed by the indefatigable showman Bill Veeck for $1.5 million. Bill DeWitt went from being president of the club to vice president under new team president Veeck.[23]

Despite much fanfare, promotions, and publicity stunts, even Veeck was unable to save the Browns. In 1953 he sold Sportsman's Park to the Cardinals, who were now owned by August A. Busch, Jr. of the Anheuser-Busch beer empire. Veeck knew he could not match the financial resources of Busch and his brewery. Veeck explored his options for moving the Browns to another city, such as Milwaukee or Baltimore, but he was prevented from doing so due by the other team owners.[24] Veeck sold his interest in the Browns at the end of the 1953 season, and the American League allowed the team to relocate to Baltimore. DeWitt stayed with the team during the transition period but the new owners hired Art Ehlers in October 1953 to be the new general manager.[25]

The resilient DeWitt was out of a job only a short time. In April 1954 the New York Yankees hired him to serve as assistant general manager under George Weiss. DeWitt was to assist Weiss in player contract negotiations and serve as a general troubleshooter. Some baseball observers speculated that DeWitt was being groomed as a successor to Weiss. The assumption was that Weiss would retire shortly and DeWitt would succeed him. But in 1956 Weiss signed a new contract, and DeWitt found another opportunity.[26] He was named the coordinator of the commissioner's Professional Baseball Fund Committee, which helped minor-league teams in economic peril. Then in September 1959 he became the president of the Detroit Tigers, who were in a tumultuous transitional period after the Briggs family sold the team. DeWitt became the fourth president of the team in three years.

In Detroit DeWitt left an indelible mark on baseball history by pulling off one of the game's most unusual trades. In August 1960, he helped engineer a trade of managers with Cleveland Indians. The Tigers' Jimmy Dykes was sent to Cleveland in exchange for Joe Gordon. Other important trades DeWitt made that had a lasting impact for the Tigers were sending Harvey Kuenn to Cleveland for slugger Rocky Colavito and acquiring Norm Cash from Cleveland in exchange for Steve Demeter.[27] One of DeWitt's unheralded but significant moves in Detroit was having the pay toilets removed from the women's restrooms at the ballpark.

Despite some improvements in the team, and a fair amount of controversy over some of his work, after only one year on the job he was forced out as president in October 1960. John Fetzer, head of the majority ownership group of the Tigers, became the president of the team. DeWitt, who was working under a three-year contract, was to be demoted. Instead, DeWitt chose to leave under amicable terms after declining the opportunity to serve as Fetzer's assistant.[28]

Once again, DeWitt was not out of a job for long. About two weeks later he became general manager of the Cincinnati Reds. With his jelp, the Reds won the National League pennant in 1961. They lost to the Yankees in the World Series. In March 1962 DeWitt purchased the Reds from the Crosley Foundation for $4.6 million. (Owner Powel Crosley, Jr. had died the previous March.) Soon after the sale a controversy developed. Ohio Attorney General Mark McElroy moved to reopen the sale of the team as part of an investigation involving the claim of Joseph F. Rippe, a Cincinnati realtor, and a group of prospective buyers who supposedly had offered $5.5 million for the Reds. Eventually the controversy died down and there was no change to DeWitt's ownership of the team.[29]

In the years to come, DeWitt planted the seeds of a team that would grow into the Big Red Machine of the 1970s, signing Pete Rose and Johnny Bench. The Reds finished in third place in 1962, and in fifth place in 1963. The team came close to winning the pennant in 1964 but fell short in a tight four-team race that was won by the Cardinals on the final day of the season. The Reds and the Phillies tied for second place. During the season, the Reds' cancer-stricken manager Fred Hutchinson, was replaced by Dick Sisler as interim manager. Hutchinson died on November 12, 1964.[30]

In 1965 the Reds fell to fourth place and DeWitt began to trade away players. During the December 1965 baseball meetings, he made a deal that will be remembered by many Reds fans as one of the worst trades in the history of the team. DeWitt traded the former National League MVP and All-Star outfielder Frank Robinson to the Baltimore Orioles in exchange for pitchers Milt Pappas and Jack Baldschun and outfielder Dick Simpson. In 1966 the Reds fell to seventh place while Robinson won the Triple Crown and led the Orioles to the American League pennant and a World Series championship. After Robinson had been named American League MVP for 1966 and World Series MVP, Arthur Daley of the *New York Times* called DeWitt's trade of Robbie to the Orioles "the most colossal trading blunder in history"

In December 1966 DeWitt sold the Reds to a local ownership group that included the *Cincinnati Inquirer* and Cincinnati Gas and Electric Company. (Another member of the ownership group was DeWitt's son, Bill DeWitt, Jr.) A major factor in DeWitt's decision to sell the team was the ongoing negotiations to build a new stadium downtown for football and baseball that would require the Reds to sign a 40-year lease. DeWitt later admitted he could not, in good faith, make such a long-term commitment in Cincinnati.[31]

DeWitt was out of a baseball for a short time, though he was not entirely out of sports. He and his son held a 40 percent share of the ownership of the Kentucky Colonels of the American Basketball Association. The two also headed a financial group that owned the Cincinnati Stingers of the World Hockey Association.[32]

During this time, DeWitt almost ended up in Seattle twice. After the expansion Seattle Pilots spent one season (1969) in Seattle, and then faced financial and legal troubles, it was proposed to the American League that DeWitt be brought in to run the team with $2 million in funds from the American League. The plan did not carry, partly because of DeWitt's other financial and business obligations at the time. Then, in 1971, after the Pilots relocated to Milwaukee, DeWitt looked at Seattle again. This time he scouted out opportunities to place another team in Seattle. DeWitt and, his former associate with the St. Louis Browns, Rudy Schaffer, explored the possibility of making Seattle the home for a National League expansion team in two or three years. One aspect of this plan involved moving Eugene of the Pacific Coast League to Sicks' Stadium in Seattle in the interim until Seattle could build a new stadium and secure a team in the National League. In the end, the DeWitt-Schaffer plan for Seattle never materialized.[33]

A few years later, in 1975, DeWitt was reunited with Bill Veeck. He was an investor and chairman of the Chicago White Sox from 1975 to 1981. DeWitt's involvement with Veeck's ownership group was instrumental in keeping the White Sox in Chicago at a time when the American League had approved moving the team to Seattle.

On March 3, 1982, DeWitt died in his adopted hometown of Cincinnati at the age of 81. His funeral was held in St. Louis and he is buried at Oak Grove Cemetery in suburban St. Louis County.[34]

Bill DeWitt was an important presence in major-league baseball for his entire adult life. He spent time in both leagues with six teams in a variety of positions. He was an owner and general manager and an executive for Organized Baseball. Teams DeWitt was involved with won nine pennants over the course of his career.

One of the hallmarks of DeWitt's career was that he always found himself behind the eight ball financially and had to innovate in order to make ends meet. St.

Louis sportswriter Bob Broeg summed it up: DeWitt "always suffered from the financial shorts, but maneuvered wisely and well to stay alive, selling off stars and picking a playing plum in the process." Along the way he generally came out all right. He built a nice nest egg for himself with the sale of the Browns in 1951 and also with the sale of the Reds in 1966. In both cases, he bought the teams when the price was low and sold them for a higher price. DeWitt also must have been good at networking in the game because when one job fell through, he was never unemployed for long. From a poor boy in North St. Louis selling soda pop at the ballpark to help his family make ends meet, to a club owner wheeling and dealing in the millions, DeWitt worked himself up the corporate ladder in the world of sports with a lot of hard work and some guidance from his mentor Branch Rickey.[35]

A testament to DeWitt's enduring legacy in the game is the fact that William O. DeWitt, Jr. and William O. DeWitt, III became the owners of the St. Louis Cardinals.

DeWitt was involved with or contributed to many charities including the Boys Club of Cincinnati, the 100 Club of Cincinnati, the Boy Scouts of America, and the St. Louis Society for the Blind. He was honored by the National Recreation and Park Association and the Hamilton County (Ohio) Hall of Fame for donating money to build youth baseball fields in the Cincinnati area.[36]

DeWitt once said, "I'm 100 percent baseball, I love the game. I've been in baseball since I was in knee pants, and don't think I could be happy in anything else." DeWitt lived those words over the course of his life, spending approximately 65 years working in the game.[37]

After DeWitt died, Bill Veeck summed up the career of his longtime friend and business partner: "Bill DeWitt was the most underrated operator in baseball. No man I can think of served longer in the game's management end."[38]

Notes

1 U.S. Census; Missouri Birth Records; Gould's City Directory for St. Louis; *The Sporting News*.

2 Arthur Mann, *Branch Rickey: American in Action* (New York: Riverside Press, 1957); Oral history interview with William O. DeWitt, Sr. for the A.B. Chandler Oral History Project of the University of Kentucky Library; *The Sporting News*, March 19, 1936.

3 *The Sporting News*, March 19, 1936.

4 Ibid.

5 *The Sporting News*, December 22, 1948, and February 9, 1949.

6 *The Sporting News*, December 28, 1944.

7 Baseball-almanac.com/players/player.php?p=deandi01; Arthur Mann, *Branch Rickey: American in Action* (New York: Houghton Mifflin, 1957); Vince Staten, *Ol' Diz: A Biography of Dizzy Dean* (New York: Harper Collins, 1992); *St. Louis Globe-Democrat*, November 23, 1934; *The Sporting News*, November 29, 1936.

8 Fred Lieb, *The Baltimore Orioles* (Carbondale, Illinois: Southern Illinois University Press, 2005); Arthur Mann, *Branch Rickey*; *The Sporting News*, November 19, 1936, and May 4, 1944.

9 *St. Louis Star-Times*, November 13, 1936; *The Sporting News*, January 7, 1937.

10 University of Kentucky Oral History Interview

11 *The Sporting News*, December 28, 1944.

12 *The Sporting News*, November 23, 1944; *The Washington Post*, November 21, 1945; retrosheet.org/boxesetc/G/Pgray101.htm

13 *St. Louis Globe-Democrat*, August 10, 1945; *St. Louis Star-Times*, August 10, 1945; *The Sporting News*, August 16, 1945.

14 *Baseball Magazine*, December 1946; *New York Times*, September 22, 1946, *The Sporting News*, September 25, 1946.

15 *St. Louis Globe-Democrat*, July 18, 1947.

16 Ibid.; *St. Louis Post-Dispatch*, July 18, 1947; *St. Louis Star-Times*, July 19, 1947.

17 *St. Louis Post-Dispatch*, November 4, 1947; *The Sporting News*, November 12, 1947.

18 *Chicago Daily Tribune*, February 3, 1949; *New York Times*, February 3, 1949; *St. Louis Star-Times*, February 3, 1949.

19 *The Sporting News*, March 20, 1982.

20 *Chicago Daily Tribune*, December 20, 1949; *New York Times*, April 19, 1949; *St. Louis Star-Times*, December 7, 1948; *The Sporting News*, March 16, 1949.

21 Associated Press, February 5, 1949; *The Sporting News*, December 17, 1947, and December 22, 1948.

22 *Los Angeles Times*, March 1, 1950; *The Sporting News*, March 15, 1950.

23 *Chicago Daily Tribune*, June 22, 1951; *New York Times*, July 4, 1951.

24 Fred Nichols, *The Final Season* (St. Louis: The St. Louis Browns Historical Society, 1991); *The Sporting News*, March 4, 1953, April 15, 1953.

25 *The Sporting News*, November 4, 1953.

26 *New York Times*, April 28, 1954; *The Sporting News*, March 20, 1982.

27 *The Sporting News*, April 20, 1960, April 27, 1960.

28 *Boston Globe*, October 21, 1960; *Chicago Daily Tribune*, October 21, 1960; *Detroit News*, October 12, 1960.

29 *Boston Globe*, March 24, 1962; *Chicago Daily Tribune*, March 21, 1962, June 4, 1962, *Hartford Courant*, March 24, 1962.

30 Frank Robinson, *Extra Innings: The Grand Slam Response to Al Campanis's Controversial Remarks about Blacks in Baseball* (New York: McGraw-Hill, 1988); *New York Times*, November 13, 1965; *The Sporting News*, November 28, 1964.

31 *Boston Globe*, October 14, 1964; *Chicago Tribune*, December 6, 1966, and March 7, 1982; *Hartford Courant*, December 6, 1966.

32 *The Sporting News*, November 22, 1975.

33 *Chicago Daily Defender*, August 18, 1971; *Los Angeles Times,* August 18, 1971; *Seattle Times,* August 17, 1971.

34 *St. Louis Globe-Democrat*, March 4, 1982.

35 *St. Louis Post-Dispatch*, March 3, 1982.

36 *Bryan* (Texas) *Times*, March 4, 1982, *The Sporting News*, May 16, 1970.

37 *The Sporting News*, December 28, 1944.

38 *Chicago Tribune*, March 7, 1982.

Branch Rickey

By Andy McCue.

BRANCH RICKEY WAS "a man of strange complexities, not to mention downright contradictions," wrote the *New York Times'* John Drebinger. The great decision to break baseball's policy of excluding blacks, for which he is justly praised, has, in recent decades, tended to overwhelm the highly negative image he had earned before that decision. He went from "El Cheapo" to moral beacon in just a few years, and richly deserved each characterization.

He was deeply religious, sowing Biblical quotations and religious axioms like Johnny Appleseed sowed apple seeds.

He was a tightwad. "Rickey believes in economy in everything except his own salary," wrote the *New York Daily Mirror's* Dan Parker. *Daily News* columnist Jimmy Powers tagged him El Cheapo after Rickey dumped a number of the Dodgers' older, and better-known, players soon after taking over.

He was politically and socially conservative. He preached on the temperance circuit as a young man and, as an older man, would regularly attack Communism, Communists, and liberal politicians.

He preached courage and honesty, yet he was devious. Bob Broeg of the *St. Louis Post-Dispatch* dubbed him Branch Richelieu. When a decision by Commissioner Kenesaw M. Landis deprived Rickey of a promising player, he could actively work to subvert the decision through fake transfers. Rickey could "think up many a little scheme that, while not dishonest, still will not leave Rickey & Co. holding the sack on the snipe hunt," wrote Bill Corum in the *New York Journal-American*.

He could bring Jackie Robinson to the majors, and tell stories of being deeply moved when an African-American player he coached in college sought to rub off his skin color to escape the prejudices of white America, but he could also relate dialect jokes. He made anti-Catholic remarks at the dinner table and characterize a potential Dodgers purchaser as "of Jewish extraction and characteristics."

He was articulate, if inclined to overdo the rhetoric and the vocabulary. "Rickey's natural element is the pulpit," wrote Red Smith. "He talks with such pontifical oratory that he could and would make a reading of batting averages sound as impressive and as stirring as Lincoln's Gettysburg Address," said the *New York Times'* Arthur Daley. Players who stumbled out of salary-negotiating sessions were amazed at the verbal rings that had been run around them, and at the salaries they had accepted.

He was absent-minded, often tossing lighted matches into trash cans filled with paper and acknowledging defeat when his five daughters all wound up with fingers next to their noses, the family code that somebody was talking too much. Jane Moulton Rickey, whom he met when she was twelve, proposed to a hundred times, and married at twenty-four, could note, "Mr. Rickey is not, and

Rickey implemented the first minor-league "farm" system while serving as the Cardinals' general manager. Many players who made up the Gashouse Gang were the first fruits off the Rickey 'bush leagues." He was posthumously elected to the Hall of Fame in 1967.

never has been, one of the ten best-groomed men in America."

He was fearsomely intelligent, well read, and thoughtful.

Wesley Branch Rickey was born on December 20, 1881, in Scioto County, on the Ohio River in south central Ohio, to the modest farming family of Jacob Franklin "Frank" Rickey and Emily Brown Rickey. Branch had an older brother, Orla, born in 1875, and a younger brother, Frank, born in 1888. As Branch's first name would indicate—John Wesley was the founder of Methodism—it was a pious, Methodist household. Rickey finished grade school in Lucasville, Ohio, but then farm labor called. With help from a sympathetic retired educator, he read as widely as the resources of Scioto County allowed in the 1890s. He educated himself enough to become the teacher at the local grade school, saving money for college. Eventually, he went off to Ohio Wesleyan University. For the next decade, Rickey's life was a welter of sporadic academics, sports, and, eventually, coaching.

He played baseball and football at Ohio Wesleyan and, realizing he could make money to pay for his studies, entered baseball's semipro summer circuit in 1902 and began to coach the university team the next spring. That summer, he moved to the minor leagues, playing in Terre Haute, Indiana; LeMars, Iowa; and Dallas, Texas. In 1904, after graduation, Rickey returned to Dallas, and was purchased by the Cincinnati Reds near the end of the season.

He spent parts of the next three seasons in the majors, earning a reputation as a marginal catcher, a poor hitter, and an odd duck for refusing to play baseball on Sundays. In Cincinnati, his refusal to play on Sundays infuriated manager Joe Kelley, who released him back to Dallas before he appeared in a league game. For the winter, Rickey moved to Allegheny College, in Meadville, Pennsylvania, where he served as football and baseball coach.

That winter, the White Sox purchased Rickey's contract, but sent him to the St. Louis Browns after deciding they could not afford a catcher who took Sundays off and would not report until his college coaching duties were done. He made his major-league debut on June 16, 1905. That one appearance was it for the year, as his mother became ill and Rickey went back to Lucasville. By the time she recovered, he went back to Dallas before heading to Allegheny for another year of coaching. There, he became disillusioned with the semiprofessional character of college football and left before the baseball season began.

When the 1906 season did begin, Rickey was back with the Browns. He had his best year that summer, playing in 65 games and hitting .284. The left-handed hitting Rickey had his first major-league safety, a single, on April 23 off Detroit southpaw Ed Killian at Sportsman's Park. The offensive highlight of his career came on August 6 against the New York Yankees. Rickey hit a two-run homer in the bottom of the second inning to chase Jack Chesbro and extend the Browns' lead to 5–0. He then hit a "fluke" inside-the-park home run off reliever Walter Clarkson in the sixth, to make the score 6–2. But by the end of the summer his arm was hurting. He returned to Ohio Wesleyan to coach and complete the courses he needed to enter law school. In late winter the shoulder pain returned.

During the offseason Rickey had been sold to the Yankees. Despite a spring training visit to Hot Springs, Arkansas, his arm did not improve. Rickey played sporadically and the league noticed his inability to throw. On June 28, 1907 the Washington Senators stole 13 consecutive bases against him, and Rickey had stopped bothering to throw by the end of the game. It's a record that stands a century later. Offensively, his average fell to .182 in 52 games. He would make a cameo two-game appearance for the Browns in 1914, but otherwise his playing career was finished. In all, he played in 120 games over four seasons and had a .239 lifetime batting average.

After marrying Jane in Lucasville in June 1906, he had turned to a laundry list of jobs. He was Ohio Wesleyan's athletic director, while also coaching football, basketball, and baseball. He was secretary of the Delaware, Ohio, YMCA, and he taught beginning law classes even while taking other law classes as a student. As 1908 rolled in Rickey threw himself into William Howard Taft's campaign for the presidency and the work of the Anti-Saloon League. By the end of 1908, perhaps run down from his schedule, Rickey was diagnosed with tuberculosis, the biggest medical killer of the time.

He spent much of 1909 in a sanatorium in upstate New York, leaving only to begin his first semester at the University of Michigan law school in the fall. By early 1910 his health had improved enough for him to supplement his savings by coaching the university's baseball team.

In 1911, nearing age thirty, Branch Rickey graduated from law school and chose Boise, Idaho, as the site of his law office. He was, by his own accounts, a miserable failure, gaining one client, who did not even want a lawyer. The impressions he had made as a baseball player and coach came to his rescue. Even while in Boise, he had spent his summer scouting for Robert Hedges, owner of the St. Louis Browns, who had been impressed with Rickey's intelligence and articulate presentations when he was a player. After his second unsuccessful winter in Boise, Rickey was only too happy to respond to Hedges' request for a meeting in Salt Lake City to discuss a full-time job with the Browns. He borrowed the train fare from Hedges and began a half-century of life in professional baseball.

Rickey's initial role was somewhere between scout and general manager. With the help of full-time scout Charley Barrett, Rickey evaluated and tracked players from the Midwest and South. In the winter of 1912 he produced a list of players the Browns could draft from minor-league teams, and thirty of the 105 players chosen that winter were taken by the Browns. By mid-1913 Rickey was the field manager of the Browns. He began teaching his players with a blend of lectures, heart-to-heart talks, and drills. He also began his lifelong fascination with statistical analysis, hiring a young man to sit behind home plate and keep track of how many bases each player made for himself and advanced his teammates. The team improved in 1914, but slid back in 1915 amid accusations that Rickey was too intellectual in dealing with his players.

That winter Hedges sold the Browns to Phil Ball, after granting Rickey a long-term contract. Ball, however, was contemptuous of Rickey's religious views and his approach to the game. He brought in Fielder Jones as field manager while Rickey chafed in his former role of finding players for the Browns. By the spring of 1917 a new ownership group for the National League's St. Louis team persuaded Ball to let Rickey out of his contract to become the Cardinals' president.

While he was still in St. Louis with his growing family, running the Cardinals was not a dream job. The new ownership was undercapitalized. The team had finished in the top half of the league once in the previous quarter-century. Rickey and Cardinals manager Miller Huggins clashed over Rickey's "theoretical" approach to the game. The 1917 Cardinals struggled to their best record since 1891, but it was good only for third place. After the season, Huggins was lured away by the New York Yankees, and Rickey hired Jack Hendricks to take his place.

In August 1918 Rickey joined the Army Chemical Corps, then a new field with cachet. He was commissioned a major and joined a unit with Captains Ty Cobb and Christy Mathewson. In the weeks leading to the November 11 armistice, Rickey's unit supported a number of American attacks on the Germans. He was back in the United States on December 23 and in Lucasville with the family for Christmas.

The Cardinals team he returned to was in serious financial trouble. Rickey borrowed Jane's family heirloom rugs to make his barren office look respectable, and made himself manager to save a salary. But he was building the foundation that would make the Cardinals a dominant team for the next three decades.

Rickey's record as manager of the Cardinals was mediocre. For his first three years, he increased the win totals each year, and the Cardinals reached third place by 1921. But in 1922, the team slipped to fourth, then fifth, then sixth, before he was replaced early in 1925. Angry and humiliated, he contemplated quitting, but eventually decided to remain as general manager. For those who questioned Rickey's ability to lead and motivate players, they had their prejudices confirmed when Rogers Hornsby took the Cardinals to the 1926 pennant.

While the critics savaged Rickey as a manager, no one doubted his abilities in the front office. It was only when Rickey was kicked upstairs from the Cardinals' dugout that he found his true role. "Rickey practically created the office of business manager as it is understood today," wrote the *New York Times'* John Drebinger in 1943.

Rickey's first great innovation was the farm system. "When the Cardinals were fighting for their life in the National League, I found that we were at a disadvantage in obtaining players of merit from the minors," Rickey said. "Other clubs could outbid. They had money. They had superior scouting machinery. In short, we had to take what was left or nothing at all.... Thus it was that we took over the Houston Club for a Class A proving ground in 1924... Still, I do not feel that the farming system we have established is the result of any inventive genius — it is the result of stark necessity. We did it to meet a question of supply and demand of young ball-players," he told *The Sporting News'* Dick Farrington.

The Cardinals eventually created a chain of minor-league teams so they could sign players cheaply, winnow the good from the great, win pennants, and make money. Rickey would sell the good to others and keep the great for the Cardinals.

Rickey proved a cold-blooded judge of talent, and a man with the knack for nurturing what talent he had. He was not the sentimentalist to hang on to an aging player who had contributed greatly to the team's past success. It is better to trade a man a year too early than a year too late, he preached. He created the concept of the "anesthetic ballplayer," the one who is good enough to be a major leaguer, but not good enough to help win a pennant or a World Series. Trading the anesthetics and the fading stars filled holes the farm system could not. And in the minors, Rickey was an innovator not just in creating, but in teaching.

He came up with sandpits to teach players to slide; a set of strings to define the strike zone and help pitchers with their control; the batting tee to help hitters hone their swings, and chalk talks. After World War II, when Rickey was with the Dodgers, he expanded on the statistical analysis he had first tried with the Browns. He hired Allan Roth, who charted where Dodgers batters' hits fell.

Rickey was observant in a way that amazed even other baseball men. There was the story of one pitch — a foul ball — while Rickey was sitting behind the plate one day. After the pitch he turned to an aide and dic-

tated the following notes: The center fielder had failed to get a jump on the ball, the pitcher had an unbalanced motion and would not be able to field his position, and the catcher had blinked as the batter swung, causing him to miss the foul tip.

Rickey's player-evaluation skills built the Cardinals' machine that dominated the National League, winning nine pennants and six World Series between 1926 and 1946. This machine, built on the ownership of minor-league clubs, did not run smoothly. Baseball commissioner Kenesaw Landis did not like to see minor leagues or teams run simply as talent suppliers for the major leagues. He wanted them to act as independent businesses. He wanted players to have the fullest freedom to exploit their talent, and not get stuck in the minor-league systems of talent-rich organizations. Rickey, whose plan had been followed by the other major-league teams, argued that major-league ownership had allowed the minor leagues to survive the Depression of the 1930s.

In 1938, in what became known as the Cedar Rapids decision, Landis freed at least seventy-four Cardinals farmhands. Landis found that the Cardinals had relationships with more than one team in some leagues, meaning it could affect pennant races by moving players between these teams. He offered no evidence that they had done so. The one released player of unusual talent was Pete Reiser, and Rickey set out to subvert Landis's decision by making sure his protégé, Larry MacPhail of the Brooklyn Dodgers, picked up Reiser with a promise to return him to the Cardinals once the hullaballoo calmed down. Reiser, however, performed so well in spring training that press and public pressure to keep the young outfielder led MacPhail to renege on his promise.

In public, Rickey's reputation as a shrewd executive and motivational speaker grew. He was asked to speak often, and was never afraid to tie his conservative religious and political beliefs with his baseball success. He befriended political figures, usually conservative Republicans. He was approached to run for governor of Missouri. He was described as one of Republican presidential candidate Thomas Dewey's closest friends and supporters and touted as his successor as New York governor if Dewey was elected president.

By late 1942 Rickey's relations with Cardinals owner Sam Breadon had become strained. The two were fighting over Rickey's bonus payments and Breadon's dismissal of Rickey protégés in the farm system. Rickey reportedly was upset at Breadon's refusal to back him over the Cedar Rapids decision and with Breadon's paying a large bonus to himself while cutting Rickey's budget for salaries. Rickey was considering a top executive post with a large insurance company.

In 1937, when Brooklyn Dodgers board member James Mulvey had first approached him, Rickey had not been prepared to leave a comfortable life in St. Louis. By late 1942 he was. The wooing was relatively quick. The *New York Times* first reported Brooklyn-Rickey talks on October 4, 1942. The move was announced on October 29, a day when Rickey was introduced as the new general manager at a lunch at the Brooklyn Club. At that lunch Rickey also was introduced to Walter O'Malley, a thirty-nine-year-old lawyer who shared the Brooklyn Trust table with him.

In Brooklyn Rickey saw a different team than the press and the fans. The fans and the reporters saw the 1941 pennant winner and a 1942 team that had finished second. Rickey saw a team that was old, with a roster about to be ravaged by the needs of military service. It was the disposal of aging stars that earned him the nickname El Cheapo. It was his response to World War II that would build the foundation of the Boys of Summer.

With the draft in place most teams cut back on signing players, bowing to the uncertainties of wartime. In response the number of minor leagues shrank to ten in 1944 from the forty-one of 1941. Rickey simply figured the war would end some day and he signed talent in buckets, seeking to repeat his success in building the Cardinals' minor-league system. Players like Gil Hodges would make token appearances in the Major Leagues before disappearing into boot camp, then emerge after the war to stock baseball's richest farm system. Rickey earned another nickname, "The Mahatma," after sportswriter Tom Meany read a portrait of Indian political leader Mohandas "Mahatma" Gandhi that described Gandhi as a combination of "your father and Tammany Hall."

In the years immediately after the war, Rickey blended prewar players like Dixie Walker, Hugh Casey, and Pee Wee Reese with the results of his player-development program. That program had led to another Rickey innovation—the spring training complex. With more than 700 players under contract, the Dodgers needed a large facility if they wanted to insure uniform training and easy analysis of their prospects. In 1947, Rickey struck a deal with the town of Vero Beach, Florida, for the use of the former U.S. Navy pilot-training base on the west edge of town. Using a complex system of colors and numbers, the minor leaguers were sorted, trained, analyzed, graded, and eventually assigned to their minor-league teams, all according to the Rickey methods.

Except for the Vero Beach facility, which would become a model for other teams, the methods were those Rickey had developed with the Cardinals. But in Brooklyn, he took another step, one that would raise him from talented baseball executive to sainted agent of progress.

Rickey's decision to seek black baseball talent came fairly soon after he joined the Dodgers. His pursuit of black players was a typical combination of motives and methods. It was a product of his religious beliefs; of his desire to win and draw fans; and of his ability to see baseball in the context of American society. It was conducted not by looking for just the best baseball talent, but for the best combination of on-field talent, maturity, and intelligence. For his African American torchbearer, he chose a college-educated man who would be twenty-seven before he played even one game in the white minor leagues. He chose Jackie Robinson in part because he was from California, in whose milder racial climate he had played most of his life on integrated athletic teams. Rickey encouraged him to marry his fiancée, a move he felt always helped a ballplayer's career. Robinson went on to justify Rickey's gamble in every way and cement a lifelong relationship between the two men.

But his relationships with his partners were not so strong. By 1950, Rickey knew his lucrative contract would not be renewed and he began the steps that would put Walter O'Malley in control of the Dodgers and himself at the general manager's desk in Pittsburgh.

In Pittsburgh Rickey set out to build the kind of dominant organization he had constructed in St. Louis and Brooklyn. Rickey's one original move in Pittsburgh came too late to save him. In 1955, he sent Howie Haak, his best scout, to begin scouring the Caribbean for talent. This move would bear immense fruit for the Pirates in the 1960s, but by then Rickey was gone

After the 1955 season Rickey stepped down as general manager, saying he would spend the rest of his ten-year contract as a senior consultant to the team. But it was clear that consulting was a cover for being at loose ends, a situation that did not change until late in 1958, when Rickey began talking with a New York lawyer named William Shea. In the wake of the Dodgers' and Giants' departures for the West Coast, New York City Mayor Robert Wagner, Jr. had asked Shea to head an effort to bring National League baseball back to New York. Shea turned for advice to George V. McLaughlin, a New York banker and civic luminary who had brought O'Malley to the Dodgers in 1940. McLaughlin suggested that Shea talk to Rickey. Rickey, who had apparently been mulling the idea for a while, suggested a third league.

For the next two years, Rickey headed the Continental League. He wooed ownership groups, promised his league would find players even while honoring major-league baseball's reserve clause, and worked through Congress to bring pressure to limit the Major Leagues' control of their players. The league collapsed in late 1960, when both the National and American leagues committed to expansion.

For two years he puttered, but then jumped at a chance to return to the Cardinals as a "senior consultant." It was an awkward relationship. General manager Bing Devine felt threatened by owner Gussie Busch's hiring of Rickey. Rickey's opposition to a trade that brought shortstop Dick Groat to the Cardinals worsened the situation. And when a strongly worded memo urging Stan Musial's forced retirement leaked to the press, Rickey's status became fragile. He was not helped when Busch decided to fire Devine in mid-1964, a move that was interpreted as interference by Rickey. The move embarrassed Busch as the Cardinals rallied to win the pennant with a team Devine had assembled. After the World Series, won by the Cardinals, Busch fired Rickey as well.

In 1965, Rickey finished his work on *The American Diamond: A Documentary of the Game of Baseball*, the closest thing to an autobiography Rickey would do. It contained portraits of a group Rickey called the sports immortals, as well as reflections from his years in the game.

He died on December 9, 1965, and was buried in Rushtown, Ohio, just across the Scioto River from Lucasville. Jane Rickey died on October 16, 1971, and is buried next to him.

Sources

Current Biography 1945, p. 497.

Polner, Murray. *Branch Rickey: A Biography*. New York: Atheneum, 1982.

Chamberlain, John, "Brains, Baseball, and Branch Rickey," *Harper's*, April, 1948.

Dexter, Charles, "Brooklyn's Sturdy Branch," *Collier's*, September 15, 1945.

Fitzgerald, Ed, "Sport's Hall of Fame: Branch Rickey, Baseball Innovator," *Sport*, May 1962.

Holland, Gerald, "Mr. Rickey and the Game," *Sports Illustrated*, March 7, 1955, p. 38.

Rice, Robert, "Profiles: Thoughts on Baseball. Two parts, *The New Yorker*, May 27 and June 30, 1950.

Farrington, Dick, "Branch Rickey, Defending Farms, Says Stark Necessity Forced System," *The Sporting News*, December 1, 1932, p. 3.

The Branch Rickey Papers at the Library of Congress.

This essay was originally published in Lyle Spatz, ed. *The Team That Changed Baseball and America Forever* (Lincoln: University of Nebraska Press, 2012).

Mike Gonzalez

By Joseph Gerard

Miguel González enjoyed a long and prolific career as a major-league catcher and coach, and along with Adolfo Luque is considered to be one of the two true patriarchs of baseball in Cuba, where he was a player, manager, and owner in the Cuban League from 1910 through 1960. He was a coach on the 1934 world champion St. Louis Cardinals, and although it was only on an interim basis, in 1938 he became the first Latin American to manage in the major leagues. He was the third-base coach who, depending on your point of view, either waved home or tried in vain to stop Enos Slaughter when the latter made his celebrated "mad dash" from first base on a double by Harry Walker to score the deciding run in Game Seven of the 1946 World Series. Despite these accomplishments and the recognition that came with them, González is probably best remembered for coining one of the most famous phrases in the lexicon of baseball while on a scouting expedition for John McGraw and the New York Giants.

Miguel Angel González Cordero was born on September 24, 1890, in the town of Regla, across the bay from Havana. Not much is known about his early life, other than that he and his family lived humbly in modest surroundings. Baseball had become enormously popular on the island by the time Miguel was a boy, as Cubans began to disavow any ties to Spanish colonialism, including its sports, while looking to the US for inspiration. Like many young Cuban boys at the time, Miguel and his friends learned the game on the fields and lots of the city, using whatever makeshift equipment they could find.

Miguel quickly grew to a height of 6-feet-1 but was extremely gaunt for his size. It was said that he resembled a long loaf of thin Cuban bread, and his physique, along with his childhood occupation delivering bread to his neighbors in Regla, earned him the nickname Pan de Flauta, after a loaf of bread so narrow as to resemble a pan flute. González had played baseball during his school years at the Institute of Havana, and he was working as a bank clerk when he was recruited by Fé, the baseball club that had originated decades earlier in the Havana neighborhood of Jesús del Monte. He made his first appearance for Fé as a shortstop in the professional Cuban League in 1910, appearing in six games and amassing 21 at-bats.

González was catching in Cuba during the following winter when he was noticed by Georges Henriquez, a physician who had purchased the Long Branch, New Jersey, club in the fledging Class D New York-New Jersey League, along with his brothers Carlos and Richard. The three brothers had emigrated from Colombia to the United States with their parents, settling in Manhattan, but evidence suggests they spent time in Cuba as well and were familiar with the brand of baseball played on the island.

They decided to stock the Long Branch club with Cuban players. In addition to González, the brothers lured Cuban stars like Adolfo Luque (at that time Gonzalez's batterymate),

Gonzalez played for five teams in a career that lasted 17 seasons, mostly as a utility man. After his playing days he was a Cardinals coach for 13 seasons.

Angel Aragón, Manuel Cueto, Luis Padrón, Tomás Romañach, and Juan Violá; the team was aptly named the Cubans. Richard Henriquez, who had played baseball at Columbia while attending medical school, joined the team himself. Long Branch quickly outclassed its opposition, winning the 1912 pennant by approximately 20 games. While Luque was undoubtedly the star attraction, González hit for an average of .333 and was behind the plate for every game.

After the summer of 1912 the Henriquez brothers sold González's contract to the Boston Braves, and he made his major-league debut on September 28, appearing in one game and walking once in three plate appearances. He was on the roster of the Braves to begin 1913, but manager George Stallings sent him down to Buffalo, which passed González along to Class B Wilkes-Barre. González refused the assignment and the Long Branch club purchased his optional release from Boston. The Braves recalled González briefly in the fall of 1913, but Long Branch subsequently purchased his outright release.

When González returned to Cuba he was traded from Fé to Habana for the 1913-14 season, which began his affiliation with the Rojos or, as they came to be known later, the Leones, a connection that lasted until the demise of the Cuban League.

At the same time, a letter from William H. Peal, secretary of the Eastern League, to Louis Heilbroner of the Baseball Statistical and Information Bureau described González as a very good hitter who is "catching great ball" in Cuba against American squads, at least one of which, the Birmingham Barons of the Southern Association, had made an offer for his services.[1] Heilbroner forwarded the letter to Garry Herrmann, president of the Cincinnati Reds, who signed González for the 1914 season.

In the fall of 1914, González, 24 years old, was named manager of Habana by new owner Abel Linares, who apparently had already taken note of the reserved, studious, and loyal nature of his protégé. González rewarded Linares with a championship in the 1914-15 season, the first of 13 Cuban League titles he would win as manager of Habana.

Meanwhile, González had appeared in 95 games for Cincinnati in 1914, catching in 83 of them and batting .233. Tommy Clarke was established as the regular backstop in Cincinnati, but in early April of 1915 the Reds traded González to the Cardinals for catcher Ivey Wingo. The Cardinals were looking to free up playing time for young catching prospect Frank "Pancho" Snyder. González played the next four seasons with the Cardinals, beginning as a backup for Snyder, who was one of the best catchers in the National League in 1915 at the age of 21, while occasionally filling in at first base.

Despite his size, González had a reputation as a stellar defensive catcher who possessed a strong, whip-like throwing arm, very quick feet, and soft hands for blocking pitches. Snyder himself was considered to be an excellent defensive catcher, one of the best of his era, yet manager Miller Huggins began to use González as his starting catcher as early as 1916, penciling him in as the starter in 84 games compared with 69 for Snyder. J.J. Ward of *Baseball Magazine* observed, "There are a few better catchers in big league ball than Miguel A. González, but they are very, very few indeed."[2]

González batted .262 in 1917. His best season with the bat came in 1918, when he hit .252 with 39 walks and 20 extra-base hits. He stole 14 bases. Despite his success, González was placed on waivers by the Cardinals in May 1919, and was selected by the New York Giants. Manager John McGraw had spent much time in Cuba and had seen González play there in winter ball. On one occasion after Gonzalez's arrival, McGraw gave his team a pep talk convincing them of victory in the 1919 season, and looked to González, the newcomer, for validation. "We won't win, Cincinnati has the best team," replied González, who turned out to be quite prescient on the matter, even if his characteristic candor did not sit well with McGraw.[3]

McGraw kept González on his roster for four seasons, but Mike's playing time diminished as the Giants used first Lew McCarty as well as Frank Snyder, whom they had brought on board in 1919, as their starters. González spent considerable time as a bullpen catcher, and McGraw often sought his input on the relative merits of the pitching staff. But by 1922, at age 31, Gonzalez was considered through as a hitter, and the Giants sold his contract to the St. Paul Saints of the American Association.

González had two good seasons with the Saints, batting .298 and .303, and his contract was purchased in the spring of 1924 by the Cincinnati Reds. The Reds subsequently sold him to Brooklyn and González spent spring training with the Robins in Clearwater. The day before the season began, Brooklyn traded González to the Cardinals for infielder Milt Stock.

González had a good season with the Cardinals in 1924, playing in 120 games and batting .296, but in May 1925 he was traded to the Chicago Cubs along with infielder Howard Freigau for catcher Bob O'Farrell, who at the time was considered to be one of the finest defensive catchers in the league. González arrived in Chicago only to find young sensation Gabby Hartnett firmly entrenched as the starting catcher for the Cubs; he served primarily as Hartnett's backup for the better part of the next two seasons.

When Joe McCarthy took over as manager of the Cubs in 1926, he created some controversy by increasing Gonzalez's playing time at Hartnett's expense. "There aren't many players who can't outhit González, and maybe he doesn't spiel our language so well, but somehow he makes those pitchers understand him and they'll learn about pitching to hitters from him," McCarthy said.[4] Of course, Hartnett eventually blossomed into a star, and González did not appear in more than 60 games in any of the next three seasons for the Cubs, although he was a member of the pennant-winning squad of 1929 and appeared twice in the 1929 World Series, won by the Philadelphia Athletics in five games, striking out as a pinch-hitter in Game Two in his lone at-bat.

Undeniably, González's career in the big leagues represented only half of his baseball life—the rest was spent in Havana. The Cuban League arranged its schedule around that of American baseball, allowing González and many other Cuban players to have dual careers. In the winter they played against fellow Cubans, the finest players from the Negro Leagues, and American major leaguers. The competition was fierce, and the level of play superb. Many major-league teams and mixed barnstorming squads visited the island each winter to play the local teams, only to be startled by the quality of play of Cuban stars like Jose "The Black Diamond" Mendez, Cristobal Torriente, Alejandro Oms, and Dolf Luque. Many of their legendary feats have lived on, such as Mendez's streak of 25 scoreless innings for Almendares against Cincinnati in a series at Almendares Park in 1908.

Professional baseball in Cuba existed as far back as 1878, but the Cuban League never represented a cross-section of the population on the island—it was centered in Havana, and for all intents and purposes, it really existed as a mechanism for perpetuating one of the greatest and most intense rivalries in the history of the sport, the battle between the Habana Leones, or the Reds, and the Almendares Alacranes, the Blues. Attempts to add clubs from the provinces over the years generally met with failure; one of the steadier teams, Cienfuegos, rarely bothered to schedule games in its own city, traveling to Havana for "home" games in search of a bigger gate.

The first glory years of the Cuban League are generally considered to have taken place between World War I and the onset of the Great Depression, and it was during this period that the two great patriarchs of the sport in Cuba, González and Luque, became the faces of the two "eternal rivals." While the league shuttled third and fourth teams in and out over a period of years, the one constant was the competition between the Reds and the Blues, between González and Luque, which literally divided the city in two.

By the time this period ended, in 1929, González had managed Habana to six championships, in the seasons of 1918-19 (notable for the participation of the Cuban Stars, a team of Cubans who played in the American Negro Leagues), 1920-21, 1921-22 (an abbreviated season of nine scheduled games, of which only five were completed), 1926-27, 1927-28, and 1928-29, while still serving as a full-time player.

His only notable absence from the league during this period was in the 1923-24 season, won by the Santa Clara Leopardas, considered by many to be the best team ever assembled in Cuba, with an outfield of Oscar Charleston, Pablo "Champion" Mesa, and Alejandro Ohms. González left Habana to form a league of his own in Matanzas, which would feature all Cuban players, and he was replaced at the helm of Habana by his rival, Luque.

There were many reasons for his defection. González was becoming increasingly disaffected with the control promoter Abel Linares exerted over the league. Linares owned all three teams—Habana, Almendares, and Santa Clara—that participated in the 1923-24 season. Also, more American players were traveling to Cuba for the winter campaign, and Gonzalez's gesture of creating an all-Cuban insurgent league was seen as a protest against this development. Finally, and most significantly, González may have been trying to avert the gaze of Major League Baseball. Commissioner Kenesaw Mountain Landis, aware that the veneer of invincibility enjoyed by the major leagues was being peeled back by losses to Latin teams, had banned barnstorming in the offseason, which could easily have been construed to include the Cuban League.

When the Roaring Twenties gave way to the Depression, the golden age of the Cuban League ended, and by this time González's major-league career seemed over as well. The Cubs released him after the 1929 season, saying he had lost his arm strength. González denied it. "I am sorry to leave the Cubs for I have many friends in Chicago, but I have changed teams so many times that one more will make no difference," he said. "I am through as a Cub, but not as a ballplayer. My arm is all right, although I will have to admit that it is not what it used to be. Someone has said that the Cubs let me go because it went back on me, but that is very funny, because I never noticed it."[5]

Unable to find a major-league job, he played for the Minneapolis Millers of the American Association, at age 39. He hit .263 in 92 games and led the league's backstops with a .993 fielding percentage.

González's performance caught the attention of Branch Rickey, the general manager of the Cardinals, who signed him for the 1931 season. González played for the Cardinals in 1931 and 1932, but had only 33 plate appearances over the two seasons, serving mostly as a bullpen coach. He did make a significant contribution to the Cardinals' world championship team in 1931. During the deciding Game Seven against the Athletics, Gonzalez walked from the bullpen to the dugout under the guise of getting a drink of water. What he had in mind was getting a good look in the eyes of starting pitcher Burleigh Grimes, who appeared to be struggling to hold a 4-0 lead late in the game. González hastened back to the bullpen and instructed left-hander Bill Hallahan to start warming up. "Burleigh, she tired," González said.[6] As it turned out, Grimes was indeed tired, and needed Hallahan to enter in the ninth inning with two outs, two runs in, and Philadelphia runners on first and second. Hallahan retired Max Bishop on a fly ball and the Cardinals held on for a 4-2 victory.

After the 1932 season González's major-league playing career came to an end. He was 41 years old. He finished with a lifetime batting average of .253, but his value was mainly on defense, where he compiled a fielding percentage of .980 and threw out 47 percent of baserunners attempting to steal. He finished within the top three in the National League in caught-stealing percentage five times. In assists as a catcher, he ranks immediately behind Hall of Famers Johnny Bench, Ernie Lombardi, and Mickey Cochrane, and just ahead of Yogi Berra.

For 1933 Rickey sent González to the Double-A Columbus Red Birds as a player-coach. González was credited with assisting in the development of the Red Birds' top pitching prospects, including Paul Dean and Bill Lee. He also managed, at 42, to accumulate 111 at-bats as a backup catcher, with a batting average of .324.

When Cardinals player-manager Frankie Frisch needed a coach for the 1934 team, he did not hesitate to select González, calling him "a great guy, loyal and true."[7] The Gas House Gang won 95 games and the National League pennant, then defeated the Detroit Tigers in seven games in the World Series.

González coached for Frisch and the Cardinals into the 1938 season as the Cardinals' fortunes faded under the Fordham Flash; they dropped from 96 wins in 1935 to 71 in 1938. Frisch was fired with 16 games remaining in 1938, and González was named interim manager, the first Latin American to manage in the big leagues. This was a bittersweet moment for González, for his promotion came at the expense of his mentor and close friend.

"I hate to see him go. He's a real pal and a good man. I didn't want him to leave," he said.[8]

In the offseason, Rickey and owner Sam Breadon sought out González for his advice on a new manager for the Cardinals, and followed his recommendation that they hire Ray Blades, his tutor at Columbus. González returned to his role as coach under Blades until June 1940, when he briefly took over the reins as manager again after Blades was fired and before Billy Southworth succeeded him. González's final record as a major-league manager was 9-13.

In Cuba, 1930 was a precursor of an extremely difficult decade for the Cuban League. A contract dispute between the teams and the owners of La Tropical Stadium in Havana reduced the schedule to a mere five games. Over the next three years, the political stability in the country deteriorated as labor strikes and other, more violent measures were taken against the ruthless, heavy-handed government of President Gerardo Machado, who was finally forced out of office in 1933. The playoffs to settle a tie in the 1932-33 season were canceled, and then the entire 1933-34 season was wiped out. The 1934-35 campaign was notoriously weak, with all three professional teams going down to defeat at the hands of the amateur Rum Havana Club.

An improvement in the Cuban economy in the mid- to late 1930s, as well as the exploits of some of the great Cuban players of the era, among them Martin Dihigo, Raymond "Jabao" Brown, and Lazaro Salazar, led to a revival of interest in the Cuban League. González, who had taken a two-year hiatus, returned for the 1938-39 campaign, but despite a pitching staff that included Dihigo, Tomás de la Cruz, Negro League great Ted "Double Duty" Radcliffe, and Luis Tiant the elder, Habana could finish no higher than second place, five games behind Santa Clara.

The revitalization of the league was also due to a rebirth of the rivalry between Habana and Almendares that began in the following season. Beginning with the 1939-40 campaign, the championship was won by either Habana or Almendares for five consecutive seasons, before Cienfuegos dethroned them in the 1945-46 season, the last to be played at La Tropical Stadium.

González had owned a tobacco and cigar business in Cuba, and was always a level-headed businessman and a good steward of his finances. When the widow of Abel Linares was ready to sell both the Almendares and Habana franchises, González put together a group of investors, and bought the Habana team for $25,000 in 1946. By 1947 he owned the team outright, and a decade later it was appraised at $500,000. But his rise to ownership directly resulted in the end of his career in American baseball.

González had continued coaching under Southworth in 1941, and the Cardinals improved to finish second behind the Brooklyn Dodgers. Beginning in 1942, the Cardinals entered the most hallowed era in their history, winning 106, 105, and 105 games in their next three seasons. In 1942 they edged out Leo Durocher's Brooklyn team to win the pennant by two games, and went on to defeat the New York Yankees in five games in the World Series. They won the pennant again in 1943 but lost to the Yankees in the World Series. The Cardinals won the Series in 1944, defeating their city rivals, the St. Louis Browns, in six games.

After leading the Cardinals to a second-place finish in 1945, Southworth signed a lucrative contract to manage the Boston Braves, and the Cardinals hired Eddie Dyer as manager. In a testament to how well González was regarded within the organization, and by owner Sam Breadon himself, he was retained and made the third-base coach, at which position he would be involved in one of the most famous plays in World Series history.

With both the Series and Game Seven knotted at 3-3, Enos Slaughter was on first base with two outs in the bottom of the eighth inning. On a 2-and-1 pitch to Harry Walker, Slaughter broke for second. Walker lined a double to left-center field, where Leon Culberson, who had just replaced the injured Dom DiMaggio, raced to his right to field it and throw to the cutoff man, shortstop Johnny Pesky. Slaughter had kept on going around third and beat the startled Pesky's throw to the plate to score the go-ahead run. The Cardinals held on and won their third World Series in five years.

The winning play was surrounded by some confusion that has caused continuing dispute. Walker's hit was called a single by some members of the media, which magnified Slaughter's achievement. Also, DiMaggio, standing on the dugout steps, had yelled to Culberson to move to his right prior to the pitch, but the crowd noise drowned him out, and Culberson did not notice. Pesky, stunned to see Slaughter heading for home, was said to have hesitated upon catching Culberson's throw, allowing Slaughter to score. The available film of the play shows that Pesky wheeled and threw home without much more than a momentary hesitation. Unfortunately for the Red Sox, his throw was well up the third-base line, allowing Slaughter to score.

Another dispute is whether González put up the stop sign or waved Slaughter home. The video is inconclusive on this matter. The video shows González coming into vision as Slaughter approached third base with his head down, and the only clearly discernible movement the coach made was to backpedal rapidly, almost as if to get out of Slaughter's way. Slaughter himself was ambivalent on the subject, siding with each point of view on different occasions. Perhaps his most telling comment on the play took place during a television interview in 2000, when he said, "I never saw Mike González, the third-base coach. Whether he tried to stop me or not, I don't know. I never looked up."[9]

For his part, González was persistent in his account of the play, insisting that with two outs and the bottom of the order coming up, he did not hesitate to wave Slaughter around third. If so, he may have been influenced by a play in the fourth inning of Game One, when Slaughter tripled to left-center field with two outs, but was left stranded, with the Cardinals losing the game in extra innings. On this occasion, Pesky fumbled the relay from DiMaggio, but González held Slaughter at third base when he clearly could have scored. González was criticized by some observers of that play for being out of position to make the proper call.

Game Seven marked the end of Miguel González's career in the major leagues. In many ways his departure was symbolic of the conflict that had arisen between the owners of Organized Baseball in the United States and the independent interests of league owners outside of their purview.

The Mexican League, which had come into existence in the 1930s, had always depended for its success on the participation of many of the greatest Latin American players, including Cubans, as well as the finest African-American players from the Negro Leagues. The president and kingpin was Jorge Pasqual, a multimillionaire who was eager to expand the influence and importance of his league in Mexico's postwar economic boom. The return from World War II of many gifted baseball players was flooding the available talent pool, and Pasqual wanted his share of the overflow. He offered exorbitant bonuses and salaries to American major leaguers in an effort to get them to jump their contracts and join his league. When his plan began to bear fruit, Commissioner Happy Chandler and the team owners were quick to take action to defend their interests.

Chandler proclaimed that any player who jumped to Mexico, as well as those who played against them in winter leagues, would be blacklisted from Organized Baseball. This was a direct blow to the Cuban League, which had for years drawn on talent from the Mexican League, including famous jumpers like Sal Maglie, Max Lanier, and Lou Klein. The two leagues had formed a summer/winter combination that was attractive to many African-American and Latin players. Many of the top Cuban players, like Dihigo, Luque, and Salazar, had played and managed in Mexico — the baseball connection between the two countries was close. Regardless, Major League Baseball was now in effect restricting Cuban players from playing in their own country.

González and Luque, as well as at least 18 other Cubans, were formally banned from Organized Baseball. On October 17, 1946, González, with eyes on purchasing the Habana franchise, resigned as a coach of the Cardinals. Owner Sam Breadon expressed disappointment, saying, "We'd like to see him come back at any time, and hope he will."[10]

As the controversy swirled throughout Cuba, "the eternal rivals" engaged in a pennant race in February 1947 that enthralled the entire nation. The 1946-47 Cuban League season was moved to the new Gran Stadium. The ballpark accommodated 35,000 fans and was centrally located in Havana, which was enjoying an outbreak of postwar tourism that had bolstered the economy. González's Leones had built a large early lead in the standings, but a tremendous late run by Luque's Alacranes that saw them win 12 of 13 games at one point, left the outcome hanging in the balance on the last day of the season. Finally, Max Lanier defeated Habana to reward Almendares with the pennant.

With the threat of further sanctions very much in mind, the executives of the Cuban League decided to seek peace. An agreement between Organized Baseball and the Cuban League in the summer of 1947 ended Cuban autonomy over its own professional baseball. The jumpers would be banned, and from then on the major leagues would have control over the flow of players between the United States and Cuba. The Cuban League would in essence become a training ground, a minor league, for developing major league players.

González continued to manage the Leones under the agreement, winning three consecutive championships, in 1950-51, 1951-52, and 1952-53. In the winter of 1953, he made the surprising announcement that he would retire as manager of Habana at the end of the season, but would remain as owner. He retired with many Cuban League managerial records that would never be eclipsed, including most games (1,525), most seasons (34), most wins (917), and most pennants (14). He was elected to the Cuban Baseball Hall of Fame in 1955. Habana never won another Cuban League title.

There are many stories about González, some certainly apocryphal and others existing in various forms. Many center on his inability to speak English well; in the perhaps unwitting racism that was commonplace at the time, most sportswriters painstakingly spelled out every word González spoke phonetically, as a rather cruel way of pointing out his problems with the language.

However, González did have a few characteristic mannerisms as well as phrases that he used throughout his baseball career, almost as calling cards. Like many Spanish speakers first learning to speak English, he had trouble with pronouns, often referring to males as "she." His stock phrase for a person of superior intelligence or intuitive wisdom was a "smart dummy," while a person who lacked those qualities was a "humpy-dumpy."[11]

González's problems with the language did lead to some challenges for his teammates. One of the most famous tales involved a play in a game against the Giants at the Polo Grounds on September 13, 1936. The Cardinals were batting in the third inning of the first game of a doubleheader before a crowd of 64,417, a record National League one-game attendance at the time. With pitcher Henry "Cotton" Pippen on second base and Terry Moore on first, Art Garibaldi hit a line drive into right-center field. Pippen took off but quickly stopped between second and third, unable to understand the instructions of his third-base coach, González. Moore had by then rounded second only to find Pippen directly in his path. The Giants tagged both Pippen and Moore out while Garibaldi, despite having ostensibly doubled, was back on first base. After the inning, an angry González stormed into the dugout. "They no understand, Frank," he told manager Frisch. "I tell Pippen go and she stop. I tell Moore stop and she go ahead. What do you do with dummies like them? I do my best, Frank, I cannot do some more."[12]

Of course, González's issues with the language resulted in his coining one of the most famous phrases in baseball. After the 1921 season, Giants manager John McGraw told González to scout a young prospect in Cuba over the winter. González, never one for verbosity, replied with a four-word telegram. It read simply, "Good field, no hit," a phrase that has lived on in the scouting community ever since.

Despite these humorous anecdotes, Gonzalez was never considered to be anything less than an astute baseball man and evaluator of talent. He was renowned among his teammates for his ability to unravel the most complicated signs of the opposing team. In particular, he was excellent at cracking the code that opposing infielders used to signal the forthcoming pitch, and discreetly informed the batter from the third-base coaching box. He had a remarkable memory that allowed him to recall the strengths and weaknesses of every player, both at bat and in the field, and he could recite batting averages at the drop of a hat.

While at first the Cuban League showed signs of surviving the revolution of 1959 that brought Fidel Castro to power, by 1961 professional baseball had been banned in Cuba. It was later reported that some of González's property was confiscated, but due to his stature and fame, he was allowed to reside in his principal residence, a marble home in the exclusive Vedado neighborhood of Havana, and maintain his car and chauffeur. Because of travel restrictions instituted by the Castro government, he became isolated from his friends and colleagues in American baseball, who quickly lost track of his whereabouts.

One of González's last reported public appearances was at the final game of the World Amateur Baseball Championship in Havana in January 1972. A Havana newspaper reporter covering the event wrote for *The Sporting News*, "Now 81 years old, Miguel Angel still has a strong voice, recalls his lifetime baseball records, and his keen eyes observe everything on the diamond."[13]

González's was last heard from when Preston Gomez returned from a visit to Cuba with pictures taken at González's 85th birthday party. He is seen smiling from behind a large birthday cake, holding a bottle of beer in each hand. He is missing his toes, suggesting that he suffered from diabetes.

González was married twice. After his first wife, Esther, died of cancer, he took his mother, Juana Cordero, into his home in the Havana suburb of Cerro. He later remarried and had a son, Miguel Jr., with his second wife, who was still alive when he died on February 19, 1977, from a heart attack at the age of 86. He is buried in the Christopher Columbus Cemetery in Havana.

Sources

Billheimer, John, *Baseball and the Blame Game: Scapegoating in the Major Leagues*. (Jefferson, North Carolina: McFarland & Co, 2007). Bjarkman, Peter C., *A History of Cuban Baseball 1864-2006* (Jefferson, North Carolina: McFarland & Co, 2007).

Figueredo, Jorge S., *Cuban Baseball: A Statistical History 1878-1961* (Jefferson, North Carolina: McFarland & Co, 2011).

Gonzalez Echevarria, Roberto, *The Pride of Havana: A History of Cuban Baseball* (New York: Oxford University Press, 2001).

McNeill, William F., *Black Baseball Out of Season: Pay for Play Outside of the Negro Leagues* (Jefferson, North Carolina: McFarland & Co, 2007).

Perez, Louis A. Jr., *On Becoming Cuban: Identity, Nationality and Culture* (Chapel Hill, North Carolina: University of North Carolina Press, 1999).

Riley, James A., *The Biographical Encyclopedia of the Negro Baseball Leagues* (New York: Carroll & Graf Publishers, 1994).

Ruck, Rob, *Raceball: How the Major Leagues Colonized the Black and Latin Game* (Boston: Beacon Press, 2011).

Stockton, J. Roy, *The Gashouse Gang* (New York: Bantam Books, 1948).

Broeg, Bob. "Ex-Cardinal Gonzalez Added Accent to Coaching," *St. Louis Post-Dispatch*, August 19, 1971.

——— "Mike Gonzalez—Smart Dummy Coach," *St. Louis Post-Dispatch*, January 29, 1972.

——— "Mike, She's Gone—Grins Linger," *St. Louis Post-Dispatch*, April 30, 1977.

Hamilton, Jim, "Gonzales (sic) Made Views Known," *Oneonta (New York) Daily Star*, August 25, 1985.

Holmes, Thomas, "Aged Gonzales (sic) Returns to St. Louis to Teach Cardinal Kid Pitchers," *Brooklyn Eagle*, January 25, 1931.

McKenna, Brian, "The Henriquez Long Branch Cubans," Baseballhistoryblog.com, accessed June 25, 2013.

Stockton, J. Roy, "Mike Gonzales (sic), He Coach Third Base and Keep Cardinals from Fumbling Around This Year," *St. Louis Post-Dispatch*, March 17, 1934.

Ward, John J., "Gonzales (sic), the Cuban Backstop," *Baseball Magazine*, February 1917.

——— "Cuba's Best Catcher With the Cubs," *Baseball Magazine*, July 1927.

"Gonzalez, Miguel Angel (Mike)," no author, title or date given. From González's file at the Baseball Hall of Fame.

Karst, Eugene F., "Cardinal Newcomers for 1931," undated press release from St. Louis Cardinals.

Peal, William H., Letter to Louis Heilbroner, February 5, 1914.

Baseball-reference.com

Notes

1. William H. Peal, letter to Louis Heilbroner. February 5, 1914.
2. John J. Ward, "Gonzales (sic), The Cuban Backstop." *Baseball Magazine*, February 1917.
3. Jim Hamilton, "Gonzales (sic) Made Views Known." *Oneonta (New York) Daily Star*, August 25, 1985.
4. Thomas Holmes, "Aged Gonzales (sic) Returns to St. Louis to Teach Cardinal Kid Pitchers," *Brooklyn Eagle*, January 25, 1931.
5. Joe Massaguer, personal interview with Miguel González. Quoted in *The Sporting News*, January 23, 1930.
6. Bob Broeg, "Mike, She's Gone—Grins Linger," *St. Louis Post-Dispatch*, April 30, 1977.
7. J.G. Taylor Spink, "Mike Gonzalez—Cuban Caballero of the Cardinals," *The Sporting News,* October 20, 1938.

8 Miguel Angel (Mike) "González," No author, title or date given. From González's file at the Baseball Hall of Fame.

9 John Billheimer, *Baseball and the Blame Game: Scapegoating in the Major Leagues*, 14.

10 United Press, "Card Coach Job Given Up by González," October 17, 1946.

11 Miguel Angel (Mike) "González," from González's file at the Baseball Hall of Fame.

12 J.G. Taylor Spink, "Mike González—Cuban Caballero of the Cardinals," *The Sporting News*, October 20, 1938.

13 J.G. Taylor Spink, "Mike González Attends Title Contest in Havana." *The Sporting News*, January 22, 1972.

Buzzy Wares

By Charles F. Faber

IN A BRIEF major-league career, he appeared in only 92 games. Yet Buzzy Wares played an important role in helping the St. Louis Cardinals win seven National League pennants and five World Series championships.

Clyde Ellsworth Wares was born on May 23, 1886, the younger of the two children of Rosa Wares and Frank Wares, a barber. He was born near the village of Vandalia in Newberg Township, Cass County, Michigan, about halfway between Kalamazoo, Michigan, and South Bend, Indiana.

At an early age the boy demonstrated a love of baseball. He first gained attention by playing on the Kalamazoo High School team. Later he played for a club representing Kalamazoo College, which he attended for one year. An apocryphal story maintains that Wares gained the nickname Buzzy by greeting a girlfriend with a joke electric buzzer hidden in the palm of his hand. According to the tale, the girl responded by slapping the young man's face. However, Wares claimed that he was known as Kiddo or Kid when he first broke into baseball, and the nickname Buzzy was bestowed on him years later by a teammate on the St. Louis Browns because he was always buzzing about baseball.[1]

Buzzy began his professional career as an infielder with Hancock of the Northern Copper Country League. A right-handed batter and thrower, the teenager stood 5-feet-10 and weighed 160 pounds. In 1906 he played for the Houghton Giants in the same league. During the seasons of 1907 through 1909, Buzzy was with Zanesville. (The Zanesville club, called the Infants, was in the Pennsylvania-Ohio-Maryland League in 1907 and moved to the Central League for the 1908 and 1909 seasons.) In 1909 Wares hit .302 for Zanesville, the only time he reached that mark as a batter.

Wares married Gertrude Jones of South Bend. At the time of the 1910 census the newlyweds were living with Buzzy's parents in Kalamazoo. Later in 1910 and 1911 Wares advanced to the Oakland Oaks in the Class A Pacific Coast League, appearing in 426 games in the two seasons, playing out the much longer PCL schedule. Then followed two years with the Montgomery (Alabama) Rebels of the Southern Association.

The St. Louis Browns used the Montgomery stadium for spring training in 1913. For six weeks Wares worked out with the Browns and thought he had acquitted himself well. When Browns manager George Stovall called the young infielder into his office on March 28, the final day of spring training, Wares was hoping to hear that he would be traveling with the club to St. Louis and the major leagues. Instead, Stovall informed him that he was leaving him in Montgomery. When Wares asked why, Stovall said, "You're the payment for our grounds rental."[2] In one of the most bizarre transactions in the history of baseball, the Browns had utilized Wares to reimburse the Rebels for use of the stadium and grounds. At the end of the Southern Association season, Wares, now 27, was called up to the majors. He made his major-

An infielder for the St. Louis Browns during the Deadball Era, Wares later coached for the Cardinals for 23 seasons.

league debut on September 15, 1913. By then Stovall had been replaced as manager because of a dispute with club owner Robert Hedges. Jimmy Austin served as interim manager for eight games. Branch Rickey took over on September 17 and managed Wares throughout his brief major-league career. Wares appeared in 11 games for the Browns that season, playing second base in nine of them and hitting for a .286 average. He scored five runs and batted in one. In 81 games the next year, 1914, Wares played shortstop most of the time. He drove in 23 runs and scored 20. His average dropped to .209, but he worked 28 bases on balls and held a .300 on-base percentage, nearly the same as in 1913. His final major-league game came on September 27, 1914. He had played in a total of 92 games, 85 in the field. Shortstop was a challenge, as his .903 fielding average indicates. (He committed 35 errors in his 68 games at short.) The highlight of Wares' career was probably on May 26, 1914, when he successfully pulled the hidden-ball trick on Amos Strunk of the defending world champion Philadelphia Athletics during a 6-5 Browns victory over the eventual AL pennant winners.

After his major-league playing career ended, Wares returned to the minor leagues. He was a player-manager for the Wichita Witches of the Western League in 1915 and held the same position fort the Little Rock Travelers of the Southern Association in 1917. In 1918 he played part of the season back with the Oakland Oaks of the Pacific Coast League before responding to Secretary of War Newton Baker's "work or fight" order by taking a job as a shipfitter for the Moore Ship Building Company in Oakland.

After the war Wares remained on the West Coast for several years. He split the 1919 season between Oakland and the Seattle Rainiers. He managed Seattle in 1920 and 1921.

It has been reported that Wares was out of baseball from 1922 to 1929.[3] Baseball-reference.com has no entries for him in the minor leagues after 1921. However, Wares was not out of baseball during all of those years. For at least four years he was player-manager of the Hanford Kings in the little-known San Joaquin Valley League.[4] Apparently, his temper had got the best of him while he was managing Seattle and he left the club. *The Sporting News* reported that Wares was suspended from Organized Baseball for playing outlaw ball until he paid a $200 fine levied against him by Commissioner Kenesaw M. Landis.[5]

By 1930 Wares was back in the major leagues, hired by general manager Branch Rickey to be a coach for the St. Louis Cardinals. The same man who had managed Wares as a player in 1913 and 1914 was responsible for helping him embark on a long and distinguished major-league coaching career. Wares served as both first-base coach and batting coach. He coached for the Cardinals for 23 consecutive years, from 1930 through 1952. He coached the club before it was known as the Gas House Gang and was still coaching the team when all of the members of that classic aggregation had played their last game on the banks of the Mississippi. Wares coached under eight different managers. He coached and was part of seven NL pennant winners and five world champion clubs. While he was coaching the Cardinals, the club claimed the World Series title in 1931, 1934, 1942, 1944, and 1946.

Wares was an excellent sign stealer and a productive teacher of the art. For a dozen years he shared coaching duties with the colorful Mike Gonzalez. Although Wares was genial and approachable, sportswriters tended to ignore him in favor of the flamboyant Cuban, who frequently rewarded them with fascinating quotes. On the other hand, Wares was described by one writer as docile.[6]

Billy Southworth, who managed the Cardinals to three consecutive pennants (1942-1944), gave equal credit to Wares and Gonzalez. "I can't put into words the part those two play in developing young players," Southworth said. "They're my right and left arms, and if I tried to sum up the number of times one of their suggestions has won a ballgame, the sum would be staggering."[7]

Despite having very different personalities, Wares and Gonzalez were good friends, and ribbed each other, as friends sometimes do. Gonzalez said jokingly of his fellow coach: "Buzzy awful dumb fellow; remind me of a blind hog sometimes. You know the one I mean, the one who sometimes finds acorn just the same."[8]

After retiring from baseball, Wares made his home in South Bend, his wife's hometown. He and Gertrude had one child, a daughter named Elizabeth Jean, born in Kings County, California, on September 28, 1921.

Following a long illness, Wares died at his home on May 26, 1964, at the age of 78. He was survived by his widow and daughter. Clyde "Buzzy" Wares was buried in South Bend's Riverview Cemetery.

Sources

Heidenry, John, *The Gashouse Gang* (New York: Public Affairs, 2007).

Lieb, Frederick G., *The St. Louis Cardinals: The Story of a Great Ball Club* (New York: G.P. Putnam's Sons, 1945).

Nash, Bruce, and Allan Zullo, *The Baseball Hall of Shame* (New York: Pocket Books, 1987).

Small, Kathleen Edwards, and J. Larry Smith, *History of Tulare County and Kings County, California*, vol. II (Chicago: S.J. Clarke Publishing Company, 1926).

Stockton, J. Roy, *The Gashouse Gang and a Couple of Other Guys* (New York: A.S. Barnes, 1945).

www.ancestry.com.

www.baseball-reference.com.

www.findagrave.com.

www.newspaperarchive.com.

Notes

1. *The Sporting News*, December 17, 1942.
2. Bruce Nash and Allan Zullo, *The Baseball Hall of Shame 3* (New York: Pocket Books, 1987), 43.
3. www.findagrave.com
4. Kathleen Edwards Small and J. Larry Smith, *History of Tulare County and Kings County, California*, vol. II (Chicago: S.J. Clarke Publishing Company, 1926).
5. *The Sporting News*, op. cit.
6. J. Roy Stockton, *The Gashouse Gang and a couple of other guys* (New York: A.S. Barnes, 1945), 162.
7. *Pittsburgh Press, August 1, 1943*.
8. Ibid.

Postscript

By Charles F. Faber

THE CHAMPIONSHIP SEASON of 1934 proved to be the swan song for the Gas House Gang. Three of the more colorful characters departed the Mound City during the season. Burleigh Grimes was released on May 15. In June both Kiddo Davis and Flint Rhem were traded away. Nineteen of the 32 men who appeared in a regular-season game played against Detroit in the 1934 World Series. None of them were still with the Cardinal club that defeated the New York Yankees in the 1942 Series.

Including the general manager, Branch Rickey, and Leo Durocher, who was honored as a Brooklyn Dodgers manager, eight members of the 1934 Cardinals have been installed in the National Baseball Hall of Fame in Cooperstown, New York. Grimes and Dazzy Vance were selected for their exploits with other clubs, but Dizzy Dean, Frankie Frisch, Jesse Haines, and Joe Medwick went in as Cardinals. Dean, Frisch, Medwick, and Vance were voted in by baseball writers; the others were selected by the Veterans Committee. Other members of the 1934 Cardinals who have received votes for the Hall of Fame include Spud Davis, Mike Gonzalez, Bill Hallahan, Pepper Martin, and Burgess Whitehead. None of them came close to the 75 percent approval necessary for induction.

Team owner Sam Breadon and Rickey had built the Cardinals well. In the seven seasons between the 1934 and 1942 titles, the Cardinals finished second four times, third once, and fourth once. Only the 1938 sixth-place club finished out of the first division. The 1942 club won 106 games, a franchise record. The club repeated as National League champs in 1943 and 1944. No other NL club has won three consecutive pennants since the 1920s. The Redbirds have continued winning, adding 11 more National League flags and six World Series titles since 1944. Their modern (since 1901) total of 19 pennants and 11 world championships are the best by any National League club.

As we go to press in 2014 baseball is alive and well in St. Louis, home of the defending 2013 National League champion Cardinals.

CONTRIBUTORS

Mark Armour is founder and chair of the SABR Baseball Biography Project and the author or editor of six books on baseball, including *The Great Eight — The 1975 Cincinnati Reds* (University of Nebraska Press, 2014.) He researches and writes from his home in the Pacific Northwest.

Eric Aron has written for various film and baseball publications, including newenglandfilm.com., *Imagine Magazine*, and throughthefence.com. He has been a SABR member since 2002 and has contributed several bios for the BioProject website and team books. Bios include Bob Uecker, Lee May, Dick Williams, Art Shamsky, and Bud Harrelson. He lives in Boston and holds a Master's degree in Public History and Museum Studies from Northeastern University.

Thomas Ayers is a lawyer who practices labour and employment law. He has earned degrees from the University of Toronto, the London School of Economics, and Queen's University. A lifelong Blue Jays fan, who was born and raised in Toronto, he has contributed several biographies to the SABR Biography Project while waiting for the Blue Jays to return to the playoffs.

Lawrence Baldassaro is professor emeritus of Italian and former director of the Honors College at the University of Wisconsin-Milwaukee. He has written for several baseball journals and is a regular contributor to *GameDay*, the Milwaukee Brewers magazine. He is the editor of *Ted Williams: Reflections on a Splendid Life* and co-editor with Richard Johnson of *The American Game: Baseball and Ethnicity*. His latest book is *Beyond DiMaggio: Italian Americans in Baseball* (University of Nebraska Press, 2011.}

Parker Bena is a lobbyist by trade. He lives in Jefferson City, Missouri, with his wife of 23 years, Karen, has three sons, Jordan, Jeremy, and Brendan, three cats, and a chocolate Lab named Shimmy. He is a devoted fan of the St. Louis Cardinals, following their doings on Fox Sports Midwest, and is especially fascinated with 19th century base ball. He contributed to SABR published books, *Sock It To 'Em Tigers* and *Inventing Baseball*.)

Alan Cohen is a retired insurance underwriter who is spending his retirement doing baseball research, working with the New Britain Rock Cats and volunteering in a local elementary school. He lives in West Hartford, Connecticut, with his wife Frances, their dog Sam, and their cats Morty and Elsie. He contributed biographies on Gino Cimoli and R. C. Stevens to *Sweet 60: The 1960 Pittsburgh Pirates*. His "History of Hearst Sandlot Classic" appeared in the Fall 2013 issue of the *Baseball Research Journal*. The Hearst Classic launched the careers of 89 major leaguers, including former Cardinals Dick Groat and Joe Torre.

Greg Erion and his wife Barbara live in South San Francisco, California. Retired from the railroad industry, he currently teaches history at Skyline Community College. Greg has contributed several articles to the on-going SABR Biography Project and is currently working on a book about the 1959 season.

Charles F. Faber is a native of Iowa, currently living in Lexington, Kentucky. He holds degrees from Coe College, Columbia University, and the University of Chicago. A retired public school and university teacher and administrator, he has contributed to numerous SABR projects. Among his publications are dozens of professional journal articles, encyclopedia entries, and research reports in fields such as educational administration, school law, and country music. In addition to textbooks, he has authored nine books (mostly on baseball), published by McFarland. His most recent book is *Major League Prodigies*. Currently he is working with co-author Zachariah Webb on a book about the 1990 Cincinnati Reds, to be published by McFarland in 2015.

Scott Ferkovich was born in Detroit. In addition to his article on Sportsman's Park, he has also written other ballpark biographies for the SABR Ballpark Project, including Bennett Park, Tiger Stadium, Wrigley Field, Lane Field, and Westgate Park. He is currently editing a book on the 1935 Detroit Tigers. He lives in Michigan along with his wife and daughter and Spenser, their English Cream Golden Retriever.

Paul Geisler grew up in San Antonio, Texas, and has been a Lutheran pastor for over 30 years. He lives in Lake Jackson, Texas, with his wife Susan, and their three children: Sarah, Brydon, and Johanna. He loves anything baseball—playing, watching, coaching, researching, and writing.

Joseph Gerard has been a lifelong Pittsburgh Pirates fan. He grew up hating the Yankees despite being born and raised in Newark, NJ. His biggest regret in life is that he was only 2 years old in 1960. Because of Roberto Clemente, he developed an interest in Latin-American baseball history and has contributed biographies of five Latin players to the SABRBioProject. He lives in New York City with his wife Ann Marie and their two children, Henry and Sophie.

Nancy Snell Griffith grew up near Pittsburgh, and came to love baseball while listening to Bob Prince and Jim Woods broadcast the Pirates' games on KDKA. She is a graduate of Dickinson College and Syracuse University and recently retired as Archives and Special Collections Librarian at Presbyterian College in Clinton, South Carolina.

Don Harrison is the author of *Connecticut Baseball: The Best of the Nutmeg State* (The History Press) and a SABR member. As sports editor of the *Waterbury Republican*, Harrison was a two-time selection as Connecticut Sportswriter of the Year. He chronicled nine World Series, including the New York Mets improbable triumph over the Baltimore Orioles in 1969 and Reggie Jackson's three home runs in the finale of the 1977 fall classic. Don is the founding editor of two publications, *Sacred Heart* (University) magazine and a weekly newspaper, *Greenwich Citizen*, the latter winning General Excellence recognition and three other awards from the New England Press Association. His free lance articles have appeared in *The New York Times, The Sporting News, Sports Quarterly/Baseball* and dozens of other publications. Don and his wife, Patti, reside in Fairfield, Connecticut.

Dwayne Isgrig lives in St. Louis (a great place to live for a student of baseball history). He is currently writing a book on the integration of the St. Louis Browns in 1947. In his spare time he uses social media to promote the rich history of the Negro Leagues with a Facebook page for the St. Louis Giants and Twitter @stlouisgiants.

Jimmy Keenan has been a SABR member since 2001. His grandfather Jimmy Lyston, along with his great-grandfather John M. Lyston and John's two brothers Marty and Bill were all professional baseball players. He is the author of the book *The Lystons: A Story of one Baltimore Family and Our National Pastime*. Jimmy has contributed articles to the 2009 and 2013 editions of SABR's annual publication *The National Pastime*. In addition, he was the writer and historian for the Forgotten Birds documentary that chronicles the 50-year history of the minor league Baltimore Orioles. His pre-recorded interview about the 1921 Baltimore Orioles can be heard at the "Second Inning" display at the Sports Legends Museum in Baltimore, Maryland. He has also written biographies for SABR's Baseball Biography Project and contributed to seven SABR book projects. Jimmy is a 2010 inductee into the Oldtimers Baseball Association of Maryland's Hall of Fame and a 2012 inductee into the Baltimore Boys of Summer Hall of Fame,

Norm King is a retired Canadian civil servant who delights in having the time to devote to SABR research. He still misses his beloved Montreal Expos and awaits the day when he will hear an umpire yell "Au jeu" again at the beginning of a ball game.

Russ Lake lives in Champaign, Illinois and is a retired Professor Emeritus. He was born in Belleville, Illinois, on the other side of the river from downtown St. Louis. The 1964 Cardinals remain his favorite team; however he was told many stories by his grandparents about the players that made up the Gas House Gang. His wife, Carol, deserves an MVP award for watching all of a 14-inning ballgame in Cincinnati with Russ in 1971—during their honeymoon. He joined SABR in 1994 and, later in that same year, was an editor for David Halberstam's *October 1964*.

Len Levin is a lifelong Red Sox fan who has admired the Cardinals for many years, but wishes they would lose to the boys from Boston a bit more often. (The 2013 World Series was a refreshing interlude for him.) Len is a retired newspaper editor and teacher in Providence, Rhode Island, and a member of the Society for American Baseball Research since 1977. He spends a lot of post-retirement time editing for various SABR projects.

Andy McCue has been a SABR member since 1982, winning the L. Robert Davids Award in 2007. He served on SABR's board for nine years, finishing with a term as president in 2009-2011. He won the SABR-Macmillan Award for *Baseball by the Books: A History and Bibliography of Baseball Fiction* and the Doug Pappas Award for a presentation on the Dodger ownership. His biography of Walter O'Malley, *Mover and Shaker*, is being published by the University of Nebraska Press in 2014.

Jeffrey Marlett grew up in southwest Missouri listening to Cardinals games. Now he teaches religious studies at The College of Saint Rose in Albany, New York. He has written SABR biographies of Leo Durocher and Mickey Owen. Currently he is writing a book comparing Leo Durocher with Vince Lombardi.

Jack Morris is a corporate librarian for a pharmaceutical company. He lives in East Coventry, Pennsylvania, with his wife and two daughters. His baseball biographies have appeared in six books, including *The Team That Forever Changed Baseball and America: The 1947 Brooklyn Dodgers* and *Bridging Two Dynasties: The 1947 New York Yankees*. He is not the Jack Morris of World Series fame, but every once in a while he wishes he was.

Bill Nowlin has been vice-president of SABR since 2004 and has helped edit several of SABR's BioProject team books. As a lifelong Red Sox fan, he was pleased to see the 2013 Red Sox draw even with the Cardinals in World Series wins when the two teams have gone head-to-head. Author or editor of more than 40 books, he is also co-founder of Rounder Records, one of America's leading independent music labels.

J. G. Preston is a freelance writer in Benicia, California, with extensive experience asa radio and television host, play-by-play broadcaster and media relations specialist. He edited the Minnesota Twins program and monthly magazine from 1988-90 and contributed to the Twins' program and yearbook for more than a decade after that. He also wrote the script for a video biography of Kirby Puckett narrated by Bob Costas. His baseball history blog is at http://prestonjg.wordpress.com.

C. Paul Rogers III is the coauthor of four baseball books, including *The Whiz Kids and the 1950 Pennant* (Temple University Press, 1996) with boyhood hero Robin Roberts, and more recently *Lucky Me: My 65 Years in Baseball* (SMU Press, 2011) with Eddie Robinson. Paul is president of the Hall-Ruggles (Dallas-Fort Worth) chapter of SABR and a frequent contributor to the SABR BioProject, but his real job is as a law professor at Southern Methodist University, where he served as dean of the law school for nine years. He has also served as SMU's Faculty athletics representative for 27 years.

Matthew Silverman is the author of numerous books on baseball, including *Swinging '73: Baseball's Wildest Season*. He and Ken Samelson co-edited the 2009 SABR book, *The Miracle Has Landed: The Amazin' Story of How the 1969 Mets Shocked the World*. The former associate publisher at Total Sports Publishing, he also served as managing editor for both *Total Baseball* and *The ESPN Baseball Encyclopedia*. He lives in High Falls, New York. He can be contacted through his blog, metsilverman.com.

The essay on Frankie Frisch was originally written by the late **Fred Stein** for the SABR BioProject and subsequently modified slightly by Charles F. Faber for inclusion in this volume. Mr. Stein was born in New York City in 1924. He earned degrees from Pennsylvania State and The Ohio State University. He joined SABR in 1975 and contributed five biographies to the BioProject. His first book, entitled *Under Coogan's Bluff: A Fan's Recollection of the Giants Under Terry and Ott*, was self-published. He then co-authored with Nick Peters *Giants Diary: A Century of Giants Baseball in New York and San Francisco*, published by North Atlantic Books. This was followed by three books published by McFarland: *Mel Ott: The Little Giant of Baseball*; *And the Shipper Bats Cleanup: A History of the Player-Manager*; and *A History of the Baseball Fan*. Fred Stein died in 2010.

Andy Sturgill, a lifelong Phillies fan, lives in suburban Philadelphia with his wife, Carrie. A college administrator by day, he enjoys reading and visiting ballparks in his free time.

Clayton Trutor is a PhD candidate in history at Boston College. He is currently working on a doctoral dissertation which deals with the impact of professional sports franchise relocations and league expansions on the politics and culture of 20th century American cities.

Cort Vitty is a resident of Maryland and a lifelong New York Yankees fan. He is a native of New Jersey and a graduate of Seton Hall University. A SABR member (Bob Davids chapter) since 1999, Vitty has contributed to the *Baseball Research Journal, Go-Go to Glory: The 1959 White Sox,* and *Bridging Two Dynasties: The 1947 New York Yankees.* Original compositions are posted at Seamheads.com and Philadelphia Athletics. org. For the SABR bio project Vitty has authored biographies of Buzz Arlett, Benny Bengough, Mickey Grasso, Goose Goslin, Billy Johnson, Babe Phelps, Dave Philley, and Suitcase Simpson.

Joseph Wancho lives in Westlake, Ohio, and is a lifelong Cleveland Indians fan. Working at AT&T since 1994 as a Process/Development manager, he has been a SABR member since 2005. He is the editor of *Pitching to the Pennant,* a BioProject book on the 1954 Cleveland Indians published by the University of Nebraska Press in 2014.

John J. Watkins, a retired law professor, is the author of three books and more than forty scholarly articles. A native Texan, he lives with his wife Joan in Fayetteville, Arkansas. His great-uncle, George "Watty" Watkins was a major league outfielder in the 1930s, primarily with the St. Louis Cardinals.

Charlie Weatherby is a lifelong Phillies fan who also follows the San Francisco Giants. A native of Wilmington, Delaware, he is a social work supervisor at the Independent Adoption Center, a domestic open adoption program. He is a softball fanatic and manages the Marin Joe's Giants Over-40 club, has a pitching record of 931-465, and counts 80 championships in the last 40 years. A periodic contributor to SABR's BioProject, he now lives in Novato, California, with his wife, Sara Duggin, and their cat, Panther.

Bob Webster grew up in Northwest Indiana and has been a Cubs fan since 1963. He has earned degrees from Linfield College and Maryhurst University. Now living in Portland, Oregon, and recently retired, Bob is currently working on putting together the history of the Northwest League and researching the West Coast League along with many other collegiate leagues. He is a member of the Northwest chapter of SABR, on the Board of Executives of the Old-Timers Baseball Association of Portland, and a manager in the Great American Fantasy League.

Gregory H. Wolf, a lifelong Pirates fan, was born in Pittsburgh, but now resides in the Chicagoland area with his wife, Margaret, and their daughter, Gabriela. A professor of German and the holder of the Dennis and Bauman endowed chair of humanities at North Central College in Naperville, Illinois, he has published articles on baseball history at *The Hardball Times*, and regularly contributes to SABR projects, including the BioProject. He is currently editing two SABR great teams books, one on the 1957 Milwaukee Braves and the other on the 1929 Chicago Cubs.

SABR BioProject Books

In 2002, the Society for American Baseball Research launched an effort to write and publish biographies of every player, manager, and individual who has made a contribution to baseball. Over the past decade, the BioProject Committee has produced over 2,200 biographical articles. Many have been part of efforts to create theme- or team-oriented books, spearheaded by chapters or other committees of SABR.

THE YEAR OF THE BLUE SNOW: The 1964 Philadelphia Phillies
Catcher Gus Triandos dubbed the Philadelphia Phillies' 1964 season "the year of the blue snow," a rare thing that happens once in a great while. This book sheds light on lingering questions about the 1964 season—but any book about a team is really about the players. This work offers life stories of all the players and others (managers, coaches, owners, and broadcasters) associated with this star-crossed team, as well as essays of analysis and history.
Edited by Mel Marmer and Bill Nowlin
$19.95 paperback (ISBN 978-1-933599-51-9)
$9.99 ebook (ISBN 978-1-933599-52-6)
8.5"x11", 356 pages, over 70 photos

DETROIT TIGERS 1984: What a Start! What a Finish!
The 1984 Detroit tigers roared out of the gate, winning their first nine games of the season and compiling an eye-popping 35-5 record after the campaign's first 40 games—still the best start ever for any team in major league history. This book brings together biographical profiles of every Tiger from that magical season, plus those of field management, top executives, the broadcasters—even venerable Tiger Stadium and the city itself.
Edited by Mark Pattison and David Raglin
$19.95 paperback (ISBN 978-1-933599-44-1)
$9.99 ebook (ISBN 978-1-933599-45-8)
8.5"x11", 250 pages (Over 230,000 words!)

SWEET '60: The 1960 Pittsburgh Pirates
A portrait of the 1960 team which pulled off one of the biggest upsets of the last 60 years. When Bill Mazeroski's home run left the park to win in Game Seven of the World Series, beating the New York Yankees, David had toppled Goliath. It was a blow that awakened a generation, one that millions of people saw on television, one of TV's first iconic World Series moments.
Edited by Clifton Blue Parker and Bill Nowlin
$19.95 paperback (ISBN 978-1-933599-48-9)
$9.99 ebook (ISBN 978-1-933599-49-6)
8.5"x11", 340 pages, 75 photos

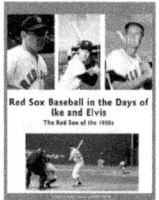

RED SOX BASEBALL IN THE DAYS OF IKE AND ELVIS: The Red Sox of the 1950s
Although the Red Sox spent most of the 1950s far out of contention, the team was filled with fascinating players who captured the heart of their fans. In Red Sox Baseball, members of SABR present 46 biographies on players such as Ted Williams and Pumpsie Green as well as season-by-season recaps.
Edited by Mark Armour and Bill Nowlin
$19.95 paperback (ISBN 978-1-933599-24-3)
$9.99 ebook (ISBN 978-1-933599-34-2)
8.5"x11", 372 pages, over 100 photos

THE MIRACLE BRAVES OF 1914
Boston's Original Worst-to-First Champions
Long before the Red Sox "Impossible Dream" season, Boston's now nearly forgotten "other" team, the 1914 Boston Braves, performed a baseball "miracle" that resounds to this very day. The "Miracle Braves" were Boston's first "worst-to-first" winners of the World Series. Refusing to throw in the towel at the midseason mark, George Stallings engineered a remarkable second-half climb in the standings all the way to first place.
Edited by Bill Nowlin
$19.95 paperback (ISBN 978-1-933599-69-4)
$9.99 ebook (ISBN 978-1-933599-70-0)
8.5"x11", 392 pages, over 100 photos

THAR'S JOY IN BRAVELAND! The 1957 Milwaukee Braves
Few teams in baseball history have captured the hearts of their fans like the Milwaukee Braves of the 1950s. During the Braves' 13-year tenure in Milwaukee (1953-1965), they had a winning record every season, won two consecutive NL pennants (1957 and 1958), lost two more in the final week of the season (1956 and 1959), and set big-league attendance records along the way.
Edited by Gregory H. Wolf
$19.95 paperback (ISBN 978-1-933599-71-7)
$9.99 ebook (ISBN 978-1-933599-72-4)
8.5"x11", 330 pages, over 60 photos

NEW CENTURY, NEW TEAM: The 1901 Boston Americans
The team now known as the Boston Red Sox played its first season in 1901. Boston had a well-established National League team, but the American League went head-to-head with the N.L. in Chicago, Philadelphia, and Boston. Chicago won the American League pennant and Boston finished second, only four games behind.
Edited by Bill Nowlin
$19.95 paperback (ISBN 978-1-933599-58-8)
$9.99 ebook (ISBN 978-1-933599-59-5)
8.5"x11", 268 pages, over 125 photos

CAN HE PLAY? A Look At Baseball Scouts and their Profession
They dig through tons of coal to find a single diamond. Here in the world of scouts, we meet the "King of Weeds," a Ph.D. we call "Baseball's Renaissance Man," a husband-and-wife team, pioneering Latin scouts, and a Japanese-American interned during World War II who became a successful scout—and many, many more.
Edited by Jim Sandoval and Bill Nowlin
$19.95 paperback (ISBN 978-1-933599-23-6)
$9.99 ebook (ISBN 978-1-933599-25-0)
8.5"x11", 200 pages, over 100 photos

SABR Members can purchase each book at a significant discount (often 50% off) and receive the ebook editions free as a member benefit. Each book is available in a trade paperback edition as well as ebooks suitable for reading on a home computer or Nook, Kindle, or iPad/tablet.

To learn more about becoming a member of SABR, visit the website: sabr.org/join

The SABR Digital Library

The Society for American Baseball Research, the top baseball research organization in the world, disseminates some of the best in baseball history, analysis, and biography through our publishing programs. The SABR Digital Library contains a mix of books old and new, and focuses on a tandem program of paperback and ebook publication, making these materials widely available for both on digital devices and as traditional printed books.

CLASSIC REPRINTS

BASE-BALL: How to Become a Player
by John Montgomery Ward
John Montgomery Ward (1860-1925) tossed the second perfect game in major league history and later became the game's best shortstop and a great, inventive manager. His classic handbook on baseball skills and strategy was published in 1888. Illustrated with woodcuts, the book is divided into chapters for each position on the field as well as chapters on the origin of the game, theory and strategy, training, base-running, and batting.
$4.99 ebook (ISBN 978-1-933599-47-2)
$9.95 paperback (ISBN 978-0910137539)
156 pages, 4.5"x7" replica edition

BATTING
by F. C. Lane
First published in 1925, Batting collects the wisdom and insights of over 250 hitters and baseball figures. Lane interviewed extensively and compiled tips and advice on everything from batting stances to beanballs. Legendary baseball figures such as Ty Cobb, Casey Stengel, Cy Young, Walter Johnson, Rogers Hornsby, and Babe Ruth reveal the secrets of such integral and interesting parts of the game as how to choose a bat, the ways to beat a slump, and how to outguess the pitcher.
$14.95 paperback (ISBN 978-0-910137-86-7)
$7.99 ebook (ISBN 978-1-933599-46-5)
240 pages, 5"x7"

RUN, RABBIT, RUN
by Walter "Rabbit" Maranville
"Rabbit" Maranville was the Joe Garagiola of Grandpa's day, the baseball comedian of the times. In a twenty-four-year career that began in 1912, Rabbit found a lot of funny situations to laugh at, and no wonder: he caused most of them! The book also includes an introduction by the late Harold Seymour and a historical account of Maranville's life and Hall-of-Fame career by Bob Carroll.
$9.95 paperback (ISBN 978-1-933599-26-7)
$5.99 ebook (ISBN 978-1-933599-27-4)
100 pages, 5.5"x8.5", 15 rare photos

MEMORIES OF A BALLPLAYER
by Bill Werber and C. Paul Rogers III
Bill Werber's claim to fame is unique: he was the last living person to have a direct connection to the 1927 Yankees, "Murderers' Row," a team hailed by many as the best of all time. Rich in anecdotes and humor, Memories of a Ballplayer is a clear-eyed memoir of the world of big-league baseball in the 1930s. Werber played with or against some of the most productive hitters of all time, including Babe Ruth, Ted Williams, Lou Gehrig, and Joe DiMaggio.
$14.95 paperback (ISNB 978-0-910137-84-3)
$6.99 ebook (ISBN 978-1-933599-47-2)
250 pages, 6"x9"

ORIGINAL SABR RESEARCH

INVENTING BASEBALL: The 100 Greatest Games of the Nineteenth Century
SABR's Nineteenth Century Committee brings to life the greatest games from the game's early years. From the "prisoner of war" game that took place among captive Union soldiers during the Civil War (immortalized in a famous lithograph), to the first intercollegiate game (Amherst versus Williams), to the first professional no-hitter, the games in this volume span 1833–1900 and detail the athletic exploits of such players as Cap Anson, Moses "Fleetwood" Walker, Charlie Comiskey, and Mike "King" Kelly.
Edited by Bill Felber
$19.95 paperback (ISBN 978-1-933599-42-7)
$9.99 ebook (ISBN 978-1-933599-43-4)
302 pages, 8"x10", 200 photos

NINETEENTH CENTURY STARS: 2012 EDITION
First published in 1989, Nineteenth Century Stars was SABR's initial attempt to capture the stories of baseball players from before 1900. With a collection of 136 fascinating biographies, SABR has re-released Nineteenth Century Stars for 2012 with revised statistics and new form. The 2012 version also includes a preface by John Thorn.
Edited by Robert L. Tiemann and Mark Rucker
$19.95 paperback (ISBN 978-1-933599-28-1)
$9.99 ebook (ISBN 978-1-933599-29-8)
300 pages, 6"x9"

GREAT HITTING PITCHERS
Published in 1979, Great Hitting Pitchers was one of SABR's early publications. Edited by SABR founder Bob Davids, the book compiles stories and records about pitchers excelling in the batter's box. Newly updated in 2012 by Mike Cook, Great Hitting Pitchers contain tables including data from 1979-2011, corrections to reflect recent records, and a new chapter on recent new members in the club of "great hitting pitchers" like Tom Glavine and Mike Hampton.
Edited by L. Robert Davids
$9.95 paperback (ISBN 978-1-933599-30-4)
$5.99 ebook (ISBN 978-1-933599-31-1)
102 pages, 5.5"x8.5"

THE FENWAY PROJECT
Sixty-four SABR members—avid fans, historians, statisticians, and game enthusiasts—recorded their experiences of a single game. Some wrote from inside the Green Monster's manual scoreboard, the Braves clubhouse, or the broadcast booth, while others took in the essence of Fenway from the grandstand or bleachers. The result is a fascinating look at the charms and challenges of Fenway Park, and the allure of being a baseball fan.
Edited by Bill Nowlin and Cecilia Tan
$9.99 ebook (ISBN 978-1-933599-50-2)
175 pages, 100 photos

SABR Members can purchase each book at a significant discount (often 50% off) and receive the ebook editions free as a member benefit. Each book is available in a trade paperback edition as well as ebooks suitable for reading on a home computer or Nook, Kindle, or iPad/tablet.

To learn more about becoming a member of SABR, visit the website: sabr.org/join

Join SABR today!

If you're interested in baseball—writing about it, reading about it, talking about it — there's a place for you in the Society for American Baseball Research. Our members include everyone from academics to professional sportswriters to amateur historians and statisticians to students and casual fans who merely enjoy reading about baseball history and occasionally gathering with other members to talk baseball.

SABR members have a variety of interests. There are dozens of groups devoted to the study of areas related to the game, from Baseball and the Arts to Statistical Analysis to the Deadball Era to Women in Baseball. In addition, many SABR members meet formally and informally in regional chapters throughout the year, and hundreds come together for the annual national convention, the organization's premier event. These meetings often include panel discussions with former major league players and presentations by members.

Why join SABR? Here are some benefits of membership:

- Two issues of the *Baseball Research Journal,* which includes articles on history, biography, statistics, personalities, book reviews, and other aspects of the game.
- One issue of *The National Pastime,* which focuses on baseball in the region where that year's national convention is held.
- Regional chapter meetings, which can include guest speakers, presentations and trips to ballgames
- "This Week in SABR" e-newsletters every Friday, with the latest news in SABR and highlighting SABR research
- Online access to back issues of *The Sporting News* and other periodicals through Paper of Record
- Access to SABR's lending library and other research resources
- Online member directory to connect you with an international network of passionate baseball experts and fans
- Discount on registration for our annual conferences
- Access to SABR-L, an e-mail discussion list of baseball questions and answers that many feel is worth the cost of membership itself
- The opportunity to be part of a passionate international community of baseball fans

SABR membership is on a "rolling" calendar system; that means your membership lasts 365 days no matter when you sign up! Enjoy all the benefits of SABR membership by signing up today at SABR.org/join or by clipping out the form below and mailing it to SABR, 4455 E. Camelback Rd., Ste. D-140, Phoenix, AZ 85018.

✂ -

SABR MEMBERSHIP FORM

Dues payable by check, money order, Visa, MasterCard or Discover Card; online at http://store.sabr.org; or by phone at (602) 343-6455

Mail to: SABR, 4455 E. Camelback Rd., Ste. D-140, Phoenix, AZ 85018

	Annual	3-year	Senior	3-yr Sr.	Under 30
U.S.:	☐ $65	☐ $175	☐ $45	☐ $129	☐ $45
Canada/Mexico:	☐ $75	☐ $205	☐ $55	☐ $159	☐ $55
Overseas:	☐ $84	☐ $232	☐ $64	☐ $186	☐ $55

Add a Family Member: $15 each family member at same address (list on back)
Senior: 65 or older before end of the current year
All dues amounts in U.S. dollars or equivalent

Participate in Our Donor Program!
I'd like to designate my gift to be used toward:
☐ General Fund ☐ Endowment Fund ☐ Research Resources
☐ Other: _____
☐ I want to maximize the impact of my gift; do not send any donor premiums
☐ I would like this gift to remain anonymous.
Note: Any donation not designated will be placed in the General Fund.
SABR is a 501 (c) (3) not-for-profit organization & donations are tax-deductible to the extent allowed by law.

NAME _____
ADDRESS _____
CITY _____ STATE _____ ZIP _____
HOME PHONE _____ BIRTHDAY _____
EMAIL _____
(Your e-mail address on file ensures you will receive the most recent SABR news.)

Dues _____ $
Donation _____ $
Total Enclosed _____ $

Do you work for a matching grant corporation? Call (602) 343-6455 for details.
☐ Check/Money Order Enclosed   ☐ VISA, Master Card, Discover

CARD # _____
EXP DATE _____ SIGNATURE _____